A History of East Asia

Charles Holcombe begins by asking the question "What is East Asia?" In the modern age, many of the features that made the region – now defined as including China, Japan, Korea, and Vietnam – distinct have been submerged by the effects of revolution, politics, or globalization. Yet, as an ancient civilization, the region had both a historical and cultural coherence. This shared past is at the heart of this extraordinarily ambitious book, which traces the story of East Asia from the dawn of history to the twenty-first century. The second edition has been imaginatively revised and expanded to include an added emphasis on cross-cultural interactions and connections, both within East Asia and beyond, new chapters on Vietnam, and new material on modern pop culture. The updated volume also features a Chinese character list, fourteen new illustrations, and seven new maps.

Charles Holcombe is professor of history at the University of Northern Iowa. His publications include *The Genesis of East Asia, 221 BC–AD 907* (2001) and *In the Shadow of the Han: Literati Thought and Society at the Start of the Southern Dynasties* (1994).

A History of East Asia

From the Origins of Civilization to the Twenty-First Century

CHARLES HOLCOMBE

CAMBRIDGE
UNIVERSITY PRESS

CAMBRIDGE
UNIVERSITY PRESS

University Printing House, Cambridge CB2 8BS, United Kingdom

One Liberty Plaza, 20th Floor, New York, NY 10006, USA

477 Williamstown Road, Port Melbourne, VIC 3207, Australia

4843/24, 2nd Floor, Ansari Road, Daryaganj, Delhi – 110002, India

79 Anson Road, #06–04/06, Singapore 079906

Cambridge University Press is part of the University of Cambridge.

It furthers the University's mission by disseminating knowledge in the pursuit of education, learning and research at the highest international levels of excellence.

www.cambridge.org
Information on this title: www.cambridge.org/9781107118737

First edition © Charles Holcombe 2011
Second edition © Charles Holcombe 2017

First edition published 2011
Reprinted 2011 (twice)
Second edition published 2017

Printed in the United States of America by Sheridan Books, Inc.

A catalogue record for this publication is available from the British Library

Library of Congress Cataloguing-in-Publication Data
Names: Holcombe, Charles, 1956- author.
Title: A history of East Asia : from the origins of civilization to the twenty-first century /
Charles Holcombe.
Description: Second edition. | Cambridge : Cambridge University Press, 2016. | Includes
bibliographical references and index.
Identifiers: LCCN 2016025900| ISBN 9781107118737 (Hardback) | ISBN 9781107544895
(Paperback)
Subjects: LCSH: East Asia–History. | East Asia–Civilization.
Classification: LCC DS511 .H65 2016 | DDC 950–dc23 LC record available at
https://lccn.loc.gov/2016025900

ISBN 978-1-107-11873-7 Hardback
ISBN 978-1-107-54489-5 Paperback

Contents

List of Illustrations

List of Maps

Pronunciation Guide

(Where not indicated otherwise, pronunciations are approximately as might be expected by American English speakers.)

Chinese

East Asians normally simply do not use the Roman alphabet, but for the purpose of transcribing the sounds of East Asian words in our alphabet a number of different spelling systems have been devised. For Mandarin Chinese, a spelling system called *pinyin* is increasingly standard. In pinyin, the vowels and diphthongs (two vowels that combine to form a single syllable) of Mandarin are pronounced approximately as follows:

a as in **ah**
ai like the **igh** in s**igh** or h**igh**
ao like the **ow** in h**ow** n**ow** br**ow**n c**ow**
e like the **u** in b**u**t
ei like the **ay** in M**ay** d**ay**
i as in pol**i**ce or like the **ee** in f**ee**t – except in the combinations *chi* (where it sounds more like the **chi** in **chi**rp), *ci* (where it sounds more like the **si** in pop**si**cle), *ri* (where it sounds more like the **ur** in **ur**ban), *shi* (where it sounds more like the **shou** in **shou**ld), *si* (where it sounds more like the **si** in **si**bling), *zhi* (where it sounds more like the **Ge** in **Ge**rman), and *zi* (where it sounds more like the **zi** in **zi**ggurat)
o like the **ou** in **ou**ght
ou like **oh**, or the **o** in **O**klahoma
u like the **o** in wh**o** or the **oo** in h**oo**t

Some exceptional combinations follow:

ui sounds more like **oo-eigh** rather than **oo-ee**
yan sounds like **yen** (rhymes with **Zen**) rather than **yahn**

-*ian* (in such words as *bian, lian, nian,* etc.) sounds like -**ee-en** (as in **Z**en) rather than -**ee-ahn**

yi sounds no different from a solitary *i* (as in po**li**ce) – in other words, the *i* sound in isolation, or at the beginning of a word, is by convention spelled *yi*

A few unusual consonants in pinyin follow:

c sounds like the **ts** in the Russian title **Ts**ar (the word *cui* therefore sounds like **ts-oo-eigh**, pronounced together quickly)

q sounds like the **ch** in **ch**ance (*Qin* therefore sounds like **cheen**)

x sounds like **hs** or the **s** in **s**ee (*Xia* therefore sounds like **hs-ee-ah**, pronounced together quickly)

zh sounds like the **j** in **j**ay (*zhou* therefore sounds just like the familiar English name **Joe**)

Each Chinese syllable also always has a distinct tone, which is not, however, normally indicated in writing and therefore cannot be guessed from the spelling.

There are a number of alternate Chinese spelling systems still in circulation (though they are not used in this book) and several old, irregular spellings (and associated pronunciations) that have become conventionally established in English usage such as Peking for Beijing, Canton for Guangzhou, Sun Yat-sen for the man more commonly known in Mandarin as Sun Zhongshan, and Chiang Kai-shek for Jiang Jieshi.

Japanese

The vowels and diphthongs in Japanese are pronounced approximately as follows:

a as in **ah**

ai like the **igh** in s**igh** or h**igh**

e as in t**e**n

ei like the **ay** in **May** d**ay**

i as in po**li**ce

o as in **oh**, or the **o** in **O**klah**o**ma

ō (with a macron) is pronounced just like *o* but is sustained for twice the duration

u is like the **o** in wh**o** or the **oo** in h**oo**t

ū (with a macron) is pronounced just like *u* but is sustained for twice the duration

When other vowels appear next to each other in Japanese, they are each pronounced separately rather than combined into a single-syllable diphthong. For example *ii* is pronounced **ee-ee**.

After an initial *s*, the *u* in Japanese is often also nearly silent. *Sukiyaki*, for example, sounds more like s'kiyaki.

Korean

The vowels and diphthongs in Korean are pronounced approximately as follows:

a as in **ah**

ae like the **a** in h**a**t

e as in t**e**n

i as in po**li**ce

o like the **o** in **o**rbit

ŏ like the **au** in c**au**ght

u like the **o** in wh**o** or the **oo** in h**oo**t

ŭ like the **u** in p**u**t

ŭi like **we**

Note also that in Korean pronunciation, the consonant pairs *ch/j, k/g, p/b, r/l, s/sh,* and *t/d* are not necessarily clearly distinguished (technically, in one widely used spelling system, they are distinguished with the aid of an apostrophe, e.g., **ch'** represents the English **ch** sound and **ch** the English **j** sound, with *tch, kk, pp, ss,* and *tt* indicating further subtle shades of difference). Chosŏn, for example, there-fore sometimes appears spelled as Joseon (with the *ŏ* sound being represented by *eo*), Koguryŏ as Goguryeo, Paekche as Baekje, and Silla as Shilla.

Vietnamese

Vietnamese is the only East Asian language that is normally written today (in modern times) using the Roman alphabet. The standard Romanization system is called *quốc ngữ,* which means "national language." In addition to special marks indicating five of the six tones (like Chinese, Vietnamese is a tonal language, but, unlike Chinese, the tones are conventionally indicated in writing), several other diacritical (accent) marks are also used to distinguish different pronunciations. For example, the letter d written with a line through it (Đ, đ) is pronounced like the English letter d, but without a line through it a d sounds more like the English letter z. Unfortunately, because the Vietnamese diacritical markings are complicated, they are frequently dispensed with in English-language publications, as is the case in the present volume. Without the diacritic markings it is not always possible to know how to correctly pronounce a Vietnamese word.

Distinctive vowels and diphthongs in Vietnamese include:

a is pronounced as **ah**, or as in f**a**ther

â and *ă* are shorter in pronunciation than *a*

e is pronounced like the **a** in **a**verage

ê is pronounced like the **ay** in s**ay**

i is pronounced as like the **e** in cr**ee**k

o is pronounced **aw**

ơ is pronounced as in **uh** or f**ur**

ô is pronounced as **oh**, or as in g**o**

u is pronounced as **ooh**, or as in r**oo**t

ư is pronounced as in sh**ou**ld

ia is pronounced as eeah

ua is pronounced as üah

ưa is pronounced ooah

Distinctive consonants and consonantal combinations include:

c, *k*, and *q* are pronounced as in **c**at, or like the **k** in than**k**
d is pronounced as **z**
ḍ is pronounced as **d**
g is pronounced as in **g**ood
kh is pronounced something like the **h** in **h**ut
ng is pronounced something like **nuhguh**
nh is pronounced something like **ny**
r is pronounced like the **zh** in Doctor **Zh**ivago
s is pronounced sh
t is unaspirated, and pronounced like the t in standard: almost a **d**ull sound
th is pronounced as the English letter **t**
tr is pronounced tch
x is pronounced as s

Timeline: Dynasties and Major Historical Periods

Timeline

China	Japan	Korea	Vietnam

BCE
1100 — Shang, ca 1570 BCE–ca 1045 BCE

1000

900 — W Zhou, ca 1045–771

800

700

Jōmon, ca 10,000 BCE ca 250 BCE

600 — Spring and Autumn, 722–481

500 — E. Zhou, 770–256

400

Dong Son ca 600 BCE–100 CE

300 — Warring States, 403–221 BCE

Old Chosŏn ? –?

200 — Qin, 221–207 BCE

Au Lac 257 BCE–ca 179 BCE

S. Yue 179–111 BCE

100 — Former Han, 202 BCE–9 CE

BCE

Yayoi, ca 250 BCE ca 250 CE

CE — Xin (usurpation) 9–23 CE

100 — Later Han, 25–220 CE

Trung Sisters, 40–42 CE

200 — Three Kingdoms, 220–280

Chinese Rule, 111 BCE–939 CE

300 — W. Jin, 266–316

16 Kingdoms (north), 304–439

Kofun (Old Tomb), ca 250–552 CE

Koguryŏ, ?– 668 CE

400

Southern Dynasties, 317–589

500

N. Wei–N. Zhou, 386–581

Paekche, ? –663

Ly Bi and effective independence, 541–602

600

Sui, 581–618

Late Yamato, 552–710

700

Silla ?–935 (unified 668)

Nara, 710–784

800

Tang, 618–907

900

Heian, 794–1185

Five Dynasties, 907–960 (10 Kingdoms in south)

1000

N. Song, 960–1127

Independence, 939–
Former Le, 980–1009

1100

Koryŏ, 918–1392

Ly, 1009–1225

1200

S. Song, 1127–1279 (Jurchen rule in N, 1127–1234)

Kamakura, 1185–1333

1300

Yuan, 1271–1368 (Mongol rule)

Tran, 1226–1400

1400

Muromachi, 1338–1573

Ho Usurpation 1400–1407
Ming Invasion 1406–1428

1500

Ming, 1368–1644

Chosŏn, 1392–1910

Later Le, 1428–1527

1600

Mac Usurpation, 1527–1592

1700

Tokugawa, 1603–1868

Trinh/Nguyen 1593–1771

Qing, 1644–1912

1800

Tay Son, 1771–1802

1900

Meiji, 1868–1912
Taishō, 1912–1926

Nguyen 1802–1945

Republic, 1912– (on Taiwan,1949–)

Shōwa, 1926–1989

Japanese rule, 1910–1945

French, 1858–1954

2000

N/S wars 1954–1975

People's Republic,1949

Heisei, 1989–

N/S Division, 1945–

Unified, 1975–

Glossary

Altaic	A major, somewhat hypothetical north Eurasian language family, possibly including the Turkic, Mongolic, Manchu, Japanese, Korean, and other languages
Amaterasu	The Japanese sun goddess
Annam	A premodern name for Vietnam (in French colonial times, specifically central Vietnam)
Bakufu	The military "tent government" of the Japanese shōguns
Bodhisattva	An altruistic enlightened Buddhist being (Sanskrit)
Bushi	A Japanese "military gentleman," or samurai
Chaebŏl	A post–World War II South Korean conglomerate (written with the same two Chinese characters as the pre–World War II Japanese word *zaibatsu*)
Cham	Austronesian-speaking people living in what is today central Vietnam
Chanoyu	The Japanese tea ceremony
Chosŏn	Korea
Cochinchina	European name for southern Vietnam
Comintern	The Communist International, an organization based in Moscow from 1919 to 1943 (English abbreviation)
Daimyō	"Great name": the lord of a regional domain in late premodern Japan
Dao Tong	The Neo-Confucian "Transmission of the Way" (in Chinese)
Dhāraṇī	A Buddhist magical formula (Sanskrit)
Enka	A popular sentimental modern Japanese musical style
Falun Gong	A new "traditional" Chinese religion, founded in 1992 and currently banned in the People's Republic of China
Guandong	Chinese for "East of the Passes," with reference to early twentieth-century Japanese military activity, usually referring to Manchuria (and frequently spelled "Kwantung" in older publications)
Guanzhong	The region "Within the Passes": a Chinese geographical area roughly corresponding to modern Shaanxi Province

Guomindang	The Chinese Nationalist Party, alternatively spelled "Kuo-Min-Tang" in the older Wade-Giles spelling system (and abbreviated either GMD or KMT)
Guoyu	The Chinese National Language, or Mandarin
Hakka	"Guest Families" (Mandarin: *Kejia*): a Chinese sub-ethnic group
Han'guk	"The Country of the Han": Korea
Han'gŭl	The Korean alphabet
Hanzi	Chinese characters or written symbols
Hiragana	A Japanese syllabary, or set of phonetic written symbols representing complete syllables
Hu	A generic Chinese name for northern non-Chinese peoples, used especially during the Age of Division
Huangdi	The Chinese term for *emperor*
Huaxia	China
Hwarang	"Flower Youths": aristocratic young warriors in Silla (Korea)
Jinshi	"Presented Scholar": the highest degree in the late imperial Chinese examination system
Juche	The modern North Korean ideology of self-reliance
Junzi	Literally the "son of a Lord" but used by Confucius to refer to anyone who behaved as a proper gentleman should (in Chinese)
Kami	Japanese gods or spirits
Kantō	Japanese for "East of the Passes," referring to the largest Japanese agricultural plain in the vicinity of modern Tōkyō
Katakana	A Japanese syllabary, or set of phonetic written symbols representing complete syllables – now chiefly used to write Western loanwords
Keigo	The Japanese "respect language"
Keiretsu	Post–World War II Japanese enterprise groups
Kokutai	Pre–World War II Japan's "national polity"
Kolp'um	Aristocratic "bone rank" in Silla (Korea)
Kuo-Min-Tang	The Chinese Nationalist Party, alternatively spelled "Guomindang" in pinyin (and abbreviated either GMD or KMT)
Kwantung	Chinese for "East of the Passes," with reference to early twentieth-century Japanese military activity, usually referring to Manchuria (and now spelled "Guandong" in pinyin)
Li	"Courtesy," "propriety," "rites," or "ceremony" (in Chinese)
Li	The organizing "principle" or "principles" for *qi*, or "matter," in Neo-Confucian philosophy (in Chinese) (note: this word *li* is written with an entirely different character from the preceding *li*, meaning "courtesy")
Lingnan	"South of the mountain ranges," a region of early imperial south China that included the modern provinces of Guangdong and Guangxi and what is now northern Vietnam
Logograph	A nonphonetic written symbol, such as a Chinese character, used to represent a word in a particular language (a newly coined English term)
Maripkan	Early native Korean royal title
Minzu	The modern Chinese word for "nation," in the sense of "a people"

MITI	The Ministry of International Trade and Industry in post–World War II Japan (English abbreviation)
Nihon	Japan
Nirvāṇa	"Extinction," or Buddhist enlightenment (Sanskrit)
Nom	A system for writing the Vietnamese language, derived from Chinese characters.
Pinyin	Literally, "to spell the sound": the modern phonetic system for spelling Chinese using the Roman alphabet that was developed in the People's Republic of China
Qaghan	A supreme Mongol and Turkic title, meaning roughly Khan of Khans, or Great Khan
Qi	The basic matter or substance of the universe according to Neo-Confucian philosophy (in Chinese)
Qipao	"Banner gown," a Chinese female fashion that derived from Manchu clothing styles (in Chinese)
Qiren	"Banner People," an alternate name for the Manchus (in the Chinese language)
Quoc ngu	System of writing Vietnamese using the Roman alphabet
Ren	The Confucian virtue of humanity (in Chinese)
Rōnin	Japanese masterless samurai
Rujiao	The "Teachings of the Ru," or Confucian scholars (in Chinese)
Saṃsāra	The cycle of existence: birth and death (Sanskrit)
Sankin kōtai	The alternate attendance system for daimyō in Tokugawa Japan
SCAP	Supreme Commander for the Allied Powers during the postwar occupation of Japan (English abbreviation)
Shangdi	"The Lord on High": the supreme ancient Chinese deity (and a term sometimes also used as a Chinese translation for the Christian God)
Shintō	"The Way of the Spirits": the indigenous Japanese religion
Shōgun	"General": the premodern Japanese military overlord
Śramaṇa	A Buddhist monk (Sanskrit)
Sūtra	A sermon attributed to the Buddha (Sanskrit)
Taigi-meibun	The moral obligation of fulfilling the role proper to one's title or status (in Japanese)
Taiji	The "supreme ultimate" in Neo-Confucian philosophy (in Chinese)
Taotie	A common design on ancient Chinese bronze vessels
Tatami	The floor matting in late premodern Japanese buildings
Tennō	"Heavenly Sovereign": the standard Japanese imperial title
Tianming	The Chinese Mandate of Heaven
Tianxia	Chinese for "Under Heaven," referring to the royal or imperial realm
Tianzi	Chinese for "Son of Heaven," referring to the supreme ruler
Tonkin	European name for northern Vietnam
Topolect	A proposed alternate term for the Chinese dialects (in English)
Tripiṭaka	The "Three Baskets," or the complete set of Buddhist Scriptures (Sanskrit)
Uji	A Japanese lineage or descent group

Viet Cong	Southern term for Vietnamese Communists
Vietminh	League for the Independence of Vietnam
Wuwei	The Daoist principle of nonaction (in Chinese)
Xiao	The Confucian virtue of filial piety (in Chinese)
Yangban	The "two orders" of premodern Korean civil and military aristocracy
Yuan	The modern Chinese currency (also known in the People's Republic of China as *renminbi*)
Zaibatsu	The great business conglomerates of pre–World War II Japan
Zhong	The Confucian virtue of loyalty (in Chinese)
Zhongguo	The "Central Country" or "Middle Kingdom," that is, China

Introduction

What Is East Asia?

The country with what is probably already now the world's single largest national economy is located in East Asia, and three of the world's five largest economies are also Asian — two of them (China and Japan) specifically East Asian.[1] In addition to having the world's largest economy, the People's Republic of China also now has the world's second largest military budget, and is clearly an emerging superpower. Although not nearly as huge as China, some of the smaller East Asian states such as South Korea can also boast astonishing recent success stories. This is a dramatic reversal of the situation that had prevailed a century ago, when a handful of Western European powers, together with the United States and Russia (with Japan already as an emerging junior player), dominated much of the planet economically, militarily, politically, and even culturally.

A hundred years ago China was a collapsed and failed state, and, within East Asia, Singapore, Taiwan, Korea, and Vietnam were all colonies of foreign powers. Only Japan appeared moderately successful. Even well into the mid-twentieth century, East Asia still remained largely preindustrial, often bitterly poor, and desperately war ravaged. Even Japan, which almost alone in the entire non-Western world had succeeded in asserting itself as a regionally significant modern power by the early 1900s, was left crushed and in ruins by the end of the Second World War in 1945. A fresh start was required in Japan, which gained momentum beginning in the 1960s. Since that time, first South Korea, Taiwan, Hong Kong, and Singapore, then the People's Republic of China, and recently even (to some extent) Vietnam have all joined Japan – though each in characteristically different ways – in achieving dramatic levels of modern economic takeoff. Beyond any doubt, the rise of East Asia has been one of the most important stories of recent world history.

An argument can be made, moreover, that rather than representing some fundamentally unprecedented departure from past human experience, the recent economic strength exhibited by East Asia is really more of a return to normal. For much of history, China – the largest single component of East Asia – enjoyed one of the most developed economies on earth. Especially after the disintegration of the western Roman Empire, for a thousand years beginning around 500 CE

China was probably the wealthiest country in the world, not merely in aggregate total but possibly also in per capita terms. Even as late as the year 1800, when the Industrial Revolution was beginning to dramatically accelerate in Great Britain, China is still estimated to have accounted for a larger share (33.3%) of total world production than all of Europe, including Russia, combined (28.1%).[2]

It is generally acknowledged that such crucial technologies as gunpowder, paper, and printing were all invented in China. Less well known is the fact that gunpowder, paper, and printing actually made a significant impact on China long before those technologies transformed Europe. Paper and printing, especially, helped to make books, and therefore also knowledge, relatively widely available in premodern China. It has been seriously suggested that China may have produced more books than all the rest of the world combined prior to about 1500.[3]

Although, when compared with China, the other countries of premodern East Asia were each much smaller in size – in 1800, China's population may have been roughly 300 million, Japan's perhaps 30 million, Korea's 8 million, and Vietnam's about 7 million – each made its own notable contributions and produced unique variants of East Asian civilization. Korea, for example, pioneered the development of metal moveable-type printing by at least 1234 (although moveable type made of baked clay rather than metal had been experimented with in China as early as the 1040s). Japan, as already mentioned, became perhaps the first non-Western society in the world to successfully modernize. Despite its relatively small size, in the modern era Japan long eclipsed China and became regionally dominant. For much of the late twentieth century Japan was a notably harmonious and peaceful society and the second most important economic power in the entire world, after the United States, and for a while even appeared poised to become "Number One."[4]

Even when East Asia was at its relative poorest and weakest in the early 1900s, it continued to be globally significant. World War II, for example, began in East Asia, at a bridge near Beijing in 1937. Today, there should no longer be any doubt about the region's importance. China is a rising superpower, and although the People's Republic of China actually still remains quite poor and underdeveloped in per capita terms (that is, on average), parts of what is sometimes called "Greater China" compare favorably with conditions almost anywhere else on the planet. Hong Kong, for example, which is now a semiautonomous region of the People's Republic of China, today enjoys a per capita income above the United States. Taiwan and Singapore are both predominantly ethnic Chinese places that have also achieved notable economic success. Singapore's per capita income is substantially higher even than Hong Kong's, and Taiwan's is above Canada and the European Union as a whole.[5] Japan, although it has recently been surpassed by China in terms of the total size of its economy, probably still remains the world's second most fully mature industrialized economy. South Korea is a breathtaking example of a modern success story, and North Korea, while decidedly less prosperous than the south, as an unpredictable and sometimes belligerent nuclear power nonetheless compels global attention. Vietnam has enjoyed rapid economic development in recent decades, and was the scene of much conflict, and a focal point of global attention, in the late twentieth century.

East Asia is therefore a critically important region of the world; but what is East Asia? Asia, in its entirety, is actually not a coherent entity. The concept of Asia is one that we have inherited from the ancient Greeks, who divided the world broadly into two major parts: Europe and Asia. For the Greeks, however, this original Asia meant primarily the Persian Empire. As the scope of Asia expanded beyond Persia and what we now call Asia Minor, Asia came to include so many different cultures and peoples that the label was drained of most of its significance. By the late 1700s, for example, two-thirds of the world's total population and 80 percent of the world's production were all located in Asia. Asia was nothing less than the entire Old World minus Europe. If Asia as a whole is not a very meaningful label, however, the word can still serve as a useful terminological anchor for certain geographic subregions, such as South Asia and East Asia, which do have more historical coherence.[6]

Even these subregions, of course, must still be somewhat arbitrarily defined. Premodern East Asians certainly did not think of themselves as either Asians or East Asians. Today the U.S. State Department lumps Southeast Asia and even Oceania together with East Asia under its Bureau of East Asian and Pacific Affairs. Geographic regions can be defined in many ways, and a variety of labels applied to suit different purposes. In historical terms, however, and especially in consideration of shared premodern culture, East Asia is most usefully defined as that region of the world that came to extensively use the Chinese writing system, and absorbed through those written words many of the ideas and values of what we call Confucianism, much of the associated legal and political structure of government, and certain specifically East Asian forms of Buddhism. At a very mundane level – but actually important in people's everyday lives precisely for that reason – East Asia is distinct as being that part of the world that eats with chopsticks. It is a fundamental premise of this book that East Asia really is a culturally and historically coherent region, deserving attention as a whole, and not just as a random group of neighboring countries or some arbitrary lines on a map.

At the same time, East Asia is also part of a universally shared human experience. One of the most significant recent changes in our understanding of premodern East Asia is a growing realization that it was not traditionally always especially closed and isolated, as was once popularly imagined. There have, indeed, been episodes of isolationism in East Asian history, but they were, if anything, more Early Modern and Modern (notably under certain recent communist regimes) than ancient tradition. Throughout much of history the whole of the Eurasian world was surprisingly interconnected.

For example, images of Heracles – the mythical Greek hero – were replicated across premodern Eurasia as far as China. In the tomb of a man buried in what is now southern Manchuria in 415 CE, archeologists have found both local Chinese and non-Chinese artifacts, the earliest firmly dateable pair of horse stirrups, and five Roman-style glass items that may have originally been crafted on the shores of the Mediterranean. Chinese silks were buried in central Sweden (in western Europe) in the late eighth–early ninth century, together with a small statue of the

Map Introduction.1 East Asia Physical

Buddha that may have come from what is now Pakistan.[7] During the first millennium CE there existed "a common grammar of diplomatic conversations from China to Byzantium," and, with the turn into the second millennium, the Mongol conquests provided a powerful model for successor empires everywhere from the Ottomans on the eastern Mediterranean to the Manchus in China.[8]

Recently, it has even been suggested that premodern China was part of a relatively exposed inner core of the Eurasian Old World, in contrast to the comparatively sheltered periphery occupied by Eurasian extremities such as Europe and Japan.[9] Perhaps it is no coincidence that the pattern of Japanese history – which included a medieval period featuring hereditary warrior elites living in castles and institutions reminiscent of vassalage and the fief – in some ways more closely resembled that of Europe than it did China. This is a healthy reminder, too, that even if we do accept East Asia as a coherent cultural area, it is still a very large region composed of several quite different cultures (each of which contains, furthermore, its own internal sub-differences).

Specifically, East Asia will be defined as today consisting of Greater China (including the People's Republic of China, Hong Kong, Taiwan, and Singapore), Japan, Korea, and Vietnam. Each of these places is different. Two of them may be considered outliers. Singapore is especially remote, located geographically in the midst of Southeast, rather than East, Asia. Because Singapore has a majority Chinese population, however, it can plausibly be considered as a distant outpost of Greater China, and therefore East Asia. Vietnam, meanwhile, also presents something of a borderline case. Although northern Vietnam was long actually part of the Chinese Empire, Vietnam as a whole occupies a transitional zone that straddles both East and Southeast Asia. Something of Vietnam's unique identity is suggested by its old French colonial label, "Indochina."

Despite considerable internal diversity, however, East Asia does have a historical coherence that is roughly equivalent to what we conventionally think of as Western Civilization. The Bronze Age prototype states that first emerged in high antiquity in the region we now call China provided approximately the same kind of core historical legacy for the modern countries of China, Japan, Korea, and Vietnam that ancient Greece and Rome left for modern Italy, France, Britain, Germany, and "the West." This volume, while paying attention to both the larger global interconnections and to local differences, will attempt to present an integrated history of East Asia as a whole. It will also focus somewhat unusually closely on that period in the first millennium CE when a coherent East Asian cultural region first emerged (and which happens, perhaps not entirely coincidentally, to be chronologically parallel to the period that also witnessed what has been called "the birth of Europe"[10]).

It should be emphasized that no "civilization" is a permanently fixed concrete reality. What we call civilizations are merely abstractions that people imagine around certain historical continuities and agglomerations that seem to us to be significant. Borders are always permeable, all cultures interact and exchange both artifacts and ideas, and multiple nested layers of distinction can be discerned everywhere within what is ultimately a single global human community.

In the present age of globalization, moreover, all such regional civilizational differences are to some extent blurring. Since the beginning of the twentieth century, many of the features that made East Asia East Asian, such as the unique writing system, Confucianism, and traditional-style monarchies, have been sometimes quite self-consciously challenged, rejected, or abandoned in the name of either (or both) universal modernization or local nationalism. The various nations of modern East Asia are today, in some ways, both more different from each other and, at the same time, paradoxically, more like every other successful modern country on the planet than may have been the case (at the level of the educated elite anyway) in premodern times. It may be well asked, therefore, how relevant the East Asian cultural region still is.

One answer is that East Asia's disproportionate recent economic success, by itself, suggests there is still something distinctive about the region. Some analysts have even invoked a "Confucian work ethic" to explain the East Asian "miracle."[11] While there are good reasons for maintaining a healthy dose of skepticism concerning any simplistic Confucian explanations for East Asian dynamism – starting with the fact that Confucianism itself is a rather nebulous concept – East Asian success has been exceptional, and is reason enough alone to take East Asia seriously. And, although access to modern Western technologies and the enormous U.S. consumer market was certainly an early key to export-led Pacific Rim economic growth, the East Asian nations have all more recently become each other's largest trading partners, and often enthusiastic consumers of each other's modern pop culture. In the post-Cold War era the East Asian region may, to some extent, even be recoalescing.

This in no way diminishes the East Asian countries' simultaneously accelerating participation in the larger global community, or the attraction of American and Western pop culture, nor does it eliminate internal East Asian rivalries. Hostilities in East Asia are frequently internal. Yet, the ghost of a long-shared logographic writing system does still hover over the region. The various East Asian languages all have extensively shared vocabularies. China, Japan, Korea, and Vietnam are each different countries having distinctive cultures, but they literally share many of the same words and ideas. South Korea, for example, is a thoroughly modern, Westernized country with especially close ties to the United States, which is nonetheless also sometimes considered the "most Confucian" country in Asia.

If East Asia is arguably still at least a moderately coherent cultural region today, on the other hand, it has also always been internally diverse. Not only are the major nations of East Asia sharply different from each other, but each nation also contains within itself cascading layers of internal differences. And East Asia has changed greatly over time, too, most obviously and abruptly in the modern period but also throughout history. There was no timeless, traditional continuity in premodern East Asia.

As an illustration of this ongoing process of change, we might ask ourselves a surprising question: how old is China? It is often supposed that Chinese civilization is the oldest continuously existing civilization in the world, having emerged out of the late Stone Age (the Neolithic), flowered into the full glory of Bronze Age civilization beginning as early as 2000 BCE, and survived thereafter without interruption to the present day. In fact, there is some truth to this popular story. Though it may be difficult to pinpoint many aspects of late Stone Age culture that can still be observed today (silk, a preference for pork among meats, and the cultivation of rice are some long-standing Chinese cultural markers), it is highly significant that the very first writing samples to be found in the area of China, dating to approximately 1200 BCE, were already written in an archaic version of the same Chinese language, and the same Chinese writing system, that is still used today. In this sense, China is very old indeed.

The earliest books written in that Chinese language, produced over the course of the last thousand years BCE, formed the nucleus of a deeply cherished literary canon that remained continuously fundamental to what we call Chinese civilization, at least until the start of the twentieth century. During the course of that same formative last millennium BCE, a discernible consciousness of being Chinese (called *Huaxia*), in opposition to neighboring alien peoples (referred to by various Chinese names), may also be said to have emerged. Thus, the Warring States of the late Zhou era (403–221 BCE), though each were independent sovereign countries, could also all be described as being different Chinese kingdoms surrounded by various non-Chinese peoples.

After the Qin unification of these Warring States into the first empire in 221 BCE, an enduring ideal of political unity under a single centralized imperial government was firmly planted. Although China's subsequent remarkable record of unity is sometimes explained in terms of presumed ethnic and cultural homogeneity (it is too easy to assume that the Chinese are naturally unified because, after all, "they are all Chinese"), it may well really have been more the other way around: China's present-day relative ethnic and cultural homogeneity is the end product of millennia of political unity. Certainly the early Chinese Empire's population was quite mixed.

Even after that first imperial unification in 221 BCE, moreover, China continued to change. There have been roughly eighty historically recognized premodern dynasties in the place we call China (although only about a dozen or so were truly major dynasties). Each dynasty was in some sense a separate state. Many had identifiably non-Chinese rulers. In addition, China has also undergone repeated periods of division since that first imperial unification, and even during extended periods of unity, fashions still changed. As Guo Maoqian (fl. 1264–1269) observed in the thirteenth century, "folk songs and national customs also have a new sound each generation."[12] Premodern China was far from static.

If China can be called an ancient civilization, at the other extreme it is also possible to argue that the very concept of a Chinese "nation" did not even exist until about 1900. It is generally believed that the nation-state is an invention of the modern West, and certainly the Chinese word for nation (*minzu*, designating a "people" rather than a country or state) was imported into the Chinese language only at the end of the nineteenth century.[13] China first attempted to reconfigure itself as a modern Western-style nation-state only with the overthrow of the empire and establishment of the Republic of China (ROC) in 1912. Moreover, the specific country that most of us think of today as "China," which is formally known as the People's Republic of China (PRC), dates only from 1949. Nor was this merely a new name for an old reality: in the entire history of the planet there can have been few revolutionary ruptures that were intended to be as total and sweeping as that of the New China following its 1949 "liberation." In hindsight, of course, many of the revolutionary changes imposed after 1949 did not prove to be very durable, and in recent years, there has even been some revival of older traditions; yet, the PRC still does mark a sharp break in the continuity of history.

Even the word China is itself, literally, not Chinese. The English word China probably derives from the Sanskrit (Indian) word *Cīna*, which in turn may have derived from the name of the important northwestern frontier Chinese kingdom and the first imperial dynasty, Qin. Not only did the Chinese people not call themselves Chinese, moreover, it could be argued that there was no precise native-language equivalent term at all, at least before modern times. One distinguished scholar has even gone so far as to claim that the concept and word China simply "did not exist, except as an alien fiction."[14]

To be sure, as already mentioned, the ancient Chinese certainly did have some reasonably coherent self-conceptions. The names by which early Chinese people identified themselves were frequently those of specific kingdoms or imperial dynasties, such as Qin, Chu, or Han, but there were also a few more all-encompassing ancient Chinese-language words that we might reasonably translate into English as "China" or "Chinese," such as *Huaxia* and *Zhongguo*. Even these, however, were not perfectly synonymous with the English word China. Initially, *Huaxia* seems to have been a somewhat elastic cultural marker, referring neither to race nor ethnicity nor any particular country but rather to "civilized," settled, literate, agricultural populations adhering to common ritual standards, in contrast to "barbarians."[15]

Zhongguo – "the central country" (or "countries," since the Chinese language has no grammatical distinction between singular and plural), a term which is often quaintly rendered as the "Middle Kingdom" – in a somewhat similar manner also contrasts the civilized countries in the center against an outer fringe of barbarians. Initially this term *Zhongguo* may have referred only to the royal capital city. Somewhat later, during the Warring States period, *Zhongguo* definitely had to be understood as plural, because there were multiple "central" countries then. This term *Zhongguo* long remained more of a geographic description rather than a proper name, referring simply to the countries in what was imagined to be the center of the world: the Central Plain in north China. Even as late as the third and fourth centuries CE, some five hundred years after the first imperial unification in 221 BCE, the entire southern half of what we would think of today as China Proper could still be explicitly excluded from the *Zhongguo*. After the northern conquest of the southern state of Wu (whose capital was the city that is today called Nanjing, just upriver from modern Shanghai) in 280 CE, for example, a children's verse predicted that someday "*Zhongguo* [the north] will be defeated and Wu [in the south] shall rise again."[16]

Today, *Zhongguo* is probably the closest Chinese-language equivalent to the English word China. Even so, both the modern People's Republic, on the mainland, and the Republic of China (confined to the island of Taiwan since 1949) are still officially known, not as *Zhongguo*, but by a hybrid combination of the two ancient terms *Zhongguo* and *Huaxia*: *Zhonghua*.

Many outsiders today find the implicit conceit that China is the "Middle Kingdom" alternately either offensively arrogant or simply ridiculous. Such ethnocentricity was hardly unique to ancient China, however. Nearly all early civilizations viewed themselves as occupying the center of the world. While China may be a little unusual in having this ancient conceit preserved in a name that is still used today, our own name for the Mediterranean Sea also comes originally from a Latin expression meaning "middle of the earth." We have merely become accustomed to the name, no longer understand much Latin, and have forgotten what it means.

Furthermore, it was Westerners who more literally referred to foreigners as barbarians. Barbarian is an English word that derives from an ancient Greek expression for those unintelligible "bar-bar" noises emitted by strangers who were so uncivilized as not to speak Greek. Not only did the ancient Chinese (quite naturally) not use this Greek word, there was no native word in classical Chinese that was exactly equivalent to it. There are, indeed, several Chinese terms that are commonly loosely translated into English as "barbarian," but this (as is often the case with translations) is a little misleading. More precisely, they are all generic Chinese names for various non-Chinese peoples. The word Yi, for example, was used for non-Chinese peoples in the east. Such names were often no more authentic than the name "Indian" that was mistakenly applied by early modern Europeans to the natives of the Americas, yet like the term American Indian they remain fundamentally names rather than words meaning "barbarian."[17]

If China is not a Chinese name, then, what about our familiar names for the other East Asian countries? The English word Japan is actually a distorted version, via Malay, of the Chinese pronunciation (*Riben* in current standard Mandarin, which can also be written *Jih-pen* using an older spelling system) of the two-character name that in Japanese is pronounced *Nihon* (or *Nippon*). This name *Nihon* – the "Origin of the Sun" – is, however, a genuine early native Japanese name for Japan, although one that could probably only have been conceived from a vantage point outside of Japan, further west, and that may have been first used by immigrants to Japan from the continent. The name was apparently consciously adopted by the Japanese court in the late seventh century for the favorable meaning of its written characters.[18]

In some ways it could be argued that Japan has been less chimerical as a country and has displayed more historical continuity since antiquity than China. Unlike China, Japan has never suffered foreign conquest. Since the dawn of reliably recorded history, Japan has had, quite uniquely in the entire world, only one ruling family. There has been only one Japanese dynasty, in contrast to China's roughly eighty dynasties and two post-dynastic republics. Yet, on the other hand, Japanese emperors have rarely wielded much real power, court and emperor have often been quite irrelevant to the overall history of the Japanese islands, and Japan, too, has been divided. Much Japanese "tradition" is, moreover, not really very ancient, and much of it ultimately can be traced to foreign origins. Japanese Zen Buddhism, for example, is an especially Chinese form of what was originally an Indian religion. The quintessentially Japanese art of the tea ceremony (*chanoyu*) was born only in the late fifteenth century (although the Japanese had learned to drink tea, from China, centuries earlier). *Sushi*, as we know it, "began as a street snack in nineteenth-century Edo-era Tokyo." The Japanese national sport of *jūdō* was invented, as such, only toward the end of the nineteenth century – and by the same man who would also serve as Japan's first member of the International Olympic Committee. Even the Japanese nation-state itself arguably only took its final shape during the nineteenth century.[19]

As for Korea, the English name derives from that of the Koryŏ Dynasty (918–1392), which in turn was an abbreviation of the name of an even older northern kingdom called Koguryŏ (roughly first-century 668 CE). In this respect, our English name Korea somewhat resembles the probable derivation of our name for China from the early dynastic name Qin. Just as Qin is not quite entirely synonymous with China, neither is Koryŏ exactly the same thing as Korea. Today, North Koreans prefer to invoke the memory of the oldest legendary Korean kingdom, Chosŏn, while South Koreans are inclined to use the name Han'guk, the "Country of the Han," the name of the peoples who were the inhabitants of the southern parts of the Korean peninsula in the early historical period. (The Chinese today are also called the Han people, but this is an entirely different word Han, written 漢, which just happens to sound like the Korean Han 韓.) Although Korea is today an exceptionally good example of an ethnically homogeneous modern nation-state (marred by political and ideological division, north vs. south, since 1945), it can be argued that Korea, as such, never really existed prior to the first unification of the peninsula under native rule in 668.

Vietnam is more of an authentic native-language name than either China, Japan, or Korea, but the story of how it got that name may still come as something of a surprise. The name was first proposed from Beijing in 1803. Prior to that time, it had commonly been called Annam, or Dai Viet (Great Viet), among other names. The new nineteenth-century name Vietnam was intended to evoke the glorious memory of an independent ancient (ca. 207–111 BCE) kingdom called Southern Viet (pronounced *Nam Viet* in Vietnamese and *Nan Yue* in modern Mandarin Chinese). Because the capital of that ancient Southern Viet kingdom had been located at the site of the modern city of Guangzhou (English: Canton), in what is now China, however, it did not seem entirely proper to revive it in 1803 for the name of a country lying south of China's border. The old name was therefore altered slightly by changing it from Southern Viet to South of Viet, an adjustment that was achieved in both Vietnamese and Chinese simply by transposing the word order from *Nam Viet* to *Viet Nam* (Mandarin: *Yue Nan*).[20]

The reason why the capital of the ancient kingdom of Southern Viet was located north of modern Vietnam in what is now China, meanwhile, was because the earliest Bronze Age kingdom that was called Viet (Mandarin: *Yue*), from which all of these names presumably ultimately derived, had been located even farther north, in the vicinity of the modern Chinese province of Zhejiang, almost halfway up the coast of what is today China. Early Chinese texts, in fact, referred to most of what is now southeast China as the land of the "Hundred Viets."

This story helps illustrate just how far from being static and unchanging traditional East Asia actually was. Not only was Vietnam a new name in 1803, but the full assemblage of territory and ethnic groups that now make up Vietnam was also new at the time. The original Annam, or Dai Viet, had been confined to the north, and the southward extension of the country since the sixteenth century has been described as creating "the least coherent territory in the world."[21]

To suggest that Vietnam did not exist before the nineteenth century is, of course, at some levels as absurd as trying to claim that China did not exist until modern times either. Yet in fact, neither China nor Vietnam really had existed previously under precisely their present names and current configurations, despite their genuinely ancient pedigrees. No country, people, or civilization exists unchanged forever. These are dynamic ancient streams that have continually been renewed. History is all about change, and East Asia has experienced as much change as almost any comparable region. This is the story of East Asian history.

For Further Reading

Different ways of defining "East Asia" are discussed in the introduction to John H. Miller, *Modern East Asia: An Introductory History* (Armonk, NY: M. E. Sharpe, 2008). A particularly valuable collection of essays addressing East Asia as a coherent cultural area is Gilbert Rozman, ed., *The East Asian Region: Confucian Heritage and Its Modern Adaptation* (Princeton University Press, 1991). For a fascinating, although now somewhat dated, exploration of how China and Asia have been geographically conceived by Western minds, see Andrew L. March, *The Idea of China: Myth and Theory in Geographical Thought* (New York: Praeger, 1974).

Standard surveys of East Asian history include Warren I. Cohen, *East Asia at the Center: Four Thousand Years of Engagement with the World* (New York: Columbia University Press, 2001); Patricia Buckley Ebrey, Anne Walthall, and James B. Palais, *East Asia: A Cultural, Social, and Political History* (Boston: Houghton Mifflin, 2006); John K. Fairbank, Edwin O. Reischauer, and Albert M. Craig, *East Asia: Tradition and Transformation*, rev. ed. (Boston: Houghton Mifflin, 1989); and Conrad Schirokauer, Miranda Brown, David Lurie, and Suzanne Gay, *A Brief History of Chinese and Japanese Civilization*, 3rd ed. (United States: Wadsworth, 2006).

1 The Origins of Civilization in East Asia

"Out of Africa": The First East Asians

According to a now lost *Old Record* cited in the thirteenth-century Korean history *Memorabilia of the Three Kingdoms* (*Samguk yusa*), the divinity Hwanung descended from heaven to Mount T'aebaek, a sacred peak at the source of the Yalu and Tumen rivers on the border between present-day Korea and China, where he mated with a she-bear he had helped transfigure into human shape. From their union was born the great Lord Tan'gun, supposedly in the year 2333 BCE, who founded the country known as Old Chosŏn and who is widely celebrated today as the father of the Korean nation.

Meanwhile, according to a quite different *Record of Ancient Matters* (the Japanese *Kojiki*, compiled in 712 CE), the grandson of the sun goddess Amaterasu was sent down to earth from heaven, bearing the three sacred Japanese imperial regalia – the curved *magatama* bead, bronze mirror, and sword – to become the founder of the Japanese imperial line (the same line that still occupies the Chrysanthemum throne in Tōkyō today) and the origin of the Japanese nation.

Much earlier, in China, various ancient royal houses also typically claimed divine or miraculous origins, although Western scholars have generally been more impressed by the relative absence of important creation myths from the dawn of Chinese history. The traditional version of China's story begins, instead, with a more apparently human age of (legendary) cultural heroes, starting with Fuxi (supposedly dating from 2852 BCE), who first domesticated animals; Shennong (from 2737 BCE), who invented farming; and the Yellow Emperor (ruling from 2697 BCE), who is popularly viewed as the ancestor of the Chinese people.

Though the Japanese emperor officially renounced his divinity after World War II, in 1946, and few people today are likely to believe literally the story of Japanese imperial descent from the sun goddess, some of these myths and legends are still quite charming.[1] It is doubtful, however, that many nonnatives, coming from different religious and cultural traditions, ever gave much literal credence to such stories of divine descent. Early modern Europeans, for example, brought their own quite different sets of expectations about possible East Asian origins. Not untypically, in a book published in Amsterdam in 1667, Athanasius Kircher speculated that the Chinese must have descended from the biblical Noah's son Ham, via Egypt, which would have also explained the apparent (but very superficial) similarity between Chinese writing and Egyptian hieroglyphics.[2]

Even after Europeans became better informed about East Asia, the theory that civilization must have diffused to China (and everywhere else) from a common universal point of origin somewhere in the Middle East long continued to be widely accepted. The implication that all civilization originated in the West (even though this was a "West" whose history began, strangely enough, in the Fertile Crescent that is now Iraq and Egypt) and that all non-Western native peoples must therefore have been incapable of achieving civilization on their own was understandably rather offensive to many non-Westerners. As new archeological evidence mounted steadily over the course of the twentieth century that Bronze Age civilization in China was actually very ancient and showed little evidence of direct importation from the West, an opposing theory of almost completely independent indigenous origin came to be preferred by many scholars. A classic 1975 study by Ping-ti Ho, for example, famously labeled China the "Cradle of the East," in conscious parallel to the so-called Cradle of (Western) Civilization in the Fertile Crescent of Egypt and Mesopotamia.[3]

It was probably always a mistake, though, to assume that the only option was a binary choice between diffusion from a single common source or entirely independent local development. In fact, these are not necessarily mutually exclusive alternatives. People have always traveled and communicated across sometimes vast distances, yet it is also true that movement was usually extremely slow and difficult in antiquity, and local communities, especially if they are relatively distant and isolated, naturally do develop independently. The most likely explanation for all the different historical civilizations of the world is a combination of common ultimate human origins and multiple ongoing processes of local diversification and exchange, in a process of interaction that has been described as "not so much diffusion as dialectic."[4]

New breakthroughs in the science of genetics, especially the study of mitochondrial DNA, make it seem increasingly likely that all modern human beings everywhere throughout the world share relatively recent common ancestors and are closely related. A currently influential theory is that modern humans spread across the planet from a shared ancestral homeland in Africa only within the last one hundred thousand years. From carbon-14 dating, we know that modern humans had reached eastern Eurasia by at least 25,000 BCE and possibly as early as fifty to sixty thousand years ago. Even leading scientific skeptics of this *out of Africa theory* acknowledge that entirely independent origins for different human populations are improbable, and suggest instead merely that local human variations developed over a much longer period of time within a loose network of genetic exchanges sufficient to maintain the overall commonality of the human species.

Globally, then, there were three major centers of late Stone Age (Neolithic) cultural development based on the critical breakthrough to agriculture: one in western Eurasia, involving wheat and barley; one in eastern Eurasia, involving rice and millet; and one in the Americas, based on maize (corn). Within eastern Eurasia, in turn, there were also multiple local late Stone Age cultures. These cultures, furthermore, did not necessarily align with modern national borders. It is misleadingly anachronistic to think of these Stone Age peoples as already being Chinese, Korean, Vietnamese, or Japanese, for example.

Merely within the territory that we think of now as China proper, there was much local variation, and also a very significant broad division between north and south. The peoples of the south cultivated rice – by at least 8000 BCE in the lower Yangzi River valley – were fond of boats, tended to elevate their houses above ground level on posts, produced pottery with impressed geometric designs, and probably spoke languages more closely related to those now spoken in Southeast Asia than to modern Chinese.

The peoples in the north, meanwhile, centering especially around the Yellow River valley and what is commonly called the Central Plain, grew millet and often lived in houses dug partially below ground level, perhaps for insulation purposes. At least some of these northern peoples must have spoken an early form of the Chinese language. The most famous of these northern cultural complexes (dating from about 5000 BCE) is called Yangshao by modern archeologists and is known for its vividly decorated "painted pottery."

Along the northernmost fringe, roughly in the region now called Inner Mongolia, the climate apparently became somewhat colder and drier beginning around 1500 BCE, and the peoples living there gradually turned away from agriculture toward the raising of livestock. Animals that can graze, feeding themselves by eating wild grass, such as sheep and cattle, began to predominate over the pigs that have traditionally provided the staple meat in the Chinese diet, but which cannot graze and require the support of an agricultural society. As mastery of the technique of horseback riding – apparently first achieved in the western reaches of that great belt of grassland called the steppe, stretching from the Hungarian Plain in Europe eastward to Mongolia – finally spread to the vicinity of China, perhaps by roughly 500 BCE, these northern peoples became true pastoral nomads.

These livestock-raising nomads became the great cultural Other, and frequent military opponent, of the Chinese people for most of premodern history. Many of these nomads actually lived within the borders of what is now China, however, in Inner Mongolia, and sometimes even farther south in China proper. The nomads interacted in a dynamic fashion with the agriculturally based Chinese civilization, forming what could alternatively even be conceived of as a single system with two opposing poles. Nomads, or at least semi-nomadic peoples, provided not a few of the ruling families of Chinese imperial dynasties. Clearly, despite their sharp differences, the pastoral nomads of Inner Mongolia and the farmers of northern China were historically bound together.

On the Korean peninsula, meanwhile, there were also multiple prehistoric cultures – some overlapping with Manchuria, in what is now China. By the end of Korean prehistory, there are also tantalizing hints of connections with the Japanese islands. What appears today to be the striking homogeneity of Korean national identity was probably originally "forged from diverse elements."[5] This present-day Korean cultural uniformity, furthermore, did not really coalesce until relatively late. Although rice cultivation was known on the Korean peninsula by at least 1000 BCE, and bronze metalworking appeared perhaps a few centuries later, the details of Korean history remain largely a mystery until the peninsula began to be mentioned in Chinese documents of the early imperial era.

Some time before those first documentary references, people from the Korean peninsula had probably begun crossing the straits south into the Japanese islands. Much earlier still, Japan may have once been connected to the mainland of Asia by a land bridge, and there may have also been some ancient maritime connections between Japan and Southeast Asia. Certainly there were humans on the Japanese islands from very early times. Japan is notable, in fact, for having produced some of the earliest known pottery on earth, from around 11,000 BCE. Yet the population of Japan in the late Stone Age always remained sparse – probably never numbering more than roughly a quarter million people throughout the islands – and extensive farming and metalworking did not appear in the Japanese islands until as late as about 300 BCE. The relatively sudden surge of major new developments after that time is associated with new arrivals from the Korean peninsula. As is the case with Korea, moreover, the earliest written description of Japan appears in a Chinese text, this one dating from the third century CE.

If all modern human beings share common ancestors, and if there has always been more contact and exchange between different population groups than is sometimes imagined, it is also the case that in antiquity mobility was commonly limited, especially for agricultural peoples bound to farmland. Everywhere there was much local independent cultural development. Within the Eurasian Old World, East Asia became a uniquely separate cultural zone. One particularly visible emblem of East Asian distinctiveness was the use throughout East Asia in pre-modern times of a writing system (a script) that is strikingly different from the Middle Eastern-derived alphabets and phonetic spelling systems that eventually came to be used everywhere else in the world.

East Asian Languages and Writing Systems

"Far more than princes, states or economies, it is language-communities who are the real players in world history," writes Nicholas Ostler.[6] It has been observed that the same Old English word that meant "people" or "nation" could also indicate "language."[7] Languages are frequently central to the self-identification of human communities (and a primary barrier to communication with others), and they constitute a vital piece of the story of East Asian civilization. Indeed, the most Chinese thing about China may very well be the language. Some basic understanding of the languages of East Asia is therefore fundamental at the outset, even though these languages are by definition foreign to native speakers of English, and any discussion of language runs the risk of quickly becoming dauntingly technical. I will try to keep it simple.

Map 1.1 Language Families, Languages, and Major Dialects of Chinese

The languages of East Asia break into separate national traditions: Chinese, Japanese, Korean, and Vietnamese. Far from being unified by its languages, East Asia is divided into four major national language systems, which are further torn between at least three wholly different language families. Each of these language families, furthermore, extends beyond the borders of East Asia. It is not the languages as spoken, but the language as written – the shared use in premodern times of a common writing system and, to a surprising degree, even a common written language – that gives East Asia much of its cultural coherence and distinctiveness as a region.

The Chinese and Japanese languages, for example, could hardly be more different. Japanese is polysyllabic, with words compounded out of simple basic syllables piled up in an agglutinative manner to make sophisticated grammatical distinctions, such as the distinction between currently doing something and having done it in the past. Perhaps its most distinctive feature is that Japanese is a *respect language* (*keigo*), meaning that word endings and honorific particles are used to indicate the relative status of speaker and listener, and also the degree of formality or informality. For example, *benkyō-shite-imasu* is a formal way of saying "I am studying," while *benkyō-shite-iru* is a more informal way of saying the same thing. Grammatical particles are also used to mark the different parts of a sentence. A typical Japanese sentence pattern takes the form subject-*wa*/ object-*o*/ verb (e.g., "I *wa*/ book *o*/ read"), with the verb invariably coming at the end.

Chinese is almost the opposite. The word order is closer to English, with the verb coming before the object (e.g., "I read [a] book"). The Chinese language is completely uninflected, having no tenses or plurals or any grammatical modification of word endings whatsoever. Chinese is also not a respect language, at least not in the Japanese sense of having status relationships built into its very grammar (although it is, of course, possible to speak respectfully in Chinese). And Chinese is monosyllabic, to the extent that every Chinese character (written symbol), without exception, is pronounced as a single syllable and is a discrete unit of meaning.

In practice, however, Modern Chinese usually then constructs the equivalent of longer compound words from combinations of two or three characters. For example, the familiar Chinese place name Tiananmen is written with three characters: *tian* 天 (heaven), *an* 安 (peace), and *men* 門 (gate), or the "Gate of Heavenly Peace." (*Tiananmen Square* adds two more characters: *guang* 廣, meaning "broad" or "spacious," and *chang* 場, meaning "an area of level ground.") Although, conceptually, we may regard *Tiananmen* as one word (and *Tiananmen Square* as two), written Chinese characters are never clustered into word groupings separated by spaces: each individual character always occupies a roughly equal square or rectangular space on the page. Traditionally, Chinese was written in vertical columns from top to bottom and then moving from right to left. Beginning as early as the late nineteenth century, the Western direction of writing, horizontally from left to right, has become increasingly common, but even today is still not universal.

Spoken Chinese is also notably different from Japanese (and English) in being a *tonal language*; that is, in speech (but not in writing), the pitch or tone with which a particular syllable is pronounced determines the word. Modern Mandarin, the standard dialect, has four tones and an additional neutral tone. Some dialects have more.

There are multiple regional dialects of Chinese. Some of these dialects are, furthermore, not mutually intelligible. They can sometimes be as different from each other as English and German – which we generally regard as being entirely separate languages rather than dialects of a single Germanic tongue. Partly for this reason, some specialists reject the label "dialects" altogether as a misleading designation for the regional varieties of Chinese speech, preferring instead something more neutral such as *regionalects* or *topolects* (from the Greek *topos*, meaning "place").[8]

As just one example of the possibilities for linguistic complexity, a solid majority (roughly 69%) of the inhabitants of the island of Taiwan today speak as their mother tongue a dialect (or topolect, if you prefer) that is technically called Southern Min and that originated in Fujian Province (on the mainland directly across the straits) but that is now usually simply called Taiwanese. This Taiwanese dialect is incomprehensible to speakers of the Mandarin that has officially been promoted on Taiwan since 1945 as the (literally so-called) National Language (*guoyu*). Perhaps another 15 percent of the current inhabitants of Taiwan are native speakers of yet another significantly different dialect called Hakka. In addition, there are also still a number of speakers of entirely non-Chinese aboriginal languages on the island.

Meanwhile, Hakka is also spoken in other places on the Chinese mainland, and Taiwanese remains at least very similar to the language spoken directly across the straits in its place of origin in Fujian Province on the mainland. Fujian dialects are also widespread among the overseas Chinese communities living scattered throughout Southeast Asia, while Fujian Province itself is home to some of the most extreme dialectical variety in all China. In general, the major variant dialects of Chinese are concentrated in the southeastern coastal region.

This all makes the linguistic situation in China seem more confusing than it really is, however. Passably standard Mandarin is now spoken almost everywhere throughout the Chinese world, and despite the sometimes bewildering diversity of local dialects (or topolects), the most remarkable feature of the Chinese spoken language overall may actually be its surprising uniformity. It has been said that nowhere else in the entire premodern world "has there ever been a linguistic unity like that of North China."[9] Some three-quarters of all Chinese people, especially in the north and west, are native speakers of a relatively uniform version of the language that we call Mandarin (in English; in Chinese it is generally referred to as either *putonghua*, "the common speech," or *guoyu*, the "national language"). The Mandarin dialect of Chinese is, in fact, by far the most commonly spoken native tongue in the world today, with approximately nine hundred million speakers. In contrast to this Chinese uniformity, consider the still highly varied linguistic map of Europe.

All the various local versions of Chinese are then, more broadly, sometimes said to belong to a larger Sino-Tibetan language family, which distantly links the

Chinese languages to Tibetan, Burmese, and certain other languages extending beyond East Asia. Within East Asia, the major contrast with this Sino-Tibetan language family is presented by Japanese and Korean, which are both sometimes said to belong to yet another, somewhat hypothetical Altaic (or Ural-Altaic) language family that extends in a belt across the north, stretching as far west as Europe, and that notably includes Manchu, Mongolic, Turkic, and possibly even Finnish.

Japanese is certainly closer to Korean than it is to any other living language. It is possible that the two may have split from a common original ancestral tongue, although, if so, they had already become mutually distinct by the dawn of the historical period, and their similarities today should not be exaggerated. Japanese, in turn, even today still includes some distinctive local dialects. The *Ōsaka-ben*, or Ōsaka dialect, sometimes heard on the streets of Japan's second largest city in the west of the main island, for example, remains different from the standard Japanese that is based on the dialect of Tōkyō in the east. Of all modern East Asian nations, Korea today may be the most homogeneous, but even in Korea, one third-century Chinese description specified that, at that time, the people living in the southeastern corner of the Korean peninsula spoke a language that was not the same as what was spoken in the southwest of the peninsula.[10]

If Japanese and Korean belong to the Altaic language family, and Chinese belongs to the Sino-Tibetan, the Vietnamese language is classified as Austroasiatic. Originally, not only Vietnam but also much of what is now southeast China may have been inhabited by speakers of languages ancestral to those spoken today in Southeast Asia, and beyond. These languages must have gradually been displaced from southeast China by the spread of Chinese, leaving behind as a residue only perhaps a contribution to the dialectical complexity of southeast China and a substratum of vocabulary items such as the word commonly used for "river" in south China, *jiang* (as in the *Yangzi jiang*, or "Yangtze River"), which contrasts with the standard northern Chinese word for river, *he* (as in the *Huang he*, or "Yellow River").[11]

East Asia is therefore split between three radically different major language families as well as four modern national languages and multiple regional dialects (not to mention some completely different other languages spoken by ethnic minorities). One linguistic feature that all of premodern East Asia shared exclusively in common, however, and that served as a powerful unifying bond, was extensive use of the Chinese writing system.

Globally, the use of written symbols to represent spoken words probably first began in Mesopotamia around 3400 BCE. The idea seems to have been independently reinvented in nearby Egypt not long thereafter. (Ancient Egypt and Mesopotamia, despite close proximity, remained strikingly different civilizations.) In China, writing did not first appear until much later, around 1200 BCE, about the time of the siege of Troy immortalized by Homer. Despite its relatively late date, however, the Chinese script seems to have been another case of independent invention.

All of the world's pristinely invented earliest writing systems – Mesopotamian cuneiform, Egyptian hieroglyphics, Chinese, and Mayan – can technically be described as *logographic*, in the sense that they were not primarily phonetic systems but represented instead the meaning of words as much as their sound. Chinese characters (called *hanzi* in Chinese, which simply means "Chinese characters") may have begun with greatly simplified, highly abstract pictures of the things they represented. The limitations of a pictographic writing system must have very soon become apparent, however, and the overwhelming majority of Chinese characters quickly came to have both a component vaguely indicating pronunciation and another component suggesting approximate meaning, such as having something to do with a hand, a mouth, water, fire, fish, and so on.

The most complete Chinese dictionaries today list nearly fifty thousand different characters, but standard desktop dictionaries commonly include only around seven thousand. Many of the characters in even these shorter dictionaries are rarely used, and functional literacy can be achieved with mastery of only a few thousand. In Japan, in 1946, the government issued an official list of 1,850 approved characters (known as the *Tōyō Kanji* list) that were intended to be sufficient for all uses. Compared to the much smaller number of symbols used in an alphabet, however, even the shortest feasible list of Chinese characters clearly poses a daunting task to memorize. The undeniable difficulty of learning the system has not prevented users of the Chinese script from achieving relatively high literacy rates in both premodern and modern eras, however, nor has it posed an insuperable obstacle to producing some of the world's finest works of literature. And it can be argued that the system does have certain inherent strengths.

There is a natural tendency to assume that the early logographic writing systems, such as Chinese, cuneiform, or hieroglyphics, represent an early stage in some universal linear progression toward the evolution of an alphabet. A glaring problem with this assumption, however, is that none of these early logographic scripts apparently ever actually did evolve directly into a purely phonetic writing system. In both the Middle East and East Asia, instead, the development of phonetic writing systems seems to have occurred only when the existing logographic scripts had to be adapted by other peoples to write languages other than the ones for which they were originally developed.[12]

In the classic instance, the original alphabet was probably invented sometime before 1500 BCE by scribes in Canaan or Byblos, along the eastern shore of the Mediterranean Sea, who were familiar with Egyptian (and possibly also cuneiform) and were attempting to devise a system more suitable than Egyptian for writing their own language. From this original Canaanite alphabet, the better-known Phoenician alphabet was soon derived (by 1000 BCE) and eventually also the Greek and Roman, Arabic, and Indian scripts and most of the other phonetic scripts that are still used in the world today.[13] In East Asia, phonetic writing systems were similarly also spun off from logographic Chinese, as both the Japanese and the Koreans eventually devised new scripts to write their own radically different languages. (In Vietnam, French missionaries, and later French colonial authorities, introduced the Roman alphabet directly from Europe.)

Most of the world's other original ancient logographic writing systems – cuneiform, hieroglyphics, and Mayan – have since fallen out of circulation, along with their associated languages. The ancient Egyptian language, for example, while it may still tenuously survive in the form of Coptic, has long since been replaced by Arabic as the national language of Egypt. But the Chinese language is not only still widely spoken, it is actually the most commonly spoken native language in the world today. There has been, accordingly, little need for the Chinese to abandon their own original writing system, which is well suited to their language.

In China, during the centuries before the first imperial unification in 221 BCE, somewhat variant regional forms of the written characters did emerge, but imperial unification thereafter standardized the writing system, and the civil service examination system that became a defining institution of late imperial China solidified and stabilized the educational curriculum to a remarkable degree, at least at the elite level. The written word, in Chinese characters, came to hold immense prestige.

In the early twentieth century, as China's status as the preeminent regional power was dramatically challenged by the industrialized modern West, China was plunged into a period of profound cultural crisis, and various Western models sometimes appeared irresistible. Many would-be modernizers, including even the communist leader Mao Zedong, at times came to the conclusion that alphabetization of Chinese writing must be an inevitable part of modernization. In the end, however, although a standardized system of spelling Chinese using our Roman alphabet (called *pinyin*) was officially approved for educational and other limited applications, all that was actually accomplished after the establishment of the People's Republic in 1949 was the simplification, to reduce the total number of strokes necessary to write them, of over two thousand characters in the 1950s and 1960s. For example, *Hanyu* (which means the "Chinese language") was simplified from 漢語 to 汉语.

In hindsight, even simplification may not have really made the system very much simpler, because it created a need for well-educated persons to learn both the old forms (which are still used in Taiwan, Hong Kong, by many overseas Chinese, and, of course, in old books) and the new forms, and because a reduction in the number of pen strokes only makes them easier to write, not easier to read, and has become somewhat irrelevant in the more recent age of computer-generated word processing. In any event, the logographic writing system still survives today in twenty-first-century China and seems to be, if anything, less seriously threatened now than it was a half-century ago.

In view of how completely different the other East Asian languages are from Chinese, it may be more remarkable not that they eventually moved away from the Chinese writing system but how tenaciously they clung to it. One modern scholar even jokes, for example, that "although no one would wish for it, it would have been far easier to write English, which is structurally similar to Chinese, with Chinese characters than to adapt this system to Japanese."[14]

The early Japanese were faced with three basic options in adapting the Chinese writing system to write Japanese: (1) they could take a Chinese character exclusively for its meaning, forgetting its Chinese pronunciation, and use it to stand for an approximately equivalent preexisting word in the spoken Japanese language, or (2) they could borrow both the meaning and the Chinese pronunciation of the Chinese character, thus importing a wholly new Chinese loanword into the Japanese language. In either of these cases, furthermore, there remained the problem of how to represent Japanese grammatical distinctions that simply do not exist in Chinese. (3) A third option was to borrow the Chinese character exclusively for its pronunciation, forgetting its meaning, and use such characters to then painstakingly "spell out" the sound of native Japanese words. Finally, of course, the Japanese could also learn to read and write directly in the foreign Chinese language itself. In practice, from the time writing first began to appear in Japan around the fifth century, the Japanese did all of the above.

Much early writing in Japan was in the Chinese language, but already in 712, Japan's oldest surviving history, the *Kojiki* (*Record of Ancient Matters*), was composed in Japanese using Chinese characters. Early efforts to transcribe the Japanese language in this manner made for extremely cumbersome reading, however. One lasting consequence of the multiple different approaches taken to using Chinese characters in Japan is that the characters still used in Japanese today nearly all have at least two completely different pronunciations, one reflecting the borrowed approximation of the Chinese sound, and one representing a roughly equivalent (but originally unrelated) native Japanese word. For example, the Chinese character *dao* 道, meaning "way" (as in Daoism) or "road," can be pronounced in Japanese either (approximately) Chinese-style as *dō* (as in the martial art *jūdō* 柔道, the "Way of Suppleness") or *tō* (as in the Japanese religion *Shintō* 神道, the "Way of the Spirits"), or native Japanese-style as *michi* 道, a common word for "road."

Over time, in a process that was completed by about the ninth or tenth century, the Chinese characters used to phonetically spell out Japanese were standardized, reduced in number, and simplified. The character 伊, for example, which is pronounced *i* in Japanese (and sounds more like the English letter *e* in "return" than the usual letter *i* in English), was simplified to イ; the character 久, which is pronounced *ku*, became ク; and the character 奈, which is pronounced *na*, became ナ. The eventual result was the creation of two separate sets of some fifty-one symbols each: the angular and "masculine" Katakana and the curved and "feminine" Hiragana (both collectively called *kana*). These *kana* symbols could then be used to fluently write the sounds of all the syllables of the Japanese language. Although these *kana* were derived from Chinese characters, they have been stripped of all meaning, and they also no longer resemble the original Chinese characters very much. It was now possible to write the Japanese language using a native Japanese phonetic script.

Japanese authors soon put these *kana* to use in producing some of the world's truly outstanding early literary masterpieces. Perhaps most famous is *The Tale of Genji* (*Genji monogatari*), written at the beginning of the eleventh century by Lady Murasaki Shikibu (978–1016). *The Tale of Genji* is often called the world's first great true novel, or extended work of prose fiction. It relates the romantic affairs of an imaginary prince at the Japanese imperial court, Prince Genji, and is infused throughout with the characteristic Japanese sentiment of the age: *mono-no-aware*, the "sadness of things," a Buddhist-inspired awareness of the impermanence and transience of all existence. The word *aware*, "sadness," in fact appears no fewer than 1,018 times in this book.[15]

Despite helping make possible the creation of several early works of striking genius and universal appeal, such as *The Tale of Genji*, the phonetic Japanese Hiragana script was at the time often condescendingly referred to as "woman's hand." In practice, the gender distinction between supposedly masculine Chinese characters and feminine Hiragana was often transgressed: men wrote phonetically in *kana*, and a number of memorable Japanese ladies were certainly literate in Chinese. But the Chinese script, and even the Chinese language itself, long remained the most prestigious vehicle for serious writing in Japan. One distinguished twelfth-century aristocrat, Fujiwara Michinori (1106–1159), for example, did not include even a single text written in the Japanese script in his library. The intellectual primacy of Chinese writing in Japan would not be fatally challenged until modern times. Even the last catalog compiled for the shōgun's library in 1864–1866 still contained 65 percent Chinese or Chinese-style material. When Japan went to war with China in 1894 – a war that would first spectacularly demonstrate Japan's success at transforming itself into a modern, Western-style power, as well as China's corresponding failure to do so – the majority of Japanese war poetry was still being written in the classical Chinese language! The movement toward writing in a standardized vernacular Japanese "national language" (*kokugo*) really only began at that surprisingly late date.[16]

Today, of course, the Japanese language is universally written everywhere throughout the Japanese islands. But Chinese characters are still quite normally used in Japan for the roots of words, with Hiragana added for grammatical matters and certain common basic words. Katakana, meanwhile, is today reserved mostly for Western loanwords, of which there are now a great many. One study conducted in the 1970s estimated that Western loanwords, especially from English, made up as much as 10 percent of the daily Japanese vocabulary. In the process of being absorbed into Japanese, however, these English words have frequently also been domesticated beyond easy recognition. Among the most common English loanwords, for example, are *biiru* (beer), *terebi* (television), *nyūsu* (news), *karā* (color), and *supōtsu* (sports).[17]

Compared to Japan, Korea is geographically closer to China, and the Chinese influence tended to be proportionately greater in premodern times. Beginning perhaps as early as the fifth century, however, Koreans had already started experimenting with adapting Chinese characters to write the native Korean language, in part phonetically, in a form known as *idu*. Despite this modest breakthrough, only a total of about fifty poems written in vernacular Korean survive today from the entire period prior to the fifteenth century, compared to thousands of Korean documents written in Chinese.[18] Even the proudly nationalistic Korean priest-historian Iryŏn (1206–1289) compiled his invaluable early history of Korea, the *Samguk yusa* (*Memorabilia of the Three Kingdoms*), in 1281, mostly in the Chinese language, although he did include some native-language poetry.

In 1446 the great Korean King Sejong is credited with introducing a unique new twenty-eight-letter Korean alphabet, known as *han'gŭl*. In contrast to the Japanese *kana*, which represented the sounds of entire syllables, the Korean *han'gŭl* is a true alphabet, representing the smallest possible units of sound. *Han'gŭl* can be used very effectively to easily write anything in Korean, without reference to Chinese characters. After its inception, a large and growing Korean-language literature did begin to emerge, but even then, members of the educated Korean elite still tended to view Chinese-language writing as more prestigious, and it was only in the twentieth century that the use of Chinese characters has largely been abandoned in Korea. Since that time, however, the rejection of Chinese characters has been much more comprehensive in Korea than in Japan.

In Vietnam, Chinese characters and the classical Chinese language continued to be used until the late nineteenth century, when French colonial rule replaced them with Vietnamese written in the Roman alphabet. Throughout East Asia, therefore, the Chinese writing system, and to a lesser (but significant) extent the classical Chinese written language itself, continued to be widely used until modern times. The astonishing durability of this apparently cumbersome Chinese logographic script owes much, of course, to its cultural prestige and the heavy weight of tradition. That the Chinese writing system had relatively few serious regional rivals until the nineteenth century surely also was a factor. But it may also be argued that the system does have some inherent strengths. Though an alphabet is certainly easier to learn, and more flexible in its applicability to a multitude of different languages, an alphabet also merely reproduces phonetically in writing the babel of those different spoken tongues – the cacophony of sound. Chinese characters, by contrast, though difficult to learn and far from providing any magic universal ideographic means of communicating ideas without the need for passing through language first, once learned, do tend always to mean approximately the same thing in every language or dialect and across all time.

This universality should not be exaggerated: for example, the character *shu* 書 that in classical Chinese once meant either "to write" or "something that is written" in modern Chinese has come nearly always to mean specifically "book," whereas in Japan, it is usually used for the verb (pronounced *kaku*) "to write." With late-twentieth-century script simplification in the People's Republic of China, but not in Taiwan or other parts of the Greater Chinese world, even native Chinese Mandarin speakers no longer all use exactly the same script. And characters are sometimes used phonetically without any reference to meaning. Despite these caveats, however, the use of the Chinese script can make written communication across dialects, languages, and centuries of time, easier. For anyone who has learned the system, moreover, it can be a thing of beauty and power.

Since new words can also be freely and easily coined by combining existing characters, Chinese characters – far from being stuck with a vocabulary dating from the Bronze Age – are actually extremely flexible in adapting to new ideas. *Computer,* for example, is "electricity + brain" (*diannao* 電腦), *democracy* is "people + master" (*minzhu* 民主), and *stock exchange* is "proof + certificate + meet + exchange +

place" (*zhengquan jiaoyisuo* 證券交易所). Another modern (or at least nineteenth-century) European concept without much precedent in traditional East Asia, *communism*, is rendered as "collective + production + ism" (*gongchan-zhuyi* 共產主義, with "-ism" in turn being "master + meaning").

Although printing was invented in East Asia, the Chinese script, with its enormous number of different characters, was never very suitable for moveable type printing, and a convenient Chinese typewriter was effectively impossible. In the post-typewriter age of digital computers, however, the Chinese script now poses considerably fewer disadvantages. Indeed, it has been predicted that Chinese may eventually pass English to become the world's most commonly used computer language, and there are already far more people online in China than in any other country in the world.

Despite the strengths of this system, in the twentieth century, under the impact of modern Western influences, Chinese characters were largely abandoned in Korea and Vietnam, while in Japan they have been so thoroughly domesticated as to seem part of traditional Japanese culture, and are ordinarily used in conjunction with native phonetic *kana*. Even within China, sweeping language reforms were implemented, including the abandonment of the classical written language in favor of a modern vernacular in the early twentieth century, and more recent script simplification in the People's Republic. It is still the case, however, that over one-third of the vocabulary items in each of the modern Japanese, Korean, and Vietnamese languages derive from Chinese, so the ghost of this once-shared premodern written language still hovers over East Asia.[19]

This should be less surprising (and less offensive to nationalist sensibilities) if we remember the equally large number of words in modern English that derive ultimately from either Greek or Latin. The prestige that Latin long enjoyed in Western Europe compares roughly to that of classical Chinese in East Asia. As late as the year 1500, some three-quarters of all books in Western Europe were still being published in Latin.[20] To the extent that Western civilization enjoys a common core of Greco-Roman heritage, in a similar way, East Asian civilization is also marked by a shared legacy of writing in classical Chinese, and the reading of a core group of common books written in that language.

Bronze Age China

Northern China, particularly the lower Yellow River area known as the Central Plain, was the location of one of the world's major early *primary civilizations*. This term refers to the indigenous development of a civilization under only limited outside influence. By contrast, Korea, Japan, Vietnam, Western Europe, the United States, and most of the other societies with which we are familiar today are *secondary states* or civilizations, meaning that they emerged chronologically somewhat later, under the influence of older neighbors or predecessors.

Because the major primary civilizations of the world developed in sometimes significantly different ecological environments – the Mayans, for example, amid the tropical forests of Central America, the Egyptians in the arid river valley of the Nile, and the Chinese in the temperate rain-watered Central Plain of north China – it is not entirely obvious why the Central Plain area should have been favored for this breakthrough. There is no evidence that large-scale irrigation was employed in early Bronze Age China, for example, so theories about how the organized mass mobilization of labor for irrigation purposes caused the rise of early civilizations do not seem to be supported in the case of China. The Central Plain is, however, a large and relatively level area suitable for dry-field agriculture (millet, and later wheat, were the principal crops of the Central Plain; wet-field rice cultivation, although equally ancient, was mostly limited to the originally semi-foreign south), centering on a major river. The Central Plain is also relatively accessible overland from western Eurasia, which may (or may not) have been a contributing factor. Compared to Mesopotamia, where what is technically defined as "civilization" is said to have emerged as early as 3500 BCE, and Egypt, which was unified circa 3100 BCE, the emergence of Bronze Age civilization in China around 2000 BCE came relatively late. By almost any other measure, however, China's civilization was indisputably ancient.

As we have seen, traditional Chinese histories begin with an age of celebrated culture heroes, including Fuxi, Shennong, the Yellow Emperor, and a series of later Sage Rulers, culminating in Great Yu (ruling from 2205 BCE), who, according to the traditional story, tamed a catastrophic flood and founded the first dynasty, called Xia. Xia then became the first of the so-called Three Dynasties, Xia (traditionally dated 2205–1766 BCE), Shang (ca. 1766–1045 BCE), and Zhou (1045–256 BCE), that form the classical age of Chinese antiquity. The problem is that all the stories concerning these great ancient cultural heroes were recorded only very long after the events they purport to describe – and necessarily had to be because writing did not appear in China until roughly 1200 BCE.

The legends concerning high antiquity were deeply revered by traditional Chinese scholars and usually accepted without question, but the enormous rupture triggered by the end of the Chinese Empire in 1912 and sweeping early twentieth-century modernization led to calls for a more scientific history, and a movement to "doubt antiquity" began in the 1920s. Everything traditional was then regarded with some skepticism. Certainly, all the stories purporting to deal with events dating from before the Zhou Dynasty were legend in the literal sense of the Chinese word for legend, *chuanshuo*: "passed-on sayings." Such orally passed-on legends could easily also be legendary in the other sense of being mythical and possibly untrue.

In 1899, however, a pair of Chinese scholars happened to notice some particularly archaic-looking Chinese writing on old turtle shells and bones that were being marketed for medicine as so-called "dragon bones." These bones were eventually traced to a source near the modern city of Anyang, in the northern province of Henan. The site was finally excavated by scientifically trained archeologists beginning in 1928, and it proved to be the ruins of an ancient Shang Dynasty capital. The dragon bones turned out actually to be shells and bones that were used for divination by Shang Dynasty rulers, and they are therefore now generally called oracle bones. The inscriptions found on some of these oracle bones are the earliest known examples of Chinese-language writing.[21]

This dramatic archeological rediscovery of the last Shang capital, together with the oracle bone inscriptions that provided unquestionable new documentary evidence for it, spectacularly verified much of the later part of the traditional Chinese story. In general, modern archeology has tended to support traditional Chinese accounts, and there is today much less of a skeptical inclination to doubt antiquity than there was in the early twentieth century. Even so, the very earliest portions of the traditional narrative should still be read with caution. They are at best unverified, and much is rather clearly mythical in flavor. The idea that the Yellow Emperor is somehow the ancestor of all Chinese people, for example, is not only scientifically dubious but also racist.

The current academic fashion is to emphasize that Chinese civilization actually had multiple origins, in contrast to the earlier assumption that it must have spread from a single point of origin in the north. Beyond any doubt, there were numerous local prehistoric cultures scattered throughout the area of what we today call China during the late Stone Age, with a particularly broad division between the wet-field rice-based cultivation of the southern Yangzi River basin and the dry-field millet-based agriculture of the northern Yellow River region. All these different cultures contributed to the brewing Chinese civilization. A degree of regional diversity, furthermore, has remained a fixture throughout history, even to the present day. However, the late Stone Age peoples of southern China appear to have spoken languages unrelated to Chinese, and it still does seem fair to say that the northern Central Plains Neolithic cultures, based on millet, sorghum, pig, dog, and silkworm raising, some of whom must have also spoken ancestral forms of the modern Chinese language, probably provided the core for what eventually became "China."

Sarah Allan has recently suggested that a standard for what became Chinese civilization may have first been set by the elite culture of what archeologists label "Erlitou" (named after an archeological type site in modern Henan Province).[22] Erlitou may be the closest archeological equivalent to what traditional sources call the Xia Dynasty, and it is radiocarbon dated to approximately 2100–1600 BCE. Erlitou is the first archeologically identified culture to show evidence of the construction of royal palaces and the first to use bronze for casting ritual vessels, which were apparently used for making offerings to the spirits of dead ancestors. Such bronze ritual vessels subsequently spread through the entire region of China. Although these bronzes were produced in enormous quantities, they were always cast in a relatively limited number of fixed standard shapes and with common decorative themes, such as the abstract and somewhat mysterious *taotie* design (see Figure 1.1). Sarah Allan compares the spread of this elite bronze ritual culture to the dispersal of McDonald's fast-food restaurants around the world today, extending everywhere from Chicago to Cairo, Tōkyō, and Beijing, in that it did not necessarily imply either a single homogenous ethnicity or centralized political control, but rather the widespread acceptance of the artifacts of a prestigious cultural model by independent local communities.

Figure 1.1. A Shang Dynasty bronze bell featuring the characteristic *taotie* design, ca. twelfth to eleventh centuries BCE, southern China. Arthur M. Sackler Gallery, Smithsonian Institution, Washington, DC: gift of Arthur M. Sackler, S1987.10.

Allan claims that the strikingly different collection of ancient bronzes found at Sanxingdui in Sichuan, in southwest China, in 1986 are all the more amazing because they are the only group of bronzes in all China that seem to spring from an entirely different cultural style (and even they are found mixed together with more standard Erlitou-derived types). The ritual behavior associated with these Erlitou bronzes eventually became the standard of Chinese decorum, known as *li*, a term which has been translated variously as "courtesy," "propriety," "rites," or "ceremony" and that unfortunately lacks any precise English equivalent. At least until the revolutionary changes of the twentieth century, *li* set an ideal standard for cultivated behavior in China and eventually throughout all East Asia, becoming a cornerstone for the cultural coherence of the region. For example, in 707 CE, one Japanese empress proclaimed that "all the ways of government take the *li* [pronounced *rei* in Japanese] as foremost."[23]

The Shang Dynasty (ca. 1766–1045 BCE), which represented a more mature development of this Erlitou culture, is commonly understood to have been an early example of a relatively large territorial state, in contrast to the alternative model of small, independent city-states familiar from ancient Mesopotamia. The Shang ruler does appear to have been the only leader in the whole area of China at that time to claim the supreme sovereign title "king" (*wang*). Even so, however, the Shang probably did not employ an extensively centralized bureaucratic government but rather delegated authority to largely autonomous local leaders based in a far-flung network of walled towns. These local leaders may have often been either directly or indirectly (through marriage) related to the Shang king. Sarah Allan points out, for example, that the names of sixty-four known wives of one particular late Shang king are recorded in oracle bone inscriptions and that most of their names include a component that is also a place name. She speculates that these probably signified royal marriage ties between the Shang king and those places, and suggests that Shang may have been at the center of a vast network of marriage affiliations.

Shang families were organized by patrilineal descent and seniority. A group tracing descent from a common (presumably often legendary) male ancestor, called a *zu*, ideally lived together in a community and performed ancestral cult rituals. (Significantly, in the nineteenth century, when a new Chinese-character translation for the Western word *nation* was coined, it was done by combining the character for "the people," *min*, with this same ancient character for descent group, *zu*, creating the new combination *minzu*.) The oldest member of the senior line headed the entire group. Married sons remained subject to their fathers' authority, and women joined their husbands' families after marriage.

Despite this obvious patriarchal male bias, Shang queens nonetheless appear to have assisted in administration, performed ancestral rituals, and even mobilized armies on occasion. There is at least some evidence to suggest that the status of women in traditional China tended to decline over time, perhaps under the growing influence of Confucian moral ideals, and possibly reaching its lowest point only in early modern times. For example, the ideal of the chaste widow (who refuses to remarry after her husband's death) may have not been especially influential prior to the Tang Dynasty (618–907 CE) and may have been most strenuously promoted only during the last imperial dynasty, Qing (1644–1912). Female foot binding does not seem to have begun before the Song (960–1279 CE).

It was the exclusive prerogative of the Shang kings to sponsor oracle bone divination, the vehicle through which questions could be asked of the spirits. In this divination, heat would be applied to the chest pieces of tortoise shells and other animal bones, causing them to crack, and the shape of the crack was interpreted as an answer from the spirits. Eventually the questions, and occasionally the answers, came to be inscribed directly on the bones, creating the famous oracle bone inscriptions that are the earliest known examples of Chinese writing.

This role of the king as a crucial intermediary between the human and the spirit worlds was hardly unique, among early civilizations, to the Shang Chinese. Mayan kings communicated with their ancestors and cosmic spirits through sometimes drug-induced trances, while ancient Egyptian pharaohs claimed a royal monopoly over religious offerings.[24] The Shang monarchy thus had a theocratic dimension in common with many other ancient societies – and one that also sets it apart, to some extent, from subsequent Chinese history.

Bronze Age civilization reached mature form in northern China under the Shang, but the Shang Dynasty that has been reconstructed by archeology is in some ways rather strange and unfamiliar by later Chinese standards. The relatively large-scale human sacrifice, for example, that the Shang kings practiced, as well as the very existence of those oracle bone inscriptions that have so strikingly confirmed the historical existence of the Shang, had been almost completely forgotten in China until they were rediscovered by archeologists in the twentieth century. Around 1045 BCE, moreover, the Shang state was decisively conquered by a foreign people, called the Zhou. The Zhou then founded a new dynasty, and it was this Zhou Dynasty that ushered in the great formative age of classical Chinese civilization.

For Further Reading

On the origins of Bronze Age civilization in China, see Sarah Allan (ed.), *The Formation of Chinese Civilization: An Archaeological Perspective* (New Haven: Yale University Press, 2005); Kwang-chih Chang, *The Archaeology of Ancient China* (4th ed.; New Haven: Yale University Press, 1986); and Kwang-chih Chang, *Shang Civilization* (New Haven: Yale University Press, 1980). An excellent comparative view of some of the world's earliest civilizations is provided by Bruce G. Trigger, in *Understanding Early Civilizations: A Comparative Study* (Cambridge University Press, 2003).

On East Asian languages and writing systems, see John DeFrancis, *The Chinese Language: Fact and Fantasy* (Honolulu: University of Hawai'i Press, 1984); Wm. C. Hannas, *Asia's Orthographic Dilemma* (Honolulu: University of Hawai'i Press, 1997); Bruno Lewin, "Japanese and Korean: The Problems and History of a Linguistic Comparison," *The Journal of Japanese Studies*, 2.2 (1976); Roy Andrew Miller, *The Japanese Language* (University of Chicago Press, 1967); and S. Robert Ramsey, *The Languages of China* (Princeton University Press, 1987).

2 The Formative Era

The Age of the Classics

Zhou Dynasty China (1045–256 BCE)

The Zhou people who conquered the Shang Dynasty around the year 1045 BCE were originally separate and distinct from the Shang. The Zhou homeland (in what is today Shaanxi) lay to the west of the core Shang territory, and they were politically independent. For a while before their conquest, however, Zhou leaders did acknowledge themselves to be subordinate vassals of the Shang king, and much of Zhou high culture, including oracle bone divination and the production and style of bronze vessels (inscribed with a shared written Chinese language), was derived from Shang. The outcome of their conquest was a new synthesis or fusion.

After the 1045 BCE conquest, the newly established Zhou Dynasty absorbed the preexisting Shang population and even allowed the former Shang royal family to maintain its identity, under the reduced title of dukes (of Song) rather than as sovereign kings, to continue their essential ancestral sacrifices. This illustrates once again the extent to which Chinese civilization was, from the beginning, a hybrid mixture, blending together multiple local cultural traditions. The late Shang had been a relatively small state existing within a field of roughly similar other cultures, and in contact with places that were much more remote, as is demonstrated by the large number of cowry sea shells that were imported from as far away as the Indian Ocean, and the introduction of the horse-drawn chariot (which had first appeared centuries earlier in what is now Kazakhstan) from the northern steppe around 1250 BCE, possibly coming via the northeast.[1] Chinese civilization may have developed largely indigenously, but it was never entirely a closed and isolated system.

As Christopher Beckwith has shown, the Zhou origin myth is strikingly similar to those of a surprising number of other Eurasian peoples, ranging from the ancient Scythians and Romans in the west to the Koguryŏ in Korea, and including the later Turks and Mongols, suggesting an unexpected degree of shared Eurasian culture.[2] According to the Zhou legend, the first ancestor of the Zhou people was conceived when a woman named Jiang Yuan stepped into the footprint of the supreme god

Shangdi (the "Lord on High") and thereby became pregnant. Jiang Yuan's name literally means "Progenitress of the Jiang" – the Jiang being yet another early people, sometimes said to be ancestral to modern Tibetans, with whom the Zhou apparently intermarried. Jiang Yuan's miraculous pregnancy, then, resulted in the birth of a son known as Hou Ji, the "Lord of Millet."

Believing that Shangdi disapproved of her pregnancy, however, Jiang Yuan abandoned her son in the countryside, only to have his life be saved by cattle and sheep that lay down beside him to keep him warm. She next tried to abandon him in a forest, where he was rescued by woodcutters, and then once more abandoned him on some ice, where birds warmed him with their wings. After his divine conception and repeated supernatural protection in childhood, the adult Hou Ji discovered agricultural techniques that he passed down to his descendants, who became the Zhou people.

The legend continues that these descendants lived a semi-nomadic existence for some years, and even temporarily gave up agriculture altogether, before finally settling in a region known as the Plain of Zhou, located some eighty miles west of the modern Chinese city of Xi'an. It was from this plain that they supposedly took their name. The Plain of Zhou, in turn, is situated in a much larger basin that has traditionally been known as the region "Within the Passes" (*Guanzhong*). This is a large, reasonably fertile agricultural area almost completely surrounded by mountains, forming a kind of vast natural fortress, which has repeatedly throughout Chinese history served as a base for the military conquest and unification of China.

The prehistoric Zhou people were themselves, from the start, apparently also the product of cultural mixing, and were obviously caught up in the interplay between farming and semi-nomadic livestock-raising lifestyles on the northwestern fringes of the Bronze Age Chinese world. The Zhou presumably emerged from a fusion of several local prehistoric cultures, under the influence of the nearby Shang civilization, as an early example of what is called *secondary state formation*. Early Zhou bronze ritual vessels were, for example, apparently copied from Shang models, although over time, somewhat unique Zhou styles did develop. The Zhou people were also literally armed by Shang technologies: Zhou chariots and composite reflex bows were identical to Shang weapons, although it has been speculated that Zhou bronze armor may have represented an improvement over Shang leather armor.

No identifiable archeological trace of Zhou culture has been found in the region "Within the Passes" until about a century before the Zhou conquest of the Shang, which supports the legend of their migration there from somewhere else. It is uncertain where that somewhere else was located, but it may have been from slightly farther northeast. On their arrival "Within the Passes," the Zhou people may have mixed with other populations already in the area. After settling "Within the Passes," the Zhou chief was invested by the Shang king as a vassal duke. Not content with that subordinate status, however, the Zhou dukes soon usurped the supreme Shang title of sovereignty, promoting themselves to kings.

According to legend, the second Zhou king was killed by the Shang, and the third Zhou king was held captive by the Shang for seven years, until he was ransomed.

After generations of such repeated provocation, the fourth Zhou king, known as King Wu – a posthumous designation that means the "Martial King" – finally declared war on the Shang, accusing the last Shang king of a lengthy list of abuses, including failure to perform the proper ceremonies to the spirits of his own ancestors. King Wu mobilized a huge coalition of other disaffected peoples and decisively defeated the Shang in battle at a place called Muye ("Shepherd's Wilderness"), south of the last Shang capital (near modern Anyang, in Henan Province). The government of the present-day People's Republic of China, regarding this as an important national heritage, has funded a special chronology project to determine the exact dates of events at the dawn of Chinese history. As best as can be determined, the Zhou conquest is now thought to have occurred around the year 1045 BCE. It is one of the most important dates in all Chinese history.

After the great battle and the Shang defeat, the story continues that the last Shang king withdrew into Deer Terrace Pavilion and burned himself to death. Eight days later, King Wu of the Zhou reported his victory to Heaven and announced his intention to assume residence in the Middle Kingdom. This term, *Middle Kingdom* (*Zhongguo*), as previously described, has today become the closest Chinese-language equivalent to our English word *China*. An inscription discovered in 1963 on a bronze ritual vessel cast by the Zhou to commemorate their victory over the Shang is believed to be the earliest known surviving example of the use of this key term.

Although the Zhou and Shang were different peoples, both were in a sense Chinese. More precisely, both fed into a Chinese identity that was still in the process of formation. Over the course of the eight centuries of the Zhou Dynasty, a conscious sense of identity as *Huaxia* (Chinese) apparently did coalesce, especially in contrast to the clearly alien semi-nomadic cultures to the north. However, many of the peoples living in what we think of today as China, including virtually the entire south, still lay outside this *Huaxia* world in Zhou times. At the same time, until surprisingly recently, some people in both Korea and Vietnam also claimed descent from the same legendary ancestors and to be part of the same great civilization as these Chinese. As one ninth-century Chinese text explained, "when Confucius composed the *Spring and Autumn Annals*, he treated the various lords who used foreign ritual as foreign, and those who approached the Chinese as Chinese."[3] This early Chinese *Huaxia* identity was obviously rather open and inclusive and defined in terms of civilization (as well as myths of common descent). It was not exactly a modern-style national identity.

King Wu of Zhou died a mere two years after his victory over Shang, and he was succeeded on the throne by his oldest son. Since the new king was still very young, and the Zhou Dynasty still somewhat insecure, the late king's brother, who is known as the Duke of Zhou, assumed power as regent on behalf of the new boy king. Other members of the royal family were suspicious of the duke's motives, however, and soon three of the duke's own brothers rebelled. In renewed military campaigns, the Duke of Zhou crushed this rebellion, killing one older brother and driving another into exile in the process.

According to a particularly treasured story preserved in the *Book of Documents* (one of the five core Confucian Classics), Heaven then sent down a great wind that flattened the crops. In search of a ritual response to this disaster, the young king was inspired to open a certain metal-bound box that had been sealed by the Duke of Zhou. In this box, the king discovered the record of an earlier ritual in which the Duke of Zhou had offered his own life in prayer as a substitute for the ailing, but not yet dead, King Wu. This previously undisclosed document revealed unexpectedly dramatic proof of the Duke of Zhou's selfless sincerity. After successfully putting the dynasty on a more stable basis, the story continues that the Duke of Zhou voluntarily relinquished his authority as regent. At least according to the traditional story, therefore, the Duke of Zhou had acted decisively and effectively on behalf of the dynasty, without any thought of personal advantage.

Such stories about the Duke of Zhou became foundational to the Chinese political tradition. They established the overriding Confucian principle of rule by virtue, and also the important corollary that if a dynasty's administration were not virtuous, it might lose its legitimacy and thus its continued right to rule. The figure of the Duke of Zhou is intimately associated with the elaboration of a particularly important Chinese political concept known as the Mandate of Heaven (*tianming*). Heaven was the supreme Zhou deity (displacing the earlier Shangdi), and Zhou kings claimed to be "Sons of Heaven" (*tianzi*), with a "Mandate from Heaven" to rule all "Under Heaven" (*tianxia*).

The Zhou veneration of Heaven as a source of royal legitimacy is strikingly reminiscent of Inner Asian steppe beliefs in a universal sky god, and may reflect northern cultural influences on early, pre-dynastic, Zhou.[4] From the beginning, however, what became the characteristic Chinese approach to the very widespread idea of the "divine right" of kings had a unique twist. While some in the Zhou royal family might have preferred to understand the Mandate of Heaven as a permanent hereditary right, the Duke of Zhou gave this a more revolutionary interpretation: the Mandate of Heaven was revocable. Dynastic survival depended on continued good government. The same Heaven looks down on all people, everywhere, and enforces universal principles. The Shang had once enjoyed Heaven's Mandate (and before the Shang, supposedly also the Xia), but because the Shang kings had become corrupt, the Mandate passed to Zhou. Zhou kings would retain the Mandate only for so long as they continued to deserve it.

Because "Heaven sees as my people see," according to the *Book of Documents*, popular discontent itself might be taken as evidence of the loss of the Mandate of Heaven. By the fourth century BCE, the great Confucian thinker Mencius (Mengzi, ca. 385–ca. 312 BCE) was so bold as to say explicitly that the overthrow of a bad ruler was no crime but as justifiable as the punishment of any ordinary thief or robber. The concept of the Mandate of Heaven therefore legitimated repeated changes of dynasty throughout premodern Chinese history and imposed an ideal standard obligation of meritorious rule on each. At the same time, the concept of a solitary Son of Heaven holding Heaven's Mandate may have also helped buttress the notion that at any given time there could only be one legitimate dynasty "Under Heaven" holding that Mandate.[5] The concept of the Mandate of Heaven remains not entirely irrelevant even today: "Change of Mandate" (*geming*) is the literal Chinese-language translation of our modern Western word *revolution*, a term that was much invoked in twentieth-century China.

The Zhou Dynasty lasted for some eight centuries, but, although the Zhou ruling house may indeed have brought the previously loose Shang network of regional affiliations into a somewhat more systematic basis, and Zhou claims to sole legitimate sovereignty "Under Heaven" may have helped establish a lasting ideal of political unity in China, the Zhou probably never enjoyed direct centralized administration over a very large area. Especially after the early Zhou capital in the west was sacked by foreign forces in 771 BCE, and the capital was relocated east to Luoyang, inaugurating the so-called Eastern Zhou period (770–256 BCE), the real power of the Zhou kings was increasingly overshadowed by the rise of regional territorial states, which eventually, during the Warring States period (479–221 BCE), became fully independent countries (*guo*) with their own sovereign kings.

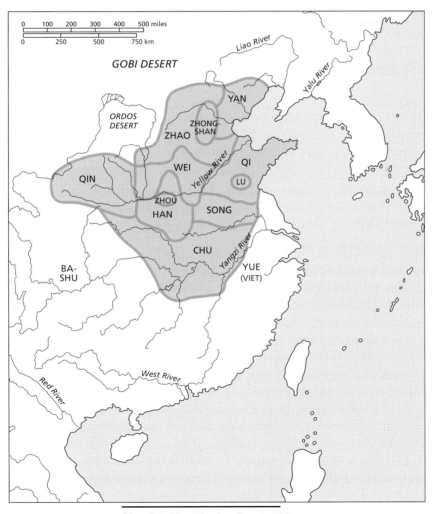

Map 2.1 The Warring States, 350 BCE

The Hundred Schools of Thought

The Zhou Dynasty is regarded as the formative era of Chinese civilization. Nearly all the classic works of Chinese literature, and major schools of indigenous thought, took shape during the Zhou. This reference to schools of thought is a little misleading, though, because one of the most characteristic features of Chinese thought has always been its open eclecticism – a willingness to borrow and incorporate whatever ideas might seem useful or good. Few premodern Chinese people ever fit neatly and exclusively into any one particular school of thought. Still, there are certain broad lines of intellectual tradition that can be usefully, if somewhat artificially, distinguished from each other. These most notably include Confucianism, Daoism (also spelled Taoism), and Legalism. As an example of the range of Zhou era thought, which was by no means limited to these three major schools, we may also mention the tradition of military specialists.

Confucianism

Confucianism is commonly considered to be the mainstream of Chinese, and East Asian, tradition. Surprisingly, however, a plausible argument can be made that Confucianism is really "a Western invention."[6] In fact, there is no Chinese word or concept that precisely corresponds with our English word *Confucian*. The closest Chinese-language approximation, *Ru*, refers more specifically to scholars who study the ancient classics (with *Confucianism* as the "Teachings of the Ru" – *Rujiao*). It was those classic texts, in particular, that were fundamental to the premodern Chinese cultural tradition.

Although the classics include what may be the oldest books in the Chinese literary tradition (not counting the slightly older inscriptions on oracle bones as "books"), the classics did not assume their final form until relatively late and did not attain venerated canonical status until the late second century BCE. There are five core Confucian Classics:

1. The *Book of Documents* (also called the *Book of History*, *Shujing*, or *Shangshu*). This is a collection of speeches, announcements, and other documents attributed to great figures of antiquity, from the legendary Sage Kings into early Zhou. Much of the Zhou material is believed to be genuine, although the authenticity of the pre-Zhou texts is more dubious.
2. The *Book of Odes* (*Shijing*), a collection of roughly three hundred early Zhou songs or poems, some of which are still of considerable literary value.
3. The *Book of Changes* (*Yijing*; sometimes spelled *I-Ching*). This is a handbook for divination, based on a set of sixty-four hexagrams (variant combinations of six broken and unbroken lines) accessed through the casting of milfoil stalks.
4. The *Rites* (*Li*), which is actually a collective name for three separate books, covering a wide range of matters. These ritual texts appear to have been compiled relatively late, despite the conventional attribution of a portion of them to high antiquity.

5. The *Spring and Autumn Annals (Chunqiu)*. This is an extremely terse history of Confucius's home state of Lu, covering the years 722–481 BCE. Because it was traditionally believed that Confucius himself had compiled this history, its entries were carefully scrutinized for presumably profound moral judgments conveyed by subtle distinctions in the choice of language.

This list of five core classics was eventually expanded to include a total of thirteen. Much of the importance that was attached to the classics was due to their presumed antiquity, as portraits of an idealized golden age in the early Zhou and the even earlier Sage Kings. From the time they first achieved canonical status in the late second century BCE until the early twentieth century CE, these texts remained at the heart of formal education in China (and to a large extent all of East Asia). Though the study of the classics often took the form of tediously dry memorization and detailed chapter and verse textual commentary, Confucius himself had personally emphasized the need for both study and critical thinking. "To learn without thinking is unavailing; to think without learning is dangerous," Confucius said.[7]

The Confucian Classics spread, together with literacy itself, to Korea, Japan, and Vietnam, where they gained increasing influence over time. In Japan, the heyday of Confucianism did not come until the early modern Tokugawa period (1603–1868 CE). In Vietnam, Confucianism blossomed especially after the fifteenth century, in some ways finally culminating under the last dynasty (Nguyen, 1802–1945) in the early nineteenth century. In Korea, the peak period of Confucian influence also coincided with the last premodern dynasty, Chosŏn (1392–1910). As late as the mid-nineteenth century, one Korean official could still proudly inform a Japanese visitor that the Korean ceremonial code was "based on the precedents" of the Zhou.[8]

East Asia can, to a large extent, even be defined in terms of this shared Confucianism, which coincided also with a shared use of the Chinese writing system and classical written language. This common literary language enabled educated premodern Koreans, Japanese, and Vietnamese to read the Confucian Classics in their original words rather than in translation. It should be emphasized, however, that the appeal of Confucianism in Korea, Japan, and Vietnam was not primarily because it was Chinese. Although the prestige of a powerful and apparently successful Chinese imperial model undoubtedly did play a critical early role in encouraging emulation, many Koreans, for example, ultimately came to see themselves as even better Confucians than the Chinese. In general, the classics were regarded as being no more uniquely Chinese than the Old Testament of the Bible is uniquely Jewish, the Koran uniquely Arab, or the Buddhist scriptures uniquely Indian. The appeal was, instead, to supposedly universal truth.

Except for the *Spring and Autumn Annals*, certain portions of the ritual texts, and the appendices, or *wings*, of the *Book of Changes*, these Confucian Classics were not usually ascribed to Confucius himself. Most were believed to be much older than Confucius, although Confucius was conventionally credited with playing some role in the editing or transmission of each. But if the study of the classics – the special activity of the *Ru* – was central to the actual practice of Confucianism in premodern East Asia, Confucianism is nonetheless named after the man we call Confucius (551–479 BCE).

"Confucius" is the Latinized (i.e., European) version of the Chinese title *Kong Fuzi* (or more simply, *Kongzi*), which means "Master Kong." His proper name was Kong Qiu, and he was born in the northeastern state of Lu, in what is now Shandong Province. In his own lifetime, Confucius remained a somewhat obscure teacher. Most of what we know reliably about both the man and his ideas derives from a single collection of his conversations that was compiled by his followers some time after his death, called the *Analects* (in Chinese, *Lunyu*).

Confucius's central message was one of leadership by moral example. He believed that any attempt to govern through regulations and punishments would only encourage people to find clever ways to evade the law, but that if you led through proper ritual (*li*) and moral force (*de*) the people would spontaneously correct themselves. Confucius, for example, once explicitly rejected capital punishment, saying, "Sir, in conducting your government, why use killing? . . . The virtue of the noble person is like the wind, and the virtue of small people is like grass. When the wind blows over the grass, the grass must bend."

The key to a good society was individual self-cultivation of moral principles by a gentleman (*junzi*), who might then hope to influence other people nearby and eventually even bring peace on earth. As Confucius said, the gentleman "cultivates himself so as to give peace to all the people." Confucius once charmingly described how this process of self-cultivation and internalization of virtue had worked in his own life: "At fifteen, my heart was set upon learning; at thirty, I had become established; at forty, I was no longer perplexed; . . . at seventy, I could follow my heart's desires without crossing the line."

Important specific virtues (among others) that a Confucian gentleman was expected to cultivate were proper observance of ritual (*li*), "humaneness" or "humanity" (*ren*), and filial piety (*xiao*). Ritual was a legacy from the dawn of Chinese civilization, when bronze ritual vessels were cast for offerings to the spirits. For Confucius himself, however, the religious beliefs underlying this ancient ritual were no longer the crucial point; ritual had become merely a standard of proper behavior and a tool for self-discipline. "Through mastering oneself and returning to ritual one becomes humane," said Confucius.

Humanity, then, was most especially the ability to empathize with other people. "As for humaneness – you want to establish yourself; then help others to establish themselves. You want to develop yourself; then help others to develop themselves. Being able to recognize oneself in others, one is on the way to being humane." Or, as Confucius put it most succinctly, "what you do not want for yourself, do not do to others."

Filial piety refers to showing proper respect to parents and ancestors. It is perhaps the most difficult Confucian value for modern Western individualists to feel much sympathy for, but Confucians traditionally viewed filial piety as the absolute bedrock of a good society. As one passage in the *Analects* put it, "Among those who are filial toward their parents and fraternal towards their brothers, those who are inclined to offend against their superiors are few indeed.... Being filial and fraternal – is this not the root of humaneness?" In Japan, in 757 CE, one empress decreed:

> The ancients, in governing the people and pacifying the country, had to use the principle of filial piety. As a source of all action, nothing takes priority over this. We should command [each] family in the [Japanese] empire to possess and diligently memorize a copy of the *Classic of Filial Piety*.[9]

The *Classic of Filial Piety* (*Xiaojing*) was one of the later additions to the Confucian canon. It is actually quite inconceivable that all, or even very many, Japanese really read this book in the eighth century. One plausible estimate of the total number of Japanese people who were engaged with Chinese-language written documents at that time is no more than twenty thousand.[10] Yet the imperial Confucian pose in Japan, and the centrality of filial piety to that interpretation of Confucianism, is still significant.

The expectation of hierarchy inherent in this ideal of serving parents filially and not offending superiors also highlights one of the key contradictions in Confucian thought. On one hand, Confucians idealized the memory of a highly aristocratic ancient Zhou social order and conservatively sought to perpetuate it. "I transmit but do not create" is one of Confucius's more famous sayings. Some of the most important Confucian virtues, moreover, such as filial piety and loyalty (*zhong*), can only be expressed through hierarchical relationships. This is one side of the Confucian equation. The other side of the equation, however, was a pointedly egalitarian and meritocratic strand of Confucian thought. Anyone, it was assumed, could potentially perfect himself or herself through self-cultivation and then lead the world by his or her example. As Confucius said, "in education there should be no class distinctions." China had ceased to have a truly hereditary aristocracy already by the third century BCE, and the meritocratic line in Confucian thinking would eventually find realization under the empire in the remarkable Chinese civil service examination system, under which government officials were selected on the basis of anonymously graded performances on written tests.

This contradiction in Confucianism is partially resolved with the realization that merit is necessarily unequal. Anyone can potentially perfect himself or herself (and seniority accrues naturally to everyone equally over time), but not everyone actually does perfect himself or herself. In addition, it may be that internal inconsistencies and variant tendencies within Confucianism allowed it a flexible vitality of interpretation and application. Whereas late imperial China may have become an exceptionally meritocratic society (by premodern standards), for example, in early modern Japan, the same Confucian ideals helped justify a rigidly hereditary social hierarchy under such slogans as *taigi meibun*, or the moral obligation of fulfilling the role proper to one's title.

About a century after Confucius's time, a second great Confucian teacher appeared, known as Mencius (mentioned already in our discussion of the Mandate of Heaven). Mencius is most famous for insisting that people are naturally good, just as water, although it can be forced in any direction, naturally inclines to flow downward. Mencius explained the undeniable fact of human misbehavior in practice with a wonderful story:

> The trees on Ox Mountain were once beautiful. But being situated on the outskirts of a large state, the trees were hewn down by axes.... [Even so] they do not fail to put forth new buds and shoots, but then cattle and sheep also come to graze. This accounts for the barren appearance of the mountain. Seeing this barrenness, people suppose that the mountain was never wooded.

In a similar way, the innate goodness of people can often be "fettered and destroyed by what one does during the day," to the point that some might even suppose that people "never had the capacity for goodness." Like the barrenness of Ox Mountain, however, this is not really humanity's natural state. Aside from persuasively making a rhetorical point, this story also reveals a notably early awareness of the process of environmental degradation due to human economic activity.

The third and final major classical era Confucian thinker was Xunzi (ca. 310–ca. 219 BCE). Xunzi lived at the end of the Warring States period and held an understandably darker opinion of human nature than Mencius. Xunzi viewed natural human desires as evil impulses that could only be tamed through conscious training and effort. Xunzi also had a notably rationalistic, nonreligious understanding of the regular order of nature:

> The processes of Heaven are constant.... Respond to them with order, and good fortune will result; respond to them with chaos, and misfortune will result. If you strengthen what is basic and are frugal in your expenditures, then Heaven cannot make you poor.

Heaven, in other words, helps those who help themselves. Although the book that bears Xunzi's name is a superb collection of deliberately crafted essays – in contrast to the scraps of remembered conversation that constitute both the *Analects* of Confucius and the *Mencius* – unlike the other two, the *Xunzi* never achieved recognition as one of the canonical expanded set of thirteen Confucian Classics.

Daoism

After Confucianism, the next most influential school of classical Chinese thought was Daoism. Compared to Confucianism, Daoism had much less influence on parts of East Asia outside China, though it was not unknown in Korea and arguably actually contributed to the founding ideology of the Japanese Empire – even providing the name of the ostensibly "native" Japanese religion *Shintō* (the "Dao of the Spirits").[11] Even by the normally eclectic Chinese standards, Daoism is remarkably diffuse and difficult to pin down. The word *dao* itself means "path" or "road." In a philosophical sense, it came to mean "The Way." The word *dao* is widely used throughout East Asia in contexts that are not particularly "Daoist." Examples include the Japanese martial art known as *kendō*, or the "Way [Dao] of the Sword," and Chinese *Daoxue*, the "Study of the Way [Dao]," which in English is called Neo-Confucianism!

Even the things that are actively considered to be "Daoist" can be surprisingly nebulous and varied. The famous yin–yang dualism, for example, is often called Daoist and even imagined as central to Daoism, but it might more usefully be regarded simply as an independent strand of traditional Chinese thought. In addition, a distinctive Daoist religion eventually emerged beginning in the second century CE that became a fairly well-defined and discrete religious tradition, with its own canonical body of scripture, liturgy, priests, and institutions. Even this institutionalized Daoist religion was internally complex: the set of Daoist religious scriptures known as the *Daozang* includes over a thousand separate texts. For the classical Zhou era, however, Daoist thought may effectively be defined in terms of just two relatively short and not overtly religious books: *Laozi* (*Lao Tzu*) and *Zhuangzi* (*Chuang Tzu*). Though short, these are two of the greatest and most profound works of world literature.

According to one tradition, the man known as Laozi (from whom the book derived its title) was an older contemporary of Confucius who served as an archivist at the Zhou capital, and who once allegedly even instructed Confucius himself. Laozi merely means "Old Master," however, and both the identity of the author of the book *Laozi* and its date of composition – which may, or may not, have been as late as the third century BCE – are uncertain. The language of the *Laozi* is simple, poetic, and enigmatic in the extreme.

Zhuangzi (Master Zhuang, whose full name was Zhuang Zhou, ca. 369–ca. 286 BCE), by contrast, is thought to have been a real historical figure. The book that bears his name is a delightful, though often linguistically and conceptually challenging, collection of parables and tall tales. A fine example of Zhuangzi's style is his story concerning Cook Ding. Cook Ding was a master butcher who, in carving, had learned to follow the natural patterns of joints, tendons, and ligaments so that "flop! The whole thing comes apart like a clod of earth crumbling." After years of practice, he no longer even saw the entire carcass itself but wielded his blade with his spirit. "A good cook changes his knife once a year – because he cuts. A mediocre cook changes his knife once a month – because he hacks. I've had this knife of mine for nineteen years and I've cut up thousands of oxen with it, and yet the blade is as good as though it had just come from the grindstone." Such a cook truly understood the Way.

The Way, or Dao, is obviously the most important central concept in Daoism, but this Dao is inexpressible in words. As the famous opening line of *Laozi* puts it, "The Way that can be spoken of is not the constant Way." The Dao is nonetheless inescapable, pervading and shaping all things. Unlike the Confucian Dao, which was specifically moral and human centered, the Daoist Dao was beyond petty, artificial human considerations. "Heaven and Earth are not humane, regarding all things as straw dogs" (expendable sacrificial tokens), says *Laozi*. In the vastness of nature, humans and human concerns are inconsequential. Daoists, appropriately, were among the first people in the world to develop a fine appreciation of the natural beauty of untamed wilderness.

It was not merely that human morality was artificial: it could even be counterproductive. It is precisely because society honors the worthy that there is competition; it is because gold, jade, and other rare precious goods are treasured that there is theft. "When everyone in the world knows beauty as beauty, ugliness appears. When everyone knows good as good, not-good arrives," cautions *Laozi*. Wisdom, therefore, lies in not pursuing such "goods":

> The sage does not hoard,
> The more he uses on behalf of others,
> The more he has himself.
> And the more he gives to others,
> The more comes back to him.
> The Way of Heaven is to bring benefit and not to harm.
> The Way of the sage is to do things without contending.

Often the best course of action is nonaction (*wuwei*). The Daoists were early advocates of what could be described as laissez-faire policies. In fact, it has seriously been suggested that the French expression *laissez-faire* may have originally been coined in the eighteenth century by certain pioneering French economists (known as the Physiocrats) who admired what they imagined to be the "minimum of government intervention in the Chinese economy."[12] Although Chinese imperial government in practice was actually quite inconsistent on this point, both Daoist and Confucian theory did tend to consciously advocate an ideally minimalist approach toward rulership. Confucians favored leadership by virtuous example over regulations and punishments and stereotypically made calls for reducing taxes and "giving rest" to the people. Daoists, from their different perspective, believed that active intervention would only make things worse. "The Way is constant: by doing nothing, nothing is left undone. If lords and kings can hold to it, all things will, of themselves, be transformed," advised *Laozi*.

Legalism

A striking contrast to the ideal of minimalist government advocated by both Confucians and Daoists is provided by the third great school of classical Chinese thought: Legalism (*Fajia*). As the name implies, Legalism emphasized techniques of government based on written law – clearly codified and strictly enforced. Legalism was even less of a formal academic philosophical "school" than Confucianism. Although there are a few important Legalist texts, notably *The Book of Lord Shang* (*Shangjun shu*, attributed to Shang Yang, d. 338 BCE) and, most especially, the *Han Feizi* ("Master Han Fei," written by a student of the Confucian Xunzi named Han Fei, d. 233 BCE), Legalism developed less out of teaching and theory than through certain tendencies in administrative practice that emerged over the course of the Warring States period.

Against Confucian morality and idealism, the Legalists are sometimes said to have offered realism. Though the virtuous example of a Sage King may, or may not, impel a few people to correct themselves, as the Confucians hoped, genuine Sage Kings are in practice rare. All people, however, are naturally driven by their pursuit of self-interest, and their behavior can therefore be modified, as desired, by drafting clear laws, backed by the powerful incentives of fixed rewards and punishments.

As *The Book of Lord Shang* explained,

> The way to administer a state well is for the laws regulating officials to be clear; one does not rely on men to be intelligent and thoughtful. The ruler makes the people single-minded so they will not scheme for selfish profit. Then the strength of the state will be consolidated, and a state whose strength has been consolidated is powerful, but a country that loves talking is dismembered.

This single-minded commitment to the state goals of building a "rich country and a strong army," as the slogan had it, helped transform the Qin Kingdom, where Lord Shang served as prime minister in the fourth century BCE, into the most powerful of the Warring States, and eventually enabled it to unite all the other kingdoms into the first Chinese Empire. The ancient Chinese Legalist slogan "rich country, strong army" was also, incidentally, consciously reinvoked in modern Japan to serve as the "formal ideological foundation of industrial and technological development" in the late nineteenth century.[13] In modern China, too, the memory of ancient Legalism was somewhat rehabilitated in the twentieth century, when it came to be viewed as a progressive movement that, more than two thousand years ago, had already argued against blindly following conservative traditions and insisted on changing with the times. People had once lived in caves, as the ancient Legalists pointed out, but it would be foolish to continue living in caves now just because that was the ancient way.

The compilation of legal codes in China may have begun as early as the ninth century BCE, and the seminal *Classic of Law* (*Fajing*) was composed in the late fifth century BCE. Legalism became the ideological foundation of the first Chinese Empire, and though explicit Legalism was soon thereafter somewhat discredited because of its alleged harshness and rigidity, the Chinese Empire long remained shaped very much around the idea of government by law. This was so much the case that in the formative stage of early Japanese history, in the eighth century CE, when a new Japanese imperial government was self-consciously establishing itself on what was perceived to be the continental Chinese model, the Japanese took codes of law to be the very essence of that model. Japanese historians today routinely label this period the "Age of Penal and Administrative Law" (*ritsuryō jidai*). In Japan, however, Chinese-style legal codes would soon lapse, to be replaced by more indigenous developments. In premodern China, too, although government by law was never entirely abandoned, over the centuries it was the more humanistic Confucianism, instead, that was increasingly ascendant.

The Art of War

Confucianism, Daoism, and Legalism were the three major schools of thought in late Zhou China, but there were also many other strains of thought. One important early group were the followers of Mozi (fifth century BCE), who advocated universal love, and trained a band of followers in the techniques of defensive warfare to help protect small countries from foreign aggression. No fewer than nine chapters of the book called *Mozi* deal with issues of military defense, including such items as scaling ladders and techniques of siege warfare. Not surprisingly, the aptly named

Warring States era produced a number of specialists in military affairs. The first military text, said to be the oldest military treatise in the world, was *Sunzi's Art of War* (*Sunzi bingfa*). This book is still studied today at military academies around the world and has also inspired certain modern politicians and businesspersons. In late imperial times in China, six ancient Zhou Dynasty military treatises were combined with one later text to form what are known as the *Seven Military Classics* (*Wujing qi shu*).[14]

As is true of many early Chinese texts, the date and authorship of the *Sunzi* are hotly debated. Suggested dates range from the late sixth century (when the alleged author, Master Sun, or Sunzi, is supposed to have lived) to the late fourth century BCE. In general, the date of composition of these early texts is a matter of interest only for specialist scholars, but in the case of *Sunzi*, it may make a considerable difference because of the rapidly changing nature of warfare in the late Zhou period.

In early Zhou, armies had typically been small, campaigns brief, and combat focused on chariot-riding aristocrats adhering to chivalric ritual ideals. If the early histories can be believed, fighting with honor was regarded as more important even than winning. As China entered the Warring States era, however, large countries increasingly organized for total war. The right to bear arms, which had once been an aristocratic monopoly and privilege, was now a universal male obligation. Military conscription – a draft army, based on compulsory household registration lists – made possible huge new armies of peasant infantrymen, numbering up to hundreds of thousands of men, armed now with deadly crossbows and sometimes mobilized for quite lengthy wars. No fewer than 590 separate wars, moreover, were recorded during the two and a half centuries of the Warring States period – an average of more than two wars every year. War had become a grim familiarity.

One consequence of the changing nature of war was a much greater ruthlessness. Winning, not fighting with honor, was now everything. *Sunzi*, notoriously, declared the military "a way (*dao*) of deception," which would seem to reflect this new Warring States ruthlessness. Surprise is essential: "Attack where he is unprepared. Emerge where he does not expect." At the same time, mask your own dispositions so that to the enemy it appears that your forces are without form or pattern. At the point of attack, then, apply overwhelming force. The objective is not glory or heroics; it is victory.

An easy victory is better than a bloody one, and a decisive triumph is best achieved by making sure of preconditions before ever striking the first blow. "Therefore, the victorious military is first victorious and after that does battle." Intelligence is critical. For *Sunzi*, a key word was *shi*. Although the standard dictionary definition of *shi* is simply "power" or "force," for *Sunzi*, it meant, more precisely, the latent disposition of potential force, like an avalanche poised to fall or a crossbow cocked and ready to be fired with a slight pull on the trigger. "Thus the *shi* of one skilled at setting people to battle is like rolling round rocks from a mountain," explained *Sunzi*.

The idea is to win with as little fighting and destruction as possible, based on intelligence rather than brute force. If you know yourself and know your enemy,

Sunzi advises, there will be no danger "in one hundred battles." Such an emphasis on intelligence (if not always on avoiding bloodshed) was also in keeping with the new Warring States approach. The huge new peasant conscript armies required massive and sophisticated logistical support, including the large-scale manufacture of arms and armor and supplies of food and clothing. Training and organization became critical, and the military treatises of the era typically emphasized the importance of discipline and planning. The commander was no longer a chariot-riding aristocrat or a warrior who heroically personally leads the charge into battle but rather a grand strategist operating behind the lines. *Sunzi*, famously, put attacking the enemy's strategies ahead of striking at his cities. Cerebral warfare took precedence over physical combat.

Sunzi suggested the intriguing ideal of possibly even winning a war without the need for any actual fighting. This is sometimes said to represent a uniquely Chinese approach to warfare, and Chinese civilization is also sometimes described as particularly unmilitaristic. It is in fact true that under the later empire, a military career was not nearly as honored as a literary one, and that even in military affairs, brains were typically valued over brawn. One of the more notable contrasts that can be drawn between the Chinese Confucian ethos and the familiar Western (and Japanese) traditions may indeed be a consistent tendency to prefer the civilian and literary (*wen*) over the martial (*wu*). According to the *Analects*, when asked about tactics, "Confucius replied, 'I have heard about sacrificial vessels but have learned nothing about the deployment of troops.' The next day he made his departure." But Confucianism was never the only strand of thought in China. One modern scholar who has carefully studied the *Seven Military Classics* and their application in late imperial warfare concludes that the central paradigm of Chinese strategic culture was actually not so very different from the Western realist's epigram: "If you want peace, prepare for war."[15] Certainly there have been many wars throughout China's long history. The first imperial unification of China, in particular, was forged in bloody war.

First Empire

"The Faults of Qin" (221–207 BCE)

The ancient Greek world of multiple small city-states was transformed into the Hellenistic age of large autocratic empires by the conquests of Alexander the Great (356–323 BCE). Roughly a century later, in eastern Eurasia, China went through a somewhat similar process. In China's case, the many small, semi-independent domains that had made up the early Zhou realm had long since been consolidated into a handful of relatively large territorial kingdoms. These kingdoms were all unified into a single empire for the first time in 221 BCE.

The man who would become the first emperor of China, Ying Zheng (260–210 BCE), was thirty-nine years old, by Chinese reckoning, when he unified what seemed to be the entire civilized world – a triumph so complete that he boasted, "Wherever there are traces of people, there are none who are not my subjects."[16]

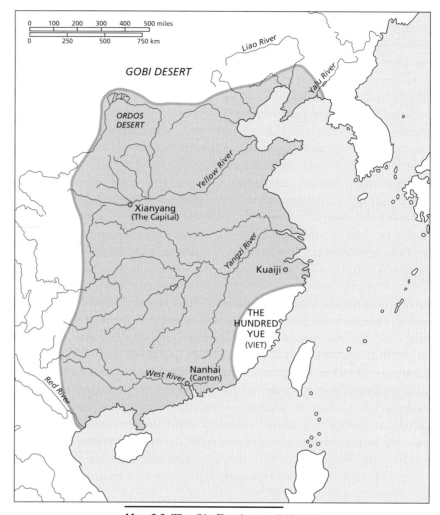

Map 2.2 The Qin Empire, ca. 210 BCE

Despite such obvious exaggeration, and continued use of the ancient expression "[All] Under Heaven" (*Tianxia*) as a designation for the realm, it was approximately what we think of today as China proper that was now, for the first time, seriously unified into a single country. As natural as this unification may seem to us now, it was probably not altogether inevitable. The early Zhou had established an ideal of a universal Son of Heaven, under Heaven's universal moral order, but had not attempted a single central government. The classical world of the ancient Chinese philosophers had been one of multiple independent countries and considerable local diversity. Even a century after the first unification in 221 BCE, there were still several different languages spoken within the empire, descended from the languages of the former Warring States.

Ironically, the kingdom that conquered all the others and founded the first version of the Chinese Empire, Qin, had begun as only a peripheral, semi-Chinese, frontier state on the edges of the Chinese world. The Qin state was officially founded (after having been a minor Zhou vassal for some time) in 770 BCE in that same region "Within the Passes" that had been the original Zhou heartland. Among the earliest distinctively Qin-style archeological artifacts, which were at first confined to an area west of the region "Within the Passes," there is clear evidence of a blending of Zhou-style Chinese and non-Chinese influences.

Until the Warring States period, Qin remained less developed than the other states on the Central Plain to its east. But the Qin location on the northwestern frontier of the Zhou world may have given it advantageous access to trade with Central Asia.[17] Its frontier location may also have encouraged warlike inclinations, and Qin's relatively weak commitment to traditional Confucian values may have made it more open to experimentation with the radical new ideas of Legalism. Qin may therefore represent an early example of what is sometimes today called the "advantages of backwardness." Qin was in a position to make a selective borrowing of useful ideas from the more advanced kingdoms in the east without being burdened by the weight of all their traditions.

The arrival in Qin, from the east, of Lord Shang in 361 BCE marks a turning point in the history of both Qin and China. One of the notable features of the Qin state was a remarkable degree of openness to immigrant talent. A scurrilous (and probably untrue) rumor even alleged that the First Emperor himself, a century later, was the illegitimate son of an immigrant merchant who had become chancellor. After his arrival in Qin, Lord Shang was given a chance to experiment with Legalist reforms in the Qin government. Over the course of the next decade, Lord Shang promulgated new law codes, unified the systems of weights and measures, established a centralized bureaucratic system of administration, and created new nonhereditary titles. Although Lord Shang himself was executed in 338 BCE because of a conflict with the royal family, he set the Qin war machine in motion.

A century later, in 247 BCE, the man who would become the first emperor of China assumed the throne as the last king of Qin. Surviving several assassination attempts, this king grew increasingly fearful of appearing in public or even of disclosing his location. In 221 BCE, his armies conquered the final remaining Warring State (Qi), and his first recorded act following this unprecedented achievement was to consult with his officials to devise a more majestic title for himself than mere "king." The result of their deliberations was the new title *huangdi*, or "emperor." This man is usually known to history as Qin Shi Huangdi, a title that literally means "First Emperor of Qin." (After ascending the throne, East Asian rulers are never supposed to be referred to by their personal names – while they remain alive, a range of euphemisms are employed, and after their death, they are referred to by various posthumous titles.) The title *huangdi* continued to be used in China until 1912, and it inspired related imperial terminology in Japan and Vietnam as well (while in premodern Korea, the humbler and older title "king" continued in use).

The First Emperor of Qin famously standardized the writing systems, legal codes, coins, and weights and measures of all the conquered kingdoms in an effort to promote a single unified imperial culture. He erected fortifications across the northern borders, which are popularly thought of as the first version of the Great Wall of China; established forty-four new administrative units north of the Ordos Desert; and relocated hundreds of thousands of people from the interior to settle the northern frontier. The First Emperor's southern conquests, which extended into what is now northern Vietnam, also brought much of what is now southeast China into the Chinese world for the first time. Altogether, according to one estimate, no fewer than 3.17 million people were relocated to both the northern and southern frontiers by the First Emperor, in the process helping to dissolve old local identities and establish new empirewide allegiances.[18]

Traditional Chinese histories portray the Qin regime as incredibly systematic and intrusive, and skeptical modern scholars have sometimes been inclined to doubt that any premodern government could have ever really exercised that degree of effective control over such a large area. In 1975, however, archeologists discovered roughly a thousand strips of wood – the principal writing material in China before the invention of paper – containing Qin era documents at a place called Yunmeng, in central China. These and other discoveries have tended to reconfirm the traditional picture of relatively efficient Legalist bureaucratic machinery. At the same time, if the Qin "reputation for Draconian punishments is not exactly controverted" by these new discoveries, "neither is it strikingly confirmed."[19] Revisionists now argue that the Qin government may not have been quite as tyrannical as later Chinese Confucians traditionally remembered it. These archeologically rediscovered Qin texts also reveal a greater diversity of thought, and evidence of a less docile subject population, than might have previously been imagined.

The First Emperor justified his conquests in the name of providing peace and uniform justice to the people, after a long period of incessant warfare. Two thousand years before Thomas Hobbes was born, a book compiled at the Qin court around 239 BCE already prefigured Hobbes's famous notion that it may be necessary for people to submit to the authority of a powerful state in the sheer interest of self-preservation: "there is no greater disorder than the absence of a Son of Heaven. Without a Son of Heaven the strong subdue the weak, the many abuse the few, and mutual destruction through the deployment of troops cannot cease." As the First Emperor himself put it, "that the whole world is tormented by warfare without cease is because there are Lords and Princes."[20]

The First Emperor initially made a display of promoting traditional values by appointing seventy scholars as advisors to the throne. Continued dissent, especially criticism of the Qin regime by comparing it unfavorably to the idealized memory of antiquity, proved intolerable, however. In 213 BCE, the First Emperor notoriously ordered the burning of all books, except for histories of the Qin state and a few useful technical treatises. In 212 BCE, he reportedly went further and ordered the execution, for subversion, of 460 scholars. In Confucian memory, these two horrifying acts became indelible emblems of Qin tyranny.

The First Emperor was also deeply interested in arcane techniques for prolonging life and may have even envisioned himself as a god figure (*di*), wielding cosmic power to align the universe.[21] Perhaps the ultimate example of his self-aggrandizement may be the enormous tomb that he had constructed for himself. The tomb, which is twenty miles in circumference, contains, as just one small part, an entire terracotta army consisting of thousands of life-sized clay soldiers, which was buried and only recently rediscovered by accident. Thus, though the First Emperor's reputation may have been darkened by Confucian biases under subsequent dynasties, the staggering scale of his ambition was real enough.

According to traditional histories, the very harshness and inflexibility of the Qin Legalist regulations soon provoked revolt. Within a year of the First Emperor's death in 210 BCE, the land was writhing with rebellion. At the same time, a power struggle at court was simultaneously also tearing it apart from within. It is said that when Qin Shi Huangdi died, a certain eunuch (eunuchs were castrated imperial household servants) conspired to briefly keep news of the emperor's death secret and forged an edict ordering the emperor's capable eldest son to commit suicide. The throne therefore passed to an incompetent younger son, who was soon reduced to a puppet. With the eunuch's encouragement, this Second Emperor began to suspect other members of his own family and ordered twelve of his own brothers and ten of his sisters executed. After three years, the Second Emperor's position had become so pathetic that he killed himself. By this time, rebels were already at the gates.

The Qin fell in 207 BCE, after only fifteen years as an imperial dynasty. The reasons for Qin's meteoric rise and fall were eloquently summarized by a man born just nine years after the First Emperor's death, Jia Yi (201–169 BCE), in a classic essay titled "The Faults of Qin." Jia Yi wrote that Qin had succeeded in "rolling up the empire like a mat, enveloping the entire universe, pocketing all within the Four Seas, and swallowing up everything in all Eight Directions." Yet Qin was then brought down abruptly by some rustic rebels. "Why? Because the ruler lacked humaneness and rightness; because preserving power differs fundamentally from seizing power."[22] The Qin suppression of dissent only compounded these errors by making it impossible for wise men to show their true loyalty by warning of the impending dangers.

Despite being a perceptive critic of the Qin Dynasty, Jia Yi ascribed the dynasty's fall to its abuses and excesses and the incompetence of the First Emperor's successors rather than to the imperial system itself. After a relatively brief civil war, a new imperial dynasty was established on the ruins of the Qin. Explicit Legalism may have been discredited by the Qin failure, but the imperial system was not, and in a more moderate form the Qin institutional model (and the imperial title *huangdi*) would survive for two thousand years, until 1912. The Qin model of China as a single, unified country survives still today and, appropriately enough, it is likely that our English word *China* derives (through Sanskrit) from the name Qin.

The Han Empire (202 BCE–220 CE)

The Qin Dynasty had unified the Warring States but only lasted fifteen years. At the time Qin fell, therefore, for many people, the old independent kingdoms were still a living memory, and a return to some version of the old Warring States multinational order might have been a not unreasonable expectation. Despite the fleeting revival of some of those kingdoms as participants in the anti-Qin rebellion, however, it was the unified imperial model that was soon restored instead.

In the long run, the most important rebel leader proved to be a man named Liu Bang (d. 195 BCE). Liu was a man of humble birth – he began his career by passing a test and becoming a local Qin Dynasty police chief – but by 207 BCE, a rebel army under his command had penetrated the region "Within the Passes" and captured the Qin capital, putting an end to the Qin Dynasty. There had been a prior agreement among the rebel leaders that whoever took the region "Within the Passes" first would become its next king, but Liu Bang nonetheless sealed up the Qin treasuries and awaited the arrival of the supreme rebel coalition commander.

In the aftermath, Liu Bang was not awarded the historically and strategically significant region "Within the Passes" but was instead made king of Han, in the Han River valley area somewhat farther south. An enduring consequence of this assignment was that Han would become not only the name of the imperial dynasty Liu Bang soon founded but, by extension from that, eventually also the standard name for all ethnic Chinese people. Today the Han people are the Chinese people.

When the king of Chu was treacherously assassinated by another commander in 206 BCE, that act gave Liu Bang a pretext to reopen the civil war. Liu's first move was to strike north and retake the region "Within the Passes." This put Liu Bang in possession of the very same base area from which both the Zhou and the Qin had previously conquered China. After several more years of seesaw conflict, by 202 BCE, Liu Bang had defeated all his rivals and made himself the founding emperor of a new dynasty, the Han. By this time, however, the land had reportedly been so devastated by years of civil war that the new emperor was unable even to assemble a team of four horses of matching color for his own carriage. (For a bronze model of a carriage from the late Han Dynasty, see Figure 2.1.)

As emperor, Liu Bang is known to history by his posthumous temple name Han Gaozu (the "High Ancestor of the Han"). Emperor Gaozu rewarded his leading lieutenants and relatives with appointments as kings (or princes) over what were initially semiautonomous principalities. Such refeudalization may have been necessary at first, but subsequent Han emperors quickly reversed the policy. Within about a half-century, semi-independent principalities had effectively been eliminated, and Qin-style centralized administration had been restored throughout the empire.

Once Han Gaozu (the former Liu Bang) achieved control of the Central Plain, he then led a huge military force, reportedly consisting of 320,000 infantrymen, against the nomadic tribes to the north. The Qin Dynasty had done much the same thing a decade or two earlier, but this time Han Gaozu encountered a rude surprise: organized opposition. The nomadic tribes to the north of China had unified into their first imperial confederation, the Xiongnu.

Despite the apparent clarity provided by the line of the Great Wall, China's northern frontier is actually more of an uneven transitional zone from Chinese-style farming to ranching and, eventually, true steppe pastoral nomadism. The Great Wall may have originally even been constructed more as a projection of

Figure 2.1. A bronze model horse and carriage, with driver and attendant, from the Eastern Han Dynasty (second century CE). Excavated in 1969 at Wuwei, Gansu. Gansu Provincial Museum, Lanzhou, China. Erich Lessing/Art Resource, New York.

Chinese imperial power onto the nomads than to keep the nomads out. In fact, the Qin walls brought some of the best Xiongnu archaeological sites inside the Qin Empire. Although the region is generally called Mongolia today, the word *Mongol* did not yet exist in Qin and Han times. Chinese sources themselves commonly make an important distinction between regions north and south of the Gobi Desert, roughly corresponding to modern Outer and Inner Mongolia. Areas south of the Gobi have frequently been included inside Chinese imperial borders, even though much of the terrain is better suited to grazing than to farming.

The rise of the first nomadic imperial confederation to the north of China may actually have been a direct military response to the challenge posed by the creation of the first Chinese Empire – a new form of political organization capable of mobilizing the military potential of the scattered steppe tribes. The Xiongnu were not a homogeneous people but a confederation of tribes, including different ethnic and linguistic groups. The Xiongnu language, if there was one, remains a mystery.

This should not be surprising. Most steppe nomadic empires were actually such mixtures. A Roman visitor to the camp of Attila the Hun (ca. 406–453 CE) in western Eurasia, for example, reported that the Huns were a mixed group, speaking the Hunnic, Gothic, and Latin languages. Attila's own name was actually Gothic. There has been a persistent theory that these Huns who so famously terrorized the Roman Empire may have been a westward-migrating splinter group of the very same Xiongnu who had earlier confronted Han Dynasty China. Since both the Xiongnu and the Huns are known to have been internally mixed groupings, however, such speculation may ultimately be rather meaningless. Nonetheless, the steppe grasslands, which stretch from north of Beijing to the Hungarian Plain in Europe, did form a single reasonably coherent cultural zone.

The early Han Dynasty, like the Qin before it, had a conscript or draft army. All adult males were required to perform two years of military service – typically one year of training and one year of active duty. This enabled the Han Dynasty to muster a truly enormous army, but also one that essentially consisted of amateur peasant infantry. Han Gaozu's forces on this occasion, as they marched north, to their surprise found themselves no match for Xiongnu mounted archers, who were accustomed to life in the saddle as warriors. The first Han emperor, Gaozu, was surrounded and trapped on a mountaintop near modern Datong, just east of the northernmost bend of the Yellow River, for a whole week in 200 BCE.

Humbled by this first encounter with Xiongnu nomadic military power, for the next half-century, the Han Dynasty pursued policies of peace with the Xiongnu, appeasing them with lavish gifts and sending Han imperial daughters to become brides for Xiongnu chieftains. This appeasement policy ended only after Wudi (Emperor Wu, the "Martial Emperor") took the throne in 141 BCE as the sixth Han emperor. Wudi would rule for fifty-four years (141–87 BCE), longer than any emperor of China prior to the eighteenth century, and his reign would be marked by both great success and controversy.

Soon after taking the throne, Wudi held formal court debates over the wisdom of the appeasement policy toward the Xiongnu. Appeasement was now rejected, if only because it had not actually prevented continued Xiongnu raiding. Moreover, the Han Dynasty had by this time developed the military resources to successfully confront the Xiongnu. At the start of the dynasty, the Han army had been conspicuously lacking in cavalry, but by the time Wudi assumed the throne, several horse-breeding stations had been established, and the Han army now had access to some three hundred thousand horses. Infantry equipped with crossbows fitted with precision triggers and fired from wagon trains had also proved effective against nomadic warriors. Even so, however, the Han still faced enormous logistical difficulties in trying to mount sustained warfare on the vast open reaches of the steppe, where the nomads could always simply pull back their tents and wait until supplies ran out for the Chinese armies.

Wudi therefore developed a new grand strategy for outflanking the Xiongnu. To the northeast, this involved the conquest and incorporation into the Han Empire of southern Manchuria and northern Korea. In the northwest, Emperor Wu began by dispatching an embassy, with a Xiongnu defector as a guide, to seek allies in the western regions. Some members of this party may have penetrated as far west as Persia, but they were twice captured by the Xiongnu, and of a hundred men, only two finally managed to return to China thirteen years later. Although this embassy forged no military alliances, it gained strategically valuable information and established more formal diplomatic and commercial exchanges with the western regions. Over the next several decades, Han military campaigns brought what are now Gansu and Xinjiang (Eastern Turkestan) into the empire as part of the western extension of the Han imperial offensive against the Xiongnu. On one occasion, crossing the Pamir Mountains into Central Asia in 101 BCE, Han armies even captured the area of Samarkand, in what is now Uzbekistan.

The Han established a chain of garrisons and fortifications in the northwest, which disrupted the oasis sources of tribute for the Xiongnu and led ultimately to the disintegration of the Xiongnu Empire (by about 73 BCE). The financial cost of this strategy also almost bankrupted the Han Dynasty, however. One recent estimate puts the total expense of Han Wudi's military operations in the northwest at 1.89 trillion Chinese cash over forty years.[23] Although the expansion of the Han Empire to the northwest helped promote what later came to be called the Silk Roads, across which camel caravans brought grapes from Persia and glass from the Mediterranean in exchange for Chinese silk, Emperor Wu's aggressive military campaigns put a severe strain on the Han economy and prompted intrusive new state economic interventions, including such measures as taxes on merchant inventories and government monopolies on mines and on the manufacture and distribution of iron, salt, alcohol, and coins. A fascinating record of a court debate in 81 BCE over the wisdom of continuing these economic policies survives, known as the *Discourses on Salt and Iron*.

Despite Han Wudi's economic interventionism and aggressive military expansionism, which might seem reminiscent of Qin Dynasty Legalism, Wudi was also ironically the emperor who first established Confucianism as imperial orthodoxy. The original Han founders had been rough military men. One famous story tells of a scholar presenting the first Han emperor with copies of the classics. Patting his mount, the emperor said that he had won his empire from horseback and had no need for books. The scholar's swift reply was, you may have conquered the empire on horseback, but can you rule it that way? With Legalism discredited by the fall of Qin, the Han Dynasty needed a new theoretical basis for its legitimization. Although Wudi himself was not exactly a Confucian, he found his source of imperial justification in that school.

The Confucian canon was first officially defined by Han Wudi in 136 BCE, when he assigned a master to teach each of the Five Classics.[24] In 124 BCE, Wudi also established an imperial academy for the study of the classics. This academy initially had only a few students, but by the end of the Han Dynasty there were reportedly thirty thousand students in 1,850 rooms. Systems of testing, and regional recommendations of students, began to be elaborated. Local officials were encouraged to recommend men with a reputation for Confucian virtue for government office. The expectation was increasingly planted, over the centuries of the Han Dynasty, that officials should be scholarly gentlemen. Ambitious families encouraged their children to study for the purpose of career advancement. Over time, schools began to be promoted even in rural communities. In late Han times, tablets were placed marking the doors of villagers who conspicuously exhibited Confucian virtues, and Confucian expectations even came to be enforced by law. For example, in the last century BCE, people who were in mourning for deceased parents, or whose parents

Map 2.3 The Han Dynasty under Emperor Wu (r. 141–87 BCE)

were aged, were exempted from compulsory labor service. In 116 CE, high officials were required to observe three years of mourning following the death of their fathers. A final consummation of Confucianism as Han Dynasty imperial orthodoxy was achieved in 175 CE, when it was decreed that correct texts of the Five Classics literally be carved on stone outside the imperial academy.

Han Dynasty Confucianism was rooted in the meticulous study of the classics. There were, however, certain aspects of Confucian thought peculiar to the Han Dynasty. These are best exemplified by a man named Dong Zhongshu (179–104 BCE). Central to Dong's interpretation of Confucianism was the idea that "Heaven and man are mutually connected." The special function of the ruler, therefore, is to harmonize relations between Heaven, earth, and man. It was believed that humane behavior could reverberate sympathetically throughout the natural order so that if only the monarch corrected his own heart, even the seasons might follow in proper order. This created an ideology that legitimized the Han Empire by linking it to the very cosmological structure of the universe, yet simultaneously also restricted autocratic conduct with threats of dire supernatural sanctions.

The dynastic *History of the Former Han*, for example, tells the story of one high government official who rode past a brawl without intervening but stopped to inquire about the panting of an ox. The official explained his seemingly bizarre behavior by saying that brawls were routine affairs that should be handled by subordinates, but an ox panting due to unseasonable heat was the responsibility of top officials, who "are charged with the task of harmonizing the yin and yang."[25] Thus Confucianism promoted a kind of autocratic imperial minimalism.

The Han Dynasty lasted for some four hundred years (interrupted briefly by the usurpation of Wang Mang in 9–23 CE), and its legacy remains so important that the Chinese are still today called the Han people. Nonetheless, the Han eventually fell. One growing problem was economic polarization. By the late Warring States period, the practice of private ownership of land had already been well established, but the Warring States and early imperial governments were founded on a tax and conscript base that consisted of many roughly equal small farmers. Over the course of the Han Dynasty, however, some wealthy families were able to acquire large estates. In the process, many smallholders were dispossessed and often reduced to tenants, servants, or even vagrants and bandits. This in turn reduced the central government's tax base and put an even heavier burden on the dwindling number of small farmers remaining on the tax rolls.

Court politics generated other problems, especially the allegedly undue influence exercised by eunuchs and the families of imperial consorts. Dissident critics of eunuch power were punished in a series of purges, stretching over some two decades beginning in 166 CE. During these purges, more that a hundred distinguished gentlemen died in prison, and some six or seven hundred others were banned from office for life. Paradoxically, this gave the pose of lofty withdrawal and disengagement from government a degree of fashionable moral cachet.

In 184 CE, a religiously inspired rebellion, known as the revolt of the Yellow Turbans, erupted. Although the Yellow Turbans themselves were soon suppressed, in the process, power passed into the hands of independent military commanders.

In 191, one of these generals carried away the heir to the throne and destroyed the late Han capital (Luoyang), looting and burning, among other things, the great imperial libraries. "The fine silks of charts and books were used by military men as curtains and sacks."[26] As warlord armies tramped across China, "beside their horses they hang the heads of men; behind their horses they carry the [captive] women."[27] The female poet who wrote these last lines was herself captured and lived with a Xiongnu prince for twelve years before being ransomed. After her ransom, she reported that the private library of four thousand rolls of books that her father had left her was all lost.

The Romance of the Three Kingdoms (220–280 CE)

By the year 196, there were thirteen major independent warlord regimes within the ruins of the Han Empire. Reportedly, some of their armies lacked plans even to see themselves through the year, plundering when they were hungry and throwing away the leftovers when they were full. One warlord, however, Cao Cao (155–220), whose father had been an adopted son of the Han Dynasty chief eunuch, gained custody over the person of the puppet Han emperor and leveraged this control over the emperor into domination of all north China. By 207, he may have controlled half the total population of China. It was not until after Cao Cao's own death in 220 that Cao's son finally had the audacity to formally depose the last Han monarch and proclaim himself the founding emperor of a new imperial dynasty, called the Wei (or Cao-Wei, to distinguish it from various other states called Wei).[28]

Before long, the situation stabilized somewhat, as the various warlord enclaves resolved themselves into three relatively substantial empires, popularly known as the Three Kingdoms (see Map 2.4). Cao Cao's family ruled the Wei Dynasty in the north (220–265); another empire called Wu (222–280) was established in the southeast, in the lower Yangzi River region, with its capital at what is now Nanjing (Nanking); and a third dynasty called Shu-Han (221–263) was formed in the southwest, in the area of modern Sichuan. The name Shu-Han is obviously a compound. Shu was an old place name for the area, and Han referred to the Han Dynasty, since the Shu-Han emperors claimed special legitimacy through descent from the old Han imperial family.

The Three Kingdoms era has been richly immortalized in Chinese fiction (and more recently in movies and video games) as the great age of Chinese military strategy and heroic warfare. One of the most beloved and widely read premodern Chinese novels was called the *Romance of the Three Kingdoms* (*Sanguo zhi tongsu yanyi*). Although it was not written until much later – the earliest surviving edition of the novel dates from 1522 – the book is a fictionalized retelling of the history of this period, with Cao Cao cast in the role of leading villain. The clever stratagems, battles, and dramatic political rivalries of the era have been much glorified on stage and in fiction. Although this warfare is what has captured the popular imagination, the Three Kingdoms period was also an age of notable awakening in thought and literature, of individualism, and of some remarkably colorful eccentrics.

Map 2.4 The Chinese Three Kingdoms and East Asia in 250 CE

The fall of the Han Dynasty brought down with it much of the ideological underpinnings of Han Confucianism. Seemingly arid classical chapter and verse scholarship became less fashionable now than elegant discussions of lofty metaphysical principles, known as Mysterious Learning (*Xuanxue*), often especially involving references to the *Laozi, Zhuangzi,* and the *Book of Changes.* Such profound questions as what existed before the universe began or what lies beyond the borders of Heaven and earth were asked, and answered, *Laozi* fashion, paradoxically, with "nothing." Nothing, therefore, it came to be argued, was the origin of all things.

A vogue emerged for retreat into libertinism, hedonism, wine, and drugs, sometimes with the cynical observation that both the Sage and the Tyrant "wind up equally dead" anyway. One amusing character was said to go out riding in a wheelbarrow with a jug of wine in his hand, and a servant following with a shovel, instructed to bury him wherever he died. For some of the more memorable figures of this era, however – such as Ruan Ji (210–263), one of the celebrated "Seven Sages of the Bamboo Grove" – the pose of habitual drunkenness and remote philosophical abstraction was chiefly a vehicle for escape from murderous political intrigue, and the deliberate flouting of the staid conventions of Confucian decorum (*li*) was in the name of a more sincere morality. In the late Han Dynasty, the need to win a local reputation for Confucian virtue in order to be recommended for office had created a powerful incentive for hypocritical pretense, and such third-century figures as Ruan Ji represent an appealing counterreaction against hypocrisy.

In 265, the Three Kingdoms Wei throne was usurped by one of its own generals, who founded a new dynasty called the Western Jin (265–316). In 280, the Western Jin then successfully completed the unification of the other Three Kingdoms with the final subjugation of Wu in the southeast. The Chinese Empire was thus reunified, but this reunification proved to be ephemeral, effectively lasting little more than a decade before it began to fragment again. Drawing a lesson from the ease with which he himself had seized the throne through a palace coup, the first Western Jin emperor tried to strengthen the position of his family by appointing twenty-seven (eventually fifty) of his close relatives as princes, often with real regional military power. Rather than solidifying the dynasty, this instead created the conditions for a vicious power struggle within the imperial family itself, after the founding Western Jin emperor died in 290. Imperial power soon tore itself apart completely in the resulting Disturbances of the Eight Princes.

These warring princes typically relied on cavalry forces drawn from semi-nomadic tribal auxiliaries. Over the course of the Han Dynasty, the practice of military conscription had lapsed, and the draft-based citizen army was replaced by more professional forces, many of whom were ethnic minorities. Much of the burden of northern frontier defense, meanwhile, had also been assumed by nomadic allies, who had settled within the borders of the Han Empire in a belt stretching from Manchuria in the east to the northern loop of the Yellow River in the west. Now, as Chinese imperial government imploded amid protracted and devastatingly self-destructive civil wars, non-Chinese warriors often found themselves in control of the battlefields. In 304, one Xiongnu chieftain proclaimed himself ruler of an independent state in north China. In 311, the Western Jin capital at Luoyang fell, and in 316, the alternate Western Jin imperial capital at Chang'an (modern Xi'an) was also captured. By this time, as a contemporary lamented, "marauding nomads watered their horses in the Yangzi."[29]

Far to the west, dramatic parallel events were also occurring. In 376, bands of Goths, fleeing the depredations of the Huns, crossed the Danube and delivered the first of several military shocks that eventually brought down the western Roman Empire. In China's case, although there were no literal invasions from beyond the borders, there were certainly similar roaming bands of "barbarian" warriors. Chinese imperial unity was shattered. Between the third century and the seventh, there would be thirty-seven historically recognized dynasties in China, twenty-two of which, moreover, had identifiably non-Chinese rulers. The greatest Age of Division in two thousand years of Chinese imperial history had begun.

For Further Reading

Comprehensive coverage of China's formative age is provided by Michael Loewe and Edward L. Shaughnessy, eds., *The Cambridge History of Ancient China: From the Origins of Civilization to 221 B.C.* (Cambridge University Press, 1999). On the Zhou Dynasty, see Cho-yun Hsu (Zhuoyun Xu), *Ancient China in Transition: An Analysis of Social Mobility, 722–222 B.C.* (Stanford University Press, [1965] 1977); and Cho-yun Hsu and Katheryn M. Linduff, *Western Chou Civilization* (New Haven, CT: Yale University Press, 1988).

An important study of the classic textual canon that became so central to Chinese and East Asian civilization is Mark Edward Lewis, *Writing and Authority in Early China* (Albany: State University of New York Press, 1999). On the Chinese classics, see also Burton Watson, *Early Chinese Literature* (New York: Columbia University Press, 1962). For the military treatises, see Ralph D. Sawyer and Mei-chün Sawyer, trans., *The Seven Military Classics of Ancient China* (New York: Basic Books, [1993] 2007).

On classical Chinese thought, see A. C. Graham, *Disputers of the Tao: Philosophical Argument in Ancient China* (La Salle, IL: Open Court, 1989), and Benjamin I. Schwartz, *The World of Thought in Ancient China* (Cambridge, MA: Harvard University Press, 1985). A somewhat dated but still valuable comprehensive survey is Yu-lan Fung, *A Short History of Chinese Philosophy*, ed. Derk Bodde (New York: Free Press, 1948).

For the early imperial Qin and Han dynasties, see Denis Twitchett and Michael Loewe, eds., *The Cambridge History of China, vol. I. The Ch'in and Han Empires, 221 B.C.–A.D. 220* (Cambridge University Press, 1986). See also Chun-shu Chang, *The Rise of the Chinese Empire*, 2 vols. (Ann Arbor: University of Michigan Press, 2007); Mark Edward Lewis, *The Early Chinese Empires: Qin and Han* (Cambridge, MA: Harvard University Press, 2007); and Michael Loewe, *Everyday Life in Early Imperial China during the Han Period 202 BC–AD 220* (Indianapolis, IN: Hackett, [1968] 2005). Early imperial relations with the steppe world are expertly explored in Nicola Di Cosmo, *Ancient China and Its Enemies: The Rise of Nomadic Power in East Asian History* (Cambridge University Press, 2002).

On the Three Kingdoms period, see Rafe de Crespigny, *Generals of the South: The Foundation and Early History of the Three Kingdoms State of Wu*, Faculty of Asian Studies Monograph 16 (Canberra: Australian National University, 1990), and, by the same author, *Imperial Warlord: A Biography of Cao Cao, 155–220 AD* (Leiden: Brill, 2010); Howard L. Goodman, *Ts'ao P'i Transcendent: The Political Culture of Dynasty-Founding in China at the End of the Han* (Seattle: Scripta Serica, 1998); and – concerning Ruan Ji and the "Seven Sages of the Bamboo Grove" – Donald Holzman, *Poetry and Politics: The Life and Works of Juan Chi, A.D. 210–263* (Cambridge University Press, 1976).

3   The Age of Cosmopolitanism

China in Division

The Sixteen Kingdoms (North China, 304–439)

In the early fourth century, centralized imperial government disintegrated almost completely in north China. For over a hundred years, the ancient Chinese cultural heartland in the north was shredded between what are conventionally known as the Sixteen Kingdoms.[1] More precisely, historians actually recognize twenty-one distinct regimes in north China between the years 304 and 439 (not to mention other independent local communities that never aspired to become states). Despite the conventional English label "Sixteen Kingdoms," moreover, these regimes were also often really empires, in the sense of being relatively large, multiethnic, military-conquest states ruled by men claiming the Chinese title "emperor" (*huangdi*). An alternate title, "heavenly king" (*tianwang*), was, however, invoked with unusual frequency during this period, possibly as a result of cultural influences coming from the steppe.[2] As it happens, most of these Sixteen Kingdoms had rulers with non-Chinese ethnic identities.

While north China plunged into chaos during the fourth century, perhaps an eighth of the entire northern Chinese population may have fled to the relative shelter and stability of the south. Many of these refugees settled in the general region of the lower Yangzi River valley, where members of the Western Jin imperial family reestablished a court in exile, known to history as the Eastern Jin Dynasty (317–420). The Eastern Jin capital was the city that is today called Nanjing (English: Nanking). This became the nucleus for a series of five (Eastern Jin, Song, Qi, Liang, and Chen) culturally and economically flourishing, but politically and militarily weak, Southern dynasties. Including the earlier third-century southern state of Three Kingdoms Wu, these Southern dynasties are sometimes also referred to as the Six Dynasties. Those people who remained in the north, meanwhile, huddled behind thousands of improvised local fortifications.

Trade and commerce ground to a virtual halt in the north during this period. No new coins were issued in north China for almost two hundred years. Much

Map 3.1 States and Peoples in 410 CE

farmland was given over to pasture (or stood vacant), and a ranching or herding economy spread deeply into north China. The raising of livestock was a fundamental part of the lifestyle of the non-Chinese peoples (generically referred to in the Chinese sources as Hu, and divided into five major different population groups[3]) who now came to dominate the northern landscape politically and militarily. Some scholars believe there may have even been millions of these originally non-Chinese people in fourth-century north China.

These people typically emphasized the raising of livestock (though they were not necessarily actual nomads) rather than Chinese-style agriculture, and they consumed much animal flesh, such as mutton, as well as quantities of the dairy products that Chinese cuisine has otherwise normally abhorred. They spoke languages that were not merely different from but completely unrelated to Chinese. Most of their languages were probably related to either Turkic or Mongolic, but it has been speculated that the core of one group (the Jie) may have even originally been speakers of an Indo-European language. At least some of these people were, furthermore, said to have a distinctive physical appearance, featuring deep-set eyes, high (i.e., protuberant) noses, and full beards (sometimes even described as "yellow," although probably really meaning brownish). Most critically, they were also clearly still conscious of having identities that were different from the majority population of the former Chinese empires, whom they began to call "Han" in the fifth or sixth century.

Nevertheless, there is also no evidence that any of them had actually come from anywhere outside of the modern borders of China anytime recently. There were not really any "barbarian invasions." During the Bronze Age, roughly contemporary to the Shang Dynasty on the Central Plain, a distinctly non-Chinese northern cultural complex had emerged that extended south as far as the northern parts of modern Shaanxi, Shanxi, and Hebei provinces of China proper, and northern-style nomadic mounted archery was famously first adopted in China in 307 BCE by a Warring State located in northern Shanxi.[4] A non-Chinese presence in this region was hardly anything new. Shanxi in particular now became something of an epicenter for non-Chinese activity.

The first of the Sixteen Kingdoms (which was initially called Han, a name that was later changed to Zhao, and which is known to history as Former Zhao; 304–329 CE) was founded by a scion of Xiongnu royalty in 304 at a preexisting Xiongnu base in southern Shanxi. Even the most exotic of the fourth-century non-Chinese state founders – the Jie – for generations now made their home in southern Shanxi, whatever their distant origins. The population group that seems to have come from farthest away most recently (and also the one that became historically the most important), the Tuoba branch of the Xianbei people, according to their own legends, came originally from what is today northeastern Inner Mongolia, inside China's modern borders. By the fourth century, moreover, even these Tuoba Xianbei had resided for some time in the area adjacent to the northern loop of the Yellow River, including northern Shanxi.

The Qin and Han empires had unified multiple local populations under a single political structure, with a single common written language and a broadly shared elite culture, but they had remained, nonetheless, significantly multicultural and multiethnic empires. The Han Dynasty had also relied heavily upon client non-Chinese tribal allies as a kind of defensive buffer along the broad and often vaguely defined northern border between the zones of Chinese-style intensive farming and steppe-style pastoral nomadism. The non-Chinese groups who appeared so suddenly on the historical scene in the fourth century had therefore, in reality, mostly already long been there. Many were at least nominally Chinese imperial subjects, spoke at least some of the Chinese language, and their elites not infrequently already had some acquaintance with the Chinese classics.

The collapse of imperial government in north China in the early 300s provided military men with an opportunity to seize power. Because the non-Chinese peoples of the north were typically already accustomed to life on horseback, they made naturally fine cavalry. When, in the fourth century, the stirrup and complete armor for both horse and man was added to their equipment, such mounted warriors became truly formidable.[5] From the fourth century until the sixth, heavy cavalry would remain militarily dominant in north China.

At the same time, political legitimacy still tended to be most convincingly defined in Chinese terms. Several of the armed bands that arose in the early

300s, whether they were ethnic Chinese or not, did so in the name of saving the throne – that is, at least nominally rallying to the defense of the legitimate but beleaguered Jin Dynasty. Significantly, also, that first Xiongnu Sixteen Kingdoms state that was formed in southern Shanxi in 304 was founded by a Xiongnu prince who also claimed descent, on the maternal side, from the Han Dynasty founder Liu Bang (Emperor Han Gaozu). The early Han Dynasty had provided imperial brides for Xiongnu leaders, and therefore the Xiongnu elite had literally intermarried with Chinese royalty. This particular Xiongnu prince even bore the Han Dynasty imperial surname Liu (his name was Liu Yuan; 251–310), had lived for years in the Chinese imperial capital, and pointedly even called his new state Han.

As another way of invoking legitimacy in Chinese terms, this same Xiongnu leader is also quoted as claiming that both Great Yu (the legendary founder of China's first Xia Dynasty) and King Wen of Zhou had also been born among non-Chinese peoples. "What is of concern" in founding dynasties worthy of the Mandate of Heaven, he concluded, "is only who has been conferred with virtue."[6] Whether such words were really uttered by this Xiongnu ruler, or merely put into his mouth later by a Chinese historian, the argument very clearly was that the Mandate of Heaven did not belong to any one particular people. As the Zhou had conquered the Shang, and the Shang had supposedly conquered the Xia before that, so, too, the legitimate Mandate could always pass again to some other group. Why not to a Xiongnu?

Perhaps even more significantly, these words, whether really spoken by this Xiongnu leader or not, were recorded in the written Chinese language. Despite the multiethnic and multilingual character of the era, and the fact that identifiably non-Chinese people were frequently the political and military rulers, Chinese remained (with minor exceptions) almost the only written language. Even a particularly barbarous Jie tribal ruler of northeast China in the mid-fourth century, Shi Hu (295–349), felt compelled to dispatch a scholar to copy the stone inscriptions of the Confucian Classics in the former imperial capital at Luoyang. Although the fourth-century Sixteen Kingdoms often had at their core a non-Chinese tribe, with conscious bonds of tribal solidarity, and administered their Chinese and non-Chinese populations separately, by the late fourth century some of those ethnic divisions were already beginning to be erased.

The Southern Dynasties (South China, 317–589)

As the Western Jin Dynasty tore itself apart amid vicious civil wars in the early fourth century, one imperial prince established a new headquarters for himself in 307, just south of the Yangzi River, in the city we now call Nanjing. After the final collapse of the Western Jin, this prince assumed the throne in 317 to become the founding emperor of an Eastern Jin Dynasty in exile, the first in a series of five Southern dynasties that claimed to represent the sole legitimate line of Chinese imperial succession. Despite a reasonably plausible claim to superior legitimacy, however, their immediate situation was precarious.

The watery terrain – with many rivers, canals, lakes, and flooded rice paddies – of the south provided a degree of natural protection against northern cavalry, but the south was thrown into confusion by a flood of refugees from the north. These recent émigrés from the north may have amounted to as much as 17 percent of the total southern population. Because refugee members of former northern Great Families carved out large new estates for themselves in the south and tended to dominate the Southern dynasty governments, there was a serious potential for resentment and conflict with the older southern Chinese natives – who themselves, meanwhile, remained distinct from the pre-Chinese aboriginal population of the south, which was also still quite large.

In the third century, Three Kingdoms Wu had experienced much conflict with so-called Mountain Viet (in Chinese, *Shan Yue*) peoples in the lower Yangzi River area. These were presumably, at least in part, descendants of the Hundred Viets who had inhabited much of southeast China in antiquity. As recently as the Han Dynasty, this southland had still been something of a frontier region. In one three-year campaign beginning in 234, Three Kingdoms Wu reportedly forced the surrender of a hundred thousand Mountain Viet people in modern Anhui Province, converting the more vigorous among them into soldiers for the Wu Dynasty and the less vigorous into ordinary tax-paying farmers. After the Three Kingdoms period, the label "Mountain Viet" ceased to be heard much, but large numbers of aborigines continued to exist, under other names, throughout the Southern dynasties.

Despite the potential for conflict between northern refugees and older native southerners, between ethnic Chinese and aborigines, and with invaders from the Sixteen Kingdoms in the north, and despite the serious weakness of its government, the Eastern Jin Dynasty enjoyed a surprisingly lengthy period of stability and prosperity. The secret of the Eastern Jin's somewhat unexpected success was compromise, conciliation, and a relatively robust balance of power, in which the threatened rise of any one Great Family to supreme power (at a time when the emperors themselves were particularly weak) stimulated all the others to rally against that family to restore stability. Much credit should also go to the adroit leadership provided by a number of outstanding statesmen such as Wang Dao (276–339). Wang Dao, although a northern émigré himself, immediately began to practice the local southern dialect to win southern support. According to one contemporary description, "there were few who could resist Wang Dao's welcome," and everyone felt that Wang Dao "met them like an old friend."[7]

The Eastern Jin Dynasty produced an astonishing cultural efflorescence in the arts, which included China's first truly famous painter, Gu Kaizhi (341–402), and arguably the most admired calligraphic genius of all time, Wang Xizhi (303–379). In a much celebrated story, Wang Xizhi once, in 353, hosted an elegant literary gathering at an orchid pavilion in Zhejiang, during which wine cups were floated down a gently winding stream. Wherever the cup touched the bank, each of forty-one guests in succession had to compose a poem or be forced to drink a penalty. The preface to the record of this gathering that Wang Xizhi brushed was so treasured for its calligraphy that a later emperor (Tang Taizong, 600–649) supposedly took the original copy of it with him to his grave.

The brilliant poet Tao Qian (Tao Yuanming, 365–427) also belongs to the Eastern Jin period. Tao is considered one of China's first great landscape poets and an extoller of the joys of a simple life of contentment in rural reclusion. He is famous also as the author of a brief pioneering work of utopian prose fiction known as "Peach Blossom Spring." This short story tells the tale of a fisherman who once followed a stream into a grove of flowering peach trees, where he found a cave. Entering and passing through this cave, he discovered an entire community filled with happy people who had been entirely cut off from the outside world for centuries. Although the residents asked the fisherman to keep their existence a secret, on his return home, he reported directly to the government. Despite much searching, however, no one was ever able to find this marvelous land again.

Another Eastern Jin artistic genius was the painter and musician Dai Kui (d. 396). Dai was known for his performances on a delicate horizontal stringed instrument called the *qin*. According to one story, around the year 345, when a certain prime minister and prince of the imperial family summoned Dai to play for him, Dai smashed his *qin* in front of the messenger instead, remarking that he was not an entertainer for princely houses. Although the prince was reportedly furious, he was unable do anything about Dai's defiance. This story illustrates the remarkable degree of independence from imperial power that gentlemen of this era enjoyed.

The amazing cultural splendor of the Southern dynasties owed much to the fact that scholarship and literary ability had become essential requirements for high social status and office holding since the late Han Dynasty. After the fall of the Han, and with the weakening of imperial government, the focus of learning and education shifted to individual private families. Literary cultivation became one of the most important criteria that separated the Great Families, who were the dominant figures throughout the age of division, from ordinary commoners.

Another contributing factor to the cultural richness of the Southern dynasties was the growing availability, and variety, of books, both in imperial and private collections. In the mid-sixth century, one imperial library is said to have contained as many as 140,000 rolls of books and charts. The possession of some thirty thousand rolls helped one early sixth-century prince to compile an influential literary anthology, the *Selections of Refined Literature* (*Wen xuan*), which "became the text from which most educated men obtained their literary education" for centuries thereafter and which was also widely read by early Korean and Japanese elites.[8] This proliferation of books was partly due, in turn, to a revolution in writing materials that had finally replaced wood, silk, and bamboo with true paper by Eastern Jin times. The vibrant marketization of the southern economy also helped make books more widely available.

Not only did agriculture expand considerably in south China during the Age of Division but the Southern dynasty economy was increasingly privatized and commercialized. By the fifth and sixth centuries, the circulation of money and commerce had penetrated nearly every level of society. Commercialization of the economy was further stimulated by a growing volume of international maritime trade, which had already linked southern Chinese ports with markets as far away as the Mediterranean by late Han times. From the Han Dynasty through the Age of Division, China's most important port was probably located, surprisingly enough, in the vicinity of modern Hanoi, in the Red River valley area of what is now northern Vietnam. Thanks to this commercial vitality, it is likely that the Southern dynasty capital (modern Nanjing) had become the largest city in the world by the early 500s, with a population of perhaps 1.4 million.[9]

The remarkable cultural and economic dynamism of Southern dynasty China stands in obvious contrast to what was happening in western Europe at about the same time, where – although the trauma associated with the fall of the Roman Empire may sometimes be exaggerated – there does seem to have been a "startling decline in western standards of living during the fifth to seventh centuries."[10] This Southern dynasty Chinese economic and cultural efflorescence also makes a striking contrast to simultaneous developments in the original heartland of Chinese civilization in the north. One sixth-century Buddhist author even marveled at how the Central Plain in the north had once been "China" but had since become a "barbarian waste," while the south had once been "barbaric" yet had now become a "Chinese" land.[11] It almost seemed as if north and south had exchanged places!

Yet the Southern dynasties also had serious weaknesses. Wealth and learning were sharply concentrated in a few hands. The exuberant process of monetization and commercialization, while greatly benefiting some, apparently also reduced many independent small farmers to abject dependency. Economic polarization seems to have become extreme. And although the first Southern dynasty, the Eastern Jin, enjoyed a degree of stability and legitimacy, it was overthrown in 420 by a military usurper. No subsequent Southern dynasty survived long, and every one was founded by an ambitious general. These upstart military houses then frequently tore themselves apart through internal rivalries and suspicions. Of twenty-eight sons of Emperor Xiaowu of the Song (r. 454–465), for example, not one died a natural death – all were killed by other members of their own family. A ditty popular around the year 454 captured something of the viciousness of the internal conflict: "First see son slaughter father, later see younger brother slaughter older brother."[12]

Not surprisingly, there may have been little popular sense of identification with these brief and less than thoroughly admirable Southern dynasties (little sense of what we might call national identity). Despite the cultural brilliance of the Southern dynasties – in the mid-sixth century, for example, one southern writer could sweepingly dismiss all but a few northern literary efforts as little more than "the braying of assess and barking of dogs" – ironically, in some ways, a conservative version of traditional Confucianism may have been better preserved by the non-Chinese regimes of the north.[13] After a devastating rebellion in 548–552, the Southern dynasties never fully recovered. In the end, reunification came from the north.

Northern Wei (North China, 386–534)

In north China, as a degree of stability began to return following the chaos of the fourth century, the most important of the various non-Chinese peoples turned out to be the Xianbei, and especially a Xianbei subgroup called the Tuoba.[14] The

Xianbei, in general, are thought to have originated roughly in the area of modern Manchuria. Tuoba Xianbei legend located their particular homeland just west of Manchuria in what is now extreme northeastern Inner Mongolia. The origins of the Tuoba Xianbei remain murky, however, and their native language (which is now extinct) cannot be identified any more precisely than as Ural-Altaic, somewhere between Turkic and Mongolic. By the late second century, the Tuoba Xianbei had established their grazing area in the belt of hilly grassland that stretches from the northernmost loop of the Yellow River in the west to just north of modern Beijing in the east. Emperor Wu of the Han Dynasty had made an effort to incorporate this area into the Han Empire, constructing fortifications and establishing agricultural colonies, but by the third century, Chinese administration had largely been evacuated. The historical Tuoba Xianbei emerged out of the mixture of populations, and cultures, in this area at this time.

In 261, a Tuoba chieftain sent his son to attend the imperial court in north China, and as Western Jin imperial government began disintegrating amid disastrous civil war, the semi-nomadic Tuoba were enlisted by one faction (and courted by others) of the ruling family as military auxiliaries. As a reward for their service, the Tuoba chieftain was invested by Western Jin as first duke, and by 315, as king of Dai (the name of a Chinese administrative unit in the vicinity of their grazing area). After the fall of the Western Jin Dynasty, the Tuoba Xianbei were themselves briefly conquered and incorporated into one of the many non-Chinese empires of the fourth-century north, but Tuoba independence was restored in 386 at a meeting of the tribes near modern Hohhot in Inner Mongolia. The Tuoba ruler then quickly elevated his title from king to emperor, and the name of his state was changed from Dai to Wei (a prestigious Chinese state name). Thus began what is known to history as the Northern Wei Dynasty (386–534).

In 398, the hitherto still semi-nomadic Northern Wei emperor established a new permanent capital near the site of modern Datong, in northern Shanxi Province, and began to develop an agricultural base in the region. In the process, Northern Wei made much use of captive labor, resettled on a truly massive scale around their capital. There are records of over a million persons being forcibly relocated there in the first half of the fifth century, including Chinese people, other subgroups of Xianbei, Xiongnu, persons from what is now northern Korea, and others. By extensively reshuffling and relocating population groups in this fashion, the Northern Wei helped dissolve older identities and began to forge a new and more cohesive Northern Wei identity.

By 439, the Northern Wei had completed the conquest and reunification of north China. Even so, Northern Wei long remained a distinctly Xianbei dynasty. The grazing of livestock remained fundamental to the Northern Wei economy, and historical records mention literally millions of head of cattle, sheep, horses, and camels. Well into the fifth century, the hunting of wild game – often with hawks or falcons – appears to have retained an actual economic significance as well as being a favorite leisure activity for the Northern Wei elite. In 415, a year when there was a poor harvest, someone proposed moving the capital farther south into the Chinese heartland. A counterargument prevailed, however, that as long as the Tuoba

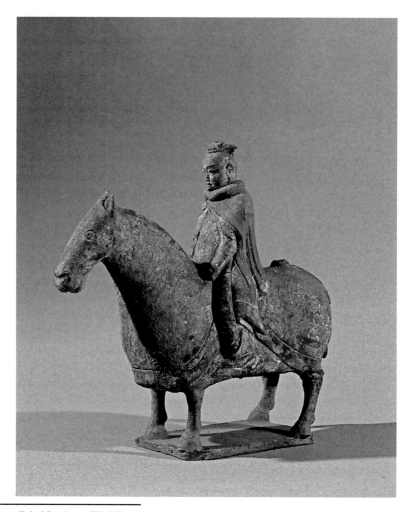

Figure 3.1. Northern Wei Dynasty terracotta funerary statuette of a horseman (fifth–sixth centuries). Musée des Artes Asiatiques, Guimet, Paris. Erich Lessing/Art Resource, New York.

Xianbei remained in the north, the Chinese would imagine them as having vast hordes of warriors. Relocating the capital south would expose their small true numbers. Better to remain in the north, from where they could strike south swiftly when necessary, and the Chinese would tremble and submit at the sight of the dust kicked up by their horses' hooves (see Figure 3.1).

In 443, the Northern Wei sent an emissary to offer sacrifices at what they believed to be the newly rediscovered "original" Tuoba Xianbei ancestral temple, in a cave in remote northeastern Inner Mongolia. Whether or not this really was the ancestral home of the Tuoba Xianbei, a commemorative inscription was then etched into the cavern wall, and the text of that inscription was recorded in the dynastic history. Amazingly, in 1980, archeologists rediscovered this same cave, complete with its fifth-century inscription. This archeological discovery strikingly confirms the traditional historical account, but with some qualifications. There are minor but interesting variations between the actual text of the rediscovered inscription and what was recorded in the dynastic history. In particular, the original inscription used the title "khan" for early Tuoba Xianbei rulers (perhaps the earliest known use of that now familiar nomadic title), whereas the dynastic history omitted that term. Khan is not a Chinese title, and this discrepancy is a reminder that the Northern Wei Dynasty may have been less thoroughly Chinese than the standard histories, which were written in the Chinese language by Chinese authors, suggest. On other hand, though, even the non-Chinese word khan in this original inscription is still written in Chinese characters.

Until the mid-fifth century, Northern Wei emperors ruled north China essentially as Xianbei-style overlords, did not apparently envision themselves as sole legitimate successors to the Chinese Mandate of Heaven, and did not display much evidence of any driving ambition to conquer the still independent Southern dynasties and reunify China. A majority of high-ranking Northern Wei officials, moreover, were still identifiably non-Chinese.[15] Eventually, however, in 494, Northern Wei actually did relocate its capital farther south to the hallowed early Chinese imperial site at Luoyang. Even before then, led first by a powerful empress dowager and then by Emperor Xiaowen (r. 471–500), the court began promulgating measures to convert Northern Wei into more of a Chinese-style regime. These included the construction of a Confucian temple with seasonal sacrifices to the spirit of Confucius, the adoption of Chinese names (for example, the non-Chinese imperial surname Tuoba was changed to the Chinese name Yuan), and mandatory court use of the Chinese language. The underlying motive for these actions was probably less due to any obvious superiority or attractiveness of Chinese culture than it was to lay the groundwork for a Northern Wei conquest of the south and reunification of China.

One of the new measures implemented at this time was a remarkable system of per capita state farmland allocation known as the Equitable Fields (*juntian*) system. This Equitable Fields system would continue in operation in China from roughly 485 to 780 and would exert an important influence on early Japanese institutions. It is also a fascinating example of an intrusive early government attempt at management of the economy. Despite drawing on ancient Chinese Confucian egalitarian ideals, however, the Northern Wei per capita assignment of farmland emerged more directly out of the non-Chinese Xianbei practice of putting captive labor to work tilling the fields. From the semi-nomadic Xianbei perspective, farming remained very much a base, servile occupation. Even the imperfect implementation of such an Equitable Fields system was also only possible because of the massive dislocation of population and extensive vacant lands that characterized war-ravaged fourth- to fifth-century north China. Despite its historical interest, the Equitable Fields system was therefore actually something of an anomaly in the overall pattern of Chinese economic history, and the private commercial development that characterized the contemporary Southern dynasties was more representative of long-term Chinese trends.

Even after the relocation of the Northern Wei capital to Luoyang in 494, there were apparently still enough Xianbei people who were not yet proficient in the

Chinese language that it was felt necessary to have the gist of the Confucian *Classic of Filial Piety* translated into Xianbei. A number of books are reported to have been written in the Xianbei language around this time (although today, nothing survives of their language except a handful of words in Chinese transcription). The Northern Wei imperial command to dress in Chinese fashion was also apparently ineffective. To the contrary, it was Chinese men who adopted Xianbei-style tunics, trousers, and boots as the new standard of Chinese male clothing.[16]

However, the Tuoba Xianbei people did come to imagine themselves as descendants of the same mythical Yellow Emperor, and other early legendary figures, as the Chinese. The Northern Wei became enough of an authentically Chinese dynasty that the original version of the classic Chinese story *Mulan* (familiar from the modern Disney animated movie) may have actually been composed under Northern Wei. The dynasty came to be considered not merely a legitimate Chinese dynasty but even (although contemporary Southern dynasties would have disputed this at the time) as the sole legitimate possessor of the Chinese Mandate of Heaven. After the reunification of China in 589, one seventh-century historian even wrote that the reason "the Dao of China did not fall" during the centuries of division was because of the efforts of Emperor Xiaowen of the Northern Wei.[17] In 601, a seventh-generation descendant of a Tuoba Xianbei chieftain actually helped compile a rhyming dictionary, called the *Qieyun*, which set an influential standard for "correct" Chinese language pronunciation! Interestingly enough, the name of the Tuoba tribe, through the Turkic variant of its pronunciation as "Tabgatch," later even became a generic Central Asian name for China.

If the Xianbei who moved south into China proper eventually joined with the preexisting population to forge a new Chinese synthesis, those Xianbei who remained in the far north (and others who joined them) did not. Northern Wei military power remained based on Xianbei-style cavalry, especially those stationed in Six Garrisons at the top of the Yellow River's northern loop. These garrisons commanded the strategic grasslands south of the Gobi Desert, where potential nomadic invaders from the steppe might launch an attack on China. But the warriors in these frontier garrisons felt increasingly neglected by the China-oriented Northern Wei court in Luoyang, and in 524 a rebellion erupted out of the Six Garrisons that ultimately resulted in splitting the Northern Wei Dynasty in half, east and west, by 534. Both these so-called Eastern and Western Wei dynasties themselves soon suffered further usurpations and changes of dynasty.

A counterreaction against the Chinese-style policies of the late Northern Wei government followed, together with a considerable revival of Xianbei culture and identity. Xianbei names were restored. Some ambitious Chinese people even took Xianbei names themselves and learned to speak the Xianbei language in the mid-sixth century. At the same time, however, the regime in the northwest, partly because of the small number of Xianbei warriors at its disposal, also began making unprecedented efforts to incorporate ethnic Chinese into its military. Perhaps because its base area also happened to be the very same region "Within the Passes" that had been the ancient Zhou (and Qin) homeland, this regime also began to consciously evoke the memory of ancient Zhou ideals and standards. In 589, after yet another usurpation and change of dynastic houses, this regime (now called the Sui Dynasty) based in the northwestern region "Within the Passes" finally reunified China.

Cosmopolitan Elite International Culture

"The most striking feature of sixth-century China was its cultural diversity."[18] In north China, as late as the 570s, the rulers, much of the army, and the language of military command were all still identifiably non-Chinese Xianbei. These non-Chinese warriors sometimes shockingly disparaged ethnic Chinese farmers and civilian officials, calling them such offensive things as "Han dogs."[19] At the same time, however, many of the Xianbei had also already absorbed a great deal of Chinese culture. One powerful mid-sixth-century northeastern warlord (Gao Huan, 496–547) – who is famous for urging his Xianbei warriors to regard the Chinese as useful servants who should therefore not be mistreated, while simultaneously telling the Chinese that the Xianbei were their defenders who should therefore be fed and clothed without resentment – is particularly interesting because it is actually difficult to say with any certainty whether he himself was Chinese or Xianbei.

According to the historical record, he was the grandson of a Chinese attendant censor from the eastern Central Plain who had been exiled to a northwestern frontier garrison in the region of the Ordos Desert. Two generations later, however, this man himself was now culturally rather Xianbei (although apparently fluent in both the Chinese and Xianbei languages). Some modern scholars have accordingly argued that his claim to Chinese descent must have been a fabrication. Such genealogical fraud might indeed have been both advantageous and possible, but it is also conceivable that he really was of Chinese descent (although perhaps not from such a distinguished family as he claimed). His claim to Chinese descent, at any rate, must have seemed plausible at the time. In the end, there is really no certain proof either way, and the very ambiguity of his identity illuminates something important about this era.

The culture of this age was something of a hybrid mixture. As early as the third century, it had already become fashionable among wealthy Chinese to adopt such foreign things as so-called Hu beds (an early type of folding chair) and cooking techniques. Foreign influences sometimes even came from surprising distances. A silver pitcher found in the grave of a garrison commander who died in northwest China (modern Ningxia) in 569 was apparently made in what is now Afghanistan, in Persian style, and decorated with scenes from the Trojan wars![20]

In the south, ethnic Chinese rule was maintained throughout the Age of Division, but the southern population was also mixed, and the south, too, was open to wide-ranging contacts. According to historical records, for example, the sixth-century Southern dynasty court was continually visited by embassies, not just from the nearby Korean peninsula but also from Southeast Asia, India, Persia, and Central Asia. Some scholars even believe that stone pillars at certain southern imperial tombs show evidence of Greek influence.

If China was extraordinarily open to outside influences during this Age of Division, and if some of those influences emanated from surprisingly distant sources, on the other hand, this was also exactly the time when certain key cultural features that make East Asia East Asian were planted. A relatively common elite culture spread throughout East Asia in this period, extending to modern China, Korea, Japan, and northern Vietnam. The various local East Asian elites of this period in some ways had more in common with each other than with the peasants in their own nearby villages. This was the age when East Asia was born. One of the key features of this new East Asian cultural community – and one that simultaneously also linked it to a much larger world – was Buddhism.

Buddhism Comes to East Asia

Indian Origins

Buddhism was the world's first great missionary religion. During precisely those same centuries when China was most divided politically, a vast swath of the planet, including much of South Asia, Central Asia, East Asia, and portions of Southeast Asia, came to be united by a shared religious faith in Buddhism. Buddhism had originated, of course, in South Asia. The historical Buddha (the "Enlightened One"), Siddhārtha Gautama, who is also called the "Sage of the Śākya tribe" (Śākyamuni), was born in the vicinity of present-day Nepal around the sixth century BCE. His breakthrough realization is said to have been that, although the realm of material existence continues endlessly (the cycle of birth and death and rebirth that the Indians called *saṃsāra*), nothing within it is permanent, and it is devoid of any higher purpose. That is, to the classic religious question, what is the meaning of life?, the Buddha's answer was that life really has no meaning. After you die, there is no permanent personal identity that is passed on to future incarnations. The various components of your identity instead scatter and recombine in new ways. Everything changes, nor is there any purposeful direction to this endless change. All things are merely the consequences of prior causes, which themselves are the cause of other effects, and so on forever. Existence is therefore ultimately empty, and meaningless, and the truly enlightened goal can only be to escape this endless cycle of misery.

This realization moved the Buddha to preach his first sermon, in which he formulated the Four Noble Truths. The first Noble Truth is that life is suffering. The second is that the cause of our suffering is our attachment to the things of this world. The third Noble Truth then follows with remorseless logic: the way to end our suffering is to break those attachments and desires. The way to do this is explained by the fourth and final Truth, which is to follow the Eightfold Path of proper living. If one succeeds in breaking all attachments, one may ultimately attain an end to reincarnation, or *nirvāṇa*.

Although the Four Noble Truths are said to represent the core of Buddhist doctrine, they have not generally been much emphasized in Chinese Buddhism. The essential Chinese approach to Buddhism may best be captured by the popular saying "The bitter sea [of existence] has no end; [but just] turn your head, and there is the shore." That is, although there is no end to the miseries of life, release can be achieved through a simple realization of the truth.

For many Chinese and other East Asian Buddhists, furthermore, the most realistic hope for salvation seemed to lie not in any rigorous path of spiritual detachment from desires or sudden burst of enlightenment, but rather simple faith that appeals to the compassionate intervention of a Bodhisattva – an enlightened being who deliberately chose to remain in the realm of existence to help save others – might bring rebirth in paradise. The most important of these Bodhisattvas was Amitābha, the Bodhisattva of Infinite Life and Infinite Light, who had taken a vow to cause anyone who invoked his name in genuine sincerity to be reborn in the western Pure Land. East Asian Buddhism is predominantly what is called Mahayana (Greater Vehicle) Buddhism, a tradition that promises universal salvation, in which the Buddha and Bodhisattvas have come to be worshipped as deities and rebirth in paradise is often seen as a more immediate goal than an end to reincarnation in *nirvāṇa*.

If this version of Buddhism seems strikingly different from what has been described earlier as the Buddha's own original realization, it must be emphasized that it is difficult to speak with any certainty about the original Buddhism, because there are no reliable records for the earliest period, and because multiple different versions of Buddhism quickly sprang up. Buddhism soon became enormously complex and sophisticated, defying easy generalization. The standard modern edition of the Chinese Buddhist canon, for example, includes some 2,184 different complete texts, and this is only one of three different major collections of Buddhist scriptures that have survived (the other two being the Tibetan and the Southeast Asian, or Pali, canons). A great many texts, furthermore, have not survived.

The earliest Buddhist community may have emerged in the Ganges River valley of northeastern India, but by the third century BCE, there were Buddhists all across South Asia, from Sri Lanka in the south to Gandhāra in the northwest (in what is now Pakistan and Afghanistan). Meanwhile, the conquests of Alexander the Great (356–323 BCE) had brought actual Greeks into that very same area of modern Pakistan and Afghanistan. Around the year 160 BCE, one Greek king in that region, Menander, supposedly converted to Buddhism. The result was something of a fertile fusion of Hellenistic, Persian, and Indian cultural influences. Because the main Silk Road trade routes also passed through this same region, some of these cultural and artistic influences began extending eastward into China.

Stone grotto temples began to appear in India by as early as the second century BCE, as places for Indian holy men to practice their austerities. In the first century CE, images of the Buddha began to be created in the Gandhāra region. Both Buddhist images and cave temples spread from there to China and East Asia. Over 120 cave temples are known in northern China, the oldest dating from the fifth century. This cave temple style extended as far east as Korea. The result was a visible expression of Buddhist cultural commonality linking together the entire region from modern Afghanistan to Korea. The world's largest Buddhist statues (until they were destroyed by the Taliban in 2001) were created at Bamiyan,

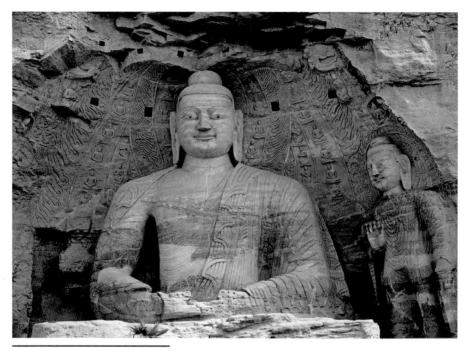

Figure 3.2. Colossal stone Buddha at Yun'gang, cave 20, Northern Wei Dynasty, 460–494 CE, near Datong, China. Werner Forman/Art Resource, New York.

Afghanistan, around the sixth century. Among the finest examples in China is the complex of Buddhist grottoes at Yun'gang, near the Northern Wei Dynasty capital at modern Datong, which was largely constructed between 460 and 494 (see Figure 3.2). The Yun'gang complex contains altogether some fifty-one thousand Buddhist images, the largest statue being roughly fifty-five feet tall.

At the same time that Buddhism united vast stretches of Asia into a single religious community, there remained important regional differences, even in specific matters of Buddhist practice. The fashion for constructing cave temples did not extend to Japan, for example, and was also rare in south China. The pagoda, a symbolic Buddhist structure that merged together older Han Dynasty Chinese-style tower architecture with imported Indian religious elements, and which matured in China by the fifth century, is uniquely East Asian.[21] Within East Asia, furthermore, Chinese pagodas were characteristically made of masonry and Japanese pagodas of wood, while Korea is famous for its stone pagodas.

In China, the spread of Buddhism was also paralleled by the simultaneous emergence of a new indigenous Chinese Daoist religion that interacted with Buddhism in complicated ways. Although this Daoist religion drew on more ancient Chinese beliefs in the possibility of physical immortality, divinely revealed texts, an underworld bureaucracy, and both the classical text and deified figure of *Laozi*, the temples, clergy, and scriptural canon of a specifically Daoist religion developed only belatedly around this time. By the fifth century, many new Daoist scriptures were being conspicuously modeled after Buddhist *sūtras*, although such originally alien Buddhist ideas as rebirth were also modified to suit the somewhat different Daoist purposes.[22] At the same time, Buddhism itself was also being transformed in China.

Buddhism's Spread to China

Buddhism spread to China along the caravan trade routes that led through Central Asia, as well as the maritime trade routes through Southeast Asia. The pre-Buddhist Indian Brahmanical teachings had forbidden sea travel, but the Buddhist Bodhisattva of compassion Avalokiteśvara became a patron saint for travelers, providing merchants with the courage to face the real and imagined dangers of distant voyages in ancient times. Perhaps for that reason, many early Indian merchants were Buddhists, and Buddhist monks not infrequently accompanied them on their journeys.

In a charming example of Buddhism's ability to adapt and transform itself locally, in China, this Indian deity Avalokiteśvara eventually came to frequently (but not always) be portrayed in female form, as the beloved goddess of mercy Guanyin (Kannon in Japanese, Kwanŭm in Korean). Chinese women frequently prayed to Guanyin in the hope that she would help them give birth to a male child. In Tibet, much later, the revered Buddhist leaders known as the Dalai Lamas (a title that dates from 1578) also came to be viewed as incarnations of Avalokiteśvara, known locally as Chenrezig.

Buddhism had unquestionably reached China by the early first century, but it did not initially have much appeal there. Although the preexisting native Chinese religious beliefs, which recognized a wide variety of different spirits, did not necessarily exclude the introduction of new foreign gods, the early Buddhist missionary monks appeared quite outlandish, begging for their existence with bare feet, shaved heads, saffron robes, and bare right shoulders. Most fundamentally, the Buddhist message of withdrawal from a world filled with misery was contrary to the characteristically optimistic Chinese tradition of active worldly participation. Confucian ideals of service to family, community, and state conflicted directly with the Buddhist goal of leaving the family and society to become a celibate monk. As a consequence, Buddhism took root only very slowly in China, and it was not until the third century that the first known Chinese person was ordained as a Buddhist monk. For roughly the first three hundred years of its existence in China, Buddhism was largely confined to the foreign community there.

It was only after the collapse of imperial government in north China in the fourth century and the beginning of a period of large-scale ethnocultural flux that Buddhism found a more receptive audience. Much of Buddhism's appeal then was because of its alleged ability to work miracles. For example, one Indian missionary in early fourth-century south China reportedly enthralled crowds by cutting his tongue off with a knife and then putting it back, and placing paper in a fire only to pull it intact from the ashes. The great missionary monk Fotucheng (d. 348) – who arrived from the western regions in the Chinese imperial capital Luoyang in 310 just in time to see the city fall to non-Chinese conquerors – was "skilled at reciting supernatural incantations and able to marshal demons. He would smear sesame oil mixed with rouge in the palm of his hand, and affairs from a thousand *li* beyond could all be observed in his palm, as though right before your face."[23] Fotucheng presented himself to one important Sixteen Kingdoms' commander and, filling his begging bowl with water, burning incense, and saying a prayer, caused a blue lotus flower to bloom miraculously from the bowl. As the wielder of such awesome supernatural powers, Fotucheng was welcomed as a trusted advisor to the throne.

It is sometimes alleged that the non-Chinese rulers of the Northern dynasties were especially receptive to Buddhism precisely because it was foreign, like themselves. In fact, textual sources do place just exactly such a claim in the mouth of at least one ruler in the fourth-century north. Nevertheless, of the four most notorious purges of Buddhism in all of Chinese history, two were conducted by non-Chinese Northern dynasties in the fifth and sixth centuries, and none by the native Chinese Southern dynasties of this era. At least one motive for these northern purges of Buddhism, moreover, may have been exactly the desire to demonstrate their credentials as legitimate Chinese-style empires. In addition, government supervision and regulation of the Buddhist clergy began in the north, in the late fourth and early fifth centuries, and the Northern dynasties were generally more rigorous in exerting control over Buddhism than the Southern dynasties. In the south, meanwhile, the philosophical sophistication and ability to engage in elegant conversation of certain distinguished fourth-century Buddhist monks had helped make Buddhism respectable. Buddhism flourished in both south and north, and among both Chinese and non-Chinese.

Unlike in medieval Europe, governments in China did at an early date assert their authority to regulate religion, and the principle of the superiority of state over church. Nevertheless, with rare exceptions, there was no official state church to which everyone was expected to belong in premodern China. The government's concern was chiefly to limit the number of religious tax exemptions and to suppress potential religiously inspired rebellions. Beyond that, the government was generally tolerant of differing faiths. Premodern Chinese people enjoyed a surprising degree of individual religious freedom. For this reason, despite the great popularity of Buddhism in China at its peak, China was never an exclusively Buddhist civilization.

If Indian Buddhists supposedly viewed the endless round of existence as a curse, and *nirvāṇa* as release from the cycle of reincarnation, in China, ironically, the previously unfamiliar Indian idea of reincarnation – of rebirth – seemed to imply a promise of eternal life, which, for many Chinese people, was not unappealing. The idea of reincarnation also solved the classic moral conundrum of why bad things seem to happen to good people: their good deeds are repaid in the next life. In China, Buddhists came to believe that, after death, one could either go to hell for a period of punishment (where Yama [in Chinese: Yan wang], the God of the Dead, judges evildoers), be doomed to haunt the land as a hungry ghost, be reborn as an animal, be reborn as a human, be reborn in a paradise (such as the Pure Land in the west), or be reborn as a kind of demon called an *asura*.

Buddhism changed as it traveled from India to China, but this should not be surprising. Not only were the cultural backgrounds very different but an enormous linguistic gulf existed between the languages of India, in which the concepts of Buddhism were first articulated, and Chinese. For centuries, the first priority of Buddhists in China was translation. In the early period, the region in far northwest China that is today called Xinjiang played a critical role in the transmission process. Many early Buddhist translators were not actually Indians but Central Asians, many of them from Xinjiang.

Xinjiang has, for good reason, been called the crossroads of Eurasia.[24] The principal Silk Road trade routes lay both north and south of the Tarim basin desert that occupies the heart of Xinjiang. Although Xinjiang was first brought into the Chinese Empire as early as the second century BCE, it was only sporadically included inside Chinese borders thereafter, and it long remained largely un-Chinese in culture and population. For example, in parts of Xinjiang such as Kuchā, an oasis community on the northern branch of the Silk Roads, an Indo-European language called Tocharian continued to be spoken until as late as the ninth century.

It was from Kuchā that the greatest of the early Buddhist translators came: Kumārajīva (344–413). Kumārajīva was born in Kuchā, reportedly to an Indian father and a local mother, and as a boy, he traveled with his mother to Kashmir, in India, learning the languages of various lands. In 384, Kuchā, and with it Kumārajīva, was captured by one of the Sixteen Kingdoms regimes in north China. It is said that on his return from Kuchā, the victorious general needed twenty thousand camels to carry all his loot. Together with this loot came the Buddhist master Kumārajīva. Eventually, Kumārajīva settled in the old Han Dynasty capital at Chang'an, in the historic region "Within the Passes." There Kumārajīva assembled a team of eight hundred scholars and embarked on a major translation project, which may have done more than any other to make the Indian scriptures readably available in Chinese, although even the vastly talented Kumārajīva still lamented that much was lost in translation.

Over time, a number of Chinese pilgrims went to India itself and other western destinations to study Buddhism at its source. The most famous early Chinese pilgrim was Faxian, who traveled throughout South Asia in 399–412 and left an important record of his journeys. Even going to India did not lessen the language barrier, however. There was simply no way to avoid having to use Chinese words to translate (or at least explain) Indian concepts – in the process, inevitably involving preexisting Chinese ideas. As Mouzi (late second century), an early Chinese apologist for Buddhism, said when asked why he responded to questions about Buddhism with answers drawn from the Confucian Classics, "If I were to speak the words of the Buddhist sūtras . . . it would be like speaking of the five colors to a blind person, or playing the five sounds to a deaf person."[25]

Buddhism had to be filtered through the lenses of existing Chinese words and ideas. Although Mouzi drew on Confucian principles, and most Chinese Buddhists were at pains to emphasize the fundamental compatibility of Buddhism with Confucianism, in the long run it was Daoist terminology that was most influential in translating the Indian Buddhist ideas and shaping Chinese interpretations of Buddhism. For example, *nirvāṇa* was sometimes translated into Chinese using Laozi's favorite expression *wuwei* (nonaction). It has been suggested that the title of an important Chinese Pure Land Buddhist text, *The Sūtra of Longevity without Measure* (*Wu liang shou jing*), betrays a Daoist-inspired quest for immortality that is quite at odds with the Indian notion of the goal of *nirvāṇa* as extinction.

A Chinese monk who has been credited with laying some of the theoretical foundations of what became Pure Land Buddhism, Tan Luan (476–542), was a northerner who sought out the immortality techniques of a famous Daoist at Mao Mountain in the south. There he received a Daoist *Classic of Immortality*, but on returning to the northern capital he supposedly encountered an Indian monk who conferred on him the allegedly superior Buddhist *Sūtra Contemplating Longevity without Measure* (*Guan wu liang shou jing*). "Longevity without measure," or "infinite life," was another name for the Bodhisattva Amitābha. This story nicely illustrates the complex swirling patterns of interaction between north and south, Chinese and non-Chinese, and Buddhism and Daoism that characterized this age of cosmopolitanism.

A milestone in the Chinese domestication of Buddhism was the claim, which began to be heard in the fifth century, that all beings already contain within themselves the Buddha Nature (*Fo xing*). The key to salvation is therefore already inherent in all things. A particularly important text for Chinese Buddhists was the *Sūtra of the Lotus of the Wonderful Law* (*Miao fa lianhua jing*), or more simply, the *Lotus Sūtra*. The actual Indian origins of this *sūtra* are obscure, but it was claimed that this *Lotus Sūtra* contained the final sermon that the Buddha had preached on Vulture Peak before he attained *nirvāṇa*. In it, the Buddha explains that what he had said previously about *nirvāṇa* was not exactly the whole truth but merely an expedient intended to elevate the consciousness of his listeners. The ultimate truth is that *nirvāṇa* is not real extinction. Because the Buddha nature is already present in all things, you need only awaken to it to be saved.

By the sixth century, a number of distinctively Chinese forms of Buddhism began to emerge, which were largely without precedent in India. In addition, approximately one-third of all the scriptures in the Chinese Buddhist canon are thought to be apocryphal, meaning that they are original Chinese compositions rather than translations from Indian texts.[26] Buddhism, in other words, was being domesticated, and becoming Chinese.

Most of the ordinary faithful, of course, were little concerned with fine scripture-based scholastic distinctions. The promise of rebirth in paradise, the threat of hell, and stories of karmic retribution – good and bad deeds being justly rewarded – excited more popular enthusiasm. Buddhism came eventually to be popularized in China through public sermons, consisting of excerpts from the *sūtras* followed by prose and poetic explanations. To enhance the appeal of the Buddhist message, the entertainment value of the stories was often highlighted. For a sermon by a famous master, an audience would be summoned by the sound of a bell, each arrival making a small cash donation to pay for incense. The priest would ascend his dais holding a *ruyi*, a Chinese-style scepter, amid clouds of incense, and the sermon would begin.

China changed Buddhism, but Buddhism also greatly changed China. The religion exercised a profound influence on Chinese art, especially statuary, as it developed during this period. Buddhist temples and pagodas became characteristic features of the Chinese, and East Asian, landscape. Buddhism enriched the scope of Chinese literary forms, introducing such things as fables, parables, and Indian-style hymns. The knowledge of Indian phonetic writing systems that was introduced with Buddhism may have contributed to the invention of a new Chinese system for indicating pronunciation (using combinations of two characters) and also for the first time to the conscious recognition and analysis of the tones of spoken Chinese. Chinese people moved from kneeling to (sometimes) sitting cross-legged during the Age of Division, apparently under Buddhist influence, and the chair was also introduced from the northwest in these centuries. The ancient practice of sacrificing live animals in religious ceremonies was ended because of the deep Buddhist abhorrence of killing. For a time, during the Age of Division, it even became quite fashionable for Chinese people to take Sanskrit or other Buddhist names. A Chinese emperor who ascended the throne in 307, for example, went by the childhood name Śramaṇa (Sanskrit for "monk"), one sixth-century man styled himself Bodhisattva, another styled himself Arhat (Sanskrit for "holy man"), and the founding emperor of one sixth-century dynasty in northwest China styled himself Dhāraṇī (Sanskrit for "magical verses"). A great many people included the Chinese character for "monk" (*seng*) in their personal names.

By the end of the Age of Division, there were thousands of Buddhist temples throughout China, and by some reports millions of monks and nuns. One devout sixth-century southern emperor donated his person to the Buddhist church four times, obliging his government to lavishly ransom him back on each occasion. A contemporary complained, perhaps with some exaggeration, that the empire had "lost almost half" its population to the Buddhist monasteries.[27] By the late sixth century, copies of the Buddhist scriptures were said to have been more numerous in China even than the Confucian Classics. As a final example of the pervasiveness of Buddhism in sixth-century China, the great emperor who would finally reunify China in 589 (Yang Jian, 541–604) was born in a Buddhist monastery and raised as a child by a Buddhist nun, who gave him a Sanskrit baby name.

Buddhism and the Birth of East Asia

It was from China that Buddhism spread to Korea and Japan – but from a China that was itself also both divided and part of a much larger Buddhist world. For example, Buddhism was first introduced to the northernmost Korean kingdom of Koguryŏ in 372 by an apparently Chinese monk (known as Sundo in Korean and Shundao in Chinese) who was sent by one of the non-Chinese regimes of fourth-century north China, whereas Buddhism was separately introduced to the southwestern Korean kingdom of Paekche in 384 by a non-Chinese monk (Mālānanda) sent by a so-called native Chinese Southern dynasty. Despite the international flavor of early East Asian Buddhism, the transmission of the religion was also intermixed, at the same time, with more specifically Chinese cultural influences.

In 541, for example, the Korean kingdom of Paekche requested and received from Southern dynasty China not only copies of the Buddhist *sūtras* but also physicians, craftsmen, painters, and specialists in the Confucian Classic *The Book of Odes*. Most critically, it was in Chinese language translation that the scriptures of Buddhism spread to both Korea and Japan, in conjunction with the introduction of writing itself.

In Korea, it apparently took some time for Buddhism to diffuse from the level of the elite to ordinary people. The known sites of Buddhist temples within the Paekche kingdom, for example, are concentrated in a limited area around its successive capitals and not in outlying regions of the realm. Meanwhile, it was from Korea, especially Paekche, that Buddhism was introduced into Japan.

The earliest Japanese Buddhist temples were constructed in Korean style, and actual Korean monks played a leading role in early Japanese Buddhism. The Hōkōji (a temple also known as Asukadera), for example, was completed in 596 by craftsmen and priests from Paekche. The first official head (*sōjō*) of the Japanese Buddhist church, in 623, was an immigrant priest from Korea. Although it is impossible to say with any certainty when the first person with knowledge of Buddhism actually landed in the Japanese islands, the dates conventionally given for the introduction of Buddhism are either 552 or 538. Interestingly, one of the earliest native Japanese histories presents the court debate that supposedly ensued in 552 over whether to accept Buddhism precisely in terms of foreign versus native, one minister arguing that because "all the Western frontier lands without exception" worship the Buddha, Japan should not alone refuse to join them, while others replied that if the Japanese began now to worship "foreign Deities, it may be feared that we should incur the wrath of our National Gods."[28]

Because this book of history was not actually compiled until 720, long after the events it describes, and because the account may be colored by special interests, it should be read with caution. There can be little doubt, however, that Buddhism was the cutting edge of a powerful wave of continental influences that swept across Japan in these centuries. These influences came most immediately from Korea, but ultimately, they were more broadly East Asian. Beyond East Asia, some degree of Indian, Persian, and even Mediterranean influences have also been claimed for Japanese art of the seventh and eighth centuries. An actual person from India supposedly officiated at the ceremony "opening the eyes" of an enormous bronze statue of the Buddha that was cast in Japan in 752.

At the same time, early Japanese Buddhism also retained aspects of local native culture. For example, many of the first Buddhist professionals in sixth-century Japan were unmarried young ladies, reflecting the indigenous tradition of shrine maidens (*miko*) in pre-Buddhist Japanese religion. Many early Japanese temples were also clan temples (*ujidera*), reflecting the importance of the clan in pre-Buddhist Japanese society and religion. And many local pre-Buddhist spirits (*kami*) were absorbed into Japanese Buddhism – a phenomenon that may also be observed everywhere the Buddhist religion spread, beginning in India itself.

By 623, there were reportedly forty-six Buddhist temples in Japan, all clustered in the vicinity of the capital. With the turn into the eighth century, a newly systematized Japanese imperial government began vigorously promoting Buddhism throughout the islands. In 741, for example, the central government ordered the construction of a Buddhist monastery and a nunnery in every province. Japan became a quite thoroughly Buddhist land – in some ways arguably eventually even more so than either China or Korea. Yet despite this important early transplantation and flourishing of Buddhism in Japan, it has been suggested that it was not until as late as the fifteenth century that Buddhism was finally domesticated to the level of the ordinary daily life of commoners, as Buddhism came to monopolize funeral services and ancestral sacrifice in Japan.

The Emergence of Korean Kingdoms

Early Korea (ca. 2000 BCE–313 CE)

By the seventh century, as Buddhism was taking firm root in Japan, the great Age of Division had finally ended in China. This Chinese Age of Division coincides with the dawn of recorded history for both Korea and Japan, and the first stirrings of a culturally coherent East Asian region. Long before this time, however, for many thousands of years human beings had already inhabited both the Korean peninsula and the Japanese islands. Both Korea and Japan enjoyed lengthy and culturally rich prehistoric eras. Pottery, for example, was being made on the Korean peninsula as early as 10,000 BCE.

In Korea, an age of megalithic (large stone) monuments, strikingly reminiscent of the dolmens of prehistoric Europe, began around 2000 BCE. Northern-style dolmens in Korea were typically formed by four upright stone slabs capped by an overhanging horizontal lid, roughly in the shape of a stone table. Some of these are very large. Though dolmens in the southern style, which did not have the large, uplifting vertical side pieces, are associated with burials, the purpose for the table-shaped dolmens is less clear. Estimates of the total number of prehistoric stone monuments in Korea range as high as an astonishing one hundred thousand.[29] While dolmens can also be found in adjacent regions beyond the Korean peninsula, they are concentrated in Korea and were evidently an indigenous development.

By the last millennium BCE, rice farming and bronze metalworking had been added to the prehistoric cultural complex in Korea. Rice cultivation probably originated in what is now southern China, but rice was little grown in the Chinese cultural heartland in the north, where the staple grain was millet (and later wheat). Bronze, meanwhile, may have been an influence from north China, but there is a notable lack of the characteristic Chinese-style bronze ritual vessels in Korea, where bronze was commonly used, instead, for daggers and mirrors. In a number of ways, therefore, late prehistoric culture in Korea was distinct from that of the Central Plain in China. Korea (which can be viewed in some ways as a peninsular extension of Manchuria, and which was closely associated with Manchuria in early times) may have also been exposed to wider influences from the Eurasian steppe, possibly including the craft of making wrought iron (in contrast to Chinese-style cast iron).

The first written accounts of what we now call Korea, however, come from Chinese sources. Little was recorded until the wars surrounding the collapse of the Qin Empire and the founding of the Han Dynasty, shortly after which a refugee named Wiman from an unstable peripheral Han client kingdom (called Yan) located in southeastern Manchuria fled to northern Korea and established a small kingdom there in 195 BCE. Wiman's new kingdom was called Chosŏn, and he ruled over a mixed population of natives and refugees (themselves probably better understood as "Yan people" than as "Han Chinese"). Over three generations, friction developed between this Chosŏn kingdom and the Han Dynasty, and in 108 BCE, Emperor Wu of the Han Dynasty invaded and conquered Chosŏn. After the Han conquest, at its peak, roughly the northern half of the Korean peninsula may have been directly incorporated into the Han Empire.

At least a portion of northern Korea would remain under Chinese rule for some four centuries, until the late third or early fourth century CE. The principal seat of Chinese rule was called Lelang (in Korean, Nangnang), an administrative city located near modern P'yŏngyang. Archeological evidence makes it clear that local cultures in the area of Korea remained distinct from the standards of the Chinese Central Plain (see Figure 3.3), but Han Dynasty Chinese administration in Korea was not necessarily any more (though also certainly no less) a matter of foreign imperial colonial rule than it was in a number of other parts of the still quite multiethnic Han Empire. Under the early Chinese Empire, it was not uncommon for local culture to vary from metropolitan imperial standards. As late as the Han Dynasty, it has even been suggested that the language spoken near what is now Beijing may have been "still foreign to the Chinese ear and rather close to the languages spoken in the northern part of the Korean peninsula."[30]

If the native populations under Han Dynasty rule in Korea remained culturally distinct from the Chinese imperial metropolitan elite, they also did not yet constitute a single unified and homogeneous Korean people either. Internally, there remained a surprising variety of different ethnic groups, and externally, the borders of anything that might be called "Korea" had yet even to be imagined. Although, as a peninsula, the geographic map of Korea might appear to have been drawn by the very hand of nature itself, the modern land border in the north, which now follows the line of the Yalu and Tumen rivers, was not actually fixed until as late as the fifteenth century CE. An influential Korean book written in 1784 could still claim that the peninsula was really only the southern part of a Korean identity that more properly extended well north into Manchuria.[31] In the south, even the water's edge was not necessarily an inevitable end point. On a clear day, the Japanese island of Tsushima can be seen from the coast of Korea, and in the third century, this appears to have been "an area connected by water" rather than separated by it, across which "one of the most common scenes must have been people going back and forth in their boats."[32]

A third-century Chinese history (the *Sanguo zhi*, or *Chronicles of the Three Kingdoms*) describes several different peoples occupying the general area that we now call Korea. The Puyŏ lived well north of the peninsula, in central Manchuria, and might not seem relevant, except that according to Korean legend the Puyŏ

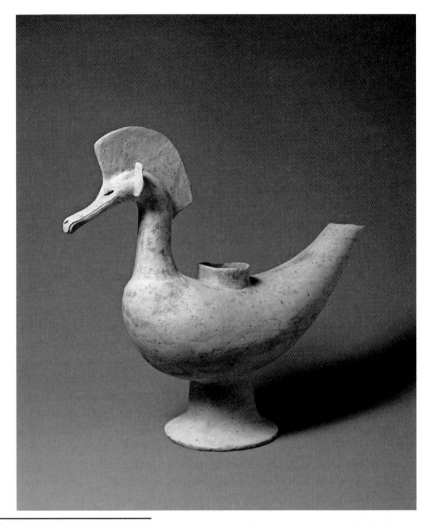

Figure 3.3. A bird-shaped earthenware vessel from Korea, ca. late second–third centuries. Purchase, Lila Acheson Wallace Gifts, 1997 (1997.34.1). The Metropolitan Museum of Art, New York. © The Metropolitan Museum of Art/Art Resource, New York.

were directly ancestral to other more obviously Korean peoples such as Koguryŏ. To the south of the Puyŏ, in southern Manchuria and in the Chinese Han Dynasty-administered area of northern Korea, the kingdom of Koguryŏ was emerging. Koguryŏ had completely replaced Chinese government in northern Korea by the early fourth century. Koguryŏ was said to be a splinter group of the Puyŏ and resembled the Puyŏ in language and culture. East of Koguryŏ, bordering on the ocean, were the Okchŏ people, whose language was said to be slightly different from that of Koguryŏ. South of the Okchŏ were the Yemaek (or Ye) people, living along the eastern seaboard of the Korean peninsula. In the southern half of the peninsula, beyond the maximum zone of Han Dynasty Chinese administration, were the Three (Korean) Han peoples. (Despite the similarity of pronunciation, the Korean name Han is written with an entirely different character from the name of the Chinese Han Dynasty.)

These Three Han (*Samhan*) peoples were probably linguistically and culturally most directly ancestral to modern Koreans, since the eventual unification of the Korean peninsula was achieved by a kingdom that emerged from one of them, in the southeast. In the third century, however, they were themselves still far from unified. The three were called Mahan in the southwest, Pyŏnhan in the center, and Chinhan in the southeast. According to the Chinese account, Chinhan and Mahan did not speak the same language. Mahan, by itself, was described as a collection of over fifty so-called countries (*guo*) in the third century. These countries were apparently small agricultural communities, scattered between the mountains and the sea, without walled cities. The largest reportedly contained over ten thousand households and the smallest only a few thousand. Pyŏnhan and Chinhan were both less populous, each having only a dozen somewhat smaller countries. In Pyŏnhan and Chinhan especially, people tattooed their bodies and used stones to compress the heads of newborn babies into an artificially narrow shape. Pyŏnhan was also notable as a major producer of iron for the entire region.

The people of Koguryŏ, in the north, were highlanders who occupied rugged mountainous terrain and lacked any very satisfactory agricultural base. In the third century, their population was reported at thirty thousand households. They were allegedly warlike and rode small ponies that were adept at clambering over the mountains. Koguryŏ is known for its hill forts, and its capitals typically combined a mountain citadel with a residential city on the plain. In striking contrast to the most typical Chinese marriage practice, in which the bride moves in with her husband's parents, in Koguryŏ it was said that the husband moved into a smaller son-in-law's house constructed behind the bride's parents' home, and the newly married couple continued to live there until their own children were adults.

Three Kingdoms Korea (313–668)

Koguryŏ, which seems to have originally coalesced just north of the Yalu River, was the first of the communities in Korea to form an organized territorial kingdom – the first of the formative Korean "Three Kingdoms" (Samguk) (see Map 3.2). In the year 32 CE, the Koguryŏ leader for the first time supposedly took the Chinese title king (*wang*). With the gradual weakening of the Chinese Han Dynasty, Koguryŏ began raiding the Han borders in the early second century. After the total collapse of the Han Dynasty by 220, southern Manchuria (not to mention northern Korea) was left a political vacuum that was filled by the rise of various non-Chinese Xianbei regimes, and Koguryŏ.

In the early third century, a subgroup of the Xianbei called the Murong moved into southwestern Manchuria (probably coming from further west), where they assisted the Chinese Three Kingdoms state of Wei in subduing local independent Chinese warlords, and began to build a Murong state. The Murong would eventually generate five different Sixteen Kingdoms-era states, all called Yan (the ruling family of the last one, Northern Yan, is said to have been of Chinese rather than Murong descent, but even it was culturally Xianbei-influenced). Despite the rise of the Murong, until as late as 353 the Murong chieftains accepted titles from the Chinese Western and Eastern Jin dynasties, thus preserving a thin pretense of continued Chinese rule in the area long after it had ceased to have much reality. Eventually, however, the Murong leaders took the (Chinese) imperial title for themselves, and for a few years the Murong-ruled Former Yan dynasty (349–370) even conquered and ruled most of northeast China.

These Murong Xianbei also interacted extensively with proto-Korean Koguryŏ, at one point reducing Koguryŏ to a vassal state. In 342, the Murong sacked Koguryŏ's capital, capturing more than fifty thousand of its people. A few years earlier, in 336, meanwhile, a man named Dong Shou (d. 357) had escaped from a factional dispute in the Murong state in southern Manchuria by fleeing to Koguryŏ, where he apparently became locally prominent. He died in 357, and was buried some distance southwest of the current North Korean capital. His impressive tomb contains an inscription written in Chinese and claiming Chinese official titles, and murals depicting, among other things, the new style of heavily armored cavalry. This tomb is a fascinating example of the complicated patterns of cultural exchange and ambiguous identity in this period. Dong Shou may (perhaps) have been of Chinese descent, and was clearly a participant in Chinese-style literate high culture, but he was probably also culturally somewhat mixed: his tomb is in the Koguryŏ style, and he had lived as an accepted member of the elite among both the non-Chinese Murong Xianbei and proto-Korean Koguryŏans.[33]

The Murong Xianbei were eventually conquered and absorbed by the Tuoba Xianbei, while Koguryŏ recovered from its setbacks and grew stronger. By the mid-fifth century, the chaos of the age of the Sixteen Kingdoms (304–439) had stabilized into two large and powerful states in northern East Asia: the Tuoba Xianbei-ruled Northern Wei Dynasty in north China, and Koguryŏ in southern Manchuria and northern Korea. Both states had non-Chinese rulers (although Northern Wei presumably had a Chinese majority subject population), but both Northern Wei and Koguryŏ had also, by this time, absorbed a substantial amount of Chinese culture, helping to convert the Tuoba Xianbei Northern Wei into a reasonable facsimile of a legitimate Chinese dynasty and touching off a process of secondary state formation in East Asia that would eventually extend the length of the Korean peninsula and across the sea to Japan.

In 372, Koguryŏ established an academy for the study of the Chinese classics, and in 373, Koguryŏ promulgated its first Chinese-style law codes. In 427, Koguryŏ moved its capital from what is today the Chinese side of the Yalu River in Manchuria to the vicinity of modern P'yŏngyang in northern Korea. The focus of Koguryŏ's attention by this time was increasingly directed toward domination of the Korean peninsula.

The second of the Korean Three Kingdoms, Paekche, was founded, according to Korean legend, by a son of the founder of Koguryŏ. Like Koguryŏ, therefore, the Paekche royal line claimed Puyŏ descent. Paekche was initially only one of the more than fifty small countries in the Mahan region of southwestern Korea, and it took shape out of the gradual consolidation of those Mahan communities, with a presumably predominantly Mahan population (whether or not its rulers really were of Puyŏ descent). Contact between Paekche and a Chinese dynasty was first recorded in 372, and by 386, the Paekche ruler had been invested with such Chinese titles as "General Garrisoning the East" and "King of Paekche." The keeping of written records also reportedly first began in Paekche around the mid-fourth century. In the fifth and sixth centuries, Paekche would enjoy particularly close relations with Southern dynasty China, becoming a highly sophisticated Chinese-style kingdom. At the same time, Paekche also had important ties with the newly emerging state in Japan.

The third Korean kingdom, Silla, developed out of a community called Saro in the Chinhan region of southeastern Korea. This was the most remote, and the slowest to develop, of all the Korean Three Kingdoms. It was not until 503 that Sillan leaders finally abandoned native titles such as *maripkan* and took the Chinese title "king" (see Figure 3.4). It was also in 503 that "Silla" was first standardized as the name of the country. In 520, Silla promulgated its first Chinese-style law codes. By around 535, opposition to Buddhism was overcome, and Buddhism was officially endorsed in Silla. In 545, by royal command, Silla began the compilation of a written history of the kingdom.

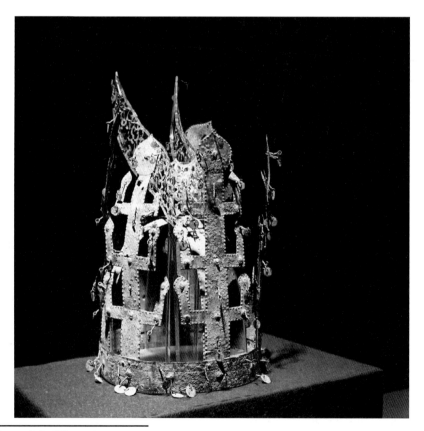

Figure 3.4. Silla period Korean silver crown, sixth century. Asian Art Museum of San Francisco. Werner Forman/Art Resource, New York.

Map 3.2 Three Kingdoms Korea, ca. 500 CE

What the Koreans were learning from China in these centuries were the institutions and techniques of state building. Despite the spread of Chinese influences, notably including writing, it should be emphasized that the Korean Three Kingdoms were all characterized by warrior aristocracies quite distinct from the Chinese literati elite, and many aspects of traditional native culture survived. Most people in Koguryŏ continued to live in simple thatched huts, with only royal palaces, government offices, and Buddhist temples adopting heavy Chinese-style tiled roofs. Simultaneously, there may have also been some even wider connections: the gold crowns and jewelry of fifth-century Silla suggest northern links with not just Koguryŏ and the Xianbei but beyond to Siberia and Afghanistan, and also exchanges with maritime South Asia.[34]

Aside from their obvious distinctions from the Chinese, these three early Korean kingdoms were also somewhat different from each other in both language and custom. Each had, for example, their own distinctive ceramic traditions.[35] The monumental tumuli called old tombs (*kobun*) that appeared in each of the Three Kingdoms between the fourth and seventh centuries had somewhat different regional styles: stone burial chambers with painted murals in Koguryŏ, arched brick chambers in Paekche, and wooden coffins piled over with stone in Silla. The Three Kingdoms were also more or less constantly at war with each other. At the same time, though, they were also continuously exchanging influences. In the seventh century, they would finally be unified for the first time in what could even be called the birth of Korea.

Yamato Japan (ca. 300–645)

Some of the earliest known pottery in the world has been found in the Japanese islands. These early ceramics mark the beginning, around 11,000 BCE, of what archeologists call the Jōmon period of Japanese prehistory. The word *jōmon* literally means "cord pattern" in Japanese. It refers to a characteristic decorative pattern produced by making impressions in the wet clay with cords. Despite Japan's remarkably early breakthrough to ceramic culture, however, the prehistoric inhabitants of Japan long remained primarily hunter-gatherers. The total population also remained quite sparse, probably never exceeding roughly a quarter million. Nevertheless, despite the fact that agriculture was little developed, Jōmon period people did eventually settle into permanent villages of perhaps thirty to fifty persons, who caught their food with bows and traps and by riding dugout canoes to fish with harpoons, hooks, and nets. They consumed so much seafood that the sites of their villages are often still marked by piles of discarded shellfish.

Certain tantalizing hints of southern cultural influences on Japan – resemblances to prehistoric southeast China and later Southeast Asia – have been observed. These include such things as the custom of building homes of wood elevated above the ground on posts. Some of these southern traits, such as rice cultivation, did not appear in Japan until the very end of the Jōmon period, and others cannot be verified until relatively late, such as the practice of tattooing the body. Some, however, can be detected already in Jōmon times, such as ritual tooth extraction (of canines or incisors), perhaps to celebrate rites of passage to puberty or marriage; a fascination with comma-shaped decorative beads (called *magatama*); and a fondness for boats and seamanship.

Japan's prehistoric culture then underwent some fairly dramatic changes beginning around 300 BCE, when the predominant direction of influence also shifted to the north – coming especially now from the Korean peninsula. These influences included significant new genetic contributions to the population of the islands, sufficient to indicate either very large numbers of new immigrants (some estimates reach as high as a million) or a relatively small group that succeeded in reproducing itself disproportionately after arrival. Other new introductions included wet-field rice cultivation and metallurgy, and possibly even the Japanese language itself, which is thought to be distantly related to Korean. This new phase of prehistoric culture is called Yayoi (roughly third century BCE–third century CE).

It was at the end of the Yayoi period that the oldest written description of Japan finally appears. As with the case of Korea, this is found in a Chinese source. The Chinese *Chronicles of the Three Kingdoms* (*Sanguo zhi*), which was compiled in the late third century, contains a fascinating brief account of Japan based on diplomatic contact. It describes a land called Yamatai, formed from a coalition of some thirty smaller entities and ruled by a princess named Himiko who excelled at magic and lived in a fortified palace with a thousand female attendants, but who was rarely seen in public. A younger brother assisted in her rule.

In modern Japan, there has been intense historical controversy over whether Himiko's realm of Yamatai was located in northern Kyūshū, the southwestern-most of Japan's four largest islands and the point of nearest approach to the Korean peninsula, or on the large plain at the eastern end of the Inland Sea on the main island. This plain has traditionally been known as the Yamato Plain, and it was home to the imperial capital for most of recorded Japanese history. The obvious similarity between the names Yamatai and Yamato is tantalizingly suggestive.[36] So, too, is mention of a great earthen tomb raised for Princess Himiko after her death, since just such tumuli began to appear roughly at this time, concentrated in the area of the Yamato Plain. The exact location of Himiko's kingdom of Yamatai remains uncertain, however. It is clear, moreover, that as of the third century, Japan was still divided among multiple small communities, although the Himiko story also indicates that some consolidation of authority was already being attempted. It may also be observed that the Yamatai described in this third-century Chinese account is in some ways already recognizably Japanese in culture.

Archeologists speak of an old tomb (*kofun*) period in Japan, covering roughly the years 250–552 CE (see Figure 3.5). The largest of these massive, earthen, old tombs is a hundred feet high and covers eighty acres. It is interesting that the exact same term, *old tomb*, is also used for the tumuli of roughly contemporary Three Kingdoms Korea. Though the word is pronounced *kofun* in Japanese and *kobun* in Korean, both are written with the same two Chinese characters. To some extent, of course, the creation of tumuli for deceased great leaders may have merely been a general phenomenon. The First Emperor of China (Qin Shi Huangdi) and other Chinese emperors also had large earthen mounds heaped over their graves. Many of the Japanese tombs, furthermore, have a unique keyhole shape – round at one end and square at the other – which distinguishes them from the Korean old tombs. Still, fourteen of these distinctively Japanese-style keyhole-shaped tombs have also been found in extreme southwestern Korea, and fairly frequent contact between the islands and the peninsula in these centuries is beyond doubt.[37]

Fierce modern nationalistic debates over whether Japan conquered Korea or Korea conquered Japan in this period are largely misguided and anachronistic, if only because neither Japan nor Korea really existed yet as a coherent identity. However, people from the Japanese islands apparently did have some presence on the Korean peninsula in these early centuries, and the Japanese islands clearly did absorb a number of highly critical influences from the peninsula, including

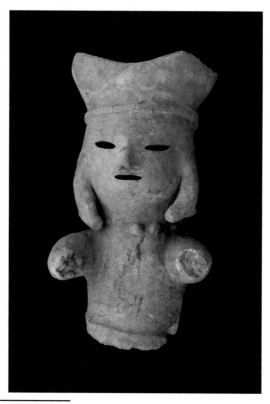

Figure 3.5. Female *Haniwa* earthenware figurine, fifth–sixth centuries, Kofun (Tumulus) period, Japan. Arthur M. Sackler Gallery, Smithsonian Institution, Washington, DC: Gift of Joseph H. Hirshhorn to the Smithsonian Institution, S1986.518.

such technologies as stirrups and armor. By the fifth century, Northern Wei (Xianbei or Chinese) and Koguryŏ-style heavily armored cavalry had appeared in Japan. There were also a significant number of actual immigrant persons from the continent. In early historical Japan, this was still openly acknowledged. In a record of 1,059 prominent families living in the capital region that was compiled in 815, for example, some 30 percent were explicitly said to be of foreign descent.[38] In these critical centuries, at the dawn of Japanese history, immigrants played a vital role in shaping the emerging Japanese state.

Japan's mountainous terrain tends to naturally divide the islands into separate local communities, but the main island of Honshū is also blessed with two significantly large plains. The largest of these, the Kantō Plain in the east, around modern Tōkyō, was too remote from continental influences to figure significantly in early state formation, but the Yamato Plain in the west (at the eastern end of the Inland Sea) was well situated to become the heart of a major agricultural civilization. By contrast, Korea's relative lack of comparably large, flat land areas may have constrained Korea's premodern development somewhat.[39] Because of the critical importance of imported continental technologies such as ironworking and wet-field rice cultivation on early Japan, the regions closest to and most accessible from the continent (northern Kyūshū and the Inland Sea area, including the Yamato Plain) quickly became the most developed areas. Archeological evidence suggests that by the 400s, the Yamato Plain had already to some degree been brought under consolidated rule.

Newly emergent East Asian rulers in Manchuria, Korea, and Japan all at various times tried to buttress their positions against possible rivals by offering tribute to Chinese dynasties and being invested in return with prestigious Chinese titles. Himiko had already been proclaimed "Queen of Wa" (the earliest written name for Japan) in 238 by the Three Kingdoms Chinese state of Wei. Between the years 413 and 502, no fewer than thirteen Japanese tribute missions are mentioned in Chinese dynastic histories. One of the titles the Chinese Southern dynasties bestowed on fifth-century Japanese rulers was "Great General Pacifying the East." This originally Chinese title "general" (*jiangjun*) is pronounced *shōgun* in Japanese, and it is a word that would have a prominent future in Japan. Even in this early period when emerging Japanese leaders were still actively seeking titles from China, however, an inscription on a sword that was buried in western Kyūshū in the late fifth or early sixth century already speaks of a Japanese Great King "ruling All Under Heaven," revealing that the Japanese were already beginning to adapt and apply continental ideas of supreme sovereignty to themselves.[40]

The rise of centralized royal authority in Yamato Japan, especially in the period from the fifth through the early seventh centuries, owed much to the court's ability to control and monopolize the distribution of imported foreign prestige goods such as iron – which was imported from Korea in the earliest period – bronze mirrors, and swords. This included also control over groups of immigrant people who possessed useful specialized skills such as writing. By the fifth century, record keeping was beginning at the Japanese court, with immigrants forming the nucleus of a literate scribal class. Immigrant artisans were often organized into special hereditary production units called *be*. Besides writing, other key crafts that tended to be dominated by immigrants in the fifth and sixth centuries included silk weaving, metalworking, and architecture.

The Yamato court also attempted to gain leverage over the major native Japanese descent groups, called *uji*, which were the primary organizational units of early Japanese society, by conferring new titles as surnames on their leaders and converting these leaders into orientations of dependency on the Yamato court. These *uji* often claimed descent from deities (called *kami* in Japanese) and cohered around shared worship of those deities. What became the Japanese imperial line, in particular, claimed descent from the sun goddess Amaterasu. Over time, the ascent of this sun goddess to the top of the religious hierarchy was successfully engineered. To a degree that is relatively unique in East Asia, politics and religion were closely interrelated in early Japan. One Japanese word for government, *matsurigoto*, actually derives from a word meaning "matters of religious ritual."[41]

Throughout this entire early phase, not only did the Yamato ruler not yet style himself (or herself – there were a striking number of female rulers in early Japan) "emperor," but even the posthumous names by which the early Japanese rulers are known today had not been conceived yet. Contemporaries apparently merely referred to the earliest Japanese rulers by the names of the palaces where they lived. By the sixth century, however, Yamato leaders had begun proclaiming themselves "true sovereigns" (*sumera mikoto*).

In 587, one Yamato ruler supposedly indicated a willingness to accept the foreign, continental, religious doctrines of Buddhism. Political opposition stiffened, and when the ruler died later that same year a coalition of five royal princes, together with the head of the powerful Soga family, marched against the leaders of the opposition and annihilated them. The Soga family had been early supporters of Buddhism and had risen to great power through attaching themselves closely to the service of the throne, eventually attaining the title of "senior minister." After their victory in this swift civil war of 587, the Soga family head emerged as the dominant personality in Japan.

In 592, the Soga leader even audaciously arranged the assassination of the reigning monarch and the installation of his own niece, who is known to history as Empress Suiko (r. 592–628), on the throne – now located in a new palace in the heart of the Soga family stronghold near Asuka, in the Yamato region. Empress Suiko, together with her renowned regent Prince Shōtoku (Shōtoku Taishi, 574–622), then became associated with a range of extremely important innovations that helped transform Yamato into a more continental-style centralized state. These new developments may have included the adoption, for the first time, of such Chinese titles as "emperor" (written with two characters that are pronounced *kōtei* in Japanese and *huangdi* in Chinese), although what would become the distinctively Japanese variant of this East Asian imperial title, "Heavenly Sovereign" (*tennō*), was not definitely first used until the end of the seventh century.[42] In 604, Prince Shōtoku also supposedly issued a landmark Seventeen-Article Constitution that outlined a new vision of an ethical and political order based on a combination of Confucian and Buddhist ideals, and asserted an unprecedented royal monopoly on ultimate authority throughout Japan, stating flatly that "in a country there are not two lords; the people have not two masters."[43]

Although Japan's two earliest native histories, the *Record of Ancient Matters* (*Kojiki*, completed in 712) and the *Chronicles of Japan* (*Nihon shoki*, also known as the *Nihongi*, completed in 720) purport to describe Japanese history from the primordial creation of the islands, and date the beginning of the alleged first Japanese emperor's reign to 660 BCE, much of this early material is clearly legendary. It is only now, roughly around the time of Empress Suiko, that we can begin to read these accounts as reasonably reliable history. Even at this time, much of the northern part of the main island of Honshū, southern Kyūshū, and other outlying islands were still largely outside the pale of Japanese civilization. In important senses, however, it may be said that in this era, Japan was born.

For Further Reading

China during the Age of Division is surveyed by Mark Edward Lewis, *China between Empires: The Northern and Southern Dynasties* (Cambridge, MA: Harvard University Press, 2009). For material culture, see Albert E. Dien, *Six Dynasties Civilization* (New Haven, CT: Yale University Press, 2007). For a lavishly illustrated catalog of artifacts from a landmark exhibition, see James C. Y. Watt et al., eds., *China: Dawn of a Golden Age, 200–750 AD* (New York: The Metropolitan Museum of Art, 2004). A fine collection of essays on the period is Scott Pearce, Audrey Spiro, and Patricia Ebrey, eds., *Culture and Power in the Reconstitution of the Chinese Realm, 200–600* (Cambridge, MA: Harvard University Press, 2001).

For aspects of literary culture and non-Buddhist religion in China during the Age of Division, see Stephen R. Bokenkamp, *Ancestors and Anxiety: Daoism and the Birth of Rebirth in China* (Berkeley: University of California Press, 2007); Robert Ford Campany, *Making Transcendents: Ascetics and Social Memory in Early Medieval China* (Honolulu: University of Hawai'i Press, 2009); Isabelle Robinet, *Taoism: Growth of a Religion*, trans. Phyllis Brooks (Stanford University Press, [1992] 1997); and Xiaofei Tian, *Beacon Fire and Shooting Star: The Literary Culture of the Liang (502–557)* (Cambridge, MA: Harvard University Asia Center, 2007).

The classic study of the arrival of Buddhism in East Asia is Erik Zürcher, *The Buddhist Conquest of China: The Spread and Adaptation of Buddhism in Early Medieval China*, 3rd ed. (Leiden, Netherlands: Brill, 2006). For a quick overview, see Arthur F. Wright, *Buddhism in Chinese History* (Stanford University Press, 1959). Robert H. Sharf, *Coming to Terms with Chinese Buddhism: A Reading of the Treasure Store Treatise* (Honolulu: University of Hawai'i Press, 2002), offers a penetrating analysis of the interaction of Buddhism with Chinese culture. See also John Kieschnick, *The Impact of Buddhism on Chinese Material Culture* (Princeton University Press, 2003). For early Korean Buddhism, see Peter H. Lee, trans., *Lives of Eminent Korean Monks: The Haedong Kosŭng Chŏn* (Cambridge, MA: Harvard University Press, 1969). For Japan, see Kōyū Sonoda, "Early Buddha Worship," in *The Cambridge History of Japan, vol. 1. Ancient Japan*, ed. Delmer M. Brown (Cambridge University Press, 1993).

For a general, overall introduction to East Asian religion, see Joseph M. Kitagawa, ed., *The Religious Traditions of Asia* (New York: Macmillan, 1987). See also H. Byron Earhart, *Religions of Japan: Many Traditions within One Sacred Way* (San Francisco: Harper and Row, 1984); Joseph M. Kitagawa, *On Understanding Japanese Religion* (Princeton University Press, [1979] 1987); Toshio Kuroda, "Shinto in the History of Japanese Religion," *Journal of Japanese Studies* 7, no. 1 (1981); Daniel Overmyer, *Religions of China: The World as a Living System* (Prospect Heights, IL: Waveland Press, [1986] 1998); and Laurence G. Thompson, *Chinese Religion: An Introduction*, 5th ed. (Belmont, NY: Wadsworth, 1996).

On the origins of an East Asian cultural community, see Gina L. Barnes, *China, Korea and Japan: The Rise of Civilization in East Asia* (London: Thames and Hudson, 1993), and Charles Holcombe, *The Genesis of East Asia, 221 B.C.–A.D. 907* (Honolulu: University of Hawai'i Press, 2001).

Concerning pre-seventh-century Korea, see Jonathan W. Best, *A History of the Early Korean Kingdom of Paekche: Together with an Annotated Translation of the Paekche Annals of the Samguk sagi* (Cambridge, MA: Harvard University Asia Center, 2006); Mark E. Byington, ed., *Early Korea 1: Reconsidering Early Korean History through Archaeology* (Cambridge, MA: Korea Institute, Harvard University, 2008), and *Early Korea 3: The Rediscovery of Kaya in History and Archaeology* (Cambridge, MA: Korea Institute, Harvard University, 2012); Kenneth H. J. Gardiner, *The Early History of Korea: The Historical Development of the Peninsula up to the Introduction of Buddhism in the Fourth Century A.D.* (Honolulu: University of Hawai'i Press, 1969); Sarah Milledge Nelson, *The Archaeology of Korea* (Cambridge

University Press, 1993); and Hyung Il Pai, *Constructing "Korean" Origins: A Critical Review of Archaeology, Historiography, and Racial Myth in Korean State-Formation Theories* (Cambridge, MA: Harvard University Asia Center, 2000).

On Japan before the seventh century, see Gina L. Barnes, *State Formation in Japan: Emergence of a 4th-Century Ruling Elite* (London: Routledge, 2007); Mark J. Hudson, *Ruins of Identity: Ethnogenesis in the Japanese Islands* (Honolulu: University of Hawai'i Press, 1999); Keiji Imamura, *Prehistoric Japan: New Perspectives on Insular East Asia* (Honolulu: University of Hawai'i Press, 1996); J. Edward Kidder, *Himiko and Japan's Elusive Chiefdom of Yamatai: Archaeology, History, and Mythology* (Honolulu: University of Hawai'i Press, 2007); and Joan R. Piggott, *The Emergence of Japanese Kingship* (Stanford University Press, 1997).

4 The Creation of a Community

China, Korea, and Japan (Seventh–Tenth Centuries)

The Sui Reunification (589) and the Founding of the Tang

In 581, a palace coup brought a new dynasty, called Sui, to power in the history-haunted region "Within the Passes" in northwest China. The founder of this dynasty was a man named Yang Jian (541–604). As emperor, he is known as Sui Wendi (the "Cultured Emperor of the Sui"). His father had been a high official, ennobled as the Duke of Sui, under the last Xianbei-ruled regime in northwest China (the Northern Zhou Dynasty). Yang Jian inherited his father's title as Duke of Sui, and his daughter was selected to be a consort for the imperial crown prince. When this crown prince, in due course, inherited the throne in 578, it made Yang Jian the father-in-law of the reigning emperor – always a potentially influential position. Because this emperor only lived two more years and was succeeded by a young boy, Yang Jian was then well placed to step in and grab supreme power for himself. After eliminating all potential legitimate heirs to the throne, and quelling a certain amount of armed opposition, Yang Jian usurped the throne outright, founding the Sui Dynasty.

A few years earlier, in 577, the last independent Xianbei-ruled dynasty in northeast China (the Northern Qi) had already been conquered by the predecessor of the Sui Dynasty in the northwest (that is, Northern Zhou), accomplishing the reunification of north China. The new Sui Dynasty now aspired to conquer the south too, and complete the reunification of a Chinese world that had been divided (with one brief exception) ever since the disintegration of the Han Dynasty that began in 184. The south, meanwhile, had never recovered from a devastating mid-century rebellion (548–552), which had severely diminished Southern dynasty imperial resources. In particular, control over the strategic upper (western) reaches of the Yangzi River had now passed from the south to the north. During the centuries of division, the north had frequently been able to field superior cavalry-based armies, but the south had always been protected, when all else failed, by the formidable natural barrier of the Yangzi River. Now the south was vulnerable to attack down the line of the river from the west. The final southern military defense also appears to have been ineptly led. Although the Sui Dynasty spent eight years preparing for its invasion of the south, a relatively small Sui expeditionary force was able to capture the southern capital (modern Nanjing) in less than one month of combat operations in 589.

The southern capital, which may have been the largest city in the world in the early sixth century, was completely destroyed. The city that we know today as Nanjing had to be rebuilt again later, almost from scratch. Nearly four centuries of southern independence also ended forever (with only fleeting temporary exceptions). Chinese dynasties would continue to rise and fall, punctuated by occasional brief periods of division, but China had now been fairly permanently reunified. The Sui completion of the Grand Canal in 611, a manmade waterway linking the Yangzi River in the south to the Yellow River in the north, can be said to have capped the Sui Dynasty's military, economic, and cultural unification of the entire Chinese world.

This spectacular Sui Dynasty success story soon unraveled, however, due to a classic example of what historian Paul Kennedy calls "imperial overstretch."[1] The second Sui emperor (Yangdi, r. 604–618), who gained the throne under a cloud of suspicion of having murdered his own father, attempted to continue the Sui imperial expansion. Most of south China had fallen quickly to Sui armies in 589, but the Red River valley area in the extreme south (in what is today northern Vietnam) was not reconquered by Sui until 602. From there, under its second emperor, the Sui launched an even more ambitious invasion farther south into the wholly foreign realm of Champa, in what is now central Vietnam, in 605. Despite some military victories, the expedition suffered heavy losses due to tropical diseases. The Sui also launched an invasion of an island that may have been Taiwan.

In the north, by 612, the Sui had subdued the Eastern Türks. The Türks — who may have originated in the southern foothills of the Altai Mountains as a small group of ironworkers in the service of another steppe qaghanate (khanate) in Mongolia — emerged from obscurity in 552 by swiftly defeating their former overlords and seizing control over Mongolia. Forging an alliance with Sassanid Persia, by around 563 the Türk empire had extended its sway westward across much of Central Asia, after which they approached the Byzantines with an offer of alliance against Persia.

This enormous Eurasian Türk empire soon split into largely separate eastern and western qaghanates. The Eastern Türks established relations with both of the rival Xianbei regimes in north China in the mid-sixth century, but tended to favor the Northern Zhou in the northwest, which may have helped strengthen Northern Zhou and contributed to its reunification of north China in 577. After the Sui Dynasty replaced the Northern Zhou in 581, the Sui was now expansively ascendant on all fronts. In the far northwest, Sui authority was extended as far as Turfan and Hami in Xinjiang. Even successful Sui military campaigns placed heavy burdens on the resources of the empire, however, and in 612 Sui began an attack on the northeastern kingdom of Koguryŏ (in northern Korea and southern Manchuria) that proved to be a fatal failure.

In 607, the second Sui emperor had discovered that Koguryŏ was making secret diplomatic contacts with the Türks. Because he felt this was improper behavior for what he haughtily regarded as a vassal state, the Sui emperor threatened that if Koguryŏ did not promptly dispatch an appropriately submissive embassy, he would personally lead an armed "inspection" into Koguryŏ. More than imperial vanity and protocol was at stake: a military alliance between Koguryŏ and the Türks might seriously threaten the Sui. In addition, much of the territory of Koguryŏ had once lain inside the Han Dynasty frontiers, and a desire to match the glories of the Han may have also fired Sui imperial ambition.

A Koguryŏ raid into Sui territory in 598 had already been met with a large but unsuccessful Sui counter-invasion that same year. In 612, a massive Sui army, reportedly involving over a million combat troops, was assembled for an invasion of Koguryŏ. Although one Sui naval contingent actually penetrated the outer walls of the Koguryŏ capital, it was quickly expelled. The Sui armies operating in northern Korea could not obtain adequate provisions and eventually were forced to retreat – or starve. Much of the Sui invasion force was annihilated during this retreat. Undeterred by this first fiasco, however, the Sui emperor called for a second attack on Koguryŏ in 613. This time, the Sui forces were obliged to turn back quickly to deal with a domestic rebellion. Yet a third invasion was ordered in 614, which achieved some limited success, but by this time, the Sui Dynasty was rapidly disintegrating from within.

The massive conscription and mobilization of resources that made possible these monstrous invasions put a severe strain on the common people, especially in northeast China. In 611, one rebel, based in the Long White Mountains of modern Shandong Province, attracted draft evaders to his camp with a song about not "rashly dying" in northeastern military campaigns. Further rebellions quickly spiraled out of control. Some of these rebellions were led by high-ranking former Sui Dynasty officials rather than by desperate peasants. Clearly, even well-placed men within the dynastic establishment were turning against it. Eventually, as many as two hundred separate identifiable rebel groups arose.

Meanwhile, in 615, the Sui emperor was encircled and trapped by Türks at a place called Wild Goose Gate (Yanmen) in northern Shanxi, near the great northward loop of the Yellow River. He was rescued from this trap by troops led by his maternal cousin Li Yuan (566–635), the Duke of Tang. On the strength of Li Yuan's proven combat effectiveness against the Türks, Li was made garrison commander of the frontline northern city today known as Taiyuan, in Shanxi, while the Sui emperor himself retreated to the comfort of his favorite refuge in the south. The Sui emperor was suspicious of his cousin Li Yuan, however, and delegated two officers to keep their eyes on him. When these men conspired with the Türks against him, Li Yuan was tipped off and trapped them instead, rising in open rebellion against the Sui emperor in 617. In 126 days, his army marched south to occupy the Sui capital in the region "Within the Passes." In 618, the second (and last) Sui emperor was strangled to death at his southern refuge by some of his own courtiers, and Li Yuan ascended the throne as the founding emperor of a new Tang Dynasty.

The Consolidation of Tang Rule

After proclaiming the establishment of this new Tang Dynasty, the name of its capital city (modern Xi'an) was restored to what it had been in the glorious days when it had served as the capital of the Former Han Dynasty (i.e., Chang'an), to invoke the memory of China's first great age of imperial unity.[2] (The actual layout of the Sui and Tang dynasty city, however, more closely followed the recent example of the Tuoba Xianbei Northern Wei capital at Luoyang.) A claim was also publicized that the spirit of the ancient Daoist sage Laozi had supernaturally revealed himself to be Li Yuan's ancestor (the "Old Master" Laozi's surname was believed to have also been Li) and divinely predicted that Li Yuan was destined to win the empire. Despite such brave assertions, however, at the time Li Yuan seized the throne he actually controlled little more than the region "Within the Passes," and years of further warfare would be necessary before all the many other rebel bands were eliminated and all China reunified again. Significantly, early Tang population figures (as of 639) show serious population decline from the heights of the Sui Dynasty just a few decades earlier. Whether or not there were actually fewer people, fewer people were being counted by the government. The years of transition from Sui to Tang witnessed much upheaval.

The second Tang emperor (Tang Taizong, r. 626–649), then, came to the throne in an especially horrifying manner. In the final stages of a power struggle with his own elder brother (during which, at one point, Taizong supposedly survived an attempted poisoning), in 626, the future emperor Taizong (keep in mind that Taizong is his posthumous temple name, and not a name by which he would have been known at that time) bribed the commander of a palace gate (the Xuanwu gate) to set up an ambush. As his older brother, accompanied by a younger brother, rode in, they discovered the trap and spurred their horses in an attempt to escape. Taizong chased them, firing arrows, and his older brother was shot and killed. Taizong himself was then knocked from his horse by some branches, but before his younger brother could take advantage of this sudden vulnerability, Taizong's men arrived and put the younger brother to death also. When the heads of the two assassinated princes were displayed, resistance ended. Taizong then dispatched a man to "safeguard" his father, the reigning emperor, who was boating on a palace lake at time. Whether out of shock and horror, or perhaps because he had all along coldly calculated that the succession would have to be determined by such ruthless competition,[3] the father soon vacated the throne, elevating himself to the ceremonial position of Retired Emperor, and Taizong became emperor of Tang.

Despite the bloody way in which he gained the throne, and the fact that just days after becoming emperor, a massive Türk army penetrated to within a few miles of the capital and had to be humiliatingly appeased before withdrawing, Tang Taizong is remembered as one of the most outstanding emperors in all of Chinese history. The reign of Taizong became a time of peak Chinese political and military power, and Taizong also presided over an age of exceptionally glorious cosmopolitanism. This cosmopolitanism extended even to the Tang imperial family itself, which was of culturally mixed descent. It has even been suggested that the fratricidal power struggle that brought Taizong to the throne may have been a lingering influence of Xianbei nomadic cultural traditions.

Until the establishment of the Sui Dynasty in 581, the rulers of north China had mostly still been identifiably non-Chinese Xianbei. In the mid-sixth century there had even been a revival of Xianbei names and language. Although the new Sui imperial family are said to have been Chinese (tracing descent through the paternal line), and they did restore the use of Chinese names after 581, they had also lived for generations in what we now call Inner Mongolia and had extensively intermarried with the Xianbei elite. Their cousins, the Tang imperial family, sprang from identical origins. Li Yuan, the Tang founder, was said to have been a great archer and hunter who "never missed his shots."[4] Elements of nomadic culture long remained noticeable at the Tang court, and during the Sui and Tang dynasties, Xianbei-style clothing even became a new standard Chinese costume.

Actual Türks gave valuable assistance to Li Yuan in establishing his Tang Dynasty, and although relations between the Tang and Türk empires then turned hostile for a generation, in 630, the Eastern Türks were decisively defeated, and Tang Taizong assumed for himself the title of "Heavenly Qaghan" as a Türkic-style supreme ruler over the eastern steppe (as well as Chinese-style emperor of China).[5] By the mid-seventh century, Tang military and political influence had penetrated deeply into Central Asia, although direct Tang administration probably never extended any farther west than Hami and Turfan in Xinjiang. The renowned Chinese pilgrim Xuanzang (ca. 596–664), who traveled to India in 629–645 to study Buddhism at its source, reported encountering an "orphan city" near the Talas River, in what is now Kazakhstan or Kyrgyzstan, where more than three hundred households of formerly Chinese inhabitants lived. By the time Xuanzang arrived, they had become acculturated to Türkic standards of dress and activity, but they still preserved the Chinese language and certain Chinese customs.[6]

Traveling in the other direction, the game of polo, which appears to have originated in Persia, became popular in Tang China. Nestorian Christianity also reached China during Taizong's reign, and a Christian church was established in the Tang capital by imperial decree in 638. A number of Nestorian Christian churches apparently existed in Tang China, although the religion never sank deep roots into Chinese society. Other exotic Western religions, such as Zoroastrianism and Manichaeism, also enjoyed official toleration and may have been more widespread.

If the Tang began as a militarily expansive, culturally mixed, and "self-consciously multi-ethnic empire," however, it ended three hundred years later, in 907, as a much more "self-consciously mono-ethnic empire united by significantly more homogenous Chinese culture." The Tang Dynasty was "perhaps *the* crucial period in the formation" of a Chinese ethnic, and even proto-national, identity.[7]

The aborigines who had lived scattered throughout south China, and who had made up a substantial portion of the total population of the Southern dynasties, largely disappeared during the Tang – absorbed into the general Chinese population (although a considerable number can still be found even today, especially near the frontiers). Many descendants of the Xianbei and of the other non-Chinese groups who had ruled north China from 304 until 581 also lost their separate identities and simply became Chinese during the Tang era. The term "Han," which had first begun to be used as an ethnic label to distinguish the conquered subject population ruled by Xianbei elites during the Northern Wei Dynasty, came to refer to all of the people of the Tang Dynasty.[8]

At least forty-three persons of traceable non-Chinese descent are known to have reached the highest government office (grand councilor) during the Tang Dynasty. The general who captured Tashkent in remote Central Asia for the Tang in 750 was a second- or third-generation descendant of an émigré from Korea. Several of the most renowned Tang Dynasty Chinese-language poets, such as Li Bai (also spelled "Li Po," 701–762), Liu Yuxi (772–842), Bai Juyi (also spelled "Po Chü-I," 772–846), and Yuan Zhen (779–831), were all of known, or suspected, non-Chinese descent. Whatever their ancestry, however, by this time, they had all effectively become Chinese, and unparalleled masters of the Chinese language. As already mentioned, a rhyming dictionary (the *Qieyun*), which set an influential standard for "correct" Chinese-language pronunciation, was compiled in 601 in part by a man of known Xianbei descent. And, even as persons of Xianbei descent became native speakers of Chinese, the Xianbei language itself became extinct. Of the many Xianbei-language songs that had frequently been performed at Northern dynasty courts, by 801, although fifty-three were still in existence, only six titles could still be understood.[9] Despite the fact that some degree of multilingualism was probably only normal throughout much of the premodern world, this was less true of Tang Dynasty China. Within the geographic place we call China, the Chinese language had triumphed.

The Harmonization of Diversity

An obscure mid-sixth-century religious figure named Lu Fahe (dates unknown) may help illustrate how the cultural diversity of the Age of Division came to merge into the relative uniformity of the late Tang. Lu Fahe first attracted notice while living in reclusion as an ascetic *śramaṇa* (Buddhist monk) on Thirty Mile Island, in the middle reaches of the Yangzi River. His place of origin was unknown, but some said he came from the centermost of the five sacred peaks in the ancient Chinese cultural heartland in the north. He spoke, however, with a southern aboriginal accent, and he appeared frequently in close association with aborigines. Lu developed a reputation for being able to predict the future and was much sought after in helping people design houses and lay out graves in such a way as to bring good fortune (what is called *fengshui*, or geomancy). He also gathered medicines to cure the many diseases of the lush southern climate, and he cast imprecations that allegedly prevented venomous insects and wild animals from biting or stinging.

Once, when someone tested a new blade on an ox, severing its head with one blow, Lu warned the man that he must perform meritorious services for the spirit of the ox or be struck by karmic retribution. The man scoffed, but died a few days later.

At the time of a major southern rebellion in 548, Lu joined loyalist imperial forces in counterattacking the rebels. He summoned eight hundred aboriginal disciples to a river ferry and set sail aboard a warship with some regular imperial troops. At a place called Red Sands Lake, they encountered the enemy. Because the wind was wrong for releasing fireships to drift down on the rebel fleet, Lu (according to the story) magically changed the direction of the wind by waving a white feather. After the defeat of the rebel forces, Lu became an imperial official, but when the southern empire split, and the southern emperor he served was killed by an invasion from the Xianbei-ruled dynasty in the northwest, Lu Fahe defected in 555 to the rival Xianbei regime in the northeast. As Lu Fahe approached the northeastern capital (Ye, near modern Anyang in Henan), the northeastern emperor, who had heard of Lu's uncanny arts, went out from his city several miles to respectfully meet him. When Lu caught sight of the distant city, he dismounted and performed the Pace of Yu. In the city, later, Lu would again rise to high office.[10]

The Pace of Yu refers to the legendary founder of the first Chinese dynasty, Great Yu. According to the legend, Great Yu traipsed the length and breadth of China taming floods that were ravaging the land and, in the process, supposedly became lame, developing a peculiar gait or pace. By the Age of Division, something called the Pace of Yu had become a potent performance in the ritual arsenal of religious Daoism.

Lu Fahe is an extremely obscure and unimportant figure, but his career is of some interest nonetheless. Aside from illustrating the role of religion in China in living practice (as opposed to scripture-based sectarian doctrine), it also nicely demonstrates the inextricable mingling of Indian Buddhism with assorted native Chinese religious ideas, and the merging of north and south, aborigines, Xianbei, and Chinese, and the possibility of bringing them all together through the invocation of the grand Chinese cultural tradition, symbolized by the legend of Great Yu. The stage was set for reunification.

The Age of Division had been marked by sweeping physical population movements, which not only brought non-Chinese people such as the Xianbei to power in north China but also dispersed large numbers of Chinese refugees from the ancient heartland in the Central Plain to new locations in the far northeast, northwest, and, above all, south of the Yangzi River. The result was to promote cultural exchange, ethnic intermixing, and a general expansion of Chinese civilization. For example, the manuscript of a set of civil service examination answers written in 408 has recently been discovered near Turfan, Xinjiang. Although the test itself had probably actually been administered in Gansu, in the somewhat less extremely remote northwest, and the literary quality of the writing is hardly outstanding, it is nonetheless noteworthy that Chinese-language written civil service examinations were being conducted at such a time and place.[11]

The last Xianbei-ruled dynasty in the northwest, based in the region "Within the Passes," initially had only a small number of Xianbei warriors at its disposal – perhaps fewer than ten thousand. After a military defeat by its northeastern rival in 543, it began recruiting ethnic Chinese into the army out of necessity and, in the process, erasing the long-standing occupational division between Xianbei warriors and Chinese (Han) farmers. When its successor dynasty, the Sui, forced many soldiers to return to civilian status and farming in 590, following its reunification of China, the division between non-Chinese warriors and Chinese farmers effectively ended.

Meanwhile, despite a revival of Xianbei names, language, clothing, and culture in the mid-sixth century, that same final northwestern Xianbei Dynasty had also, paradoxically, simultaneously revived an idealized memory of ancient Chinese Zhou Dynasty institutions, and pointedly called itself [Northern] Zhou. This may have been in part simply because the regime happened to be based in the ancient Zhou homeland "Within the Passes," and also because it needed some unifying ideology to rally an otherwise decidedly mixed population. The Sui Dynasty emerged directly out of this regime in 581, and reunified China in 589.

The reunified Sui and Tang dynasties then transformed the empire into a single, centralized country. The Tang, for example, established a network of 1,639 post stations along the main roads leading to the capital to facilitate communications. Beyond mere administrative centralization, moreover, Tang also began promoting a more uniform Chinese culture. Near the beginning of his reign, in 619, the Tang founder established temples to the Duke of Zhou and Confucius at the Imperial Academy, with seasonal sacrifices to their spirits. In 628, Confucius was elevated to a position of superiority over the Duke of Zhou, and in 630, every province and county in the empire was ordered to establish such Confucian temples. Although the practice of offering sacrifices to the spirit of Confucius at his own home state of Lu (in modern Shandong) dates back to at least the beginning of the Han Dynasty, and a Confucian temple may have first been erected at the Imperial Academy in the capital in 386, these seasonal rites at Confucian temples, which became a hallmark of traditional Chinese civilization, reached mature form only in the Tang Dynasty.

The early Tang also established empirewide standard editions of the Confucian Classics and went to unprecedented efforts to construct a continuous narrative history of the Chinese past. In 593, the Sui Dynasty had imposed a ban on the private composition of state histories, which did not begin to be relaxed until the middle of the Tang. History writing was therefore concentrated at the imperial court, as a great affair of state. The Tang Dynasty then sponsored major imperial history-writing projects. Of the unparalleled sequence of "Twenty-four Dynastic Histories" that provide the standard version of the story of China from the time of the legendary Sage Kings to the end of the premodern era, eight, exactly one-third of the total (including two that were somewhat unofficial), were compiled within roughly a twenty-year period at Tang Taizong's court.

Education is a particularly powerful tool for promoting a common cultural identity. Emperor Wu of the Han Dynasty had, to a large extent, first defined the Confucian canon and established Confucianism as state orthodoxy when he appointed teachers and established an Imperial Academy in the second century BCE. Now, in 624, the Tang founder ordered every province and county in the empire to establish schools. By 738, at least on paper, there were nineteen thousand official schools in Tang China.[12]

Before long, official state-run schools came to be eclipsed by private education. Such late-Tang literary giants as Li Bai, Du Fu (712–770), and Han Yu (768–824) all received their educations privately. The result of this privatization may have only been to further universalize education in late Tang, however. Many people undoubtedly were still illiterate or poorly educated, but in 824, it was nonetheless claimed that the latest fashionable poetry was in the mouths of every "prince, duke, concubine and wife, child tending cattle, and passerby on horseback."[13] What had once been exclusively elite cultural standards were increasingly diffused to become universal Chinese norms, and in the process, the old divisions between Great Families and commoners, and between Chinese and non-Chinese, were collapsing into a more universal Chinese civilization. For example, in a cache of old texts preserved by the arid climate of remote northwestern Dunhuang, over a thousand anonymous popular lyrics from the Tang period have been found, many of which may have been written by fairly ordinary folk.

The new technology of woodblock printing was also already beginning to play a role in this process of diffusing a common Chinese culture by the end of the Tang Dynasty. The origins of printing are obscure, and the oldest known surviving printed text is a Buddhist charm discovered in Korea dating from sometime before 751. By the early ninth century, however, a complaint was already heard in Tang China that printed calendars were on sale in the markets throughout the empire even before the Bureau of Astronomy issued its official calendar each year.[14] Although a genuine explosion in the availability of books due to printing would have to wait until the next dynasty, such humble printed items as calendars were already becoming available for use by ordinary people in late Tang, and were helping to promote a common Chinese culture in the process.

Even private education in Tang times was, furthermore, directed toward specifically imperial goals by the civil service examination system. Tests had been used in the selection of Chinese officials since at least the beginning of the empire, but only as part of a selection process that was driven mostly by personal recommendation. During the Age of Division, beginning in 220, a so-called Nine Ranks system had been introduced, under which specially designated regional administrators evaluated potential candidates for office and ranked them – in practice, largely based on family background. The result was to deeply entrench the status of a few Great Families, who acquired something even of an aristocratic aura. In the early sixth century, however, one Southern dynasty emperor asserted the radical idea that officials should be selected purely based on ability as demonstrated through examination, without regard to family background. In 587, the Sui Dynasty terminated the evaluating authority of the Nine Ranks administrators and began to move toward a system based more on examinations.

Several different academic degrees came to be offered. For the Understanding the Classics (*ming jing*) degree, all but one line of a selected passage from one of the

Confucian Classics would be covered up, and several characters of the remaining line would also be concealed. The candidate was then expected to be able to supply the missing characters from memory. After this, there would also be an oral examination and answers to test questions. During the reign of the second Sui emperor, another new degree, called *jinshi* (Presented Scholar), was introduced, which put more emphasis on questions of current relevance, as well as poetry and literature, and less on memorization of the classics. The *jinshi* quickly became by far the most esteemed degree, and in later dynasties it would eventually come to be the highest of a standard sequence of three successive degrees. During the late Tang Dynasty, an annual average of about thirty *jinshi* degrees were awarded, and the degree's prestige was incomparable.

Obtaining a degree such as the *jinshi* conferred status and qualified a man to potentially hold government office, but to actually be appointed to office it was still necessary to be further examined by the Ministry of Personnel. In the Tang, this examination paid special regard to physical appearance and deportment, speaking ability, calligraphy, and ability to pronounce judgments. Under the growing authority of Empress Wu Zetian (624–705) in the late seventh century, anyone who believed they had talent – even commoners – were encouraged to recommend themselves for advancement, and the practice of testing candidates anonymously may have first been introduced.

The civil service examination system, which reached full maturity only after the Tang, became perhaps *the* defining institution of late imperial China (until it was abolished in the name of modernization in 1905). Although the system always had its critics, it may be said that it did promote a relatively fluid and apparently meritocratic social and political order, and it was certainly a powerful force for cultural homogenization. For example, several grandsons of one eighth-century Türk from the remote northwest, who had himself attained distinction through military service to the Tang, "all became known for Confucianism" and achieved success through the examination system.[15]

Commercial exchange also contributed to Tang Dynasty cultural integration, as will be examined in more detail later. One new product circulated by the Tang commercial markets was tea. Tea had been mentioned as early as the Han Dynasty, and during the Age of Division tea drinking became popular in the south. In the north, meanwhile, the prevalence of livestock raising had made dairy products the beverage of choice (for perhaps the only time in Chinese history). Under the reunified Tang Dynasty, the passion for drinking tea spread from the tea-producing regions in the southeast to the entire country. One explanation for tea's new popularity was that it was promoted as an aid to staying awake during Buddhist meditation.

Domesticating Chinese Buddhism

Although the reunified Sui and Tang dynasties depicted themselves as restorations of the earlier Han Dynasty imperial unity, in many ways, China was now a substantially different place. The spread of tea, and chairs, during Tang times are but two examples of such innovations. The most glaring difference was probably Buddhism. Buddhism had been unknown in China at the start of the Han Dynasty, and even at the end of the Han it was still very much a religion for foreigners. By the time of the Sui reunification in 589, however, there were reportedly more copies of the Buddhist *sūtras* in China than of the Confucian Classics. China had become a thoroughly Buddhist land.

In Sui and Tang, monks from the major capital monasteries took turns contemplating the Buddha in a place of worship within the imperial palace, day and night without cease. Once under the Sui, and four times under the Tang, empirewide networks of Buddhist temples were ordered constructed, with obligations to perform services for the imperial family and recite *sūtras* for the religious protection of the state. Public preaching reached a large popular audience by late Tang, and ordinary people sometimes bankrupted themselves making religious donations. By late Tang times, even criticism of Buddhism was frequently couched in Buddhist terms. For example, if all earthly activity is an illusory dream – the mere "shadow of a bubble," as the Buddhists liked to say – then a counterargument could be offered that expenditure and labor on behalf of Buddhist temples is also in vain, and that efforts might more appropriately be diverted to the relief of the poor and the service of the state. Although there never was a time when all Chinese people universally were Buddhist – there were always other religious traditions, and belief remained largely a matter of individual choice – by Tang times, China had become deeply Buddhist. At the same time, though, Buddhism had also become thoroughly Chinese.

Buddhist monks in China frequently resided in permanent, sometimes magnificent, monasteries. By Sui and Tang times, some of these monasteries had grown into complex tax-exempt economic institutions with their own estates, slaves, pawnshops, and sometimes even floating high-interest loans. Following the secular Chinese family model, the Chinese Buddhist abbot handed monastic property down to a chosen successor, establishing patriarchal lines of succession. This, combined with certain doctrinal variations, helped generate what are often called the sects of Chinese Buddhism. It should be emphasized that while these sects did become formally distinct in Japanese Buddhism, in China, especially through Tang times, the situation remained more fluid.[16] Nonetheless, there were certain subdivisions in Chinese Buddhism that can loosely be considered as sects. In particular, through long resonance with native Daoist language and ideas, the Chinese domestication of Buddhism reached a kind of culmination in something called Chan (in Japanese, Zen; in Korean, Sŏn).

From the early Chinese conviction that there was a Buddha Nature in every person, it began to be supposed that this Buddha Nature was everywhere and that salvation could be attained in this life merely through realization of this truth. In Chan Buddhism, enlightenment may be sought not by escaping from the world but by awakening to the reality of the world around you. The word *Chan* literally means "meditation" (from the Sanskrit *dhyāna*), and meditation was central to Chan: not merely as a way to enlightenment but as enlightenment itself in practice. Chan meditation – the stripping away of thoughts and sensations and the elimination of superficial distinctions to realize the fundamental unity of all things – was aided by characteristically enigmatic riddles intended to stimulate awakening. The study of scripture, on the other hand, was said to be useless, because ultimate truth simply cannot be reduced to words. Chan Buddhism famously has been described as "a special transmission outside the scriptures, not founded upon words and letters" but rather "pointing directly to [one's] mind."[17] Appropriately enough, the renowned Sixth Chan Patriarch Huineng (638–713) began life as an illiterate firewood seller and apparently never learned to read.

By the end of the Tang Dynasty, and especially under the next dynasty (Song, 960–1279), Chan had become perhaps the mainstream of Chinese Buddhism. Chan, by this time, was quite thoroughly Chinese, and most of its actual development can be traced back to that Chinese Sixth Patriarch Huineng. Even with Chan, however, a legendary Indian origin was still obligatory. According to tradition, the Chan transmission had passed through twenty-eight generations in India, starting from Śākyamuni Buddha himself, until an Indian Brahman known as Bodhidharma brought it to China sometime around the year 500. This Bodhidharma was a real historical figure, but most of the legends associated with him developed only later. He is best known for supposedly introducing the meditative technique of "wall watching" as a method of calming the mind. Bodhidharma is regarded as the First Chan Patriarch.

Despite the Chinese domestication of Buddhism, genuine Indian connections still existed. The great Chinese pilgrim Xuanzang went on a seventeen-year journey to India and the western regions in early Tang. He returned in 645 and presided over the translation into Chinese of more than thirteen hundred rolls of Indian scriptures he had brought back. In the middle of the Tang Dynasty, three prominent South Asian missionary monks, Śubhakarasiṃha (637–735), Vajrabodhi (671–741), and Amoghavajra (705–774), introduced Esoteric (Tantric) Buddhism to the Tang court. Amoghavajra (who had come to China while still a child) was especially influential, enjoying the support of three Tang emperors. In 765, when the Tang capital was threatened by an invading enemy army, the emperor, instead of organizing military resistance, sent copies of Amoghavajra's new version of the *Sūtra for Benevolent Kings* to two temples, where priests recited the scripture and officials burnt incense for the protection of the state. When the invasion failed, Amoghavajra was credited with the victory.

Among Amoghavajra's Chinese disciples was the monk Huiguo (d. 805), who in turn instructed the visiting Japanese monk Kūkai (774–835) as well as at least one monk from Korea and another from what may have been the island of Java. Kūkai was then responsible for introducing Esoteric Buddhism to Japan, where it is called Shingon. In Japan, this Esoteric Buddhism became much more important than it was in China, largely as a result of Kūkai's incomparable talents. As Kūkai described it, a direct sequence of transmission from Vairocana (the first of the five celestial Buddhas) linked Esoteric Buddhism directly to Amoghavajra, then Huiguo, and finally Kūkai himself. Despite such claims, however, Kūkai actually studied under the Chinese master Huiguo a mere six months. Any real transmission of learning must have been somewhat tenuous.

Chinese contacts with India continued during the Tang and afterward, and the volume of maritime trade with Indian ports actually accelerated. But the center of gravity for Chinese (and East Asian) Buddhism had shifted now to China, and Chinese Buddhism developed thereafter almost exclusively in the Chinese language. A number of late Tang monks, such as Huaisu (b. 737), are best known for their achievements in calligraphy, which is not only a quintessentially Chinese art form but is also necessarily writing in the Chinese language. Other late Tang monks are famous for their Chinese-language poetry, including Jiaoran (ca. 734–ca. 792), who once playfully wrote, "I don't like foreign languages; I won't study them; And I've never translated barbarian words."[18] Given the extreme importance placed on translating Indian scriptures in the early phase of Chinese Buddhism, this represents a remarkable loss of interest in anything foreign. Such self-absorption, however, is entirely consistent with the general monolingual self-confidence that Chinese civilization was beginning to display.

Watershed: The Mid-Tang Crisis

Tang Taizong was succeeded on the throne in 649 by a weaker son, who was (inappropriately) attracted to one of his father's former concubines, Wu Zetian (624–705). This Lady Wu soon became the real power behind the throne, and after the emperor's death, she placed two of her own sons on the throne in quick succession. In 690, drawing on the support of the Buddhist *Great Cloud Sūtra*, which predicted that the Future Buddha Maitreya would one day be reincarnated as a female ruler, she broke completely with precedent and proclaimed herself the founding emperor of a new Zhou Dynasty. Although there have been several women in Chinese history who exercised actual supreme power, typically from the position of empress dowager, Wu Zetian is the only woman to ever officially hold the title "emperor." Wu Zetian was ruthless (and undeniably a usurper), but she was also a dynamic individual and a capable monarch, and she has understandably been the subject of considerable fascination ever since.

In her old age, however, when Empress Wu was about eighty, power finally slipped from her hands. Not long before her death, she was compelled to restore the Tang Dynasty in 705 and allow her son to resume the throne. After several more years of palace intrigue, in 712, another great Tang emperor, Xuanzong (r. 712–756), ascended the throne (see Figure 4.1). The reign of Emperor Xuanzong is commonly regarded as the golden age of the Tang – the most glorious period of a generally glorious dynasty – and is especially celebrated for the outstanding poets it produced. Xuanzong's reign ended, nonetheless, in disaster.

For roughly a century, the Tang Empire had remained militarily dominant. In 647, a Tang army had been able to intervene as far away as India to suppress a rebellion. In 659, the Tang defeated the Western Türks (having already defeated those in the east). In 668, in alliance with Silla, Tang crushed the northern Korean kingdom of Koguryŏ. The ultimate Tang military high water mark did not come until as late as 750, when Tang armies captured Tashkent in Central Asia. Long before that time, however, the military tide had already begun to turn. Korea,

Figure 4.1. Han Gan (active ca. 742–756), "Night-Shining White," a horse belonging to Emperor Xuanzong (r. 712–756). Handscroll, ink on paper. The Metropolitan Museum of Art, New York. © The Metropolitan Museum of Art/Art Resource, New York.

under unified Sillan rule, proved stubbornly independent. Around 679, the Eastern Türks restored their independence in Mongolia as what is sometimes called the second Türk Qaghanate. By the end of the seventh century, there were also the first stirrings of Khitan power in the northeast. Most dangerous, however, was the rising new Tibetan Empire.

The various tribes of Tibet were first unified under King Songtsen Gampo (Srong-btsan sgam-po, r. ca. 618–641). The royal seat was initially in the southeast, at Yarlung, and then later at Lhasa. Songtsen Gampo's reign also coincides with the introduction of Buddhism into Tibet, from both Tang China in the east and India in the south. The king accepted a royal Chinese bride, who supposedly discouraged the Tibetan practice of smearing their faces with red ochre, but the king also married a princess from Nepal and adopted an Indian, rather than the Chinese, writing system, laying the foundations for the emergence of a distinctive Tibetan civilization. Beginning around 665, this new Tibetan Empire overran Khotan, Kuchā, Karashar, and Kashgar in previously Tang-dominated Xinjiang and, shortly before that time, also captured the area of modern Qinghai. Although Tang counteroffensives recaptured some of these outposts, the Tang now confronted a highly formidable imperial military rival in the west.

In 747, a Tang general of Korean descent named Gao Xianzhi (Ko Sŏnji in Korean; d. 756) won a victory in the vicinity of Gilgit, Kashmir. Growing

Map 4.1 East Asia in 650 CE

overconfident, he began offensive operations against the small kingdoms in the western regions, and in 750, he took Tashkent. The captive king of Tashkent was sent to the Chinese capital, where he was executed, but the king's son fled west, where he gained the assistance of an Arab army. In 751, these Arabs defeated Tang forces at the Talas River in what proved to be one of the great pivotal battles of world history. This Arab victory marked the beginning of the rise of the new religion of Islam in Central Asia and a permanent end to Chinese influence west of the Pamir Mountains.

Meanwhile, the Tang emperor Xuanzong had become besotted by the beautiful Yang Guifei ("Precious Consort Yang"; 719–756). Yang Guifei extended patronage to her own favorites at court, among whom was a certain military general of mixed Central Asian (Sogdian) and Türkic parentage named An Lushan (ca. 703–757). An Lushan was supposedly so fat that he caused more than one horse to collapse and die beneath him. Thanks to Yang Guifei's support, An Lushan came to control the major Tang frontier armies in the northeast, in the vicinity of modern Beijing. After a dispute with Yang Guifei's brother, however, An Lushan rebelled in 755.[19] The Tang capital quickly fell to the rebels. Emperor Xuanzong fled, and was forced to execute his beloved Yang Guifei along the road.

Emperor Xuanzong's heir reorganized the loyalist imperial forces and proclaimed himself the new emperor, and in 757 both Tang capitals (Chang'an and Luoyang) were retaken with the aid of Uighur Türk and Arab allies. Although An Lushan was killed in 757 by his own son, the warfare touched off by his rebellion was not finally quelled until 762. To hasten the peace, rebel generals were confirmed in positions of independent power on the condition that they at least nominally surrender. Effective centralized Tang imperial authority was never entirely restored.

After An Lushan's rebellion, as much as 80 percent of the country's military force fell under the control of largely independent frontier commands. The central imperial government was unable to collect taxes from large swathes of China. Even within the imperial court itself, eunuchs (a eunuch was a castrated imperial household servant), through their control of the Imperial Guard and the Palace Secretariat, became the real power holders. From 821 to the end of the dynasty, seven out of eight emperors were enthroned by eunuchs, and two may have even been killed by the eunuchs. Politically, the Tang Dynasty had been greatly weakened.

The "Transmission of the Way," and Growing Commercialization

An Lushan's rebellion in 755 is commonly thought to mark an important watershed, not merely in the history of the Tang Dynasty but also for the entire course of Chinese history. Conventional wisdom has it that the exotic foreign origins of the rebel An Lushan provoked increased suspicion of foreigners thereafter. Although Uighur Türks and other non-Chinese forces helped Tang loyalists suppress the rebellion, they also unleashed much looting and slaughter of the Chinese population in the process. Despite these developments, however, the volume of foreign trade actually increased after the rebellion, bringing with it, among other things, increasing numbers of Arabs and Persians to Chinese coastal ports. China definitely did not retreat into economic isolationism after An Lushan. But the great age of Chinese cultural cosmopolitanism really was over, whether or not An Lushan was to blame.

Part of the reason for the decline of the old cosmopolitanism may have been because, not only was China itself becoming more homogeneous, but also, for the first time in history, it was coming to be surrounded by comparably organized foreign countries. China could no longer very credibly pretend to be a universal civilization surrounded merely by barbarian tribes. Some of these new foreign countries, moreover, were militarily threatening. During An Lushan's rebellion, for example, the Tibetan Empire took advantage of the distraction to resume its offensive, briefly even capturing the Tang capital in 763. From 780 to 848, the Tibetans controlled the important northwestern Silk Road oasis at Dunhuang, in Gansu.

After about 842, the Tibetan Empire began to split apart due to internal disputes. Tibet would not be reunified again until the era of Mongol domination in the thirteenth century, and would never again be a major military power. But the Tibetan imperial presence in the northwest was replaced by the new forces of the Uighurs and Tanguts. A Uighur Türkic Empire (744–840) had succeeded the second Türk Qaghanate on the steppe directly to the north of China (in what is today called Mongolia), but in 840, the Uighurs were scattered by yet another steppe tribe, the Kirghiz, and the center of Uighur power relocated west to Xinjiang.[20] This brought Uighur Türkic-language speakers in substantial numbers to Xinjiang for the first time, and is the source of Xinjiang's modern alternative English-language designation as Eastern Turkestan. Much of the population of Xinjiang today is still Uighur. The Tanguts, for their part, did not establish a formal empire, called Xia (or "Western Xia," Xi Xia), in the Ordos region of northwestern China until 1038 (–1227), but they were already mentioned in Chinese sources from early Tang times.

In the northeast, in eastern Inner Mongolia, Manchuria, and extending into parts of China proper, a people called the Khitan (whose language may have been related to Mongolic) had formed a powerful imperial state by 907 (–1125), which formally adopted the Chinese-style dynastic name Liao in 947. Also in Manchuria, an independent kingdom called Parhae (which had both Chinese and Korean influences) lasted from 698 until it fell to Khitan forces in 926. Korea, meanwhile, had been unified under independent native rule since 668.

In the southwest, in modern China's Yunnan Province, a regionally powerful kingdom called Nanzhao flourished from about 738 to 937, and was succeeded by another independent kingdom called Dali (937–1253). In the southeast, Vietnam (then called Annam or Dai Viet) gained permanent independence in 939, becoming a foreign country. By late Tang times, China was increasingly, therefore, becoming just one country among other roughly equivalent countries. Some of these foreign countries were organized in fashions similar to the Chinese Empire, and some posed serious military threats. The result was a multistate international system, fostering some of the preconditions for what might even be called proto-national identity formation. Two short Tang Dynasty essays written in the late ninth century explicitly considered the issue of what was Chinese identity, and both concluded that political loyalty and adherence to Confucian ideals were the main criteria for being Chinese.[21]

Another reason for the end of the great age of cultural cosmopolitanism in China may have been because, as described earlier, Chinese culture was by this time becoming increasingly standardized. The extension of formal Chinese-language education and the spread of common cultural expectations during the Tang Dynasty may have been more responsible for a growing consciousness of difference between Chinese and foreigners than any fear inspired by An Lushan's rebellion. Central to this more unified culture of late Tang were the first stirrings of a great Confucian revival, which would color all the remainder of premodern Chinese and East Asian history. This Confucian revival began with a call to reject the ornate literary parallelism of recent prose writing and return to the simpler so-called ancient writing of the classics. A new emphasis was placed on fundamental philo-sophical principles, such as human nature and "principle" itself (*li*), and on understanding the broad meaning of the Confucian Classics rather than narrow textual study.

Two authors in particular prefigure what has come to be known as Neo-Confucianism: Han Yu (768–824) and Li Ao (d. ca. 844). In their writings, they fabricated a new vision of an "orthodox transmission" of the Confucian Way, or *Dao*, that began with the legendary Sage Kings Yao, Shun, and Yu and was passed to the founders of the Shang and Zhou dynasties, the Duke of Zhou, and finally to Confucius and Mencius. As Han Yu wrote in a letter in 820, this Orthodox Dao then went into decline after the time of Confucius and never completely recovered from the First Emperor of Qin's notorious book-burning campaign, hanging at times by only a thread.[22] The implicit claim was that this Confucian Dao had now been rediscovered and revitalized in a kind of Chinese Renaissance. The explicit claim, unambiguously, was that there is only a single line of correct succession and a unitary Confucian truth. Under the next dynasty (the Song), this would begin to be called the *Dao tong*: the "Transmission of the Way."

Despite the claim to origins in remote antiquity, this was actually a rather new idea that may furthermore have even been influenced by contemporary Buddhist concepts of patriarchal lines of transmission. Neo-Confucianism, in fact, was deeply shaped by Buddhist and Daoist influences. However innovative it may have been, however, this idea of the *Dao tong* helped cement in place a powerful vision of a unitary China that had supposedly existed since the dawn of time.

The circulation of material goods through trade, even as it brought China into more extensive contact with foreigners, also helped create a more uniform Chinese market and provided expanded opportunities for both physical and social mobility throughout the empire. Late Tang China was becoming highly commercialized. Following An Lushan's rebellion, the Equitable Fields farmland allocation system that had first been put into operation by the Northern Wei collapsed, together with many of the other old government economic regulations. Agriculture came increasingly to be performed by tenant farmers, based on written contracts. Trade and commerce boomed. Even the government turned toward sources of commercial profit to sustain its finances, and state monopolies on such products as salt and alcohol relied increasingly on the operations of expert merchants and market forces.

The story of Dou Yi (d. ca. 840) may help illustrate the new entrepreneurial energy of late Tang China, as well as some of its limitations. As a youth, Dou Yi had some female relatives in the imperial palace and an uncle who was a high official, with a family temple in the capital. When Dou was a teenager, he received a pair of fine silk shoes as a gift, which he promptly sold in the market for 500 cash, beginning a small accumulation of capital. In spring, when there were many winged elm seeds floating in the city air, Dou collected some and planted them in his uncle's family temple. The trees that grew from these he cultivated and sold in various forms, beginning to amass real wealth. After various other clever initiatives, Dou purchased some inexpensive, apparently worthless, low-lying swampland in the city's western market. He set up stalls around the edges of the depression, where he sold fried pastries and dumplings, and he encouraged children to throw bits of rubble at a flag he planted in the middle of the mire, rewarding those who hit the flag with pastry treats. The rubble they threw into the muck quickly filled it in, and Dou then built a handsome shop with twenty rooms on the newly reclaimed land. Dou went on to cultivate good relations with officials and become a broker in government offices and an investor, dying a wealthy man.[23]

This story of Dou Yi does not come from an orthodox history and may even be more what we would today consider fiction than an accurate record of actual events. The story was recorded already in the ninth century, however, so the type of entrepreneurial behavior it describes must at least have not seemed entirely implausible to a late Tang audience. Clearly Dou Yi's brand of enterprise is not modern-style industrial capitalism, but the tale is nonetheless colorful testimony to the kind of urban business energy and acumen that was fueling unprecedented economic development by late Tang times. The market-based commercial development that began in late Tang and culminated in the subsequent Song Dynasty was "so remarkable that some scholars . . . view it as an early stage of protocapitalism."[24]

By the end of the Tang Dynasty in 907, although modern nationalism and the nation-state were still far in the future, something like an emergent Chinese national identity may have already been prefigured. The economy was highly commercialized and largely market based. The social order was becoming surprisingly fluid, with a nonhereditary meritocratic elite increasingly determined by anonymously graded performance on written tests. Even the technology of woodblock printing was beginning to have an impact. The obvious contrast is with what was happening in Western Europe, where, although Charlemagne was anointed "Emperor of the Romans" in 800 and promoted a justly famous "Carolingian renaissance," Charlemagne himself was scarcely literate, the former unity of the Roman Empire throughout the Mediterranean was never restored, status was becoming rigidly hereditary, and there had been a long-term decline in the production and commercial exchange of material goods. This was a time in human history when Western Europe became a relative backwater, and China, which may have contained one-third of the world's total population by the tenth century, strode to global center stage.

The Birth of Korea: Unified Silla (668–935)

Unification of the Korean Peninsula (668)

Among the new countries that emerged along the borders of the Tang Empire was the one we call Korea. The early histories of both Korea and Japan would be incomprehensible except as parts of a larger East Asian community. During the centuries of division in China following the collapse of the Han Dynasty, and continuing on through the reunified Sui and Tang dynasties, a degree of shared international aristocratic culture had developed throughout East Asia. This was a time when elites in China, Korea, and Japan (as well as northern Vietnam, which remained part of the Chinese Empire until 939) in some ways had more in common with each other than they did with their own peasants living in nearby villages. In particular, educated East Asians shared a common written language and literary canon. The glories of Tang poetry were as much admired by contemporary elites in Korea and Japan as they were in China. In fact, Bai Juyi was arguably even more highly regarded in Japan than he was at home in China – a healthy reminder that even direct cultural influences can take different local forms, based on local variances in taste and experience and the almost universal human desire for self-assertion.

Particularly vital to the formation of a shared East Asian cultural community were the connections provided by Buddhism. (See Figure 4.2.) When the Sui Dynasty in China ordered the establishment of a network of Buddhist reliquary pagodas in every province, for example, ambassadors from the Three Korean Kingdoms all requested relics from the Sui court and erected similar pagodas in their own states. A monk from Koguryŏ called Hyegwan (J: Ekan; fl. 625–672) studied in China under the master who is credited with founding the Three Treatise school of Buddhist doctrine. After returning to Koguryŏ, he traveled to Japan in 625, where he is considered to have formally introduced the Three Treatise school (although he may not really have been the first to bring its ideas to Japan), and eventually even became official head (*sōjō*) of the Japanese Buddhist church.

The sacred scriptures of East Asian Buddhism came to Korea and Japan in Chinese-language translation. Almost imperceptibly, this Buddhist transmission was a lubricant bringing with it other Chinese influences as well. For example, the Sillan monk Chajang went to Tang China in 636 to study Buddhism. In 643, he was summoned home by the king of Silla. It was at his suggestion, then, that in 649, Silla officially adopted Tang-style clothing and, in 650, the Tang calendar and reign periods for dating purposes.

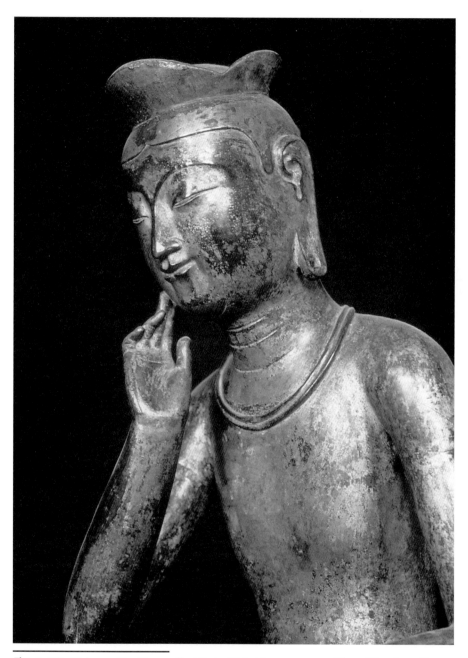

Figure 4.2. Maitreya (the Future Buddha). Gilded bronze statue. Three Kingdoms Korea, seventh century. National Museum, Seoul. © DeA Picture Library/Art Resource, New York.

Another Sillan monk, Wŏn'gwang (d. 640), studied for eleven years in Tang and was subsequently honored at the Sillan court, lecturing frequently on the scriptures. Wŏn'gwang is credited with formulating, in 602, a highly influential Sillan secular code of conduct in five precepts: (1) serve one's lord with loyalty, (2) serve one's parents with filial piety, (3) interact with friends in good faith, (4) do not retreat from battle, and (5) exercise discretion in the killing of living things. The first two of these precepts are explicitly Confucian, even using the standard Chinese characters for *loyalty* and *filial piety*. Only the last precept can be called Buddhist, and even it appears somewhat modified, since, presumably, a proper Buddhist should refrain from killing altogether. The fourth precept, enjoining fearlessness in battle, may represent native Korean tradition. Altogether, these five precepts constitute a classic example of cultural interaction. Wŏn'gwang is also credited with drafting a successful Chinese-language written request on behalf of the Sillan king for Chinese military assistance against the rival Korean kingdom of Koguryŏ.[25]

In the early seventh century, each of the Three Korean Kingdoms sent envoys requesting Chinese military assistance against their Korean neighbors. Somewhat surprisingly, it was Silla that proved successful. There had been little contact between Silla and China until the end of the sixth century. According to one sixth-century Chinese report, Silla was still preliterate, and all communication had to go through Paekche. Over the course of the sixth century, however, Silla was reorganized along more familiar East Asian lines. Sillan Buddhist monks began to make the journey west to China in search of the dharma. In 631, the new Chinese Tang Dynasty constructed expanded school facilities in its capital, and thousands of foreign students were reportedly attracted there from the Three Korean Kingdoms, Tibet, Turfan, and elsewhere. Beginning in 640, members of the Sillan royal family itself went to study at the Tang capital.

There had been repeated conflicts between China and Koguryŏ throughout the Sui and early Tang dynasties. The first Sui clash with Koguryŏ had come in 598. The massive series of disastrous Sui invasions of Koguryŏ that began in 612 are conventionally blamed for the rapid disintegration and fall of the Sui Dynasty. In 618, Tang replaced Sui, and after Tang rule was stabilized, conflicts with Koguryŏ reignited. Between 644 and 658, Tang conducted five substantial campaigns against Koguryŏ. The repeated Chinese inability to defeat Koguryŏ by direct invasion, and the stiffness of Koguryŏ resistance, may have finally persuaded Tang to adopt a new strategy: outflanking Koguryŏ with an attack from the south, in alliance with Silla.

This shifted the immediate point of attack to the southwestern Korean kingdom of Paekche. In 650, a Sillan emissary (the future King Muyŏl, r. 654–661) was sent on a mission to personally ask the Tang emperor for military assistance against Paekche. In 651, a member of the Sillan royal family named Kim In-mun (d. 694) began service in the Tang imperial bodyguard. Kim In-mun was then able to use his position as an intermediary with a foot in both the Tang and Sillan courts to help coordinate a successful military alliance between Tang and Silla. Kim finally died at the Tang capital in 694, after helping to smooth over later ruptures between the two allies.

With guidance from Kim In-mun, and a hundred Sillan warships to convey Tang troops to the battlefield, a combined Tang and Sillan attack on Paekche in 660 successfully captured its capital. The Paekche royal family was brought back to

China as prisoners, but a Paekche prince who had been away in attendance at the court in Japan was proclaimed by the Japanese as the new king, and with Japanese support, an expedition was launched to restore Paekche. At a great river battle fought in 663, the combined Tang and Sillan navies reportedly sank four hundred Japanese warships, sealing the fate of Paekche and ending Japanese influence on the continent for almost a millennium.

Meanwhile, Koguryŏ had been weakened by internal conflict. In 642, the Koguryŏ aristocrat Yŏn Kaesomun killed the king and, appointing a figurehead monarch, assumed the role of strongman himself. When he died in 666, his sons quarreled among themselves. One of these sons, Chŏn Namsaeng, eventually defected to Tang, bringing with him a powerful force. This last strongman of Koguryŏ then contributed to the final Tang and Sillan conquest of his own former kingdom in 668, for which he was rewarded with an appointment as a Tang general.

After the fall of Koguryŏ in 668, the Tang Dynasty is reported to have relocated as much as 5 percent of its total population to sparsely inhabited areas of China.[26] A surprising number of persons from both Koguryŏ and Paekche are known to have subsequently served with distinction in the Tang military – the most famous being the second- or third-generation descendant of a Koguryŏ émigré who captured Tashkent for the Tang in 750. In Korea, the victorious Tang Dynasty apparently expected to incorporate the peninsula directly into the Chinese Empire. Tang governors were appointed, but the Tang did not station sufficient occupation forces on the peninsula to maintain control against determined resistance. By 676, Silla had expelled the Tang presence, and the Korean peninsula (up to a line somewhere north of modern P'yŏngyang) was now unified, for the first time ever, under native rule.

Silla

Silla may have originated as a cluster of six tribes governed by a council of tribal elders. Although Silla gradually became a more centralized (and larger) state, acquiring a single hereditary ruler known as the *maripkan* by the fourth century, and reportedly adopting the Chinese title "king" (*wang*) in 503, a degree of collective decision making by the top aristocracy always remained a distinctive feature of Sillan society. A Council of Nobles (*Hwabaek*) decided such crucial issues as the royal succession. Sillan society also remained highly aristocratic, graded in terms of something called bone rank (*kolp'um*). The framework of a Chinese-style bureaucratic government had been proclaimed in 520 with new legal codes that established seventeen official titles, but these titles were awarded strictly according to hereditary bone rank. Bone rank determined the highest possible title to which a man could aspire, the maximum size of his home, and even what clothing he could wear.

There is some evidence to suggest that the status of women in Sillan society may have been somewhat higher than it was in contemporary China (or later Korean history). There were, for example, three reigning Sillan female kings (*yŏwang*), as distinct from queens, who were merely consorts of male rulers. In general, descent continued to be traced through both paternal and maternal lines throughout the Sillan era, which naturally also made the inheritance of family names awkward. The Sillan royal Kim and royal consort Pak families may have been among the first in Korea to adopt hereditary surnames, by perhaps the sixth century, but the use of patrilineal surnames remained inconsistent even among royalty until as late as the tenth century – a clear indication that Silla was still a very different society from neighboring China. China, by contrast, may have been the first place on earth where hereditary family names were universal.

Also unlike nearby China, Silla had a warrior culture. Particularly renowned were the young aristocratic warriors called *Hwarang*, or Flower Youths. The *Hwarang* cultivated military skills and a heroic image. They also traveled to sacred mountains and rivers to perform ceremonial songs and dances and appear to have had multiple dimensions beyond mere fighting ability. In addition, in 583, a new oath banner system was implemented, organizing some of Silla's military forces around flags with differently colored borders (an intriguing organizational forerunner of the much later seventeenth-century Manchu banner system). Since top aristocrats of True Bone status sometimes still controlled their own private armies, this oath banner system may have helped bring military force more closely under centralized royal control.

After a Sillan king died in 632 without leaving any direct heir, and following two subsequent female kings, the exclusively royal bone rank of *sŏnggol*, or Hallowed Bone, became extinct, and Sillan kings thereafter shared the next lower True Bone rank (*chin'gol*) with the top aristocracy. This may be one reason why later Korean kings never claimed the pretensions to divinity that Japanese emperors did and why Korean kings also never (except briefly in the tenth century, and again in 1897) assumed the supreme East Asian title of "emperor" (unlike Japanese and Vietnamese as well as Chinese monarchs). This may also help explain why Korean kings, despite their determined and ultimately successful struggle for independence from Tang China, remained more willing than Japanese rulers to accept the nominal status of tributaries to the Chinese emperor, since the delegation of their status from a Chinese sovereign gave Korean kings some leverage against the otherwise powerful domestic Korean aristocracy.

In a phenomenon that has been observed in many other monarchies throughout world history, Sillan kings also aligned themselves domestically with persons of relatively humble rank against the independent power of the top nobility. In the case of Silla, that meant especially persons of Head Rank Six, which was the next highest rank below True Bone. Here, again, the Chinese bureaucratic model, with its ideal of possible upward mobility based on demonstrated merit (and service to the throne) rather than heredity, may have been useful in supporting the interests of the Korean kings.

After the unification of the Korean peninsula and the expulsion of Tang forces, Sillan contact with Tang China, ironically, seems to have actually increased. Much of this contact was commercial. In late Tang times, Sillans came to dominate the maritime trade of northern East Asia, despite the fact that Silla produced no coins

of its own and used Chinese money instead. With a favorable breeze, it was a two-
or three-day voyage by boat from the west coast of Korea to China, and there seems
to have been a large Korean presence in late Tang China. Several Tang cities had
"Sillan wards," or "Sillan villages" in the suburbs.

There was also a "Sillan Office" in the Tang capital, designated to house Korean
embassies. Sillans remained probably the most numerous group of foreign students
studying in late Tang Chinese schools. Some eighty-eight Sillans are known to
have passed the civil service examinations in China during roughly the last century
of the Tang Dynasty. Several of them served in Tang government office before
returning to Korea, where they became voices for the promotion of Confucian
ideals.

Confucianism in Korea was still only in its infancy, however. In 682, Silla
established a National Academy, where a small number of young Koreans were
instructed in a Chinese-style curriculum that included the Confucian Classics,
Chinese history, and Chinese literature. In 788, Silla inaugurated its first Chinese-
style civil service examinations. The examination model had obvious attraction for
both strong monarchs and ambitious men born into anything less than the highest
ranks of the nobility. The role of examinations remained quite limited in Sillan
times, but the introduction of Chinese-language education had profound implications for Korea (as well as Japan). The use of the Chinese writing system brought
Korea into a distinctive East Asian cultural sphere to which some of Tang China's
other neighbors – such as Tibet, with its Indian-derived script – did not equally
belong.

At the same time, although the Chinese written language prevailed in Korea
(only twenty-five native Korean-language poems survive from the tenth century or
earlier, and even they had to be written using Chinese characters), the spoken
language was overwhelmingly Korean. The modern Korean language, which is
spoken today fairly uniformly throughout the peninsula, probably derives from
Sillan. Before Silla unified the peninsula in 668, there had certainly been at least
some regional linguistic diversity. After the Sillan unification, however, everyone
on the peninsula gradually came to speak the same language. This Korean language is, furthermore, entirely unrelated to Chinese and quite unlike even
its probable closest relative, Japanese. Despite significant Chinese influences,
therefore, the people of the peninsula became very distinctively Korean.

After about 780, the rising power of local warlords caused Sillan central government to enter a period of decline. Between 800 and 890, Silla experienced no fewer
than fourteen revolts or coups by members of the royal family. Few Sillan kings
died natural deaths in those years. Perhaps the most colorful figure from this age of
warlordism was Chang Po-go (d. 846). Chang was an apparently Sillan-born
swashbuckler of obscure origin who had traveled to Tang China, where he had
served as a minor officer in the Tang army. Later, returning to Silla, he reported to
the king that he had observed Sillans serving as slaves everywhere in China. Chang
Po-go proposed establishing a garrison on what is now called Wando (Wan Island),
off the southwestern tip the Korean coast, from where he could dominate the sea
lanes and prevent further slave raids. The island base was duly established in 828,

and Chang Po-go became a powerful sea lord, dominating the entire Yellow Sea region. When Chang Po-go tried to arrange a wedding between his daughter and the Sillan king, however, he was murdered by an outraged member of the aristocracy in 846.

As the Sillan state weakened, between 901 and 935, the Korean peninsula was temporarily divided once more into three kingdoms, which briefly even revived the old names Paekche and Koguryŏ. This division did not last, however, and in 935, the peninsula was again reunified under a new kingdom called Koryŏ. This name was an abbreviation of Koguryŏ (written with two characters instead of three) and is the origin of our English word *Korea*. The dynasty's founder was a man named Wang Kŏn (King T'aejo, r. 918–943). The subtlety of his position as the ruler of a fiercely independent country with a uniquely Korean culture that was nonetheless also simultaneously firmly part of a larger East Asian cultural sphere is nicely expressed by his injunction to his heirs in 943:

> We in the east have long admired the Tang style. Our literary matters, ritual, and music all follow their institutions. Yet, in strange regions and different lands, peoples' natures are each different. They need not improperly be made the same.[27]

Imperial Japan: Nara (710–784) and Early Heian (794–ca. Tenth Century [–1185])

The Taika Coup (645)

The reunification of the Chinese Empire under the Sui Dynasty in 589 dramatically altered the strategic balance in East Asia. For the first time in centuries, a resurgent, unified China was asserting its traditional nominal claim to authority over all "Under Heaven" and aggressively expanding its empire beyond the nuclear area of the Chinese heartland. This had serious implications for China's neighbors, and when the Sui Dynasty began to threaten offensive operations against the Korean peninsula, the Yamato court in Japan felt compelled to open direct contact with the Sui at the start of the seventh century. Within a period of just fourteen years after 607, Yamato dispatched no fewer than five embassies to first Sui and then Tang China. By this time, however, the Japanese court was no longer interested in buttressing its domestic authority with delegated Chinese titles, nor was it willing to play the humble Chinese-allotted role of tributary. Instead, the Yamato court was now claiming rival – if not actually superior – imperial status. The credentials of the embassy that was sent to Sui in 607 were notoriously addressed from the "Son of Heaven in the place where the sun rises to the Son of Heaven in the place where the sun sets."[28]

Japanese rivalry was inseparable from a certain degree of imperial imitation, however. Leading figures at the Japanese court were now consciously trying to build a powerful centralized state, somewhat like the model provided by Sui and Tang China. Japanese monks who had been sent to study in China with the early embassies began returning home in the 630s, bringing with them firsthand knowledge of conditions in the Tang Dynasty. A coalition developed involving some of these returned masters of Chinese learning, centering around the royal figure of Prince Naka no Ōe (who ruled later as Emperor Tenji, r. 662–671) and led by a man named Nakatomi Kamatari (614–669). According to tradition, Nakatomi Kamatari carefully weighed the ability of all the royal princes and judged Naka no Ōe the most promising for the purpose of promoting his cherished project of government centralization. Kamatari still lacked a personal relationship with Prince Naka no Ōe, but one day (the story goes), when the prince was playing kickball, he accidentally threw off a shoe, and Kamatari, respectfully retrieving the shoe, was finally able to establish the necessary connection. Only one thing now stood in the way of continental-style imperial centralization: the power of the Soga family.

After the death of the great Prince Regent Shōtoku in 622, the Soga, who had already been the most powerful court family for more than thirty years, began casting a lengthening shadow over the Yamato court. The Soga were even suspected of harboring ambitions to usurp the throne. Then, at a state ceremony in 645, in the presence of the empress herself, Prince Naka no Ōe and his co-conspirators struck suddenly, assassinating the leaders of the Soga family. A new Chinese-style imperial reign period was proclaimed, Taika (645–650), which literally means "Great Change" (although it is possible that this highly symbolic reign period name may have actually been chosen only retroactively, a few years later), and a momentous program of reforms was initiated. As a reward for his crucial service in this Taika coup d'état, a new family name was bestowed on Nakatomi Kamatari: Fujiwara. The name Fujiwara literally means "Wisteria Plain," and it supposedly commemorates the place where the conspirators first met to plot the removal of the Soga. This Fujiwara family would later become the leading family in Japan.

Traditional Japanese accounts probably paint a somewhat idealized portrait of the Taika reforms that were implemented after 645, but there is little doubt that a radical new centralization of power began to be rapidly asserted in the middle to late seventh century. As of the early 600s, it is likely that many local Japanese chieftains had still been really little more than "autonomous allies of the king," and the reach of the Yamato court may not have extended very far beyond the palace itself, except for some direct royal estates and certain groups of workers.[29] After the Taika coup d'état, the process of centralized state development in Japan accelerated and intensified. Part of the urgency behind this drive may have been fear of invasion from Tang China.

The Taika coup in Japan in 645 happened to coincide with the beginning of a new series of Tang Dynasty attacks on Koguryŏ, in Korea. When the Tang strategy shifted from direct frontal assault from the north to an alliance with Silla and an attack on Koguryŏ from the south, through Paekche, Yamato sent an expeditionary force to assist Paekche. The Japanese expeditionary force was annihilated in 663, however, with the reported loss of four hundred boats and ten thousand men. Paekche ceased to exist, and in 668, Koguryŏ was obliterated also. For a few years after 668, it even appeared as though the entire Korean peninsula might be brought under Tang control, which would have put Japan within easy reach as the next potential target of Tang conquest. Efforts to strengthen the Japanese state in this moment of crisis took the form of an accelerated adoption of Chinese-style imperial institutions, which was simply the most impressive administrative model then available. This Chinese model was probably mostly introduced only indirectly, through the intermediary of Silla in Korea rather than directly from Tang, but even the Sillans and Japanese sometimes communicated with each other using the Chinese written language.[30]

These late seventh-century innovations included a new name for Japan. In speech, the old name Yamato probably long continued to be used, but Yamato was not a written word. The oldest written name for Japan was Wa. But, although the origins of this name Wa are obscure and it did not become flagrantly offensive until much later, by the late 600s the Japanese court had already apparently become dissatisfied with Wa and favored a new written name, chosen for the meaning of its Chinese characters: Nihon ("Origin of the Sun," sometimes also pronounced *Nippon*). Nihon is still the standard Japanese name for Japan today. It was also about this time that the rulers of Japan definitely began using what has since become the standard Japanese title for "emperor," *tennō* (literally, "Heavenly Sovereign"). This is a variant of the Chinese imperial title, and the complete set of standard Chinese imperial titles were also officially adopted in Japan.

These Chinese titles were originally used only in writing, however. The commentary to an eighth-century Japanese law code specified that in speech, Japanese monarchs should continue to be referred to by native-language titles such as *sumera mikoto*.[31] Oral pronouncements, in Japanese, remained central to the self-representation of the Japanese monarchy. The uniquely Japanese cult of imperial descent from the sun goddess Amaterasu, and imperial worship at the shrine in Ise, may have also only really crystallized at the end of the seventh century, and in the seventh and eighth centuries the conception of Japanese emperors as manifest deities (*arahitogami*) was also clarified. In these centuries, Japan was refashioning itself as a Chinese-style centralized empire, but in a manner very much of its own choosing.

Nara (710–784)

The administration of this newly organized Japanese Empire received its clearest expression in a series of Chinese-style penal and administrative law codes. The earliest of these Japanese legal codes may have been issued in 668, but the system reached maturity with the Taihō Code of 701. Eight or nine of the nineteen persons who drafted this Taihō Code came from immigrant families, and some had participated in embassies to the continent, so its authors must have been reasonably familiar with continental precedents. The Japanese imperial bureaucracy that was structured by these codes included a state council, eight ministries, and forty-six bureaus. A comprehensive administrative hierarchy of provinces, districts, and villages was established throughout the empire. Household registration began in 670 as the basis for government-directed farmland allocation, tax collection, and military conscription. A new census was intended to be conducted every six years, and rice paddies were to be reallocated after each census, roughly along the lines of the Equitable Fields system that was then still in effect in China. Mandatory military service for all adult males was instituted, coins began to be minted, and the preparation of Japan's first written national histories began (resulting in the *Kojiki* and the *Nihongi*). Japan had now become a unified empire, even though some of the outlying islands still remained beyond imperial reach, and the far northeastern tip of the main island also remained largely independent until the twelfth century or even later.

At the heart of this newly centralized Japanese Empire was a great new capital city, Nara, which was planned and built between 708 and 712. Early Japanese capitals had changed with each ruler and often consisted of little more than a thatch-roofed wooden palace, not much different from the halls of other local Japanese chieftains. By the early seventh century, more impressive structures were being constructed, and Japan's first true Chinese-style capital city was at Fujiwara, just south of Nara, which was occupied from 694 to 710. Nara was not exactly, therefore, really Japan's first capital, nor did it serve as capital very long. But Nara was a permanent city that still exists today. Notably, Nara's eighth-century Tōdai-ji (Eastern Great Temple) is still operational in its current reconstruction. In typical Chinese fashion, Nara was laid out in a regular grid design, orientated north to south, although Nara differed notably from most traditional Chinese cities in not being surrounded by a wall. The significance of this city is so great that it has given its name to what is conventionally called the Nara period of Japanese history.

Standard textbook descriptions of the Nara period emphasize the functional administrative aspects of the law codes, and Buddhism. Confucianism, however, was inseparable from the contemporary Chinese model, and written Japanese sources (at least) also do contain much Confucian-style rhetoric about rule by virtuous example. In 757, for example, Empress Kōken (r. 749–758) proclaimed, "To secure the rulers and govern the people, nothing is better than the [Confucian] Rites."[32] In the same year, she also ordered every household to maintain and study a copy of the *Classic of Filial Piety*, in imitation of an earlier Tang decree. Because it is inconceivable that many eighth-century Japanese households could have actually satisfied this command, this may also illustrate the extent to which continental influences were often a rather thin façade.

An academy was established in Nara, near the palace gate, where instruction was provided in the Confucian Classics, calligraphy, law, mathematics, and Chinese-language pronunciation (necessary for orally reciting books written in Chinese). A network of schools, extending to every province, was also ordered opened. Twice-annual sacrifices to the spirit of Confucius were mandated at the academy, by law, beginning in 701. In ninth-century Japan, after participating in a spring sacrifice to Confucius and attending a lecture on the *Classic of Filial Piety*, Sugawara Michizane (845–903) exclaimed that the spirit of "the Sage [Confucius] was never far away."[33]

Ironically, however, this same Sugawara Michizane is more famous for recommending the abandonment of the last official Japanese embassy to Tang

China in 894. Unlike in Korea or Vietnam, a Chinese-style examination-based meritocracy never matured in Japan, and growing frustration at the poor chances for bureaucratic promotion through the academy caused Miyoshi Kiyotsura (847–918) to lament in 914 that the academy had become "a pit of disappointment," to the extent that "parents warned each other not to let their children mention school."[34] In the eighth century, out of a total Japanese population of perhaps six million, it has been estimated that only about twenty thousand participated in elite literate culture, and the academy had only four hundred students. Provincial schools had difficulty finding qualified instructors, and even in the capital teaching positions gradually became hereditary. In the twelfth century, the academy burned down and was not replaced.

Chinese influences had always been limited, and they were often wielded, moreover, in a conscious spirit of rivalry. Japan became, not part of the Chinese imperial order, but the center of its own independent Chinese-style imperial order. Highlighting this is the fact that, although the Nara period is conventionally considered to have been the peak period of continental influence on Japanese institutions and culture, paradoxically, compared with both earlier and later periods, "the country was in fact relatively closed."[35] Following the defeat of the Japanese expeditionary force to Korea in 663, an office was established on the southwestern island of Kyūshū, at the point of closest approach to Korea, which was intended to regulate all international contact, and for the first time effectively sealed Japan's borders.

Rather than a regional superpower (in this case, Tang China) simply "influencing" its neighbors, what actually happened was that elements of the powerful Chinese model were selectively borrowed by China's East Asian neighbors and domesticated, often becoming ingredients of their own "native" culture having independent dynamics. Some continental influences were also obviously inadvertent. A disastrous epidemic of smallpox introduced from the continent, for example, spread from Kyūshū to all the major population centers of Japan in 735–737 and may have killed a quarter or more of the entire Japanese population.[36] Buddhism, although it came to Japan from the continent in Chinese-language translation, and often in specifically Chinese forms, nonetheless functioned as an independent variable. Buddhism had, moreover, originally been a foreign influence in China too, and it stimulated complex patterns of interaction. For one thing, Buddhism arguably became a more powerful presence in Nara Japan than it did in Tang China.

After 746, the Buddhist Tōdai-ji (Eastern Great Temple) Construction Office in Nara became the largest Japanese government office. Tōdai-ji served as the headquarters for an empirewide Japanese system of state-sponsored Buddhism, with a branch temple in every province. For this there was Sui and Tang Dynasty Chinese precedent, but no temple in the Tang capital overshadowed the city in quite the way Tōdai-ji did in Nara. The temple's awesome influence was symbolized by the completion of the sixty-four-foot-tall bronze Great Buddha at Tōdai-ji in 752 (see Figure 4.3). This Great Buddha also illustrates the international range of Buddhist connections. The grandson of a Korean who had fled to Japan

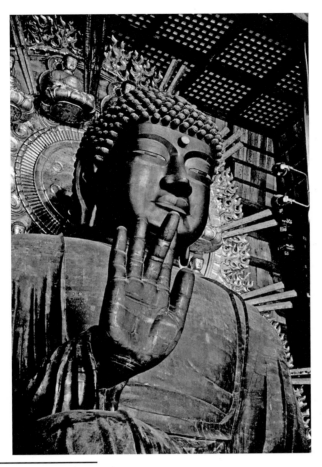

Figure 4.3. The Great Buddha (*Daibutsu*) at Tōdai-ji in Nara, Japan, bronze statue, 748–751 CE. Vanni/Art Resource, New York.

after the fall of Paekche in 663, Kuninaka Kimimaro (d. 774), played a role in the casting of the Great Buddha, and the ceremonial opening of its eyes in 752 is said to have been performed by an actual Brahman from India named Bodhisena (704–760).

Chinese may have been the language of the Buddhist scriptures throughout East Asia, but the Indian Sanskrit language retained an aura of at least potentially superior sanctity. Around 770, one Japanese empress had a million copies of a *dhāraṇī* charm, written in Sanskrit using Chinese characters, printed and placed in miniature wooden pagodas.[37] Shortly after the end of the Nara period, the renowned Japanese monk Kūkai was motivated to pursue Buddhist studies in China in part because he could not obtain a satisfactory explanation of the Sanskrit mantras and other esoteric symbolism in Japan, and he carefully brought forty-four rolls of Sanskrit texts back to Japan as evidence of his interest in Sanskrit. We may doubt that Kūkai really learned much Sanskrit, but as far as that is concerned, it is unlikely that he became very fluent in spoken Chinese either. After only one year in the Tang capital, Kūkai petitioned to be allowed to return to Japan with the embassy of 806. In Japan, Kūkai then played a decisive role in shaping the Japanese Shingon (Esoteric) sect, and put his religion to the service of the Japanese state.

Early Heian (794–ca. Tenth Century [–1185])

In 764, a Buddhist nun and retired female emperor resumed the throne again, and in 766 she elevated a Buddhist monk to a position of virtual co-ruler, awarding him the title "dharma king." In 769, an oracle was even presented to the court suggesting that it might be auspicious if this monk himself were to become emperor – threatening to turn Japan into an outright Buddhist theocracy (and simultaneously also entailing a change of dynasty, and of ruling family). This must have alarmed many people at court, and the interpretation of this oracle was quickly reversed. The nun emperor promptly died in 770, and a greater distance was soon introduced between the sources of imperial legitimacy (rooted especially in the claim to descent from the native sun goddess Amaterasu) and Buddhism.

It may have been in part to escape the influence of the powerful Nara Buddhist temples that the imperial capital was permanently moved away from Nara in 784, although at the time, frequent shifts of capital were also still simply customary. After an abortive effort to build a capital somewhere else, a small village was chosen as the location for the new capital in 794, and the site was renamed Heian. This new city of Heian, known today as Kyōto (which literally means "capital"), would serve as the imperial capital of Japan for over a thousand years, until 1869. After 1185, however, real political power shifted for many years away from the imperial court, and historians therefore refer to the years between 794 and 1185, when Heian was the functioning center of Japan, as the Heian period.

Over the course of these four Heian centuries, the pattern of Japanese history profoundly shifted, and it also diverged fairly pointedly from the continental trajectory. The early Heian period can be viewed to some extent as a continuation of the Nara period from a different location. In some ways, Chinese influences were still only increasing in late Nara and into early Heian times, especially in matters of aristocratic high culture. The frequency of female monarchs in early Japanese history (between 593 and 770 there had been six female rulers), which stands in sharp contrast to the Chinese patrilineal imperial model, came to an abrupt end in 770, for example.[38] There would be none in Heian times, and in all of Japanese history thereafter there would only be two more reigning female emperors (Meishō, r. 1630–1643, and Go-Sakuramachi, r. 1762–1771). In the early Nara period some of the palace buildings had still been constructed in native Japanese style – which typically featured cedar bark roofs, plain untreated wood, and elevation above the ground on posts – but in the mid-eighth century the Nara palace and administrative center was entirely rebuilt in the Chinese style, with heavy tiled roofs. Although the Nara period produced one magnificent collection of native Japanese-language poems, the *Manyōshū* (*Collection of Ten Thousand Leaves*, ca. 760), much of the literary energy in early Heian times was directed toward writing poetry in Chinese. By late Heian, however, the balance was reversing itself, and more uniquely Japanese styles and themes began to emerge.

In general, the tipping point between two quite different eras in Japanese history fell in mid-Heian, roughly around the tenth century, although most changes occurred only gradually and almost imperceptibly. Two particularly critical Heian era developments were the long-term weakening – to the point of virtual irrele-vance – of centralized imperial government, and the rise of a new class of provincial warriors, who would come to be known as *bushi* or *samurai*. Both developments were largely without parallel in China. Another notable divergence was the almost complete triumph in Japan of a Buddhist-centered worldview, even as China was experiencing its great Neo-Confucian renaissance and the beginning of a relative decline in the pervasiveness of Chinese Buddhism.[39] The roots of all these uniquely Japanese developments, which came to full fruition in late Heian, can be traced as far back as Nara times.

After the anticipated invasion from Tang China never materialized in the seventh century, for example, Japan no longer faced any serious foreign military threats, and the conscript army was allowed to lapse by as early as 792. Eventually, even the business of policing the Japanese countryside was abandoned by the central government and was delegated (or fell by default) to local warriors – the embryonic samurai. Meanwhile, the Nara system of direct imperial farmland allocation also began to fray in as little as half a century. The minting of copper coins, which had begun in 708, ended in 958. Japan had largely reverted to direct commodity exchange by the ninth century, due to inflation and other problems with the use of money, and many government-imposed market regulations also lapsed around that time. This did not mean that commerce necessarily declined – in fact, there is some evidence that commerce may have actually been increasing – but it did coincide with a weakening of the central government. Diminishing government revenue also encouraged powerful nobles to find other, private, sources of income beyond their official stipends. These especially took the form of private landed estates, which, over time, characteristically became exempt from taxation and even entry by government officials.

Already in the Nara period, great noble families typically employed large private household staffs, and increasingly these private aristocratic family administrations came to be the real bases of power. Even the imperial family itself eventually came to exercise its greatest authority privately, through the offices of so-called "Retired Emperors," by the end of the Heian period in the twelfth century. Among the small group of court nobles who came to dominate Heian politics and society, the Fujiwara family that had been founded by Nakatomi Kamatari at the time of the seventh-century Taika coup emerged as absolutely preeminent.

The formal basis of Fujiwara power was appointment as regent over either minor or adult emperors (two different titles in Japanese), but the real secret of Fujiwara success was intermarriage with the imperial family. Especially in a society such as Heian Japan, where children were commonly raised in the homes of their mother's (not their father's) families, the father-in-law or maternal grandfather of an emperor could wield great authority. The most renowned member of the Fujiwara family, Fujiwara Michinaga (966–1028), for example, actually held the title of regent for only one year, but four of his daughters married emperors, who gave birth to three more emperors, and at one point, Michinaga was simultaneously both grandfather and father-in-law to the same emperor![40]

While these political and economic structural changes were occurring, there were also important new developments in Japanese culture. As direct centralized imperial administration of the provinces was increasingly abandoned to custodial governors who collected taxes and forwarded them to the court, the perspective of the great Heian aristocrats increasingly shrank, until it was effectively confined to the capital city alone. The lives of aristocratic women were especially sedentary and secluded. This was not because the status of Heian women was unusually low – Heian women, for example, retained their family name after marriage and had the right to initiate divorce – but they were expected to stay at home, secluded from prying eyes behind screens. If they ventured out, they traveled in covered oxcarts and generally did not go far. Though the mansions of leading Heian aristocrats could be very large, including multiple buildings and gardens with artificial hills and lakes, this was still a very circumscribed existence. For entertainment, some women turned to literature and developed it into a fine art.

By the tenth and eleventh centuries, self-consciously literary diaries began to be compiled, which were sometimes deliberately intended for others to read. In one famous case, Sei Shōnagon (b. ca. 965) claimed that her so-called *Pillow Book* began as private jottings that were accidentally discovered by a visitor and passed around at court.[41] Fictional tales were also composed to entertain the household and circulated in manuscript form. This newly developing Heian women's literature was written in the Japanese language, using the new Japanese syllabic writing system.

The Japanese Hiragana script, which had come into use by the start of the tenth century, was largely reserved for informal documents, frivolous entertainments, and women's writing. Serious texts were still expected to be written in Chinese. Hiragana was, in fact, commonly known as women's hand (*onnade*). This was so much the case that, although the first great literary diary in Japanese, Ki no Tsurayuki's (883–946) *Tosa Diary*, was actually written by a man (around 936), he apparently felt obliged to adopt the pose in writing it of being a woman. The *Tosa Diary* is an account of a fifty-five-day return journey by the governor of Tosa, on the southern island of Shikoku, to the capital. The diary is introspective and self-consciously artistic, with a generous admixture of poetry, and it ends with the governor returning to his old home in Heian to find his garden in ruins – evoking the artistic melancholy and sensitivity to the mutability of all things that was the favorite sentiment of Heian Japan.

The full-length fictional prose novel also emerged from this Heian women's literature. The titles of some eighty tales survive from the ninth and tenth centuries, but the renowned *Tale of Genji* overshadows all other Heian productions and puts its stamp on the age. Lady Murasaki's (978–1016) lengthy fictional narration of the life and loves of the Shining Prince Genji is the consummate example of the exquisitely refined aesthetic taste perfected by the Heian court at its eleventh-century peak. This Heian period women's literature, moreover, although not without references to China, was uniquely and thoroughly Japanese. From the late ninth century, a distinctively Japanese high culture had emerged that was not so much a return to ancient pre-Taika native traditions as a dynamic new creation, revealing itself in cooking, clothing, and painting styles as well as the new Japanese-language literature.

Between 607 and 894, the Japanese government commissioned twenty official embassies to China. Of these, three never left Japan, and four got no farther than Korea. Perhaps three thousand people altogether participated in these embassies, but by one estimate, only about 130 Japanese pursued longer-term study in China during these centuries. China remained a very remote place for even the best-educated Heian aristocrats. It took, for example, three years for news of An Lushan's rebellion to reach the Japanese court. In 839, three people who had been assigned to accompany an embassy to China as students ran away and hid rather than obey the terrifying order.[42] In 894, the last embassy was simply cancelled.

The six great Chinese-style Japanese national histories (*Rikkokushi*) that were compiled, beginning with the *Nihongi* in 720, came to an end in 887. Under the reign of Emperor Murakami (r. 946–967), one more official national history was commissioned but never finished, and the last Chinese-style legal code was begun but was also never completed.[43] The last Japanese coins were minted in 958. Meanwhile, after a lengthy period when Chinese-language poetry had been favored, the first imperial collection of Japanese-language poems, the *Kokinshū* (*Collection of Ancient and Modern [Poetry]*) was compiled in 905. Clearly the early tenth century, which witnessed the fall of the Tang Dynasty in China and of Silla in Korea, and the permanent independence of Vietnam, was also an important watershed for Japan.

The cancellation of the last Japanese embassy to China in 894 did not mean an end to all contact with the continent. Trade would actually continue to grow, continental cultural influences remained strong, and China may have even gradually come to seem somewhat less remote. After about 850, private Chinese and Korean merchants developed maritime trade with Japan, often becoming residents of a port in northern Kyūshū. By the mid-thirteenth century it was reported that forty to fifty ships came from China to Japan each year.[44] Zen Buddhism (in Chinese, Chan) had made only a limited impact on Japan before the tenth century. The first recognized Chinese Zen master arrived in Japan only in 1246, and during the thirteenth century the full array of Chinese-style Zen practices was eagerly embraced by the new Japanese warrior elite.[45] But this warrior elite itself, which had no counterpart in China, and even the growing dominance of Zen culture in medieval Japan – unlike its position in contemporary China, and despite its self-proclaimed Chinese sources – was eloquent testimony that the broad course of Japanese history had begun to follow a distinctly independent trajectory.

For Further Reading

Authoritative coverage of China during this period is provided by Denis Twitchett, ed., *The Cambridge History of China, vol. III. Sui and T'ang China, 589–906, Part 1* (Cambridge University Press, 1979). On the Sui Dynasty, see Arthur F. Wright, *The Sui Dynasty* (New York: Alfred A. Knopf, 1978), and Victor Cunrui Xiong, *Emperor Yang of the Sui Dynasty: His Life, Times, and Legacy* (Albany: State University of New York Press, 2006). On the Tang, see Marc S. Abramson, *Ethnic Identity in Tang China* (Philadelphia: University of Pennsylvania Press, 2008); S. A. M. Adshead, *T'ang China: The Rise of the East in World History* (New York: Palgrave Macmillan, 2004); and Arthur F. Wright and Denis Twitchett, eds., *Perspectives on the T'ang* (New Haven, CT: Yale University Press, 1973). A somewhat revisionist view of the importance of the Tuoba Xianbei in Tang and Chinese history may be found in Sanping Chen, *Multicultural China in the Early Middle Ages* (Philadelphia: University of Pennsylvania Press, 2012). For Tang Dynasty religion, see Stanley Weinstein, *Buddhism under the T'ang* (Cambridge University Press, 1987).

On the controversial figure of Empress Wu Zetian, see Jo-shui Chen, "Empress Wu and Proto-Feminist Sentiments in T'ang China," in *Imperial Rulership and Cultural Change in Traditional China*, ed. Frederick P. Brandauer and Chun-chieh Huang (Seattle: University of Washington Press, 1994); R. W. L. Guisso, *Wu Tse-t'ien and the Politics of Legitimation in T'ang China* (Bellingham: Western Washington University, 1978); and Norman Harry Rothschild, "The Mother of Laozi and the Female Emperor Wu Zhao: From One Grand Dowager to Another," in *China and Beyond in the Mediaeval Period: Cultural Crossings and Inter-Regional Connections*, ed. Dorothy C. Wong and Gustav Heldt (New Delhi: Manohar, 2014). On Empress Wu and the invention of printing, see also Timothy H. Barrett, *The Woman Who Discovered Printing* (New Haven, CT: Yale University Press, 2008).

The "Silk Roads" were perhaps most flourishing during the Tang. See Valerie Hansen, *The Silk Road: A New History* (Oxford University Press, 2012); Xinru Liu, *The Silk Road in World History* (Oxford University Press, 2010); and, for a strongly argued revisionist approach, Christopher I. Beckwith, *Empires of the Silk Road: A History of Central Eurasia from the Bronze Age to the Present* (Princeton University Press, 2009). For interactions with the steppe, see Jonathan Karam Skaff, *Sui-Tang China and its Turko-Mongol Neighbors: Culture, Power, and Connections, 580–800* (Oxford University Press, 2012).

The Tang Dynasty is considered to have been the golden age of Chinese poetry. The glories of Tang poetry may perhaps best be encountered through a series of books by Stephen Owen: *The Poetry of the Early T'ang* (New Haven, CT: Yale University Press, 1977), *The Great Age of Chinese Poetry: The High T'ang* (New Haven, CT: Yale University Press, 1981), and *The Late Tang: Chinese Poetry of the Mid-Ninth Century (827–860)* (Cambridge, MA: Harvard University Asia Center, 2006). For an innovative study of how poetry may have circulated at the time, see Christopher M. B. Nugent, *Manifest in Words, Written on Paper: Producing and Circulating Poetry in Tang Dynasty China* (Cambridge, MA: Harvard University Asia Center, 2010).

An excellent general introduction to Korean history is Ki-baik Lee, *A New History of Korea*, trans. Edward W. Wagner (Cambridge, MA: Harvard University Press, 1984). For pre-modern Korea, see also the more recent volume by Michael J. Seth, *A Concise History of Korea: From the Neolithic Period through the Nineteenth Century* (Lanham, MD: Rowman and Littlefield, 2006).

On Japan's relations with China in this era, see Zhenping Wang, *Ambassadors from the Islands of Immortals: China–Japan Relations in the Han-Tang Period* (Honolulu: University of Hawai'i Press, 2005).

Valuable studies of pre-Heian Japan include Herman Ooms, *Imperial Politics and Symbolics in Ancient Japan: The Tenmu Dynasty, 650–800* (Honolulu: University of Hawai'i Press, 2009), and Joan R. Piggott, *The Emergence of Japanese Kingship* (Stanford University Press, 1997). See also Bruce L. Batten, "Foreign Threat and Domestic Reform: The Emergence of the Ritsuryō State," *Monumenta Nipponica* 41, no. 2 (1986). On pre-Heian Japanese Buddhism, see also Kyoko Motomochi Nakamura, trans., *Miraculous Stories from the Japanese Buddhist Tradition: The Nihon Ryoiki of the Monk Kyōkai* (Cambridge, MA: Harvard University Press, 1973). On the development of writing, consult David B. Lurie, *Realms of Literacy: Early Japan and the History of Writing* (Cambridge, MA: Harvard University Asia Center, 2011).

For Heian Japan, Donald H. Shively and William H. McCullough, eds., *The Cambridge History of Japan*, vol. 2. *Heian Japan* (Cambridge University Press, 1999), is authoritative. See also Mikael Adolphson, Edward Kamens, and Stacie Matsumoto, eds., *Heian Japan, Centers and Peripheries* (Honolulu: University of Hawai'i Press, 2007); Robert Borgen, *Sugawara no Michizane and the Early Heian Court* (Cambridge, MA: Harvard University Press, 1986); Paul Groner, *Saichō: The Establishment of the Japanese Tendai School* (Seoul: Berkeley Buddhist Studies Series, 1984); and Ivan Morris, *The World of the Shining Prince: Court Life in Ancient Japan* (Harmondsworth, UK: Penguin Books, [1964] 1985).

5 Mature Independent Trajectories (Tenth–Sixteenth Centuries)

Late Imperial China: The Song (960–1279), Yuan (1271–1368), and Early Ming Dynasties (1368–ca. Sixteenth Century [–1644])

The Song Dynasty Situation

In 907, an upstart military commander dethroned the last Tang emperor and proclaimed himself the founder of a (brief, as it turned out) new dynasty. Once again, China was plunged into a period of division. In north China, Five Dynasties followed each other in rapid succession – three of them founded by Shatuo Türks rather than ethnic Chinese – while southern China was simultaneously partitioned into ten separate regimes. This time, however, the division was only temporary. In 960, the mother of the seven-year-old boy emperor of the last of the northern Five Dynasties, acting in the capacity of a regent, ordered the commander of the Palace Guard, Zhao Kuangyin (927–976), to lead an army north against a rumored Khitan invasion. On the second morning of their march, some of Zhao's officers entered his residence with swords drawn and hailed him as emperor.

The result was a bloodless coup that brought a major new dynasty, the Song, onto the stage. Zhao Kuangyin is known to history as Emperor Taizu of the Song (r. 960–976). Because this Emperor Taizu was acutely aware of the fragmentation that had been caused by warlordism since the middle of the Tang Dynasty, and of the frequency of military coups like the one that had brought him to power, as emperor, he was determined to clearly separate military command from civilian administration. Emperor Taizu hosted a legendary palace banquet for his senior generals at which, with a toast, he relieved them of their military commands and retired them to lives of civilian comfort in the capital.

Emperor Taizu's policies would be successful enough that dynastic change would thereafter be very much less frequent and would never again be the result of an internal military coup. Although there were roughly eighty dynasties in premodern Chinese history, only three of them came after the Song (not counting peripheral alien regimes that sometimes extended into Chinese territory). Each of

132

the relatively few remaining changes of dynasty, furthermore, can be attributed to foreign invasion. The premodern Chinese sociopolitical order became rather remarkably stable in the thousand years remaining after the Song Dynasty began in 960 – but the flip side of this same coin was also a long-term decline in the prestige of military service and relative military weakness. China would thereafter repeatedly be threatened with foreign conquest.

The paradox of the Song Dynasty is that, although it was a time when China led the world in technology, commercial prosperity, and sophisticated culture and the arts – and a time when China may have held a third of the world's total population – yet even after the Song reunification was complete (by about 978), it was still a somewhat diminished, militarily more vulnerable China. The loss of control over Inner Asian borderlands not only made the Song a geographically smaller empire, but also deprived it of horses and high quality cavalry supplied from the borderlands (cavalry that was, furthermore, less expensive than regular imperial garrisons because it was composed of self-sustaining pastoral nomads), forcing the Song to spend more of its revenue on the military than the Tang Dynasty, even as it was militarily weaker.[1] At the same time, Song China was also now surrounded by significant foreign powers.

Most formidably among the Song Dynasty's neighbors, a nomadic people called the Khitan had organized a semi-Chinese-style Liao Dynasty stretching across the northern steppes, which included sixteen prefectures of northeastern China proper. After a treaty that was concluded in 1005, the Song Dynasty was even compelled to make annual payments to the Liao of two hundred thousand bolts of silk and one hundred thousand ounces of silver and to treat the Khitan Liao Dynasty as an equal. Another dynasty formed by the Tangut people, called Western Xia (Xi Xia, 1038–1227), controlled substantial territory in what is now northwest China.[2] In addition, the area that is now northern Vietnam — after more than a thousand years as part of the Chinese Empire — became independent during the post-Tang period of division and was never successfully brought back inside the Chinese Empire.

Independent Vietnam at least played along with the (nominal) role of being a Chinese tributary, but other Song neighbors were less compliant. Notably, the Khitan Liao Dynasty and the Tangut Western Xia developed their own writing systems (as the Tibetans in the west had also already done) rather than use Chinese. Their use of non-Chinese scripts placed these societies largely outside the sphere of shared East Asian civilization. At the same time, however, the Khitan Liao Dynasty did, to some extent, adopt the Chinese political model. The Khitan dynastic founder – the same man who ordered the adoption of the first version of the distinctive Khitan writing system in 920 – could speak the Chinese language, and had himself enthroned twice: once as a native Khitan-style leader in 907, and again later as a Chinese-style emperor in 915.[3] In fact, ironically enough, *Khitan* is actually the ultimate source of our English word *Cathay*, which is today a somewhat poetic alternative name for China. It has been perceptively observed that an "increasing emphasis on differences between" the Khitan north and the Chinese south "coincided with a growing political similarity between the two," suggesting that international rivalry may even be intensified by a degree of comparability in political form.[4]

Map 5.1 East Asia in 1050 CE

The Khitan Liao Dynasty, meanwhile, ruled over a variety of different tribes and peoples, including several Jurchen tribes in the area of modern Manchuria. Beyond the Jurchen who submitted to the Liao Dynasty were still other so-called wild Jurchen living farther east, in the area of the Amur, Ussuri, and Sungari rivers in Manchuria. These Jurchen tribes – a name that first appears in the early 900s – were speakers of Tungusic languages that were ancestral to what we now call Manchu. Although the Jurchen were forest-dwelling semiagricultural villagers, not nomads, they learned from the Khitan the techniques of nomadic cavalry warfare and became skilled horsemen.

In 1114, Jurchen warriors under a dynamic tribal leader named Aguda (1068–1123) rebelled and attacked the Khitan Liao Dynasty, soon taking the Chinese-language dynastic title Jin ("Gold") for themselves. By 1122, this new Jurchen-ruled Jin Dynasty (1115–1234) had effectively destroyed the Khitan Liao regime, at which point they came into conflict with Song Dynasty China farther south. These Jurchen proved to be even more deadly foes for the Song than the Khitan had ever been. By 1127, a Song emperor had personally been captured and the Jurchen Jin Dynasty had overrun all of north China. A younger brother of the captive Song emperor then took the Chinese throne, and the Song Dynasty continued, withdrawing south to a temporary capital at Hangzhou and beginning what is known to history as the Southern Song (1127–1279). After some further military action, the border between the Jurchen Jin Dynasty and the Southern Song stabilized along the line of the Huai River, about a hundred miles north of the Yangzi.

The Jurchen-ruled Jin Dynasty for a time "became the most powerful state in East Asia."[5] Following their lightning conquest of north China, many of the Jurchen people moved down from Manchuria into China proper. In 1153, the Jurchen Jin capital was also relocated from Manchuria to what is now Beijing. The Jurchen people remained a minority, however, perhaps 10 percent of the total Jin Dynasty population: two or three million Jurchen ruled over some thirty million Chinese. Initially, the ethnic Jurchen and the Chinese populations of the Jin Dynasty were organized separately, and there was even some conscious revival of Jurchen cultural practices later in the dynasty, following a bout of Chinese-style imperial centralization. From their new homes scattered across north China, however, the Jurchen soon began intermarrying with the Chinese and speaking the Chinese language. Leading Chinese Confucian scholars living under the dynasty fully accepted its legitimacy.[6] In some senses, this Jin Dynasty even became what could legitimately be called a Chinese dynasty. Yet the Jurchen-ruled Jin Dynasty's rivalry with the Southern Song did not diminish. Some scholars have even seen in Song Dynasty Chinese hostility to the Jurchen an early stage in the development of a spirit of Chinese nationalism.[7] Then, in 1234, the Jurchen Jin Dynasty was inundated by an even greater new menace from the north: the Mongols.

Economic and Social Change

Compounding the paradox of a militarily weak Song Dynasty that nonetheless managed to flourish culturally and economically, after the loss of the north in 1127, the geographically much diminished Southern Song in some respects may have actually even entered the most flourishing phase of the whole dynasty. Although the land area controlled by the Song had shrunk dramatically, the Southern Song was the period when what has been called China's "medieval economic revolution" reached its climax.[8]

Archeologists have uncovered large quantities of Chinese porcelain and other artifacts on the islands of Java and Sumatra (in what is now Indonesia), in what is now Malaysia, in the Philippines, in India, in East Africa, in the suburbs of Cairo in Egypt, and in the Persian Gulf, dating from late Tang times and swelling in volume during the Song. Song China enjoyed a flourishing maritime trade with the entire Islamic world, reaching as far west as Moorish Spain and almost everywhere in between.

In the earliest phase of China's international maritime trade, much of the shipping that arrived in Chinese ports had been foreign – at first mostly Southeast Asian and then later Arab and Persian. As early as 750, a Chinese Buddhist monk traveling on his way to Japan reported seeing numerous Persian and Arab, as well as South and Southeast Asian, merchants in Guangzhou.[9] By 902, Arab and Persian merchants were so prominent in Asian waters that it was reported that on the island of Sumatra even the parrots spoke Persian and Arabic, as well as other languages.[10] But, by Song times, the Chinese themselves were now actively engaging in maritime trade, and China's ships were the largest and finest in the world. With watertight compartments, sternpost rudders, and guided by magnetic compasses since at least the twelfth century, Song Dynasty Chinese ships became regular visitors to Indian ports and sometimes even appeared in the Persian Gulf and the Red Sea. The fourteenth-century Arab traveler Ibn Baṭṭūṭa, observing large Chinese ships with four decks and up to a dozen sails on the southwestern coast of India, concluded, "There is no people in the world wealthier than the Chinese."[11]

By Song times, the high-value, low-bulk luxury goods that had traditionally been the staple of long-distance world trade were yielding to more bulky and inexpensive commodities such as textiles, porcelain, pepper, rice, sugar, and even lumber, which could now be economically transported great distances in quantity for a profit. A number of Song ports were active in international trade, but the most important was Quanzhou (located on the mainland across from Taiwan). Although much of the Old World was incorporated into these trade routes, the largest importer of Chinese porcelains and coins in these centuries was probably Japan.[12] One fourteenth-century shipwreck off the Korean coast, explored by modern archeologists, sank on the way from China to Japan while carrying 18,600 pieces of ceramics, sandalwood, and several tons of Chinese coins. It had an apparently mixed crew of Chinese, Koreans, and Japanese, with a Japanese captain.[13]

Song Dynasty Chinese society was commercialized, technologically sophisticated, and urban. The city-dwelling population of Song China may have even been equal to the entire urban population of the whole rest of the world at the time.[14] It was not uncommon for wealthy merchants to combine their capital for fixed periods of investment, credit was available on commission from local brokers, and even futures contracts with commissioned agents were already being signed.

Commercialization had become so pervasive that market forces determined even such activities as the sale of concubines (secondary wives) and religious behavior. For example, it was now normal to hire different types of religious professionals to perform different specific religious services, as a kind of market transaction, and to abandon any god who did not appear able to deliver tangible blessings. Coal-fired blast furnaces were producing iron in quantities that may have peaked in the eleventh century at levels nearly equal to that of all Europe combined as late as 1700.[15] Gunpowder was put to at least limited military application, for example, as an igniter for naphtha-based flame throwers. Paper money – which had first appeared in late Tang – was in wide circulation, and the technology of woodblock printing was promoting a revolution in the availability of books.

The first imperially printed edition of the Confucian Classics was completed in 953. The first complete printing of the standard East Asian Buddhist scriptures (the *Tripiṭaka*) was completed in 983, in 5,048 chapters. Soon after the establishment of the Song Dynasty, the Song law code was also ordered printed and distributed throughout the empire in 963, using the new technology of printing to help legitimize the new dynasty.[16] Not just central and local governments but also private academies, individuals, and professional bookshops all contributed to a (relative) explosion of printed books.

Among other literary achievements, the Song Dynasty is notable for the compilation of a number of encyclopedias that are still valuable today, such as the *Taiping yulan* ([Encyclopedia Assembled for] Imperial Inspection during the Taiping Era [976–984]), which was completed in 983 in a thousand chapters. This encyclopedia arranges quotations from some two thousand different pre-Song texts, many of which are now lost, according to topic. Although the very earliest Chinese encyclopedias had appeared at the end of the Han Dynasty and in the Age of Division, and some still survive from the Tang, the Song represents a major step forward in this useful form of assembled and ordered human knowledge.

The increased availability of books may have also contributed to a major social transformation. In late imperial China, beginning with the Song, although there certainly were other ways of becoming wealthy, there was to a very large extent only one true elite career path: that of the scholar-official, or mandarin. The word *mandarin* is English, not Chinese. It is derived from Portuguese (and ultimately Sanskrit), but it is nonetheless used to describe a very uniquely Chinese sociopolitical class. In China, of course, there was nothing new about an association between elite status and a career in government, but the late imperial mandarins now – unlike their ancient predecessors – held office overwhelmingly on the strength of academic degrees obtained through anonymously graded written tests. The Chinese imperial civil service examination system finally came of age in the Song Dynasty.

If an annual average of only thirty *jinshi* degrees were awarded in late Tang, by the Southern Song Dynasty, the average was four or five hundred. Roughly 95 percent of all men (i.e., virtually all) were eligible to participate in what was now an empirewide series of examinations that began with qualifying tests in every county. Although the examination route was never the only way to become a government official in imperial China, it had, by Song times, become both the

Figure 5.1. Examination compound, Guangzhou (Canton), China, showing a few of the twelve thousand examination cells (photographed in 1900, but characteristic of late imperial China). Library of Congress, LC-USZ62-54326.

normal and the most prestigious path.[17] And, although the number of government offices always remained strikingly few – in 1800, under the last dynasty, there were only about twenty thousand posts in the entire regular civilian bureaucracy – merely participating in the examination system marked one as a member of the elite, even if one never actually passed any tests. By the final two dynasties, Ming and Qing, about a million men at any given time were actively engaged in taking examinations, and the holders of the lowest-level academic degrees made up perhaps 1 or 2 percent of the total population (see Figure 5.1).

For better or for worse, the examination system helped shape the kind of society late imperial China became. To a remarkable degree, it was a society focused on education and book learning. The elite were scholars. According to Confucian notions of rule by moral example, government itself is essentially an act of educating people to improve themselves. Confucius is regarded as China's first teacher.

On balance, the examination system never really permitted as much upward social mobility as is sometimes imagined by enthusiasts. True rags-to-riches cases were rare, and a large stratum of relatively wealthy families produced most degree holders. The system also did not reward technological or scientific innovation. But by any premodern standard, this was a relatively fluid social order, with elite status not directly hereditary and opportunities for advancement through ability and effort clearly visible (if not always actually attainable). The examination system provided at least the appearance of fairness of opportunity, and at the same time ensured that the elite were extremely well educated and steeped in common Confucian values. This, too, helps explain why late imperial Chinese society was exceptionally stable.

The ethical values that were spread by this pervasive education were not always necessarily ones of which we might approve today. For example, the renewed emphasis on the study of the Confucian Classics is sometimes blamed for a perceptible deterioration in the status of women. It would actually be a little unfair to blame Neo-Confucian moralists for the foot-binding fashion that just happened to begin spreading in Song times, and the late imperial spread of the ideal of the chaste widow may have been due in part to a Chinese reaction to the peculiar circumstances of Mongol rule in the fourteenth century. But, nonetheless, Neo-Confucianism did reaffirm patrilineal principles and patriarchal ideals such as the chaste widow and gender separation. The Neo-Confucian revival may have contributed to a hardening of patriarchal attitudes in late imperial China.[18]

Neo-Confucianism

The economic prosperity of the Song Dynasty coincided, unsurprisingly, with a period of great cultural vitality, both in the realm of popular street culture and in the fine arts. Chinese painting, for example, reached a level of exquisite perfection in the Song Dynasty that has never been surpassed, though it may sometimes have been equaled (see Figure 5.2). The most important intellectual development during the Song Dynasty was undoubtedly the great Confucian revival we call Neo-Confucianism.

The Neo-Confucian movement grew out of the late Tang, matured in the Song, and continued to dominate East Asian higher culture until the early twentieth century. Though "Neo-Confucianism" is a convenient English label for this broad movement, there was actually no single Chinese name for it, and the Chinese tended to perceive it instead in terms of multiple schools associated with individual scholars or groups of scholars. By far the most influential single figure was Zhu Xi (1130–1200), whose approach was sometimes called *Daoxue*, or the "Learning of the [Confucian] Dao." Zhu Xi's writings became so widely influential that they "served as the common denominator of education in premodern East Asia" after this time.[19]

This Neo-Confucianism is notable for transcending the meticulous textual commentary that had dominated earlier Confucian studies to ask more grand philosophical questions, and for a new interest in metaphysics and cosmology. As

Figure 5.2. Ma Yuan (active ca. 1190–1225), "Viewing Plum Blossoms by Moonlight." Fan mounted on an album leaf. Ink and color on silk. The Metropolitan Museum of Art, New York. © The Metropolitan Museum of Art/Art Resource, New York.

is so often the case, broad generalization is likely to be misleading, but it may be said that the underlying vision of much Neo-Confucianism was a kind of organic holistic understanding of the universe, on the grounds that all things in the universe are supposedly composed of the same basic substance, *qi*, which is given unique specific shape according to principle(s), called *li*. A further elaboration was the idea, derived from the classic *Book of Changes*, that all of the endless transformations of the material stuff in this universe are ultimately driven by a single common "supreme ultimate" (*taiji* – sometimes spelled *T'ai-chi*, as in "supreme ultimate boxing," the well-known therapeutic martial arts exercise). These ideas resulted in the famous "diagram of the supreme ultimate," a schematic representation of how this *taiji*, as the pivotal point of alternation between yin and yang, ultimately produces all things in the universe.

This new Confucian interest in cosmology reflects the continuing influence of Buddhism and Daoism. The private Confucian academies that began to be built in the countryside during the Song Dynasty "closely resembled Buddhist monasteries in their architecture and physical layout."[20] Their regulations for community life, style of lecturing, and practice of venerating portraits of former patriarchs were also all similar to those of Buddhist monasteries. Yet, if some early Song Buddhists did try to make the argument that Buddhism was now simply part of Chinese civilization, the Neo-Confucian mainstream nonetheless rejected Buddhism explicitly.[21]

The fundamental Confucian objection to Buddhism was the idea that personal pursuit of individual religious salvation was inherently selfish – the abandonment of essential social responsibilities. Confucians continued to insist on an obligation to work for the larger public good. The Neo-Confucian reconciliation of this secular imperative with Buddhist-inspired influences was deftly achieved with a new emphasis on a short text drawn from one of the ancient classics, now often published and studied separately, called the *Great Learning* (*Daxue*). This text made individual self-cultivation (which, in the particular form of the Neo-Confucian practice called quiet sitting, might not differ all that much from Buddhist meditation) the first step toward world peace:

> The ancients who wished to illustrate illustrious virtue throughout the kingdom, first ordered well their own states. Wishing to order well their states, they first regulated their families. Wishing to regulate their families, they first cultivated their persons. . . . From the Son of Heaven down to the mass of the people, all must consider the cultivation of the person the root of *everything*.[22]

Despite this great Neo-Confucian revival, the standard textbook tendency to depict the triumph of Neo-Confucianism over previously dominant Buddhism and Daoism during the Song Dynasty is an exaggerated caricature. All three remained influential, and the Buddhist and Daoist religious establishments were themselves part of Song Dynasty elite society, below which were other levels of religious orientation extending down to humble village spirit mediums. A huge Song Dynasty collection titled the *Record of Hearsay* (*Yijian zhi*), compiled by Hong Mai (1123–1202), for example, contains roughly two hundred accounts of spirit possession.[23] China was a big place, and late imperial Chinese society remained richly complicated.

Mongol Tempest: Chinggis Khan (ca. 1162–1227)

The Mongols were largely unknown before the twelfth century. There are some obscure references in Tang period sources to a tribe whose name, although written differently, might have been pronounced something like "Mongol," but it is uncertain whether this was really the same group.[24] In any case, as of the mid-twelfth century, the Mongols were still only one obscure steppe nomadic tribe living among others. The legendary story of their rise to earth-shaking prominence begins with the fatal poisoning of a Mongol leader at what was expected to be a friendly meal with the neighboring Tatar tribe around 1167. After this murder, the Mongol tribe temporarily scattered. The dead chieftain's son, Temüjin, fled with his mother to the mountains, where they survived by hunting and fishing. Gradually, after many exploits, Temüjin built up a personal following of sworn companions, who supposedly pricked their fingers and mixed their blood to become blood brothers. Eventually, Temüjin won recognition as khan, or leader, of the Mongol tribe and took the title Chinggis ("Boundless") Khan (also spelled Genghis Khan).

Meanwhile, Tatar power had been growing in the area of the eastern Gobi Desert. To oppose these Tatars, Chinggis Khan sought an alliance with another nomadic tribal confederation, the Kereyids, many of whom happened to be Nestorian Christians. Around the year 1198, this Mongol–Kereyid alliance went to war with the Tatars, and Chinggis Khan was finally able to avenge his father's murder. In the process, Chinggis Khan also emerged as a remarkably successful warrior leader. By 1206, Chinggis Khan's army numbered around ninety-five thousand men, and at an assembly of tribal notables (known as a *khuriltai*) in that year he received recognition as Great Khan over "all those who live in felt tents."

Many of the warriors who fought for Chinggis Khan were actually speakers of Turkic languages rather than Mongolic, and they were certainly not all members of the original Mongol tribe, but as Chinggis Khan's star rose dramatically, the Mongol identity also began to spread. Chinggis Khan became the founder of a great new imperial ruling family that would continue to provide Great Khans in direct male line of descent until the death of Ligdan Khan (1588–1634) in 1634. And the Mongol imperial model would long echo across Eurasia in the form of such later examples as the Mughals, Ottomans, and Manchus.

Throughout imperial Chinese history, since the early Han Dynasty in the second century BCE, the military superiority of nomadic cavalry had posed a recurring threat. As we have seen, semi-nomadic emperors ruled many of the Northern dynasties during China's great Age of Division, and the reunified Sui and Tang dynasties sprang from culturally mixed origins. It has even been claimed that semi-nomads or nomadized persons actually ruled a majority of all the dynasties in imperial Chinese history. But these various ruling groups had nearly all begun as frontiersmen in China's immediate border areas. They were commonly already thoroughly exposed to Chinese civilization, and in some senses often could be considered Chinese. The Mongols were different.

In general, the nomadic lifestyle, which is based on the mobile raising of goats, sheep, cattle, horses, and camels, is fundamentally different from the stereotypical Chinese lifestyle based on intensive sedentary farming. The ecological boundary between steppe grassland and fertile farmland is, furthermore, relatively sharp along the frontier between Mongolia and China. In other parts of Eurasia bordering on the steppe the ecological division may be less pronounced, and especially where both nomads and farmers were Muslim, the sources of conflict may have been reduced. Confrontations between nomads and farmers on the frontier of China may have therefore been especially acute. But not all Chinese are really necessarily farmers. There have always been ranchers and semi-nomadic tribes living inside the Chinese Empire, which frequently extended northward to include at least Inner Mongolia. Frontier warriors often played a useful role in the service of the Chinese Empire, and a degree of occupational specialization for different groups always existed inside China.

Chinggis Khan's Mongols were the exception. They came more truly from outside the Chinese world and remained more permanently outsiders. Their conquests were also unparalleled. The explanation for their sudden eruption from the steppe at this particular moment has always been something of an historical puzzle. Some scholars have attempted to explain the Mongol invasions as a result of climate change, arguing that there was a decrease in average temperature in the years 1180–1220, leading to shorter growing seasons and driving the nomads off the steppe in search of other resources. In this case, however, the much maligned "great-man" approach to history may also explain a great deal. The dynamic personality of Chinggis Khan himself, a vigorous commander who believed that the sky god Tenggeri had given him a mission to bring the entire world under one sword, may have been much of the reason for the explosive Mongol conquests. Although the entire population of the Mongolian steppes in the twelfth century may have been only about one million, the hardiness of the nomads and their skill with horse and bow made them an almost unstoppable force.

After consolidating his command over the tribes of the Mongolian steppe, in 1210, Chinggis Khan struck south at the Jurchen-ruled Jin Dynasty in northern China. Between this first assault and about 1260, however, the Mongols made little serious attempt to occupy and rule the territory they overran in north China, resulting in widespread and lasting devastation. Chinggis Khan next turned west, leading an attack on Central Asia. In 1220, he captured the Central Asian city of Bukhara. Legend has it that on entering the great mosque in Bukhara, Chinggis Khan proclaimed himself the "scourge of God."

Chinggis Khan died in 1227, before the Mongols had completed their destruction of the Jurchen Jin Dynasty in north China in 1234, and before the Mongol attack on Southern Song had even begun in 1235. But the Mongol onslaught continued after Chinggis Khan's death. Previous nomadic cavalry armies had always been stopped by the barrier of the Yangzi River and the rice paddies and generally wet terrain of south China. To conquer the Southern Song, the Mongols had to learn the techniques of naval and siege warfare and such novel Chinese technologies as the use of gunpowder. They also made good use of the classic strategy for conquering the lower Yangzi River valley by outflanking it and attacking down the line of the river from the west. By 1279, the last pretender to the Song throne had drowned off the southeast coast, and the Mongols had completed their conquest of China.

The Mongols conquered the largest land empire in the history of the world. In the west, they overran parts of Poland and Hungary and pushed as far as the Adriatic Sea. In the south, they raided into India, although they did not then attempt to occupy it. In the northeast, the Mongols won the submission of Korea. Two huge amphibious invasions of the Japanese islands were both scattered by typhoons, with disastrous results, however, and repeated strikes southeast into the region of Vietnam became mired in tropical jungles and fierce resistance. Even the Mongol Empire eventually reached its limits. While the Mongol conquests were

Map 5.2 The Mongol World Empire, ca. 1300

still accumulating, meanwhile, Chinggis Khan's grandson, Khubilai Khan (1215–1294), was acclaimed as Qaghan – that is, Khan of Khans, or Great Khan – in 1260 and began to consolidate a semi-Chinese-style Yuan Dynasty based at Beijing, in the east.[25]

The Yuan Dynasty (1271–1368)

Although Khubilai Khan styled himself Great Khan, his position as supreme leader of the Mongols was contested by a younger brother and later by a cousin. Cracks were already beginning to appear in the vast Mongol world empire. These fissures can be traced all the way back to the time of Chinggis Khan's death, when each of his four principal lines of descent received their own separate territorial bases. These evolved into what became four effectively independent Mongol khanates: the Golden Horde in the area of Russia, the Il-khanate in the area of Persia, the Chaghadai Khanate in Central Asia, and the Yuan Dynasty in East Asia. The conversion of the Mongol khans in the west to Islam in 1295 – just sixteen years after the Mongols had finished conquering Southern Song Dynasty China – can be said to mark the effective end of any unified Mongol world empire.

Chinggis Khan had not been Chinese, had not spent much time in China, and did not speak the Chinese language. His grandson Khubilai Khan, on the other hand, lived most of his life in, and ruled primarily over, China. Although he probably never learned to read Chinese, and relied on Chinese interpreters, he did learn to speak enough Chinese that he sometimes pointedly corrected those interpreters. Khubilai Khan frequently dressed in Chinese-style clothing, and in 1266, he built a magnificent new Chinese-style capital at Beijing (then known as Dadu, the "Great Capital"). Khubilai Khan attempted to conciliate his Chinese subjects by forbidding nomads from grazing their herds on Chinese farmland. In 1271, he also took the Chinese-language dynastic title "Yuan" (which means, roughly, "Beginning"). To some extent, Khubilai Khan did rule China in Chinese style.

But the Mongol Yuan Dynasty was more than just China. The Mongols had, for example, subdued Tibet in 1252, for the first time establishing a patron–priest relationship between an empire based in China and Tibetan lamas. The implications of this relationship, first established in the Yuan Dynasty, remain controversial today. Tens of thousands of Russian troops were stationed in fourteenth-century north China, some of them near what is now Beijing, while thousands of Chinese people were relocated as far west as what is now Iran to help develop the economy, and a unit of "one thousand households" of Chinese artillerymen mobilized by the Mongols after 1251 introduced Chinese gunpowder to western Asia.[26]

Khubilai Khan divided the population of his multiethnic and multilingual Yuan Empire into four hierarchical ethnic categories, with the Mongols themselves on top. Western and Central Asians (known as *semuren*) occupied the second most privileged position, while subjects of the former Jin Dynasty in north China were next, referred to as Han people. Ironically, while the word Han today specifically means ethnic Chinese, these Yuan Dynasty "Han people" included ethnic

Jurchens, Khitans, and others long resident in the north, while the ethnically Chinese former subjects of the Southern Song Dynasty in the south were not called Han, but "southern people," and consigned to the bottom of the ethnic hierarchy. In Yuan times, north and south China were regarded as different places.

Most high-level positions in the Yuan Empire were held by non-Chinese. The last Yuan emperor, Toghan-Temür (1320–1370, r. 1333–1370), had a Korean-born wife who has been called "the most powerful woman in Eurasia." Under the late Yuan Dynasty the capital (what is now Beijing), interestingly enough, may have been more closely connected to Korea than it was to southern China.[27] Throughout the Yuan Empire, many people adopted Mongol personal names, and even southern Chinese gentlemen reportedly tried to speak the Mongol language and favored Mongol clothing and hairstyles.[28]

Despite all this, the Yuan Dynasty did not prove very enduring. By the time he had completed his conquest of the Southern Song in 1279, Khubilai Khan was already in his late sixties. He was old by the standards of the day, and his final years were dogged by failures. Khubilai Khan, for example, attempted to impose a new universal writing system, based on Tibetan, which simply failed to win acceptance. His two invasions of Japan were disasters. In 1294, he died. Within a few years after his death, the Mongol empire in China began to tear itself apart amid succession disputes. Such struggles over succession were a frequent feature of steppe history. Although the steppe tradition was that leadership should be broadly hereditary within a single family, there were no fixed rules for selection, and descent could just as easily pass from older brother to younger brother or from father to younger son, as from father to eldest son. The result was that when a khan died, it was normal for there to be a power struggle.

In addition, and catastrophically, the bubonic plague (or something like it – the identification remains controversial) also made its appearance in the Mongol-ruled Yuan Empire sometime around the 1320s. From there, the plague may have spread along the newly established transcontinental Mongol trade routes to the Mediterranean and Europe, where the resulting Black Death had a major impact on medieval European history. In China, it has been estimated that as much as a third of the entire population may have died of the plague. For many, it seemed as if the end of the world was at hand.

The chaos was interpreted by some people as foretelling the apocalyptic arrival of the Future Buddha Maitreya. When Mongol authorities reacted fearfully by trying to suppress these apocalyptic religious beliefs, the faithful began to arm themselves and go into rebellion. Meanwhile, a certain teenage boy named Zhu Yuanzhang (1328–1398) had been orphaned and taken into a Buddhist monastery, where he prepared to become a monk. When the monastery where he had lived was destroyed by Mongol troops, he joined a religiously inspired rebel band called the Red Turbans. As a rebel, Zhu Yuanzhang demonstrated military talent, and he quickly rose through the ranks, eventually becoming a king with his own independent forces. In 1368, at the age of forty, Zhu's armies succeeded in capturing Beijing and reunifying China. Zhu Yuanzhang now proclaimed himself the founding emperor of a new dynasty, which he called Ming.

The word *ming* means "bright," and the title was chosen to signify the supposed victory of the forces of light. Despite the natural tendency of modern nationalists to see the Ming as a restoration of native Chinese rule following a dark interlude of foreign conquest, however, people did not necessarily see it in quite those terms at the time. Many Chinese families who had served the Mongol Yuan Dynasty had come to see it as the legitimate object of Confucian loyalty. It took years before everyone in China entirely accepted the legitimacy of this new "native Chinese" Ming Dynasty. In his accession decree, even the Ming founder himself acknowledged the century-long legitimacy of the Mongol Yuan Dynasty, though he insisted it had now come to end.[29]

Bubonic plague aside, the years of Mongol rule in China had not been altogether terrible. They were, for example, something of a golden age for Chinese painting and theater. And the Mongols did promote trade and cultural exchange. These were the years when the Arab traveler Ibn Baṭṭūṭa and the Italian Marco Polo both visited China, and Nestorian Christians from China had audiences with the Pope and the kings of England and France. Italian merchants sought profits in Beijing and Quanzhou.[30] Elements of Mongol clothing style, "including fabric with small patterns, vests, and fur trim," spread everywhere from China and Central Asia to northern India, Iran, Egypt, and even to fourteenth-century England.[31] The century of the Mongol Peace (ca. 1250–1350) saw increased global connections and helped inspire a later age of European world exploration. Marco Polo's account of his twenty-four years traveling in the Far East revolutionized European knowledge of world geography. Whether or not Christopher Columbus had actually read Polo before setting sail on his epochal voyage of discovery, Columbus was certainly familiar with the Polo story.[32]

In China, the Ming Dynasty reaction to the memory of Mongol rule may have been somewhat the opposite of the Western European reaction: to retreat into defensive isolationism. Of perhaps greater significance for world history, however, was that both China and Western Europe recovered from the crisis of Mongol conquest and bubonic plague more successfully than the Islamic Middle East. After the Mongol capture of Baghdad in 1258, the Middle East, which had until then arguably always been the leading world center of human civilization, entered a phase of long-term relative economic decline, and Europe, India, and China emerged as the world's principal new economic leaders.[33]

The Early Ming (1368–ca. Sixteenth Century [–1644])

Both out of reaction to the memory of Mongol rule, and perhaps also due to sensitivity about his own extremely humble origins, the Ming founder Zhu Yuanzhang (known as emperor by the posthumous temple name Ming Taizu, r. 1368–1398) was notoriously paranoid and despotic. Paradoxically, however, he also upheld as never before a Confucian ideal of puritanical austerity and of limited government by means of moral example. His vision of the empire was one of a vast collection of semiautonomous peasant villages. Taxes were deliberately held low and paid in kind (i.e., in rice or some other commodity rather than money). The total civilian government bureaucracy was initially kept to only about eight thousand. Physical movement was also restricted. Under the Ming founder, an official certificate was required for anyone to travel more than thirty miles from home, and travel beyond the Ming borders without official permission was punishable by death.

Despite the stereotype of Ming isolationism, however, throughout the dynasty the Ming was actively engaged in foreign wars. The Ming waged a total of 308 external wars, or an average of more than one war every year.[34] Most of these wars were against the Mongols. At first, furthermore, the Ming took the offensive against the Mongols, but by the mid-1400s Mongol power had revived considerably under the leadership of the great Oirat Mongol Esen (d. 1455).[35] In 1449, Esen even captured a Ming emperor and penetrated to the walls of Beijing. This Mongol resurgence led to a Ming strategic shift from the offensive to the defensive and resulted in the Ming reconstruction of the Great Wall of China in its now familiar form. A more brooding symbol of Ming defensive isolationism could hardly be imagined.

Yet the late Ming Dynasty would also paradoxically become conspicuous for its growing commercial prosperity and participation in international trade, and even the early Ming sponsored China's single most famous episode of world exploration. The Ming founder's fourth son (born of a Mongol consort) seized the throne by force from his own nephew in 1402, becoming the third Ming emperor, known to history as the Yongle Emperor (r. 1403–1425). This Yongle Emperor had some astoundingly grandiose ambitions. Most notably, he commissioned a series of naval expeditions under the command of a Chinese Muslim eunuch named Zheng He (1371–1433). For the first expedition in 1405, a fleet of sixty-two large ships – some as large as approximately four hundred feet in length – was assembled, carrying some 27,800 persons. By 1433, seven major voyages had been launched, which sailed up the eastern seaboard of Africa, cruised past Hormuz into the Persian Gulf, and ventured into the Red Sea. A small party apparently even made it to Mecca. These voyages brought back tribute from Hormuz, Mogadishu, Bengal, and other places; a king from Ceylon was taken back to China; and also such exotic beasts for the imperial menagerie as giraffes from Africa.[36]

The scale of these immense naval expeditions, which dwarfed anything European monarchs could have put to sea at that time, is breathtaking. Nonetheless, they were not actually voyages of exploration, since they followed trade routes that had already been well known since Roman times. Zheng He's father, a Muslim, had apparently already even made the pilgrimage to Mecca. The voyages did not make any significant new discoveries, nor were they intended to promote trade because the Ming government was not much interested in trade (and private commerce was developing on its own initiative, anyway). The voyages were expensive and put a considerable strain on imperial resources. Confucian officials, always concerned with reducing taxes and "giving rest to the people," were convinced that such expeditions were not worth the cost. After 1433, the expeditions stopped entirely.

In the early fifteenth century, the Ming Dynasty had the most powerful navy in the world, but over the next hundred years, this mighty fleet shriveled away. In

1525, there was even an imperial edict ordering the destruction of all oceangoing ships. Ironically, however, even as the Ming government was apparently retreating into conservative isolationism, private Chinese commerce was entering a new age of dynamic growth by the sixteenth century. China was approaching the threshold of its early modern era.

These were also times of exciting new intellectual developments. A particularly important Ming Dynasty departure from the Neo-Confucian orthodoxy of Zhu Xi emerged, for example, in the teachings of Wang Yangming (1472–1529). Wang Yangming was a man of considerable practical accomplishment in government and military service, who insisted that knowledge must be realized through action – that "filial piety cannot be learned by mere talk," for example, but must be achieved through practice. Yet the core of his philosophy was a Buddhist-style sudden enlightenment (in the middle of the night in 1508) and realization that all principles are inherent already in one's own mind. Understanding, therefore, can be achieved simply through introspection, requiring no external authority for validation. In contrast to Zhu Xi, who had believed it was necessary to first studiously acquire the knowledge to distinguish between right and wrong, Wang Yangming believed in the preexistence within everyone of intuitive knowledge, or innate conscience (*liang zhi*, a term that Wang borrowed from Mencius), of right and wrong.[37] In extreme form, this faith in instinctive knowledge foreshadowed the development of what came to be known as "wild Chan" (or "wild Zen") in late Ming, a freethinking movement that contributed much to the intellectual open-mindedness, and sometimes eccentric individualism, of China's early modern seventeenth century.

Confucian Korea: Koryŏ (918–1392) and Early Chosŏn (1392–ca. Sixteenth Century [–1910])

Koryŏ (918–1392)

The Koryŏ Dynasty was founded in 918 with a rebellion led by Wang Kŏn, a man from a locally powerful northwestern Korean mercantile and naval family. As ruler of Koryŏ, Wang Kŏn is known to history as King T'aejo (r. 918–943). Although he founded the dynasty in 918, it was not until 935 that the last king of Silla abdicated in his favor, and a period of rivalry between the so-called Later Three Kingdoms ended with the reunification of the Korean peninsula under Koryŏ.

The Koryŏ Dynasty, as its choice of names implies, to some extent presented itself as heir to the old Koguryŏ kingdom that had once straddled both sides of what is today the Korean border with Manchuria. Whatever ambitions Koryŏ may have cherished for Manchuria, however, were thwarted by the rise of Khitan nomadic military power (and later, Jurchen and Mongol). After the Khitan conquest of the partially Korean-influenced independent state of Parhae in Manchuria in 926, Koryŏ found itself locked into the peninsula, and the geographic shape of what we think of today as Korea was confirmed. The very real threat posed by Khitan and later Jurchen military power may have also been an incentive to Korean political and cultural consolidation.

Wang Kŏn's (King T'aejo's) rebellion, which established the Koryŏ Dynasty, was explicitly justified with reference to Chinese Mandate of Heaven theory and the revered Chinese historical example of the eleventh-century BCE Zhou conquest of the Shang. Political, legal, and economic institutions in Koryŏ also continued to be structured after the now vanished Tang Chinese imperial model. But, at the same time, Korea also achieved greater distance from China during this period and, in a sense, became more Korean. After the fall of the Tang Dynasty in China in 907, and with the rise of intervening powers such as the Khitan Liao Dynasty and the Jurchen Jin, contact between Korea and China was interrupted. The early Koryŏ period "vibrates with Korean tremors of independence and assertiveness," and the founder Wang Kŏn's "instructions emphasize Korea's unique culture and values."[38]

The Koryŏ approach to rule reflected the continuing hold of native traditions. Wang Kŏn, for example, sought marriage alliances with local lords to strengthen his position. Altogether, he took twenty-nine queens. Of the nine daughters to whom they gave birth, Wang Kŏn married two to the last Sillan king, and others were married to their own half-brothers. In China, where there was an ancient and total taboo on any marriage between people having the same family name (whether or not they were actually related), this would have been shocking. But the earliest Koreans did not have family names at all, and marriage between cousins and even half-brothers and -sisters was not unusual in antiquity, at least among the Korean aristocracy. Although family names had already been introduced by Koryŏ times, some of theses older native marriage practices continued. For example, a young married man quite commonly lived with his wife's family, and if a man had several wives, they were all regular wives, rather than Chinese-style secondary wives or concubines. Koryŏ women were also still commonly entitled to an equal share with their brothers of the family inheritance.

As the elder statesman Ch'oe Sŭng-no (927–989) summarized the balance at the end of the tenth century, "although Chinese systems are good to follow, as the customs of each area have their own characteristics, it would be difficult to change every custom. . . . We need not be like China in everything."[39] Even direct Chinese influences were adapted in uniquely Korean ways. For example, connoisseurs regard Koryŏ "china" (i.e., celadon porcelain) as even finer than the Chinese. Printing may have been invented in China, and most documents in Korea may have long continued to be written in the Chinese language, but the world's first use of metal moveable-type printing was in Korea, by at least 1234. And, if Buddhism was transmitted to Korea from China, often in specifically Chinese forms, the Koreans consistently took a more interdenominational, syncretistic approach. This culminated with the great monk Chinul (1158–1210), one of the few leading Korean Buddhist masters who never studied in China, who synthesized the divergent scriptural and meditative wings of Korean Buddhism with his formula of sudden enlightenment followed by gradual cultivation. In this way, Chinul reconciled the seemingly irreconcilable differences between the careful doctrinal study of the *sūtras* and Chan (in Korean, Sŏn; in Japanese, Zen) views on the inexpressible nature of ultimate truth.[40] Koreans, despite immersion in a shared general East Asian pattern of civilization, consistently displayed unique streaks of innovation.

Rather than a highly centralized Chinese-style imperial bureaucracy, local administration under Koryŏ was initially left largely in the hands of local lords. These lords often controlled their own private armies, and the central government merely recognized the fact of their preexisting local authority by conferring official titles on them. The old bone rank system of the Silla period gave way, however, to a new system in which aristocratic families were closely identified with the particular place where their lineage was based. Accompanying this change, the use of family names also spread.

In tension with this native Korean aristocratic system, however, in 958 Koryŏ also implemented Chinese-style civil service examinations, with the assistance of an advisor who had come from the last of the northern Five Dynasties in post-Tang China. Although the examinations began on a small scale, in the long run most Korean officials came to be selected through such testing. Even this did not eliminate aristocratic dominance in Korea, but it did give the Korean aristocracy a more bureaucratic and Confucian orientation. The examination system may have also encouraged greater prestige for the civil aristocracy over the military. By Koryŏ times, the Korean aristocracy was coming to be known collectively as *yangban*, which refers to the "two orders" of civil and military officials.

Military dissatisfaction with this civilian preference may have contributed to a coup in 1170. In that year, a commander of the Royal Guard massacred many of the court officials and exiled the king, later executing him. After this, real power was long held by generals and their private household retainers. This rise of a military dictatorship in Korea intriguingly parallels the almost simultaneous establishment of the Shogunate, and warrior domination, in Japan. Centralized, civilian, bureaucratic institutions remained more vigorous in Korea than in Japan, however, and the period of military domination in Korea was, in any case, soon terminated by the Mongol conquest.[41]

The Era of Mongol Domination (1270–1356)

Mongol attacks on the Jurchen-ruled Jin Dynasty in north China had begun in 1210, and Mongol strikes at Korea began in 1231. Although the assaults were sporadic, Mongol armies overran and laid waste to almost the entire peninsula. Amid the general destruction, for example, the first edition of the Korean Buddhist *Tripiṭaka* was burned. The Koryŏ government nonetheless stubbornly continued to resist the Mongols from a base on a small island off the western coast, and fighting continued off and on until 1270, when a pro-Mongol government was finally established in Korea.

Even after that, the Mongols allowed the Koryŏ kings to retain the form of having their own Korean dynasty. But, although Korean kings continued to rule the peninsula, from 1270 to 1356 they did so in subordination to Mongol overlords, at first under the watchful eyes of resident Mongol commissioners known as *darughachi*, and, after 1280, overseen by a Mongol institution known as the Eastern Expedition Field Headquarters. During these years, the Mongols dethroned Koryŏ kings no fewer than seven times. The Mongols also literally established family ties with their Koryŏ vassals. The Korean king's son married a daughter of Khubilai Khan, and generations of Koryŏ princes grew up in the Mongol capital (modern Beijing) with Mongol mothers, often serving in the Great Khan's bodyguard, the *keshig*, which had become "the training ground for Eurasia's elite." Koryŏ has been colorfully described as a "son-in-law" state to the Mongol Yuan Dynasty. Thousands of Koreans lived in the Mongol capital, and many Koreans took Mongol names, spoke the Mongol language, and adopted Mongol clothing and hairstyles.[42]

Under the Yuan Dynasty, the city that is today called Beijing was the capital of a vast transcontinental Mongol Empire. It was more than just a Chinese city. At the same time, nonetheless, it was also still a largely Chinese city. In Beijing, visiting Koreans encountered Neo-Confucianism. In 1313, one Korean king, after spending much of his five-year reign living in Beijing, retired there and founded a Sino-Korean-Mongol Neo-Confucian salon called the "Hall of Ten Thousand Volumes." Meanwhile, in Korea the academy was rebuilt and the Korean national shrine to Confucius restored. Leading Confucian scholars were appointed as teachers in the academy, and they gathered dedicated followings, spurning the old-style textual studies for more stimulating discussions of the true meaning of the classics. Paradoxically, Mongol overlordship in Korea did much to promote a Neo-Confucian revival in Korea.

As Mongol rule began disintegrating in China, in 1356, King Kongmin (whose Mongol name was Bayan-Temür; r. 1351–1374) broke with the pro-Mongol faction in Korea and reasserted Korean independence, but even then he continued to cooperate militarily with the Yuan against rebel forces. After the Chinese rebel leader Zhu Yuanzhang drove the Mongols out of Beijing and founded his new Ming Dynasty in China in 1368, a reduced Mongol power continued to exist on the steppe, and complicated patterns of diplomacy emerged. Although King Kongmin was able to successfully assert and maintain Korean independence, he was less successful in his attempt to extend royal authority over the powerful Korean families. In 1374, he was assassinated by a Korean aristocrat.

Early Chosŏn (1392–ca. Sixteenth Century [–1910])

With the weakening of Mongol power, Koryŏ regained independence, but the dynasty confronted many challenges. A military hero named Yi Sŏng-gye (1335–1408), who had risen to prominence fighting Japanese pirates, was dispatched in 1388 at the head of a Koryŏ army to resist Ming Dynasty Chinese claims to disputed territory in the north. After reaching the Yalu River, however, Yi Sŏng-gye turned his army around and marched back, overthrowing the Koryŏ king instead. In 1390, he dramatically burned all the land registries and enacted land reforms, which may have helped weaken the Koryŏ Great Families. With the enthusiastic support of Neo-Confucian scholars, in 1392, he then established his own new dynasty.

At the suggestion of the Ming emperor, the name of the legendary ancient Korean state of Chosŏn was resurrected for the title of this new Korean dynasty. This Chosŏn Dynasty is also sometimes referred to as the Yi Dynasty, after the name of its ruling family. Exactly like the founder of the previous Koryŏ Dynasty, as ruler, Yi Sŏng-gye is also known to history as King T'aejo (r. 1392–1398). The explanation for this repetition is because T'aejo means "Great Founder" or "Grand Progenitor" and is a common posthumous title for founders of East Asian dynasties. In fact, the contemporary founder of the Chinese Ming Dynasty, Zhu Yuanzhang, is also known by the same posthumous title (pronounced "Taizu" in Chinese). This new Korean Chosŏn Dynasty would endure a remarkable 518 years, until 1910, although we will only discuss the early Chosŏn period in this chapter.

At the start of the fifteenth century, the Chosŏn capital was moved from Kaesŏng to what is today called Seoul. Under the new dynasty, private military forces were finally eliminated, and armed might was brought under central command. During the reign of the especially renowned King Sejong (r. 1418–1450), the northern border was finally permanently stabilized at the line of the Yalu and Tumen rivers. The native Korean alphabet, commonly called *han'gŭl*, was also officially promulgated by King Sejong in 1446. Unlike the Japanese *kana* syllabaries, this is a true alphabet, with twenty-eight symbols, and it is furthermore an entirely independent invention, not derived from Chinese characters like the Japanese *kana*. Among other accomplishments during the reign of King Sejong, a system of rain gauges was established in the kingdom in 1442, providing Korea with "the longest records of measured rainfall in the world."[43] In the sixteenth century, Korean inventiveness would reveal itself again in the world's first use of ironclad warships.

Chosŏn officials were selected through Chinese-style civil service examinations conducted in written Chinese. Because, in Korea, ancestry was scrutinized before men were allowed to take the examinations, however, and because the Korean *yangban* – the "two orders" of civil and military officials – married only other *yangban*, unlike in late imperial China, the Korean elite remained a closed hereditary group, perhaps 10 percent of the total population, despite the meritocratic aspect of the Chinese-style examination system. Beneath the *yangban* elite were the majority of commoners, most of whom were poor peasants, and beneath these commoners was yet another relatively large group of hereditary slaves. Slaves may have even made up as much as 30 percent of the total population. They did not work in teams on large plantations but often farmed small plots without much direct supervision, not altogether unlike ordinary peasants.

Through their study of the Chinese Classics, zealous Korean Neo-Confucians came to adopt ancient China as an idealized model. Chosŏn Korea went further than anywhere else in East Asia, including China, in actually attempting to recreate the golden age of Chinese antiquity, as they understood it from the classics. The Chosŏn reforms, which were literally written into a series of legal codes, included an attempt to legislate a restructuring of the Korean family according to the supposedly universal Confucian moral order of patrilineal descent, ancestor veneration, and fixed mourning obligations. A 1390 law, for example, required Korean officials to perform ancestral sacrifices in each season.[44]

As late as Koryŏ times, family descent in Korea had still been traced through both male and female lines, but in the fifteenth century, mourning requirements for matrilineal relatives were downgraded. Women gradually lost their inheritance rights, and after 1402, women were legally forbidden to ride horses. The principle of primogeniture was increasingly promoted, tracing inheritance from eldest son to eldest son by the sole legal wife, and reducing the status of secondary sons and of all daughters. Sons born to secondary wives (concubines) eventually became ineligible to take the civil service examinations. Intermarriage between persons with the same family name was banned. Although the implementation and enforcement of all these measures was gradual, at least among the *yangban* elite Chinese-style marriage and family patterns eventually became pervasive.

In the early Chosŏn Dynasty, the pressure to conform to Confucian family ideals came largely from the government, but by the seventeenth century, Confucian values were being privately promoted through popular literature and the private academies that had begun to emerge in the countryside. The first Neo-Confucian private academy (*sŏwŏn*) in Korea was founded in 1543. By the end of the eighteenth century, 823 had been established.[45] The result was what is now often regarded as "traditional" Korean society: patrilineal families sharing surnames and ancestral seats, claiming descent from and venerating a common male ancestor, and with the main line of descent carried through the first-born son of the primary wife. By about the eighteenth century, Korea had become a thoroughly Confucian society. These Confucian ideals were understood as universal truths, however, rather than necessarily as Chinese influences. In fact, late Chosŏn Koreans even came to feel that they were better custodians of proper Confucian civilization than the degenerate Chinese, who had fallen under foreign Manchu rule.[46]

Confucianization was not the whole story, however. There continued to be flickers of Korean innovation, as we have seen. Female shamans, known as *mudang*, testify to the lingering strength of older native traditions. Even Confucian influences were domesticated in uniquely Korean ways. And Buddhism remained influential, despite Neo-Confucian disdain. Under the Chosŏn Dynasty, Buddhist temples were excluded from the capital and lost their official support and tax exemptions. In 1395, Buddhist-style cremation of the dead was prohibited in favor of Confucian-style burial. Over the course of the Chosŏn Dynasty, Buddhist funeral practices were gradually displaced even at the lowest levels of society. Yet when government forces were driven back by a great invasion from Japan (led by the warlord Hideyoshi) in 1592–1598, bands of Korean Buddhist monks still played a prominent role in waging fierce guerrilla resistance.

Warrior Japan: Late Heian ([794–] Tenth Century–1185), Kamakura (1185–1333), and Muromachi (1333–1568)

The Rise of the Warriors

From Japanese literature of the Heian period (794–1185), it is easy to get the impression that the aesthetically refined aristocrats of the capital, Heian (modern Kyōto), were scarcely even aware of life beyond the outskirts of the city. The aristocracy lived off taxes collected in the provinces, but was otherwise not much interested in them. Parallel to this elite inattention, the central government's ability to exercise actual administrative control over the countryside also progressively diminished. In the beginning, the performances of provincial governors had been carefully audited by their successors. By the eleventh century, however, it was rare for governors even to visit their assigned provinces at all – local administrative responsibilities were instead passed to deputies.

In the meantime, out in the provinces, new types of local strongmen were emerging. A major intention of the sweeping reorganization of the Japanese state that had followed the Taika coup d'état in the late seventh and eighth centuries had been to create a Chinese-style centralized empire, not the least of whose enhanced capabilities would be to mobilize a large army – like the huge continental armies that had fought the seventh-century wars for the unification of the Korean peninsula. Military conscription was introduced in Japan, and an army of peasant foot soldiers was created, armed with crossbows and organized into provincial units under the command of governors. But the threat of an invasion from the continent quickly receded. Military conscription put a heavy burden on ordinary farm families, and the draft was abandoned by as early as 792.

Japan would not face another serious foreign enemy for many years, but external peace did not eliminate the need for internal, domestic armed forces. For one thing, non-Japanese people called the Emishi still lived in the extreme northeast of the main island. These Emishi raided Japanese settlements, and significant conflict with the Emishi did not end until 811. In addition, local security – law and order – was always a concern. Even at its height in the eighth century, the conscript peasant infantry had already been supplemented by mounted warriors drawn from elite rural families. The art of mounted archery had been practiced in Japan since about the fifth century, and especially in eastern Japan, there was a long tradition among the local elite of hunting from horseback and of bearing arms.

The Japanese warriors who began to emerge at this time were not yet quite the familiar samurai. The word *samurai* originally only meant "attendant," and in the eighth century, it typically referred literally to household servants. By the early Heian period, the word had begun to be applied to armed household guards in attendance on court nobles. Such private guards had become necessary because of the deteriorating security situation even in the capital. Another relatively familiar term for the warriors, *bushi*, or "military gentleman," did not come into use until about the twelfth century. In the early period, Japanese warriors were most commonly called *tsuwamono*. The evolution of these relatively rustic warrior farmers into the familiar hereditary elite samurai class was not completed until as late as the sixteenth century.[47]

Early Japanese warriors were most especially mounted archers. The Way of the Warrior was "the way of the bow and horse." The cult of the sword was a later development. In the eighth century, Japanese peasant infantry armies had made the crossbow their principal weapon. But, though a crossbow is relatively easy to point and shoot, it is difficult to manufacture. By the ninth century, the crossbow had largely been abandoned in Japan. The longbow, by contrast, is easier to make but requires very much more skill to use effectively, especially from horseback.[48] At least if we can believe the Japanese warrior tales, single mounted combat became the preferred style of fighting. Combat would begin with a ritualized exchange in which the names, age, rank, and genealogy of the combatants were announced to establish suitable adversaries. A warrior's reward was then calculated by his taking of enemy heads.

Initially, Japanese warriors were only part-time warriors and part-time farmers who joined into relatively unstable rural armed bands. Warriors in the east began fortifying their homes with ditches and palisades, and in the late eleventh century, these eastern warriors also began forming groups aligned, notably, with either the Taira or Minamoto families. The Taira and Minamoto families were junior branches of the imperial line. The Japanese imperial family was quite large: as of the early tenth century, there were roughly seven hundred members who were entitled to public support.[49] To help reduce the strain on diminishing central government resources, in the ninth century junior descendants of emperors began being reduced from imperial to merely noble status, and given new family names such as Minamoto or Taira. (The Japanese imperial family does not have a family name.) Although no longer royalty, these new houses still enjoyed immense prestige, especially in rural areas outside the capital.

At roughly the same time that warrior bands began to form around the Taira and Minamoto families in the countryside, the domination of the imperial court by the Fujiwara family, which had endured for nearly two centuries, was also challenged by the institution of the Retired Emperor; that is, the hold that had been exerted over emperors by their Fujiwara mother's father or brother was now replaced by that of their own fathers. In 1068, the first emperor in 170 years whose mother was not a Fujiwara took the throne. For roughly a century thereafter, a succession of three emperors each abdicated early and then established administrative offices out of their households as Retired Emperors, from which they exercised effectively supreme power. Emperor Shirakawa (1053–1129, r. 1072–1086), for example, abdicated the throne in 1086 but did not die until 1129. These Retired Emperors took Buddhist orders, and are also therefore sometimes referred to as Cloistered Emperors. Between 1068 and 1180, there were ten reigning emperors, but a mere three Retired Emperors were the truly dominant figures for most of that period. This institution of the Retired Emperor proved to be an effective device for enhancing the economic and political position of the imperial family, but it naturally also created a potential for tension between the officially reigning emperor and the Retired Emperor.

In the early twelfth century, one branch of the Taira family demonstrated its military capability by quelling piracy on the Inland Sea, and became attached to the Retired Emperor as his personal armed escort. In 1156, for the first time in centuries, military force was called in to settle a dispute within the imperial family. A Taira family leader named Kiyomori (1118–1181) backed the reigning emperor Go-Shirakawa (1127–1192, r. 1155–1158) against a Retired Emperor, whose own armed forces were largely drawn from the Minamoto family. Although in practice battle lines were never precisely drawn into separate family camps – it was quite normal for some family members to fight against other members of their own family – a great rivalry between the Taira and Minamoto clans began, which was destined to change forever the course of Japanese history.

The Gempei War (1180–1185)

In the conflict of 1156, the Taira-backed Emperor Go-Shirakawa prevailed. He then abdicated in 1158, becoming Retired Emperor himself. Following yet another armed dispute in 1159–1160 (see Figure 5.3), the principal remaining Minamoto family leader was treacherously murdered in his bath. The lives of two of his sons were unexpectedly spared, however. One was spared, the story goes, because Taira Kiyomori was captivated by his mother's beauty, while the other, the older brother, Minamoto Yoritomo (1147–1199), was spared because Taira Kiyomori's step-mother was sentimentally reminded by him of her own lost son. Although Mina-moto Yoritomo's life was spared, he was banished to a peninsula in the distant east, where he spent the next two decades in exile. The east – the great Kantō plain surrounding what is now Tōkyō – would become his permanent new home.

Taira Kiyomori now commanded an almost unchallengeable military force at the Heian capital. Although he long remained a client attached to the authority of the Retired Emperor, by 1167 Kiyomori had risen to the top court office. In 1171, Kiyomori engineered the marriage of his daughter to the emperor, and after this daughter bore the emperor a son, in 1180, that grandson of Taira Kiyomori himself

Figure 5.3. Detail from one of the *Heiji Scrolls*, illustrating a Japanese warrior tale narrating the story of the Heiji conflict, 1159–1160. Kamakura period, 1185–1333. Museum of Fine Arts, Boston. Werner Forman/Art Resource, New York.

became the reigning emperor (Antoku, r. 1180–1183). At the peak of Taira Kiyomori's power, his family seemed to exercise a stranglehold over the entire court. "Altogether more than sixty governors of provinces, military zones, and districts, as well as sixteen nobles and more than thirty courtiers, derived from his clan. It seemed that the whole world was ruled by his kinsmen alone."[50]

The one remaining restraint on Taira Kiyomori's power had been eliminated by a coup in 1179, during which the Retired Emperor Go-Shirakawa was dismissed and placed under house arrest. This proved to be one coup too many, however, because it aroused opposition within the imperial family. In 1180, Go-Shirakawa's son issued a call to arms against the Taira. This imperial prince had been deprived of his own chance to become emperor because of Kiyomori's maneuvering to put a Taira grandson on the throne. Although the rebellious prince was soon killed, his call was answered by a now adult Minamoto Yoritomo from the remote eastern Kantō region.

Yoritomo declared the Kantō independent, and local warriors eagerly stepped in to replace officials appointed from the imperial capital. By rewarding his warrior followers with land confiscated from the enemy or confirming their existing land titles, Minamoto Yoritomo was able to raise a huge army. He soon established his headquarters at a place called Kamakura, at the base of a peninsula in the Kantō. The war that was now unleashed between the Minamoto warriors of the east and the court-based Taira forces in the west is known as the Gempei War (1180–1185). (The name Gempei derives, confusingly enough, from alternate Japanese pronunciations of the Chinese characters with which Minamoto and Taira are written.) The story of this war unfolds in what may be the greatest of all the Japanese warrior tales, the *Tale of the Heike*, a book that developed out of a tradition of oral storytelling by blind itinerant monks in the thirteenth century.

Almost immediately, the Taira launched an expeditionary probe into the Kantō to suppress the Minamoto-led rebellion. The Taira troops were spooked by the noise made by some birds at night, however, which they mistakenly thought indicated an imminent surprise attack, and the Taira forces fled without even joining battle. For the next three years, then, there was something of a phony war, as Minamoto Yoritomo preoccupied himself with consolidating his hold over the Kantō. For a time, it even seemed possible that Japan might be divided between east and west. In the twelfth century, the Kantō plain in the east and Japan's other great plain in the west near the capital, between them, together held about 40 percent of the total population of the Japanese islands.

In 1183, the war finally resumed in earnest as Minamoto Yoritomo now took the offensive, although Yoritomo personally remained behind in Kamakura and allowed others to assume tactical command on the battlefield. Taira Kiyomori had meanwhile died of a fever at the outset of the war in 1181. The Taira were quickly dislodged from the capital and retreated slowly west to the farthest tip of the main island, where, in a climactic naval battle from a multitude of small craft in 1185 at a place called Dan no Ura, the last remnants of the Taira were wiped out and the boy emperor drowned. The winner, Minamoto Yoritomo, then did a remarkable thing: he stayed in Kamakura and did not move to the imperial capital.[51]

The Kamakura Shogunate (1185–1333)

The Gempei War proved to be a great turning point in Japanese history. The victor, Minamoto Yoritomo, remained in his eastern headquarters at Kamakura, which came to be known as a *bakufu*, or military "tent government." The imperial court remained far away to the west, in the old capital Kyōto (Heian). Yet Japan was not divided between them – at least, not into two separate parts, although the erosion of central government power continued. Yoritomo claimed direct authority only over his own network of vassal warriors, or "housemen." He solidified his hold over these warriors by also claiming the right to reward them with appointments as estate stewards throughout Japan. But the emperor, in Kyōto, remained the font of legitimate government.

In 1192, Yoritomo received from the emperor the title *Sei-i tai-shōgun*, or "Great General Pacifying the Barbarians." This is commonly shortened simply to shogun (*shōgun*). Yoritomo was Japan's first shogun. It is clear that in the last decades of the twelfth century, Japan had crossed some important threshold, moving from the Heian age of centralized, civilian, aristocratic rule to a time of increasingly decentralized military rule in the age of the shoguns. As a sign of the radically changed times, between 1200 and 1840, no Japanese emperor appears to have actually held what we think of now as the standard imperial title, *Tennō*.[52]

These changes were not necessarily perceived at the time as what we might call "progress." Quite the contrary: there was a pervasive feeling of decline. It became common for Buddhists to speak of having entered the "last age of the law," when the Buddha's teachings had reached a final stage of human decay. The melancholy theme of the *Tale of the Heike* was of the victory of rough eastern warriors over the culturally sophisticated Taira of the imperial court. Japanese warriors still had no special privileged monopoly over the carrying of arms or the riding of horses, and were often still quite rustic fellows. Court nobles still epitomized cultural polish and social prestige. Minamoto Yoritomo owed his own towering stature more to his imperial descent than to any particular abilities as a warrior.

Perceptions are not necessarily realities, though. There were also signs of more positive developments in the Kamakura period, including a narrowing of the gap between elite high culture and that of ordinary commoners through the medium of popular Buddhist preaching and the new, often oral literature of the warrior tales. An especially attractive Japanese custom – regular bathing – also first manifested itself now with the appearance of public baths in monasteries, beginning in the thirteenth century. Local markets began to spread in the thirteenth century, and a new agricultural surplus accumulated and began to be sold in what was an increasingly monetized cash economy.[53]

The cash came in the form of Chinese copper coins, imported from the continent in large quantities. It would not be until the sixteenth century that coins would again be minted in Japan. Despite the unique trajectory taken by developments in Japanese history during the age of the shoguns and the samurai, contact with other parts of East Asia remained important. Japanese warrior society was, in fact, arguably more deeply Confucian in its ethical values than the old Heian aristocracy had been. The war tales, for example, emphasized warrior relations with their lords in terms of the Confucian ideal of loyalty. Even the Buddhist idea of the "last age of the law" had been developed first in China.

Important developments in Japanese Buddhism in this period were often extensions of Chinese influences. For example, Hōnen (1133–1212) was a Japanese monk from the great Tendai sect temple complex on Mt. Hiei, the tallest mountain overlooking Kyōto in the northeast. Living at the time of the Gempei War, he found it very easy to believe that the "last age of the law" was at hand, a time when salvation was no longer possible except through faith in the compassion of the Bodhisattvas. Hōnen began to preach an inspired message of universal salvation through the intervention of the Bodhisattva Amitābha, with his promise of rebirth for the faithful in the Pure Land. All that was necessary was to sincerely recite, "I put my faith in Amitābha Buddha" (in Japanese, *namu Amida Butsu*). Although Hōnen was expelled from Mt. Hiei because of controversy in 1207, his exile only served to further spread his message of faith as he traveled and preached beyond the capital. After his death, although belief in Amitābha and the Pure Land had long been widespread throughout East Asia, Hōnen's followers established a distinctive Pure Land sect (*Jōdo*), which eventually acquired the largest Buddhist following in Japan.

Zen Buddhism (in Chinese, Chan) was especially welcomed by the Shogunate in Kamakura as a way of transforming the rough warriors of the eastern Kantō into trendsetters in sophisticated new fashions, both secular and sacred, imported from the continent. At the end of the Kamakura period, there were more than two hundred Chinese monks living in Japan, and hundreds of Japanese monks had made the trip to China.[54] This Zen Buddhism did much to establish what we think of today as characteristically "Japanese" tastes for poetry, rock gardens, tea, monochromatic painting, and architecture.

Despite these ongoing continental contacts, though, it should be emphasized that all this occurred in the context of a still quite uniquely Japanese culture that was, furthermore, currently evolving along independent lines that curiously, in some ways, might even be said to better echo developments in contemporary medieval Western Europe than in China. The Japanese islands remained detached from the mainland of East Asia. Yet the Mongol invasions of 1274 and 1281, though they were successfully repulsed, were also reminders that the islands did not exist in isolation. In the aftermath, the Japanese began to become somewhat more active again overseas.

Initially, much of this activity took the form of piracy, directed first especially against the Korean peninsula. In 1350, a fleet of one hundred Japanese pirate ships descended on the Korean coast, and Japanese pirates returned to Korea five more times that same year. As we have already seen, Japanese piracy played a role in the establishment of the new Korean Chosŏn Dynasty in 1392. The legacy of the Mongol invasions also left much domestic dissatisfaction in Japan because there were very few spoils of victory with which to reward the warriors who had beaten the Mongols. Driving away Mongol invaders, after all, did not produce any new land to give away.

Minamoto Yoritomo died in 1199, and his widow lived on for another quarter-century. She became the real power – sometimes called the "Nun Shogun." She was ruthless, and is even suspected of engineering the end of Minamoto Yorito-mo's direct line of descent with the murder of her own younger son in 1219. The end of Yoritomo's line left her own family, the Hōjō, in a position from which to control the Kamakura Shogunate as regents. Naturally, however, other leading Kamakura vassals were inclined to resent such Hōjō family domination.

Muromachi (1333–1568)

Circumstances must indeed be unusual for an emperor to rebel, but that is what happened next. A succession dispute had emerged between two branches of the imperial family, which had been resolved with an agreement to alternate the throne between the two lines after 1290. Rather than abdicate to that other branch of his own family, however, in 1331, Emperor Go-Daigo (r. 1318–1339) rebelled. The Kamakura Shogunate might have had the military resources to contain this rebel emperor, but too many warriors rallied to the imperial cause instead. Even some of Kamakura's own leading vassals defected, including a man named Ashikaga Takauji (1305–1358). Takauji's mother was from the Hōjō family of Kamakura regents, and he claimed descent from a branch of the Minamoto family. With such leading vassals turning against it, in 1333, the city of Kamakura was burned, the Hōjō family and its remaining faithful retainers committed mass suicide, and the Kamakura Shogunate came to an end.

Emperor Go-Daigo's aspiration was not merely to keep the throne but to achieve a genuine imperial restoration: a return of real power from the military headquarters of the shoguns to the central imperial government. Emperor Go-Daigo therefore made his own son shogun, and combined the previously separate offices of civilian and military provincial governor into a single new office that was to be appointed by the emperor rather than by the shogun. Leading warriors were naturally dissatisfied with being excluded by this imperial arrangement, however, and rivalries between great warriors also created fissures at the court. In 1336, Ashikaga Takauji forcefully expelled the emperor from Kyōto, enthroned a new emperor of his own choosing, and had himself appointed shogun in 1338. Takauji thus became the first in a new line of Ashikaga shoguns. This Ashikaga Shogunate is also called the Muromachi period, after the name of the section of Kyōto where the Ashikaga shoguns established their headquarters.

But Emperor Go-Daigo did not relent. After being driven from the capital, he took refuge at a location south of Kyōto called Yoshino. There were now two imperial courts, and sporadic warfare between these "Northern and Southern dynasties" would continue for more than half a century, until 1392. Questions of imperial legitimacy were now subsidiary to personal ambition, however, as warriors used the pretext of loyalty to one or the other emperor to raid their neighbors and acquire land. In 1351, Ashikaga Takauji himself even changed sides, after his brother had temporarily gained the upper hand in Kyōto. Once Takauji had defeated and killed his brother, he changed sides again. It has been observed that

Takauji's rise was accomplished through three betrayals: first of Kamakura, then of Emperor Go-Daigo, and finally of his own brother. Japan was entering an age of instability, when it became commonplace for vassals to treacherously overthrow their lords.

Ashikaga Takauji returned the seat of power to the imperial capital Kyōto, though he made sure that real power remained in the shogun's hands rather than the emperor's. Kyōto flourished once again, and the Ashikaga shoguns were now able to tap into a growing urban commercial economy. By the time the Northern and Southern dynasty courts were reunified in 1392, under the third Ashikaga Shogun Yoshimitsu (1358–1408), most of the Shogunate's revenue actually came from trade: from taxes on shipping, at barrier gates and markets, and on wealthy money lenders and sake brewers. Yoshimitsu also sponsored trade with China, approaching the Ming Dynasty with a request for a resumption of friendly relations in 1401. The Ming Dynasty interpreted his lavish gifts as tribute, and in 1403, the Ming even conferred on Yoshimitsu the title "king of Japan" (the memory of which has outraged modern Japanese nationalists because it disregards the legitimate Japanese emperor). It was this commercial prosperity that made possible Yoshimitsu's construction of his fabled Golden Pavilion (*Kinkaku-ji*) in 1397, a literally gilded retreat in the northwestern suburbs of Kyōto (see Figure 5.4).

Even at its peak, however, the Ashikaga Shogunate's control over the countryside beyond Kyōto had been limited. Ashikaga Takauji had worked to appoint

Figure 5.4. Temple of the Golden Pavilion (*Kinkaku-ji*), originally built in 1397 but burned and reconstructed in the twentieth century. Kyōto, Japan. Werner Forman/Art Resource, New York.

many of his own relatives as provincial governors (or "constables"), but this was an age when even family loyalty could not be depended on, and the provincial governors – or their deputies – tended to become independent regional lords. After the assassination of the sixth Ashikaga Shogun in 1441, the power of the shoguns effectively ended. As the Shogun Yoshimasa (1435–1490) explained in 1482, "the daimyo do as they please and do not follow orders. This means there can be no government."[55]

This word, *daimyō*, was a relatively new term that would continue to be important in Japan until the late nineteenth century. Literally, it means "great name," and it refers to the holders of many rice fields. Unlike the old aristocratic estates of the Heian and Kamakura periods, which had been scattered across many locations and involved a complicated hierarchy of production rights culminating in great court nobles or temples, the lands of these new *daimyō* were now compactly consolidated territories dominated by on-the-spot warlords from heavily fortified castles. These *daimyō* exercised largely independent authority over domains that even came to be referred to as "countries" (*kokka*).

A dispute between the Hosokawa and Yamana families over who should succeed Yoshimasa as shogun resulted in the outbreak of the so-called Ōnin War (1467–1477) in 1467. This war lasted for a decade and involved hundreds of thousands of warriors, yet it was fought mostly in the streets of Kyōto, and neither the shogun nor the emperor involved himself in its conduct. Amid the battles, Kyōto was reduced to two separate walled and moated camps about a half mile apart. Much of the rest of the city was destroyed by fire. As one contemporary recorded, "across our charred land, all human traces have been extinguished. For blocks on end, birds are the sole sign of life."[56]

Having been notably ineffectual in handling the warrior squabbles that devastated his capital, in the wake of the Ōnin War the Shogun Yoshimasa retired to his villa in the Eastern Mountains (Higashiyama) section of northeastern Kyōto. There he cultivated the arts, and constructed an intentionally rustic Silver Pavilion (*Ginkaku-ji*), into which he moved in 1483. Although it is called the Silver Pavilion, it was never in fact coated with silver leaf – an omission that only intensifies the contrast with the garishness of Yoshimitsu's older and more ostentatious Golden Pavilion on the other side of town.

If Yoshimasa was a failure as a warrior leader, he was an outstanding patron of the arts. Yoshimasa actually helped establish many of the cultural styles that we have come to think of as "traditionally Japanese." These included a conscious aesthetic of rustic simplicity. Yoshimasa's Silver Pavilion became something of a model for the "traditional" Japanese house, including such characteristic touches as *tatami* matting on the floors (which became widespread only in the fifteenth century), sliding internal papered partitions called *shōji*, a special alcove for the display of artwork (the *tokonoma*), and staggered wall shelves. Other features of traditional Japanese culture that were particularly cultivated, if not actually invented, in this period include Nō theater (developed in the late fourteenth and early fifteenth centuries out of older entertainments), the art of flower arranging (*ikebana*), raked-sand gardens, and linked-verse poetry (*renga*). Although tea drinking had been introduced from China centuries earlier, the first known use of the Japanese word for the tea ceremony, *chanoyu*, appears in 1469, and the characteristically Japanese art of tea matured in the time, and in the company, of the Shogun Yoshimasa.[57] (Still other aspects of "traditional" Japanese culture are even more recent, such as Kabuki theater, the geisha girl, the "Way of the Warrior" *bushidō*, and such cooking styles as tempura and sushi.)

Kyōto was ravaged by the Ōnin War, and in the war's aftermath the great lords and their warriors returned to the provinces, leaving behind a now powerless shogun and emperor. Although the last Ashikaga Shogun would not be driven from Kyōto until 1573, after 1467 there simply was no effective central government in Japan. The century following the Ōnin War is often called the Warring States period. It was a century of conflict and of almost total decentralization. In the provinces, governors found themselves unable to control their own subordinates, who were often themselves confronted with similar insubordination from below. As one European observer reported in 1580, Japan was "continually torn by civil wars and treasons, nor is there any lord who is secure in his domain. This is why Japan is never a firm whole, but is always revolving like a wheel; for he who today is a great lord, may be a penniless nobody tomorrow."[58]

Rural society, meanwhile, reorganized itself from scattered farm residences into more compact villages, often initially with a defensive orientation. Although the samurai had originally been household attendants of top court nobles, now many wealthy peasants who happened to possess swords, a little land, and ties of vassalage to some lord began to call themselves samurai. At least in places, samurai may have made up as much as 20 percent of the rural population.

Even as decentralization reached an extreme, however, some of the more successful and energetic of the two or three hundred *daimyō* who divided the Japanese islands between themselves at the start of the sixteenth century began reversing the process and consolidating their control over surrounding land and warriors. Some *daimyō* began conducting systematic land surveys to convert their domains into more closely integrated economic units. The income of vassals gradually began to be assessed in regular standardized units (called *koku*), and this was eventually translated into an actual paid salary, as *daimyō* began to pull their samurai off the land and into permanent residence as garrisons in the *daimyō*'s castle. In the sixteenth century, some *daimyō* even began to issue their own money, and the increasing monetization of the economy enabled the mobilization of still larger armed forces and the construction of even greater fortifications. In 1568, one *daimyō* named Oda Nobunaga (1534–1582) marched into Kyōto, and the great age of Japanese reunification began.

For Further Reading

An excellent comprehensive survey of the entire late imperial period in China is Frederick W. Mote, *Imperial China: 900–1800* (Cambridge, MA: Harvard University Press, 1999). For a collection of insightful essays on this period, see Paul Jakov Smith and Richard von Glahn, eds., *The Song–Yuan–Ming Transition in Chinese History* (Cambridge, MA: Harvard University Asia Center, 2003).

On Song Dynasty China and the major late imperial cultural, social, economic, and intellectual transformations, see Peter K. Bol, *"This Culture of Ours": Intellectual Transitions in T'ang and Sung China* (Stanford University Press, 1992); John W. Chaffee, *The Thorny Gates of Learning in Sung China: A Social History of the Examinations*, new ed. (Binghamton: State University of New York Press, 1995); Edward L. Davis, *Society and the Supernatural in Song China* (Honolulu: University of Hawai'i Press, 2001); Dieter Kuhn, *The Age of Confucian Rule: The Song Transformation of China* (Cambridge, MA: Harvard University Press, 2009); and Linda A. Walton, *Academies and Society in Southern Sung China* (Honolulu: University of Hawai'i Press, 1999). For women in late imperial China, see in particular Patricia Buckley Ebrey, *The Inner Quarters: Marriage and the Lives of Chinese Women in the Sung Period* (Berkeley: University of California Press, 1993).

On Song foreign relations, see Morris Rossabi, ed., *China among Equals: The Middle Kingdom and its Neighbors, 10th–14th Centuries* (Berkeley: University of California Press, 1983); Naomi Standen, *Unbounded Loyalty: Frontier Crossing in Liao China* (Honolulu: University of Hawai'i Press, 2007); and David Curtis Wright, *From War to Diplomatic Parity in Eleventh-Century China: Sung's Foreign Relations with Kitan Liao* (Leiden, Netherlands: Brill, 2005).

On painting and the fine arts, which reached a high state of perfection in the Song Dynasty, see James Cahill, *Chinese Painting* (New York: Rizzoli, [1960] 1985), and Sherman E. Lee, *A History of Far Eastern Art*, 5th ed. (New York: Prentice Hall, 1994).

On the Mongol period, see Herbert Franke and Denis Twitchett, eds., *The Cambridge History of China, vol. VI: Alien Regimes and Border States, 907–1368* (Cambridge University Press, 1994). See also John W. Dardess, *Conquerors and Confucians: Aspects of Political Change in Late Yüan China* (New York: Columbia University Press, 1973); David M. Robinson, *Empire's Twilight: Northeast Asia under the Mongols* (Cambridge, MA: Harvard University Asia Center, 2009); and Morris Rossabi, *Khubilai Khan: His Life and Times* (Berkeley: University of California Press, 1988).

For the early Ming Dynasty, see Edward L. Farmer, *Early Ming Government: The Evolution of Dual Capitals* (Cambridge, MA: East Asian Research Center, Harvard University, 1976), and Louise Levathes, *When China Ruled the Seas: The Treasure Fleet of the Dragon Throne, 1405–1433* (New York: Oxford University Press, 1994).

Concerning Korea in the tenth–sixteenth centuries, see Robert E. Buswell Jr., trans., *The Korean Approach to Zen: The Collected Works of Chinul* (Honolulu: University of Hawai'i Press, 1983); Martina Deuchler, *The Confucian Transformation of Korea: A Study of Society and Ideology* (Cambridge, MA: Harvard University Press, 1992); Kichung Kim, *An Introduction to Classical Korean Literature: From Hyangga to P'ansori* (Armonk, NY: M. E. Sharpe, 1996); and Michael C. Rogers, "National Consciousness in Medieval Korea: The Impact of Liao and Chin on Koryŏ," in *China among Equals: The Middle Kingdom and Its Neighbors, 10th–14th Centuries*, ed. Morris Rossabi (Berkeley: University of California Press, 1983).

A splendid general overview of Japan in this period is Pierre François Souyri, *The World Turned Upside Down: Medieval Japanese Society*, trans. Käthe Roth (New York: Columbia University Press, [1998] 2001). For a much narrower but fascinating case study, see Mimi Hall Yiengpruksawan, *Hiraizumi: Buddhist Art and Regional Politics in Twelfth-Century Japan* (Cambridge, MA: Harvard University Asia Center, 1998).

Studies focusing on the rise of the Japanese warrior class include William Wayne Farris, *Heavenly Warriors: The Evolution of Japan's Military, 500–1300* (Cambridge, MA: Harvard University Press, 1992); Karl F. Friday, *Hired Swords: The Rise of Private Warrior Power in Early Japan* (Stanford University Press, 1992); Rizō Takeuchi, "The Rise of the Warriors," in *The Cambridge History of Japan; vol. II, Heian Japan*, ed. Donald H. Shively and William H. McCullough (Cambridge University Press, 1999); and H. Paul Varley, *Warriors of Japan as Portrayed in the War Tales* (Honolulu: University of Hawai'i Press, 1994).

The leading English-speaking authority on Kamakura period Japan is Jeffrey P. Mass. See his *Yoritomo and the Founding of the First Bakufu: The Origins of Dual Government in Japan* (Stanford University Press, 1999). For the Muromachi period, see Mary Elizabeth Berry, *The Culture of Civil War in Kyoto* (Berkeley: University of California Press, 1994); Kenneth A. Grossberg, *Japan's Renaissance: The Politics of the Muromachi Bakufu* (Ithaca, NY: Cornell University Press, [1981] 2000); and John Whitney Hall and Toyoda Takeshi, eds., *Japan in the Muromachi Age* (Berkeley: University of California Press, 1977).

For Japanese institutional history, see Martin Collcutt, *Five Mountains: The Rinzai Zen Monastic Institution in Medieval Japan* (Cambridge, MA: Council on East Asian Studies, Harvard University, 1981), and John W. Hall and Jeffrey P. Mass, eds., *Medieval Japan: Essays in Institutional History* (Stanford University Press, 1974).

For Japanese culture during this period, the following books are highly recommended: Donald Keene, *Yoshimasa and the Silver Pavilion: The Creation of the Soul of Japan* (New York: Columbia University Press, 2003), and William R. LaFleur, *The Karma of Words: Buddhism and the Literary Arts in Medieval Japan* (Berkeley: University of California Press, 1983).

6 Early Modern East Asia (Sixteenth–Eighteenth Centuries)

Late Ming Consumer Culture

Even to suggest that East Asia had an early modern period remains somewhat controversial. The word *modern* comes from Late Latin, and the entire concept of modernity emerged originally in the specific context of European history.[1] There is, furthermore, no denying the driving role that was played by western Europe (and its overseas colonial offspring, including the United States) in giving shape to what we think of as the modern world. With regard to non-Western civilizations, there is still a tendency to prefer imagining them as societies that had always been changelessly traditional, from some primordial beginning until relatively recently, when the process of modernization (often assumed to be synonymous with Westernization) finally started as a direct consequence of contact with the modern West. East Asian history is still commonly divided into only two major parts, premodern and modern, with the point of transition placed somewhere in the nineteenth century. Yet, paradoxically, the use of paper money, printing, gunpowder, urbanization, market-based commercialization, complex bureaucratic administration, and a relatively fluid meritocratic sociopolitical order based on the examination system all make Song Dynasty China (960–1279) seem curiously modern already a thousand years ago! The idea of a changelessly static East Asia, at any rate, is a fantasy, sustained only by lack of historical knowledge.

If long-term historical change is acknowledged for the non-Western world, another common approach has been to assume that it must naturally have followed the familiar three-stage European historical sequence of ancient, medieval, and modern. This sequence is often presumed to be universal, and applied rather mechanically to East Asian history. As it happens, within East Asia, the case of Japan actually does provide one of the closest parallels to this European developmental curve that can be found anywhere in world history. Between Japan's age of classical antiquity and modern times, Japan did experience a feudal middle phase that was uncannily (though imperfectly) reminiscent of the European Middle Ages.[2] Neither China nor Korea nor Vietnam, however, fits this three-stage European formula nearly as well. While there have indeed been many commonalities in global human history – especially in the Eurasian Old World, where some degree of exchange was always continuous – it is probably a mistake to assume that a universal model can be constructed based exclusively on the details of any one particular case. Each local society is to some degree unique, and it may be presumptuous to think that any one represents a universal norm.

Still, perhaps because of that continuous (if often slow and limited) ongoing process of cross-cultural interaction, there do appear to have been some overarching common trajectories in the history of the Eurasian Old World. Beginning in the sixteenth century, for example, there are a few tantalizing similarities between western Europe and both China and Japan that make an argument that they were all part of some more general Eurasian early modern age seem at least plausible. These parallels include points of both apparent convergence and also actual contact. In China, the signs of such early modernity include the appearance of a commercialized consumer culture in the late Ming and the forging of a vast new "gunpowder empire" under the subsequent Qing Dynasty.

The conventional verdict on the early Ming Dynasty had been that it was hopelessly isolationistic. Under the first Ming emperor, a special document was required authorizing travel more than thirty miles from home, and travel abroad without official permission was theoretically punishable by death. The early Ming Dynasty may have also experienced depressed markets and urbanization rates, and one influential interpretation sees this as the beginning of a lengthy period of more limited foreign contact and reduced technological and scientific innovation.[3] In fact, Confucian moralists in China were actually inclined to decry the growing commercialization of the later Ming Dynasty as a decline from the austerely ideal order established by the dynastic founder. Yet, whether the government and Confucian moralists approved or not, private commerce did blossom in the late Ming.

Precisely because the government neither understood nor approved, much of this late Ming commerce took place outside the sphere of government surveillance. Ming commercialization therefore could be described as laissez-faire in approach partly by default. In some cases, however, the Ming government's attitude may have even been deliberately laissez-faire: one late Ming official, writing in the 1580s, boasted, for example, of how a reduction in commercial tax rates in Nanjing not only resulted in increased trade but also caused a net increase in tax receipts![4]

Given China's huge size, most of China's trade has always been domestic. The Ming government inadvertently helped facilitate internal trade by reopening and maintaining the Grand Canal. Some twelve thousand government barges plied this canal to bring tax grain from the south to the capital at Beijing in the north, and the private vessels that also took advantage of this manmade waterway, as well as of the many other rivers and canals of south China, were beyond count. Increasing regional economic specialization further stimulated interregional domestic trade. For example, concentration on the cultivation of cotton for textile production in the lower Yangzi River area created a local demand for imported food grain that was satisfied by shipments of rice from further upriver. By the 1730s such shipments had reached a volume in excess of a billion pounds a year.[5] The invention, by at least Ming times, of that invaluable tool of trade, the abacus, is another indication of growing commercialization. The mobility made possible by ease of transportation also encouraged increasingly large-scale recreational tourism. By late Ming, it had become common to complain that "crowds of tourists" and souvenir vendors were spoiling the tourist attractions.[6]

At sea off the Ming coast, in any single day, there might be as many as 1,200 ships.[7] Although much coastal shipping was for domestic purposes, the volume of foreign trade was also substantial. Since the Ming government viewed foreign trade with suspicion, however, a large portion of this traffic operated outside the law, including both smuggling and piracy. The contradiction between growing trade and government restriction of it reached its climax in a period of so-called "Japanese pirate" raiding (in Japanese, *Wakō*; in Chinese, *Wokou*) along the Ming coast, especially in the 1540s–1550s. Although actual Japanese people were certainly among these pirates, many of the seaborne marauders were really Chinese or Korean.

Officially authorized trade between the Ming Dynasty and Japan was initiated by the Shogun Yoshimitsu in 1401, but this authorized trade was very limited in scale, and merchants who did not have the necessary official seals were probably always much more numerous. They developed a flourishing contraband trade with the Ming. Imported luxury goods from Japan, especially lacquerware and metalwork, became notably fashionable items of late Ming consumption. In addition to the Japanese imports, there were also other even more exotic items such as edible sea slugs from eastern Indonesia and Australia and even turkeys from America.[8]

The turkey has always remained a somewhat exotic creature in China, but another product native to the Americas, tobacco, was beginning to become genuinely popular in China by as early as the seventeenth century. For the first 142 years of the Ming Dynasty, the only legally acknowledged foreign trade had been that which was conducted under the rubric of formal diplomatic tribute missions (though these were sometimes merely fictitious pretexts for trade, and there was much extralegal activity), but in 1509, Guangzhou (in English, Canton) was legally opened to private merchants from tributary countries, and in 1567, a port in Fujian Province was opened to private Chinese traders.[9] By that date, there was also already a permanent Portuguese presence on the southeast coast of China. Conditions were significantly changing, and China was being swept up into the now, for the first time, truly global trade routes that had been opened by the great early modern European Age of Exploration.

The first Portuguese landfall in south China was probably made in 1513 (although the earliest Portuguese apparently came as passengers aboard Asian vessels, and the first actual European ship may not have arrived until 1517). Because of mutual misunderstandings, Portuguese relations with Ming China got off to a poor start, but by 1557 the Portuguese had a permanent base on Chinese soil at Macao, a small peninsula near the mouth of the river leading up to

Guangzhou, across from what would later become the British colony of Hong Kong (see Map 14.2 in Chapter 14). Macao would remain under Portuguese jurisdiction until the end of the twentieth century. By the 1560s, official Ming restrictions on overseas trade were beginning to relax, and the Portuguese were soon joined by the Spanish, who had established a base at Manila in the Philippines in 1571.

In the sixteenth century, most Portuguese profits from their Asian trade came from handling shipping between destinations within Asia rather than from trade between Asia and Europe. With their seafaring and navigation skills (and heavy seaborne firepower), the Europeans had carved an important niche for themselves among ancient Asian maritime trade routes, alongside Southeast Asians, Indians, Arabs, Persians, and Chinese, but at this point, the Europeans were still far from dominant, at least as far as volume was concerned. When Portuguese firearms were famously first introduced to Japan in 1543, for example, it was by three Portuguese merchants who just happened to be aboard a Chinese ship that was blown off course to a Japanese island (Tanegashima). It is not even certain if the guns they introduced were of European or Middle Eastern manufacture. The pioneering Christian missionary to Japan, Saint Francis Xavier (1506–1552), also arrived in Japan aboard a Chinese rather than a European ship.[10]

Early Ming policies may have discouraged foreign ships from coming to China, causing Muslim traders to withdraw from China's coasts and weakening the linkage between the Indian Ocean and South Sea (that is, Southeast Asian) trade – which had included even a Chinese commercial presence in southern India – that had developed under Mongol hegemony. But the early Ming restrictions also had the unintended consequence of giving Chinese merchants a near monopoly of China's maritime foreign trade. Chinese people, who had already been active in Southeast Asian trade since late Tang times, fanned out across Southeast Asia in increasing numbers beginning especially after about 1500.[11] These ethnic Chinese merchants may have often been unattached to any particular Chinese government (refugees from the seventeenth-century Manchu conquest of Ming Dynasty China, for example, played a significant role in the history of southern Vietnam), but they were very active throughout Southeast Asia, and usually retained some sense of Chinese identity. In Spanish Manila, between 1571 and 1600, there was an annual average of seven thousand Chinese visitors, in comparison with a resident ruling Spanish and Mexican population of fewer than one thousand.[12] In Thailand, the son of one Chinese immigrant even became king (Taksin, r. 1768–1782), although he failed to establish a lasting dynasty. Before Japan imposed its own fairly rigorous exclusion policies around 1639, the Japanese were also active in maritime trade, notably with Vietnam.

Andre Gunder Frank has recently argued that Europe, in its early modern Age of Exploration, did not really pull the rest of the world into a European-centered economic system – at least, not initially. "Instead, Europe belatedly joined ... an already exiting world economy," in which, if any location could truly be called "central" prior to about 1800, "it was China." Early modern Europeans, moreover, still had no product that would sell consistently in China, except for money itself.

But in the matter of cash, the Europeans were fortunate. Between 1492 and 1800, some 85 percent of the world's total silver supply, and 70 percent of its gold, came from the new European colonies in the Americas.[13] In Ming China, raw silver literally was money, and early modern Europeans used a substantial portion of their New World silver to pay for imported Chinese luxury products such as porcelain, silk, lacquerware, and (later) tea.

In the seventeenth century, the Dutch East India Company (the VOC) was the largest company in the world, and the Dutch became the most dynamic European presence in Pacific waters. Although the focus of their attention came to be directed at what is now called Indonesia, the Dutch also attempted to trade with China. In the first half of the seventeenth century, the Dutch imported some three million pieces of Chinese porcelain (which was often simply called "china," or chinaware) into Europe and established a successful outpost on the island of Taiwan. On Taiwan the Dutch erected their second-largest fortress in Asia, and there they purchased silk from Chinese merchants to exchange for silver in Japan.[14]

This Dutch base on Taiwan survived for four decades (1624–1662) and was, ironically enough, responsible for encouraging the ancestors of the people we now call "Taiwanese" (as distinct from the aborigines, who were there already) to begin settling the island from the mainland of China. The Dutch were forcibly driven off Taiwan in 1662, however, by a colorful Chinese freebooter named Zheng Chenggong (known in Europe as Koxinga, 1624–1662), the son of a Chinese Christian and a Japanese mother, who became the first Chinese ruler of Taiwan.[15] After about 1690, the Dutch generally stopped even trying to trade directly with China, finding it easier simply to allow Chinese and Portuguese merchants to come to the Dutch base on Java (in what is now Indonesia) to conduct trade.

Europeans were therefore among the participants in China's overseas trade by the seventeenth century, but they hardly constituted a dominant presence. Even so, Europe had already begun to make an impact on China. The telescope, for example, was introduced to China by 1618, within thirty years of its European invention around 1590.[16] A European-style world map, with captions written in Chinese, was prepared by the Italian Catholic missionary Matteo Ricci (1552–1610) in 1584. This was quickly copied and printed by the Chinese. A copy of a revised version of this map was eventually even hung in large panels on the wall of the emperor's palace in Beijing. In addition to his mapmaking contributions, Ricci also worked with the Chinese scholar Xu Guangqi (1562–1633) to produce the first good Chinese translation of Euclid in 1607.[17] This same Chinese scholar, Xu Guangqi, later rose to the highest office in the Ming government and became a baptized Christian, taking the Christian name Paul.

Matteo Ricci was a Jesuit. The Jesuits were a Roman Catholic counterreformation order that produced some of the best-educated minds in seventeenth-century Europe. Jesuits were expected to undergo a nine-year course of study that included mathematics and astronomy, classical philosophy, art, and the humanities as well as Christian theology. The first Jesuit missionary came to China – from Japan, as it happens – in 1552, when the Spanish (Basque) missionary Saint Francis Xavier arrived on an island off the southeast coast. He died later that same year without ever making it to the mainland, but other Jesuits followed. In 1601, Matteo Ricci became the first European Christian missionary since Mongol times to be allowed to reside in Beijing. Ricci may have also been the first European ever to learn to speak the Chinese language proficiently. With his profound erudition, scientific knowledge, and accommodating approach, Matteo Ricci made a favorable impression on many Chinese. The Jesuit mission to China enjoyed a measure of real success, and by the end of the seventeenth century, there may have been two hundred thousand Chinese Christian converts.

Arguably, however, the Jesuit reports from China had as much impact on Europe as their missionary activity had on the Chinese. Matteo Ricci drew on Chinese as well as European sources for his famous world map, and native Chinese and Japanese maps were of great interest to contemporary Europeans.[18] Curious early modern Europeans were amazed to learn of China's reported antiquity – which supposedly, and very perplexingly, extended back even before the widely accepted date of the biblical flood. Europeans were also impressed by China's enormous size and apparent good government. Ideas about China and Confucius had explicit influences on such important European Enlightenment figures as Leibniz (1646–1716), Voltaire (1694–1778), and the eighteenth-century French school of pioneering economists known as the Physiocrats. There was, in addition, a long-standing vogue in Europe for Chinese-style art objects, called chinoiserie, which, among other things, had a significant impact on English gardening styles.[19]

In China, the seventeenth century was a time of remarkable tolerance, individualism, and open-minded intellectual inquiry. Li Yu (1611–80), for example, has been called "China's first professional writer," meaning someone who intentionally made "writing a profit-making business venture." Li was best known as a writer of fiction – short stories and plays – but he was also an authority on gardening and interior design, a theater manager, critic, publisher (with his own publishing firm), and the inventor of a heated chair for use in winter. In his writing, he expressed some curiously modern-sounding opinions, such as protofeminist views about the equality of women with men. In his fiction, he portrayed thieves, beggars, prostitutes, and homosexuals sympathetically, as characters to be judged by their behavior as human beings rather than as stereotypical moral categories automatically to be condemned.[20]

The new age of commercial wealth, which began roughly in the mid-1500s, supported an affluent consumer lifestyle of conspicuous consumption. As one Ming author observed in the 1570s, "long skirts and wide collars, broad belts and narrow pleats – they change without warning. It's what they call fashion."[21] Word of the latest fashions was spread throughout China by books on connoisseurship and etiquette guides, which described even such things as the most tasteful way to display fruit on a plate, and which circulated widely, even to persons of relatively modest means in rural villages. (The male literacy rate in seventeenth-century China has been estimated at between 40 and 50 percent.)[22] Anxiety to follow constantly changing fashions also produced a large market for cheap imitations and outright fakes. For fashion-conscious shoppers who feared they might not be discriminating enough to judge product quality on their own, the maker's marks

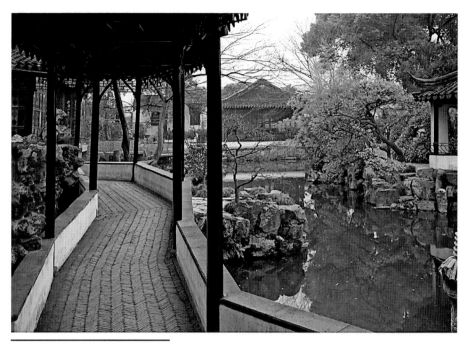

Figure 6.1. Covered walkway at the Humble Administrator's Garden (Zhuozheng yuan), Suzhou, China. Originally built in 1509–1513 and restored in the seventeenth–eighteenth centuries, this is an example of the style of magnificent garden houses that became characteristic of late Ming Dynasty China. Vanni/Art Resource, New York.

of well-regarded craftsmen and workshops began to function as an early form of reliable "brand names."

All this seems strangely modern and reminiscent of Western developments. Because newly wealthy merchants in China wished to be seen as men of good taste, however, many of their favored collectors' items were drawn from the scholar's study, including the paraphernalia of writing itself: brushes, ink, and ink stones (necessary for grinding the solid cakes of ink). Such fashions reflected a uniquely Chinese sociopolitical order, in which academic degree holders were the admired elite. Wealthy merchants emulated the lifestyle of scholars. Other fashionable collectors' items included paintings and calligraphy, musical instruments, antique bronzes, and curios of every description. Perhaps the finest coordinated displays of late Ming taste and commercial wealth were the exquisite garden homes that began to be landscaped in extravagant numbers, most famously in Suzhou (see Figure 6.1).

If late Ming China seems in some ways surprisingly modern, therefore, it was an early modernity that took characteristically Chinese forms. European cultural influences were a minor undercurrent, and European cash (in the form of silver) served a still predominantly Chinese economy. Despite the appearance of prosperity, moreover, the Ming government itself was bankrupt and disintegrating by mid-century. The Manchu conquest of China that began in 1644 would usher in a more conservative reaction, and the open-minded tolerance that gave Li Yu's seventeenth-century fiction such a surprisingly modern flavor would be banned as immoral in the eighteenth century. Manchu conquerors took China in other directions after 1644.

The Manchu, Qing, "Gunpowder Empire" (1644–Eighteenth Century [–1912])

Some of the greatest empires in the early modern world were not western European. Examples include the Ottoman Empire (1300–1919), which captured Constantinople in 1453 and besieged Vienna in 1529, and yet again in 1683; the Safavid Empire in Persia (1501–1722); the Mughal Empire in India (which flourished ca. 1556–1707); and the Russian Empire. Moscow fully escaped from Mongol domination only in the 1460s, and then embarked on a course of explosive expansion that eventually made Russia the largest country in the world. These early modern empires were typically distinguished by military reliance on the new artillery technology, and have sometimes therefore been described as "gunpowder empires." While the early modern empires of western Europe were characteristically seafaring adventures, these others were mostly continental land empires. Either directly or indirectly, they also often claimed some connection to the memory of Chinggis Khan. Among the greatest of all these early modern empires was the one forged by the Manchus, based in China.

Before the seventeenth century, there literally were no Manchus. The first known use of the word *Manchu* was in 1613, and the name was not officially adopted until 1635.[23] Nor was Manchu just a new name for an older reality; the Manchus were a significantly new group, with a new corporate identity. The core around which this new Manchu identity coalesced did consist, however, of much older Jurchen tribes. The Jurchen people had inhabited the region we now call Manchuria for centuries, and what became the Manchu language was indeed essentially another name for Jurchen. Jurchen was a Tungusic language, related to others spoken in eastern Siberia, and more distantly perhaps also to that northern belt of so-called Altaic languages that includes Turkic, Mongolic, and possibly even Korean and Japanese.

In the late sixteenth and early seventeenth centuries, the land we now call Manchuria was sparsely inhabited, with a total population of less than half a million. This thin scattering of people was divided among various tribes – some of whom did not submit to the new Manchu Empire until long after most Chinese people had. Parts of southern Manchuria had been included, off and on, inside Chinese imperial dynasties since the first one, but Manchuria was also separated from China proper by the line of the Great Wall. If Manchuria's southern border was fixed by the Great Wall, its northern border, on the other hand, would remain open and ill defined until the end of the seventeenth century. This was a rough frontier land, with every residence surrounded by some sort of defensive stockade. Among the local strongmen at the turn of the seventeenth century was a man named Nurgaci (1559–1626). Nurgaci founded what was to become the Manchu imperial lineage (the Aisin Gioro) and began the process of empire building. He started with only a few hundred men, however, and for many years, he accepted the role of Ming tributary.

Nurgaci introduced the device of different colored banners (in Manchu, *gūsa*) as an organizational tool to cut across the old tribal allegiances and assemble larger forces. In Chinese, the Manchus were in fact commonly referred to simply as the Banner People (*qiren*). This banner system was a form of military and political mobilization, and over the course of the seventeenth century it brought together people of surprisingly diverse origin, including persons of Chinese, Korean, Mongolic, Turkic, Tibetan, and even some of Russian descent, as well as the core group of Jurchen. Once established, however, banner status became hereditary and closed. A degree of uniformity in such matters as hairstyle and clothing was imposed upon the Banner People, and all were expected to learn to speak the Manchu language. These Manchus therefore soon acquired an unmistakable ethnic identity.[24]

In 1635, Nurgaci's successor officially adopted the name Manchu for his following. Soon afterwards, he also took the Chinese-language dynastic name Qing (which means "pure" or "clear") for his state, and the Chinese title "emperor" (although, in the Manchu language, rulers continued to be referred to as khans). As several other frontier peoples had before in the past, the Manchus thus began constructing a native Manchu dynasty roughly along Chinese imperial lines.

But this Qing Empire was not simply Chinese, or even East Asian. "The Qing dynasty represents the culminating phase of the unification of Inner and East Asia," and its remarkable success in building a vast and stable empire – one that, by 1800, may have contained twice the population of Europe, and which would serve as a template for the map of the People's Republic of China today – arguably owed much to its cultural and institutional hybridity.[25] The Manchus were not steppe nomads, but from the beginning they interacted closely with the eastern Mongols. Nurgaci's family intermarried extensively with Mongol nobility, the Mongol language was frequently spoken at the early Manchu court, and the Manchu writing system, which was developed in the sixteenth and seventeenth centuries, was adapted from Mongol. The capture of the Mongol Great Seal in 1635 also allowed the Manchu emperors to make the potent claim that they were the legitimate successors to Chinggis Khan.

Meanwhile, in the 1640s, the western Mongols – based on marriage alliances between tribes, shared faith in Tibetan Buddhism, and a new universal Mongol law code – were once again constructing a mighty Mongol empire, this time called the Zunghar Empire. The Zunghar Mongols were based in the grasslands of the Yili River region of northern Xinjiang, in the remote northwest of what is now China. Their rise was an obvious challenge to the Manchu Qing Dynasty that was also rising at that same time in the northeast. One common thread linking them all was Tibetan Buddhism. In 1578, an eastern Mongol khan had bestowed a new title on a leader of the reformed sect of Tibetan Buddhism: "Dalai Lama." *Dalai* was originally a Mongol rather than a Tibetan word, and is a translation of the Tibetan *gyatso*, meaning "ocean." The Tibetan Dalai Lamas and Mongol khans were

Figure 6.2. Portrait of the Manchu, Qing Dynasty, Qianlong Emperor of China (r. 1735–1796) as the Buddhist Bodhisattva Mañjuśrī, in the style of a Tibetan *thangka* but with the face painted by the Italian Giuseppe Castiglione (1688–1766). Freer Gallery of Art, Smithsonian Institution, Washington, DC: Purchase – anonymous donor and museum funds, F2000.4.

therefore linked from the beginning, and important priest–patron relationships were cultivated between them. Thanks in part to spiritual support provided by the Dalai Lama, by 1680 the Zunghar Mongols in the northwest had expanded their empire to gain control over all of Xinjiang.

The Manchu rulers in the northeast, meanwhile, also presented themselves as patrons of Tibetan lamas (see Figure 6.2). As an indication of the importance of

Tibetan Buddhism in the overall Manchu empire-building project, there would eventually be no fewer than thirty-five separate buildings in the Manchu imperial palace in Beijing dedicated specifically to Tibetan Buddhism, and ten more Tibetan shrines elsewhere in the palace complex.[26] In a dispute over the Dalai Lama's succession, the Manchus soon managed to outmaneuver the Zunghar Mongols and bring Tibet into the orbit of the Qing Dynasty as a Manchu protectorate. A Qing garrison was installed in the Tibetan capital at Lhasa in 1720, although it was soon reduced to a mere one hundred troops and two officials, who only loosely supervised a decentralized Tibetan society and government, headed (after 1751) by the Dalai Lama.[27] With its leverage over Tibet relatively secure, the Qing then unleashed a series of major military campaigns against the western Mongols and completely obliterated the Zunghar Mongol Empire by 1759.

More Zunghar Mongols may have died from smallpox – a disease to which Mongols were shockingly vulnerable – than from Qing military action. Others fled to the Russians and Kazakhs. The Zungharian steppes were depopulated and the few remaining survivors reduced to Qing servitude.[28] The Zunghar Mongols were gone, and elsewhere in Mongolia, nomadic military ferocity may have also been tamed somewhat by the fact that about one-third of all Mongol men were now peaceful Buddhist monks. Mongol nobles were given Qing imperial titles, and Mongol tribes were assigned fixed separate pasturelands to limit their mobility. Mongolia, including Outer Mongolia, was incorporated into the Qing Dynasty.

Xinjiang was also incorporated, and in the late eighteenth century finally actually began being called Xinjiang (which means "New Frontier") for the first time. The Manchus initiated a major project to map and record the details of Xinjiang history and ethnography. Qing rule in Xinjiang remained fairly indirect, however, conducted through native Turkic officials called *begs* (a Uighur Türk word for "noble"), under the loose supervision of Manchu officials known as *ambans*. The Manchus ruled Xinjiang and Mongolia largely as inner-Asian-style khans, and their patronage of Tibetan Buddhism was something of an extension of the previous Mongol role.

The Manchu population of the Qing Dynasty continued to be administered by its separate banner system, and Mongols, Uighurs, and Tibetans were supervised by a Court of Colonial Affairs rather than the regular central imperial bureaucracy. The vast majority of the population of the empire was governed by that regular bureaucracy, however, because by this time the Qing Empire also included, and was largely based in, China proper. Even as the Manchus were beginning their imperial expansion, the Ming Dynasty in China had been collapsing. The fabulous commercial wealth of the late Ming period was enjoyed mainly by a fortunate few, and there was simultaneously also much economic distress. Spanish trade with Ming China declined after 1620, as Spain's supply of silver from the Americas took a sharp downturn. The expulsion of the Portuguese from Japan after 1639 also ended their profitable role as middlemen in the trade between China and Japan. For these and other reasons, by the mid-seventeenth century the Ming government was bankrupt. Communications were disrupted, government offices went unfilled, and troops went unpaid. Unrest erupted into rebellion, and in 1644, one Chinese rebel (Li Zicheng, ca. 1605–1645) captured the Ming capital at Beijing.

A loyal Ming general commanding the strategic pass in the northeast where the Great Wall comes down to meet the sea refused to submit to these rebels, however, and sent a letter requesting military assistance from the Manchus. A young boy sat on the Manchu throne at this decisive moment, but the fourteenth son of Nurgaci (Dorgon, 1612–1650), acting on the emperor's behalf as regent, accepted the invitation and attacked, routing the Chinese rebel army. On June 5, 1644, Manchu forces entered Beijing. There they took immediate measures to win Chinese popular support by announcing tax cuts, burying the last Ming emperor with full ceremonial protocol, and making the claim that the traditional Chinese Mandate of Heaven had legitimately passed to them.

After having rather swiftly subdued north China and occupied Beijing, the Manchu expansion of their conquest to south China proved much more difficult. Resistance was, at times, stiff. A shocking total of over eight hundred thousand bodies reportedly were cremated after the fall of a single southern city (Yangzhou). Manchu rule over China proper was not fully consolidated and stabilized until after the Qing conquest of Taiwan in 1683. Even then, the slogan "overthrow the Qing and restore the Ming" long remained popular among secret societies such as the Triads. Manchu rule in China was never entirely secure, and the Qing emperors were always suspicious and fearful of rebellion. Partly for this reason, there were more literary inquisitions and books banned by the Qing Dynasty than by any other dynasty in Chinese history.

On the other hand, though, throughout the premodern world, it had never been all that unusual for the king or the ruling elite to be strangers to their subject population. In England, for example, a French-speaking Norman aristocracy ruled the land after 1066, and a House of Hanover from Germany occupied the British throne after 1714. Global examples could easily be multiplied. In China, furthermore, Chinese civilization had always been a multiethnic fusion from the beginning. Since the time of the Zhou conquest of the Shang three thousand years ago, a number of different peoples have been viewed as perfectly legitimate holders of the Mandate of Heaven. It is only in the modern age of nation-states and representative self-government that "foreign rule" became objectionable by definition. Manchu rule over China, from 1644 to 1912, was therefore not altogether an aberration, either by world or by traditional Chinese standards. It also came to be fairly widely accepted.

The Manchu Banner People did impose themselves on China as a consciously separate ruling elite, however. Banner soldiers were stationed throughout the empire in over ninety walled garrisons. The largest Manchu concentration was in Beijing, where Banner men and their dependants may have made up as much as half the city's population in the mid-eighteenth century. Ethnic Chinese residents of Beijing were confined to the southern suburbs, although by the early nineteenth century significant numbers of Chinese people were already moving into the (Manchu) Inner City.[29] Banner men were initially only permitted to serve as soldiers or officials, and were paid a regular government stipend.

A disproportionate share of top government offices were also always held by Manchus. The Banner People were distinguished from their subject populations by their "national language" (which was Manchu, not Chinese) and by their practice of the art of mounted archery. Mounted archery, in fact, became so central to the Manchu identity that when the mounted archery requirement for Banner men was finally lifted in 1905 – by which time it had already long lost any real military value – one British observer reported that the decree was still greeted with much indignation by Beijing Banner men.[30] Manchus were also distinguished by their polysyllabic non-Chinese names and by the fact that Manchu women did not practice foot binding. Manchus and ethnic Chinese were also kept separate by a number of prohibitions. They were forbidden to intermarry, and ethnic Chinese were forbidden to move to Manchuria.

The Qing Dynasty was a vast multiethnic conquest empire that, by the eighteenth century, may have ruled over as much as 40 percent of the world's total population. It had three official languages, Manchu, Mongol, and Chinese, with Tibetan also enjoying considerable prominence. The eighteenth-century Qianlong Emperor (r. 1736–1796) reportedly was able to speak Manchu, Mongol, Chinese, Tibetan, Uighur, and Tangut. During the seventeenth century, the Manchu language remained dominant in government, and even in the eighteenth century Manchu was still commonly spoken at meetings of the Grand Council. But the Banner People made up only about 1 percent of the total population of their empire, and it became a struggle for many of them to maintain competence in their own language. The Chinese language tended to prevail, and today Manchu is nearly extinct as a living language.

Nonetheless, the Manchus retained their position as a distinctly separate ruling group until the very end of the dynasty in 1912. Manchu culture also had some impact in setting standards for the entire empire. The Manchu hairstyle – the queue – was strictly imposed on all male subjects by law, and the Manchu banner gown (qipao) ironically became what many people think of today as traditional Chinese women's clothing. At least at the start of the dynasty, the Qing was also surprisingly open and cosmopolitan.

The great Kangxi Emperor (r. 1661–1722) was personally of mixed Manchu, Chinese, and Mongol ancestry, because of intermarriage. His avid interest in hunting and military exploits reflects his Manchu heritage, but he also promoted Chinese literary culture, and it was he who first established a special clientage relationship with the Dalai Lama in Tibet. At the same time, the Kangxi Emperor also studied Latin from Jesuit missionaries and collected European clocks. Unlike the Tokugawa Shogunate in Japan (1603–1868), with its relatively strict exclusion policy after 1639, the Qing Dynasty in China after 1644 did not try to shut off European contact.

Quite the opposite: the Qing Dynasty made early use of the most advanced European mapmaking experts (who had recently developed methods to accurately chart both latitude and longitude) in an imperial mapping project very similar to those sponsored by early modern European governments. The Qing actually completed its early modern mapmaking project before either France or Russia.[31]

Less than two months after Manchu forces first entered Beijing in 1644, the German Jesuit missionary Johann Adam Schall von Bell (1591–1666) offered to submit to a public test of the accuracy of his prediction of a solar eclipse anticipated for that September. Schall's calculations proved more accurate than the traditional Chinese methods, and Schall was rewarded with appointment as director of the Qing Bureau of Astronomy. Schall even became a respected senior intimate of one young Manchu emperor. In 1664, Schall's fortunes abruptly fell when he was accused of spying, after which he lived under house arrest until his death in 1666. However, the Belgian missionary Ferdinand Verbiest (1623–1688) posthumously vindicated Schall with yet another dramatic astronomical challenge, and Verbiest, too, was made director of the Qing Astronomical Bureau.[32] Into the eighteenth century, Europeans were still designing buildings for the Qing summer palace on the outskirts of Beijing and painting Qing court portraits (see Figure 6.2).

The total number of Jesuit missionaries who came to China remained small, however, and they were reluctant to increase their numbers by ordaining native Chinese priests, making it difficult to adequately serve a large Chinese Christian population. By the eighteenth century, moreover, the Jesuit order was under assault in Europe itself. In East Asia, the Jesuits had made a conscious decision to adopt local manners and culture, in a policy known as cultural accommodation, to make themselves more acceptable to East Asians (see Figure 6.3). In China, the Jesuits also chose to treat Confucianism as a secular philosophy rather than a religion, and therefore viewed it as somewhat compatible with Christianity. The argument was that reading Confucius should be no more objectionable for a good Christian than studying such other great pagan philosophers as Plato or Aristotle. Even the traditional Chinese offerings of food at household ancestral tablets, and some of the rituals conducted for the spirit of Confucius, might be tolerated as purely social obligations rather than heathen religion.

Other Catholic orders, however, particularly the Dominicans and Franciscans, were outraged by this Jesuit tolerance of Confucian rites. Serious criticism of the Jesuit approach began as early as the 1640s, and altogether, no fewer than eight popes became involved in deciding the so-called rites controversy. In 1704, a Vatican decree banned Christian participation in Confucian rites, and a papal bull (*Ex illa die*) in 1715 further reinforced this decision. In 1773, the Jesuit order was even (temporarily) suppressed altogether by the Roman Catholic Church. In 1724, meanwhile, a Qing emperor had condemned Christianity. The unraveling of the once promising Jesuit mission to China is symptomatic of an apparently widening gap in mutual appreciation between China and Europe in the eighteenth and nineteenth centuries.

After the establishment of the Qing Dynasty in 1644, meanwhile, although a scattering of embassies came to China from the Netherlands, Portugal, Russia, and the Vatican, there was little formal diplomatic contact between China and the major western European countries. Substantial private trade, however, resumed after the consolidation of Manchu authority. The leading European traders were now the British, who, according to one story, in 1664 first imported two pounds of

leading European trade were the British

Figure 6.3. Portrait of the Belgian Jesuit missionary to China Nicholas Trigault (1577–1628), in Chinese costume, by Peter Paul Rubens (1577–1640). Purchase, Carl Selden Trust, several members of the Chairman's Council, Gail and Parker Gilbert, and Lila Acheson Wallace Gifts, 1999 (1999.222). The Metropolitan Museum of Art, New York. © The Metropolitan Museum of Art/Art Resource, New York.

a curious Chinese leaf thought to have medicinal properties. In a local southeastern Chinese dialect, this substance was called something that sounded like "tea" to British ears. The British tea trade would soon grow to enormous importance. By the early 1830s the British were annually exporting thirty million pounds of tea from China, taxes on which "provided about one-tenth of the total revenue of England."[33] In the meantime, however, a new restriction had been placed on European trade with China. Beginning in 1757, the Qing Dynasty limited all Western maritime trade to only one port: Guangzhou (Canton).

Despite this new restriction on European trade, the Qing Dynasty was still not really especially closed and isolationistic – nor was it obviously in decline in the eighteenth century. In forging their vast gunpowder empire, the Manchus may have directed attention from the southeast coast to the northwest continental

Map 6.1 East Asia in 1800

interior, and in the process became more interested in Mongols and Tibetans than in Europeans. In promoting stability and traditional Chinese culture, they may have also reaffirmed conservative values, putting, for example, unprecedented emphasis on the Confucian ideal of widow chastity. But the Qing Empire was still an active major participant in world trade, and in terms of such things as average life expectancy, level of commercial development, legal property rights, and overall standard of living, Qing China still compared favorably with western Europe until as late as 1800, when the industrial revolution began to accelerate in Great Britain. Even in 1800, China may still have produced a larger share of total world manufacturing output than all Europe, including Russia, combined.[34]

The Hermit Kingdom: Late Chosŏn Korea ([1392–] Sixteenth–Nineteenth Centuries [–1910])

Ironically, Korea was still only just settling into what we normally think of as "traditional" cultural patterns when the early modern age began.[35] The process of creating "traditional" Korea had, to a large extent, only begun with institutional reforms in the early Chosŏn period, after 1392, and took a couple of centuries to fully mature. Any overarching shared Eurasian early modern tendencies remained relatively muted in Korea during this period. Instead, Korean history followed its own unique trajectory, in which the participation of Europeans, world trade, and commercialization figured less prominently than in either contemporary China or Japan. If it is relatively difficult to convincingly see late Chosŏn Korea as in any sense being early modern, however, that is a healthy reminder of both the diversity of local experience and the arbitrariness of our historical labels.

Since the history of the late Chosŏn Dynasty is commonly treated separately from the early Chosŏn, it is not merely for the purpose of (approximately) synchronizing our presentation of Korean history with Chinese and Japanese history that a brief summary of the late Chosŏn is presented here, even though the late Chosŏn may not really seem very "early modern." An especially convenient dividing point in the lengthy history – more than five hundred years – of the Chosŏn Dynasty is provided by the Japanese invasions that began in 1592.

Following an age of extreme decentralization, which will be explained later, Japan was reunified in the late sixteenth century by a series of three great warlords, including, in particular, one named Hideyoshi (1536–1598). Having completed his conquest of the Japanese islands, Hideyoshi boasted that he would conquer China too. Invading China involved going through Korea first, and in 1592, Hideyoshi landed a massive force of over 158,000 men on the southeastern tip of the Korean peninsula. The Koreans were unprepared for the assault, and within three weeks, the fierce Japanese warriors had taken the capital, Seoul. The Korean court fled to the Yalu River on their northern frontier, and Japanese samurai overran virtually the entire peninsula. However, a resourceful Korean admiral named Yi Sun-sin (1545–1598) was able to disrupt Japanese shipping, making use of the world's first iron-plated warships (called turtle ships), and win a stunning series of naval victories. The Ming Chinese, meanwhile, somewhat belatedly also sent a relief force of fifty thousand men to assist Chosŏn, and anti-Japanese guerrilla warfare erupted in many places throughout the Korean countryside.

Under these pressures, the Japanese invaders were driven back to a foothold on the southeast coast, and diplomatic negotiations began. When diplomacy stalled, Hideyoshi ordered yet a second invasion in 1597, but this time, the defenders were better prepared, and the Japanese enjoyed little success. Hideyoshi then died in 1598, and the Japanese warriors soon withdrew from the Korean peninsula. But seven years of bloody warfare had, in the meantime, laid waste to much of Korea. Notoriously, between one and two hundred thousand severed Korean and Chinese human noses (which were more easily portable across the water than the enemy heads that samurai had traditionally collected) had been sent back to Japan as tokens of Japanese martial achievement. Many of these were heaped into a (somewhat mistakenly so-called) Mound of Ears (Mimizuka) in Kyōto.[36] Despite emerging as the winner, therefore, Korea had been devastated by these invasions, and the seeds of lasting bitter antagonism were planted between Korea and Japan.

It was presumably also in partial reaction to these Japanese invasions that late Chosŏn Korea became the most genuinely isolationistic country in East Asia. Westerners would later come to picturesquely describe it as the "hermit" kingdom.[37] Although Chosŏn continued its regular tributary relations with China, private trade with China across the Yalu River was forbidden. Trade with Japan, through the lords of Tsushima Island, did resume, but it was limited to some twenty-one ships annually during the years between 1609 and the 1870s. Japanese merchants in Korea, moreover, were confined to a single walled compound at Pusan. Contact with the wider world was relatively nonexistent.

Even relations with China were soon significantly altered. In the early seventeenth century, the new Manchu empire had begun to emerge – beginning precisely in Manchuria in the Yalu River area adjacent to Korea. Early Manchu demands for Chosŏn support put the Koreans in an awkward position because of Korea's long-standing tributary relationship with the Ming Dynasty (not to mention Korean gratitude for the recent Ming assistance in defeating Hideyoshi's invasions). The Manchus responded by invading Korea in 1627 and again in 1637, taking the Korean crown prince hostage for eight years and reducing Chosŏn Korea to a tributary of the Manchu Qing Dynasty. This was even before the Manchus took Beijing and assumed the Mandate of Heaven in China proper in 1644. Although Korea remained thereafter a tributary of the Qing Dynasty, many Koreans looked down on the Manchu rulers of the Qing with disdain as barbarians.

With the long-acknowledged center of the civilized world in China trampled now under Manchu barbarian hooves, many Koreans came to perceive their own land as the sole remaining outpost of proper (Confucian) civilization. As King Yŏngjo (r. 1724–1776) explained, "the Central Plains [China] exude the stenches of barbarians and our Green Hills [Korea] are alone."[38] Despite being tributaries of the Qing Dynasty, Chosŏn Koreans continued to use the Ming rather than the Qing calendar and to wear Ming-style clothing and hairstyles (even as Chinese men were forced to adopt the Manchu queue). Even before the Manchu conquest of

China, some Koreans had already disapproved of certain Ming Chinese departures from Zhu Xi's Neo-Confucian orthodoxy (such as the thought of Wang Yangming). After the Ming had fallen, Chosŏn Korea envisioned itself as the last bastion of Neo-Confucian truth. Paradoxically, this also helped promote a new sense of pride in, and awareness of, Korean identity.

In addition to the sophisticated elaboration of Neo-Confucian metaphysics, which continued to be written in the classical Chinese language, the seventeenth and eighteenth centuries also saw a large increase in the amount of literature written in the native Korean language, in the new *han'gŭl* alphabet. This included, notably, much fiction. The arts also continued to be richly cultivated in late Chosŏn Korea (see Figure 6.4), and there does appear to have been at least some economic development in this period. In the seventeenth century, agricultural production increased due to improved irrigation and the spread of the technique of transplanting rice seedlings. By planting rice in a small seedbed first, and later transplanting the seedlings, a prior crop of barley was able to ripen earlier in the same fields. Farming also became somewhat less for subsistence and more for

Figure 6.4. Wrestling, from an *Album of Scenes from Daily Life* after Kim Hong-do (ca. 1745–ca. 1806), late Chosŏn Dynasty Korea (nineteenth century). British Museum, London. © The Trustees of the British Museum/Art Resource, New York.

commercial markets. Coins came into wider circulation. In 1801, most official slaves were freed, although slavery in Korea was not completely abolished until as late as 1894. Despite these developments, however, Korea remained much less commercially developed than either China or Japan. Seoul remained Korea's only major city, with a population of about two hundred thousand in the early nineteenth century.

Part of the reason for the low level of commercialization was the lack of convenient water transportation. There was nothing comparable in Korea to the dense network of rivers and canals in southern China or the Inland Sea in Japan. Aristocratic and Confucian elite disdain for commerce, and official policies of seclusion, surely also played a role. Yet even the hermit kingdom of Korea was not completely isolated from developments in the outside world. One of the major new Chosŏn commercial crops, for example, was tobacco – introduced from the Americas in the seventeenth century. Chili peppers, which were also introduced from the Americas, completely transformed Korean cuisine. Today, the characteristic and outstandingly delicious Korean cooking style would be almost unimaginable without hot peppers. A European telescope and clock were also brought to Korea (from China) as early as 1631.

In 1784, one Korean returned from an embassy to Beijing as a baptized Catholic Christian. Even in the absence of European missionaries, a number of Koreans converted themselves to Catholicism through reading Christian texts written in the Chinese language. Amazingly, only Italy, France, and Spain have produced more canonized Catholic saints than Korea! But, although Confucianism was generally tolerant of differing religious beliefs, such toleration did not extend to religious practices that contradicted what were believed to be fundamental secular moral obligations. Once it became clear in Korea, after 1790, that the Catholic Church had forbidden the performance of Confucian ancestral rites, one Korean Christian responded by burning all of his family's ancestral tablets. He was arrested for violation of the mourning laws and executed.[39] Especially after the turn into the nineteenth century, there were serious, if sporadic, persecutions of Christians in Korea.

In 1866, a U.S. merchant schooner called the *General Sherman* sailed up the Taedong River toward P'yŏngyang with the intention of forcing trade. Grounded by low tide, the ship was mobbed and burned and all of its crew killed. That same year, a punitive expedition consisting of seven French warships was dispatched in reaction to the earlier execution of nine French missionaries, and a detachment of French soldiers was put ashore on Kanghwa Island. When large Korean forces were mobilized against the French, the French withdrew, and the Koreans interpreted this as a victory. In 1871, a squadron of five U.S. warships arrived in belated response to the burning of the *General Sherman*. When the Koreans refused to negotiate, the Americans bombarded the city of Kanghwa and destroyed Korean fortifications. When the American eventually withdrew, however, the Koreans were again convinced that they had militarily prevailed. Long after British naval power had compelled Qing China to open new ports for Western trade (in 1842), and the U.S. Navy, under Commodore Perry, had opened Japan (in 1854), Chosŏn Korea still had serious hopes of being able to forcibly keep unwelcome foreigners out.

The Reunification of Japan (1568–1600) and the Tokugawa Shogunate (1603–1868)

Three Reunifiers

If the Qing Dynasty in China was a classic example of an early modern gunpowder empire, the term might also be applied to contemporary Japan, although in some ways Japan was certainly an exceptional case. After the accidental introduction of firearms to the southern Japanese island of Tanegashima by stranded Portuguese in 1543, the Japanese immediately appreciated the usefulness of the deadly new technology, and skilled Japanese artisans quickly began reproducing these new weapons. Gunfire proved to be decisive in combat, and matchlocks became a vital tool in the military reunification of the Japanese islands. Attempts to extend this wave of military conquests beyond the zone of Japanese culture and forge a genuinely multiethnic empire, such as Hideyoshi's invasions of Korea, were not successful, however. Japan's emperors also remained quite powerless under the surveillance of shogunal military authority, and the island empire soon closed its borders and imposed relatively strict policies of isolation. So Japan was a somewhat unusual example of an early modern empire. Yet Japan did experience significant early modern economic development, and at the beginning of this period central-ized political control was rapidly extended across a large area, thanks in no small part to the availability of guns. Not entirely coincidentally, Europeans also figured prominently in the early phases of this story.

Sixteenth-century Europeans introduced more than just firearms into Japan. They also, for example, introduced tobacco, which soon began to be cultivated domestically. The habit of smoking became fairly widespread in early modern Japan. Another European influence may have been the cooking style known as tempura: batter-fried seafood and vegetables. The Japanese word *tempura* is thought to derive from Portuguese *temporada*, or "season," referring to periods when Catholics were expected to abstain from eating meat. Christianity, too, was a sixteenth-century European introduction, which briefly was quite influential.

The Jesuit missionary Saint Francis Xavier landed in Japan in 1549, on the southwestern island of Kyūshū. Perhaps because there were some striking similar-ities between sixteenth-century Europe and Japan – including such features as regional lords and a hereditary military elite living in castles, and widespread faith in a religion of salvation (Christianity was initially even sometimes mistaken by the Japanese for a variant of Buddhism) – Japanese and Europeans greeted each other with a fair measure of initial mutual respect. The Japanese port at Nagasaki was developed after 1568 specifically for European trade, and the city was actually founded in 1571 by Jesuit missionaries, who continued to administer it for some years thereafter. For a time, it was fashionable in Japan to wear a cross and rosary. At its peak in the early seventeenth century, there may have been as many as three hundred thousand Japanese Christian converts.

The arrival of the Portuguese also brought increased foreign trade. Japanese mines just happened to be producing unprecedented quantities of silver in the sixteenth century, and because the Portuguese had a base in China at Macao, where raw silver was literally money, a flourishing trade developed between China and Japan, with the Portuguese serving as middlemen. This contributed to the ostentatious ornamentation of what was something of a literally gilded age in Japanese art history. The new wealth also helped great *daimyō* construct ever more massive fortifications and field ever larger armies. Guns, moreover, meant that the days of single combat between gallant mounted warriors, as portrayed in the old war tales, were over, and simple mountaintop castles were no longer secure. Massed ranks of infantry carrying guns, and huge fortifications with moats and earthen ramparts capable of withstanding artillery fire, were necessary. Amid the intense competition to survive a quintessentially Darwinian struggle for survival of the fittest, the process of political decentralization began to reverse itself.

In the middle of the sixteenth century, Japan was divided into roughly 120 *daimyō* domains, each of which was virtually an independent state. One relatively minor domain at Owari, in central Japan, belonged to Oda Nobunaga (1534–1582). The Oda family had emerged from obscurity while serving as deputies for the military governors of the province, and following the Ōnin War (1467–1477), they seized outright control of the domain for themselves. Oda Nobunaga was then catapulted into greater prominence in 1560, when he surprised the vastly superior forces of a neighbor in pouring rain and soundly defeated them. In 1568, an Ashikaga Shogun requested Oda's assistance in regaining shogunal control in Kyōto, and Oda's march into the imperial capital in that year is sometimes said to mark the beginning of the reunification of Japan.

Oda had no intention of merely providing military support for Ashikaga shoguns. He assumed personal decision-making authority and, in 1573, drove the last Ashikaga Shogun into exile. Thereafter, Oda simply left the position of shogun vacant. Oda scorned the trappings of formal legitimization and was content to rule by military force alone. As one European observer described Oda in 1569, he "treats all the Kings and Princes of Iapan with scorn, & speaks to them over his shoulder as though to inferiors."[40]

Oda Nobunaga's most intractable opponents in his rise to power were the Buddhists of the True Pure Land League (*Ikkō ikki*), based at the league's temple-fortress Ishiyama Honganji in Ōsaka, at the eastern end of the Inland Sea. Such leagues had emerged during the Japanese Warring States period as collective defense organizations, in an alternative to the form of a domain ruled by a single *daimyō*. Participants typically took an oath signed in blood, with their names written in a circle so that no one name came first. Most of these leagues dissolved fairly quickly, however, or transformed themselves into more conventional *daimyō* domains. By this time, the True Pure Land League itself was also no longer really very greatly different from a typical *daimyō* domain, except that it was specifically religious. Oda Nobunaga's conflict with this Buddhist sect raged for ten years before its great fortress at Ōsaka finally fell in 1580.

Since Buddhist religious institutions were particularly resistant to accepting subordination to his command, Oda Nobunaga could be especially ruthless in his assaults on them. In one shocking incident in 1571, for example, Oda destroyed the Tendai sect's ancient headquarters on Mount Hiei, overlooking Kyōto. Thousands of monastic buildings were burned and their inhabitants put to the sword.

As his headquarters, Oda built a great new castle for himself at Azuchi, on the shores of Japan's largest lake, Lake Biwa, just east of Kyōto, in 1576. Although moats and ramparts formed the most useful fortifications in this age of gunpowder, Japanese castles of the period also typically contained soaring central towers. When completed, the tower at Azuchi was 138 feet high, gilded at the top and white-washed below, and decorated inside by screen paintings from the hands of master artists. By 1582, Oda Nobunaga controlled about one-third of all Japan. In that year, however, he was surprised after taking tea in a Kyōto monastery and murdered by a treacherous vassal, and his great castle at Azuchi was demolished.

Little survived of Oda's castle, but his accumulated conquests remained as a base on which others could build. At the time of Oda's death, his top lieutenant had been Hideyoshi. Hideyoshi sprang from such humble ancestry that he originally did not even have a family name (although the surname Toyotomi would eventually be bestowed on him by the emperor). He rose from the ranks of warrior farmers, at a time when the samurai class was still poorly defined, on the strength of his ability. When Hideyoshi learned of Oda Nobunaga's treacherous murder, he moved quickly to punish the assassin, putting him to death within eleven days. Hideyoshi was then well poised to assume command over Oda's forces and continue the process of reunification. Within eight more years, the reunification of Japan was complete.

Hideyoshi not only completed the military reunification of Japan but also lived to die of old age. Part of the explanation for his striking success was that some of the most difficult fighting had already been accomplished by Oda Nobunaga, but Hideyoshi was also more willing than Oda had been to compromise.[41] Many of Hideyoshi's most powerful rivals simply were converted into his vassals. The price Hideyoshi paid for this successful approach, however, was that not only did many of the old *daimyō* continue to exist but some of the strongest were made even stronger, because the most generous rewards often had to be given to the lords who were already most powerful.

For example, Hideyoshi's foremost ally, Tokugawa Ieyasu (1542–1616), was ultimately assigned control over the lands of Hideyoshi's greatest defeated enemy, the Hōjō family of Odawara, in the eastern Kantō region, after they were crushed in 1590. Tokugawa Ieyasu then became the largest landholder in Japan, with holdings rated at 2,402,000 *koku* – greater even than Hideyoshi's own total. Inevitably, this made Ieyasu a serious potential threat to Hideyoshi, but at least in the short run, it also moved Ieyasu far away from the vital western region near the imperial capital and confronted Tokugawa Ieyasu with tremendous initial administrative challenges in bringing his new, and still potentially hostile, eastern domain under control. Tokugawa Ieyasu moved to the Kantō and established his headquarters at a small castle town called Edo (modern Tōkyō).

Because of Hideyoshi's humble birth, he was unqualified to receive the title "shogun," which still required a plausible claim to Minamoto descent. Instead, Hideyoshi engineered his adoption into the ancient aristocratic Fujiwara family and revived the traditional Fujiwara position of regent. Hideyoshi went on to publish regulations for *daimyō* conduct, survey the rice land of all Japan, and, through so-called sword hunts beginning in 1588, to disarm the peasantry. For the first time a clear line began to be drawn between peasants and samurai. An edict of 1591 was intended to permanently fix Japanese class identity.

Having subdued Japan, Hideyoshi boasted that he would conquer China and twice launched massive invasions of Korea. Hideyoshi not only failed in his invasion of the continent, however, but also failed to establish an enduring dynasty – chiefly because his heir was still too young to take active command at the time of his own death. Hideyoshi's first son had died early. Lacking an heir, Hideyoshi designated a nephew as his successor. In his old age, however, Hideyoshi unexpectedly produced another son, Hideyori (1593–1615). Hideyoshi then ruthlessly eliminated the nephew, but this meant that his son and heir was still only five years old when Hideyoshi died in 1598. From his deathbed, Hideyoshi maneuvered to safeguard the succession. He appointed a board of five elders to act as the boy's guardians until he came of age, with the idea that these five men would at least balance each other so that none of them could become dominant. The plan failed, however, when one of the most reliable of these five elders promptly died himself in 1599, after which the balance of power tilted swiftly in favor of Tokugawa Ieyasu. An anti-Tokugawa coalition was hastily assembled, but it collapsed on the battlefield, largely because of defections. After his victory at the crucial battle of Sekigahara in 1600, the "Old Badger" Tokugawa Ieyasu emerged with unchallengeable military supremacy.

Since he had sworn an oath to protect Hideyoshi's son, despite his military victory Tokugawa Ieyasu still felt obliged to allow Hideyori to continue living comfortably in his castle at Ōsaka. On the strength of a distant claim to Minamoto descent, though, Ieyasu was granted the title "shogun" in 1603, founding what is known as the Tokugawa Shogunate. Finally, in 1614, claiming that a somewhat ambiguous inscription Hideyori had cast on a bronze bell was a veiled insult, and accusing Hideyori of assembling masterless samurai (*rōnin*) in his castle in preparation for a coup, Tokugawa Ieyasu besieged Ōsaka castle. The castle's defenses proved formidable, but it fell eventually in 1615, and Hideyori and his mother were forced to commit suicide. The destruction of Hideyori's castle in Ōsaka in 1615 would be the last major military conflict in Japan for two and a half centuries.

The Tokugawa Shogunate (1603–1868)

The most significant exception to this sustained record of Tokugawa peace came early, in a bloody rebellion by Japanese Christians at Shimabara, near Nagasaki, in 1637–1638. This Christian rebellion undoubtedly helped harden the Tokugawa resolve to strictly limit all sources of possible foreign interference. After a century and a half of incessant warfare, and as a fundamentally military regime, the Tokugawa Shogunate was understandably obsessed with maintaining order. One way of strengthening internal security was to restrict external contact. For that purpose, foreign travel by Japanese people was banned in 1635. Christianity appeared to be a particularly destabilizing source of outside influences, and a mounting series of proscriptions and persecutions were directed against that foreign religion (beginning as early as 1587 under Hideyoshi). In 1624, the Spanish were expelled from Japan altogether, and following the Christian rebellion at Shimabara, the Portuguese were also expelled in 1639. From that time on, all Japanese people were required to register with a Buddhist temple and verify that they were not Christian. After 1639, the Dutch were the only Europeans who were allowed a presence in Japan, and in 1641 even the Dutch were restricted to a small manmade island called Deshima, in Nagasaki harbor.

The Dutch remained, but their walled island at Deshima was guarded at night, and by day a pass was required to venture in or out. Contact between the Dutch and Japanese was therefore limited, and, although as many as twenty-two Dutch ships each year had sailed for Japan and Taiwan in the early seventeenth century, by the early nineteenth century an average of only one Dutch ship per year visited Japan.[42] This Japanese seclusion policy was therefore relatively extreme, but even Japan was not actually totally cut off from world developments in these centuries. For example, Japan did not, popular myth to the contrary, abandon firearms. When a U.S. Navy expedition opened Japan and ended its seclusion in 1854, the fortifications at Nagasaki already included 137 cannon. The sophisticated modern technology of the pocket watch introduced by the Americans in 1854 also sparked little interest – because pocket watches were already familiar in Japan.[43]

If some news of Western developments managed to penetrate Tokugawa Japan, contacts with other parts of East Asia were naturally even greater. In fact, it has been claimed that Tokugawa Japan was "oriented more than ever before toward the language and classical culture of continental China"[44] (see Figure 6.5). Higher education in Japan was still conceived primarily as mastery of the written Chinese

Figure 6.5. Calligraphy by the Chinese-born (in Fujian Province) Zen Buddhist monk Nangen (1631–1692), from the predominantly Chinese Mampuku-ji (Mampuku Temple) that was completed in Japan in 1669 near Uji (not far from Kyōto). Until as late as 1740, all of Mampuku-ji's abbots came from China. Private collection. Werner Forman/Art Resource, New York.

language and the Confucian Classics. Tokugawa Ieyasu himself founded a Confucian academy. Thrust suddenly into an age of peace, Japan's samurai warriors pondered how to justify their continued privileges in an age when there were no more wars to fight. In the seventeenth century, this led some samurai to formulate what is known as *bushidō*: the "Way of the Military Gentleman." Yamaga Sokō (1622–1685), for example, argued that samurai justified their economically nonproductive existence because leisure from work allowed them to cultivate the Confucian values of loyalty, duty, and service and to lead the common people in the classic Confucian fashion by setting a virtuous example.

The Tokugawa period, in fact, became the acknowledged golden age of Confucianism in Japan. Hayashi Razan (1583–1657) reportedly drew crowds with his public lectures on Neo-Confucian interpretations of the *Analects*. In the great western Japanese commercial city of Ōsaka, where 95 percent of the population were not samurai, the Kaitokudō (Hall of Embracing Virtue) academy introduced all classes of Japanese people to Confucian values, but most especially merchants, who were supposed to be concerned with putting their businesses on a Confucian ethical foundation.[45]

Somewhat predictably, though, there were also nativist counterreactions against all this Confucianism. A school of National Learning emerged, eager to emphasize Japan's distinctive native traditions. The greatest of these National Learning scholars was Motoori Norinaga (1730–1801), who devoted his life to a careful study of the oldest Japanese history, the *Kojiki*, in search of a more purely Japanese national essence uncontaminated by foreign Chinese influences.

Even more fundamentally essential to the Tokugawa peace than excluding foreign sources of instability was the formulation of new methods for maintaining domestic order. The Tokugawa Shogunate did not attempt to eliminate the *daimyō* or their independent authority over their own domains. At the end of the Tokugawa period in 1868, there were still 276 *daimyō* of varying degrees of wealth and power. But the Tokugawa shoguns did attempt to subordinate these *daimyō* to themselves, using oaths of allegiance, a claimed right to confirm *daimyō* holdings or transfer them to other domains (which happened quite often in the early years), supervision of marriage alliances, and restrictions over how many armed men and castles they could maintain. Most importantly, all *daimyō* were required to spend half their time in Edo, in a system of alternate attendance (*sankin kōtai*) between their own domains and the shogun's city. This oriented all the *daimyō* toward the shogun, left crucial family members as hostages beneath the shogun's castle, drained *daimyō* resources in maintaining expensive dual establishments in Edo and in their own domains, and incidentally, helped develop networks of roads and communications centering on Edo, in the process promoting the development of a more integrated national economy. Merchants, too, converged on Edo and the other castle towns to satisfy the needs of the *daimyō* and their samurai attendants.

At the start of the sixteenth century, most samurai had still lived in rural villages, where they collected taxes, administered justice, and served as local authorities. During the wars of reunification in the second half of the sixteenth century, however, the *daimyō* consolidated their resources, built enormous new castles, and pulled samurai off the land to garrison them. No longer able to support themselves from their own lands, the samurai were instead paid stipends by their lords. Merchants, artisans, and craftsmen were also drawn in to serve the large military establishments, creating whole new castle towns. Many of Japan's modern cities began this way, as castle towns, in a great spurt between about 1580 and 1610, notably including Edo (modern Tōkyō).

In the early eighteenth century, the largest city in Europe was Paris, with a population of over half a million. At that time Edo held over a million.[46] Ōsaka, in western Japan, had also become a very large city, but Ōsaka was a merchant's town and prospered as a commercial center. Edo was the shogun's city. Half the population of Edo were samurai. All *daimyō* were required to spend half their time in Edo, and direct retainers of the shogun were not permitted to travel more than ten miles from the shogun's castle without official permission. There was, therefore, a large captive warrior audience that needed to be fed, housed, clothed, and entertained. While the shogun, *daimyō*, and samurai continued to cultivate the older traditional elite culture, the other half of the city – the townspeople (*chōnin*) – patronized a newly emerging popular culture. This was Japan's first true pop culture, a mass-production culture of the marketplace.

The relatively flashy Kabuki theater, for example, catered to the tastes of townspeople and dates almost precisely from the beginning of the Tokugawa period.[47] Because of its somewhat disreputable moral tone, the Shogunate soon banned women from the stage (much as in Shakespeare's England), and female roles came to be performed by male specialists known as *onnagata*, who mimicked the movements of women. Like most occupations in Tokugawa Japan, acting became a hereditary profession, with performers often carrying on lengthy family acting traditions, playing the same roles their ancestors had first made famous. Kabuki sets, costumes, and makeup were lavish, and a revolving stage was introduced to provide quick scene changes.

Surprisingly enough, some of the finest Tokugawa playwrights preferred to write for the puppet theater (*bunraku* or *jōruri*), which, for a time, seriously rivaled live theater. Puppets sometimes became huge, as large as three or four feet tall and requiring three manipulators to operate. These puppets were obviously capable of stunts and special effects no human actor could perform live on stage. Perhaps the most renowned Tokugawa playwright was Chikamatsu Monzaemon (1653–1725), who perceptively observed that the art of the puppet theater lay "in the slender margin between the real and the unreal."[48]

The best-loved Tokugawa play, written by a trio of other authors, was called *Chūshingura* ("The Treasury of Loyal Retainers") – popularly known as the story of the "forty-seven *rōnin*." It was first performed in 1748. A complete performance of *Chūshingura* requires about eleven hours, but the outlines of the story are quickly told. It was based on actual events that had taken place in 1701–1703. A certain *daimyō* had been assigned to help receive an imperial emissary in the shogun's castle in Edo, but because he had neglected to present adequate gifts to the man responsible for teaching him the necessary protocol, he did not know how to properly perform his duties. In humiliation and rage, he finally drew his sword and wounded his uncooperative instructor. The punishment for drawing a sword in the shogun's castle was death, and this lord was obliged to commit suicide that same evening. With his death, his retainers became *rōnin*, or masterless samurai. Samurai ideals of loyalty and duty dictated that they should seek vengeance, but to put their enemy off his guard they first pretended to become dissolute and debauched. Then one night they assaulted the villain's mansion and killed him. This satisfied the demands of duty and honor, but, unfortunately, they had in the process also committed the unpardonable crime of murder. The Shogunate's elegant solution was to allow them all to commit honorable suicide, making the forty-seven *rōnin* tragic heroes.

The Tokugawa Shogunate attempted to strictly legislate a separation between elite and popular culture. Townspeople were forbidden to stage performances of the refined Nō drama, and samurai were not supposed to attend Kabuki. In practice, however, many samurai became avid patrons of Kabuki, even if they had to attend the theater in secret. At the same time, even commercial pop culture to some extent reflected supposedly elite Neo-Confucian values. For example, one of the perennial grand themes of Tokugawa theater was the conflict between duty (*giri*) and human feeling (*ninjō*) – most famously in stories of star-crossed lovers driven by the pressure of events to commit suicide.

Books, many of them now written in the Japanese language rather than in classical Chinese, were suddenly being published in great numbers. These were intended for a relatively wide popular audience and included such things as manuals for household management and bookkeeping guides as well as novels and other entertainments. By 1692, there were some seven thousand titles in print in Kyōto.[49]

The Shogunate apparently regarded entertainment as something of a necessary evil, to be regulated and restricted but nonetheless permitted. The Shogunate therefore designated specially licensed pleasure quarters, often referred to poetically as the "floating world" (*ukiyo*). These were centers of teahouses, theaters, and brothels. After some fires in the 1650s, the theaters in Edo came to be clustered in the area of Nihonbashi (the "Bridge of Japan," from which all distances were supposedly measured), east of the shogun's castle, while other entertainments were moved northeast to the region of the city now called Asakusa. The geisha (literally, "artists"), who were skilled dancers, singers, musicians, conversationalists, and consummate female entertainers, were the heart of this floating world.

From these licensed pleasure quarters, the popular woodblock print art form known as *ukiyoe* also took its name: "pictures from the floating world." These prints – scarcely viewed as art at the time but much appreciated in the modern West – typically drew their subjects from the entertainment quarters, depicting such themes as geisha, Kabuki actors, and *sumō* wrestlers. Many of the most superb prints were landscapes, however, such as those by (Andō) Hiroshige (1797–1858) and (Katsushika) Hokusai (1760–1849). Hokusai reportedly produced an astonishing thirty-five thousand different designs during his long life, although he is best known for his set of *Thirty-six Views of Mount Fuji*, which includes the famous "Great Wave at Kanagawa" (see Figure 6.6).

Figure 6.6. Katsushika Hokusai (1760–1849), "The Great Wave at Kanagawa" (from a series of "Thirty-six Views of Mount Fuji"), Japanese woodblock print, ca. 1830–1832. Bequest of Mrs. H. O. Havemeyer, 1929. The Metropolitan Museum of Art, New York. © The Metropolitan Museum of Art/Art Resource, New York.

The World Turned Upside Down: Early Modern Economic Development

In the first century of the Tokugawa period the population of Japan more than doubled, and castle towns swelled in size. Population growth then stopped, however, and from 1721 to 1846 remained constant at roughly twenty-six million. Many castle towns even saw their populations decrease. This long-term population stability seems to have been at least partially the result of deliberate choices by individual families, such as restricting marriage to only one son in each generation to preserve the family farm intact. At the same time, however, technology was also gradually improving, education was spreading, and rural trade and production were increasing. Per capita income therefore increased, but the center of activity shifted from the castle towns to the countryside. One reason for this shift, perhaps, was the relative inability of governments based in castle towns to enforce monopoly restrictions, impose taxes, and regulate prices outside those towns. As one late eighteenth-century Japanese statute complained, "now people from the castle-town go to the country to shop."[50]

By the end of the Tokugawa period, some farm families were earning more than half their income from nonagricultural sidelines. In addition to sideline production of textiles and other activities on the farms themselves, there was also much new rural industry – such things as *sake* (alcohol) or soy sauce brewing, ceramics, and iron production – worked by part-time or seasonal labor. One result was that Japanese work habits were already relatively well prepared for the late nineteenth-century onset of modern mechanized industrialization.

Figure 6.7. A samurai in Yokohama, Japan, 1864–1865. Photographed by Felice Beato (1832–1909). The Metropolitan Museum of Art, New York. © The Metropolitan Museum of Art/Art Resource, New York.

Another result, however, was to gradually undermine the position of the warrior elite. Samurai status was now fixed and hereditary, and marked by such privileges as the exclusive right to wear two swords and to have a family name. The samurai were also paid regular stipends by their lords. But the samurai were a relatively large group, roughly 7 percent of the total population, and in an age of prolonged peace, their employment possibilities as professional warriors were obviously limited. Some samurai served their lords as domain officials, but many samurai did not really have much to do. (See Figure 6.7.)

The *daimyō*, meanwhile, collected their taxes in rice, which they shipped to Ōsaka or Edo for marketing and conversion into the cash they needed to meet domain expenses. Through servicing this trade, great merchant houses emerged and prospered, and a money-based economy flourished. Since the land tax rates remained relatively flat after 1700, however, while expenses naturally always tended to increase, *daimyō* were sometimes forced to borrow from wealthy merchants. Some lords fell deeply into debt. Merchants and other townspeople were forbidden by law from aspiring to samurai status, but despite their official inferiority, their growing economic clout to some extent reversed what the warrior elite felt should be the proper social order. To economize, many *daimyō* reduced samurai stipends (which would have remained stagnant at best anyway), typically by as much as 30–40 percent, leaving many of the lower samurai seriously impoverished and creating much samurai discontent.

Paradoxically, therefore, while Tokugawa Japan saw significant early modern economic growth, which may have helped prepare Japan for rapid industrialization in the late nineteenth century, the ideal social order had also been substantially undermined. By the nineteenth century, there was widespread evidence of contempt for established authority. As one early nineteenth-century author observed, "the shogunate's proclamations and ordinances are called 'three-day laws.' No one fears them, and no one pays any attention to them. . . . They are disregarded after that short period of time."[51] Significantly, among the most discontented and disenfranchised by these long-term developments were lower-ranking members of the samurai elite.

For Further Reading

An innovative look at early modern interactions between China, Korea, and Japan is provided by Evelyn S. Rawski, *Early Modern China and Northeast Asia: Cross-Border Perspectives* (Cambridge University Press, 2015).

Early modern European encounters with East Asia are described in Tonio Andrade, *Lost Colony: The Untold Story of China's First Great Victory over the West* (Princeton University Press, 2011); Charles Ralph Boxer, *The Christian Century in Japan, 1549–1650* (Berkeley: University of California Press, 1967); Reinier H. Hesselink, *Prisoners from Nambu: Reality and Make-Believe in 17ᵗʰ-Century Japanese Diplomacy* (Honolulu: University of Hawai'i Press, 2002); David E. Mungello, *The Great Encounter of China and the West, 1500–1800* (Lanham: Rowman and Littlefield, 1999); and Jonathan D. Spence, *The Memory Palace of Matteo Ricci* (Harmondsworth: Penguin Books, 1983). On the 1793 British embassy to China that may be said to mark the last major "traditional" encounter, see James Louis Hevia, *Cherishing Men from Afar: Qing Guest Ritual and the Macartney Embassy of 1793* (Durham: Duke University Press, 1995).

On the conjuncture of cultural, commercial, and political developments in late Ming China, see Timothy Brook, *The Confusions of Pleasure: Commerce and Culture in Ming China* (Berkeley: University of California Press, 1998); Chun-shu Chang and Shelley Hsueh-lun Chang, *Crisis and Transformation in Seventeenth-Century China: Society, Culture, and Modernity in Li Yü's World* (1992; Ann Arbor: University of Michigan Press, 1998); Craig Clunas, *Empire of Great Brightness: Visual and Material Cultures of Ming China, 1368–1644* (Honolulu: University of Hawai'i Press, 2007); Craig Clunas, *Superfluous Things: Material Culture and Social Status in Early Modern China* (1991; Honolulu: University of Hawai'i

Press, 2004); Ray Huang, *1587, a Year of no Significance: The Ming Dynasty in Decline* (New Haven: Yale University Press, 1981); and David Johnson, Andrew J. Nathan, and Evelyn S. Rawski (eds.), *Popular Culture in Late Imperial China* (Berkeley: University of California Press, 1985). Andrew H. Plaks argues that the sixteenth century witnessed the crystallization of full-length serious Chinese prose fiction in *The Four Masterworks of the Ming Novel: Ssu ta ch'i shu* (Princeton University Press, 1987).

For Qing Dynasty China, see Pamela Kyle Crossley, *The Manchus* (Oxford: Blackwell, 1997); Mark C. Elliott, *The Manchu Way: The Eight Banners and Ethnic Identity in Late Imperial China* (Stanford University Press, 2001); Laura Hostetler, *Qing Colonial Enterprise: Ethnography and Cartography in Early Modern China* (University of Chicago Press, 2001); Evelyn S. Rawski, *The Last Emperors: A Social History of Qing Imperial Institutions* (Berkeley: University of California Press, 1998); William T. Rowe, *China's Last Empire: The Great Qing* (Cambridge: Harvard University Press, 2009); and Frederic Wakeman, Jr., *The Great Enterprise: The Manchu Reconstruction of Imperial Order in Seventeenth-Century China* (2 vols., Berkeley: University of California Press, 1985). A fascinating study of the intersection of art, religion, culture, and power under the Qing Dynasty is Patricia Berger, *Empire of Emptiness: Buddhist Art and Political Authority in Qing China* (Honolulu: University of Hawai'i Press, 2003).

On late Chosŏn Korea, see JaHyun Kim Haboush and Martina Deuchler (eds.), *Culture and the State in Late Chosŏn Korea* (Cambridge: Harvard University Asia Center, 1999); James B. Palais, *Confucian Statecraft and Korean Institutions: Yu Hyŏngwŏn and the Late Chosŏn Dynasty* (Seattle: University of Washington Press, 1996); and Michael J. Seth, *A Concise History of Korea: From the Neolithic Period through the Nineteenth Century* (Lanham: Rowman and Littlefield, 2006), chapter 8.

Comprehensive treatment of early modern Japanese history is provided by Conrad D. Totman, in *Early Modern Japan* (Berkeley: University of California Press, 1993).

For early modern Japan before the establishment of the Tokugawa Shogunate, see Mary Elizabeth Berry, *Hideyoshi* (Cambridge: Harvard University Press, 1982); and George Elison and Bardwell L. Smith (eds.), *Warlords, Artists, and Commoners: Japan in the Sixteenth Century* (Honolulu: University of Hawai'i Press, 1981).

On Tokugawa era intellectual developments, see Masao Maruyama, *Studies in the Intellectual History of Tokugawa Japan*, trans. by Mikiso Hane (Princeton University Press, 1974); Tetsuo Najita, *Visions of Virtue in Tokugawa Japan: The Kaitokudō Merchant Academy of Osaka* (University of Chicago Press, 1987); and Herman Ooms, *Tokugawa Ideology: Early Constructs, 1570–1680* (Princeton University Press, 1985). For Tokugawa literature, see Donald Keene, *World within Walls: Japanese Literature of the Pre-Modern Era, 1600–1867* (New York: Grove Press, 1976). Mary Elizabeth Berry describes a Tokugawa period revolution in the dissemination of printed knowledge in *Japan in Print: Information and Nation in the Early Modern Period* (Berkeley: University of California Press, 2006). For excellent essays covering a wide range of Tokugawa period topics, see John W. Hall and Marius Jansen (eds.), *Studies in the Institutional History of Early Modern Japan* (Princeton University Press, 1968).

For aspects of Tokugawa culture that may have been conducive to later Japanese modernization and industrialization, see Robert Bellah, *Tokugawa Religion: The Cultural Roots of Modern Japan* (1957; New York: The Free Press, 1985); and Thomas C. Smith, *Native Sources of Japanese Industrialization, 1750–1920* (Berkeley: University of California Press, 1988).

7 Dai Viet (Vietnam before the Nineteenth Century)

When a new Vietnamese dynasty, the Nguyen (1802–1945), was established in 1802 in several important senses it was a realm "that had never before existed."[1] Never before had the whole of what we think of today as Vietnam been brought together under unified rule, and only now (from 1803), for the first time, did it actually begin to be called "Vietnam." A glance at any map of modern Vietnam also reveals a country with a somewhat peculiar configuration, which is partly a result of that surprisingly late political culmination and partly a natural consequence of physical geography. There are two large population centers: one in the north in the Red River delta, and one in the south along the Mekong River delta, awkwardly joined together by a long narrow neck of coastland squeezed between the mountains and the sea. Another consequence of Vietnam's historical evolution as a country is that it today contains some fifty-four different recognized ethnic minority populations (although ethnic diversity is hardly unique to Vietnam, and ethnic Vietnamese do constitute a large majority of the total population). Yet, despite some significant late developments, in other important senses Vietnam is truly ancient.

The Origins of Civilization in Vietnam

Wet-field rice agriculture may have been introduced (from farther north, having probably originated in the Yangzi River region of what is today China) into the Red River area shortly after 2500 BCE. Bronze metallurgy in the Red River region dates from perhaps 1500 BCE. By about 500 BCE, the Dong Son culture (ca. 600 BCE– 200 CE) – so named by modern archeologists because of a type-site located in northern Vietnam – had begun producing magnificent bronze drums of a characteristic style known as Heger I, demonstrating considerable cultural sophistication (see Figure 7.1). With Dong Son, the region also enters the Iron Age. Although these remarkable Dong Son bronze drums are commonly identified with Vietnam, they have been found widely scattered throughout Southeast Asia, and it is still a matter of debate whether their manufacture began in the Red River area of what is today Vietnam or in Yunnan Province of what is today southwest China. The

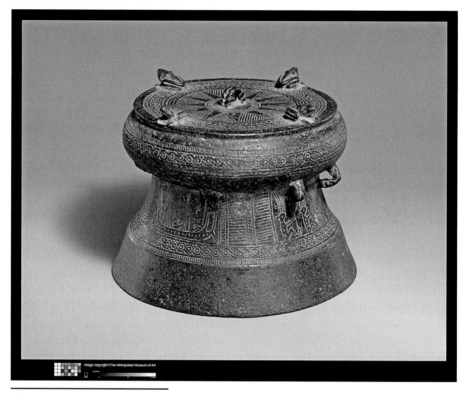

Figure 7.1. Dong Son bronze drum with four frogs, Vietnam, ca. 500 BCE–300 CE. The Metropolitan Museum of Art, New York. © The Metropolitan Museum of Art/Art Resource, New York.

largest concentration of these bronze drums, moreover (of a somewhat later and larger type known as Heger II), are found in Guangdong and Guangxi provinces in south China.[2] A distinctive type of earlier Neolithic (late Stone Age) pottery, decorated with impressed cord marks, has also been found widely distributed throughout the entire region from southeastern China to Southeast Asia.

The simple explanation for such apparently surprising distributions is that what today is southeast China, as far north as roughly the line of the Yangzi River, was, in late prehistory, culturally and linguistically more aligned with what is now Southeast Asia than with China. The word Viet (pronounced Yue in modern Mandarin) seems to have originated as the name of a mid-Zhou era Warring States kingdom (circa seventh century to 333 BCE) located in the vicinity of modern Zhejiang, on what was then the southern margins of the Chinese cultural horizon. Yue (Vietnamese: Viet) subsequently became a generic Chinese name for all of the various prehistoric non-Chinese peoples of the southeast, extending from Zhejiang (in what is now China) to the Red River (in what is now Vietnam). Independent non-Chinese kingdoms in what is today Fujian Province (across the straits from the island of Taiwan) were not conquered by the Chinese Han Dynasty until 110 BCE, and Fujian was not extensively settled by Chinese people until as late as the mid-eighth century CE[3] – although eventually Fujian became so thoroughly Sini-cized that it was home to the towering Neo-Confucian master Zhu Xi (1130–1200). Yunnan Province in southwest China, meanwhile, is directly con-nected to Vietnam by the Red River, and was the last province of China proper to be permanently brought into the empire – by Mongol conquerors in the thirteenth century (who, of course, were themselves not Chinese).

The prehistoric Yue (Viet) peoples were known for growing wet-field rice (unlike the dry-field-millet-cultivating "Chinese" of the northern Central Plain), tattooing their bodies, raising their houses above the ground on posts, riding boats, and chewing betel nuts (a mild stimulant still commonly used today in Taiwan, for example).[4] These Yue (Viet) were themselves internally quite diverse, as demon-strated by the standard Chinese label "the Hundred Yue." In the southernmost Yue (Viet) region that includes modern Guangdong, Guangxi, and northern Vietnam alone, even four and a half centuries after the initial Chinese imperial conquest in the third century BCE, in 231 CE it was still reported that their "customs are not uniform and languages are mutually unintelligible so that several interpreters are needed to communicate."[5]

According to Vietnamese legend, which was not recorded, however, until the fourteenth century CE, since the time of the mythical ancient Yellow Emperor in China there had been fifteen tribes in the Red River area of northern Vietnam. In the seventh century BCE, a man from one of these tribes used magic to subdue the others and establish a kingdom known as Van-lang, which was thereafter ruled by eighteen generations of Hung kings. A fifteenth-century CE Vietnamese history soon pushed the purported origins of these Hung kings back to 2879 BCE, and claimed that their rule had extended as far north as modern Hunan and Sichuan. According to another particularly cherished foundation myth (recorded as early as the fourteenth century CE), a Dragon Lord and a beautiful female mountain immortal named Au Co gave birth to a hundred eggs, the Dragon Lord eventually taking fifty back with him to the southern sea, and Au Co taking the remaining fifty to the lands of the Red River delta in the north, producing the line of Hung kings.[6] This legendary marriage of land and sea, and north and south, nicely captures the essence of a uniquely Vietnamese civilization.

Modern Vietnamese nationalists, naturally, like to see the realm of Van-lang and its Hung kings as the origins of the Vietnamese nation. Prehistoric culture in the region certainly did feed into what eventually became Vietnam, but, like all other nations in the world, Vietnam is not a primordial unchanging fixture but rather an evolving historical construct. The best recent archeological evidence seems to confirm the emergence of a sophisticated indigenous Bronze Age civilization in the Red River delta, having significant links to other societies in what are now Yunnan and Guangxi, and which was probably still organized around "relatively autonomous" villages. These may have consolidated into larger chiefdoms during the Dong Son period, and then finally generated the first true state in the Red River delta by around 300 BCE – perhaps in part as a ripple effect from the intense competition among the contemporary Warring States on the Central Plain in the distant north.[7]

Vietnamese prehistory begins to shade into more reliably recorded history around 258 BCE, when a ruler (reportedly from what is now Sichuan) supposedly overthrew the Van-lang kingdom and established a new kingdom called Au Lac in the Red River delta. He built a great capital city near modern Hanoi in the shape of a spiral, known as the "Ancient Spiral" (Co Loa). Around 179 BCE (although the exact date is uncertain), Au Lac is thought to have been conquered and absorbed into the somewhat more solidly historical kingdom of Nam Viet (Mandarin: Nan Yue, which means Southern Yue), based further north with its capital at what is now Guangzhou. But, while the ruins of an ancient city called Co Loa still indisputably remain today, and have been dated to roughly 300 BCE, it remains unverifiable whether they really should be identified with the semi-legendary kingdom of Au Lac, and also whether or not the city was really incorporated into the Guangzhou-based regime of Nam Viet (which, itself, should not too easily be assumed to mean "China" – Nam Viet was independent of the Han Dynasty and only partially Sinicized).[8] With the arrival of Chinese-language writing around this time, however, we do begin to finally have written records for the region.

Chinese Imperial Frontier

From the perspective of early imperial Chinese history, the most relevant geographic unit was not what is known today as Vietnam, but what the Chinese called Lingnan ("south of the mountain ranges"), a region that included modern Guangdong and Guangxi as well as northern Vietnam. The whole of Lingnan lay outside the original ancient Chinese cultural sphere, but in 214 BCE the First Emperor of Qin, attracted by the value of Lingnan's rhinoceros horn, ivory, kingfisher feathers, and pearls, supposedly marched a half million men into Lingnan and conquered it. After the death of the First Emperor, his Qin Dynasty began rapidly unraveling, and a local Qin official named Zhao Tuo (Vietnamese: Trieu Da; dates uncertain) proclaimed himself the independent king of Nam Viet (Southern Yue) in 207 BCE. This Nam Viet, with its capital at Guangzhou, was a breakaway fragment of the Qin Empire, and its first king, Zhao Tuo, supposedly came from the northern Central Plain, but he was also influenced by local customs and greeted emissaries from the Chinese Han Dynasty like a native, with his hair in a bun and squatting on the ground.[9]

The kingdom of Nam Viet (Southern Yue) retained its effective independence for almost a century, sometimes even invoking Chinese-style imperial titles, until it was conquered and absorbed into the Han Dynasty in 111 BCE. It was then administratively subdivided into nine commanderies, including two on Hainan Island and three within the borders of modern Vietnam. Local native culture and society seem to have been little affected by this incorporation into the Han Empire, however – and this native culture extended across both sides of the modern China–Vietnam border. In 40 CE two sisters, Trung Trac and Trung Nhi, who were daughters of a Lac general (the Lac were a regional Viet identity) in the Red River area, had become ensnared in some kind of legal entanglement by a local Han official and angrily rose in rebellion. Native populations across an area stretching from what is today southern Guangxi to central Vietnam responded, and Trung Trac briefly established herself as ruler over some sixty-five towns.[10] It was only after the suppression of this rebellion in 43 CE that the victorious Han Dynasty finally began vigorously enforcing Han law and Han cultural standards. Significant numbers of colonists from the north may have also begun arriving around this time, and archeological evidence confirms that Han-style brick tombs began to replace the Dong Son style in the Red River area.

After the Han Dynasty conquest of the kingdom of Nam Viet in 111 BCE, the entire region of Lingnan had been organized into an imperial administrative unit called Jiaozhi (Vietnamese: Giao-chi). The Han governor's seat was at first located on the Red River in what is now Vietnam, but, after only a few years, in 106 BCE, it was moved north to modern Guangxi. The Red River, meanwhile, may have been the principal terminus for Han Dynasty maritime trade, and, as of 2 CE, the registered population of the Red River delta greatly exceeded that of the area near modern Guangzhou.[11]

In 187 CE, as the Han Dynasty began its final descent into warlordism and political fragmentation, a man named Shi Xie (137–226) was appointed administrator of the commandery, or subregion, located in the lower Red River. Although his ancestors had supposedly come from the north and he had studied at the Han imperial capital, his family had lived in Lingnan for seven generations, and he was in some senses a local. Over the next few decades he and his relatives governed the whole of Lingnan so effectively that the region became a haven for refugees from the war-torn north, and autonomously enough that Shi Xie sometimes even came to be referred to as "king." Nonetheless, Shi was careful to send annual gifts of local products, and eventually even a son to serve as a hostage, to the emerging Three Kingdoms state of Wu (located in south China, but north of Lingnan, with its capital at the site of modern Nanjing).

Three Kingdoms Wu took advantage of Shi Xie's death in 226 to bring Lingnan more directly under central control, for the first time dividing the region between the part that is now in China, which was named Guangzhou (meaning "Guang Province" – the origin of the modern city name Guangzhou, owing to the practice of referring to the urban seats of early Chinese administrative regions by the same name as the entire region), and what is today the Red River region of Vietnam, which was then called Jiaozhou ("Jiao Province"). After resistance to Three Kingdoms Wu rule by Shi Xie's son was suppressed and the Shi family slaughtered, Guangzhou and Jiaozhou were briefly reunited, but in 264 the division was renewed – this time permanently. Wu, and subsequent Chinese Southern dynasties, were motivated to try to bring Lingnan under greater central control in order to tap the profitable South Sea trade that congregated there. Beginning around 227, Wu also dispatched several naval expeditions to explore Hainan Island, some other now unidentifiable islands, and to the Cham and Khmer regions even further south, as an indication of Wu's interest in South Sea maritime possibilities. (See Map 7.1.)

Map 7.1. Lingnan, ca. 400 CE

From the mid-fifth century, however, the Red River area grew increasingly autonomous, and even came to be described (metaphorically, since it was actually a river delta) as "a completely isolated island."[12] In 541, a man named Li Bi (Vietnamese: Ly Bi; d. 548) led a great revolt against Chinese administration. Although northern descent was claimed for Li Bi, and he had been a disappointed office seeker at the Chinese Southern dynasty capital, in 544 he proclaimed himself an independent sovereign emperor of Nam Viet (Southern Yue). Li Bi was killed in 548, but under his successors the Red River region continued to enjoy de facto independence for more than a half-century (a total of some sixty-one years), until it was finally reconquered by the Sui Dynasty, based in north China, in 602. Not content with retaking the Red River delta, in 605 the Sui also launched an invasion of the Cham regions further south in what is now central Vietnam, but suffered heavy losses due to tropical disease.

Under the Sui and Tang dynasties, the Red River delta was once again part of a newly reunified Chinese Empire, but as late as the seventh century the whole of Lingnan (including modern Guangdong and Guangxi as well as the Red River) could still be described as lying outside the natural borders of China.[13] To the end of the Tang Dynasty in 907, much of Lingnan remained remote and undeveloped – home to non-Chinese aboriginal peoples. The outstanding exceptions were the two great port cities that served as the capitals of the two major administrative subdivisions of Lingnan: Guangzhou (modern Guangzhou city) and Jiaozhou (near modern Hanoi). Thanks to a thriving South Sea trade, these had become prosperous Chinese cities. As a seventh-century history reported, "Merchants who go there often become rich."[14]

During the Han Dynasty, the Red River delta had contained a much larger total registered population than Guangzhou and was probably a more important center of maritime trade, but by the Tang Dynasty these relative positions had been reversed, and Guangzhou was now far more important. This reversal was probably the result of several developments: from about the fourth century shipping was increasingly striking out boldly across the ocean rather than crawling up the coast (which had previously made the Red River both the first and last port of call within the Chinese Empire); the Red River region was cut off and isolated from the bulk of the Chinese Empire by strong non-Chinese aboriginal chiefdoms in the intervening highland regions of southern Guangxi and Guangdong; the massive Chinese southward population migration that began in the fourth century was mostly directed to what is now southeast China (rather than the extreme south that is now Vietnam); and the Southern dynasty Chinese imperial capital, which was located at modern Nanjing, was more conveniently oriented towards Guangzhou than the Red River.

In 679, Tang Dynasty Jiaozhou (the Red River area) was redesignated as the Protectorate of Annan (Vietnamese: Annam), meaning "the Pacified South." Annam would thereafter remain a common name for Vietnam until modern times. Parallel Tang Dynasty protectorates were also established at roughly the same time in the "Pacified West," "Pacified East," and "Pacified North," and officials known as Protector-Generals were assigned to pacify, subjugate, and patrol the "foreigners" in these frontier regions.[15] This designation as Annam is a fairly unmistakable acknowledgment that the Red River area was viewed as a remote and not very thoroughly Chinese frontier under the Tang Dynasty. Among the mid-Tang Dynasty Protector-Generals of Annam were a Central Asian merchant, and a man who had been born in Japan named Abe no Nakamaro (ca. 698–770), who had come to Tang China as a student and stayed, becoming a high-ranking Chinese official.[16]

By the late 800s, Tang imperial authority over Annam had weakened, and the Red River area came under the control of local great families. After 907, the Tang Dynasty had ceased to exist altogether, and China lapsed into another period of division, known as the Five Dynasties (in the north, 907–960), and the Ten Kingdoms (in the south, 907–979). One of the southern regimes, Southern Han (917–971), which was based at Guangzhou, attempted to incorporate the Red

River delta. From the perspective of Guangzhou, the whole of Lingnan probably still appeared to constitute a kind of natural unit. Despite its evocation of the hallowed Chinese dynastic name Han, however, the Southern Han ruling family may not have even been ethnic "Han Chinese," but rather indigenous southern tribal chieftains.[17] In 931, a local general drove the Southern Han forces out of Annam. In 938, a Southern Han invasion fleet attempting to reconquer Annam was annihilated by the Red River strongman of the day, Ngo Quyen (d. 944), who proclaimed himself king in 939.

Dai Viet

Annam was now independent, but after Ngo Quyen's death in 944 it quickly disintegrated into warlordism, and was only reunified in 963 by Dinh Bo Linh (924–979). In 968, Dinh Bo Linh promoted himself from king to emperor, invoking the Chinese imperial title (Mandarin Chinese: *huangdi*; Vietnamese: *hoang de*), and calling his new dynasty Dai Co Viet ("Great Viet"). Dai was the local pronunciation of a Chinese character meaning "great," while Co was an indigenous non-Chinese term meaning essentially the same thing. The name was therefore redundant, and after 1054 the Co was dropped, becoming simply Dai Viet.

The Chinese title "emperor" indicated a supposedly universal supreme sovereign, and theoretically there could only be one legitimate emperor in the entire world at any given time. After most of the Chinese mainland had been reunified under the new Song Dynasty, therefore, the Song court naturally did not acknowledge Viet imperial pretensions. But the Song Dynasty, which was founded in 960, did not subdue the independent Southern Han regime in Guangzhou until 971. Having finally extended its power to the far south of what is today China, in 975 the Song recognized Dinh Bo Linh in Annam as a subordinate vassal king of the administrative region in the Red River delta, using the old Han-era name for the region: Jiaozhi (Vietnamese: Giao Chi).

Not content with that, in 980–981 the Song Dynasty attempted an outright invasion and annexation of the Red River area, but the invasion was incompetently led, and failed. After the failed invasion, both Song and Great Viet lapsed into acceptance of a nominal vassalage relationship, with Great Viet actually independent (and, for internal purposes, ruled by its own sovereign emperor), but for outward diplomatic purposes represented as a subordinate vassal king of the Chinese emperor. The second Song emperor was persuaded that further efforts at reconquest of the Red River delta would not be cost-effective, because Annam "is burning hot and pestilential, and twenty to thirty percent of our troops will die before seeing combat. Even if we get it, we will be unable to hold it."[18] In 1174, the Song Dynasty elevated its Viet vassal's title to King of the Country of Annam (Annam quoc vuong) – that is, from a mere administrative subregion of the Chinese Empire to a fully-fledged "country" (Mandarin: *guo*; Vietnamese: *quoc*).

The prehistoric natives of the lowland Red River area had most likely been speakers of an Austroasiatic language, related to other languages spoken in mainland Southeast Asia, but completely unrelated to Chinese. Over the millennium of Chinese rule, however, the distinction that was most obviously visible to contemporaries had not been between "Chinese" and "Vietnamese" people, but between "civilized" imperial subjects and marginalized aboriginal tribespeople.[19] Even after independence in the tenth century, those aboriginal tribespeople did not suddenly reassert some long-suppressed primordial Vietnamese identity and take over the newly independent state of Great Viet. It was, instead, the former "civilized" imperial subjects who continued to be the elite of the new country. At the time of independence, many of them may have actually been native speakers of a local variant of the Chinese language. However, these elite families were surrounded by humble villagers who were less proficient in Chinese, and still spoke the old languages. Before long, the elite switched to speaking the dominant surrounding non-Chinese language, but imported much Chinese vocabulary and other features of the Chinese language in the process, thereby creating what we know today as Vietnamese. (A similar thing happened to the French-speaking Norman conquerors of England after 1066, who eventually shifted to speaking English, but brought with them much French vocabulary.)[20]

Written Chinese remained the predominant language of writing in Vietnam until the nineteenth century, although newly coined characters and other characters employed for their phonetic value rather than their meaning began to be used by the thirteenth century, if not earlier, to write the native Vietnamese language, in a system known as *Nom*. By the seventeenth century, vernacular Vietnamese language writing had produced an impressive body of native literature. In the twentieth century, French colonial rule in Vietnam eliminated Chinese characters altogether. The result today is a Vietnamese language that is unrelated to Chinese and written in the (European) Roman alphabet, but which still shares a great deal of vocabulary (perhaps 60 percent, or even more) with Chinese.[21]

Although Dinh Bo Linh is regarded as the first Vietnamese emperor, his death in 979 left a young child as heir. Facing invasion from the Chinese Song Dynasty, a military leader named Le Hoan (941–1005) deposed the child ruler and married its mother, making himself the new emperor. He defeated the Song invasion, and founded what is known as the Former Le Dynasty (980–1009).[22] After Le Hoan died, he was followed through two brief reigns by other Le family members, but when the last of those died in 1009 without an adult heir, a commander of the imperial guard named Ly Cong Uan (974–1028) seized power. Ly moved the capital to the site of modern Hanoi (then called Thang-long), and under his new Ly Dynasty (1009–1225) the independent state in northern Vietnam at last achieved stability. (See Map 7.2.)

Ly Cong Uan had been orphaned as a child and raised by a Buddhist monk, from whom he obtained the surname Ly. As emperor, he maintained a close relationship with the Buddhist establishment, and Buddhist monks organized much of the economic activity of the early Viet state. Viet Buddhism was broadly of the East Asian variety, but Indian deities such as Indra were more prominent

Map 7.2 Dai Viet, ca. 1200 CE

than elsewhere in East Asia, and early Ly rulers also incorporated non-Buddhist native cults and spirits to buttress their authority, giving the regime a local Vietnamese flavor.

The country of Dai Viet began actively engaging in maritime trade with Java and other parts of Southeast Asia, and, after another war with the Song Dynasty, the northern border with China was fixed in 1088 essentially where it still is today. In 1070, a shrine was built in the capital to the Duke of Zhou and Confucius, which later came to be known as the Temple of Literature (Van mieu), and which is today sometimes described as Vietnam's first university. In 1075, Chinese-style examinations were conducted for the first time. These examinations covered Buddhist and Daoist material as well as Confucian, however, and despite some Chinese-style elements the Ly regime was less bureaucratically organized and centralized than the Chinese Empire. During the Ly Dynasty, what were still largely autonomous local leaders were bound to the emperor by personal ties and (animal) blood oaths of allegiance.

Eventually, Ly Dynasty monarchs fell under the influence of their mothers' families, especially the powerful Tran family who held large estates in the coastal Red River area. The last Ly emperor, who was married to a Tran woman, abdicated to a young daughter in 1224 and retired to a temple (where he was compelled to commit suicide in 1226). His daughter (despite having a Tran mother) then married a Tran boy, and two months later she abdicated in her husband's favor. He became the first Tran monarch in 1225, founding a Tran Dynasty that would last from 1225 to 1400.

To avoid the danger of domination by maternal families that had so plagued the late Ly Dynasty, Tran monarchs frequently married into their own family. Four generations of Tran rulers married their own cousins. They also ensured a stable succession by adopting the practice of abdicating the throne to an adult heir, and then continuing to exercise a degree of authority as retired emperors, creating simultaneous junior and senior rulers. Despite taking such measures to ensure internal stability, the new Tran Dynasty was soon challenged from outside by no fewer than three invasions by the world-conquering Mongols.

In January of 1258, a Mongol army first arrived on the border of Dai Viet from Yunnan in the northwest, possibly with the idea of using Dai Viet as an invasion route to outflank the Southern Song Dynasty from the south and finish the conquest of China (Southern Song was not fully subjugated by the Mongols until 1279). The Mongol invasion force encountered resistance led by the Dai Viet emperor riding an elephant, and, although the Mongols captured the capital, they were forced by disease and hunger to withdraw back to Yunnan after only nine days. In 1283, a massive Mongol naval invasion fleet captured a Cham port in what is now central Vietnam, south of Dai Viet, but Dai Viet supported the Chams on this occasion and refused land passage to Mongol armies, isolating the Mongol forces in the southern Cham regions. In response, in 1285, Khubilai Khan's own son led a land invasion of Dai Viet from the north, and Dai Viet was caught in a pincer attack between the two Mongol armies in the north and in the south. The Dai Viet capital fell to the Mongols a second time, but once again the Mongols were soon forced to withdraw to escape disease and the oppressive tropical climate, and the Dai Viet capital was recaptured within six months. In 1287, there was yet a third Mongol invasion of Dai Viet by both land and sea, but after some Mongol supply ships were sunk, the Mongols withdrew again. Dai Viet now offered tribute to Khubilai Khan, based in China, and after Khubilai Khan's death in 1294, plans for further Mongol invasions were abandoned.

Under the Tran Dynasty, Dai Viet heroically repulsed three Mongol assaults, but from the later perspective of a more thoroughly Confucianized fifteenth-century Vietnam, Tran royal family intermarriage (which was shockingly incestuous by Chinese standards), Tran identification with bodily tattoos (an ancient Viet tradition that was alien to Chinese eyes), and Tran gambling, drunkenness, and other deviations from Confucian norms, all appeared disturbingly unorthodox.[23] By the late 1300s, the Tran Dynasty began to be plagued by droughts, pestilence, rural distress, and rebellion. In 1400, a regent named Ho Quy Ly (1336–1407) usurped the throne. The Tran family appealed to what was by then the Ming Dynasty in China for support against this usurper, and the third Ming emperor (who had grand ambitions – this was the same emperor who also sponsored the famous Ming voyages of world exploration under Zheng He) began an intervention in 1406 to restore the Tran family. After the Tran claimant to the throne died, however, the Ming attempted to reorganize the Viet lands into a regular part of the Chinese Empire, reviving for them the old administrative name Jiaozhi (Vietnamese: Giao-chi). The Ming also implemented a deliberate policy of destroying or removing to China all unorthodox written material, including everything written in the native Vietnamese language, which had the unfortunate consequence that few Vietnamese books survive from before the fifteenth century.

The attempt to directly reincorporate the Viet lands into Ming Dynasty China turned out to be a net drain on Ming imperial resources, however, even as corrupt Ming officials alienated the local population by enriching themselves at local expense. Resistance smoldered for several years, and then reignited in 1418 into guerrilla warfare, especially in the mountains, under a new leader named Le Loi (1385–1433). After the death of the third Ming emperor in 1424, the Ming invasion lost its imperial sponsor, and by 1428 the Ming occupation forces had been expelled, and a new Le Dynasty established (known as Later Le; 1428–1527, or, including periods of disruption and division, 1428–1788). By 1431, even the Ming had recognized Le Loi as king.

The rural distress of the late 1300s had provoked criticism of alleged Buddhist neglect of secular obligations and aristocratic indifference to the lives of commoners, and encouraged the spread of Confucian thinking. Although Chinese-style examinations had begun as early as the eleventh century, top Dai Viet officials long continued to be drawn from wellborn families. It was only now, under the Le Dynasty in the fifteenth century, that the examinations were opened up to most men, and a Chinese-style Confucian mandarinate began to be recruited. It was also in the fifteenth century that Dai Viet began to seriously expand its territory into the south, in 1471 capturing the important Cham city of Vijaya on the south central coast.

Champa

The people of Champa were seafaring Austronesian language speakers, linguistically related to the later Malays, some of whose ancestors may have settled in what is now central Vietnam around 500 BCE. The prehistoric culture in this area, circa 500 BCE–100 CE, contemporary with the northern Dong Son culture, is notable for its jar burials, and shows archeological evidence of trade with China, India, and possibly the Philippines, Thailand, and Myanmar, as well as with Dong Son in the Red River delta.[24] Chinese records tell of the founding of a state that the Chinese called Linyi near modern Hue around 192 CE, when, as the Han Dynasty was collapsing into chaos, the son of a minor local official killed the magistrate of the southernmost Han frontier county and proclaimed himself king.

It is uncertain whether or not the state that the Chinese sources called Linyi was the same entity that later definitely called itself Champa. Chinese written sources continued to use the name Linyi until 758, when it was replaced by other Chinese-language names. A Chinese name that seems to phonetically transcribe a word pronounced like "Champa" does not appear until 875. The oldest known native use of the name Champa, meanwhile, appears on an inscription found not far from modern Da Nang dating from the late 500s.[25] Early Chinese descriptions of Linyi culture report that the people wrote on tree leaves, went barefoot and wore sarongs, and valued women above men. It was also said that they worshiped Buddha, wrote in an Indian script, and had notables they called Brahmans.[26] (See Figure 7.2.)

In the early centuries of the Common Era merchants from the Indian subcontinent had fanned out across much of Southeast Asia, bringing with them educated Buddhist monks and Hindu Brahmans. Sanskrit became the language of courts and of sacred ceremonies throughout the region (although it is doubtful whether Sanskrit was ever actually much used as a language of daily life). In the Cham regions of what is now central Vietnam, from the earliest known inscriptions, dating from perhaps the second century, until the ninth century, all are written in Sanskrit (except for one: a fourth-century inscription in the Cham language that is the oldest known example in any Southeast Asian language). Not for nothing did French colonialists later call the region "Indochina." The Indian influences were significant. Cham kings erected stone *linga* and identified with Shiva, the Lord of the Universe, and with other Indian divinities, who were often eclectically worshipped side-by-side with Buddhist and indigenous spirits.

The geography of Champa lacked the kind of big agricultural plain that is conducive to large-scale early state-building. Rather than understanding Champa as a single centralized kingdom, some recent scholars have re-envisioned it "as a multi-ethnic, multi-centered" realm.[27] Champa seems to have consisted of a loosely affiliated network of riverine centers that grew rice, and exchanged salt and other goods with highland peoples in exchange for rhinoceros horn, ivory, sandalwood, and camphor, with which they engaged in maritime trade.

The strong Indian influence seems to have gradually faded. Between the eleventh and thirteenth centuries, Sanskrit inscriptions were increasingly replaced by the Cham language, and after the thirteenth century all are written in Cham.

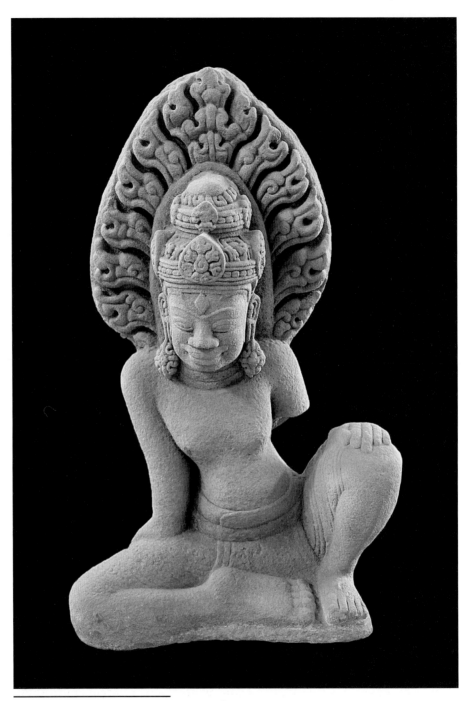

Figure 7.2. A Cham Bodhisattva in the Rajalilasana position, ninth to tenth century. Cham Museum, Danang, Vietnam. Pictures from History/David Henley/Bridgeman Images.

By this time there was also an important Islamic and Arab trading presence. Champa, meanwhile, had frequently warred with Dai Viet to its north. Neither Dai Viet nor Champa achieved lasting military supremacy until the fall of the Cham center at Vijaya in 1471, which is an event that is often thought to mark the Viet conquest of Champa. The new Viet military advantage over Champa in the fifteenth century may have been partly due to the Viet use of Chinese-style muskets and artillery (an advantage that was only accelerated by the introduction of European firearms in the seventeenth century). Nonetheless, a Cham kingdom in the south, known as Panduranga, survived until 1832, and the last Cham vassal king was not deposed until 1835. Today, the relatively small number of identifiable surviving Chams constitute one of the minority populations of Vietnam.

Vietnam Reaches the Mekong

Another of the minority peoples of modern Vietnam are the Khmers. In the early centuries of the Common Era a realm that is referred to in Chinese texts as Funan emerged in the lower Mekong River delta, in the far south. Like Champa, Funan adopted many aspects of Indian culture, and, also like Champa, it may not have really been a single centralized kingdom. For several centuries Funan was a vital entrepôt in Eurasian trade. Artifacts from Rome, Persia, Greece, and India have all been found at Funan sites. With the development by the fifth century of entirely maritime trade routes through the Straits of Malacca (which avoided the need for an overland portage across the neck of the Malay peninsula), Funan may have to some extent been bypassed by east–west shipping, and, accompanying a local shift in emphasis from coastal trade to inland rice cultivation, the name Funan disappeared from Chinese textual sources and was replaced by a different name after about the sixth century. By the ninth century, the well-known Khmer state of Angkor had emerged, based on the northwest shore of the great lake Tonle Sap in the upper Mekong River region of what is today Cambodia. The lower Mekong delta, however, remained under Khmer (that is, Cambodian) control until the seventeenth century. It also remained sparsely populated.

In 1623, the Nguyen family lord of southern Dai Viet obtained permission from the Khmer king (in exchange for support against the growing Thai influence in the region) to establish a customs post at what later became the city known as Saigon. In 1679, some three thousand Ming Dynasty loyalists, fleeing the Manchu conquest of China, settled on the lower Mekong and further developed international trade. In the late 1600s, a Chinese immigrant from Guangdong known as Mac Cuu (Mandarin: Mo Jiu; 1655–1735) settled on the Gulf of Siam at what is today the Vietnamese coastal border with Cambodia, under the sponsorship of the Khmer king. In 1708, he switched his allegiance to the Nguyen lord of southern Dai Viet, bringing his port under Viet overlordship. By 1779, Nguyen family dominance was ascendant throughout virtually the entire lower Mekong delta.

Dai Viet, meanwhile, had long been internally divided. In 1527, an imperial guardsman named Mac Dang Dung (1483–1541) had usurped the throne, forcing the Le emperor to commit suicide. Le family pretenders continued to claim legitimacy, however, part of the time from a base in exile in what is now Laos. In 1593, they finally defeated the Mac family and restored the Le Dynasty, but by that time two different families of Le Dynasty loyalist supporters had emerged as the real powers: the Trinh and Nguyen families. While the Le Dynasty nominally continued to rule, the Trinh family actually controlled the imperial court in the north, and the Nguyen family became viceroys farther south, based at Hue, from where they presided over a Viet expansion south into the Mekong delta in the seventeenth century. In 1630, the Nguyen built fortified walls between the Trinh and Nguyen spheres of control at a point where the mountains came down to only about six miles from the sea, and from 1627 to 1672 the two regimes were frequently at war. In 1744, the Nguyen lord promoted his title to king, although Le Dynasty reign periods continued to be used for dating purposes in acknowledgment of nominal Le imperial legitimacy.

When European Catholic missionaries began arriving in Vietnam in the seventeenth century, they therefore found what appeared to be two separate warring countries. The northern country they called Tonkin (a Europeanization of the Le Dynasty name for what is now Hanoi, Dong Kinh, meaning "Eastern Capital"), and the southern country they called Cochinchina (a term derived from the old Chinese administrative place name that the Europeans had picked up from the Malays and Arabs, Jiaozhi – which, ironically, had originally been located in the north but which now referred to the south – with "China" added to distinguish it from the state in India that was also called Cochin).[28] The Nguyen family regime in the south initially thrived on maritime trade with Japan, Southeast Asia, China, and Europe. The first Nguyen lord even took a Japanese merchant as an adopted son. The Trinh-dominated regime in the north, by comparison, was less commercially inclined.

The first Portuguese ship arrived near Da Nang in 1535, and a Catholic mission began in 1615. Although the first missionaries were Portuguese and Spanish, eventually the French Society of Foreign Missions became the dominant missionary presence. Early secular European interests in Vietnam were largely disappointed, because Vietnam was too strongly organized to easily succumb to colonization and lacked the rich commercial opportunities presented by China or the Spice Islands (in present-day Indonesia). The Christian missionary effort continued, therefore, but by the end of the seventeenth century most of the European business offices (known as "factories") in Dai Viet had closed.

The Last Dynasty

Inflation in the eighteenth century, due to the rising value of the copper that was used in making coins and a switch to zinc coinage in 1746, impoverished the southern Viet economy, while the north had never been especially commercially active. The Nguyen court in the south responded to inflation by increasing the taxes on foreign shipping, which had an especially large impact on the port at Hoi

An, south of the Nguyen capital at Hue, where the harbor was also suffering from siltation. All this contributed to a shift of shipping patterns from Hoi An to the more remote southern Mekong River. Economic distress was therefore particularly acute in the central portion of the Nguyen realm, and it erupted into violence in 1771, when three brothers from Tay Son village (about midway between Hue and the Mekong delta) began a rebellion, known as the Tay Son Rebellion, with support from minority highlanders and Chams. By 1776, one of the rebels had proclaimed himself king. Much of the Nguyen family was killed, but a young nephew of the last Nguyen king, Nguyen Phuc Anh (1762–1820), escaped to an island that may have been either in the Gulf of Thailand or in the South China Sea, and eventually to Thailand.

In the north, the Trinh lords were also defeated by the rebels, and the oldest of the three rebel brother leaders married a daughter of the Le emperor, claiming to restore the Le Dynasty. The Le emperor appealed to Beijing for assistance against the rebels, however, and Beijing dispatched an army to intervene in 1788. The rebels then deposed the Le emperor and founded a new dynasty, successfully repulsing the Qing Dynasty expeditionary force from China. The Qing subsequently recognized the Tay Son leader as king, and, in 1790, the Tay Son king was pressured to personally participate in an embassy to Beijing to congratulate the Qianlong emperor on the occasion of his eightieth birthday. In an amazing story, the Tay Son sent an imposter to Beijing rather than the real king.[29]

Meanwhile, the refugee prince Nguyen Phuc Anh experienced fluctuating fortunes, but gained the support of a local French missionary (the Bishop Pierre Pigneau de Behaine; 1741–1799), who, in 1787, took Anh's eldest son with him to Paris. A treaty was obtained from France, but no tangible assistance was available (the French monarchy was in the midst of a severe financial crisis, and would fall to the Revolution in 1789), so, in 1788, the bishop raised private funds from French bases in India, obtaining two French ships and a small group of French adventurers. By 1788, Nguyen Phuc Anh had permanently retaken Saigon, and, partly thanks to this French assistance, by 1802 he had unified all of Vietnam – for the first time.

Nguyen Phuc Anh became the Gia Long emperor (r. 1802–1820) of a new Nguyen Dynasty (1802–1945), establishing his imperial capital at Hue, midway between the population centers in the Red River and Mekong deltas. Hue had been the seat of Nguyen family power since the seventeenth century. The Tay Son rebels had attempted to make vernacular Vietnamese *Nom* the official language of writing, but the prestige of literary Chinese writing was now officially restored. By this time, many of the features of what we think of as "traditional" Vietnamese culture had reached maturity.

The Vietnamese emperor and his mandarins appeared Chinese-style and East Asian, while by contrast the Vietnamese peasantry often "looked Southeast Asian."[30] Since the fifteenth or sixteenth century, village life had centered upon a characteristic Vietnamese-style community hall. An emphasis on village-based wet-field rice cultivation had sharpened the contrast between lowland Vietnamese and highland minority peoples, and, unlike Champa and many of the islands of

Southeast Asia, Vietnam had a heavily agricultural civilization that was relatively little oriented toward maritime trade. And, although Frenchmen had played some role in the establishment of the new Nguyen Dynasty, because they had not been directly backed by the French government the Nguyen emperor did not feel the need to make concessions to France. Indeed, after the first Nguyen emperor's death, his successors viewed Europeans with some suspicion. At the same time, however, the early nineteenth-century Nguyen army was already about half European-style in equipment and training.[31] "Premodern" Vietnam was already, in some ways, modernizing.

For Further Reading

Premodern Vietnam remains insufficiently studied. An important pioneering volume on early Vietnam is Keith Weller Taylor, *The Birth of Vietnam* (Berkeley: University of California Press, 1983). An archeological perspective is provided by Nam C. Kim, *The Origins of Ancient Vietnam* (Oxford University Press, 2015). For the period of Chinese rule, see Jennifer Holmgren, *Chinese Colonization of Northern Vietnam: Administrative Geography and Political Development in the Tongking Delta, First to Sixth Centuries* AD (Canberra: Australian National University, 1980). For Nguyen Dynasty Vietnam, see Alexander Barton Woodside, *Vietnam and the Chinese Model: A Comparative Study of Nguyên and Ch'ing Civil Government in the First Half of the Nineteenth Century* (Cambridge, MA: Harvard University Press, 1971).

The most comprehensive account of the whole of Vietnamese history is Keith Weller Taylor, *A History of the Vietnamese* (Cambridge University Press, 2013). Another valuable recent effort is Vu Hong Lien and Peter D. Sharrock, *Descending Dragon, Rising Tiger: A History of Vietnam* (London: Reaktion Books, 2014).

On Champa, see Trần Kỳ Phương and Bruce M. Lockhart, eds., *The Cham of Vietnam: History, Society and Art* (National University of Singapore, 2011).

For an overview of premodern Vietnam as part of Southeast Asia, see Nicholas Tarling, ed., *The Cambridge History of Southeast Asia, vol. I. From Early Times to c. 1800* (Cambridge University Pres, 1992). A fascinating perspective on premodern Vietnam in relation to the whole of Eurasia is provided by Victor Lieberman, *Strange Parallels: Southeast Asia in Global Context, c. 800–1830*, 2 vols. (Cambridge University Press, 2003–2009).

8 The Nineteenth-Century Encounter of Civilizations

Industrialization and the Rise of New Great Powers

The world was fundamentally transformed in the nineteenth century by the Promethean new powers unleashed by the industrial and scientific revolutions. Modern transportation and communications technologies, such as the steamship, the railway, and the telegraph (a telegraphic link between China and Europe was first established in 1871), knit the planet together more tightly than ever before. New military technologies – including ironclad steam warships and machine guns – gave industrialized countries unprecedented military superiority over nonindustrialized peoples. The power and wealth of these industrialized countries also made them widely attractive models, although a perceptible time lag occurred before many peoples outside the early-industrializing core perceived the apparent irresistibility of modernization, and many never welcomed it. "From 1860 to 1914, the web of steel [railways] spread throughout the world, and so did the political, financial, and engineering techniques that had evolved along with it," yet "among non-Western peoples, only the Japanese showed real enthusiasm for railways," and even in Japan, the first eighteen-mile stretch of rail line was not laid until 1872 (see Figure 8.1).[1] In China, the first short rail line was built by a British firm in 1876, and then was purchased by the local Chinese government the following year and dismantled.

Despite this delayed start, by the end of the nineteenth century a virtual tidal wave of Westernization was beginning to sweep the world. Consciously Western-style clothing and hairstyles became widely fashionable, especially among elites. In the 1870s, for example, Japanese samurai cut their topknots and tentatively began adopting Western fashions. By 1900, it is said that most Japanese men owned at least one Western-style suit and hat. Representative democratic government also seemed to be the irresistible trend of the times by the end of the century. By 1890, Japan had a written modern Western-style constitution and an elected legislature (called the Diet in English, *kokkai* in Japanese). Soon after the turn into the twentieth century, even China adopted a formal constitution and held elections

Figure 8.1. Hiroshige III (ca. 1843–1894), "Picture of a Steam Locomotive along the Yokohama Waterfront," ca. 1874, Japanese woodblock print. Arthur M. Sackler Gallery, Smithsonian Institution, Washington, DC: Gift of the Daval Foundation, from the Collection of Ambassador and Mrs. William Leonhart, S1991.151a-c.

for provincial assemblies, and in 1912–1913, China experimented with its first nationwide democratic elections.

In many ways, this nineteenth-century wave of Westernization foreshadowed the current phenomenon of globalization in the late twentieth and early twenty-first centuries. Transportation and communications became not only much more rapid but also more standardized. The newly constructed railroads were everywhere quite similar operations, and typically employed standard gauges of track. An International Telegraph Union was established in 1865 and a Universal Postal Union in 1875. A global modern business culture also emerged, based on shared technology and managerial techniques. By the end of the nineteenth century, there were integrated global capital markets, nearly instantaneous communications via the telegraph, refrigerated shipping of perishable food from farms and ranches in the far-flung corners of the world, and new global markets for such things as coffee, bananas, rubber, copper, and tin. Indeed, as a percentage of gross national product, international capital flows peaked in the early twentieth century (from Britain) and have never been matched again since, while international trade as a percentage of total output did not return to its 1913 (that is, pre-World War I) levels again until as late as the 1980s.[2]

Some predicted that growing international economic integration would make war between developed countries impossible. The outbreak of World War I in 1914 proved this assumption rather spectacularly wrong, and also dealt a blow to the interdependent international financial system, especially in Europe. The onset of the Great Depression and rise of fascism and communism by the 1930s then brought this earlier age of globalization to a close. But before that happened, much of the world had already been irrevocably changed. In East Asia, the peak period of Westernization actually did not arrive until the early twentieth century, but the deep forces underlying these changes had intruded much earlier.

Industrialization was the key. Although the early achievements of the European scientific revolution are justly much celebrated, the extent to which pure science contributed to early industrialization remains a matter of debate. Pioneering breakthroughs in technological invention, and early examples of relatively large-scale production, also did not necessarily automatically lead to an industrial revolution. The premodern porcelain workshops at Jingdezhen in southeast China, for example, which employed some seventy thousand workers, have been called "the largest industrial complex anywhere in the world prior to the eighteenth century," and in the seventeenth and eighteenth centuries, China exported over a hundred million pieces of porcelain to Europe alone.[3] The Chinese had also learned to burn coal as a fuel at a very early date, and developed most of the key mechanisms for a steam engine, such as double-acting piston/cylinder arrays and methods for the transfer of rotary to linear motion.[4] Yet the Industrial Revolution did not begin in China. Instead, it was in Great Britain in the early nineteenth century that all the necessary contributing factors were first harnessed into a true industrial revolution.

Early coal-fired steam engines were so inefficient that they were almost useless, except at the sites of coal mines themselves, where coal was relatively cheap and abundant. There steam engines were initially used to pump water out of the mines to enable deeper mining. As the engines became more efficient, they began to be used also to haul the coal aboveground, and eventually, in 1825, in northern England, the world's first operational railway line was constructed. It just happened that nineteenth-century Britain combined some of Europe's largest coal reserves with a serious firewood shortage, encouraging the switch to coal for fuel. Britain also enjoyed a high level of commercialization and convenient water transportation, as well as, of course, individuals with considerable mechanical ingenuity and entrepreneurial flare.[5]

The conversion to fossil fuel–powered mechanization was the signature moment in the Industrial Revolution, but Britain's earlier development of a global trading network (and empire) was also an important precondition. Colonies and trading partners in America and elsewhere provided both markets for the products of British manufacturing and essential supplies of raw materials such as sugar and cotton. The development of worldwide trade also provided the framework for experimenting with large-scale business formats such as the joint-stock corporation.

As early as 1795, David Davies remarked on the peculiarity of the English working-class habit of drinking tea sweetened with sugar: "After all, it appears a very strange thing, that the common people of any European nation should be obliged to use, as part of their daily diet, two articles imported from opposite sides of the earth."[6] Indeed, at the time, all of the British tea came from China, and most of the sugar came from the Caribbean. This is striking testimony to the global reach of British commerce.

In the seventeenth century, a new kind of private chartered trading company had emerged to become the leading edge of European business activity in Asia. Especially important initially was the Dutch VOC (Vereenigde Oost-Indische Compagnie, or East India Company), which was founded in 1602. The Dutch established a base at Batavia (modern Jakarta) on the island of Java in 1619 and soon achieved a near-monopoly of the still vital spice trade among the islands of what is now Indonesia. Thanks to the actions of the Japanese Tokugawa Shogunate in excluding other Europeans, the Dutch also gained a complete monopoly on European trade with Japan after 1639. Meanwhile, the French Compagnie des Indies for a time seriously rivaled British interests in India, but after British military victories in such battles as Plassey, in 1757, and Pondicherry, in 1760, it was the British East India Company (EIC) that emerged as the dominant force in India. From its bases in India, the EIC then began projecting British interests to China.

The British EIC had been founded in 1599, when a group of London merchants acquired a royal charter from Queen Elizabeth I. The EIC enjoyed a monopoly over all British trade east of the Cape of Good Hope and soon became the largest British chartered company doing business outside of England. The "East India" in its title originally referred to the "East Indies" (modern Indonesia), but the British were driven from there by the Dutch, and the focus of EIC activity turned to the Indian subcontinent. As of the start of the nineteenth century, all British imports from the Far East were required to be deposited and sold from EIC warehouses. The EIC docks and warehouses in London employed fifty thousand persons, the company owned some 115 ships, and it had the largest standing army in Asia. In fact, as of the 1830s, the EIC army was more than twice the size of the regular British government army. The Crown granted the EIC the right to coin money and administer justice, and it was actually the EIC rather than the British government that first brought India under British control.

Victory in the Napoleonic wars in the early nineteenth century established overwhelming global British naval superiority and, together with the early British lead in mechanized industry, made Britain the sole global superpower of the nineteenth century – and the largest empire in the history of the world. British success stimulated imitation, however, and before long, a second wave of late-industrializing countries arose, including the United States, Germany, Russia, and Japan. The United States and Germany, in particular, had seriously eroded Britain's industrial lead by the early twentieth century. These countries (together with France, which, although now in relative decline, was still a major player) became the new great powers, and they soon engaged in a frantic competition for empire. Between 1876 and 1915, a quarter of the world was colonized by these roughly half dozen major modern powers.[7] Many older powers found themselves eclipsed by these developments. China and the Ottoman Empire were especially diminished, becoming the so-called "sick men" of Asia and Europe, respectively.

The Nineteenth-Century Impact on China

In the eighteenth century, China had enjoyed a standard of living roughly equivalent to that of western Europe. By some estimates, China actually consumed more sugar per person and produced at least comparable volumes of textiles as Europe at that time, and "western European land, labor, and product markets, even as late as 1789, were on the whole probably *further* from perfect competition . . . than those in most of China."[8] In the aggregate, if no longer in per capita terms, China was probably still the richest country in world as late as 1800, with something like one-third of the world's total production. Even well into the nineteenth century, conditions in China did not necessarily appear all that bleak to European observers. Robert Fortune, for example, a botanist sent to China by the EIC, still insisted in 1857 that although, "as their farms are all small," Chinese farmers "are probably less wealthy than our farmers in England," yet those Chinese farmers still "live well, dress plainly, and are industrious, without being in any way oppressed. I doubt if there is a happier race anywhere than the Chinese farmer and peasantry."[9]

By 1900, however, China's share of world production had fallen to only 6 percent. This was probably not the result of any absolute decline but instead was only relative to the explosive new growth of the industrialized economies. Yet, to the considerable bewilderment of many people in China, China was rapidly becoming globally marginalized, relatively impoverished, and surrounded by dynamically expanding new empires. Neighboring countries that had formerly been tributaries of the Chinese Empire were, one by one, pulled into new foreign imperial configurations: Burma was ceded to Britain in 1886, and Nepal became a British protectorate in 1815; France acquired Vietnam, Laos, and Cambodia in stages between 1862 and 1885; Japan successfully claimed the Ryūkyū (in Chinese, Liuqiu) island chain in 1878 and, in 1895, pulled Korea into the Japanese orbit and acquired Taiwan as an outright colony. Except for Taiwan (and tracts of northern borderland lost to Russia), actual Chinese territory was not directly colonized by these modern empires, but many Chinese people did eventually conclude that China was being reduced to at least "semi-colonial" status under the terms of a so-called treaty port system. This treaty port system referred, literally, to ports opened by formal diplomatic treaties, starting with the treaty that ended the first Opium War in 1842.

The Opium Wars

Beginning in 1757, all Western maritime commercial activity in China was confined by the Qing Dynasty to the single port of Guangzhou (in English, Canton). Guangzhou is a river port, lying about eighty miles up the Pearl River from the sea. In antiquity, when it was already an important port, it had actually been located on the ocean, but in late imperial times (particularly after the fourteenth century) the bay had silted up, creating today's Pearl River delta.[10] The restriction of European shipping to only one port was not some ancient Chinese tradition but a new policy – an application of imperial border control policies that had recently proved successful against the nomads of the northwest.[11] The policy also did not apply to the Russians, who could travel overland to Beijing, nor to Chinese merchants themselves, who came and went relatively freely. But Western shipping was limited to Guangzhou, where a number of Chinese firms joined to form a monopolistic association (called the Co-hong by the English) that handled every aspect of contact with the Western merchants.

Most prominent, now, among those Western merchants were the British, who had developed a considerable appetite for a Chinese product called tea, which they were beginning to purchase in substantial quantities. Even in Guangzhou, Westerners were not allowed inside the city walls. They were confined, instead, during the six-month trading season, to a cluster of so-called factories southwest of the city walls near the Pearl River. More permanent foreign residences were downriver in Portuguese Macao. Repeated British efforts to renegotiate these restricted terms of trade, most famously during the mission led by Lord George Macartney in 1793, were simply rebuffed by Beijing.

Although Western merchants sold many different products in exchange for Chinese tea, silk, porcelain, and lacquerware, only rarely could they sell enough to balance the exchange. The deficit, or trade imbalance, had to be made up with payments in cash (which, in China, meant silver). One contemporary American, for example, estimated that between 1805 and 1825, a net sixty-two million U.S. dollars in cash was transferred from the United States to China.[12] Western merchants were naturally, therefore, interested in finding a product that they could market successfully in China, and in the late 1700s, they finally did: opium.[13]

Opium is a narcotic drug produced from the sap of a flower called the poppy. Opium had long been a familiar substance throughout the Old World. It may have even been grown in ancient Egypt. What was new was the technique of smoking opium, which appears to have begun as a spin-off from the practice of smoking New World tobacco. Although opium smoking may have started simply by mixing tobacco and opium together, ultimately, instead of actually setting the opium alight and directly inhaling the smoke, the technique became to apply heat to a bead of opium in a special pipe until it vaporized and then inhale the vapor. Opium smoking became especially widespread in China, but the Chinese government also took a global lead in outlawing the practice, banning nonmedicinal use of opium by as early as 1729. Elsewhere in the world, opium use was far from universally illegal prior to the twentieth century. Indeed, nineteenth-century British mothers not uncommonly dosed their own children with a liquid tincture of opium called laudanum.

Initially, there was not very much opium in China. Only two hundred chests were imported in 1729, and domestic cultivation was minimal. In 1770, however, a famine in Bengal, in northeastern India, caused the EIC to petition Parliament for assistance, resulting in the Tea Act of 1773, which allowed the EIC to sell its products tax-free in the British colonies. This provoked some irate colonists in Boston, Massachusetts, to react angrily by dumping EIC tea into the ocean – the so-called Boston Tea Party – in December 1773. Also in 1773, and as a result of that same Indian famine, the EIC gained a monopoly on the sale and production of opium in Bengal. This opium was shaped into balls bearing the EIC seal and marketed in China. During the decade 1780–1790, imports of Indian opium into China quadrupled, and by the early nineteenth century, opium is said to have become the most valuable commercial crop in the world.

The obvious problem with this lucrative opium trade was that it was illegal in China, although it was not illegal elsewhere. In a concession to Chinese government pressure, therefore, in 1800, the EIC agreed to stop selling opium in China.

This made little difference, however, because the EIC continued to grow and manufacture opium in India, where it was perfectly legal, and auction the opium off to private firms, who then shipped it to China. The EIC's British monopoly on trade with the Far East applied only to trade between Asia and Britain and never to trade between different ports within Asia. Opium imports into China therefore continued unabated.

Then, in 1834, the EIC British monopoly expired and was not renewed. Like most other contemporary European countries, early modern Britain had favored policies of mercantilism, or protected trade, but in the early nineteenth century a new ideal of free trade was taking hold. In 1776, Adam Smith, in *The Wealth of Nations*, coined his famous phrase about the "invisible hand," suggesting that the free exchange of goods through market forces was the most efficient means of organizing an economy. In 1817, David Ricardo further developed the idea of comparative advantage, using the example of Portuguese specialization in wine production, which could then be exchanged for English cloth to mutual profit. Nineteenth-century British "classical" economists came to believe that government interference with the operation of market forces was likely to do more harm than good and advocated a laissez-faire approach and free trade. The inherent intellectual persuasiveness of this argument was underwritten by the rapidly increasing productivity of British industry – by 1840, Britain enjoyed about one-third of the world's total international trade – and Britain now moved decisively toward a goal of free trade.

The expiration of the EIC monopoly on British trade with China in 1834 was a step in this direction, and it brought increased British trade – but, correspondingly, also increased sales of opium. Between 1830 and 1836, the annual number of chests of (British-controlled) Indian opium imported into China increased from 18,956 to 30,302. Because the balance of trade had now shifted against China, and silver was now pouring out to pay for opium imports, Beijing perceived a mounting economic as well as a criminal and moral crisis. Although a number of proposals were considered, Beijing resolved to crack down and end the illegal drug trade. In 1839, a special imperial commissioner named Lin Zexu (1785–1850) was sent to Guangzhou to eliminate opium smuggling.

Lin arrived in March, and by July he had arrested some seventeen hundred Chinese involved in the drug trade and confiscated seventy thousand opium pipes. Smugglers found it almost impossible to sell opium at any price. But Lin was not content with this and surrounded the Western factories, demanding that they surrender all of their opium supplies. The highest-ranking official in the Western community in Guangzhou, the British Superintendent of Trade, was placed in an awkward position because his authority over the private businessmen was limited. He also could hardly wait for instructions from London because, at that time, it still took six months before he could expect a reply. On his own initiative, therefore, he promised the merchants that the British government would reimburse them for any opium confiscated by the Chinese. With that encouragement, the foreign merchants turned over twenty-one thousand chests, or two and a half million pounds, of opium to Commissioner Lin, who had it carefully dissolved in specially dug trenches.

Because the British home government proved unwilling, in the end, to pay for the confiscated opium, the huge financial loss involved then became an issue. In addition, Commissioner Lin was not satisfied with merely confiscating the existing opium supplies and also demanded that any foreign merchant wishing to do business in China must sign an oath, on penalty of death, never to bring opium into China again. The British, as a group, refused to sign, arguing that it would subject British citizens to what they viewed as a barbaric Chinese criminal justice system, exposing them to possible extortion and the probability of torture and execution if accused, whether falsely or not. Before long, shots were fired, and in early 1840, a British fleet arrived to enforce British interests. China and Great Britain went to war.

The Qing Dynasty had no real oceangoing navy at all, whereas Britain had the most powerful navy in the world. The British fleet also already included a pioneering iron steam warship called the *Nemesis*. The war at sea was therefore entirely one-sided. On land, however, there were not enough British troops to have much impact on the huge Chinese Empire. Eventually, the British fleet managed to sail up the Yangzi River and cut the Grand Canal, which transported vital tax grain from the south to the capital at Beijing in the north. The Qing Dynasty was then compelled to agree to terms, signing the Treaty of Nanjing (Nanking) in August 1842. This treaty opened five ports to British trade (including Shanghai, which at the time was still a relatively modest-sized city with a population of only a couple hundred thousand) and gave the island of Hong Kong permanently to Great Britain (it was the surrounding New Territories that were merely leased, for a term of ninety-nine years beginning in 1898, the expiration of which triggered the return of Hong Kong to Chinese rule in 1997), and the Qing Dynasty also agreed to pay reparations amounting to some twenty-one million dollars.

After the war, opium remained illegal in China, while the volume of legal British sales in China remained disappointing. As Britain industrialized, British manufacturers entertained visions of China as the largest potential market in the world, but such hopes were never fully realized. At the end of the nineteenth century, China was still importing fewer manufactured goods from Britain than from the Netherlands.[14] Although the reasons for this are complicated, British "old China hands" were inclined to blame their frustration on continuing unfair Chinese trade restrictions. At least initially, moreover, this was not entirely without reason. The British were still not actually being allowed inside the city of Guangzhou, there were still only five ports open to British trade, and taxes on British imports were collected erratically. British merchants therefore pressured their government to take more vigorous steps to pry open the tantalizingly vast China market.

An opportunity arrived in October 1856, when Chinese authorities at Guangzhou arrested some crewmembers of a ship called the *Arrow*. The owner of the ship was Chinese, the arrested crewmen were also "natives," and her Hong Kong British registration had technically expired eleven days previously, but the ship's master was British, and it was the British flag that was allegedly hauled down. The British governor of Hong Kong used this occasion to press further demands for the opening of China. The result was a second Opium War, in which Britain was this time joined by France – provoked to war by the execution of a French Christian missionary. The prosecution of this second war was delayed by the eruption of the bloody Sepoy Mutiny in India (1857–1858), but eventually, in 1860, a large British and French army landed on the northern coast near Beijing, the Chinese coastal defenses were stormed, and British and French troops marched into Beijing. The imperial Summer Palace in the northwestern suburbs of Beijing was burned and looted, and the emperor fled to Manchuria, where he died the next year. A five-year-old boy, known as the Tongzhi Emperor (r. 1862–1874), ascended the throne of a dynasty that appeared on the verge of collapse.

Domestic Rebellions

Even as the Qing Dynasty was waging two losing wars against European powers between 1840 and 1860, it was simultaneously also confronted with multiple domestic rebellions, some of which were on a vastly larger scale of destructiveness. The most devastating of all was the Christian Taiping Rebellion (1850–1864). The origins of this Christian rebellion were linked to those same recent foreign activities on the southeastern Chinese coast. The region around Guangzhou had been most affected by the fighting in the first Opium War (1840–1842), and the opening of other ports that resulted from that war ended Guangzhou's monopoly on Western trade. Guangzhou soon also found itself eclipsed by the rise of Shanghai in importance. For these and other reasons, there were regional economic disloca-tions, distress, and banditry. Banditry led to the formation of local self-defense militias, which then tended to represent local majority populations in confron-tations with minorities.

It happened that southernmost China had some especially large minority groups, including such aboriginal peoples as the Miao, Yao, and Zhuang. Among the ethnic Chinese, there were also significant subethnic differences, including occu-pational groups like the so-called boat people (who spent their entire lives afloat) and, most critically, a division between the Cantonese "natives" (*bendi*, sometimes spelled *punti*) of Guangdong and the Hakka (in Mandarin, *Kejia*) "guest families." While these Hakka are unquestionably Chinese (for a time in the 1980s–1990s, the leaders of the People's Republic of China, Taiwan, and Singapore were all three simultaneously Hakka), they are distinguished by speaking a unique dialect of the Chinese language. They were also relatively late migrants into the far south, often relegated to marginal farmland, and felt much discriminated against by the local Cantonese majority in the nineteenth century.[15]

The founder of the Taiping movement was a Guangdong Hakka named Hong Xiuquan (1814–1864).[16] Hong Xiuquan had made the thirty-mile journey from his native village to Guangzhou city four times between 1827 and 1843 to sit for the imperial civil service examinations, but though he passed the preliminary exams, he never obtained even the lowest degree. During his second visit to Guangzhou in 1836, he was exposed to Christian street preaching and accepted some Christian pamphlets. After his third examination failure, he suffered a nervous breakdown and experienced mysterious visions of, among other things, an old man who gave him a divine sword. After his fourth examination failure in 1843, he finally read those Christian pamphlets and came to the conclusion, based on them, that his visions were of God and Jesus Christ – who, as his father and older brother, had commissioned him to "restore" Christianity to China.

Although Hong did spend two months in 1847 studying at a Southern Baptist mission in Guangzhou under the Reverend Issachar Roberts of Tennessee, and a complete Chinese-language translation of the Bible was available to him, his training in Christian theology was obviously limited, and he developed a somewhat eccentric individual form of the faith, much influenced by his otherwise fairly conventional Chinese upbringing. The very name Taiping (great peace), for example, was drawn from ancient Chinese Daoist religious texts. There is no denying the sincerity of Hong's Christian zeal, however. Evangelizing in the countryside, he won some ten thousand converts by 1849. These were mainly, like Hong himself, Hakka or members of other minorities. They formed a God-Worshippers Society that practiced baptism and congregational worship and strictly enforced the Ten Commandments.

These God-Worshippers clashed with Cantonese self-defense militias, and early military successes inspired Hong Xiuquan to declare open rebellion against the Qing Dynasty in 1851, from a base on Thistle Mountain in the Yao aboriginal area of Guangxi Province. Hong pronounced himself the Heavenly King of a Heavenly Kingdom of Great Peace (*Taiping tianguo*). From this starting point in the far south, Taiping armies smashed their way through encircling imperial forces and marched north, picking up new recruits along the way. The Taiping soldiers maintained impressively taut discipline – they were forbidden to smoke, drink alcohol, loot, or have sexual relations – and the Qing imperial armies seemed unable to resist them. By 1853, the Taipings had captured Nanjing (Nanking) and made it their capital.

Many Westerners were at first excited by the idea of a Christian rebellion in China, especially one that appeared likely to emerge victorious and overthrow the Qing Dynasty. An early British fact-finding mission to the Taiping capital at Nanjing in 1853, however, was bluntly informed that the Taiping Heavenly King, Hong Xiuquan, was "the Lord of the whole world; he is the second son of God and all people in the whole world must obey and follow him.... The True Lord is not merely the Lord of China ... he is your Lord also."[17] Such haughty attitudes understandably tended to alienate Western opinion, not least among Christian missionaries, who were especially displeased by Hong's claim to be the literal younger brother of Jesus Christ. Up through their seizure of Nanjing in 1853, the Taiping rebels appeared unstoppable, but thereafter their offensives stalled, and an internal power struggle in 1856 led to much mutual Taiping slaughter. After 1856, Taiping cohesion and élan dissipated, and Qing imperial counteroffensives began to gain ground.

The Western powers quickly adopted postures of neutrality in this Chinese civil war and, after the Anglo-French victory in the second Opium War in 1860, even openly supported the Qing imperial side. An American mercenary named Frederick Townsend Ward (1831–1862), though he had originally dreamed of becoming a Taiping prince, instead organized an "ever victorious army," trained European-style, on behalf of the Qing Dynasty. When Ward was killed, he was replaced by a regular British army officer, Charles Gordon (1833–1885). Although this Western contribution was colorful, it actually played only a small part in the massive imperial effort to suppress the Taipings. By 1864, Nanjing was recaptured by the Qing Dynasty, and great effort was made to eradicate every trace that the Taiping movement had ever existed. The Taiping Rebellion was therefore ultimately a complete failure, and it left some twenty million people dead in its wake, together with widespread devastation. But because the imperial armies that eventually suppressed the Taipings were regionally rather than centrally organized, it contributed to the long-term decentralization of the Qing Dynasty, and the Taiping Rebellion also served as a conscious inspiration for more successful twentieth-century Chinese revolutionaries.

This Taiping Rebellion was merely the largest of several mid-century rebellions. To mention only one other, in 1864, Muslims in the far northwestern province of Xinjiang rebelled, echoing earlier Muslim rebellions in Gansu, Ningxia, and Shaanxi. The ruler of a small Islamic state on the opposite side of the Pamir Mountains, Khokand, sent a detachment of sixty-eight men across the mountains to intervene, under the command of Ya'qub Beg (ca. 1820–1877). ("Beg" is a Uighur Türkic title meaning "noble.") Ya'qub Beg soon brought all of the Tarim basin area of southern Xinjiang under his control, and after the fall of Khokand to the expanding Russian Empire, he became an independent force. While managing to remain autonomous, Ya'qub Beg accepted the title of "emir" from the Ottoman Empire and received substantial Ottoman military assistance. The British, who hoped that Ya'qub Beg's emirate might serve as a buffer in the great game of imperial rivalry between Britain and Russia, also granted Ya'qub Beg diplomatic recognition and allowed him to open an embassy in London.

Ya'qub Beg portrayed himself as a defender of the Islamic faith against the infidel Chinese, and strictly enforced Sharia law. Women were required to be veiled, for example, and drinking alcohol and eating pork were banned. Since the core of Ya'qub Beg's forces were outsiders from the other side of the Pamir Mountains, and because of such harshly puritanical regulations as well as the closing off of trade with China, the Muslim population of Xinjiang, which had initially supported Ya'qub Beg, grew disaffected over time. The Qing Dynasty, meanwhile, resolved to make a massive commitment of resources to retake Xinjiang, and after about a decade and a half of independence, the Qing reconquest of Xinjiang (except for a small pocket in the northwest that had been occupied by Russia) was completed by the end of 1877.[18] This was to be the last major successful military campaign ever waged by the Chinese Empire.

The Tongzhi Restoration (1862–1874)

The Qing Dynasty had confronted multiple serious crises in the mid-nineteenth century. As a foreign conquest dynasty, ruled by a relatively small hereditary ethnic minority elite, the Manchu position in China was also inherently vulnerable.

During the first British diplomatic mission to China in 1793, Lord George Macartney had concluded that Manchu rule was "the tyranny of a handful of Tartars [a word the British sometimes used for Manchus] over more than three hundred millions of Chinese" and predicted the dynasty's inevitable collapse, perhaps even during his own lifetime.[19] Yet the Qing Dynasty not only outlived Lord Macartney, it also survived all the mid-nineteenth-century wars and rebellions and even experienced a burst of renewed vigor. This period of revitalization is known as the Tongzhi Restoration, named after the reign period (1862–1874) of a young new emperor.[20]

For a generation beginning in the 1860s, China experienced relative peace, and the Qing Dynasty began making some pragmatic adjustments to the dramatically altered circumstances of the late nineteenth-century world. Although, when compared to the Meiji Restoration in contemporary Japan (1868–1912), the Chinese Tongzhi Restoration was visibly less successful in transforming China into a modern Western-style nation-state and industrialized power, when compared with almost everywhere else in the non-Western world, "China's Response to the West" was actually relatively effective.[21] To the extent that China's response to the challenge of the modern West was different from Japan's, this may have been partly because the domestic threats in China initially absorbed more attention. Unlike Japan, it was also harder for Chinese people to rally patriotically in modern nationalist fashion around the figure of the emperor, because the Qing emperors were not Han Chinese but Manchus. China's opening to the West was also not as abrupt as Japan's, with the result that changes in China may have been more gradual and imperceptible. Yet there were changes.

If China's opening to the West was not as sudden as Japan's, on the other hand, China's capital city, unlike Japan's, was actually occupied by hostile foreign military forces at the end of the second Opium War. Even while the court in Beijing was still preoccupied with suppressing the massive domestic Taiping Rebellion, it had little choice but to make concessions to the new Western ways. When British and French troops marched into Beijing in 1860, the emperor retreated to Manchuria, leaving the emperor's brother, Prince Gong, to deal with the foreigners. Prince Gong responded pragmatically.

In 1861, China's first ever government agency for handling foreign affairs (the *Zongli Yamen*) was established. After defeat in two Opium Wars, the need for military modernization was particularly obvious. Not content with merely purchasing advanced foreign weapons, under the slogan of "self-strengthening," new Western-style arsenals and shipyards began to be constructed in China. Because some Qing reformers concluded that modern Western military superiority was ultimately rooted in math and science, the study of those subjects – so different from the preparation in the humanities for the traditional Confucian examinations – began to be promoted in the 1860s.

A College of Foreign Languages (the *Tongwen guan*) was opened in 1862 to teach such unfamiliar Western languages as English, French, Russian, and German. Considerable effort was invested into translating Western books, and in 1872, the first group of 120 Chinese students made the journey to Hartford,

Connecticut, for a modern Western education. This project came under conservative criticism, however, and it was abandoned in 1881. As of 1879, there were only 163 students enrolled in the College of Foreign Languages. For a country the size of China, these were not impressive numbers.

Yet China's slowness to modernize, like its isolationism, is too often exaggerated. The notorious story of China's first short railway, which was built by a British firm in 1876 and soon afterwards bought out by local Chinese officials and dismantled, is a little misleading. It is not the whole story. The British firm had obtained approval to build a road, not a railroad, and had blatantly exceeded its authorization. The issue was therefore one of sovereignty and due process, rather than blind refusal to modernize. Ordinary Chinese people "embraced the railway as they had the steamships and the telegraph," and leading Chinese officials actually appreciated the value of railroads, but also feared foreign control and the danger of "railway imperialism."[22]

The Qing military reforms were successful enough that the dynasty managed to fight France to an effective draw in a war over Vietnam in 1883–1885 (though a Qing fleet caught at anchor in Fuzhou harbor was annihilated by a French attack). In the end, the Qing Dynasty's greatest military weakness was its lack of unity. There was no single national army, only fairly independent regional forces (and the now obsolete Banners). The modernizing Qing navy was divided into four separate fleets, and during the war against France the most powerful northern fleet remained neutral. A decade later, in a war with Japan, the southern fleets reciprocated and did not participate.[23] The Qing lack of national coordination and strategic military vision is, in the end, perhaps its biggest contrast with Meiji Japan.

Individual Chinese people exhibited considerable commercial drive and capitalistic enterprise. As one British official complained in 1865, "nine-tenths of the whole of the foreign trade are under the sole control, ownership, and combination of the Chinese." By the 1890s, it is estimated that Chinese people "owned about 40 percent of the stock of Western firms in shipping, cotton spinning, and banking, and held shares in roughly 60 percent of all foreign firms in China." Even in the British colony of Hong Kong, by 1880, of the eighteen largest property-tax payers, all but one were Chinese.[24] Although the vast majority of the Chinese people did remain poor farmers, even agriculture was extensively market oriented, and Chinese businesspeople were indisputably industrious.

Yet the abundant availability of cheap labor, the tendency for production to be performed as a sideline activity by individual households for just a little extra cash, and the inherent risks and uncertainties of large-scale modern ventures reduced the private incentive to purchase costly labor-saving machinery or build large and expensive factories. Commercial law was underdeveloped, and all the necessary surrounding infrastructure of a modern economy was still largely nonexistent. The late imperial Chinese government may have also carried laissez-faire well beyond the point of diminishing returns, since the central government no longer maintained roads, guaranteed much security, set uniform standards for weights and measures, or even issued a standard national currency beyond small-denomination copper cash (this in the land that had first invented paper money centuries earlier!). And, finally, there was simple inertia: the forms of modern industry that had been pioneered elsewhere took time to develop in China.

Modern industrial technologies were introduced into China. China's first steamship company was formed in 1872, for example, and a scattering of cotton mills and other modern facilities were constructed, in addition to government arsenals. But, outside of the Western-dominated treaty ports, these long remained little more than isolated experiments that were not always entirely successful. As late as 1933, the modern manufacturing, mining, transportation, and utilities sectors combined still produced only 7 percent of China's gross domestic product.[25]

The Treaty Ports

The Treaty of Nanking that ended the first Opium War in 1842 opened five Chinese ports to British trade. To these initial five, other ports (and similar treaties with other countries) were soon added, and by the early twentieth century there were ninety-two treaty ports, including both ocean and river ports and inland railway junctions. All that such treaty port status really meant, however, was that citizens of the countries that had signed treaties with China were allowed to reside and do business there. In most of the treaty ports, moreover, the foreign presence remained small. But some of the larger treaty ports did become major centers of Western activity. Foremost among these was Shanghai, which quickly became the largest and most modern city in China.

Shanghai's abrupt rise from relative obscurity was mainly due to its location, midway down the Chinese coast and near the mouth of the Yangzi River, which was the principal premodern commercial artery reaching into the interior of China, and also near the major tea- and silk-producing regions. Shanghai was a city built on trade, and the British – or more precisely Anglo-Indians, because they operated extensively from bases in British colonial India and included a fair number of Indians – were the dominant presence. One 1881 estimate put Britain's share of China's total foreign trade at 77.5 percent.[26] Shanghai became a thoroughly international city, however, with residents from all around the world. English-, French-, German-, and Russian-language newspapers were published, and special schools were established for the children of the foreigners.

The Shanghai International Settlement was originally intended exclusively for foreign residents, but when the Taiping Rebellion threatened to overrun the area, large numbers of Chinese people sought refuge inside the International Settlement. Thereafter Chinese people always remained the overwhelming majority of its population. By the early twentieth century, more Chinese-language daily newspapers were being printed inside the International Settlement at Shanghai than in all the rest of China combined.[27] Yet the International Settlement remained a foreign concession, a kind of autonomous merchant republic that was inside China but not under Chinese control. Some twenty-seven hundred of the wealthiest foreign property-tax payers annually elected a nine-member municipal council that governed the International Settlement. In addition, there was a separate French

Map 8.1 Shanghai and Vicinity, ca. 1930

Concession, under direct French administration. Only the suburbs and the old city were under Chinese jurisdiction.

Modern Shanghai became one of the great cities of the world (see Figure 8.2). By the end of the nineteenth century, the International Settlement in Shanghai boasted paved roads, streetlights, running water, telephones, and electricity.

Figure 8.2. A panoramic view of the Bund, or waterfront (Waitan), Shanghai, ca. 1932. Pictures from History/Bridgeman Images.

The mansions of the great foreign *taipans* (a regional slang expression meaning "big bosses") lined Bubbling Well Road with their tennis courts and gardens. Western entertainments included the club, amateur theater, golf, horse racing, and cricket. If wealthy foreigners lived comfortably in Shanghai, moreover, Shanghai was also a magnet for ambitious Chinese, who were attracted by the promise of security and economic opportunity. By about 1870, some of the Chinese agents of foreign businesses were already beginning to invest in their own modern enterprises, forming the nucleus of an emerging modern Chinese business class.

Yet Shanghai's modern success had an unmistakably dark underside. Shanghai "was literally built on the opium trade," and by the early twentieth century, there were some eighty opium shops and fifteen hundred opium dens inside the city.[28] Shanghai's somewhat shady reputation was notorious. For a time in the early twentieth century, the leading gangster in the French Concession was simultaneously also chief superintendent of the Chinese police squad. Continued foreign administration of the International Settlement and French Concession was also a potentially explosive affront to the growing sense of Chinese nationalism. The first Chinese member of the Shanghai Municipal Council was not seated until 1928.

The Boxer Rebellion (1898–1900)

The Tongzhi Emperor died young in 1874, providing his mother, the Empress Dowager Cixi (1835–1908), with an opportunity to place yet another pliable minor, this time her nephew, the Guangxu Emperor (r. 1875–1908), on the throne.

Figure 8.3. The Qing Dynasty Empress Dowager Cixi with foreign envoys' wives, 1903–1905. Freer Gallery of Art and Arthur M. Sackler Gallery Archives, Smithsonian Institution, Washington, DC: Negative # SC-GR 249.

As the real power behind the throne, this empress dowager balanced conservative and reformist factions against each other, with her chief concern being simply the preservation of her dynasty (see Figure 8.3). Despite the steps that had been taken toward "self-strengthening" during the Tongzhi Restoration, the Qing Dynasty was militarily humiliated when it became embroiled in a war with Japan, over Korea, in 1894–1895 – even though, on paper, the Chinese army was nearly six times the size of the Japanese army, and the Chinese navy had twice as many ships. The indemnity that China was forced to pay Japan as a result of its defeat was equal to 15 percent of Japan's total gross national product in that year, and this massive transfer of financial spoils then helped underwrite Japan's further industrialization. In China, the defeat came as a great shock.

The war with Japan severed China's ancient tributary relationship with Korea, transferred the island of Taiwan from China to the Japanese empire, and initially threatened to make further inroads into China's northeastern territories. Although Russia, France, and Germany intervened to prevent that from happening (to the outrage of the Japanese), just three years later, these very same Western great powers themselves began extracting leaseholds from Chinese soil. In 1898, Russia began building a naval base, called Port Arthur, at the tip of Liaodong peninsula in Manchuria. Germany acquired the port of Qingdao on the Shandong peninsula, France leased a harbor in far south China, and Britain leased a port in Shandong (Weihaiwei) and signed a ninety-nine-year lease on the New Territories surrounding Hong Kong. The Russians began constructing railways across Manchuria, and despite Shanghai's undisputed preeminence among the treaty ports, the city in China that soon had both the largest total number and the highest percentage of resident foreigners became Harbin, which was founded in 1898 as a Russian railway town in the very center of Manchuria.[29] At its peak, more than half of Harbin's population was Russian, and it boasted a Russian university, schools, courts, and churches.

Alarmed by these concessions, and also by the extension of even larger, more nebulous, foreign "spheres of influence" into the interior of China, the youthful Guangxu Emperor was emboldened to take radical action and embarked on the so-called one hundred days of reform in 1898. As the name implies, however, these reforms quickly proved abortive. Conservatives were horrified, and the empress dowager staged a palace coup, placed the emperor under house arrest in the rebuilt Summer Palace, executed six reformers and drove others into exile, and declared herself regent.

In the next year, 1899, north China began to suffer from a severe drought. A mysterious group called the *Yihequan* (Boxers United in Righteousness, or simply Boxers) provided an explanation: the alien religion of Christianity was causing the people to abandon their traditional gods, and in retribution, the gods were withholding the life-giving rain. This Boxer movement emerged from the variety of religious and martial arts self-defense groups that were widespread in the Chinese countryside. Many Boxers apparently were quite young boys. As the senior U.S. diplomat in Beijing explained to the Secretary of State in 1900, "a number of teachers go through the country, gather together the idle young men at the various villages and organize them into companies and pretend if they will, under their direction, go through certain gymnastic movements and repeat certain incantations, that they will become impervious to all weapons and nothing can harm them."[30]

Though the Boxers were anti-Christian and antiforeign, they were at least potentially also anti-Manchu and anti-Qing. Conservatives at the Qing court in Beijing were sympathetic, though, and on June 21, 1900, Empress Dowager Cixi issued a sweeping declaration of war against foreigners in China. This declaration was less inexplicably foolish than it might at first seem, because Allied forces had already captured the Qing forts guarding the coastal approaches to the important northern port city of Tianjin, and their attack could reasonably have been understood as an act of war that required a Qing response.[31]

The foreign Legation Quarter in Beijing was besieged by the Boxers, as was the foreign community in Tianjin, which at the time consisted of some nine hundred foreign civilians, including the future president of the United States Herbert Hoover. Cooperation between the Boxers and regular Qing imperial officials was poor, however, and most Qing officials, including those in the entire south of China, simply chose not to participate. Ironically, in view of their antiforeignism, the Boxers were generally less active in areas where the Western presence was strongest. Most of the relatively small number of foreign deaths (a much larger number of Chinese Christian converts were killed) were in remote northwestern Shanxi Province and Inner Mongolia.

Figure 8.4. The Ninth U.S. Infantry lined up before the imperial palace in Beijing, 1901, following the suppression of the Boxer Rebellion. Library of Congress, LC-USZ62-68813.

In August 1900, a multinational Allied army marched into Beijing and relieved the siege of the foreign community there (see Figure 8.4). The Boxers were crushed, and a so-called Boxer Protocol was imposed on the Qing Dynasty, which included the payment of an indemnity equal to nearly twice the annual tax revenue of the dynasty. In the aftermath, even the empress dowager belatedly recognized the need for Western-style reforms, and with the turn into the twentieth century, the Qing Dynasty embarked on a conscious course of rapid modernization.

The Nineteenth-Century Opening of Korea

At the start of the nineteenth century, Korea's only foreign contacts were with Qing Dynasty China and Tokugawa Japan. Chosŏn Korea was a self-acknowledged tributary of China. This meant that Korean kings were expected to use the Chinese calendar and seek confirmation of their enthronement from the emperor of China (who at the time technically happened to be Manchu rather than Han Chinese), who also issued approximately annual proclamations to Korea. Over the course of the Qing Dynasty, Seoul sent an average of nearly three embassies each year to Beijing. The Koreans called this "serving the great" (*sadae*). However, the Korean elite also retained deep feelings of loyalty to the previous Chinese Ming Dynasty, which had come to Korea's aid during Hideyoshi's invasions, and felt considerable disdain for the alien Manchu rulers of the Qing. The Qing border with Korea was sealed with a palisade, boat traffic between China and Korea was forbidden (Korean fishermen were, in any case, confined to coastal waters), and contact was limited to only official embassies.

Although Korea was an acknowledged tributary of the Chinese Empire, as one Chinese official explained in 1876, this really meant that except for the obligatory ceremonial tribute missions, Korea was entirely autonomous in both its domestic and foreign affairs.[32] The peculiar ambiguity of Korea's relationship with China even became a convenient excuse for rebuffing early Western approaches. When the British attempted to advance trade proposals with Korea in 1845, it was explained that this would be impossible because Korea "could not be opened to trade by China, for it was not a part of China," and it also "could not open itself to trade, for it was not independent."[33]

Korea's relationship with Japan was also somewhat complicated. Following Hideyoshi's failed invasions of Korea and the subsequent establishment of the Tokugawa Shogunate in Japan, contact with Korea was restored by a trade agreement in 1609. The Koreans viewed the Tokugawa shogun as equal in status to their own king, and a small number of Korean embassies were sent to the shogun's castle in Edo, but no Japanese embassies traveled to Korea, and direct Korean contact with the Tokugawa Shogunate ended in 1811. Instead of the shogun (or the Japanese emperor), it was the *daimyō* (lord) of Tsushima, a small island midway between the main islands of Japan and the Korean peninsula, who enjoyed a monopoly of Korean trade. This lord of Tsushima acted simultaneously as a vassal of the Japanese shogun and as a kind of tributary of the Korean king, having been granted official titles by the Korean court. Approximately a thousand persons from Tsushima traveled to Korea each year, but they were confined to a strictly monitored Japan House in the single port of Pusan.

The 1860s were a decade of restorations in East Asia. China had its Tongzhi Restoration, Japan had its Meiji Restoration, and there was also a royal restoration of sorts in Korea as well. (In Vietnam, however, the 1860s, which saw the beginning of French colonization, could hardly be described as a restoration.) Two different Chinese and Japanese terms are translated by the single English word "restoration" (while in Korea no such label is conventionally applied at all), and there were obviously significant differences of detail, but there were also some rough parallels between the midcentury situations in China, Korea, and Japan. These parallels may be explained by the fact that the ruling elites in each country were imbued with many of the same Confucian ideas and confronting some of the same challenges. All three countries also had youthful new monarchs in the 1860s.

In Korea, King Kojong (r. 1864–1907) came to the throne in 1864 at the age of twelve (see Figure 8.5). The king's father, who was known as the Taewŏn'gun (the "Lord of the Great Court"), was still alive (he had not himself ever been king), and he acted as an informal regent from 1864 to 1873 on his son's behalf. As regent, the

Figure 8.5. Kojong (1852–1919), emperor, and previously king, of Korea, ca. 1904. Library of Congress, LC-USZ62-72798.

Taewŏn'gun attempted to promote reforms that would invigorate the Korean monarchy by reducing corruption, inefficiency, and *yangban* aristocratic privileges. At the same time, he also intensified the crackdown on Christianity and hardened Korea's resolve in fending off the growing number of Western approaches. Korea's apparent successes in driving off a French fleet in 1866, and then a U.S. naval squadron in 1871, encouraged Koreans to believe that this was still militarily possible. If the Tokugawa Shogunate in Japan reacted to news of the Opium War in China by concluding that resistance to modern Western military power would be futile, the Taewŏn'gun in Korea drew the opposite conclusion: the way to avoid humiliation was to stand firm and resolutely reject all foreign demands for trade.

After the Meiji Restoration of imperial rule in Japan in 1868, and the dissolution of the Tokugawa Shogunate, Japan's new Western-style Imperial Foreign Office officially assumed jurisdiction over Korean relations from the *daimyō* of Tsushima in 1871. The Korean government, however, refused to accept these changes. Among other things, the Koreans objected to Japanese officials now dressing in

Western-style clothing, but most especially, the Koreans refused to acknowledge the position of the Japanese emperor. This was because the East Asian imperial title designated a theoretically universal supreme sovereign, and as a tributary of Qing China, the Koreans could not recognize another emperor. Furthermore, recognition of the Japanese emperor would have implied Japanese superiority over the lower-ranking Korean king. Indeed, many of Japan's Meiji Restoration leaders actively hoped that the restoration of imperial rule in Japan would also bring a "restoration" of what they believed to have been Korea's ancient (but mythical) subordination to Japan.

Korea's refusal to recognize the imperial government in Japan was regarded as an outrage by many patriotic Japanese and provoked debate over the desirability of immediate war with Korea. Although cooler heads initially prevailed, in 1875, a Japanese navy warship engaged in surveying off the coast of Korea's Kanghwa Island attempted to put a small boat ashore for fresh water. Korean shore batteries fired some shots, which may have been intended only as warnings, and the Japanese returned fire and landed troops. In 1876, Japan further signaled the firmness of its intentions by dispatching three warships, four transports, and eight hundred soldiers to Korea. King Kojong had, meanwhile, begun to rule in his own name as an adult, ending the regency of the Taewŏn'gun in 1873. King Kojong was less resolute in his opposition to all foreign contacts than the Taewŏn'gun had been, and under the looming threat of a Japanese invasion, and acting under Chinese advice, in 1876, Korea signed a modern Western-style treaty (the Treaty of Kanghwa) with Japan. This treaty formally declared Korea to be an independent country (supposedly clarifying its ambiguous relationship with China) and granted Japan various treaty port-style concessions.

While Korean conservatives looked to China to balance the growing Japanese influence, some Korean modernizers aligned themselves with Meiji Japan. In 1884, a handful of Korean reformers plotted a coup, in consultation with the Japanese minister in Seoul. On December 4, during a banquet celebrating the opening of a modern post office, the conspirators struck. Seven Korean officials were assassinated, and guards from the Japanese legation took the Korean king and queen into "protective" custody. A new Korean government was proclaimed, and modernizing reforms were outlined. Chinese troops counterattacked the palace immediately, however, regaining custody of the king. The result of this failed coup, which only lasted two days, was to tarnish the reputations of both the reform and the pro-Japanese positions.

The Qing Dynasty in China, meanwhile, which supported certain self-strengthening modernizing efforts in Korea and had actually negotiated modern treaties on Korea's behalf with the United States, Great Britain, and Germany in 1882, had by this time broken with its traditional posture of noninterference and was now actively intervening in Korea. In 1885, the Qing appointed a resident commissioner to Korea (a man named Yuan Shikai, who would later become the first non-provisional president of the Republic of China). The tensions resulting from the conflicting Chinese and Japanese ambitions in Korea were temporarily cooled by an agreement in 1885 that both China and Japan would withdraw their troops. This uneasy peace was brought to an abrupt end, however, by a religiously inspired Korean rebellion in 1894.

In the 1850s, a Korean named Ch'oe Che-u (1824–1864), who was ineligible to take the Korean civil service examinations because his mother had remarried, received what he claimed was a revelation from the Lord of Heaven. This inspired him to formulate a new religion, which was something of an eclectic mixture of traditional East Asian ideas and was called *Tonghak* (Eastern Learning), in conscious opposition to the alien ideas of the West. Although Ch'oe was executed in 1864, *Tonghak* beliefs continued to simmer in the Korean countryside. In 1894, a local *Tonghak* uprising swept across southwest Korea, fueled by popular discontent with heavy taxes and high interest rates. This became the most massive rebellion in recorded Korean history. An anxious Korean king asked China for military assistance, and the Qing Dynasty responded by sending a small detachment of soldiers. Japan countered by deploying a much larger force of its own. Although the Korean authorities, alarmed by the possibilities unleashed by this dual foreign intervention, quickly offered concessions to the *Tonghak* rebels, who agreed to lay down their arms, the Japanese troops remained. On July 23, a Japanese infantry regiment seized the Korean palace. On August 1, 1894, war was declared between China and Japan.

Over the following nine months, the Japanese army easily expelled Chinese troops from Korea, captured territory in Manchuria, and even gained a foothold in coastal China proper. Qing Dynasty Chinese forces proved to be badly led, undermined by corruption, and split by faction and regionalism. A substantial portion of the Chinese navy refused to participate in a war they considered beyond their concern. Japan won this Sino-Japanese War (1894–1895) with surprising ease. The war was much celebrated in the modern Japanese press but came as a tremendous shock, and a wake-up call, to China. Under the terms of the resulting Treaty of Shimonoseki that ended the hostilities, China was forced to transfer the island of Taiwan to Japan (as well, initially, as a strategic peninsula in southern Manchuria, which intervention by Russia, France, and Germany promptly compelled Japan to return) and to pay Japan an enormous indemnity equal to roughly 15 percent of Japan's total gross national product. In addition, China formally acknowledged the independence of Korea, which in practice meant the ascent of Japanese influence there.

During the Sino-Japanese War, Japan moved quickly to assume a dominant position in Korea, extracting the right to begin constructing railways on the peninsula and to provide advisors for Korean domestic affairs. Even while the war with China was still raging, pro-Japanese Korean officials reorganized the government, introducing sweeping modernizing reforms (known as the Kabo reforms) in 1894–1895. The Chinese calendar was dropped from official Korean documents and a new Korean calendar substituted in its place. The Confucian civil service examination system was abolished, as were the institution of slavery and formal distinctions between the aristocratic *yangban* classes and commoners. Western-style clothing and hairstyles were forcibly promoted. Altogether, there were 208 new laws, culminating in a new constitution in January 1895.

Despite Japanese victory in the war with China, Korea once again temporarily eluded reduction to an outright Japanese protectorate, partly because of the blatant contradiction inherent in the Japanese policy of pursuing domination in Korea while proclaiming a goal of promoting Korean "independence" from the archaic Chinese tributary system. The modernizing command that all Korean men cut their topknots and adopt Western hairstyles provoked great popular discontent, and when, in October 1895, a Japanese-backed coup assassinated the Korean queen and restored pro-Japanese officials to power, this assassination outraged and horrified Korean opinion. In February 1896, King Kojong, seeking to escape Japanese control, allowed himself to be smuggled out of the palace by Russian marines in the palanquin of a court lady. The king took refuge in the Russian legation, where he spent the next year.[34]

By playing off Russian interests against the Japanese, as he had previously used the Chinese against the Japanese, King Kojong was able to retain a measure of Korean independence. In 1897, the king returned to his palace and formally assumed the supreme East Asian title of "emperor" (in Korean, *hwangje*), asserting his sovereign equality with both the Chinese and Japanese monarchs. Over the next few years, modern army units were organized, postage stamps issued, and street-cars and electric lights introduced into the capital (see Figure 8.6), and in 1902, the newly renamed Korean Empire even acquired a Western-style national anthem. The Christian mission to Korea, meanwhile, was among the most successful in East Asia, and modern Western-style education began exerting a profound effect on Korean thought. A newspaper published by the Independence Club beginning in 1897 was the first to be published entirely in the Korean alphabet (*han'gŭl*), without any Chinese characters. A new spirit of modern Korean nationalism began to glimmer, and the hope kindled that Korea might successfully be transformed into an independent, modern, Western-style nation-state.[35] The degree of material modernization remained limited, however (see Figure 8.7), and in the early twentieth century, the dream of Korean independence would prove to be a false hope, as the lengthening shadow of the Japanese Empire stretched across the land.

The Meiji Restoration (1868–1912): Japan "Leaves Asia"

In the early nineteenth century, Western contact with Japan was limited to an annual average of only one Dutch ship. In Japan, the Dutch were confined to the single port of Nagasaki, where they were effectively quarantined on a small island, surrounded by a high fence topped with iron spikes, and linked to shore by one bridge. Yet, even so, Japan's isolation should not be exaggerated. After 1716, official permission resumed for the study of Western books, with a particular interest in books concerning medical and military science. This became a specialized form of learning known as Dutch studies (*Rangaku*). In 1811, the Tokugawa Shogunate itself set up an agency to translate selected Dutch works. By the 1840s and 1850s, even before the arrival of Commodore Perry, a few *daimyō* domains

Figure 8.6. The West Gate of Seoul, Korea, ca. 1904, showing an American electric tramway. Library of Congress, LC-USZ62-72552.

were already independently constructing foundries for the casting of modern Western-style munitions.

Commodore Perry and the Opening of Japan (1853–1854)

Because Japan appeared to be a poor country, unlikely to buy significant amounts of any European goods and having no known local products that were particularly in demand in Europe – and because the Japanese islands were also remote and out of the way for European shipping coming from the west – Great Britain and the other major European powers had been relatively content to leave Japan in its self-imposed isolation. Two of the newly emerging modern great powers, however, did have special interests in the Pacific Ocean that made opening relations with Japan seem more crucial: the United States and Russia. In the eighteenth and nineteenth centuries, the Russians had made repeated efforts to establish relations with Japan, without success. The United States, meanwhile, had expanded to the shores of the

Figure 8.7. Korean women with a sedan chair, 1919. Library of Congress, LC-USZ62-72675.

Pacific with the acquisition of California in 1848. American clipper ships, on the voyage from California to Guangzhou (Canton), often came within sight of the Japanese islands, and American whalers frequently found themselves in Japanese waters by the 1840s. In the age of sail, shipwrecks were an all too common occurrence, and the U.S. government was concerned about the treatment of American sailors shipwrecked in Japan. As steam navigation was increasing in importance, moreover, there was also a growing need for widespread and strategically located coaling stations. And, of course, there was always the possibility of trade.

At least twenty-five times before the arrival of Commodore Perry's squadron, U.S. ships, either officially or privately, had attempted to establish contact with Japan. In 1846, an official U.S. mission under the command of Commodore Biddle had failed – according to the interpretation prevailing in Washington, because Commodore Biddle had not made a forceful enough impression on the Japanese. When the decision was reached to send another expedition in 1851, therefore, its commander, Commodore Mathew Calbraith Perry (1794–1858), was encouraged to be firm.

Commodore Perry gathered what little information he could find about a Japan that was still largely unknown to the West and approached cautiously. In July 1853, Perry arrived in what is now called Tōkyō Bay with four ominous black warships, including the powerful steam frigates *Mississippi* and *Susquehanna*. Perry's flagship, the *Mississippi*, mounted eight large eight-inch guns and two even larger ten-inch cannon. Precisely because Japanese officials were not entirely ignorant of developments in the outside world and were well aware of China's humiliating defeat in the Opium War in 1842, these big guns left a sobering impression. On arrival, Commodore Perry remained in his cabin and refused to meet with junior Japanese officials, demanding instead that he be allowed to deliver a letter from President Fillmore into the hands of senior officials ashore.

Because the Americans were unclear about the institution of the Japanese military overlord known as the shogun, the president's letter was addressed to the Japanese emperor. In fact, however, a young shogunal chief councilor handled the negotiations. The shogun himself, who was on his deathbed, was not even told of the American arrival, and the emperor was quite powerless. Perry's men went ashore with loaded weapons, while the Japanese concealed armed samurai under the floorboards of the reception room, in mutual anticipation of trouble. An American missionary who had learned a few words of Japanese while living in China had been brought along to serve as interpreter, but most negotiations were actually conducted in the Dutch language. After delivering his letter stating the American demands, Commodore Perry departed, promising to return again next spring with an even larger squadron to receive the Japanese answer.

Armed resistance appeared futile, but yielding to foreign demands would mean a great loss of shogunal prestige, so the shogunal authorities took the unprecedented step of asking for *daimyō* advice. In the mid-nineteenth century, Japan was still divided into some 276 *daimyō* domains, each of which, despite acknowledging Tokugawa overlordship, retained its own independent government, armed forces, and sometimes even currency. Since most *daimyō* now urged the Shogunate not to give in to foreign demands, but also cautioned against war, the act of seeking *daimyō* advice only made the Shogunate's position even more awkward. Financially, the Tokugawa treasury was empty. Shogunal authority had also recently been threatened by the economic revival of some of the more powerful outlying domains. Although most *daimyō*, like the Shogunate itself, were now deeply in debt, a few key domains had succeeded in restructuring their economies and putting their finances on relatively sound footing. These included, in particular, the domains of Chōshū, at the western tip of Japan's main island, and Satsuma, in southern Kyūshū.[36] Satsuma, for example, in part because of its southern climate, had achieved something of a monopoly on sugar production in Japan.

In February, 1854, Commodore Perry returned with ten warships, and the Tokugawa Shogunate abruptly yielded, signing a treaty (the Treaty of Kanagawa) with the United States. Before long, other countries had also signed treaties, and a treaty port system very similar to what had previously been established in China was now extended to Japan as well. Foreign residence in Edo (the Shogun's castle town, modern Tōkyō) was permitted beginning in 1859. Nagasaki, Yokohama,

Kobe, and other ports were opened, the standard treaty port privilege of extraterritoriality (foreign exemption from local law) was conferred, and fixed low tax rates on foreign imports were established. In the process, shogunal military power had been exposed as hollow for everyone to see. Since shogunal authority had no real ideological basis for legitimacy apart from its military dominance, the Tokugawa position now became precarious.

The Meiji Restoration (1868)

In the eighteenth century, the school of National Learning, whose most famous representative was Motoori Norinaga (1730–1801), had revived an interest in ancient native Japanese myths and literature, especially the imperial mythology enshrined in the oldest Japanese history, the *Kojiki*. Tokugawa shogunal authority had theoretically been justified from the beginning merely as a delegation of power from the emperor, and with the Shogunate now demonstrating obvious weakness in the face of foreign threats, the slogan "revere the emperor and expel the barbarians" (*sonnō jōi*; more literally, "revere the king," since this was a four-character Chinese expression traceable to the pre-imperial era) began to rally patriotic opposition both to the foreign concessions and, at least implicitly, to the Tokugawa Shogunate itself, in the name of loyalty to the Japanese emperor.

Yoshida Shoin (1830–1859), a samurai from Chōshū, had attempted to stow away aboard one of Commodore Perry's ships to learn more about the mysterious foreigners. He was caught, however, and placed under arrest. After his release, he organized an influential patriotic school. Yoshida blamed the Shogunate for its failure to expel the foreigners and decided that the Tokugawa Shogunate must be overthrown. He plotted to assassinate a shogunal emissary to the imperial capital, Kyōto, in 1858, but was caught once again and this time beheaded. Yoshida became, however, a hero for many Japanese patriots. In 1860, furthermore, the shogunal grand councilor actually was assassinated while entering Edo castle by warriors from the domains of Mito and Satsuma.

The years following the signing of the first foreign treaties were marked by several outbursts of patriotic terrorism, as samurai vented their indignation through individual acts of violence. Two Russian sailors were killed in 1859. The American consul's Dutch interpreter was murdered in 1861. In 1862, the *daimyō* of Satsuma delivered an imperial command to the shogun, demanding that the shogun report to Kyōto in person to explain his concessions to the foreigners. As this *daimyō* was returning from delivering the message, his procession encountered a small group of British people on the road near Yokohama who failed to dismount in token of respect for the *daimyō*. Outraged samurai attendants attacked the foreigners, killing one Englishman and wounding two others. In 1863, the British legation in Edo was burned by arsonists (including Itō Hirobumi, who would later become one of Meiji Japan's leading statesmen).

By 1863, extremists had gained control of the imperial court and compelled the Shogunate to agree to set a date for the expulsion of all foreigners. This was to be June 25, 1863. Although most of Japan failed to take any action on that date, fortifications in the western domain of Chōshū did begin firing on passing ships. In retaliation, in 1864, a combined British, French, Dutch, and American fleet stormed the forts and destroyed them. The previous year, in 1863, a British squadron had also shelled the castle town in Satsuma, in retribution for the earlier attack on Englishmen on the road near Yokohama. Tokugawa Japan's defenselessness against modern firepower was fully exposed.

Thereafter, attempts to forcefully expel the foreigners were abandoned as futile, and a new patriotic slogan began to replace "revere the emperor and expel the barbarians": "enrich the country and strengthen the army" (*fukoku kyōhei*, also a four-character expression drawn originally from ancient Warring States China). By the late 1860s, the situation had changed from one of conflict between patriotic Japanese and foreigners to one of competition between different groups of Japanese, each often with its own sources of foreign assistance. The Shogunate, for example, was leaning toward France, while the domains of Satsuma and Chōshū were dealing especially with the British.

In the meantime, the requirement of alternate attendance at the shogun's castle in Edo had been effectively lifted in 1862, and *daimyō* families departed Edo for their own domains. In 1864, a radical faction gained control in Chōshū and began promoting its agenda at the imperial court in Kyōto. When fighting in July reduced much of Kyōto to ashes, the imperial court ordered the Shogunate to launch a punitive expedition against Chōshū. This was supported by other domains and initially was moderately successful, but when a second campaign was begun against the recalcitrant Chōshū in 1866, this time many other domains remained neutral. A secret agreement was arranged for mutual support between Satsuma and Chōshū in March, which brought together the two most powerful "outside" domains, and a shogunal attack on Chōshū that month was militarily defeated. The Tokugawa Shogunate was crumbling.

The death of the Shogun Iemochi in 1866 (at age twenty-one, apparently of beriberi) provided a suitable pretext for the Shogunate to call off its war with Chōshū, but soon thereafter an order was issued in the name of the emperor calling upon Chōshū and Satsuma to assume the offensive against the Tokugawa Shogunate. At this juncture, samurai from the domain of Tosa (on the smaller southern island of Shikoku) prevailed on the new shogun, who had been reluctant to accept the title in the first place, to resign. Amazingly, the shogun did exactly that, petitioning the emperor in November 1867 to accept a reversion of shogunal authority back to the imperial throne. The ex-shogun retained vast landholdings, however, and remained a powerful *daimyō*. Anti-Tokugawa forces were not satisfied, therefore, and on January 3, 1868, samurai, primarily from Satsuma, seized the imperial palace and proclaimed an imperial restoration. This is known to history as the Meiji Restoration, after the name of the Meiji imperial reign period (1868–1912). Although the ex-shogun did resist this coup d'état, his army was defeated by imperial forces in four days of heavy fighting. The ex-shogun soon surrendered and was generously treated by the victors, eventually even receiving the highest rank in a newly created modern peerage. In November, the young Meiji emperor departed the ancient capital, Kyōto, in western Japan and took up

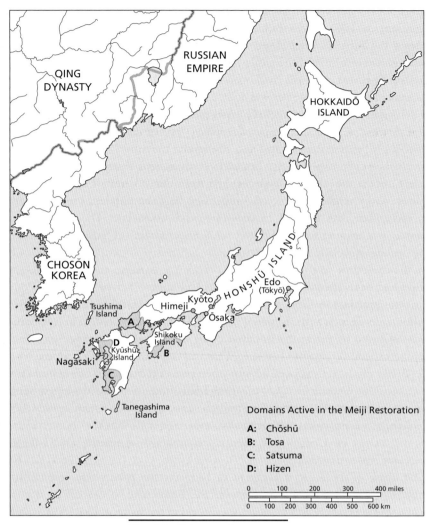

Map 8.2 Tokugawa Japan, ca. 1860

residence in the former shogun's castle in Edo, which now became known as Tōkyō (Eastern Capital).

In theory, this was a restoration of the sole legitimate ancient Japanese imperial government after centuries of improper domination by military usurpers (the shoguns), performed in the name of the quintessentially traditional Confucian virtue of loyalty. In the early years of the Meiji Restoration, there was even some actual revival of ancient court titles. The mid-ranking samurai who led this Meiji Restoration, moreover, had for many years been indignant at the incompetence of the few thousand hereditary families who monopolized Tokugawa wealth and power, and the corresponding lack of career opportunities for the much larger number of, often bitterly impoverished, lower-ranking samurai. In some ways, the meritocratic ideals underlying this revolutionary change were as traditionally Confucian as they were modern and Western.[37]

Despite these traditional and even conservative aspects, however, this Meiji Restoration was also a quite revolutionary break from the past. The Meiji Charter Oath that was issued in the name of the emperor in April 1868, which famously urged that "evil customs of the past shall be broken off and ... Knowledge shall be sought throughout the world so as to strengthen the foundations of imperial rule," provides what one historian has called "a perfect example of this blending of tradition with intended change." New foreign ideas were to be openly considered, but to buttress an allegedly primordial Japanese imperial throne.[38] Another striking example of this process of blending tradition with novelty is provided by the composition of Japan's modern Western-style national anthem in the 1870s: by a German bandmaster, who set verses from the tenth-century *Kokinshū* to music. A modern Japanese nation-state was created that was in many ways new, but popularly imagined as ancient. Into modern Japan's frontiers, also, certain peoples who had formerly often been viewed as foreign, such as the Okinawans of the Ryūkyū Islands in the south and the Ainu of the far north, were reconceived now, not as foreign but as more pristine survivals of the ancient Japanese.[39]

Despite a patina of tradition, the first two decades of the Meiji reign period were a time of considerable enthusiasm for foreign Western ideas, which came to be flatly labeled "civilization and enlightenment" (*bunmei kaika*). Abandoning the use of Chinese characters in writing was seriously debated, and the possibility of moving to a Western-style alphabet was considered. One future minister of education even suggested, in 1872–1873, replacing Japanese with English as the national language. In the end, although neither Chinese characters nor the native Japanese *kana* syllabaries were abandoned (to say nothing of the Japanese language itself), a new standard modern vernacular Japanese written national language did take shape by the end of the nineteenth century.[40]

Among the most ardent popular Westernizers of the age was Fukuzawa Yūkichi (1835–1901), who, in 1885, went so far as to editorialize that Japan should culturally "leave Asia" and distance itself from its more backward neighbors. "It is better for us to leave the ranks of Asian nations and cast our lot with civilized nations of the West," wrote Fukuzawa.[41] Fukuzawa Yūkichi had begun life as a student of Dutch learning. In the 1860s, he visited Europe and the United States and published a best-selling book based on his experiences called *Conditions in the West* in 1866.

Even Fukuzawa could be described as a vigorous Japanese nationalist, however, and, in a predictable reaction to some of the more extreme Westernizing initiatives, conservative Japanese became incensed that the Meiji government was seemingly outdoing the old Tokugawa Shogunate in making concessions to the foreigners. Meiji Restoration leaders sometimes, therefore, found themselves the targets of patriotic attacks, among them that very same minister of education who had once proposed abolishing the Japanese language and replacing it with English. He was stabbed to death in 1889 because of his allegedly disrespectful behavior at the Imperial Grand Shrine in Ise.[42]

Meiji Modernization

In the immediate aftermath of the Meiji Restoration, institutions were in considerable flux in Japan, shifting uncertainly from American to British, French, or German models. As Fukuzawa Yūkichi described the Japan of the 1870s, "there was a government but no nation." It would not be until the late 1880s that the certainty of a (supposedly primordial) Japanese national, or more grandly, imperial identity firmly gripped the popular consciousness.[43] Indeed, as of 1868, it was not even obvious that the new government would survive. It was so closely associated with the southwestern domains of Chōshū and Satsuma, and to a lesser extent, also Tosa and Hizen, that certain other domains in the northeast rebelled in July. The rebellion was put down, but by what was still essentially a Chōshū and Satsuma rather than a truly national army.

Although the four domains that had led the Meiji Restoration contained only about 7 percent of the total Japanese population, as late as 1890 they still provided some 30 percent of the central government's leaders and filled roughly half of all the top positions.[44] Despite the Meiji slogan of "personal rule by the emperor," real power was wielded in the emperor's name by a handful of senior officials. A narrow circle of some twenty individuals came to be known as the Meiji oligarchy. As elder statesmen (genrō), these Meiji oligarchs continued to dominate Japanese politics well into the twentieth century. The new Meiji government did have the clear-sighted practical objective, however, of transforming Japan into a strong, modern, centralized nation-state.

In July, 1869, all the *daimyō* were ordered to transfer their domains to the central imperial government. The former *daimyō* were initially well compensated with substantial revenue and new government titles as local governors. In 1871, however, these same governors were stripped, without advance notice, of those titles and forced to retire to Tōkyō. The underlying regional uniformity that had already emerged during the centuries of the Tokugawa Shogunate, and that had already succeeded in imposing a degree of early modern bureaucratic centralization, made the transition from aristocratic domains to a centralized system of administrative prefectures a relatively smooth process. By 1871, the new imperial government appeared stable enough that half of the leading oligarchs confidently embarked on an extended tour of the West. While they were gone, however, a diplomatic crisis emerged over Korea's refusal to recognize Japanese imperial titles. Several of the Meiji leaders wanted to dispatch a punitive force against Korea immediately. When a more cautious approach against Korea was finally adopted, the oligarchs Saigō Takamori (1827–1877), Itagaki Taisuke (1837–1919), and others resigned in protest in 1873.

Saigō, who had been one of the heroes of the Meiji Restoration, now returned to his old domain in Satsuma and became a leading figure representing samurai class discontent. After the abolition of the *daimyō* domains in 1871, the central government had assumed the responsibility for paying all samurai stipends. This was an enormous financial obligation, however, which absorbed approximately one-third of all government revenue. It was clearly unsustainable, and the payment of samurai stipends was permanently suspended in 1876: converted into interest-bearing bonds. In that same year, the samurai privilege of wearing two swords was also banned. One by one, all the special samurai privileges were abolished, until none remained. In 1870, commoners had been granted surnames; in 1871, commoners were permitted to ride horses, travel freely, and marry samurai; in 1873, a new conscription law obligated commoners to serve in the army. Whereas commoners had once been actively forbidden to bear arms, they were now required to do so, in the service of the new Japanese nation-state.

The 1876 ban on carrying two swords, the government's failure to avenge the alleged Korean insults, and general unease at the rapid pace of change and Westernization fed samurai discontent, especially in the very domains that had led the Meiji Restoration, where samurai expectations were often most acutely disappointed. In Satsuma, neither the ban on carrying swords nor the elimination of samurai stipends was enforced. Notable samurai rebellions occurred in Saga in 1874, in Chōshū in 1876, and finally in Satsuma in 1877, this one led by Saigō Takamori himself.

A year earlier, the central imperial government, then under the domination of the oligarch Ōkubo Toshimichi (1830–1878) – himself originally a samurai from Satsuma – had sent agents to disarm the arsenal in Satsuma's castle town. Captured by local men, one agent "confessed" under torture that he had been sent to assassinate Saigō. Declaring that he had questions to ask the central government, in February 1877 Saigō led a large force of fifteen thousand samurai on a march toward Tōkyō. Though they never got off the southwestern island of Kyūshū, and their samurai army, with its lingering regional loyalties, ultimately proved no match for the modern conscript army of the central government, it still took six months for the full weight of the imperial army to put this samurai rebellion down. In September, his cause a failure, Saigō Takamori committed ritual suicide (*seppuku*). In a sense, the entire samurai class died with him. Although the Meiji oligarch Ōkubo was himself assassinated the very next year, in 1878, the old warrior class never again posed a serious threat to the new Meiji order.

The Meiji Constitution

Like Saigō Takamori, the oligarch Itagaki Taisuke had also resigned from the government over the dispute involving Korea, but unlike Saigō, he adopted a dissident approach based not on samurai nostalgia but on modern Western liberal political ideals. Itagaki began to lobby for the creation of a representative government assembly. This was the origin of what is known as the popular rights movement. In the decade of the 1870s, no fewer than 130 petitions were submitted to the emperor, calling for the establishment of representative self-government. Self-government seemed to be one of those irresistible Western trends of the times, and even the Meiji government itself encouraged some degree of modern popular participation. The oligarch Ōkubo Toshimichi took a conservative stance, however. Under his watch, a press law in 1875 imposed advance censorship and restricted political criticism.

Figure 8.8. Itō Hirobumi (1841–1909), the first prime minister of Japan. National Diet Library web site.

After the assassination of Ōkubo in 1878, the Meiji government made some concessions, and it soon publicly pledged to put a written Western-style constitution and an elected national assembly in place by 1890. In anticipation of this, the first Japanese political parties began to form in 1881. Because the trend toward representative government seemed unstoppable, the Meiji oligarchs concluded that their best course of action was to quickly adopt an acceptably conservative version of a modern constitution rather than be outrun by the pace of liberal expectations from outside the government. In 1881, a list of minimally acceptable conditions was drawn up, which included the stipulations that the new constitution be conferred from above as a gift from the emperor, and that if the elected assembly refused to pass a proposed budget the last year's budget would take effect automatically (thereby, if not denying, at least limiting, the power of the purse to the elected legislature).

In 1882, the oligarch Itō Hirobumi (1841–1909) went to Europe to study various modern constitutional models directly (see Figure 8.8). Although Itō did stop in Britain, and an associate went to France, Itō spent seven months in Germany, and the Meiji oligarchs appear to have, from the beginning, favored the German model. This was the newly unified imperial Germany of the kaiser and the Iron Chancellor, Prince Otto von Bismarck (1815–1898), which, although it made significant concessions to representative self-government, also retained firm central imperial control. Returning to Japan, Itō Hirobumi was then placed in charge of drafting the new Meiji constitution.

As a further countermeasure against suspiciously liberal Anglo-American democratic ideas, German influences were now combined with ancient East Asian tradition in the formation of a new Japanese peerage in 1884, which was designed to fill a hereditary Upper House that was intended to balance the popularly elected lower chamber of the future legislature. The legal framework was German, but most of the members of this newly created nobility were former Tokugawa *daimyō* or old court nobles, and the titles for this new aristocracy were actually drawn from the ancient Zhou Dynasty Chinese classics.[45] A cabinet, or modern Western-style executive branch, was established in 1885 (before the election of the first legislature), with the idea that it might function as a "transcendent" cabinet, answerable only to the emperor rather than to the legislature. Itō Hirobumi became Japan's first prime minister.

Meanwhile, under tight secrecy, and in consultation with a German legal advisor on the faculty of Tōkyō Imperial University, Itō and his assistants produced a draft constitution. On February 11, 1889, this new Meiji constitution was formally promulgated. On the German model, it was a gift from the emperor to the people, with the emperor remaining "above the clouds." In addition, the army and navy ministers were answerable to the emperor alone and independent of civilian control. The awesome potency of the imperial symbol was, furthermore, deliberately renewed and strengthened. In 1888, an engraving of the Meiji emperor was distributed to all public schools and official buildings, making the emperor's image a ubiquitous presence throughout the new Japanese nation. In 1890, an "Imperial Rescript on Education" was issued, urging students that "should any emergency arise, offer yourselves courageously to the state; and thus guard and maintain the prosperity of our Imperial throne, coeval with heaven and earth."[46] Japanese schoolchildren were obliged to bow to the imperial portrait and hear the "Rescript on Education" recited regularly. Once again, this was a blending of allegedly ancient Japanese traditions with the forms of modern, Western-style nation building.

The first election for the Lower House of the new national legislature (the Diet) was held in 1890. Since the franchise was limited to relatively wealthy taxpayers, only a little over 1 percent of the population were actually eligible to vote, and the government continued in practice to be largely directed by the same handful of Meiji oligarchs, in the name of the emperor. Still, Japan had become the first nation east of Suez to have a modern Western-style constitution and an elected legislature. This was a conservative constitutional order that would soon be put to the service of expansive imperialism, but it was nonetheless an unmistakable emblem of modernity. In addition, Japan was also on its way to becoming the first non-Western society in the world to successfully industrialize.

Industrialization

One of the major reasons for nineteenth-century Japanese modernizing success was the sharp clarity with which the Meiji oligarchs perceived the strategic urgency of the situation and moved swiftly to implement necessary, even if sometimes painful, measures to achieve their overarching goals of national security. Though their most pressing concern was to duplicate modern Western military power, there was also a quick recognition that the secret underlying modern military power was modern economic productivity. The Meiji government managed to put its new national economy on a sound footing, in part by keeping foreign debt minimal and by eliminating the payment of samurai stipends. In 1871–1872, a new standardized currency system, based on the yen, was established, and a modern banking system modeled on the U.S. Federal Reserve was implemented. In 1882, a central Bank of Japan was established.

Initially, some Japanese leaders were under the impression that trade and commerce alone were the source of modern national wealth, but by the 1870s the Meiji oligarchs had realized that mechanized industrialization was the magic key that unlocked the secrets to exponential increases in productivity. The Meiji elite therefore determined that rapid industrialization would be necessary, not only for strategic military considerations but also to prevent Japan from slipping into poverty and becoming a mere supplier of raw materials for industrialized foreign countries. Early attempts to stimulate private investment in modern industry were not particularly successful, however, in part because of the aversion to risky new business ventures by conservative old merchant houses, and in part because the amount of capital necessary for industrialization was simply too large. The Meiji government was furthermore unable to protect domestic industrial development by placing a wall of high taxes on competing foreign imports because import taxes had been fixed at low rates by treaty. The Meiji government decided to compensate, therefore, by itself deliberately promoting domestic industrialization. The Tomioka silk-reeling factory, for example, was built by the government in 1872, both to provide employment and to encourage private mechanization by demonstrating how (see Figure 8.9). The first modern industries in Japan were mostly built and administered by the government itself.[47]

The Meiji government even backed the development, from 1876, of Sapporo, the first domestic brand of the newly introduced Western alcoholic beverage, beer. (Another brewery had been established a little earlier in Yokohama as a foreign business, which was later acquired by the Japanese, becoming Kirin beer in 1907.)[48] However, much of the focus of the Meiji government-led industrialization was explicitly strategic and military. The modern arms industry was initially owned and operated by the government, and though private light textile manufacturing soon prospered and became more important in foreign trade, generating much critically needed foreign exchange, even some of the technology used in private textile production derived from spinoffs of military applications. In the 1880s, for example, an absolute majority of private cotton textile mills in Japan were powered by steam engines made by a government arsenal. "Virtually every major firm in

Figure 8.9. The model industrial silk-reeling factory that was built in 1872 in Tomioka, Gunma Prefecture, Japan (woodblock print). Snark/Art Resource, New York.

Japan benefited from the Meiji military industrial program ... including Toshiba and Nikon, which were created directly by and for the Meiji military."[49]

On the other hand, however, Japan's success in industrialization also owed much to the skills, attitudes, and commercial practices that had already developed indigenously in late Tokugawa times, and the actual takeoff of the industrial economy was led by small-scale private textile manufacturing.[50] And, if government initiative was critical for technological borrowing and the early development of large-scale (and initially often unprofitable) heavy industry, the government's resources themselves were also far from infinite. Because taxes on imports were fixed at relatively low rates by treaty, and the Meiji oligarchs were deeply concerned to avoid incurring any debilitating foreign debt, the principal source of government funding was the land tax, which, in the 1870s, contributed some 90 percent of all government revenue.

The serious economic constraints facing the Meiji government led to a program of enforced austerity in the 1880s, which imposed much hardship but also may have strengthened the overall economy. By the mid-1880s, the government was financially solvent. Also in the 1880s, the government deliberately began to transfer its infant industrial plant into private hands. The government-built silk mill at Tomioka, for example, was sold to the private firm Mitsui in 1893. Sapporo beer was acquired by private entrepreneurs in 1887.

Since the early Meiji "government could not afford the luxury of a gestation period during which the shipping industry might build a 'model' organization" naturally, after several failed experiments the government moved toward a policy of official support for a single favored private firm. In the shipping industry, that favored firm was Mitsubishi. Mitsubishi had begun under another name in 1866 as an industrial promotion agency belonging to the domain of Tosa, but it was subsequently reorganized into a private firm and, in 1873, renamed Mitsubishi. After Mitsubishi successfully provided military transport during the government's punitive expedition against the aborigines in Taiwan in 1874, the government gave thirteen large steamships to Mitsubishi and began providing it with an annual government subsidy. Among other things, "the financial reports made necessary by the subsidy led to Mitsubishi's rapid adoption of Western accounting techniques." Mitsubishi developed and prospered, with government backing, to meet the Meiji government's strategic needs in providing transport in war and in competing with the West, which was perceived as an urgent national concern due to the fact that Western shipping long continued to dominate Japan's foreign trade.[51]

Mitsubishi became one of the distinctively Japanese conglomerates called *zaibatsu*, which dominated the modern sector of the Japanese economy in the years between the Meiji Restoration and World War II. The word *zaibatsu* might loosely be translated as "wealth lord," in an expression parallel to *gunbatsu*, or "warlord." There were perhaps a score of *zaibatsu* in pre-World War II Japan, but by every reckoning, there were four particularly great *zaibatsu*: Mitsubishi, Sumitomo, Yasuda, and Mitsui. Although Mitsui dated from early Tokugawa times, the *zaibatsu* as a whole were a significantly new kind of business enterprise. In part, they merely reflected a general worldwide trend toward larger businesses in the later nineteenth century. Mergers, monopolies, trusts, syndicates, and cartels seemed to be the order of the day: in 1880, for example, Standard Oil controlled some 90 percent of all U.S. oil refining. The Japanese *zaibatsu*, however, rarely monopolized a given market sector, but instead duplicated and competed with each other through extensive diversification into a wide range of endeavors, typically including manufacturing, banking, and trade.

Japan became the first non-Western society to successfully industrialize, but the takeoff of Japan's modern economy was far from instantaneous. In the 1880s, Japan's foreign trade was still only about a quarter of the volume of China's, and much of Japan's foreign trade was still controlled by Western merchants. As late as 1900, an approximately equal percentage of China's population (to say nothing of absolute numbers) was employed in industry as in Japan.[52] Traditional-style enterprises continued to produce most of the commodities for the Japanese domestic market. As late as 1898, 82 percent of the Japanese population was still rural, and Japan remained a largely poor country. Despite the Meiji Restoration, for most people, lifestyles did not change all that dramatically in the second half of the nineteenth century. The rickshaw, a two-wheeled vehicle pulled by human muscle power, far from being an ancient East Asian tradition, was actually not invented until after the Meiji Restoration in Japan, and the emperor did not enjoy his first ride in a horse-drawn carriage until 1871. (Roads had been poorly developed in premodern Japan, and wheeled vehicles had been rare.) The first short railway line, linking Tōkyō to nearby Yokohama, did not commence operations until 1872. Electric light service in Tōkyō only began in 1887.[53]

Yet Japan was already becoming militarily strong. By 1880, Japan was producing its first modern rifle of its own design. In 1899, a renegotiated treaty with Great Britain took effect, ending many of the more objectionable features of the treaty port system that had been in place since the 1850s (although Japan did not regain the right to set its own taxes on imports until 1911). In 1895, Japan defeated China in war. In 1902, Japan officially became a British ally, and in 1905, Japan defeated a major modern great power, Russia, in war. By this time, Japan had convincingly demonstrated its claim to the status of being a modern world power.

The French Colonization of Vietnam

In Vietnam, the anti-Christian polices adopted by the Nguyen court in the early nineteenth century prompted Catholic appeals to the French government to do more to actively support the mission. Together with the allure of commercial opportunities, and also a desire not to be left out of the acquisition of colonies in Asia by the other modern great powers, this led to the dispatch to Vietnam of a French fleet of fourteen ships (already in Asian waters because of French participation in the second Opium War against the Qing Dynasty), which landed at Da Nang, near the Nguyen imperial capital Hue, in 1858. This French toehold was besieged by Vietnamese defenders and stricken by cholera and typhus, however, and Da Nang was abandoned after only half a year. The French fleet then sailed south, seizing Saigon in early 1859.

The French had initially hoped that the Mekong River might provide a lucrative trade route from southern Vietnam into south China, but, although the Mekong does indeed originate in the Tibetan Plateau and pass through Yunnan Province in China on its long journey to the sea, it has too many rapids and waterfalls to be easily navigable. The Mekong flows into Vietnam out of Cambodia, and French expeditions into Cambodia soon won recognition of French overlordship there. By 1867, the entire Mekong delta was under French control.

The Red River in the north of Vietnam, meanwhile, really did provide a navigable passage into southwest China, and in 1872 the French Governor in Saigon sent a warship to explore the river. There, the French military made contact with a

French merchant-adventurer who had some previous experience shipping arms up the Red River into Yunnan in exchange for salt and rice. When friction developed with the Vietnamese authorities, a French captain sent from Saigon to resolve the problem instead attacked and captured the citadel at Hanoi. The Vietnamese army, joined by a Chinese rebel militia known as the Black Flags (a mixture of Triads and former Taipings), counterattacked, and the French captain was killed. The result of this conflict was a treaty in 1874 that recognized French control over the south, and opened the Red River to French trade.

Turmoil in the Red River area continued to disrupt French trade, however, and in 1882 a small French force, consisting initially of only 233 men, seized Hanoi. The Qing Dynasty in China felt obligated to intervene to protect its traditional

Map 8.3 French Indochina

Vietnamese tributary, and, although the resulting war between China and France was relatively inconclusive, by 1885 the Qing was compelled by treaty to recognize a French protectorate extending all the way north to the border with China, and authorize the French to construct a railway leading from Hanoi into Yunnan. Although the last Vietnamese armed resistance was not finally suppressed until 1913, all of Vietnam was now effectively under French rule.

Under French control, Vietnam was divided into three parts: Cochinchina in the south, which was an outright French colony; Tonkin in the north, which was a French protectorate; and Annam in the center, which was still nominally ruled by the Nguyen emperor. In 1885, however, that emperor was chosen and appointed by the French, and French Resident-Generals were established in each of Saigon, Hanoi, and Hue. In 1887, an Indochinese Union was organized under French administration, which joined Cambodia together with the three French subdivisions of Vietnam, to which Laos was also added in 1893. The Vietnamese Empire had become French Indochina. Travel between Cochinchina, Tonkin, and Annam required a passport, moreover, so that even the Vietnamese regions of French Indochina were internally separated.

For Further Reading

On comparative industrialization and economic development in China and Europe, see Lloyd E. Eastman, *Family, Fields, and Ancestors: Constancy and Change in China's Social and Economic History, 1550–1949* (New York: Oxford University Press, 1988), esp. chaps. 6–8; Andre Gunder Frank, *ReOrient: Global Economy in the Asian Age* (Berkeley: University of California Press, 1998); Robert B. Marks, *The Origins of the Modern World: A Global and Ecological Narrative from the Fifteenth to the Twenty-First Century*, 2nd ed. (Lanham, MD: Rowman and Littlefield, 2007); and Kenneth Pomeranz, *The Great Divergence: China, Europe, and the Making of the Modern World Economy* (Princeton University Press, 2000).

On the Opium Wars, see Peter Ward Fay, *The Opium War, 1840–1842: Barbarians in the Celestial Empire in the Early Part of the Nineteenth Century and the War by Which They Forced Her Gates Ajar* (New York: W. W. Norton, 1975), and Harry G. Gelber, *Opium, Soldiers, and Evangelicals: England's 1840–42 War with China, and Its Aftermath* (New York: Palgrave Macmillan, 2004).

For the Taiping and other nineteenth-century Chinese domestic rebellions, see Albert Feuerwerker, *Rebellion in Nineteenth-Century China* (Ann Arbor: Center for Chinese Studies, University of Michigan, 1975); Philip A. Kuhn, *Rebellion and Its Enemies in Late Imperial China: Militarization and Social Structure, 1796–1864* (Cambridge, MA: Harvard University Press, 1970); Franz Michael, in collaboration with Chung-li Chang, *The Taiping Rebellion: History and Documents*, 3 vols. (Seattle: University of Washington Press, [1966] 1972); Elizabeth J. Perry, *Rebels and Revolutionaries in North China, 1845–1945* (Stanford University Press, 1980); and Jonathan D. Spence, *God's Chinese Son: The Taiping Heavenly Kingdom of Hong Xiuquan* (New York: W. W. Norton, 1996).

A classic study of the Tongzhi Restoration is Mary Clabaugh Wright, *The Last Stand of Chinese Conservatism: The T'ung-Chih Restoration, 1862–1874* (Stanford University Press, 1957).

The treaty ports and Sino-Western contact are dealt with in Robert Bickers, *The Scramble for China: Foreign Devils in the Qing Empire, 1832–1914* (London: Penguin Books, 2011); John King Fairbank, *Trade and Diplomacy on the China Coast: The Opening of the Treaty Ports,*

1842–1854 (1953; Stanford University Press, [1953] 1969); Michael Greenberg, *British Trade and the Opening of China, 1800–42* (Cambridge University Press, [1951] 1969); and Rhoads Murphey, *The Outsiders: The Western Experience in India and China* (Ann Arbor: University of Michigan Press, 1977). On the final phase of the mature treaty port system in Shanghai, see Nicholas R. Clifford, *Spoilt Children of Empire: Westerners in Shanghai and the Chinese Revolution of the 1920s* (Hanover, NH: Middlebury College Press, 1991).

Concerning the Boxer Rebellion, see Paul A. Cohen, *History in Three Keys: The Boxers as Event, Experience, and Myth* (New York: Columbia University Press, 1997), and Joseph W. Esherick, *The Origins of the Boxer Uprising* (Berkeley: University of California Press, 1987).

The end of the traditional order in Korea is described in Martina Deuchler, *Confucian Gentlemen and Barbarian Envoys: The Opening of Korea, 1875–1885* (Seattle: University of Washington Press, 1977); Peter Duus, *The Abacus and the Sword: The Japanese Penetration of Korea, 1895–1910* (Berkeley: University of California Press, 1995); and Key-Hiuk Kim, *The Last Phase of the East Asian World Order: Korea, Japan, and the Chinese Empire, 1860–1882* (Berkeley: University of California Press, 1980).

Indispensable sources for the Meiji Restoration in Japan include Marius B. Jansen, *The Making of Modern Japan* (Cambridge, MA: Harvard University Press, 2000), and Marius B. Jansen, *Sakamoto Ryōma and the Meiji Restoration* (New York: Columbia University Press, [1961] 1994). A detailed narrative of events preceding the Meiji Restoration is provided by Conrad D. Totman, *The Collapse of the Tokugawa Bakufu, 1862–1868* (Honolulu: University of Hawai'i Press, 1980). The doomed samurai rebellion of Saigō Takamori is narrated in chapter 9 of Ivan I. Morris, *The Nobility of Failure: Tragic Heroes in the History of Japan* (New York: Holt, Rinehart, and Winston, 1975). For a study of one important Meiji oligarch, see Roger F. Hackett, *Yamagata Aritomo in the Rise of Modern Japan, 1838–1922* (Cambridge, MA: Harvard University Press, 1971).

The changing self-image of the Japanese nation in this period is skillfully surveyed by Carol Gluck, *Japan's Modern Myths: Ideology in the Late Meiji Period* (Princeton University Press, 1985). Changing Chinese perceptions of Japan during the 1870s–1880s, as East Asia's premodern cultural community was seriously shaken by rapid Japanese modernization, are examined in D. R. Howland, *Borders of Chinese Civilization: Geography and History at Empire's End* (Durham, NC: Duke University Press, 1996).

For Meiji Japan's precocious economic modernization, see Johannes Hirschmeier, *The Origins of Entrepreneurship in Meiji Japan* (Cambridge, MA: Harvard University Press, 1964); Byron K. Marshall, *Capitalism and Nationalism in Prewar Japan: The Ideology of the Business Elite, 1868–1941* (Stanford University Press, 1967); Thomas C. Smith, *Political Change and Industrial Development in Japan: Government Enterprise, 1868–1880* (Stanford University Press, 1955); and Kozo Yamamura, ed., *The Economic Emergence of Modern Japan* (Cambridge University Press, 1997). Mikiso Hane provides a rare glimpse into the impact of modernization on the lives of ordinary Japanese in *Peasants, Rebels, and Outcastes: The Underside of Modern Japan* (New York: Pantheon Books, 1982).

For nineteenth-century Vietnam, see Joseph Buttinger, *The Smaller Dragon: A Political History of Vietnam* (New York: Frederick A. Praeger, 1958); and Alexander Barton Woodside, *Vietnam and the Chinese Model: A Comparative Study of Nguyên and Ch'ing Civil Government in the First Half of the Nineteenth Century* (Cambridge, MA: Harvard University Press, 1971).

9 The Age of Westernization (1900–1929)

Empire's End: Republican Revolution in China

Defeat at the hands of Japan in the Sino-Japanese War of 1895 irrevocably shattered China's traditional sense of self-assurance, and what remained of the premodern Chinese world order was rapidly undermined thereafter. In 1891 and 1897, the reformer Kang Youwei (1858–1927) published two controversial (and repeatedly banned) books that argued that the existing texts of the Confucian Classics had been distorted by forgeries dating from the first century, and that Confucius, far from being a conservative transmitter of ancient traditions, had actually been a reformer in his own day.[1] Despite this attempt to rejuvenate the Sage Confucius in the modernizing guise of a reformer, such scholarship already betrayed a profound loss of faith in tradition.

In 1898, one important official, while apparently arguing conservatively for maintaining "Chinese learning for the fundamental principles," simultaneously also acknowledged that in a time of "drastic transformation" substantial modernizing reforms were appropriate. After 1898, even this relatively moderate approach tended to be abandoned in favor of more radical modernization.[2] The Japanese victory in 1895 had sounded an alarm, and following the Boxer disaster in 1900, even the Qing government recognized the need for rapid reform. China had been exposed as vulnerable – a once mighty empire reduced to being the "sick man of Asia" – and in need of some fairly dramatic measures to pull itself out of the past and adjust to modern world realities (see Figure 9.1). *New* (*xin*) suddenly became a highly fashionable buzzword in early twentieth-century China, beginning with the Qing Dynasty's "new policies" and "new schools" in the first decade and reaching its climax with the "new culture" of the May Fourth Movement in the second decade of the century – epitomized by the title of its most famous journal, *New Youth*.[3]

In 1902, the Empress Dowager Cixi authorized an edict ordering the abolition of foot binding (a painful and disabling custom that had been widespread among Chinese women since about the Song Dynasty). Although foot binding took

Figure 9.1. The last days of the Chinese Empire. A lone rider at the Ming tombs in north China, 1907. Library of Congress, LC-USZ62-56190.

decades to thoroughly eradicate everywhere, the abolition of the traditional examination system in 1905 was immediately effective and dealt a fatal blow to the old examination-selected Mandarin elite. Also in 1905, a group of imperial commissioners traveled for eight months in Japan, the United States, and Europe to study models of modern constitutional government. After their return, a nine-year program of constitutional reform was announced in 1908 that included the installation of elected provincial representative assemblies by 1909 and a promise of gradual transition to "self-government."

Yet even these dramatic reforms were no longer enough. The "new schools" were often simply converted temples or former Confucian academies that remained far from universally accessible and that were not necessarily really very different from their premodern predecessors. The electorate for the 1909 provincial elections was no more than half of 1 percent of the population.[4] The Meiji Japanese and imperial German model that was favored for the Qing Dynasty reforms, with its assertive role for centralized authoritarian imperial government, also disappointed would-be local leaders as well as reformers who held more liberal Anglo-American-style aspirations. In addition, breaking with long-standing Qing Dynasty precedent, princes from the imperial family began to play a more active role in government, and the number of ethnic Manchus in high office actually increased. For example, although the Manchu Banner People were only a little over 1 percent of China's population, they held eight of thirteen heads of ministries in 1906 and five of nine governor-general positions in 1907.[5]

This was particularly unfortunate because it coincided with the introduction of modern Western ideas of national self-determination. After some two centuries of widespread acceptance of Manchu rule under the Qing Dynasty, at the turn of the twentieth century many Chinese people suddenly awoke to the idea that they were the conquered subjects of "foreign" Manchus. Ending Manchu rule became a first priority of the new Chinese nationalism.

Something like the nation, of course, is an ancient phenomenon. But premodern states, in China and elsewhere, were often defined more by their ruling elites than by their peoples. It has been argued that true modern nationalism had its origins in sixteenth-century England, when the people first began to be conceived as the ultimate source of legitimate sovereignty. As the spread of print technology promoted increasingly standardized national languages (High German and Parisian French, for example, gained prestige over local dialects as national standards), a new sense of participation in a shared national community began to take shape among the reading public.[6]

The first East Asian invocation of this originally European concept of "nation" apparently came during the Meiji era Japanese popular rights movement, when a new two-character Japanese expression *minzoku* (meaning, roughly, the "people clan") was coined to translate the *nationale* in French expressions such as *Assemblée Nationale* – in this case, obviously, still referring to popular sovereignty. By the end of the nineteenth century, however, this Japanese word was coming to be used more commonly in approximation of the German word *Volk*, indicating a community with supposedly shared linguistic, cultural, historical, and other ties.[7] Nations in that sense, as peoples possessing allegedly distinctive characteristics, and ideally independently self-governing, came to be widely viewed as the natural divisions of humanity in nineteenth-century Europe, and Germany itself became a classic example of modern nation-state building, as the Prussian Kingdom expanded between 1866 and 1871 to forge the first-ever unified Germany.

Like many other modern Japanese translations of European terms, this new word for "nation" soon made its way to China, where the same two-character combination (pronounced *minzu* in Mandarin Chinese) could be imported and easily understood directly in written form.[8] Both in the political sense of popular sovereignty and in the communal sense of *Volk*, this new idea of nationalism demanded an end in China to hereditary rule by non-Chinese Manchu emperors. Because such nationalism was originally a Western idea, in China as elsewhere, the earliest nationalists tended to emerge from the ranks of persons who were deeply exposed to modern Western thought. In China's case, appropriately, the first great nationalist revolutionary was also one of the most thoroughly Westernized major figures in all of Chinese history: Dr. Sun Yat-sen (1866–1925).

Figure 9.2. Dr. and Mrs. Sun Yat-sen. Photograph signed and dated by Mrs. Sun, Canton, January 14, 1926. Hoover Institution Archives. Paul Myron Wentworth Linebarger papers.

Sun Yat-sen (see Figure 9.2) was a Cantonese peasant by birth – born, that is, far from the traditional centers of Chinese culture and power and speaking an unintelligible local southern dialect – but in 1879, he was sent to join an older brother in Hawai'i. In Hawai'i, Sun was placed in a boarding school where the language of instruction was English. Sun became fluent in English, and he also became a Christian. He completed his formal education in Hong Kong with training in Western-style medicine. Altogether, Sun spent some thirteen years as a student or protégé of Western Protestant missionaries, and until age forty-six he lived most of his life outside China.[9] Inspired by his intimate knowledge of the modern West, Sun hoped to create a Western-style nation-state and republic in China, sometimes specifically taking the United States as his model.

The 1911 Revolution

Sun Yat-sen organized his first revolutionary group in Hawai'i in 1894. In 1895, he attempted his first armed revolutionary uprising in Guangzhou. This came immediately after the Qing defeat in the Sino-Japanese War, which might have presented a timely opportunity to overthrow the Qing, but the uprising was delayed for two days because its preparations were incomplete, and during the interval, the police discovered the plot. Forty-eight conspirators were arrested, and 205 revolvers were confiscated. Sun Yat-sen escaped to British Hong Kong and then traveled on to Japan. From this time until the final success of the Republican Revolution in 1911, Sun spent a total of only one night in China.

Sun Yat-sen spent much of his time abroad in Japan, where he acquired the alias by which he is still most commonly known to Chinese-language speakers: (Sun) Zhongshan, the Mandarin Chinese pronunciation of the Japanese surname Nakayama. But Sun also spent some time in French colonial Vietnam, and he was particularly active with fund-raising in the United States and Britain. In a famous episode in 1896, Sun was kidnapped and held prisoner in the Qing legation in London. Fortunately for Sun, he was able to smuggle a message out to a British friend, who raised a clamor in the English press that forced his release. This incident catapulted Sun to a certain degree of international notoriety, but most Chinese people were probably still largely unaware of Sun and his revolutionary movement as late as the beginning of the twentieth century. However, in Tōkyō, Japan, in 1905, a loose coalition of Chinese revolutionary groups was formed called the Revolutionary Alliance (*Tongmenghui*), with Sun Yat-sen as a central figure.

Over the next few years, this Revolutionary Alliance sponsored several armed uprisings in China, all of which failed dismally. As the litany of defeats lengthened, the revolutionaries turned with growing fascination to the tactics of terrorism, including bombings and assassinations. On October 9, 1911, as some revolutionaries were making bombs in the headquarters of a group called the Forward Together Society, located in the Russian concession in the cluster of three mid-Yangzi River cities collectively known as Wuhan, some ashes from a cigarette they were smoking fell and accidentally detonated one of those bombs. The police came and uncovered a list of members in the rubble and immediately arrested dozens. Three revolutionaries were executed early the very next day, October 10, which precipitated an unplanned mutiny in the local New Army garrison. The mutinous troops seized control of the arsenal, the Manchu governor-general fled, and on October 11, the president of the local provincial assembly met with the rebels and declared his support. This was the beginning of the Republican, or Nationalist, Revolution in China.

Ironically enough, the modern Western-style New Armies that had been created by the Qing to save the dynasty instead provided the military force that overthrew it. The first four provinces that rebelled were all led by New Army uprisings, and New Army support was also critical in most of the other provinces that joined the revolution later.[10] Before long, fifteen provinces, mostly concentrated in the south, had declared independence from the Qing. Although there was some locally fierce combat, within about a month the fighting had reached a stalemate, and negotiations began in Shanghai. Dr. Sun Yat-sen, meanwhile, was in Colorado at the time this unplanned revolution erupted and read about it in the news while traveling by train from Denver to Kansas City. Sun eventually made his way from the United States back to China, where he was appointed provisional president of the new republic. He held that title for only forty-five days, however, because Sun soon joined in offering the presidency to another man: Yuan Shikai (1859–1916).

Yuan Shikai had been a crucial player in the formation of the main modern army in north China, and his ability to control that armed force now made him a pivotal figure. Initially, he was recruited by the imperial court in Beijing to try to rescue the Qing Dynasty, but the republican revolutionaries made him a tempting counteroffer. After some negotiations, Yuan switched sides, and on February 12, 1912 – just four months after the revolution had begun – the last emperor of China abdicated the throne. The five-year-old ex-emperor was given favorable treatment, including a generous government subsidy and permission to continue living in the old imperial palace. Yuan Shikai then became the first official president of the new Republic of China. Three days after the abdication of the last emperor, Sun Yat-sen visited the tomb of the founder of the last ethnically Chinese dynasty (the Ming) to announce the restoration of Chinese rule after three centuries of subjugation under the "alien" Manchus.

The May Fourth Movement: Science and Democracy

It was not merely Manchu rule that abruptly came to an end with the revolution in 1912: an imperial system that had lasted for more than two thousand years also ended forever. With it, in important senses, also died traditional China. Even the classical Chinese written language was now fairly rapidly replaced by a modern vernacular (roughly comparable to switching from Latin to Italian). By 1921, the Ministry of Education required all primary school textbooks to be written in the vernacular. Building a modern Chinese nation-state meant, paradoxically, a rejection of much Chinese tradition. Sun Yat-sen, for example, insisted on switching immediately to the Western solar calendar as "the first important reform of our successful revolution."[11] Most Chinese men immediately cut their Manchu-imposed queues in 1912, and rather than revert to older pre-Manchu Chinese hairstyles, modern Western-influenced hairstyles and clothing were widely adopted.

Contrary to the popular stereotype of a closed and isolationistic and deeply traditional China, China had long been heavily involved in world trade, and in the late nineteenth century many Chinese people were already surprisingly receptive to new things. Those who could afford it, especially in the big coastal cities, took fairly quickly to new technologies such as electric fans and photography, and even many of the humblest rural peasants also welcomed modern kerosene lamps, machine-manufactured enamel wash basins, and mass-produced inexpensive mirrors – although these modern mirrors might then be placed outside doorways to frighten away "traditional" evil spirits. By 1935, half of all Chinese villagers regularly used imported foreign kerosene. China's continuingly disappointing low volume of imports of manufactured goods from the West was due less to a stubborn refusal to accept new products than to the speed with which locally made substitutes began to compete with foreign goods. Especially after the suppression of the Boxer Rebellion, by 1901 even in a city deep in the interior such as Changsha, foreign kerosene, clocks, tinned vegetables and fruit from America, and European beer were easily available. The first motion picture to be shown in China was in 1897. The empress dowager received an automobile, a Benz, in 1902 (although she apparently never rode in it), and the first privately Chinese-owned automobile may have been in 1909. In 1911, China acquired its first two airplanes. Typically, one American journalist was disappointed on arrival in 1925 to find that his first glimpse of China was a billboard advertising chewing gum.[12]

For many, the revolution of 1911 brought a sweeping repudiation of the entire old order. The most famous statement of this almost complete reversal of attitudes may be a passage in an experimental short story – one of the first to be published in the new vernacular – called "A Madman's Diary," written in 1918 by modern China's most widely admired man of letters, Lu Xun (1881–1936). The main character in this story begins reading China's histories, only to find that "my history has no chronology, and scrawled all over each page are the words: 'Virtue and Morality' [i.e., traditional Confucian values]. Since I could not sleep anyway, I read intently half the night, until I began to see words between the lines, the whole book being filled with the two words – 'Eat people.'"[13] That is, unlike the dynamic modern West, China's premodern history had no progress, and all the lofty rhetoric about Confucian virtue merely concealed the hidden reality of metaphorical cannibalism and exploitation.

What suddenly now appeared to be the "bad customs" of old China were denounced, including such things as foot binding, opium addiction, arranged marriages, the sale of female bondservants, uncleanliness, spitting in public, and "superstition." Superstition (mixin, another new word in China) referred to traditional Chinese religions, which many in the educated Chinese elite, whether they were Christian or not, now felt were embarrassing signs of backwardness. Of roughly a million temples in China at the start of the twentieth century, more than half had been closed down by the 1930s.[14] Confucianism itself, moreover, now seemed to be the biggest obstacle to modernization of all. The idea of progress rendered antiquity obsolete, and tradition now seemed sweepingly discredited because it had left China so obviously weak and impoverished. As a result of the Industrial Revolution, by 1913, Europe and the United States together accounted for 88.6 percent of world manufacturing, while China's share had been reduced to only 3.6 percent.[15] The proven wealth and power of the West made Westernization attractive, especially to the young, urban, and educated. Although "the West" is something of an elastic, value-laden concept rather than a concrete, permanent, clearly defined reality, as an idea it has sometimes been undeniably powerful.

There was a fair amount of conscious Westernization, but even this still had to be on Chinese terms, suiting Chinese tastes (and, for Chinese patriots, to be in the service of the Chinese nation). The result was a complicated pattern of hybridization: a mix of old and new, Chinese and Western (see Figure 9.3). When the British-American Tobacco Company, for example, transplanted modern American commercial advertisements directly to China in 1902, the Chinese reaction was bewilderment. But when the same company installed advanced printing

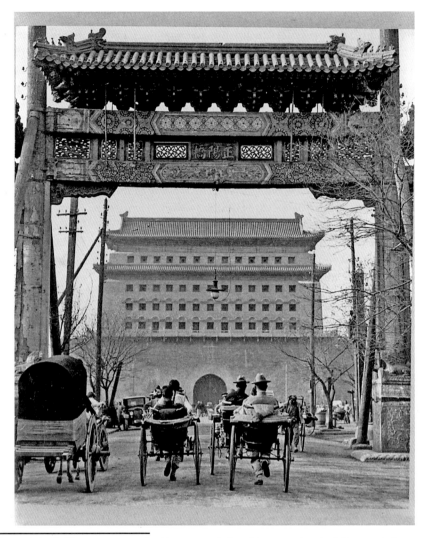

Figure 9.3. Beijing, ca. 1925, looking toward the Qianmen (gate). Library of Congress, LC-USZ62-137036.

presses in Shanghai in 1905 and began producing modern advertising designed by Chinese people, and tailored to Chinese sensibilities, this modified advertising campaign soon penetrated every corner of China with remarkable success.[16]

Although genuinely traditional clothing and hairstyles were largely abandoned after 1912, in the 1920s a major new fashion for Chinese men became the Sun Yat-sen suit (an early form of what later came to be known as the Mao suit). This was adapted from modern student uniforms and represented neither tradition nor a slavish imitation of the West but rather a distinctly Chinese version of modernity. Although the Western solar calendar was widely accepted, and also the foreign idea of a seven-day week with a regular day of rest on Sunday, the old lunar calendar simultaneously continued to be used for the celebration of holidays such as the New Year.[17] Significantly, under the Republic, dates were (really, in actual practice) calculated not from the birth of Christ but instead taking the foundation of the Republic of China in 1912 as the year 1.

Also significantly, China's greatest burst of popular enthusiasm for sweeping Westernization takes its name from what began as anti-Western (though most especially anti-Japanese) student protests: the May Fourth Movement. China had participated on the Allied side in World War I, and perhaps as many as two hundred thousand Chinese people had labored abroad as China's contribution to the Allied war effort. Because China had therefore been on the winning side, and especially in view of the American president Woodrow Wilson's stirring evocations of the ideal of national self-determination, Chinese students felt encouraged to hope that former German concessions in China would revert to Chinese rule after the war. Instead, the German base in Shandong was granted to Japan at the Versailles peace conference in 1919. When the news reached Beijing on May 4, 1919, many students felt betrayed, and several thousand gathered at Tiananmen (the old Gate of Heavenly Peace, not the Square, which did not yet exist) to stage protests.

The May Fourth Movement that began with these patriotic student demonstrations in 1919 then gave its name, more broadly, to an entire age of enthusiasm for New Culture. For the "new youth" of the May Fourth generation, "science and democracy" became the most revered mantra. Some young people even hoped for total Westernization. It was a time of youthful excitement and the discovery of new ideas. The American educator John Dewey lectured to eager audiences in China in 1919–1921. The renowned British philosopher Bertrand Russell was invited to Peking University in 1920. Hundreds of new magazines and periodicals began to be published. A modernizing attack on the entire patriarchal Confucian values system was unleashed in the name of freedom and equality, and the 1910s–1920s became the great age of Chinese individualism, feminism, and other modern Western ideals.

At the start of the twentieth century, modernizers throughout East Asia had often looked to Japan as a successful model. Japan had, after all, shaken off the treaty port system and defeated Russia in war by 1905. By 1914, Japan was one of only five countries in the entire world that were self-sufficient in railway locomotive production (a key index of early industrialization), together with Britain, France, Germany, and the United States.[18] For this, as well as reasons of convenience, the largest number of Chinese students studying abroad in the early twentieth century went to Japan – by 1906, about thirteen thousand. A truly impressive number of important early Chinese revolutionaries spent time in Japan, including both Sun Yat-sen and the future president of the Republic of China Chiang Kai-shek (in Mandarin, Jiang Jieshi, 1887–1975), who trained at a Japanese military academy in 1908–1911 (see Figure 14.3).

By World War I, however, Japan was already beginning to be viewed with suspicion as an imperialist aggressor by many Chinese people, and Japan had always served chiefly, anyway, only as a convenient filter through which modern Western ideas could be communicated. It was "the West" that fired the youthful May Fourth imagination. In particular, "the political thought of the French Revolution had an almost unrivaled vogue among young Chinese revolutionaries and reformers."

Figure 9.4. Deng Xiaoping as a sixteen-year-old student, during his study in France, 1920. New China Pictures. Magnum Photos.

Chen Duxiu (1879–1942), for example, who may have been in France between 1907 and 1910, used French rather than English for the Western-language alternate title of the extremely influential journal he founded, *La Jeunesse Nouvelle* (*New Youth*, or *Xin Qingnian* in Chinese), and for its first issue, he also wrote an article on "The French and Modern Civilization."[19] Chen Duxiu would later become the first leader of the Chinese Communist Party, when it was founded in 1921.

A surprising number of early leaders of the Chinese communist movement went to France, many in connection with a work-study program developed during World War I. The list includes Zhou Enlai (1898–1976), who became a Communist Party member while in France in 1920–1922, and who later served as premier of the People's Republic and was Mao Zedong's single most distinguished associate. Deng Xiaoping (1904–1997), who succeeded Mao as leader of the People's Republic in 1978, was in France from 1920 to 1926 (see Figure 9.4), where he also joined the Communist Party. Li Lisan (1899–1967), who was the Comintern's (an abbreviation for Communist International, headquartered in Moscow) pick to head the Chinese Communist Party in a time of crisis after 1927, before Mao Zedong's rise to power, was in France between 1919 and 1921. Mao's close friend (before his execution in 1931) Cai Hesen (1895–1931) also was in France in 1919–1921. Chen Yi (1901–1972), a future foreign minister, was in France from 1919 to 1921. In fact, during the first decade after the establishment of the communist People's Republic of China in 1949, nearly a quarter of the top leadership had been in France during this formative moment at the end of World War I.[20]

One exception was Zhu De (1886–1976), who joined the Communist Party in Germany rather than France in 1922. Zhu was the first commander of the Chinese Red Army and was the military genius probably most responsible for developing its successful tactics of guerrilla warfare.[21] In fact, among the top early Chinese revolutionaries (both Communist and Nationalist), it may have been Mao Zedong (1893–1976) who was most conspicuous for his lack of cosmopolitan experience. Mao never became proficient in any foreign language, and he never traveled outside China until after he had become head of state, when he finally made a trip to Moscow in 1949. Since Mao eventually rose to become the supreme figure in China's communist revolution, his lack of international experience is telling. Yet even Mao was a graduate of a modern-style provincial teacher's college, read numerous Western books in Chinese translation, and happened to be in Beijing at the height of the May Fourth Movement. By 1920, Mao was calling himself a Marxist.[22]

English-speaking readers may find it incredible that one of the principal outcomes of the first great wave of Westernization in China was the rise of communism. The enthusiasm with which some educated young Chinese embraced Westernization was fired, however, by a confidence that it represented a universal pattern of human progress rather than something exclusively European. Nowhere were these universalistic assumptions articulated more explicitly (or more rigidly) than in the theoretical Marxist sequence of stages, or "modes of production," through which all societies supposedly advanced. Of particular relevance, these included a transition from feudalism to capitalism, and then from capitalism to communism in the supposedly inevitable future. Communism was modern, Western (Karl Marx, after all, was a German who did much of his work in England), ostensibly scientific, and Marxism-Leninism also offered a scathing critique of great power imperialism that could be comforting to those who felt victimized, or at least humiliated, by it. And communist organization provided a tightly disciplined program of action that made it more effective than other, initially more appealing, Western ideologies such as anarchism (which, by definition, was not well organized).

The Chinese Communists were committed to a goal of industrialized (socialist) modernity, and this remained true even after Mao Zedong, for reasons of tactical necessity (and very awkwardly for Marxist theory), shifted the base of his revolution from urban industrial workers (the proletariat) to rural peasants. By the time of the final Communist victory in 1949, a large majority of party members were in fact peasants, yet the party never endorsed a so-called peasant mentality. Peasants were regarded as perhaps the most backward segment of a generally backward and feudal old regime from which the revolution was supposed to liberate China, and under the communist People's Republic, peasants even came to be treated, according to some observers, as second-class citizens.[23]

In any case, interest in communism in China was long confined to relatively narrow intellectual circles, and it was not until after the global descent into the "dark valley" of economic depression, fascism, and war during the 1930s and 1940s that communism threatened to gain control in China. Yet despite much genuine youthful Chinese interest in individualism, democracy, and other Western ideals during the May Fourth era, there was also an overriding sense of concern at China's palpable weakness and vulnerability, and a patriotic desire to regenerate national strength. Nationalists as well as Communists tended to see the solution in terms of political centralization and national unity. The Nationalist revolutionary Sun Yat-sen's most famous lament was that the Chinese people were "like loose sand," and his conclusion was that what China needed was discipline more than freedom.[24] Such discipline and unity seemed especially crucial because, after the initial success of the Republican Revolution in 1912, China had dissolved into warlordism. China became a failed state.

The Warlord Era, 1916–1928

In the early twentieth century, representative self-government seemed to be an irresistible trend that was sweeping the entire planet and an essential component of modernization. Following the success of the Republican Revolution in 1912, nationwide elections were scheduled almost immediately for a planned constitutional assembly. In this first Chinese experiment with democracy at the national level, some forty million men were eligible to vote – fully a fifth of the entire adult male population.[25] The elections went reasonably smoothly, and a newly organized, modern, Western-style political party known as the Nationalist Party (*Guomindang* in Chinese, alternatively spelled *Kuo-Min-Tang* and abbreviated either GMD or KMT) emerged as the clear winner. The first president of the Republic (Yuan Shikai), who had gained office through a deal rather than through the ballot box, was apparently alarmed by this Nationalist Party success, however, and is suspected of being implicated in the assassination of the party's dynamic young leader in 1913. President Yuan ordered the Nationalist Party dissolved later that same year, and in 1914, he dismissed the elected legislature.

In 1915, then, the president "allowed" himself to be declared emperor. He held the imperial title for only eighty-three days, however, because even some of his own officers took up arms against this attempt to revive the empire, and he was soon compelled to step down. In 1916, this first president died. Unfortunately, by that time, the constitutional process was also thoroughly bankrupt. Effective central government in China virtually ceased to exist for a dozen years after 1916. Purely for diplomatic convenience, foreign governments continued to address whichever warlord regime happened to control Beijing as if it were the government of China, but in practice, local authorities at various levels became independent. Chambers of commerce in some cities, for example, maintained their own armed forces, constructed railways, and sometimes even conducted negotiations with foreign governments.

Shanghai, the largest city in China, remained substantially under foreign administration. Because police in each of the three administrative jurisdictions (the International Settlement, the French Concession, and the Chinese city) had no authority in the other two, Shanghai was particularly ripe for the emergence of modern organized crime, especially after the re-prohibition of opium (which had been legalized in 1860) in 1919 provided opportunities for large illegal profits. Most notorious was the Green Gang, which came to be led by "Big-eared" Du Yuesheng (1888–1951). Du had been born on the wrong side of the river in a Pudong slum and began life as a fruit vendor's helper. After joining a gang as a teenager, he developed a new crime cartel to more efficiently distribute illegal profits, and he eventually even became prominent in legitimate public and charitable activities. Among his other titles, Du became deputy chairman of the Chinese Red Cross, chairman of the Shanghai Chinese Municipal Council, and director of the Shanghai Stock Exchange.[26] Du was perhaps the single best example of those colorfully sinister figures who gave pre-World War II Shanghai its rather shady reputation.

In the countryside, there was also widespread more traditional banditry. In a particularly notorious incident in 1923, bandits in Shandong derailed an express train and took twenty Westerners hostage, including a member of the wealthy American Rockefeller family. This drew international attention, and the incident was resolved by giving the bandits positions in the regular Chinese army, the bandit leader becoming a brigadier general. The line between bandits and soldiers was, in fact, often unclear, and few of China's armies were under effective central control.

As the Qing Dynasty had begun to modernize its military in the late nineteenth century, curiously, it did not attempt to forge a single, unified national army. In the aftermath of the revolution, the armed forces of the early republican era remained essentially separate provincial armies. With the collapse of clearly legitimate civilian central authority after 1916, military commanders stepped into the vacuum and became locally independent forces, or warlords.

Among these various military commanders, perhaps the most successful overall was the warlord of Manchuria, Zhang Zuolin (ca. 1875–1928). Zhang had begun his career as a bandit, and he gained control over Manchuria at the time of the 1911 Republican Revolution as a would-be Qing Dynasty imperial loyalist. After the fall of the Qing, he operated independently, and in 1922, he openly declared the independence of the three Manchurian provinces. Because Manchuria was, at this time, rapidly falling under Japanese domination, Zhang was obliged to coexist with rising Japanese power. By 1928, there may have been as many as fifty Japanese advisors attached to Zhang's Chinese army in Manchuria. But Zhang was also attended by a scattering of English, American, French, and White Russian advisors.[27] In his own way, moreover, Zhang was a Chinese patriot, and he may have even envisioned himself as the great reunifier who would rebuild China. In 1924, he gained control of Beijing and soon made it his headquarters. In 1928, he was assassinated by rogue Japanese army officers.

In the meantime, Sun Yat-sen had been driven back into exile in Japan by the authoritarian actions of the first president. After President Yuan Shikai's death, in 1917 Sun returned to China and attempted to establish a regional base in Guangzhou. Sun was joined there by 130 members of the dissolved legislature and also the minister of the Navy, who resigned and brought with him fifteen warships. The warlord commanders of the surrounding countryside were intermittently hostile, however, and Sun's effort to revive the republic, and the Nationalist Party, remained fragile. Seeking foreign aid – a recurrent theme throughout Sun Yat-sen's career – Sun now found that the only available source was the Soviet Union.

The apparent success of the Russian October Revolution in 1917, the newly established Soviet Union's public stance of avowed opposition to imperialism, and the fact that China and the Soviet Union shared the longest land border in the world all naturally drew Chinese attention to the north. Although Sun Yat-sen did not embrace communism, in 1923 Sun did reach a formal agreement with the Soviet Union. For its part, Moscow agreed that China was not yet ready for communism and pledged to assist the cause of the Nationalist revolution, while Sun Yat-sen permitted individual members of the Chinese Communist Party (CCP) also to join the Nationalist Party. Young Mao Zedong, for example, served as director of the Nationalist Party Propaganda Bureau.

Because military reunification of a China torn between contending warlord armies now seemed necessary, it was decided to create a new Nationalist Party army. In 1924, a Nationalist military academy was established (known as Huangpu or Whampoa). Moscow provided the bulk of the funds, and this new military academy was unique in China at the time for its incorporation of political as well as military instruction. On the model of the Soviet commissar system, Nationalist Party representatives were appointed to the army.[28] The man who was to be the first commandant of this Nationalist military academy was then sent to Moscow for three months of training. His name was Chiang Kai-shek.

In 1925, Sun Yat-sen died and was soon succeeded as leader of the Nationalist Party by Chiang Kai-shek. Acting swiftly, in 1926 Chiang launched a Northern Expedition to reunify China militarily from the Nationalist base in the far south at Guangzhou. Although John Pratt, a brother of the famous Hollywood actor Boris Karloff, predicted in a lecture to the British Imperial Defense College in February 1928 that China still might not have an effective central government "perhaps for a generation or two," by late 1928 Chiang Kai-shek's Northern Expedition had in fact succeeded in reunifying most of China proper, up to about the line of the Great Wall.[29]

After being admitted on an individual basis into the Nationalist Party following their 1923 agreement to cooperate, Chinese Communists had quickly become active in labor and political organization. During the Northern Expedition, a General Labor Union under leftist direction actually gained control of the city of Shanghai before Chiang Kai-shek's troops arrived. Chiang was unhappy with this leftist orientation, however, and in April 1927, while the Northern Expedition was only about half completed, Chiang broke suddenly with the leftists, striking at communist and labor organizations. Perhaps as many as twenty-five thousand Chinese Communists were killed in the first few months after this purge, and Chiang Kai-shek now emerged as a staunchly anti-communist figure.

By the end of 1928, therefore, with the completion of the Northern Expedition, a reunified Republic of China had been restored, led by Chiang Kai-shek and a now firmly anti-communist Nationalist Party, from a new capital at Nanjing (Nanking). But, in reality, most of China still remained beyond effective central government control, and the revived republic was also now reconfigured as a single-party state. Sun Yat-sen had originally anticipated a three-stage process, beginning with the military reunification of China, followed by a supposedly brief period of Nationalist Party tutelage preparing the people for representative self-government, and then a transition to democracy. But the formation of opposition parties was banned after 1928, and the republic settled into a protracted period of Nationalist Party rule. Although the ban was initially only supposed to last for six years, the formation of opposition political parties in the Republic of China would not actually be legalized again until 1987 (by that time on the island of Taiwan, where the transition to genuine multiparty democracy was finally achieved). Despite Chiang Kai-shek's purge of the Communists in 1927 and turn to the political Right, however, this did not immediately mark a complete end to the May Fourth spirit. The Nationalist Party was still a self-proclaimed modernizing revolutionary party, and official documents in Chiang Kai-shek's new government were still stamped "the revolution is not yet complete."[30]

Korea under Japanese Rule, 1905–1945

The emperor (and former king) of Korea was able to temporarily maintain Korean independence by playing Russian interests off against Japan, but room for any further maneuver evaporated suddenly after Japan defeated Russia in war in 1905. From the Japanese perspective, the Korean peninsula – which reached to just fifty miles from Japan's shores, like "a dagger pointed at the heart of Japan" in one threatening image – was understandably perceived as strategically vital. The Chinese had been expelled from Korea after the Sino-Japanese War in 1895, but in the meantime, the Russians had begun building their Trans-Siberian Railway in 1891 and acquired a naval base at Port Arthur on the tip of Liaodong peninsula in southern Manchuria in 1898. To oppose this approaching Russian power, instead of demobilizing after the Sino-Japanese War, the Japanese budget of 1896 actually called for doubling the size of the military.

Russia's primary interests lay in Manchuria, while Japan's lay in Korea, but neither power was willing to renounce its wider ambitions in order to reach an accommodation. In part to counter the Russian threat, Japan signed a formal alliance in 1902 with Russia's foremost global imperial rival, Great Britain. Under the terms of this Anglo-Japanese treaty, both countries pledged to aid the other if it became involved in a war with more than one adversary. This gave the Japanese a

Figure 9.5. "Naval Battle of the Russo-Japanese War at Chinmulpo," 1904, by Migita Toshihide (1863–1925), Japanese woodblock print. Arthur M. Sackler Gallery, Smithsonian Institution, Washington, DC: Gift of Gregory and Patricia Kruglak, S2001.37a-c.

freer hand to confront Russia in Korea. Negotiations with Russia broke off on February 6, 1904, and war was declared four days later (see Figure 9.5). Active hostilities began a day before the formal declaration of war with a surprise Japanese night attack on the naval base at Port Arthur, during which two Russian battleships and a cruiser were struck by torpedoes.

Russia was a major world power with vastly superior potential resources than newly industrializing little Japan, and although the Japanese scored some early victories on the battlefield, none were decisive. The cost of the war to Japan was staggering, both in the number of lives lost (81,455 Japanese dead) and in the skyrocketing debt necessary to fund it. Russia, on the other hand, was large enough to suffer heavy losses and continue fighting. The Japanese high command therefore grew anxious to negotiate an end to the war quickly, and an opportunity to seek peace on favorable terms came after a smashing Japanese naval victory at Tsushima on May 27, 1905. The Russian Baltic fleet, consisting of eleven battleships, had sailed halfway around the world to reinforce the Russian forces in the Pacific, but it was intercepted toward the end of its long voyage near Tsushima, an island lying midway between Korea and Japan, by a fleet of five Japanese battleships. The Japanese performed the classic naval maneuver known as "crossing the T," sailing across the head of the enemy battle line and making it possible for all of the Japanese big guns to fire broadsides at the oncoming Russian ships, while the Russians could only bring their forward guns to bear. In just forty-five minutes of action the Russian fleet was annihilated, while the Japanese suffered only minimal losses.

Japan was now in a position to approach the president of the United States, Theodore Roosevelt, with a request to mediate, and the war was ended by the Treaty of Portsmouth (New Hampshire) in September 1905. As a result of the war, Russia ceded its concessions in southern Manchuria to Japan and renounced Russian interests in Korea, but the Russian bargaining position was still strong enough that Russia could not be compelled to pay war reparations to Japan. Although Japan had won the war, therefore, many Japanese people felt deeply disappointed, and serious rioting broke out, especially in Hibiya Park in Tōkyō. A majority of Tōkyō's police boxes were reportedly destroyed, troops had to be brought in, martial law was declared, and some two thousand Japanese rioters were arrested.

Meanwhile, at the start of the war, the Korean government had attempted to remain neutral, but Japanese troops occupied Seoul and the Koreans were obliged to accept advisors recommended by the Japanese – with the power to approve Korean cabinet-level decisions. After the war, in 1905, Korea was reduced to a formal Japanese protectorate. The Meiji oligarch Itō Hirobumi – architect of the Meiji constitution and Japan's first prime minister – was brought in to serve as Japan's first resident-general in Korea. But Emperor Kojong had agreed to the Japanese protectorate only under duress, if at all, and in 1906 and 1907 he publicly appealed for world support against Japan, in particular with a mission to a peace conference at The Hague, in the Netherlands.

Japanese domination was now irreversible, however, and in 1907 Emperor Kojong abdicated in favor of his son. By now, all laws, important decisions, and appointments of high officials required the Japanese resident-general's approval. The Korean army was disbanded, and many former Korean soldiers joined anti-Japanese guerrillas in the countryside. According to a Japanese count, between 1907 and 1910, there were 2,819 armed clashes with Korean guerrillas, and in 1907, in a coordinated attack on the headquarters of the Japanese residency-general, one particularly large guerrilla force penetrated to within eight miles of Seoul.[31] The modern Japanese army was too powerful for disorganized guerrillas to overcome, however, and the overall Japanese presence in Korea was, meanwhile, expanding rapidly, multiplying tenfold between 1900 and 1910. In the southern port city of Pusan, half the population became Japanese, and much of the town was Japanese built.[32]

In the years after the establishment of the protectorate, the Japanese residency-general financed its program for the creation of modern banking facilities and roads in Korea through Japanese loans to the Korean government. This put the Koreans heavily in debt to Japan. Partly on the pretext of these unpaid debts, and after the assassination of Itō Hirobumi by a Korean nationalist in 1909, Japan openly annexed Korea as a formal colony in 1910.

By the early twentieth century, in the heyday of what is called the new imperialism, much of the entire world had been reduced to colonial status. The Japanese colony in Korea was exceptional, even so, because of the extremely large number of resident Japanese colonists and because of the high degree of intrusiveness of its colonial regime. By the 1930s, there was one policeman for roughly every four hundred Koreans, and the number of Japanese colonists in Korea was more than twenty times the number of French colonists in Vietnam.[33] Japanese rule in Korea was, moreover, at first extremely ironfisted. After annexation, all the Japanese governors-general of Korea were active-duty generals in the imperial army, with one exception, who was a retired navy admiral. From 1910 to 1920, no Korean-owned newspapers were permitted, and all Korean political meetings and public assemblies were banned. Colonial economic policy also focused initially on the exploitation of raw materials and agriculture, and little development of modern business was envisioned, especially if it was not Japanese owned.

On March 1, 1919, Korean resentment erupted in mass protest. Inspired by Wilsonian ideals of national self-determination, and coordinated with the upcoming funeral of former Emperor Kojong, demonstrations – ultimately involving as many as one million Koreans – began with the reading of a Korean "Declaration of Independence." Although these demonstrations were brutally suppressed, the Japanese colonial regime did shift to a somewhat gentler approach afterward, introducing some reforms that treated Koreans less harshly. New business start-ups no longer required government permission, and the Japanese government even began providing subsidies to certain Korean companies. The military police were replaced by civilians who no longer routinely carried swords. Censorship was relaxed, and Korean-language newspaper and magazine publishing flourished. Yet it has also been observed that even as the external appearance of the police force softened, their numbers also increased.[34]

Paradoxically, Japanese colonization of Korea in some ways did promote modernization and even Westernization. For example, although Korea's nonagricultural commercial economy had been notably less developed than either China's or Japan's in the nineteenth century, by the end of the colonial period in 1945 Korea was more thoroughly industrialized than any other part of East Asia except for Japan itself. Modern Western-style consumer culture also arrived in Korea together with Japanese rule. The cinema, phonographic records, radio, commercial advertising, magazines, department stores, and modern Western-style fashions in clothing all made their appearance in Korea's larger cities during the period of Japanese rule. Modernization in Korea thus followed a complicated trajectory, including simultaneous Japanese-ization, Westernization, and also the maturation of a new sense of Korean nationalism.

Since the beginning of the twentieth century, with the aid of a modern Korean-language press (recall that until the end of the nineteenth century much elite writing in Korea had still been in classical Chinese), Korean national consciousness had been brewing. The same new two-character word for "nation" that was used in both Japan and China (pronounced *minjok* in Korean) was adopted, and Korean history began to be conceived as the history of a Korean *Volk*, or "people." In 1921, the Korean Language Research Society was founded to promote and standardize grammatical and *han'gŭl* spelling rules for the Korean language and compile a pioneering Korean-language dictionary. In an example of the complexity of modernizing impulses, the colonial Japanese government's subsidy of radio broadcasting in Korea also helped substantially to promote the spread of the Seoul dialect as a standard pronunciation for the Korean national language.[35] Despite some early toleration of this pioneering Korean linguistic activity, however, the promotion of the Korean language eventually came to be seen as subversive of the Japanese goal of assimilation, and during World War II many Korean linguists found themselves under arrest.

From quite an early date, much of the Korean nationalist movement was driven abroad into exile. The future president of the Republic of Korea, Syngman Rhee (Yi Sŭngman, 1875–1965), for example, went into exile after 1904, and a few years later founded the Korean National Association in Hawai'i. Inside Korea, the Japanese colonial regime favored assimilation. As early as 1910, the Japanese language was officially designated Korea's "national language." The Japanese regarded Koreans as racially and culturally akin to themselves and therefore potentially as fellow "imperial peoples." At the same time, however, and with a fatal contradiction, they also stereotypically imagined Koreans as backward and underdeveloped. Koreans were therefore allowed to remain unrepresented in the Japanese legislature, intermarriage between Japanese and Koreans was discouraged, and Koreans continued to be treated with offensive condescension by many Japanese.[36] Despite the official policy of assimilation, Korean ethnicity was also still specified on identity cards.

The attempted integration of Korea into the Japanese Empire began to accelerate after Manchuria was brought into the Japanese-led yen-bloc in 1931, and even more rapidly after the outbreak of World War II in China in 1937. Beginning in 1935, Korean worship at Japanese-style *Shintō* shrines became mandatory – which was particularly objectionable to the relatively large number of monotheistic Korean Christians. In 1939, all Koreans were required to take Japanese-style names. Most officially did so, although it is questionable how many ever came to identify closely with these new Japanese names. Between 1937 and 1939 the use of the Korean language was progressively banned in a series of stages, in government, public schools, and finally in the private press. In spite of all this coerced assimilation, however, it has been estimated that as of 1942 only about 20 percent of the Korean people could actually understand the Japanese language.[37]

Increased integration into the Japanese Empire brought rapid industrialization and economic modernization. Although some Korean businesses certainly did benefit, however, this industrialization was not only Japanese dominated but also largely led by the Japanese state, for strategic military purposes. After 1937, industrial mobilization even included compulsory conscription of Korean labor. In a negative parallel to this swift industrialization, a fairly drastic decline in per capita Korean consumption of rice has also been observed in this period, because much of Korea's rice crop was now exported to Japan, while Korean agriculture saw relatively few improvements in productivity.[38]

Beginning in 1943, Koreans could be drafted into the wartime Japanese imperial army. Notoriously, more than one hundred thousand Korean women were pressured into becoming "comfort women," providing sexual services for the Japanese military. The combination of rapid industrialization and forced mobilization for Japan's war effort in World War II created enormous dislocations in what had previously been a settled agrarian Korean society. By the end of World War II, perhaps 20 percent of the entire Korean population had been uprooted and moved away from their native province or even beyond the borders of Korea altogether, many going to Manchuria or the Japanese home islands.[39] In the midst of Japan's rapidly deteriorating military situation in late World War II, all this population dislocation, hardship, and forced assimilation of a proud people who were simultaneously faced with continuing discrimination planted bitter seeds of lasting anti-Japanese resentment in Korea.

Japan: Taishō Democracy

Explicitly Western things had begun to be fashionable in Japan from early in the Meiji era. For example, reading and writing in horizontal lines from left to right, Western-style, as opposed to the traditional East Asian vertical columns marching from right to left, was introduced in Meiji times (though the practice remains inconsistent even today); chairs began to be used in government buildings as early as 1871 (although, at home, many Japanese still sit today – and also sleep, quite comfortably – on their *tatami*-matted floors); and the modern department store, complete with commercial advertising, had appeared in Japan by the early twentieth century (see Figure 9.6). The game of baseball was introduced in early Meiji, and the first international game may have been played in 1896, when a Japanese school team beat an American team.[40] Beer had been introduced from Europe very early in the Meiji period, although up until WW II it remained a consciously Western-, and most especially German-, style item of consumption in Japan (see figure 9.7). Military service on the continent at the start of the twentieth century introduced large numbers of Japanese soldiers to more Western-style foods, including beef (as in *sukiyaki*), which had rarely been consumed in premodern Japan. Pseudo Indian-style curry rice was popularized during World War I and

Figure 9.6. Showroom of the Mitsukoshi Dry-Goods Store, Japan, 1911. National Diet Library Web site.

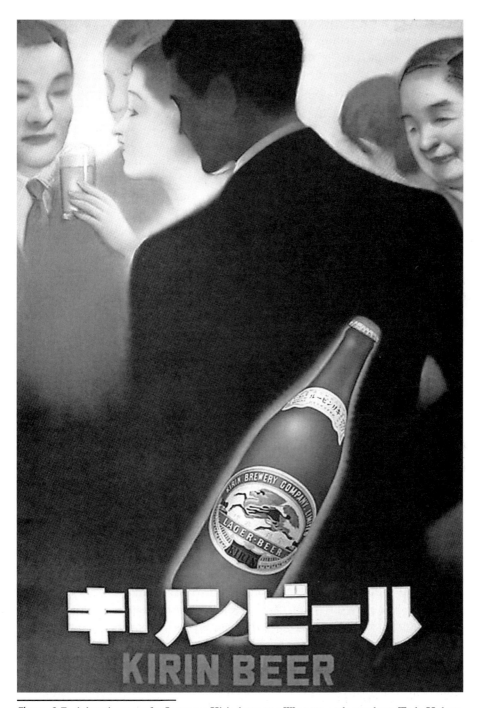

Figure 9.7. Advertisement for Japanese Kirin beer as a Western-style product. Tada Hokuu, 1937. Pictures from History/Bridgeman Images.

eventually became a Japanese staple. The now ubiquitous breaded pork cutlet (*tonkatsu*) made its debut in the Japanese national diet shortly thereafter. Despite the early date of some of these adoptions, though, daily life for most Japanese people did not really significantly begin to alter until the World War I period.[41]

There was, moreover, even something of a nationalistic counterreaction to the early Meiji enthusiasm for Westernization, beginning around 1887.[42] Interest in traditional Japanese art, literature, history, and Confucian morality was revived, and the idea of an enduring Japanese "national polity" (*kokutai*), closely identified with an unbroken and supposedly divine ancient imperial line, began to be sometimes stridently promoted. Yet, although there were countercurrents, in Japan, as in China, the first great wave of Westernization in many ways only peaked in the 1910s–1920s.

It was also during roughly this period that the modern Japanese industrial economy finally matured. A huge government steel mill had been opened at Yawata (in northern Kyūshū) in 1901, but during its first decade of operation, it suffered heavy financial losses, and as late as 1914 Japan was still only producing about a third of its own domestic steel requirements. Up to the outbreak of World War I in 1914, the Japanese government continued to provide 30–40 percent of the total capital investment in the modern sector of the economy.[43] The start of World War I, however, not only brought war-related orders to Japanese factories but also caused the withdrawal of much European and American competition, opening up new Asian and African markets for Japan. Japan's exports tripled in four years, and during the war years (1914–1918) Japan's gross national product increased by 9 percent annually.

The number of Japanese factory workers doubled during the war, but this also led to a labor shortage and rising prices, which strained the resources of those on fixed incomes. Food prices tripled during World War I, and the increased cost provoked major rice riots in 1918. Over a million persons participated, there were twenty-five thousand arrests, and the prime minister was obliged to step down. The end of World War I, then, brought resumed European and American competition and a postwar slump. The Japanese stock market crashed in 1920, and many companies went bankrupt. Plummeting prices for agricultural products led to deep, endemic rural poverty. This contributed to an already "growing chasm between the life-styles of the 'two Japans,'" urban and rural.[44] Work conditions in many of the new factories were also often grim. The development of the Japanese textile industry, for example, depended heavily on cheap labor, and a large majority of the labor force was female, typically employed only temporarily and working twelve-hour shifts under often harsh conditions.

In 1923, the great Kantō earthquake struck in the vicinity of Tōkyō, destroying half a million homes and killing 105,000 people. A bank panic in 1927 led to the withdrawal of some 11 percent of all deposits. Major banking institutions failed, including the imperial household's own bank. Thirty-two banks closed their doors. The 1920s were therefore a decade of repeated economic crises. Yet despite this, Japan's overall real economic growth rate in the period 1913–1938 was more than three times that of the United States. A critical threshold in the industrialization process seems to have been crossed, and certain developments in this era are said to have already foreshadowed the spectacular post–World War II Japanese economic "miracle."[45]

Not only did the industrialized economy mature, but parliamentary democracy also came of age in the aftermath of World War I, as rule by unelected oligarchs was finally replaced by a regular parliamentary-style political party system. The Meiji Emperor died in 1912, and the reign period of his successor, the Taishō Emperor (r. 1912–1926), was known as an age of relatively liberal "Taishō democracy." From 1918 to 1932, the prime minister was usually the head of one of the political parties elected to the Diet, and in 1925 all Japanese men aged twenty-five or older were given the vote: universal adult male suffrage.

The old Meiji period ideal of "transcendent" government – that is, an administration that was supposedly above party politics – had broken down in the early twentieth century, as cabinet after cabinet was obliged to seek the support of politicians in the legislature. After 1905, no prime minister was able to govern entirely without party support. Meanwhile, the elder statesman Itō Hirobumi had joined with the leading faction in the Diet to form a political party of his own in 1900 (called the Seiyūkai). The rice riots in 1918, then, were the largest such disturbances in recorded Japanese history and led to the fall of the current administration. In this moment of crisis, the surviving Meiji era oligarchs (acting in the name of the emperor) turned to the then president of the Seiyūkai Party, Hara Kei (also known as Hara Takashi, 1856–1921), to form the first-ever Japanese party government in September 1918. Although Hara's ancestry was samurai, he had renounced his former samurai status and refused a peerage, and he is therefore also considered to be the first commoner ever to serve as prime minister of Japan.

In 1921, Hara was stabbed to death at a Tōkyō train station by a man who was enraged by the naval arms limitations agreed to at the Washington Conference earlier that year. After Hara's death, there followed four brief administrations in quick succession, three of them non-party, but in 1924, another party politician was made prime minister, and this now became the norm (until a new age of militarism began in the 1930s). "Taishō democracy" reached its height at this time. Military expenditures were reduced in 1924, and four divisions were cut from the army. In March 1925 the movement toward democracy culminated in the implementation of universal adult male suffrage. Although the Taishō Emperor died in 1926, technically putting an end to the Taishō era, his successor, the Shōwa Emperor (former prince regent Hirohito, 1901–1989, r. 1925–1989), had visited Europe and enjoyed a reputation for Western-style interests such as golf and marine biology.

As in contemporary China, the 1920s were an era of modernity and often consciously Western-style fashions in Japan. Giant multistory department stores, with solid Western-style floors (so that it was no longer necessary to follow the custom of leaving shoes at the door), and featuring such modern goods as Shiseido cosmetics, became places of entertainment as well as commerce. Neon lights lit the streets of major cities at night, and the first Tōkyō subway line began operations in 1927.

Movies had begun to be shown in Japan as early as the 1890s, but cinema especially flourished in the 1920s. Japanese women styled their hair to resemble international movie stars like Gloria Swanson and Greta Garbo. A few experimental radio stations were already broadcasting by 1922, and Tōkyō Broadcasting Station began operations in 1925. Panel-narrative comic strips began to be published in the 1920s – ancestors of today's ubiquitous *manga*. At the more consciously elevated cultural level, Western-style avant-garde art also found a niche. There was an enormous reading public, for serious books as well as for light entertainment. At the start of World War I, Japan was publishing twice as many different book titles as the United States.[46] Today, Japan may actually provide the largest per capita audience for the quintessentially American-style jazz music in the world, and in the 1920s, Japanese musicians were consciously performing in the style of American jazz legends (although later, during the World War II years, there was an attempt to find a "native" Japanese jazz style).[47] Individualism was fashionable in the Japan of the 1920s, and feminism also took root in this era with the founding of the New Woman's Association in 1920 and the beginnings of a women's suffrage movement. The 1920s were popularly known as an age of "modern boys" and "modern girls."

The sudden swing toward militarism and ultranationalism that emerged in the 1930s might therefore appear surprising. This dramatic change of direction was driven in large part by the onset of the Great Depression and other major world trends and conditions. However, as we have already remarked, there had been an earlier period of nationalistic reaction in the late 1880s and 1890s, much of Japan's rural population had been left out of the heady urban modernization and Westernization of the 1920s, strategic military considerations had always been paramount from the beginning of the Meiji Restoration, and expansionist overseas imperial ambitions had also been a recurrent theme. Even at the peak of Taishō democracy, there were powerful countercurrents. At the very moment that the vote was being extended to all adult males, for example, a new peace preservation law in 1925 also made it illegal to advocate any change in Japan's somewhat mystical emperor-centered "national polity" (*kokutai*), or the abolition of private property.[48] Midnight raids on March 15, 1928 – provoked by leftist gains in an election the previous month – arrested some sixteen hundred persons suspected of being communists. In that same year, five professors were dismissed from imperial universities because they were suspected of harboring "dangerous thoughts."

In 1924, just as party government was stabilizing in Japan, the U.S. Congress passed legislation preventing immigration by persons ineligible for U.S. citizenship, which at that time pointedly included all Japanese.[49] This deeply insulted many Japanese people, including some of those who found Western ideals most attractive. Many in the army, especially those from impoverished rural villages, had already, in the 1920s, begun contemplating the need for a military coup to return power and wealth from the allegedly corrupt and self-interested capitalists and party politicians to the emperor, in a so-called Shōwa Restoration. The modern mass media that had matured in the 1920s could, furthermore, perhaps just as easily be turned to mobilize ultranationalist patriotic sentiments as to promote liberal democracy.

The banking crisis of 1927 brought down the cabinet, and a conservative retired army general was made prime minister. Viewing Chiang Kai-shek's Northern

Expedition to reunify China as a threat to Japanese interests on the continent, in 1927–1928 his government intervened militarily three times in China to protect Japanese interests and to prevent Manchuria from being included in the reunified Republic of China. To stimulate the economy, this prime minister also increased military expenditures. Yet even this conservative ex-soldier was also the president of a political party and a party politician himself. In 1928, his government signed the Kellogg–Briand Pact that attempted to formally renounce war as an instrument of national policy.

Also in 1928, however, the Chinese warlord of Manchuria, Zhang Zuolin, was blown up and killed in his railway car by Japanese army officers – acting without the knowledge of the home government in Tōkyō – who apparently hoped to create an incident that would provide a pretext for Japanese seizure of Manchuria. The Japanese prime minister was outraged by these actions and resolved to bring the assassins to a court-martial. The army refused to cooperate, however, with the result that the prime minister was forced to resign in 1929.[50]

Ironically, this brought a temporary return to more liberal policies under the next administration in 1929, which became the first in Japan to support women's suffrage. A proposal was actually drafted to let women have the vote in local elections, though it did not become law. But this new prime minister was fatally shot in 1930 by an outraged nationalist, because of the government's acceptance of an arms limitation agreement reached at the London Naval Conference. The political climate in Japan was suddenly becoming very chilly. With the onset of the global Great Depression, and the successful seizure of southern Manchuria by the Japanese army in 1931 (after yet another staged explosion), and after one more brief and ineffectual liberal cabinet, in 1931 a new and more conservative prime minister (Inukai Tsuyoshi, 1855–1932) took office. He survived in office only five months before he, too, was struck down by assassins – this time Japanese naval and army officers. After his death, there would be no more prime ministers from political parties. Japan had begun its descent into the "dark valley" of militarism and war.

"Our Ancestors the Gauls": French Colonial Indochina

The nineteenth-century French Christian missionary impulse in Vietnam may have been somewhat overshadowed by pragmatic French imperial and commercial ambitions, but by the late nineteenth century France was also increasingly motivated by a secular variety of missionary faith in France's "civilizing mission" (*mission civilisatrice*) to bring the benefits of modern civilization to backward lands. While such convictions are easy to ridicule today – "an ironic byproduct of the educational system under French colonial administration is that generations of Vietnamese and African children also grew up reciting the phrase 'our ancestors the Gauls,'" for example – they were often undoubtedly sincere.[51] And ideas of "progress" were not entirely an illusion. The 1920s brought accelerating French investment in Vietnam, and, as in contemporary China and Japan, this was a peak period of modernization and Westernization in Vietnam, bringing everything from Hollywood movies to Marxism (see Figure 9.8). The graduation of one of the first

Figure 9.8. Vietnamese Nationalist caricature of a Europeanized Vietnamese playing tennis. The caption reads (in Chinese characters), "Progress in Civilization." Pictures from History/Bridgeman Images.

three Vietnamese students from Hanoi's modern College of Law in 1924 was celebrated, for example, with a band playing the *Marseillaise*.[52]

The years between the two World Wars brought profound changes in Vietnamese consciousness, with the late 1920s being a time of especially intense intellectual ferment. During those years, full-length Vietnamese biographies were published of Sun Yat-sen, Christopher Columbus, Abraham Lincoln, Vladimir Lenin, Jean-Jacques Rousseau, and other world historical figures, as well as of numerous Vietnamese personalities. As of 1937, there were some 39,000 Europeans living in the Vietnamese portions of colonial Indochina (amid a total population of about nineteen million), and there were 1,556 Vietnamese studying in France itself in 1930 (although, after 1930, colonial authorities, fearing radicalization, began to limit opportunities for Vietnamese education in France). The elder generation had bequeathed upon Vietnamese youth a traditional Confucian respect for learning, confidence in human perfectibility, and a deep sense of national crisis. The necessity of translating unfamiliar new European ideas into Vietnamese by itself also compelled innovation: "The act of writing in Vietnamese forced members of the intelligentsia to go beyond simple imitation, to experiment culturally, to overcome conceptual problems never dreamt of by their Western mentors."[53]

Although the French language was widely spoken in colonial Indochina – French was the official language in Cochinchina (southern Vietnam) from 1903 – the French authorities also promoted writing Vietnamese in the Roman alphabet. A system for spelling Vietnamese with the alphabet had been invented in the seventeenth century by Catholic missionaries as an aid in spreading Christianity (it is known as *quoc ngu*, the "national language"), and it sweepingly replaced Chinese characters in the early twentieth century (although traditional Confucian examinations continued at the vestigial Nguyen court in central Vietnam until 1919, fourteen years after the examination system had been abolished in China itself). Alongside elite colonial use of French, by the mid-twentieth century alphabetized Vietnamese had emerged as the clear standard (at least for non-Europeans) even in writing, and the Vietnamese language quite naturally remained the norm in spoken conversations among Vietnamese.

Despite the French "civilizing mission," there was some ambivalence in French colonial attitudes about whether they really wanted to convert the Vietnamese into fully enfranchised Frenchmen or continue ruling over them as native subjects. As of the mid-1920s, only about 10 percent of the Vietnamese school-age population actually was in school.[54] Native Vietnamese industrialization was also not very enthusiastically encouraged by the French. As of 1939, almost 90 percent of capital investment in Vietnam was tied to only three syndicates, and a relatively small number of French businesses came to dominate the modern sector of the Vietnamese economy.[55] Advisory Vietnamese legislative assemblies were established, but both their power, and the scope of their electorate, were severely limited. Western ideals of democracy and material progress held real appeal, but many Vietnamese felt excluded by French colonial rule.

Resentment of French rule could be especially acutely felt precisely by educated, French-speaking Vietnamese who were inspired by French ideals of liberty, equality, and fraternity, but blocked from admission to the pinnacles of colonial society. A secret Vietnamese Nationalist Party, modeled after the Chinese Nationalist Party, was organized in Hanoi in 1927. Facing arrest by French colonial authorities, in 1930 it attempted uprisings in the north, which were quickly suppressed. Its leaders were arrested and several were put to death. To some extent, ironically, the eventual triumph of the communists in Vietnam may have even been the result of French success at eliminating more moderate anti-colonial alternatives.

Ho Chi Minh (the best-known of several aliases taken by a man named Nguyen Sinh Cung; 1890–1969) had studied at the National Academy in Hue, but in 1911 he shipped aboard a French freighter as a galley hand. He spent some three years at sea, lived for almost a year in New York and Boston, worked in a hotel in London, and then went to Paris for six years. In France, he became a founding member of the French Communist Party in 1920. In 1924 he went to Moscow, from where he was sent as a Comintern agent to Guangzhou, China, in 1925, to work with the Chinese Nationalist and Communist Party united front that was then in effect. When Chiang Kai-shek split with the leftists in China in 1927, Ho Chi Minh returned to Moscow and Europe. For a while he ran a school in Thailand. In 1930, he helped organize the Indochinese Communist Party among Vietnamese exiles in Hong Kong and southern China.[56] As a result of all these developments, the Vietnamese communists would thereafter be in a strong position to take advantage of the vastly changed circumstances created by WW II.

For Further Reading

On China's Nationalist Revolution, see Marie-Claire Bergère, *Sun Yat-sen*, trans. Janet Lloyd (Stanford University Press, [1994] 1998); John Fitzgerald, *Awakening China: Politics, Culture, and Class in the Nationalist Revolution* (Stanford University Press, 1996); Edward J. M. Rhoads, *Manchus and Han: Ethnic Relations and Political Power in Late Qing and Early Republican China, 1861–1928* (Seattle: University of Washington Press, 2000); and Mary Clabaugh Wright, ed., *China in Revolution: The First Phase, 1900–1913* (New Haven, CT: Yale University Press, 1968).

A fine extended essay on the problem of modernization in China is Rana Mitter, *A Bitter Revolution: China's Struggle with the Modern World* (Oxford University Press, 2004). On the early twentieth-century modern transformation of China, see Sherman Cochran, ed., *Inventing Nanjing Road: Commercial Culture in Shanghai, 1900–1945* (Ithaca, NY: Cornell University East Asia Program, 1999); Frank Dikötter, *Exotic Commodities: Modern Objects and Everyday Life in China* (New York: Columbia University Press, 2006); and Leo Ou-fan Lee, *Shanghai Modern: The Flowering of a New Urban Culture in China, 1930–1945* (Cambridge, MA: Harvard University Press, 1999). The still-classic study of China's May Fourth movement is Tse-tsung Chow, *The May Fourth Movement: Intellectual Revolution in Modern China* (Stanford University Press, 1960).

On the warlord era in China, see Edward A. McCord, *The Power of the Gun: The Emergence of Modern Chinese Warlordism* (Berkeley: University of California Press, 1993), and Gavan McCormack, *Chang Tso-lin in Northeast China, 1911–1928: China, Japan, and the Manchurian Idea* (Stanford University Press, 1977).

For Korea under Japanese rule, see Ramon H. Myers and Mark R. Peattie, eds., *The Japanese Colonial Empire, 1895–1945* (Princeton University Press, 1984), and Michael

Edson Robinson, *Cultural Nationalism in Colonial Korea, 1920–1925* (Seattle: University of Washington Press, 1988).
On early twentieth-century Japan, see Marius B. Jansen, *The Making of Modern Japan* (Cambridge, MA: Harvard University Press, 2000); Tetsuo Najita, *Hara Kei and the Politics of Compromise, 1905–1915* (Cambridge, MA: Harvard University Press, 1967); and Edward Seidensticker, *Low City, High City: Tokyo from Edo to the Earthquake* (New York: Alfred A. Knopf, 1983). Stephen Vlastos, ed., *Mirror of Modernity: Invented Traditions of Modern Japan* (Berkeley: University of California Press, 1998), provides a fascinating collection of essays on the modern reimagination of Japanese tradition.
For Vietnam, see Chapter 13.

10 The Dark Valley (1930–1945)

The Rise of Japanese Ultranationalism

The first great wave of modern globalization (which, because of the industrialized West's initial leading role in defining global modernity, in its early phase culturally overlapped fairly closely with what might also be described as Westernization) had begun in the late nineteenth century. In East Asia, it culminated in the 1910s–1920s with China's May Fourth Movement and Japan's Taishō democracy. During these same years, French colonial rule also promoted a degree of Westernization in Vietnam, while Japanese colonial rule in Korea encouraged a curious combination of modernization, Westernization, and forced Japanese-ization. The high tide of globalization receded rapidly after the disastrous collapse of the U.S. stock market in 1929, however. By the 1930s, the world was descending into what some Japanese historians have aptly dubbed a "dark valley." As a result of the Great Depression, in the United States, real gross domestic product had declined 35 percent by 1933, a quarter of American workers were out of work, and there were calls for the newly inaugurated president Franklin D. Roosevelt to assume dictatorial powers. Even socialism no longer seemed entirely unthinkable in America. In Germany, the Weimar Republic gave way to Adolph Hitler. In China, the Nationalist Republic became an authoritarian single-party state with an increasingly nationalized economy. In Japan, Taishō democracy was thrust aside by the rise of ultranationalistic militarism.

Surprisingly, the industrial sector of Japan's economy recovered fairly quickly from the depths of the Great Depression, thanks to a sharp devaluation in the exchange value of the yen (which made the price of Japanese exports globally more competitive), low interest rates, and increased government spending on public works and armaments. The volume of Japanese exports actually doubled between 1930 and 1936. But, as much of the world responded to the Great Depression by adopting protectionist measures – such as high taxes or outright quotas on imports, which threatened Japan's ability to continue exporting – the argument began to resonate that what Japan really needed was to create an economically self-sufficient

Figure 10.1. The Japanese battleship *Yamato* running trials, 1941. It and its sister ship, *Musashi*, were the largest battleships ever built. National Archives.

yen-bloc that would be independent, and under Japan's own control. Manchuria, in particular, came be viewed as a potential economic "lifeline" for Japan.

The purely economic argument for self-sufficiency was also reinforced by the strategic military lessons of World War I, which seemed to suggest that future wars would be protracted and total, pitting the entire available resources of one adversary against another. To prepare for such a total war, it was thought that Japan needed to build a self-sufficient "National Defense State."[1] To safeguard Japan's perceived vital interests, military expenditures accelerated rapidly. In 1934, Japan departed from the Washington and London naval arms limitation agreements, and in 1937, Japan began construction of what would become the largest battleships (the Yamato class) in the history of the world (see Figure 10.1).

The modern national public school system in Japan promoted ideals of patriotic loyalty to the emperor and military valor.[2] Organized state *Shintō* religion, although as an institution it was largely a modern creation of the Meiji era, nonetheless emphasized the ancient mythology of imperial descent from the sun goddess Amaterasu, from before the dawn of history. This supposedly divine imperial line was proclaimed to be the core of Japan's unique national polity (*kokutai*), which invested modern Japanese imperialism with a special sense of sacred mission. Exaltation of the imperial majesty reached a crescendo in the late 1930s, when over two million copies of the Ministry of Education's *Cardinal Principles of the National Polity* were published (beginning in 1937), and it became required reading in Japanese schools.[3]

The sense of a special divine mission also coincided with a romantic idealization of the remembered "traditional" virtues of village life, and much criticism of alleged capitalist greed and the corrupt special interests of party politicians. The idea that Anglo-American-style "selfish" individualism should give way to a more native Japanese spirit of harmony was emotionally appealing to many people. Rather than representing a genuine return to premodern tradition, though, much of this ultranationalist celebration of the "spirit of Japan" was really a new phenomenon. It was also much encouraged by the modern mass media and modern expectations of popular mass mobilization. Combined with considerable real rural economic distress in the early 1930s, these ideas fostered radical plots and conspiracies, and Japan was wracked by a staggering series of high-level assassinations and attempted military coups.

In 1930, Prime Minister Hamaguchi Osachi (1870–1931) was shot, and later died of his wounds, for his role in agreeing to naval arms limitations. Efforts in 1931 by the civilian government in Tōkyō to bring the conflict in Manchuria to a peaceful resolution proved so unpopular at home that it contributed, together with the onset of the Great Depression, to bringing down the administration. Despite the fact that the next prime minister, Inukai Tsuyoshi, was relatively hawkish, on May 15, 1932, a group of naval officers and army cadets burst into his residence and shot him to death. After the assassination, incredibly enough, the war minister publicly praised the selfless sincerity of the killers, and the chief of military police actually called them patriots, suggesting that they should have coordinated their attack with the military police! Earlier that same year, a former minister of finance and a leading businessman were also assassinated.[4]

The wave of violence and military disobedience climaxed on the morning of February 26, 1936, when the army's First Division, stationed in Tōkyō, mutinied. The rebels seized important government buildings and assassinated former Prime Minster Saitō Makoto (1858–1936), the Minister of Finance (who was also a former prime minister), and the Inspector General of Military Education. The grand chamberlain, Admiral Suzuki Kantarō (1868–1948), was seriously wounded and left for dead. Prime Minster Okada Keisuke (1868–1952) escaped only because the mutineers shot his brother-in-law by mistake. An attempted takeover of the imperial palace was blocked, however, by alert palace guards.

After the assassinations, the rebels issued a manifesto proclaiming the virtuous motives for their actions and calling for a "Shōwa Restoration" (the name of the current imperial reign period), in a hoped-for echo of the glorious nineteenth-century Meiji Restoration. The mutiny was not universally supported even in the army, however, and encountered direct opposition from the Shōwa Emperor himself (often somewhat disrespectfully referred to outside of Japan by his personal name, Hirohito), who had the mutineers surrounded with loyal troops and ordered the rebels to return to barracks. On February 29, they surrendered. Two rebel leaders committed suicide immediately, and seventeen others were quickly condemned and executed, without being given an opportunity to publicize their message.

This turned out to be the last great act of unauthorized pre-World War II violence by the imperial Japanese army. By now, however, civilian politicians were effectively intimidated, and a turn to less radical military leaders seemed a natural alternative. In the 1937 Japanese cabinet, there would not be a single party politician. Even after the final dissolution of political parties in 1940, elections continued to be held and the forms of parliamentary government maintained, but the era of Taishō democracy had ended, and a new age of ultranationalistic militarism had begun.

Manchukuo

Until the late nineteenth century, much of Manchuria – with the exception of the southern agricultural regions that, although they lay beyond the Great Wall, had long functioned as something of an extension of China proper – remained a sparsely populated frontier. This was at least partially intentional, since the Manchu rulers of the Qing Dynasty had forbidden Chinese migration into Manchuria to preserve the integrity of their homeland. Meanwhile, however, Russian Cossacks in search of furs had begun to appear in the area as early as the seventeenth century. A formal border between the Chinese and Russian empires, along the line of the Amur River, was first fixed by treaty in 1689.

By the nineteenth century, the Russians had become a dynamic presence in the far northeast. Russia obtained a port on the Pacific Ocean at Vladivostok in 1858. In 1896, thanks to Russian intervention (together with France and Germany) to prevent Manchuria's Liaodong peninsula from being ceded to Japan after the Sino-Japanese War, a deal was signed with the Qing Dynasty conceding to Russia the right to build a railway straight across Manchuria – a considerable shortcut in the Trans-Siberian route between Vladivostok and Moscow. In 1898, the Russians also obtained from the Qing Dynasty a leasehold on some territory at the tip of Liaodong peninsula and began constructing a Russian naval base (Port Arthur) and civilian port facilities there, with a rail connection joining the main Russian rail line at Harbin, in central Manchuria. After the Boxer debacle in 1900, for a time, the Russians were the dominant power in Manchuria.

But Russia was defeated by Japan in a war, largely fought on Manchurian soil, in 1905. As a result of this victory, Japan acquired control over Russian installations in southern Manchuria. These included the leasehold at the tip of Liaodong peninsula and that portion of the railway leading north from there as far as Changchun. This line now became known as the South Manchurian Railway (in Japanese, *Mantetsu*), and it became the single largest Japanese corporation of the early twentieth century. The Japanese government provided half of its initial capitalization, and although the balance came from private investors, it was government controlled. In addition to the railway itself, the South Manchurian Railway also handled the administration of policing, taxation, schooling, and other important public functions along the line of the tracks. Its first president (Gotō Shimpei, 1857–1929) had previously served as Japanese colonial head of civilian affairs in Taiwan. He had trained in Germany as a physician, and was a progressive-minded administrator concerned especially with matters of public health. Whatever other criticisms may be leveled at early twentieth-century

Map 10.1 Manchuria, ca. 1920

Japanese imperialism, it did accomplish certain modernizing improvements. Under Japanese colonial rule, for example, the death rate in both Taiwan and Korea declined significantly in the early twentieth century.[5]

Dreams of massive Japanese settlement of the new frontier opening up to them in Manchuria – supposedly thereby relieving population pressure in the crowded Japanese home islands – were never fully realized. Relatively few Japanese people found the idea of becoming peasant farmers in a remote (and foreign) frontier very attractive. The number of Japanese who did migrate to Manchuria, moreover, were eclipsed by a flood of new Chinese arrivals. The Qing Dynasty had only belatedly realized that to cement its claim to the region against the growing Russian presence Manchuria would have to be more thickly settled by Qing subjects, and lifted its ban on Chinese migration in the late nineteenth century. Large-scale Chinese in-migration then caused the population of Manchuria to explode.

The Manchurian economy also boomed in the early twentieth century, although in this case it was chiefly the result of Japanese investment. By 1932, when Manchuria first became a Japanese-controlled puppet state, 64 percent of the total capital invested in Manchurian industry was already Japanese.[6] Thereafter, the pace of Japanese investment only accelerated. In the single decade between 1931 and 1941, Japanese investment in Manchuria multiplied more than fivefold. Although actual production results did not entirely match expectations, Manchuria became the most industrialized region of China by the end of World War II.[7]

The Chinese warlord in Manchuria, Zhang Zuolin, had cooperated with the growing Japanese interests there, but he also moved his headquarters to Beijing in 1926 and exhibited signs of increasingly national Chinese ambitions. When Chiang Kai-shek's Northern Expedition for the military reunification of China approached Beijing from the south in 1928, Zhang Zuolin was informed by his Japanese advisors that he must either withdraw to Manchuria immediately or be disarmed by Japanese guards at the pass separating Manchuria from China proper if he tried to do so later. He accepted the Japanese warning and returned to Mukden (the Manchu name for the capital of Manchuria; Chinese Shenyang) immediately, but was blown up and killed in his railway car anyway by the unauthorized action of rogue Japanese army officers. His assassination was presumably intended to provoke an incident that might allow the Japanese Kwantung Army (a now conventional old spelling of the Chinese term *Guandong*, which means "East of the Passes" – in this case referring to the passes separating Manchuria from China proper) to seize control over Manchuria. The attempt backfired, however (this time). Both the emperor and the prime minister of Japan were outraged, and Zhang Zuolin's son, now understandably hostile to Japan, inherited his position. This son reached an agreement with Chiang Kai-shek's Nationalist Chinese government to bring Manchuria into the reunified Chinese Republic, which in 1931 also announced a goal of regaining Chinese control over the Japanese Liaodong leasehold and the South Manchurian Railway.

The combination of this new Chinese Nationalist threat to Japanese holdings in Manchuria, the global economic crisis created by the Great Depression, and changing domestic Japanese politics, all made a second attempt in 1931 to provoke a Japanese military takeover in Manchuria by staging an explosion much more successful. Lieutenant Colonel Ishiwara Kanji (1889–1949), who had studied for three years in Germany and was considered by many to be Japan's most brilliant military theoretician, envisioned a future apocalyptic "final war" between Asia, led by Japan, and the West, led by the United States. In preparation for that cataclysmic final showdown, Ishiwara believed that Japan needed access to the vital resources of Manchuria. He, and like-minded other officers, therefore carefully planned a Japanese takeover.[8]

On September 18, 1931, a senior officer from the Japanese general staff arrived in Mukden with orders to restrain the Kwantung Army from taking any unauthorized rash actions. Forewarned, however, the conspirators decided to strike before they were ordered not to. The distinguished visitor from the Tōkyō general staff was taken immediately on arrival to a restaurant to be entertained. While he was thus diverted, around ten o'clock that evening a bomb exploded on the tracks of the South Manchurian Railway north of Mukden. The damage was so slight that a train was able to pass over it soon afterward with little difficulty, but the explosion was blamed on Chinese saboteurs, and the Kwantung Army sprang into action, swiftly grabbing control over a growing portion of the northeast.

The Japanese Kwantung Army, which had originally been established to defend the Liaodong leasehold won from Russia in 1905, had a total force of only about ten thousand men. Japanese media now enthusiastically celebrated the ease with which such a relative handful of Japanese troops defeated the much larger force of two hundred thousand Chinese soldiers stationed in Manchuria – conveniently ignoring the fact that the Chinese were under orders not to resist. The modern mass media in Japan, notably the still new radio, found the eager popular hunger for war news to be a valuable commercial opportunity and helped generate a burst of patriotic war fever in Japan following the Manchurian incident in 1931.[9] For now, at least, the actions of the Kwantung Army on the continent were highly popular back home in Japan.

Elsewhere in the world, however, the Japanese occupation of Manchuria was widely condemned as a violation of the Kellogg–Briand Pact (a 1928 agreement that had attempted to outlaw aggressive warfare which was ultimately signed by sixty-three countries). The Japanese tried to justify their actions before the League of Nations with the argument that China did not have an organized central government and was therefore not a genuinely sovereign nation, and that Manchuria, furthermore, was not necessarily a part of China. The League of Nations was not persuaded, however, and in February 1933, it adopted a resolution, 42–1, condemning Japanese behavior. The Japanese delegation walked out, and in March 1933 Japan officially withdrew from the League of Nations.

In the aftermath, rather than attempt to directly colonize Manchuria, the Japanese reorganized it into a nominally independent new country called Manchukuo ("kuo" being an old spelling of the standard Chinese word *guo*, meaning "country"). The former last emperor of the Manchu-ruled Qing Dynasty in China, Puyi (1906–1976), was brought in to serve as head of state. In 1934, his title was elevated to "emperor of Manchukuo." In reality, however, the Japanese Kwantung Army was the real power now in Manchuria.

In Manchukuo, Japanese planners envisioned building a showcase of modernity, which would, furthermore, intentionally exclude what they considered to be the corrupt special interests of party politicians and big private business, and that they hoped might become a shining example of state-planned economic development. State-run, or joint state and private, corporations were created to administer different sectors of the economy. Despite the army's suspicions of big business, the Kwantung Army eventually did find it necessary to welcome much private investment in Manchukuo. The army was especially cordial toward so-called new *zaibatsu* such as Nissan. Yet even the private investment went overwhelmingly into state-controlled enterprises, because they provided risk-free, guaranteed returns.

The centerpiece of modern state building in Manchukuo was to be the city that was now literally renamed the New Capital (Xinjing, the former Changchun). Xinjing was rapidly transformed, with many magnificent new public buildings, wide, tree-lined avenues, numerous parks, and the novelty of universal indoor plumbing.[10] After 1934, Xinjing was linked to the ports of the original Liaodong leasehold by an ultra-high-speed Asia Express, which featured streamlined, futuristic locomotives and air-conditioned coaches.[11]

In Manchukuo, the Japanese sought to portray themselves as saving the common people from brutal warlords, as upholders of an ideal Confucian "Kingly Way," and as promoters of a new order of ethnic harmony among the Chinese, Manchu,

Mongol, Korean, and Japanese populations of the region. The Japanese Empire differed from most other colonial empires of that era in acknowledging a degree of racial and cultural commonality with its East Asian subjects. "Co-prosperity" became an important slogan in the 1930s, and many individual Japanese people were undoubtedly sincerely inspired by a genuine sense of idealism. The Concordia Association that was established in Manchukuo, for example, was intended to transcend not only the old-style imperialist exploitation of the colonized but also the enforced mass uniformity of modern nationalism by creating a harmonious multicultural new nation composed of many ethnicities. Such ideals were fatally undermined, however, by pervasive (and highly contradictory) Japanese assumptions of their own racial superiority. In practice, the Concordia Association merely became another tool of Kwantung Army rule.[12]

Despite enormous Japanese capital investments, moreover, Manchukuo became more of a net drain on the Japanese economy than the hoped-for lifeline. The integrated yen-bloc that was supposed to make the Japanese Empire economically and strategically self-sufficient failed to materialize. Instead, especially after full-scale war erupted with China in 1937 and the economy shifted to an emergency war footing, Japan found itself, ironically, even more critically dependent on imported resources from the United States and elsewhere.

Nationalist China

By 1928, Chiang Kai-shek's Northern Expedition had been successfully completed, and a nominally reunified Republic of China had been restored. Nanjing (Nanking) was chosen for the site of its new capital, as the "Father of the Chinese Republic" Sun Yat-sen had originally intended at the time of the 1912 revolution. Unlike Beijing in the northeast, Nanjing was centrally located and conveniently accessible, it was unburdened by the legacy of "foreign" Manchu rule symbolized by Beijing, and it had a glorious ancient Chinese tradition of its own as capital of the Southern dynasties – when it may have even been the largest city in the world – and of the early Ming. As an added attraction, Nanjing also held much vacant land that would be available for new construction, since the city had never entirely recovered after being laid waste by Qing forces during their suppression of the Taiping Rebellion in 1864. Plans were drawn up to rebuild Nanjing as a gleaming, modern, world-class capital, a Chinese Washington DC or Paris. Owing to a chronic shortage of funds – and, as it would transpire, a desperate shortage of time before the outbreak of World War II – most of these dreams were, unfortunately, never realized.[13]

The new government of the Republic of China also had highly ambitious plans for the rapid development of a modern, industrialized, and technologically advanced Chinese nation. Through funding by the National Economic Council, a network of modern motorways, railways, and air transportation links was rapidly expanded. Science and engineering were energetically promoted. But, again, the actual results fell far short of the hopes. Following the Japanese takeover of Manchuria in 1931–1932, the Chinese government also felt increasingly threatened, and responded with militarization. Building a strong national defense economy, under central government control, became the driving goal. By 1942, more than half of all industry in Nationalist China was state run.[14]

In addition to extending state control over the modern sector of the economy, the reconstituted Republic of China after 1928 was from the beginning – unlike the abortive multiparty parliamentary republic that had briefly followed the overthrow of the Qing Dynasty in 1912 – a single-party state. In 1928, opposition political parties (other than the ruling Nationalist Party, or *Guomindang*) were banned. Both free-enterprise capitalism and political democracy faced constraints, therefore, in the Nationalist China of the 1930s. But, if the Chinese Republic is viewed in the general context of world trends in the 1930s, these developments appear considerably less shocking.

The 1930s were difficult and complicated times, and Nationalist China was confronted by a swirl of challenges, influences, and pressures. Chiang Kai-shek's wife, Soong May-ling (Song Meiling, 1898–2003; see Figure 14.3), had gone to college in the United States and spoke impeccable English. Both she and her husband were also Christians. But Chiang, personally, had attended a military academy in Japan and had visited Moscow. One of his sons, Chiang Ching-kuo (Jiang Jingguo, 1910–1988; see Figure 14.3), spent twelve years in the Soviet Union and married a Russian woman. As future president of Taiwan (1978–1988), after his father's death, this man would become a key figure in the transition to genuine multiparty democracy there. Another son, Chiang Wei-kuo (Jiang Weiguo, 1916–1997), graduated from a military academy in Germany and, as an officer candidate there, participated in the 1938 *Anschluss*, or Nazi takeover of Austria.[15]

In fact, after Chiang Kai-shek broke with the Communists in 1927 and sent his Russian advisors packing, for the next decade Nationalist China had especially close relations with Germany. This was partly because Germany had lost its treaty port privileges in China (a sensitive issue for Chinese nationalists) after Germany's defeat in World War I, and partly because of the mutual convergence of interests between Germany's search for markets and sources of industrial raw material and China's search for a successful model for rapid modernization. This friendly relationship with Germany terminated abruptly after the start of full-scale war between China and Japan, however, when Germany opted to align with Japan. German aid and advisors were withdrawn from China in 1938. Thereafter, Nationalist China developed its closest relationship with the United States.[16]

Although this growing American influence probably did play a role in the eventual democratization of the Republic of China on Taiwan in the 1980s–1990s, as of the mid-twentieth century Nationalist China was an authoritarian single-party state. It was also heavily militarized. Forty-three percent of the central Nationalist Party leaders were military men as of 1935, and twenty-five of thirty-three provincial chairmen were also generals during the decade of feeble peace between the nominal Nationalist reunification of China in 1928 and the outbreak of World War II in 1937.[17]

Yet, despite this authoritarianism, in many ways the Nationalist Republic's most outstanding characteristic was really weakness. "Far from being a dictator," observed U.S. General Albert C. Wedemeyer, Chiang Kai-shek "was in fact only the head of a loose coalition." The Nationalist Party was heavily factionalized, and its control over the Chinese countryside was extremely limited. At the height of World War II in 1944, the government of Nationalist China was only able to mobilize about 3–5 percent of China's gross national product for the war effort, compared to the 47 percent that was mobilized by the United States.[18] Some Chinese provinces long continued to print their own separate currencies. One province (Shanxi) built its railways on a different gauge than the rest of China. Much of China's military force also remained under local rather than central control. Despite the nominal reunification of China in 1928, many of the former warlords had actually merely declared their allegiance to the Republic of China and continued doing business as usual, as effectively independent powers. We will never be able to know what might eventually have emerged from this unpromising beginning, if only China had been left in peace. Instead, however, the outbreak of full-scale war with Japan in 1937 effectively sealed Nationalist China's fate on the mainland.

The Rise of Mao Zedong

"Science and democracy" had been the great slogan of China's May Fourth Movement, and as late as the end of 1919 the man who would become the first leader of the Chinese Communist Party, Chen Duxiu, was still advocating an Anglo-American model of democracy in China. By 1920, however, he had become a self-proclaimed Marxist.[19] During a period of profound disillusionment among many of the more radical May Fourth intellectuals, in the spring of 1920 a Comintern agent arrived in Beijing from Moscow with details of the Bolshevik model for revolutionary organization. It was the organizational effectiveness of Bolshevik discipline more than any theoretical appeal of Marxism that resulted in the rise of the Chinese Communist Party.[20] The first Chinese Marxist cells emerged out of study groups in Beijing in 1920. By 1921, there were roughly fifty Chinese Communists, and the First Congress of the Chinese Communist Party convened in secret that summer, holding its opening session in a girls' school in the French Concession in Shanghai.

In its early years, the Chinese Communist Party remained under the general direction of the Comintern in Moscow, and because the Soviet Union had also reached an agreement with Sun Yat-sen and the Chinese Nationalist Party in 1923, there followed a brief period of cooperation between these two Chinese political parties. Chiang Kai-shek's sudden purge of leftists in April 1927, however, dealt the Communists a devastating blow. The disaster was compounded by misguided Communist efforts to stage uprisings in several cities that year, in a desperate effort to maintain some connection with the urban industrial working class – the so-called proletariat – which, according to Marxist theory, the Communist Party was supposed to represent. All these uprisings failed, however. During the last one, the so-called Canton Commune in December 1927, participants wore red scarves or armbands as a kind of uniform. After the uprising was crushed, these were hastily removed, but anyone discovered with telltale red stains on their skin was executed on the spot.[21] In the chaos after Chiang's purge, at one point even Mao Zedong was caught by Nationalist soldiers and only narrowly managed to escape.[22]

The Chinese Communists were driven underground or out into the countryside. As devastating as this purge was, however, it also gave young Mao Zedong a chance to try a radically unorthodox approach to Marxism: peasant revolution. Mao's faith in the revolutionary potential of peasants stood orthodox Marxism on its head. In theory, the communist revolution was supposed to be driven by objective material conditions at a particular stage of historical development, through class struggle between workers and wealthy industrialists in the most advanced modern capitalist economies. But Mao believed he could adapt the general Marxist-Leninist principles to China's unique circumstances and tap into the explosive desires of the peasantry as a force that might bring communism to power even before material conditions made it "inevitable." Mao had faith that with the right leadership and indoctrination, a "proletarian consciousness" could then be instilled into the peasantry and advanced socialist goals eventually realized.[23]

Chiang Kai-shek's purge in 1927 gave Mao a chance to put his theories to the test. At Mt. Jinggang, Jiangxi, in southeastern China, Mao led about two thousand followers to begin developing a rural Communist base in late 1927. There they began experimenting with techniques for gaining the support of poorer farmers through a program of forced land redistribution, backed by the guns of the newly created Red Army. They also began developing innovative tactics of guerrilla warfare to compensate for the Red Army's conventional military weakness. Although this style of peasant revolution was criticized by the Chinese Communist Central Committee, Mao was, for a time, beyond their effective reach and free to experiment. Details are murky, but Mao's rural Jiangxi base was successful enough that it eventually expanded to include several million people.

Success brought unwanted attention, however. Chinese Communist Party leaders began drifting into the rural Jiangxi base from their beleaguered urban headquarters in Shanghai around 1932. These newly arriving leaders were still oriented toward Moscow and critical of Mao's peasant deviations from orthodox Marxist theory. Before long, Mao was removed from real decision-making power in the Communist Party. There are even rumors that at one point Mao may have been placed under house arrest, although this has been denied.[24]

Chiang Kai-shek's attention had also been caught by Mao's rural experiment, and Chiang's Nationalist armies now launched a series of military campaigns against this agrarian Communist base in the southeast. The first Nationalist attacks were repulsed by Communist guerrilla tactics, but in 1934 Nationalist forces finally succeeded in totally destroying the Communist base in Jiangxi. Before it was overrun, however, in October 1934, a core group of about eighty-six thousand Communist cadres and Red Army soldiers managed to break out of the Nationalist encirclement and begin what is known to history as the Long March. Initially, this was something of an aimless flight from disaster, but eventually, a preexisting Communist base area in Shaanxi Province, in the arid and poor northwest, was decided upon as a destination. Of the large number who had begun the Long

Figure 10.2. Mao Zedong at an airfield in north China – probably Shaanxi – in 1936. Collection J. A. Fox. Magnum Photos.

March, only about seven or eight thousand finally arrived in Shaanxi the next year, in October 1935. Along the way, however, Mao Zedong was able to blame the disastrous collapse of the "Jiangxi Soviet" on mistakes made by others and for the first time establish himself as the dominant figure in Chinese communism (see Figure 10.2).[25] It was, ironically, Chiang Kai-shek's near-success in exterminating the Chinese Communists at the time of the Long March that helped raise Mao to the top Communist leadership, and it would be the Japanese invasion, and World War II, that would provide the context for a final Communist victory.

World War II in China

In 1936, Mao Zedong's little Communist group settled on the remote Shaanxi market town of Yan'an for its new headquarters. By this time, Chiang Kai-shek felt that he had the Communists cornered and ordered his generals in the area to finish them off. Public opinion in China, however, was now generally much more alarmed by the growing Japanese menace than by the internal communist threat. It also happened that one of the principal Nationalist commanders in Shaanxi was none other than the son of the Manchurian warlord Zhang Zuolin, who had been assassinated by the Japanese in 1928. This son had been driven out of Manchuria by the Japanese establishment of their puppet state there. The Chinese Communists had, meanwhile, astutely changed their tactics. They were now promoting a truce in the domestic civil war with Chiang Kai-shek's Nationalist Party and the formation of a United Front against Japan. When his generals in Shaanxi did not pursue the war against the Communists as aggressively as Chiang would have liked, Chiang Kai-shek flew in person to the largest city in Shaanxi Province, Xi'an (sometimes spelled "Sian"), to encourage them to make greater efforts. There, at a hot springs located in the outskirts of the city, in what is known as the "Xi'an incident," in December 1936 Chiang Kai-shek was kidnapped by his own troops, forced to negotiate with the Communists, and agree to the formation of a United Front with them against Japan.

This Xi'an incident is important because it led to the start of World War II a few months later. During the night of July 7, 1937, a small detachment of Japanese troops were on maneuvers at Marco Polo Bridge, just a few miles outside of Beijing (which was then called Beiping, "Northern Peace," rather than Beijing, "Northern Capital," since it was not the capital of the Nationalist Republic), when some shots were fired. This might easily have remained a relatively insignificant incident, except that because of the formation of the United Front and Chiang Kai-shek's new determination to resist further Japanese aggression, Nationalist China responded by reinforcing its troops in the Beijing area. The Japanese also sent reinforcements, and by July 25 full-scale war had erupted.

Based on the ease with which a small number of Japanese soldiers had earlier overrun Manchuria, and widespread Japanese feelings of contempt for warlord China, the Japanese anticipated a quick victory. The war minister assured the Shōwa Emperor that this China incident would be over in a month, and in July 1937 the Japanese cabinet authorized operations for only three divisions for three months. Although Chinese Nationalist armies did put up surprisingly stiff resistance, especially in the Shanghai area (see Figure 10.3), by December 13 the Nationalist capital at Nanjing (Nanking) had in fact fallen to the Japanese. There the Japanese soldiers, who had behaved with notably good discipline during the earlier war with Russia, went on a notorious rampage known as the Rape of Nanking.[26]

Although it took somewhat longer than originally anticipated, the Japanese did swiftly capture most of the major Chinese coastal cities and the principal agricultural plains of eastern China. But the Nationalist Chinese capital merely retreated farther up the line of the Yangzi River, finally settling in the city of Chongqing (in English, Chungking), in Sichuan Province – a vast natural fortress protected by steep encircling mountains. Despite prolonged Japanese aerial bombing of Chongqing, the Chinese Nationalists continued to resist and stubbornly refused to surrender.

Although they won repeated battlefield victories, the Japanese found themselves unable to inflict a decisive defeat on Chiang Kai-shek's Nationalist China. To the

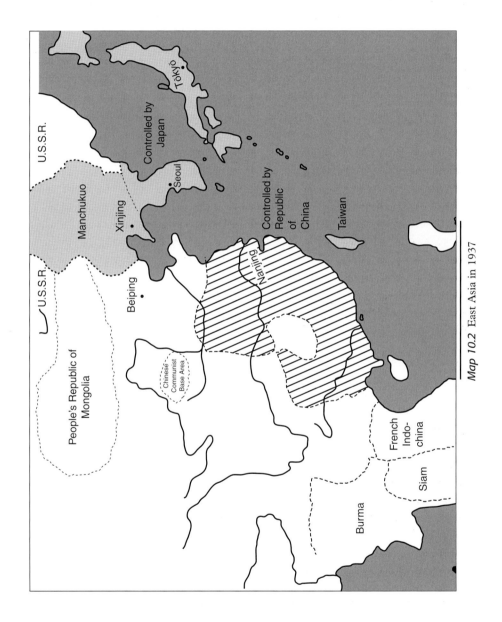

Map 10.2 East Asia in 1937

Figure 10.3. A terrified baby in Shanghai's South Station following a Japanese bombing at the start of World War II, August 28, 1937. National Archives.

end of World War II, the Japanese found it necessary to continue to station about half of all their total available forces in China, yet even that was not enough to achieve conclusive success. After the Japanese offensive stalled, however, Chiang Kai-shek's ability to launch a counteroffensive was also seriously limited.

Roughly one million Japanese troops held strategic central positions in China, while some four million Chinese troops were spread out in a vast surrounding arc, often in highly mountainous terrain and linked together only by crude roads and inadequate transportation facilities. Much of China's industrial capacity (only modest to begin with) had been overrun by the Japanese, and the Nationalist Chinese government's arsenals were now only able to produce about four bullets per soldier per month. As a result of unresolved residual warlordism, furthermore, at one point half of Chiang Kai-shek's frontline military commanders were men who had previously been in conflict with him. The result was a stalemate. Neither the Chinese nor the Japanese were able to achieve a final victory. This stalemate degenerated into an increasingly cynical phony war, lubricated by pervasive smuggling across enemy lines, and a growing cloud of corruption.[27]

Nationalist China's loss of the developed modern sector of its economy, which had been almost exclusively confined to the large coastal cities, especially Shanghai, and which had been the government's principal source of tax revenue before the war, led the Nationalist government to issue mountains of poorly backed paper money. This resulted in catastrophic hyperinflation. Between 1937 and 1945, average prices in Nationalist China increased by more than two-thousand-fold. In the end, it has been suggested that "inflation did more than any other single issue to undermine public confidence" in the Nationalist government and cause it to eventually lose control of mainland China.[28]

The Japanese had hoped that Chiang Kai-shek could quickly be brought to terms, but they were disappointed by Chiang's continued stubborn defiance. In exasperation, the Japanese government announced in January 1938 that they would have no further dealings with Chiang Kai-shek. Because they had never seriously contemplated assuming direct Japanese administration over all of China, the Japanese were therefore obliged to find other Chinese collaborators. Aside from the nominally independent country of Manchukuo in the northeast, the chief collaborator in central China turned out, ironically, to be a former Chinese nationalist hero: Wang Jingwei (1883–1944).

In 1910, toward the end of the Qing Dynasty, Wang had attempted to assassinate the Manchu prince regent. He failed, was caught, and was sentenced to death. Rather than create a revolutionary martyr, however, the Qing Dynasty commuted his death sentence to life in prison. After the sudden success of the Republican Revolution in 1912, Wang was released to a hero's welcome. When Sun Yat-sen died in 1925, Wang even briefly became Sun's successor as head of the Nationalist Party. But when cadets from the Nationalist military academy, headed by Chiang Kai-shek, moved suddenly in 1926 to end a nine-month-long antiforeign boycott in Guangzhou (Canton) without even consulting Wang, Wang Jingwei resigned in humiliation and went off to Paris.

After the Japanese stopped negotiating with Chiang Kai-shek in 1938, they established what they euphemistically called a Reformed Government of the Republic of China at Nanjing. By 1940, they had persuaded Wang Jingwei to serve as its leader. Although the verdict of history is undoubtedly that Wang collaborated with the enemy during wartime, he appears to have been no simple opportunist. Wang seems to have sincerely believed that cooperation with Japan was the best way to protect Chinese interests in a time of extreme vulnerability. At her war crimes trial after the war, Wang's widow (Wang himself having already died) still vigorously defended her husband's record – to the applause of her courtroom audience – arguing that he had not given up an inch of Chinese territory that had not already been lost and that he had done all he could to defend China's sovereignty.[29]

Elsewhere in Asia, in the former European colonies, cooperation with Japan during World War II could actually have some nationalistic appeal. In the Dutch East Indies (now Indonesia), for example, wartime association with Japan did little to damage Sukarno's credentials as a nationalist hero. In China, though, the focus of nationalist outrage was not Western imperialism but Japanese. Aside from great atrocities like the Rape of Nanking and the mounting horrors of a war that eventually cost China some twenty million dead, there were also routine humiliations like the need to bow to Japanese sentries on the streets of China's occupied coastal cities. These wartime memories planted lasting seeds of bitterness in China.

But for Japan, too, the war was hardly going very well either. Predictions of a quick and easy victory had proved false. Even before the attack on Pearl Harbor added the weight of U.S. and other Allied military power into the balance against Japan, Japan had already lost 185,000 dead in China, and Japan's economy was already under severe strain. It was in growing exasperation with this "quagmire" in China that Japanese strategists began to look south.

World War II in the Pacific

The huge costs of waging war on a continental scale in China, especially when combined with Japan's strategic ambition to simultaneously gear up quickly for military self-sufficiency, drove Japan from a surprisingly robust export-led recovery from the Great Depression in the early 1930s to what would turn out to be a fatal dependency on heavy industrial imports by the end of the decade. Increased military spending after 1936 led to inflation, which raised the cost of Japanese products and made them less competitive as exports. Government controls over imported raw materials favored those with military applications rather than materials, such as cotton, that could be used to manufacture textiles for reexport. Government control also funneled new investments into war industries rather than consumer or export-oriented businesses. As a direct result of her quest for self-sufficiency, ironically, Japan only became more critically dependent on such imported things as machine tools, iron, and oil.[30]

A February 1938 National Mobilization Act put all economic resources in Japan under government control. One of the first effects was the imposition of rationing and other austerity measures. Beginning in 1938, gasoline was strictly rationed in Japan. Rice, matches, sugar, and charcoal had joined the list of rationed items by 1940, and in May 1940 Japanese stores were forbidden to sell any nonessential goods. Not only Western-style clothing but even traditional Japanese kimonos were replaced by khaki "people's uniforms" and peasant pantaloons for women.[31]

Ever since defeating Russia in war in 1905, Japanese army planners had anticipated a future war of revenge with the Russians. The communist revolution in Russia only seemed to make such a war more inevitable. Some Japanese army officers, notably Ishiwara Kanji, the mastermind of the takeover in Manchuria, had even opposed intervention in China south of the Great Wall because it would deplete vital resources and distract Japan from the more important confrontation with Russia (which he expected would precede the final showdown with the United States). In fact, Japan actually did engage the Soviet Union in a little-known but bitter struggle during the summer of 1939, at a place called (in Japanese) Nomonhan on the border between Mongolia and Manchuria. Soviet armored forces proved disconcertingly effective in this action, however, and Japan suffered heavy losses. Even as Japan was being mauled by the Soviets at Nomonhan, meanwhile, Germany signed a nonaggression pact with the Soviet Union in August 1939. Japan, which had already signed an anti-Comintern pact (opposing communism without specifically mentioning Russia) with Germany in 1936, and reached a formal alliance with the Axis powers Germany and Italy in 1940, responded by arranging its own neutrality pact with the Soviet Union in 1941. Despite Hitler's betrayal of his pact with Stalin and invasion of Russia soon afterward, the Soviet agreement with Japan held. The Soviet Union would remain neutral in World War II in the Pacific until the very last days.

Meanwhile, Japan hoped that its Axis alliance with Germany and Italy would make other powers (such as the United States) reluctant to intervene against Japanese interests in Asia. Largely in an effort to cut off supplies to Nationalist China, by July 1941 Japanese troops had occupied French colonial Indochina (Vietnam). The French, who by this time had been defeated and forced into cooperation with Hitler's Germany in Europe, did not resist in Vietnam, but the United States, Great Britain, and the Netherlands imposed stiff economic sanctions on Japan, notably including embargoes on oil and scrap metal. These sanctions had real teeth. In 1940, 80 percent of Japan's total oil supply came from the United States.[32] Japan's principal alternative to American oil was Dutch colonial Java (in what is now Indonesia). Japan's predicament, therefore, had become daunting.

Going to war against Japan's own largest supplier of vital war materials (the United States) hardly seemed sensible, especially since the United States was also much more populous and more extensively industrialized than Japan as of 1941. But Japan's options were limited. By late 1941, Japan's stockpiles of oil were dwindling alarmingly, while the United States was already beginning a massive military buildup. If Japan was to have any chance of victory in a war with the United States, it would have to begin soon. Some leaders in the Japanese army were, moreover, confident that Japanese fighting spirit would overcome the material disadvantages. At an imperial conference on November 5, 1941, a decision was made to go to war if no settlement had been reached by December. The imperial navy drew up plans to temporarily paralyze U.S. forces by striking at the U.S. Pacific Fleet based in Hawai'i. A Japanese aircraft carrier task force sailed for that purpose on November 26 and struck at Pearl Harbor on December 7.

The attack achieved complete surprise, and most of the American battleships anchored in Pearl Harbor were at least temporarily put out of action. A simultaneous Japanese invasion of British Malaya also began. British Hong Kong fell to the Japanese on Christmas Day, and on December 26, Manila, in the American-controlled Philippines, was declared an open city. On the Malay peninsula, Japanese troops hacked their way through the jungle to attack the British fortress at Singapore from its relatively unguarded rear. Singapore fell to the Japanese on February 8, 1942. On March 9, the most valuable prize of all, the Dutch island of Java, with its rich supplies of oil, rubber, and tin, surrendered. In May 1942, the last American holdouts in the Philippines, on the island of Corregidor, surrendered. By this time, there were even rumors of a possible Japanese invasion of British colonial India and talk of evacuating all of northern Australia.

Japan needed just a few more victories to complete the ring of defensive island fortresses it envisioned in preparation for the expected eventual Allied

Map 10.3 World War II in East Asia and the Pacific

counteroffensive. These last few victories were denied to Japan, however. All the American aircraft carriers had miraculously escaped the slaughter at Pearl Harbor simply by being out of port at the time of the attack. On May 8, 1942, an American aircraft carrier task force intercepted a Japanese invasion fleet heading for Port Moresby, New Guinea. In the resulting naval air battle of the Coral Sea, located between Australia and New Guinea, although neither side won a decisive victory, the Japanese were forced to cancel their invasion of Port Moresby. In June 1942, Japanese forces staged successful amphibious landings on actual U.S. soil in the Aleutian Islands, Alaska. This was only intended as a diversion, however, as part of an elaborate plan to lure out and sink the remainder of the U.S. Pacific Fleet. Thanks to some good luck, and the fact that the Americans had broken the Japanese code and were able to decipher Japanese messages, the U.S. fleet surprised the Japanese instead. In the ensuing naval air battle of Midway Island, beginning June 4, 1942, four Japanese aircraft carriers were sunk to the American loss of only one. This battle of Midway became the crucial turning point of the war in the Pacific.

Instead of serving as an impenetrable defensive shield, Japan's island empire in the Pacific proved to be full of holes. U.S. submarines, sailing deep into Japanese waters with relative impunity, almost immediately began to wage an aggressive campaign to cut off the flow of essential raw materials from Java, and elsewhere, to the factories on the Japanese home islands. As a result, Japan's industrial economy ground to a standstill, and Japan was increasingly unable to replace the ships and planes it lost in battle. Japanese-held islands in the Pacific that were especially strongly fortified could furthermore simply be bypassed, or skipped over, in the Allied counteroffensive, in a process called "island hopping."

The Allied counteroffensive began with landings on Guadalcanal, in the Solomon Islands, in August 1942. A fiercely fought battle for supremacy there raged for some six months before the Allies finally drove the Japanese from Guadalcanal in February 1943. From there, the Japanese Pacific island empire was rolled up in a two-pronged counteroffensive, with Allied land forces (under the command of General Douglas MacArthur) driving up from the south through New Guinea to the Philippines, and the navy island-hopping across the central Pacific from the Marianas to Okinawa.

American industrial productivity, meanwhile, was unleashing a *tsunami* of steel against the Japanese Empire. Until late 1943, the U.S. Pacific Fleet never had more than four aircraft carriers at any given time, but by the end of 1944 the U.S. Navy had nearly a hundred aircraft carriers in operation (worldwide, and including smaller escort carriers).[33] By October 1944, General MacArthur had assembled a massive fleet consisting of some seven hundred ships for his long-promised return to the Philippines. Japan committed her last remaining warships to their defense, and in the naval battle of Leyte Gulf – the largest naval battle in world history – the Japanese were decisively defeated. In desperation, Japan even began to resort to suicide (*kamikaze*, or "Divine Wind," a reference to the typhoons that had scattered the thirteenth-century Mongol invasion fleets) attacks on Allied ships.

In November 1944, air raids on the Japanese home islands began with long-range B-29 bombers based in the Marianas. Altogether, some sixty-six Japanese cities were reduced to charred rubble. Incendiary bombs ignited raging conflagrations among the mostly wooden Japanese houses. Of Japan's major cities, only the ancient imperial capital of Kyōto was spared. Before long, Allied aircraft enjoyed almost complete command of the air above Japan. Yet the unconditional surrender demand that had been adopted by the Allies at the Casablanca conference in 1943 remained unacceptable to Japanese authorities. Some Japanese leaders still hoped that by winning one last major battle, and inflicting unacceptably heavy casualties on the Allies, Japan might be able to obtain better terms. The bottom line for many Japanese authorities was a deeply felt need to preserve the national polity embodied in the imperial institution.

After Germany was defeated in May 1945, Japan found herself fighting alone against almost the entire world. During the summer of 1945 the Japanese made a futile attempt to request Soviet mediation in negotiating an end to the war, not realizing that Stalin had already pledged, at the Yalta Conference in February, that Russia would enter the war against Japan after Germany surrendered. On August 6, an atomic bomb was dropped on Hiroshima. On August 8, the Soviet Union unleashed a massive assault on Japanese forces in Manchuria. On August 9, a second atomic bomb was detonated at Nagasaki. Even then, on August 10, the Japanese government still broadcast a message indicating that Japan would be willing to accept Allied surrender terms only if the preservation of the emperor could be guaranteed. The U.S. response, approved by both Britain and the Soviet Union, was to agree, but with the crucial modification that "the authority of the Emperor . . . shall be subject to the Supreme Commander of the Allied Powers."[34]

This answer was still unsatisfactory to many in the Japanese army. After considerable more debate, however, the emperor himself finally broke the deadlock on August 14 with a decision to surrender. Even then, the night before the emperor's prerecorded surrender speech was scheduled to be broadcast, a group of army officers rebelled and attempted to destroy the recording. They failed, however, and at noon on August 15, 1945, the Japanese people heard the voice of their emperor for the first time, speaking in hard-to-comprehend formal court language. Without ever actually using the word surrender, and noting (with considerable understatement) that recent developments in the war "did not turn in Japan's favor," the emperor called on his people to "endure the unendurable."[35]

Formal surrender documents were signed aboard the American battleship *Missouri* on September 2, 1945 (see Figure 10.4). World War II was over. In East Asia, Japan had been catastrophically defeated and lay in smoldering ruins, having suffered some 2.7 million war dead. Korea was to be liberated from Japanese colonial rule but would initially be subject to divided zones of Soviet and American military occupation. China had been on the winning side. But China, where World War II first began in 1937, had also suffered horribly from the war, and the postwar situation in China remained unencouraging. Almost alone in the world, the United States emerged from World War II actively strengthened. In the aftermath of

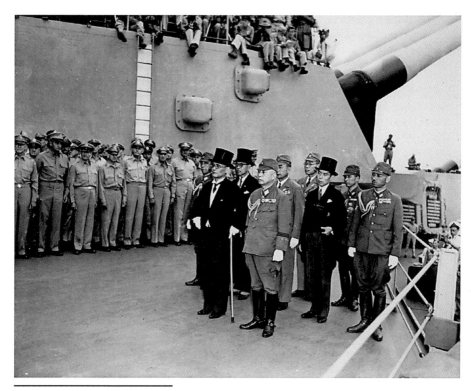

Figure 10.4. Japanese representatives arrive aboard the battleship USS *Missouri* in Tōkyō Bay to participate in surrender ceremonies at the end of World War II, September 2, 1945. National Archives.

World War II, the U.S. economy accounted for an astonishing 50 percent of all goods and services on earth.[36] Few people could have predicted then that in the following decades, East Asia would reemerge to become (at least in purely economic terms) perhaps the single most successful region of the planet, or that it would be Japan that would lead this spectacular economic "miracle."

For Further Reading

On the rise of ultranationalism in prewar Japan, see Michael A. Barnhart, *Japan Prepares for Total War: The Search for Economic Security, 1919–1941* (Ithaca, NY: Cornell University Press, 1987); W. G. Beasley, *Japanese Imperialism, 1894–1945* (Oxford: Clarendon Press, [1987] 1991); Mark R. Peattie, *Ishiwara Kanji and Japan's Confrontation with the West* (Princeton University Press, 1975); Ben-Ami Shillony, *Revolt in Japan: The Young Officers and the February 26, 1936 Incident* (Princeton University Press, 1973); and George M. Wilson, *Radical Nationalist in Japan: Kita Ikki, 1883–1937* (Cambridge, MA: Harvard University Press, 1969). Concerning Manchukuo, an excellent volume is Louise Young, *Japan's Total Empire: Manchuria and the Culture of Wartime Imperialism* (Berkeley: University of California Press, 1998).

On Nationalist China, see the fine biography of Chiang Kai-shek by Jay Taylor, *The Generalissimo: Chiang Kai-shek and the Struggle for Modern China* (Cambridge, MA: Harvard University Press, 2009). See also Parks M. Coble Jr., *The Shanghai Capitalists and the Nationalist Government, 1927–1937* (Cambridge, MA: Harvard University Press, [1980]

1986); Lloyd E. Eastman, Jerome Ch'en, Suzanne Pepper, and Lyman P. Van Slyke, eds., *The Nationalist Era in China, 1927–1949* (Cambridge University Press, 1991); and James E. Sheridan, *China in Disintegration: The Republican Era in Chinese History, 1912–1949* (New York: Free Press, 1975).

Studies of early Chinese communism and the rise of Mao Zedong include Arif Dirlik, *The Origins of Chinese Communism* (New York: Oxford University Press, 1989); Benjamin I. Schwartz, *Chinese Communism and the Rise of Mao* (Cambridge, MA: Harvard University Press, [1951] 1979); and the short biography by Jonathan D. Spence, *Mao Zedong* (New York: Viking, 1999). Edgar Snow was an American journalist who scooped an early interview with the guerrilla leader Mao Zedong and published a still extremely valuable account of Mao's early years as *Red Star over China* (New York: Grove Press, [1938] 1968).

For World War II in China and Japan, see John Hunter Boyle, *China and Japan at War, 1937–1945: The Politics of Collaboration* (Stanford University Press, 1972); Iris Chang, *The Rape of Nanking: The Forgotten Holocaust of World War II* (New York: Penguin Books, 1997); Thomas R. H. Havens, *Valley of Darkness: The Japanese People and World War Two* (Lanham, MD: University Press of America, 1986); Saburō Ienaga, *The Pacific War, 1931–1945* (New York: Pantheon Books, [1968] 1978); and Barbara W. Tuchman, *Stilwell and the American Experience in China, 1911–1945* (New York: Bantam Books, 1972). A still-valuable account by contemporary American journalists reporting from China is Theodore H. White and Annalee Jacoby, *Thunder out of China* (New York: William Sloan Associates, [1946] 1961).

World War II in the Pacific is covered by John W. Dower, *War without Mercy: Race and Power in the Pacific War* (New York: Pantheon Books, 1986); Max Hastings, *Retribution: The Battle for Japan, 1944–45* (New York: Alfred A. Knopf, 2008); and Ronald H. Spector, *Eagle against the Sun: The American War with Japan* (New York: Free Press, 1985).

11 Japan since 1945

The Postwar Allied Occupation

The Shōwa Emperor's surrender speech was broadcast over the radio airwaves on August 15, 1945, and on August 28, a few days before the formal surrender ceremonies were conducted aboard the battleship *Missouri* on September 2, the first small advance party of what would eventually become an Allied occupation force reaching up to a quarter million persons touched down in a C-47 transport plane at an airport outside Tōkyō. These first Allied arrivals were uncertain what sort of reception they might encounter. The Japanese, too, were anxious and uncertain what sort of behavior to expect from the arriving foreign army of occupation, whose soldiers had until recently been such bitter enemies. Many Japanese were relieved that the war was finally over, but many were also, understandably, apprehensive. With relatively few exceptions, however, the arriving Allied forces were treated with respect and even privilege – until 1951, for example, the Japanese government provided occupation authorities with free servants – whereas the occupation authorities, for their part, behaved with magnanimity toward their defeated foes. Not a few participants in the occupation discovered a lifelong love and fascination for Japanese culture.[1] In retrospect, the usual verdict is that the postwar Allied occupation of Japan was an overall great success.

Although it is referred to as an "Allied" occupation, it was overwhelmingly really an American affair. Unlike postwar Germany (and also the former Japanese colony in Korea), defeated Japan was not divided into separate zones of occupation by the different Allied powers. A multinational Far Eastern Commission was eventually established in Washington, DC, and a four-power Allied Council for Japan was sent to Tōkyō, which included British, Chinese, and Soviet representatives, but a single, unified, Supreme Commander for the Allied Powers (SCAP) was appointed to actively supervise the entire region. The officer assigned this command was the senior American general Douglas MacArthur (1880–1964), who set up his headquarters in the Daiichi building in Tōkyō at the end of August 1945. Most of the occupation personnel were also American.

President Truman initially instructed General MacArthur that, inside defeated Japan, "your authority is supreme," and MacArthur envisioned his own role in Japan as nothing less than "a sovereign."[2] MacArthur took a grandly imperious view of his position as a kind of military proconsul presiding over postwar Japan, and he was fond of claiming that he had some special understanding of the "Oriental mind" – based, presumably, on his early years of experience living in the Philippines. However, the Southeast Asian and largely Christian (Catholic) Filipinos had little in common with the East Asian Japanese, and MacArthur had very little real familiarity with Japan. Nevertheless, MacArthur's paternalistic attitude did generate some well-intentioned efforts to benefit the Japanese people. This was crucial because initially, amid the desolation of Japan's bombed-out cities, there were desperate shortages of almost everything.

Food was rationed, but the rations were less than the minimum normal nutritional requirements necessary to sustain life. Nearly everyone was forced, therefore, to turn to illegal black markets just to get enough food to survive. Black marketeering was so pervasive that one magazine observed with dark humor in 1948 that "the only people who are not living illegally are those in jail."[3] MacArthur responded quickly to the emergency by requesting relief supplies of food and medicine, which undoubtedly saved many lives, even though it could not begin to eliminate all the hardships of the early postwar years. MacArthur also seems to have felt some empathy for the Japanese emperor.

At the time of Japan's surrender, American opinion was seriously divided over the question of how completely Japan would have to be forcibly reconstructed so that it would never again be a threat to world peace. Some felt that the old militaristic Japan would have to be almost entirely obliterated, and a great many of the Allies felt that Japan should quite properly be punished for its wartime aggression. Initially, plans were drawn up to dismantle Japan's remaining industrial plants and ship them abroad as war reparations. All of Japan's overseas colonial possessions, including Korea, Taiwan, and Manchuria (which had not technically been a colony but had been effectively dominated by the Japanese), were liberated, and some six and a half million Japanese people were returned from overseas to the home islands.

War crime trials also soon began, intended to punish specific alleged culprits. Twenty-eight Class A prisoners were charged with major "crimes against peace" and tried by the International Military Tribunal for the Far East. Seven of these were convicted and sentenced to death by hanging. In addition (not counting those captured by the Soviet Union and Chinese Communists), some fifty-seven hundred other Japanese were tried by Allied international military tribunals, and accused of more "conventional" war crimes such as mistreatment of prisoners. Of these, 4,405 were convicted and 984 executed. Beyond the punishment of specific war criminals, during the first three years of the occupation more than two hundred thousand former military officers, politicians, and business leaders were also purged by the occupation authorities.

Many Americans felt that the individual most responsible for the war in the Pacific had been the Japanese emperor himself. The U.S. Senate passed a resolution in 1945 calling for the emperor also to be tried as a war criminal. In January 1946, however, General MacArthur cabled Washington from Tōkyō with a forceful assertion of the idea that putting the emperor on trial for war crimes would be counterproductive, and would probably even provoke guerrilla warfare against the Allied occupation. A plausible argument could be made that the emperor of Japan had always been more a symbol of the nation than an active ruler; that the emperor's individual responsibility for specific government policies, including military action, had been limited; and that, precisely as a symbol of Japan, the prestige of the throne could be wielded now in the cause of peace and stability just as easily as it previously had been used for war. In the end, MacArthur's position prevailed. Not only was the institution of the emperor preserved, but the same wartime Shōwa Emperor (Hirohito) was allowed to remain seated on the chrysanthemum throne, and the question of his war guilt was largely forgotten.

Even after the surrender, the Japanese government continued to function and handle routine administration. SCAP's authority was ultimately final, but technically the occupation authorities were there only in a supervisory capacity. In spring 1946, Japan conducted its first postwar election, which was also the first ever in which women were allowed to vote. Yoshida Shigeru (1878–1967) became prime minister, and Yoshida would continue to play a leading role throughout the occupation era. The story goes that Yoshida began his first cabinet meeting with the observation that it might be possible for Japan to lose the war and still win the peace.[4]

SCAP's ability to supervise the details of postwar Japan was handicapped by a scarcity of competent Japanese-language speakers and of specialists familiar with Japanese culture. During the war, a number of crash courses in Japanese language training had sprung up in the United States. Soon after the Japanese struck Pearl Harbor, for example, Harvard University decided to offer elementary intensive Japanese language instruction in the spring semester of 1942, instead of waiting for the normal beginning of the academic year in September. Its teachers were "stunned when we found close to a hundred students cramming the small classroom" instead of "the usual five or ten." At the start of World War II, the U.S. Navy had only twelve officers who could speak Japanese, but by the end of the war the U.S. Navy Japanese Language School alone had graduated eleven hundred new translators.[5] Even so, the number of fluent Japanese speakers among the occupation personnel was limited. This made the occupation authorities heavily reliant on English-speaking translators provided by the Japanese Central Liaison Office, and opened the door for accidental, or occasionally perhaps even deliberate, misunderstandings.

Nonetheless, SCAP had both the leverage and determination to prod the Japanese Diet (the English-language name for the Japanese legislature) into making sweeping reforms that would have been otherwise entirely unthinkable. Because of the Roosevelt era New Deal background of many Americans at the end of World War II, the initial thrust of these reforms emphasized the unionization of factory labor, farmland redistribution, trust busting, and equality of rights. For example, a trade union law was passed in December 1945 that guaranteed Japanese workers the right to organize, strike, and engage in collective bargaining. Antimonopoly and antitrust laws were passed, which forced the breakup of the giant *zaibatsu*. A 1946 farmland reform law prohibited absentee landlordism and strictly limited the amount of farmland that could be rented out to tenant farmers. This land reform, combined with rapid urbanization, was of fundamental importance in finally completing the almost total dissolution of the traditional rural social order. Political prisoners, including communists, were released from jail. State *Shintō* religion was also disestablished, the emperor renounced his claim to be a manifest deity, and the principle of religious freedom was proclaimed.

Not content with specific new laws or policies, a conviction began to grow that Japan needed an entirely new constitution to replace the nineteenth-century Meiji era document. Since official Japanese proposals for constitutional revision did not go far enough to suit the occupation authorities (whereas some unofficial Japanese proposals went too far, threatening, for example, to eliminate the emperor), the Americans stepped in and wrote the new constitution themselves, originally in English. A small team from the Government Section of SCAP drafted it in roughly a week (February 4–12, 1946) of intense effort, based on guidelines sketched out for them by General MacArthur. After a few revisions, this new constitution was approved by the Japanese Diet in November 1946 and took effect in May 1947. It is still in effect today.

Although, to a large extent, the Japanese emperor had really always only been something of a figurehead, his once theoretically supreme authority was now officially reduced in the new constitution to being merely a "symbol of the State." Sovereign power was now vested, instead, in "the people." Japan became a genuine Western-style democracy, where all citizens twenty years of age and older are eligible to vote. This includes women – a right that was not introduced in France until 1945 and in Switzerland until as late as the 1970s.[6] Despite the American authorship of this document, a British-style parliamentary system was maintained rather than an American-style presidency. Unlike the prewar Japanese system, however, under which the prime minister had been chosen by the emperor (or more accurately, by senior statesmen acting in the name of the emperor), the postwar prime minister is now responsible to, and chosen by, the Diet. The former upper House of Peers, and the peerage itself, were eliminated and replaced by an Upper House filled with elected councilors.

Because the prime minister was now chosen by the legislators, this meant that he was usually the head of the leading party in the Diet. In practice, this leading party has nearly always been the Liberal Democratic Party (LDP). Despite the continuous existence of multiple opposition parties, from the original formation of the LDP in 1955 until today, with fairly brief exceptions only in 1993–1996, and 2009–2012, the LDP has effectively been the permanent ruling party of postwar Japan. In other words, postwar Japan experienced a somewhat peculiar form of multiparty democracy in which the same one party nearly always won. The explanation for this seemingly odd situation is that the main opposition to the ruling LDP – which, despite its misleading name is actually the more conservative major party – for a long time came from the Socialists. Although the Socialists did enjoy a fairly solid core constituency, because they rejected the mutual security treaty with the United States and held to a generally Marxist line during the cold war years, their popular appeal was also always relatively limited. In contrast, the LDP long delivered undeniable peace and prosperity, and promised benefits for nearly everyone.

Since LDP rule was so entrenched, this meant that the real politics of postwar Japan commonly involved factions within the LDP, resulting in the prime minister often being chosen through deals struck between various faction leaders. Also, because LDP members still frequently had to compete against each other to get elected, election campaigns remained expensive, and corruption scandals became shockingly endemic. The LDP provided nineteen consecutive prime ministers until 1993, but in that year, when the LDP was rocked by yet another scandal involving the head of its largest faction (who was arrested and accused of taking fifty million dollars in illegal campaign contributions), the LDP splintered. In August 1993, a coalition of seven different political parties put into office the first non-LDP prime minister in thirty-eight years. This man also enjoyed the highest popularity rating of any Japanese prime minister since World War II. His government was, however, paralyzed by disagreements between the wildly divergent blocs that formed its coalition, and when he, too, soon became embroiled in accusations of campaign contribution irregularities, he resigned in April 1994, after only eight months in office. The next prime minister survived in office only two months. Then, in June 1994, a truly bizarre three-party coalition bringing the conservative LDP together with the Socialists provided Japan with its first Socialist prime minister since 1948. By January 1996, however, the LDP was back in power once again.

In 2009, after Japan's long-stagnant economy had been further afflicted by the onset of a major global recession, criticism of ineffective LDP economic policies combined with a growing loss of LDP appeal to younger voters led to a convincing LDP electoral defeat at the hands of the opposition Democratic Party of Japan (DPJ). There was some speculation at that time that this defeat might finally mark the end of LDP dominance, but in 2012 (and continuing to the present) the LDP regained the prime minister's office again.

Japan's postwar constitution quite unintentionally, therefore, enshrined a form of parliamentary democracy that has been dominated most of the time by a single political party. More intentionally, the constitution also promoted an imposing array of new popular rights, reflecting the American New Deal thinking of the 1940s. These included the rights to social welfare and security, public health, minimum standards of living, and gender equality. In an attempt to promote so-called democratic (or at least, less patriarchal) ideals, during the 1950s Japanese government agencies, together with certain private organizations, conducted a campaign to encourage Japanese families to, among other things, rotate the family bathing order so that the father did not always get to bathe first.[7]

The most remarkable feature of Japan's postwar constitution is undoubtedly Article 9, which asserts that "the Japanese people forever renounce war as a sovereign right of the nation" and flatly states that military forces "will never be maintained."

This seems to have originally been MacArthur's idea, and is entirely in keeping with the initial concern of the occupation authorities to prevent Japan from ever again becoming a threat to world peace. Ironically, however, many Americans soon began to regret this sweeping degree of Japanese demilitarization, as Japan quickly turned from being an enemy during World War II into an important American ally in the Cold War against communism.

MacArthur himself helped Japan create a new police reserve, which later became the Self-Defense Forces. Eventually, Japan came to invest fairly heavily in self-defense capability. Nevertheless, many Japanese sincerely felt deep revulsion against the militarism that had led them to disaster in 1945, and postwar Japan has genuinely long remained an almost uniquely pacifistic country.[8] Today, however, as many Japanese are increasingly worried by the dramatic rise of Chinese power, the current LDP prime minister Abe Shinzō (1954–; prime minister 2012–), a relatively conservative nationalist, would like to at least modestly revise the constitutional restrictions on military activity. This is, perhaps, an indication that the post-WW II era may finally be coming to an end in Japan.

The early Allied occupation reforms had begun in the lingering afterglow of U.S. president Roosevelt's liberal New Deal, and emphasized such things as the release of political prisoners and the passage of a trade union law. But, in February 1947, SCAP intervened to prevent a general strike that had been organized by a coalition of Japanese labor unions. With the mounting tensions of the Cold War, and a Socialist victory in the April 1947 Japanese elections, a "reverse course" in American policy has sometimes been alleged. Certainly, the overriding American strategic concern was shifting rapidly from preventing a militaristic Japan from ever again becoming a threat to world peace to the global containment of communism. Because a strong, capitalist, and democratic Japan might contribute to that Cold War effort, plans to make Japan pay war reparations were abandoned by 1948 (although Japan did eventually make some quite substantial payments anyway).

At first, there had been some expectation that the postwar occupation might continue for a long time, but MacArthur believed that a prolonged military occupation would be counterproductive. Work on a peace treaty to end the occupation began as early as 1950. The resulting treaty was officially signed in San Francisco in September 1951. In a revealing indication of the extent to which postwar Japan was now firmly in the American-oriented Cold War camp, neither the Soviet Union nor the People's Republic of China (PRC) attended the peace ceremonies, and a separate peace between Japan and China would not be concluded until 1972. Nevertheless, the San Francisco Peace Treaty took effect on April 28, 1952, officially ending the postwar occupation. In June, the Shōwa Emperor was able to report the restoration of Japanese independence to the sun goddess Amaterasu at the imperial shrine in Ise.

The official end of the occupation did not mean the end of the American military presence. Under the terms of a mutual security agreement, the United States assumed much of the responsibility for the military defense of Japan, and was allowed to maintain bases on the Japanese home islands as well as outright American control over the island of Okinawa (until 1972). In 1960, the revision and extension of this U.S.-Japan Security Treaty provoked the largest political demonstrations in Japanese history, which forced the cancellation of a planned visit to Japan by U.S. president Dwight D. Eisenhower. The American military presence continues today, and the American-drafted constitution still stands. Since 1945, in fact, Japan has remained one of the staunchest American allies in the world. After Japan regained her independence, though, in 1957 the sentences of war criminals of all classes were commuted, and for many years after 1954 Japanese prime ministers were frequently men who had once been purged by the occupation.

Economic Recovery and the "Developmental State"

For many people in Japan, the first winter after the end of World War II was the hardest. As a result of wartime firebombing, millions of persons were homeless and obliged to sleep in subway stations or whatever other improvised shelter they could find. Industrial production stood at a fraction of its prewar levels, and some five million Japanese were unemployed. Japan recovered only very slowly from this devastation. Recovery had scarcely even begun by the end of the occupation. Real per capita gross national product (GNP) in Japan did not regain its pre-World War II level until 1953.[9] The difficulty of Japan's economic recovery was compounded by the almost complete lack of industrial raw materials in the home islands. The outbreak of the Korean War in 1950 – during the fighting of which United Nations forces used Japan for invaluable forward bases – sparked a minor boom in the Japanese economy, but it would not be until the end of the 1950s that the Japanese economy really took off.

From 1955 until 1973, then, the average annual growth in Japan's GNP exceeded 10 percent. In two decades, from 1950 to 1970, Japan's GNP multiplied some twenty times. By 1968, Japan had passed West Germany to become the world's third largest economy. At the same time, the industrial sector of Japan's economy finally became one of the most developed on earth. In the 1950s, for consumers in America, the label "made in Japan" had still frequently been perceived as synonymous with "cheap." But Japan moved swiftly from its initial base in textiles and other light industries to more advanced consumer electronics. The transistor, for example, was invented by the American Bell Laboratories in 1948, and during the 1950s Japan's Sony Corporation adapted this new technology to create a whole new generation of lightweight portable radios. As a result, Japan soon dominated the world market for transistor radios. Not content to stop there, Japanese corporations moved on to become major producers of ever larger and more sophisticated products. The first Japanese-exported Toyota Toyopet automobiles were unloaded in the United States in 1957 (see Figure 11.1). By 1981, Japan had become the world's largest automaker and an authentic global economic superpower.

One reason for Japan's remarkable postwar economic success may have been the total devastation of the war itself, which provided a clean slate from which to begin with the latest technologies and newest facilities, obtained through generous

Figure 11.1. The Toyota Toyopet, shown arriving in San Francisco in 1957, was Japan's first export automobile. © Bettmann/Corbis.

(though not free) agreements for technology transfer from the United States and other developed countries. The transistor radio is one such classic example of technology transfer. Japan also enjoyed the immense advantage of relatively unrestricted export access to the huge American consumer market, although Japan was hardly alone in that position. But Japan also had the benefit of well-trained and experienced human capital surviving from before the war, and much of the credit for Japan's success is certainly due to the hard work and determination of the Japanese people.

In the early postwar years there was a general popular consensus in Japan about the importance of economic growth as a national priority. Partly as a result of occupation-imposed reforms such as farmland redistribution and the breakup of the *zaibatsu*, it also happened that during its period of rapid economic growth Japan was the industrialized nation with the most equal income distribution in the world (although by the end of the twentieth century, this had become less true). The postwar Japanese population was overwhelmingly middle class.[10] Some uniquely Japanese features of the postwar economy were also notably egalitarian. These included an expectation of secure lifetime employment (at least for the employees of larger corporations) and pay that was based mostly on seniority. This restricted individual career mobility and scope for personal ambition, but also limited competition between coworkers and allegedly encouraged a spirit of cooperation. So-called bottom-up decision making allowed even low-ranking managers a say in formulating corporate policy, while top executives typically worked their way up through the ranks at their companies and remained content with relatively modest salaries (as well as high income tax rates).

Another critical element in Japan's industrial growth was the relative abundance of capital for investment. This was possible because of Japan's exceptionally high rates of personal savings. While the Japanese inclination to save was certainly encouraged by specific government tax policies, some analysts are also, more controversially, inclined to credit something in Confucian culture. This is certainly debatable, but it is a fact that high savings rates have been a strikingly common characteristic throughout modern East Asia.

Although their effectiveness may also be disputed, deliberate government policies were a factor, too. Japan was the original East Asian "developmental state." In the 1970s, Japanese officials openly described their country as having a "plan-oriented market economy."[11] A little historical background helps explain this situation. Following the initial period of state-fostered industrialization in the late nineteenth-century Meiji era, Japan had moved in the direction of Anglo-American-style laissez-faire market capitalism. But the Japanese economic deadlock of the 1920s, the bank panic of 1927, and soon after that the onset of the global Great Depression had given birth to an impulse in Japan toward so-called industrial rationalization. This involved an odd mix of influences, ranging from American-style efficiency experts to Soviet Russian-style five-year plans, but most especially it focused on the German model. In 1930, for example, a Japanese bureaucrat named Kishi Nobusuke (1896–1987) spent seven months in Berlin studying industrial rationalization. In Japan, rationalization was interpreted to mean replacing so-called excessive competition with cooperation. Kishi Nobusuke subsequently served as a deputy director in the Industrial Department of Manchukuo (the principal laboratory for Japan's prewar experiment with state-led industrialization) in the 1930s, and then later as the home government's Minister of Commerce and Industry during World War II. After the war, Kishi was temporarily imprisoned as a war crimes suspect, but following his release, he served as prime minister in 1957–1960, at the beginning of Japan's postwar economic "miracle."[12]

The state-guided capitalism that became characteristic of post-World War II Japan was, however, in some ways a curious hybrid of the prewar Japanese experience with postwar Allied occupation practices. As SCAP began to shift its priorities toward economic reconstruction, for example, by 1947 the occupation authorities were deliberately promoting strategic industries in Japan, using such administrative tools as the directed allocation of resources, loans from the Reconstruction Finance Bank, and outright government subsidies. Although SCAP had broken up the *zaibatsu* and purged former military officers, politicians, and business leaders, relatively few Japanese bureaucrats were purged after World War II, and the level of bureaucratic control, ironically, reached an all-time peak during the American-led occupation.[13]

The prewar Ministry of Commerce and Industry (which had been reorganized during World War II as the Ministry of Munitions) was reorganized yet again in 1949, during the Allied occupation, as the Ministry of International Trade and Industry (MITI). In the late 1950s, MITI began to target designated key sectors of industry, such as oil refining, petrochemicals, and electronics, for deliberate development. To promote such targeted industries, MITI could directly approve credit for low-interest loans from the Japan Development Bank or the Japan Export Import Bank, and also offer outright government subsidies or tax breaks on such things as the portion of corporate income derived from exports. MITI also controlled access to foreign technology and foreign exchange and held licensing authority over key industries. To protect strategic industries from foreign competition, the government sometimes also resorted to outright quotas on imports. Import quotas on foreign-made automobiles were in effect until 1965, for example.

Aside from initially limiting imported foreign manufactured goods, Japan has also remained stubbornly resistant to foreign direct investment. Even after decades of economic liberalization, at the beginning of the twenty-first century in 2001, foreign direct investment in Japan was still only 0.4 percent of gross domestic product (GDP).[14] This reluctance to accept foreign investment meant that Japan has been heavily reliant on domestic sources of capital, and because the Japanese stock market, as of 1963, provided only about 10 percent of the total necessary capital, most of the money for Japan's early postwar industrial growth came in the form of bank loans. Because the Bank of Japan, the ultimate source of much of the lending, was under the supervision of the Ministry of Finance, this meant that there was a degree of indirect government supervision over most investment decisions. Perhaps even more important than government guidance, however, was the fact that, since Japanese industry obtained so much of its capital from bank loans, Japanese firms were under relatively little pressure to attract stock market investors by showing regular quarterly profit increases, and were free to concentrate more on long-term growth, market share, and stability.

In the meantime, perhaps reflecting the key role played by banks in this postwar system, giant new bank-centered enterprise groups known as *keiretsu* took shape, notably around the Fuji, Sanwa, Daiichi, Mitsui, Mitsubishi, and Sumitomo banks. These *keiretsu* typically consisted of one large bank, one general trading company, and several industrial firms. They differed from the prewar *zaibatsu* in that they no longer had central boards or holding companies and functioned instead as networks of mutual stock ownership, financing, and preferred (or even obligatory) trading partners.

These enterprise groups then competed fiercely with each other, in what was, despite some bureaucratic government guidance, clearly a predominantly capitalist economy. Bureaucratic administration of the economy had in fact peaked during the occupation years and tended to decline thereafter. As early as 1951, tax concessions began to replace direct government subsidies as a tool for the promotion of industrial development. Significant liberalization of the Japanese economy began around 1961, and vaguer (more easily disregarded) administrative guidance replaced direct bureaucratic controls. By the 1980s, Japan actually had a proportionately much smaller central and local government bureaucracy than the United States, or most other industrialized democracies.[15]

Trade Wars, and the End of the Japanese Miracle

The success of the Japanese economic miracle was so spectacular that, in 1979, an influential book was published with the unsettling title *Japan as Number One: Lessons for America*.[16] Per capita income in Japan actually passed the United States in 1988 (although it has since sunk again below the U.S. level, and a truly meaningful comparative standard of living is, in any case, much more difficult to measure). By the end of the 1980s, Japan appeared seriously poised to emerge as the world's foremost economy. By 1991, Japan had become the world's leading donor of foreign aid, and Japan had also eclipsed the United States as a source of foreign investment in Asia.

While some Americans looked to the Japanese model for possible lessons, other Americans simply felt that the playing field was unfairly skewed against them. Japan, it was alleged, was practicing predatory neo-mercantilist, or protectionist, trade policies. Though the United States had for decades provided Japan with military protection and free access to the American consumer market, Japan supposedly had not reciprocated by opening its own domestic market to foreign products. The 1980s became a decade of often highly emotionally charged trade wars between Japan and its leading allies. Tensions between Japan and the United States were reflected in books such as Clyde Prestowitz's *Trading Places: How We Allowed Japan to Take the Lead*, with its disturbing first chapter title: "The End of the American Century."[17]

One difficulty with accusations of unfair trading practices was that by the 1980s most of Japan's early postwar protectionist restrictions had already been lifted (except in the sensitive category of food), yet the Japanese market remained strangely resistant to penetration by foreign products. A partial explanation for this may have been the dense networks of preferred customers and preferential business relationships within the Japanese system, and the complicated distribution patterns involving numerous middlemen and many small, mom-and-pop, stores. At the end of the twentieth century, half of all Japan's retail outlets still had no more than two employees. Determined to force the issue, however, in 1988 the U.S. Congress passed an omnibus trade law containing a so-called Super 301 provision calling for the citation of unfair trading partners. Even earlier, in September 1985, finance ministers from the United States, Great Britain, France, Germany, and Japan met at the Plaza Hotel in New York to develop a plan to reduce the American trade deficit by decreasing the currency exchange value of the dollar, which would make American exports (priced in dollars) cheaper and theoretically therefore more competitive. The resulting Plaza Accord caused the value of the Japanese yen (which had been fixed at 360 to the dollar from the Allied occupation until 1971) to soar from 239 per dollar at the time of the Plaza Accord in 1985 to as high as 79 yen per dollar by 1995.

In Japan, officials responded to the trade wars of the 1980s with much talk about the need to internationalize and adjust to meet world standards and expectations. Curiously paralleling this, however, was also a revived interest in Japanese national identity (called *Nihonjinron* or "discourses on Japanese people"). Japan was popularly imagined as possessing a unique culture that could be traced back to Stone Age origins, and there was even a somewhat resurgent spirit of Japanese nationalism, exemplified by a 1989 Ministry of Education requirement that schools fly the "Rising Sun" national flag and sing the national anthem during ceremonies. Although the simultaneous calls for internationalization and reawakened interest in Japaneseness were seemingly contradictory impulses, the contradiction is partially explained by the emerging conceit that Japan's exceptional economic success was just exactly because of Japan's unique national character.[18]

As Japan had prospered, aspects of allegedly traditional Japanese culture, such as a preference for family-style groupings (for example, viewing the business as a fictive family), a preference for harmony over competition, decision making by consensus, and others, had come to be celebrated (by some) as reasons for Japan's success. "Spiritual training," which had been to some extent discredited by defeat in World War II, saw a revival by the early 1970s. Many companies instituted spiritual training programs for their employees, in which trainees built character by enduring physical labor, military-style exercises, long hikes, and sitting in Zen meditation.[19]

The Japanese had good reason to feel somewhat self-satisfied by the late 1980s. A new era literally began in 1989 with the death of the Shōwa Emperor (Hirohito) in January, after a lengthy sixty-three-year reign. The new emperor's reign period is called Heisei, which means "achieving peace." This new era almost immediately encountered difficulties, however. The 1985 Plaza Accord had sharply increased the exchange value of the yen, but for a few years Japanese industry had been able to successfully compensate for the increased relative cost of its exports with accelerated investments. This, however, led to inflated asset values and a bubble economy. The Japanese stock market soared, and real estate prices reached fantastic levels. By the late 1980s, the land on which the imperial palace stands in downtown Tōkyō was equal in value to all of California, and a popular joke claimed that if you were to fold the largest denomination of currency the Japanese government issued – the ten thousand yen note – as tightly as possible and drop it in the pricey Ginza district of Tōkyō, it would not pay for the cost of the ground it covered.[20]

Almost inevitably, these real estate and stock market bubbles eventually burst. It happened in 1990. Commercial real estate prices in Japan's major cities fell by as much as 85 percent, and, as of 1992, the Nikkei stock index was down 60 percent from its 1989 high. This left Japan with much excess industrial capacity and enormous bad debts. By the early twenty-first century, Japanese banks may have held as much as a hundred trillion yen in problem debt, or nearly 20 percent of GDP. The former exhilarating rates of economic growth seem unlikely now to ever return. Japan's quandary is that it can produce more than its own domestic market can consume, and with the rise of new rival Asian manufacturing powers (such as China) and the "hollowing" of Japan's own manufacturing due to the transfer of production overseas, export-led growth can no longer generate the kind of dynamic expansion of the Japanese economy it once did.

If the Japanese economy is stagnant, the Japanese population is also graying. The combination of a less-than-replacement birthrate with the longest average life expectancy in the world makes Japan now the most rapidly aging society on earth. The Japanese workforce peaked in size in 1998, and there are dire predictions that the population may even decline by as much as half over the next century. More than a quarter of the Japanese people are already over 65 years old. Because Japanese culture also remains resistant to large-scale immigration and the possible creation of new Japanese citizens via naturalization, any resumption of miraculous rates of economic growth seems unlikely.

As it happened, the apparent end of the Japanese miracle also coincided with the fall of the Berlin Wall in 1989 and the lowering of the red flag of the Soviet Union over the Kremlin walls in Moscow for the last time in 1991. The former Soviet bloc dissolved, and the world's largest remaining communist country, the People's Republic of China, had already begun experimenting with a market economy several years earlier and by the 1990s sometimes seemed even more capitalistic than the capitalists themselves. With the end of the Cold War, deregulation, privatization, free trade, and globalization were in fashion everywhere. An important milestone in this post-Cold War Age of Globalization was the creation of a new World Trade Organization (WTO) in 1995. Fueled by the Internet and other new information technologies, in the 1990s the U.S. economy embarked on what has been called the longest sustained peacetime expansion in American history. American self-confidence was resurgent, and Japan seemed more subdued.

Japan and Globalization

In March 2011, the most powerful earthquake ever recorded in Japan – a magnitude nine quake centered off the northeast coast of the main island – produced a massive *tsunami* (tidal wave) that swept across Japan's shores. This devastating *tsunami* triggered a meltdown in three of the six reactors at the Fukushima Number 1 nuclear power plant, resulting in the world's worst nuclear disaster since the accident at Chernobyl in 1986. It is, of course, ironic that the only country in the world ever to have atomic weapons actually used against it in war should also come to be heavily reliant on peacetime nuclear power generation, but Japan has very little domestic oil, and all forms of energy production have their disadvantages. Although there were no known immediate fatalities due to radiation exposure from the Fukushima meltdown, the supervisor of damage control did die from cancer in 2013. The evacuation itself reportedly resulted in numerous deaths, and the earthquake and *tsunami* killed almost sixteen thousand people.

Despite this terrible disaster, and also the end of dramatic economic growth rates, Japan today is still a prosperous, highly developed, thoroughly modern society – in many ways a very attractive place to live. Unrestrained economic development in the early postwar years had incurred costs, or downsides, of its own, such as making Japan one of the most heavily polluted countries on earth. A growing awareness of the dangers of pollution, and civic activism, brought new controls and regulations in the 1970s, and the beginning of environmental improvements. Some relaxation of the intense pressure for constant economic growth since the 1990s may also make it easier simply to enjoy life a little.

Unlike as recently as the end of World War II, when half the population had still been rural, Japan is now an overwhelmingly urban society, with an urbanization rate that is now over 90 percent. Tōkyō (then called Edo) may have already been the largest city in the world by the eighteenth century. Today, the greater Tōkyō metropolitan region is still the world's largest urban area, home to almost thirty-eight million people in 2015. (If only the more confined administrative zone composed by the city proper is considered, however, Shanghai may now be the city with the world's largest population.) Despite its great size, apart from a few scattered clusters of skyscrapers the Tōkyō skyline is relatively unremarkable. Tōkyō has been described as resembling a seemingly endless series of urban villages, each centering around a shopping arcade and connected together by a remarkably efficient network of subway lines. Thanks to the American firebombing in 1945, and relentless construction, it is almost entirely new.

Tōkyō is new, modern, and largely "Western" in appearance. Japan had, of course, already begun self-consciously Westernizing in the late nineteenth century, but the American-led postwar occupation greatly accelerated the pace, and the influences were now often specifically American. During the Cold War, as a "bamboo curtain" divided East Asia (parallel to the "iron curtain" in Cold War Europe), it was the portions of East Asia that, like Japan, looked even farther east – across the Pacific toward the United States – that proved especially dynamic. On balance, it is possible to argue that the American presence has been generally beneficial, and that "most people in East Asia are far better off today than they would have been if the Americans had stayed home."[21] Beyond the indisputably growing economic interconnectedness of the Pacific Rim, there has also been a fair amount of cultural Americanization.

If Japan today is, in many ways, just another modern, industrialized, Western society, its face is often specifically American. Baseball is enormously popular in Japan. In 2007, when the premier of the People's Republic of China visited Japan in an effort to improve Sino-Japanese relations, one of his more publicized activities was to play a game of softball at a Japanese university. If McDonald's fast-food restaurants epitomize modern American consumer culture, after the opening of the first Tōkyō outlet in 1971, McDonald's became the top restaurant in Japan by customer volume (with Kentucky Fried Chicken as number two), and so much a part of Japanese culture that according to an often-told (and maybe not even apocryphal) story, young Japanese on vacation in the United States have sometimes been "pleasantly surprised" to discover that there are McDonald's in America, too.[22] There had already been coffee shops lining the streets of Japanese cities long before the appearance of the American Starbucks chain, but the world's busiest Starbucks was soon located in Tōkyō.[23] Tōkyō Disneyland opened in 1984, and before long the Japanese were spending more money at that attraction than the Americans themselves were spending at either the California or the Florida Disney theme parks.[24]

The rising tide of American popular culture even threatened to swamp Japan's own native culture, to the alarm of some cultural conservatives. In the mid-1980s, for example, there was a flap in the Japanese media when it was reported that young

Japanese were forgetting how to use chopsticks. The use of chopsticks, which are called *hashi* in Japanese and *kuaizi* in Chinese, is another – trivial, but in its own way distinctive – East Asian cultural marker. In Greater China, chopsticks remain largely unthreatened by knives and forks, and in truth the rumors of their demise in Japan are also greatly exaggerated.

Yet, if "Japan is unmistakably westernized," it is also true that "Westerners who visit Japan do not necessarily find what they see familiar."[25] Not only are individual Western influences sometimes modified during the process of domestication, but the juxtaposition of influences, sometimes coming from totally different sources, can also be unexpected. Not all the Western influences are American. For example, during the early years of the postwar occupation, in spite of the overwhelming American military presence at that time, Japanese translations of books from French, German, Russian, and British authors each outnumbered those from American writers.[26] French, rather than English, has been the standard international language used by the postwar Japanese post office. And, even though the current Japanese constitution was actually written by Americans, as mentioned previously, Japan still has a British-style parliamentary system, and the Japanese drive on the left-hand side of the street, British style.

If McDonald's is the leading restaurant in Japan, that is mainly because most restaurants in Japan are small independent operations, not large corporate chains. The vast majority of restaurants are actually (modern) Japanese style. There are also many Chinese, Italian, French, Indian, and other restaurants. Baseball and golf are genuinely popular, but *sumō* wrestling also retains a following. Many Japanese homes still have floors with *tatami* matting rather than solid Western-style floors. It is not uncommon for Japanese people to dress occasionally in semi-traditional-style *kimono*, and significant numbers of Japanese people actually do practice such traditions as the tea ceremony or the art of flower arranging (*ikebana*). Precisely because Japan did take a conservative approach to modernization, the Japanese have sometimes quite self-consciously preserved elements of tradition. Visitors to Japan frequently find themselves presented with an explicit choice between "Japanese style" or "Western style" (*Wafū* or *Yōfū*). Despite the almost universal study of English as a second language in Japan, moreover, and although there are now many Japanese who are genuinely fluent in English, English is still not really very widely spoken on the street. In other words, despite all the modernization, Westernization, and Americanization, Japan remains, somehow, Japanese.

Moreover, if Japan today is culturally globalizing – which some interpret to mean Americanizing – Japan has become a major alternative center of globalizing influences in its own right. This includes, but is not limited to, the material products of Japanese industry (which may not always appear to be very obviously "Japanese"). Concealed beneath the superficial stagnation of the Japanese economy since 1990, there was a spike in Japanese investment elsewhere in Asia. The number of Japanese companies operating in China, for example, increased by a factor of fifteen in the decade between 1988 and 1997.[27] Japanese brands, such as Sony, Panasonic (formerly known as Matsushita), Nintendō, Nissan, Isuzu, Mitsubishi,

Honda, Toyota, and Lexus (the luxury vehicle division of Toyota) are all globally familiar and world-renowned for quality. Beyond these industrial products, moreover, Japan also exerts a powerful cultural attraction. One recent English-language book, *The Sushi Economy*, takes the consumption of Japanese *sushi* (vinegared rice with fresh seafood and other delicacies) as an index of globalization.[28] Douglas McGray even suggested that Japan might become the next cultural superpower – a center of global "cool."[29]

The Japanese children's television program *The Mighty Morphin Power Rangers* was being shown in eighty different countries as of the mid-1990s, and at its peak claimed to be the most watched children's show in the world.[30] A majority of the world's animated cartoons came to be made in Japan, and the specifically Japanese style called *anime* attracted something of a global cult following (familiar titles include *Sailor Moon*, *Speed Racer*, *Astro Boy*, and *Doraemon*). Despite sometimes bitter lingering memories of early twentieth-century Japanese imperialism (South Korea, for example, officially prohibited the importation of Japanese popular culture products until 1998), Japanese pop culture has made special inroads among young Asians. Hello Kitty and *karaoke* have been infinitely more popular in East Asia than they have been in the West, and Japanese video games, TV programs, and pop music can be found everywhere. The fiction of the Japanese novelist Murakami Haruki (1949–), although popular worldwide, seems to resonate especially with East Asians. Nearly three million copies of his books were in print in the People's Republic of China alone as of 2005. And, despite his often overtly global, Westernized, and cosmopolitan themes, Murakami's writing "brings Japan to the world every bit as much as the other way around."[31]

In Taipei, the capital of Taiwan, the first major skyscraper ever constructed (in 1993) housed a Japanese Mitsukoshi department store. Although it has since been eclipsed by the newer Taipei 101 (which for a few years in the early twenty-first century was the tallest skyscraper on the planet), the Mitsukoshi building still towers over the skyline of the old Taipei city center. Japanese cultural influences on Taiwan are not merely a fading old colonial legacy, moreover. They began to surge anew with Japan's postwar economic boom. By the mid-1980s, Japanese-language publications in Taiwan were outselling those written in English, and, despite an official ban on Japanese songs and movies imposed by the Chinese Nationalist Party-ruled government of Taiwan, 31 percent of all Taiwan's video rentals were Japanese productions.[32] In 2005, the Taiwanese airline EVA Air began colorfully decorating a number of its aircraft with Hello Kitty motifs. In recent years it has even been alleged that Japanese ties have been reemphasized in order to help distinguish (the Republic of China on) Taiwan from the People's Republic of China on the mainland. For example, a number of recent Taiwanese television programs have featured Japanese themes, such as the 2016 comedy "Xingfu bu er jia," which displays a Japanese-language (rather than the more typical English) alternative title, "Shiawase" ("happiness"), and is the story of a young Japanese woman who opens a family-style Japanese restaurant in Taipei and recruits three down-on-their-luck Taiwanese to, hilariously if quite implausibly, pretend to be her Japanese family.

Figure 11.2. The Taipei 101, in Taiwan, was the tallest skyscraper in the world from 2003 to 2009. The white sign prominent on the street in the right foreground of this picture advertises (in Chinese) "Japanese-style Ramen [Noodles]." This is an interesting example not only of modern Japanese popular culture influences on Taiwan (and Greater China) but also – since Ramen noodles are actually a modern Japanese adaptation of what was once originally a Chinese dish – of Chinese influences on Japan. Dried instant Ramen noodles have also now become an inexpensive staple of the worldwide diet, illustrating the sometimes surprisingly complex, circular patterns of what we call globalization. © Louie Psihoyos/Corbis.

One twenty-first-century Taipei restaurant advertised authentic Japanese-style curry. This may appear strange, because curry is usually considered Indian rather than Japanese. Curry was, however, broadly popularized by the British in modern times, and curry became a staple of the Japanese diet that is widely available in Japanese coffee shops and inexpensive restaurants. Another Taipei restaurant explicitly advertised Japanese-style *ramen* noodle soup (see Figure 11.2). At first glance this may not seem to be as peculiar as Japanese-style curry, but, rather than being quintessentially Japanese, *ramen* are actually a modern Japanese adaptation of Chinese-style (*lamian*) noodles. A similar, often circular, process of hybridization is at the core of much cultural globalization.

Many modern Japanese products were arguably originally Western ideas – including everything from automobiles to transistors, pop music videos, and animated cartoons – that now merely happen to be manufactured in Japan. This might simply be taken as further evidence of the Westernization of Japan, except that these things are often given a Japanese twist in the process, and sometimes then even return to influence the West. The Japanese word *anime* (pronounced "ah-nee-may"), for example, comes from the English "animation." This nicely illustrates the often complex crosscurrents of cultural globalization.

Beer was introduced into Japan in the late nineteenth century as a consciously Western product, and continued to be marketed as such up until WW II. During the war, however, Japan lost access to German technical advisors and imported ingredients, and Japanese brewing was forced to become completely self-sufficient. The Ministry of Finance took over and reorganized the beer industry as part of Japan's coordinated wartime planned economy, and by 1943 beer in Japan had been reduced to a single brand-less product. The Western-derived word *biiru* (beer) was even replaced by a "native" Japanese word for beer, *bakushu*. In the process, also, distinctively new Japanese beer flavors began to be created. After WW II, needless to say, different brands and private businesses returned, and by the late 1950s sales of beer in Japan had surpassed traditional *sake*.[33] Beer – which is commonly sold (like coffee and even whiskey) from vending machines on the street – had become one of Japan's standard adult beverages, and part of Japanese culture. Today, quite excellent Japanese brands are marketed and sold around the world as "Japanese beer."

Jūdō is, of course, a Japanese martial art. Even today, even as practiced in the United States, *jūdō* still usually involves a certain amount of Japanese-style clothing, ritual, and Japanese-language vocabulary. Yet *jūdō* was, from the start, a modern hybrid. *Jūdō* was invented in the 1880s (based, to be sure, on older styles of weaponless combat) by Japan's first member of the International Olympic Committee. It may have been inspired in part by the ancient Chinese Daoist philosophy of yielding – "using the soft to conquer the hard" – but it was also inspired by modern European ideas concerning sports and the importance of physical exercise. With its acceptance as an Olympic sport in 1960, *jūdō* became increasingly international. By the end of the twentieth century there were more *jūdō* practitioners in Europe than in Japan, Europeans were competing for the majority of A-level titles, and the official languages of the International Judo Federation were English and French, not Japanese.[34]

As one final illustration of the complicated patterns in which global and local, traditional and new, intertwine in the formation of modern pop culture, something called *enka*-style music is often considered to be the very embodiment of native popular (as opposed to elite) Japanese musical traditions. Yet *enka* combines modern Western instruments with Japanese musical scales and techniques, and although the word *enka* can be traced as far back as the 1880s, the familiar *enka* style did not really emerge until the 1920s or even later. Despite its popular association with the "soul of the Japanese," moreover, such non-Japanese artists as Teresa Teng (Deng Lijun, 1953–1995) have also been described as *enka* singers. Teresa Teng frequently recorded in Japanese – but more commonly in her native Mandarin Chinese. Teresa (notice also the assumed Western-language first name) was a "mainlander" Chinese, born and raised on Taiwan, whose clear sweet voice and numerous hit tunes played a role that "cannot be underestimated" in reintroducing modern "Western-style" commercial pop music to the mainland People's Republic of China, as it began to emerge from Maoist isolationism after 1978. She remains, even after her tragic premature death from asthma in 1995, one of the most beloved pop singers in the entire Chinese-speaking world. Somehow she managed to simultaneously combine being a singer from Taiwan who was quintessentially Chinese with also being both Western style and Japanese style.[35]

The world increasingly intermingles. In late 2014, for example, when hackers – allegedly sponsored by North Korea – maliciously hacked into the computer systems of Sony Pictures and made terrorist threats against the Sony movie "The Interview" (which presented an unflattering depiction of North Korea), the incident was widely viewed as an attack on America, in spite of the fact that Sony Pictures is a subsidiary of the Japanese conglomerate Sony. This is globalization indeed.

Yet, anyone who travels to Japan will recognize instantly that they are not in America. Japan has been called the first non-Western society on earth to successfully modernize, and it remains perhaps overall the most successful. But, despite more than a century and a half of Westernization, and although it is difficult to define or explain precisely what this means, Japan somehow remains uniquely Japanese.

For Further Reading

The postwar Allied occupation of Japan is covered by John W. Dower, *Embracing Defeat: Japan in the Wake of World War II* (New York: W. H. Norton, 1999). For a critical look at the prosecutions of Japanese defendants for war crimes, see Richard H. Minear, *Victors' Justice: The Tokyo War Crimes Trial* (Princeton University Press, 1971).

On postwar Japanese politics, see Takeshi Ishida and Ellis S. Krauss, eds., *Democracy in Japan* (University of Pittsburgh Press, 1989), and Tetsuya Kataoka, ed., *Creating Single-Party Democracy: Japan's Postwar Political System* (Stanford, CA: Hoover Institution Press, 1992).

The classic study of Japan's postwar economic recovery is Chalmers Johnson, *MITI and the Japanese Miracle: The Growth of Industrial Policy, 1925–1975* (Stanford University Press, 1982).

For contemporary Japanese life, see Theodore C. Bestor, *Neighborhood Tokyo* (Stanford University Press, 1989); Edward Seidensticker, *Tokyo Rising: The City since the Great Earthquake* (Cambridge, MA: Harvard University Press, 1991); and Christine R. Yano, *Tears of Longing: Nostalgia and the Nation in Japanese Popular Song* (Cambridge, MA: Harvard University Asia Center, 2002).

On Japanese pop culture and globalization, see Harumi Befu and Sylvie Guichard-Anguis, eds., *Globalizing Japan: Ethnography of the Japanese Presence in Asia, Europe, and America* (London: RoutledgeCurzon, 2001); Timothy J. Craig, ed., *Japan Pop! Inside the World of Japanese Popular Culture* (Armonk, NY: M. E. Sharpe, 2000); Joseph J. Tobin, ed., *Remade in Japan: Everyday Life and Consumer Taste in a Changing Society* (New Haven, CT: Yale University Press, 1992); and William M. Tsutsui, *Japanese Popular Culture and Globalization* (Ann Arbor: Association for Asian Studies, 2010).

12 Korea since 1945

The Korean War

The Cold War first erupted into heated conflict on the Korean peninsula, and the Cold War lingers on still today in Korea long after it has passed into history almost everywhere else. That the first great global crisis of the Cold War era began in Korea was a direct consequence of Allied dispositions at the end of World War II. During that war, the U.S. State Department had contemplated the possibility of a four-power trusteeship to administer the Korean peninsula following its anticipated postwar liberation from Japanese colonial rule. President Roosevelt briefly discussed such plans with the Soviet leader Joseph Stalin at their wartime Yalta conference – President Roosevelt even suggesting that such a trusteeship might need to continue for some twenty or thirty years. But Korea received so little wartime American attention that in 1945 the U.S. Secretary of State reportedly even had to ask someone where Korea is.[1] Japan then surrendered sooner than many people had expected, leaving the United States almost totally unprepared for any immediate action in Korea. Meanwhile, Soviet Russian troops had already entered the peninsula from the north on August 9, 1945, during the final days of World War II. The first U.S. occupation forces in Korea did not arrive in the south until September 8, a full month later. The arriving American GIs found, as one report to the State Department concluded on September 15, "a powder keg ready to explode at the application of a spark."[2]

Amid the gathering signs of what would soon become an open cold war rivalry between the two former World War II Allies, the United States and the Soviet Union, there was a not unreasonable fear in Washington that the Soviets might press their early advantage to overrun the entire Korean peninsula. A joint partition of Korea was therefore hastily arranged, and it was actually the U.S. Pentagon that somewhat arbitrarily decided on the thirty-eighth parallel – a mere line on a Pentagon office wall map, reflecting no particular preexisting cultural or geographic conditions – as the point of division between the U.S. and Soviet zones.[3] Meanwhile, throughout the Korean peninsula, so-called People's Committees had quickly organized themselves in the wake of Japan's surrender. Given the bitter poverty of most Korean peasants, and the taint of collaboration with Japanese colonial rule that, to some degree or another, unavoidably haunted almost all of the preexisting Korean elite, American forces in southern Korea were chiefly concerned to identify and give their support to Korean leaders who would be reliably anti-communist. Some of the most likely candidates were found among returning Korean nationalists who had evaded collaboration with the Japanese by living for extended periods in exile abroad. Most notable among these was Syngman Rhee (Yi Sŭng-man, 1875–1965), who now came home to Korea after thirty-five years in the United States.

After the attempt to negotiate a trusteeship with the Soviet Union failed, the United States appealed to the newly formed United Nations (UN), and in May 1948 the UN supervised the first general democratic election in Korean history. This was conducted only in the southern, U.S.-occupied zone. The newly elected Korean National Assembly then selected Syngman Rhee to serve as the first president in July, and on August 15, 1948, the establishment of the Republic of Korea (commonly known as South Korea) was formally proclaimed. Less than a month later, on September 9, a rival Democratic People's Republic of Korea (North Korea) was created in the north. Kim Il Sung (Kim Il-sŏng, 1912–1994), who had returned after World War II from his own period of anti-Japanese exile in Manchuria and the Soviet Union, was designated premier (later, president). By early 1949, both the Soviet Union and the United States had withdrawn their troops from Korea, and the postwar Allied military occupation of Korea was over.

Despite the sharp ideological opposition between these two new Korean governments, few Korean people saw this north–south division as at all natural or desirable, or expected it to be permanent. Many were quite eager to reunify their nation. There were, consequently, several exchanges of gunfire and mutual provocations over the next few years, but the superpower patrons of these two rival Korean governments, the United States and the Soviet Union, were both anxious to avoid being dragged into any new World War III with each other and acted to restrain their respective protégés.

However, as a communist victory in China's civil war grew increasingly more certain, the United States declined to actively intervene in the fighting on the Chinese mainland (despite substantial U.S. noncombatant assistance to Chiang Kai-shek's Chinese Nationalists). After Chiang Kai-shek's Nationalist government retreated to the island of Taiwan in 1949, for a time there were even some indications that President Truman might terminate U.S. support for Chiang. In a speech at the National Press Club on January 12, 1950, Secretary of State Dean Acheson publicly described America's defensive perimeter in Asia in such a way as to seemingly pointedly leave out both Taiwan and Korea. All these seemed to be signals that the United States might not actively intervene in a Korean civil war, or be willing to shed vast quantities of American blood to prevent a forcible North Korean reunification of the peninsula. In 1950, therefore, Joseph Stalin finally gave his approval to Kim Il Sung's ambitious plan of attack – with the understanding that there would be no active Russian participation. In hindsight, this was obviously an enormous miscalculation. What the various communist leaders did not realize was that the political backlash in the United States against the perceived "loss of China" was hardening American political resolve to contain the spread of communism and prevent any further such losses.

South Korea had a larger population than the north – approximately two-thirds of Korea's total – but most of Korea's existing heavy industry was located in the north. The northern military forces were also better equipped, with 242 new Soviet Russian-made T-34 tanks and a small combat air force, in opposition to which the south could field no tanks at all and only a handful of training aircraft. In addition, as many as one hundred thousand North Korean soldiers had previous combat experience fighting with the Chinese communist forces during China's civil war. These troops were already battle hardened, and their prior service in the Chinese communist cause also established an ominous burden of debt that the Chinese communists felt obliged to repay. Despite these northern advantages, at the time, few people in the south realized how inadequate their own military forces actually were.

In the early morning hours before dawn on June 25, 1950, North Korean forces staged a massive offensive south across the line of the thirty-eighth parallel. President Truman was home in Independence, Missouri, at the time, and it was Secretary of State Acheson who made the initial decision to engage American troops in the defense of South Korea. With characteristic determination, however, President Truman fully committed U.S. forces in Korea and also ordered the American Seventh Fleet into the Taiwan Straits to prevent a possible communist invasion of Taiwan. As a permanent member of the UN Security Council, the Soviet Union would have ordinarily been in a position to veto any intervention by the UN, but it happened that the Soviets were just then boycotting the UN (from January to August 1950) to protest China's UN seat still being held by Chiang Kai-shek's Republic of China (by then located on Taiwan) rather than by Mao Zedong's People's Republic (on the mainland). As a result, the UN was able to react quickly and decisively to condemn the North Korean attack. The defense of South Korea became a UN action. Eventually, some fifteen countries would contribute soldiers to the war effort, although by far the largest foreign contingent came from the United States, and the American general Douglas MacArthur (then still Supreme Commander for the Allied Powers in Japan) assumed overall command.

The South Korean capital, Seoul, was only sixty miles south of the thirty-eighth parallel, and Seoul fell to northern forces in just three days. By the third week of the war, over half of South Korea had been captured by northern armies. With only light handheld weapons to confront the northern armored vehicles, the first American units that engaged the enemy also fell back quickly. Eventually, however, UN forces were able to dig in and hold a defensive perimeter of about fifty square miles around the southeastern Korean port city of Pusan, which provided an essential base for resupply and the buildup for a counteroffensive. By about mid-August, the balance of firepower had shifted, with the UN increasingly having a large advantage in heavy weapons, especially airpower. By the end of active combat, UN aircrews had flown over a million sorties against the north.

Next, in a daring gamble, General MacArthur staged an amphibious landing farther up the west coast at Inch'ŏn, on September 15. Inch'ŏn is an important port city, serving the southern capital Seoul, but it has no nice sandy beaches and features one of the world's most extreme tidal ranges. At low tide, an amphibious invasion must confront miles of mudflats. Inch'ŏn could very easily have become a deathtrap for the UN soldiers, and MacArthur decided to strike there against much contrary advice – but he was fortunate, this time. Inch'ŏn turned out to be perhaps the single greatest triumph in General MacArthur's long and distinguished military career. A mighty invasion armada consisting of 261 ships put the American X Corps ashore with the loss of only 536 men. By the end of September, the North Korean forces had been driven back to the place from which they had started, across the thirty-eighth parallel.

Encouraged by this success, UN forces then proceeded from the containment of communism to its rollback. Even before the Inch'ŏn landings, President Truman had authorized General MacArthur to continue his advance into North Korea – as long as there was no sign of intervention by either the Soviet Union or the People's Republic of China. This time, it was the anti-communist world leaders who miscalculated.

On September 30, the first South Korean troops passed north across the thirty-eighth parallel. On October 2, the Chinese premier (Zhou Enlai) formally notified the Indian ambassador that China would intervene if any American troops crossed the parallel. Because the United States did not recognize the People's Republic of China and had no direct communications with it, indirect diplomacy was the only possible way to signal China's intentions. Although this Chinese message was repeated through several channels, it was evidently not taken seriously. On October 7, the American First Cavalry crossed the thirty-eighth parallel heading into North Korea. On October 19, the North Korean capital fell, and by October 26 advanced units of the UN forces had reached as far as the Yalu River, which marks the border between Korea and China. A few days earlier, on October 15, at an historic meeting on Wake Island in the middle of the Pacific Ocean, General MacArthur personally assured President Truman that there was "very little" chance of Chinese intervention in the war. Even if the Chinese did intervene, MacArthur boasted that they would be easily crushed in what he predicted would be "the greatest slaughter in the history of mankind."[4]

The very next day, on October 16, Chinese so-called "volunteers" began crossing the Yalu River into North Korea, undetected by UN observers. Given the vast disparity in military firepower between the United States and China at that time (this was, furthermore, a People's Republic of China that was still scarcely a year old), China's decision to enter the war was an enormous gamble. At the time of Chinese entry, "as many as two-thirds of some infantry units" did not have even small arms. At the end of active combat in Korea, despite receiving new supplies from the Soviet Union, the Chinese were still only equipped with a motley assortment of weapons from ten different countries, with captured American weapons (26%) still apparently outnumbering those obtained from the Soviet Union (20%).[5] Most senior Chinese leaders were reluctant to go to war against the powerful American armed forces, especially after Joseph Stalin belatedly informed them that the Soviet Union would not provide air support.[6] But Mao Zedong calculated that the U.S. would be unwilling to wage an unlimited total war, and Mao was also confident in his doctrine of "people's war," which relied on huge Chinese resources of manpower rather than technology.

On October 26 – the same day that UN troops began to arrive on the banks of the Yalu River – Chinese People's Volunteers struck at South Korean columns, hitting American forces a few days later, on November 1, and overrunning U.S. cavalry positions at Unsan. After this, however, the Chinese withdrew again into concealment in North Korea's rugged terrain, and although the American president and Joint Chiefs of Staff were cautious and anxious to avoid a major war with China, General MacArthur remained confident and inclined to downplay the Chinese intervention as merely token interference.

MacArthur, in fact, felt optimistic enough to launch a "home by Christmas" offensive on November 24, in an effort to finish the war quickly. What MacArthur did not realize was that some two hundred thousand Chinese soldiers lay hidden in the mountains separating the two main UN columns in the east and west. On November 27, the Chinese struck in full force. Within a week, the center of the UN line had fallen back again some fifty miles. By January 4, 1951, the South Korean capital at Seoul had fallen to the enemy for a second time.

General MacArthur seems to have felt at this point that the best military response to Chinese intervention in Korea would be to escalate the war by taking the offensive to the Chinese homeland. President Truman and the Joint Chiefs, however, sensibly enough, did not relish the idea of turning a limited, if nasty, war in Korea into a general World War III. China's lack of industry would have rendered attempts to bomb it into rubble futile, and China's vast population and extensive land area (coupled with the Chinese communists' considerable prior experience at guerrilla warfare) would have drawn any American ground invasion of China into a costly quagmire – and there was always the danger of sparking a true world war with the rival superpower, the Soviet Union.

When President Truman ordered that all future public statements concerning the Korean War be cleared through the State Department, General MacArthur proceeded to violate this presidential directive repeatedly. MacArthur's complaint was that the restraints being imposed on his war effort by civilian politicians were preventing him from winning total victory. In March 1951, MacArthur even wrote a letter endorsing the idea of "unleashing" Chiang Kai-shek's Nationalist Chinese from Taiwan to open a second front against the Chinese communists. When this letter was read aloud on the floor of the U.S. House of Representatives, the U.S. president viewed it as outright insubordination, and on April 11 President Truman officially relieved General MacArthur of his command.

The bloodiest phase of the combat in Korea was still yet to come, but by June 1951 the war had reached an effective stalemate not far from its original starting point at the thirty-eighth parallel. Cease-fire talks began, and a truce was declared on July 27, 1953. The war in Korea had cost the United States some thirty-three thousand lives. China lost roughly eight hundred thousand, including Chairman

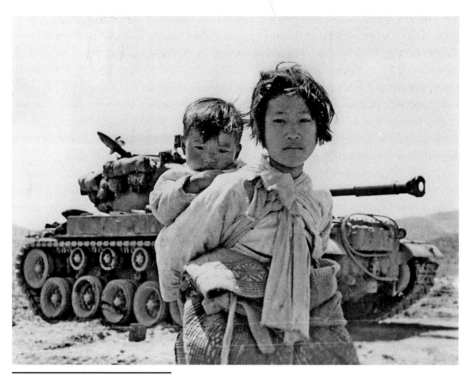

Figure 12.1. "With her brother on her back a war weary Korean girl tiredly trudges by a stalled M-26 tank, at Haengju, Korea," June 9, 1951. National Archives.

Mao's own son. The conflict left a staggering three million Koreans killed, wounded, or missing – one out of every ten (see Figure 12.1). In the north, the war provided Kim Il Sung with an opportunity to further consolidate his power. In South Korea, it helped pave the way for three decades of authoritarian military rule. In China, the war greatly increased the prestige of the infant People's Republic, which had taken on the world's leading military superpower and not been clearly defeated. To the present day, two mutually hostile Koreas still confront each other across a heavily fortified demilitarized zone (DMZ). An official end to the war has yet to be arranged. The United States still has some thirty-eight thousand troops stationed in South Korea. Yet, ironically, the by now globally engaged manufacturing powerhouse known as the People's Republic of China (PRC) today has much closer relations with South Korea than it does with the strange, isolated, Korean communist regime in the north.

North Korea

In the immediate aftermath of the war, with substantial Soviet assistance, and through energetic mass mobilization of its population, the Democratic People's Republic of Korea recovered from the extensive destruction surprisingly quickly. For many years, the North Korean economy even appeared to be more vigorous than that of the south. But the North Koreans were reluctant to fully acknowledge the massive contribution that had been made by China in saving them from defeat during the war, or the important Soviet role in establishing Kim Il Sung as leader in the first place, and North Korea began charting a resolutely independent course. After the death of Joseph Stalin in 1953, this independent streak became even more pronounced, and after the split between Russia and China in 1960, North Korean independence became extreme. Soviet assistance dwindled. After the final collapse of the Soviet Union in 1991, while much of the rest of the world entered a new post-Cold War era of globalization, North Korea's independence (another word for which is isolation) became almost total.

During the period when Korea was a Japanese colony, Kim Il Sung had grown up on the other side of the border, in Manchuria, where there was a large Korean population. There Kim became the leader of a small (fifty to three hundred men) anti-Japanese guerrilla band, operating in cooperation with the growing forces of the Chinese communists. Overwhelming conventional Japanese military advantage eventually forced Kim's guerrillas to retreat to bases in the Soviet Union in 1941, where Kim spent the remainder of World War II. After Japan's surrender, Kim returned to Korea along with Soviet Russian forces, where, initially very much as a Soviet protégé, he overcame all challengers for leadership of the North Korean communists. Once in power, and after his disastrously failed attempt to conquer the south and reunify Korea, he developed his own unique philosophy of *juche*, or "self-reliance," beginning around 1955. *Juche* became the core ideology of North Korea, to a large extent replacing orthodox Marxism. This ideology was then drummed into the entire population through morning-to-night loudspeaker broadcasts and obligatory political study sessions. The growing personality cult of the Great Leader Kim Il Sung "became a kind of secular religion" in which Kim Il Sung performed the role of "a living sage-king or god."[7]

Although it is in some ways obviously a Stalinist-style regime, the Democratic People's Republic of Korea is also quite unique. Images of the Great Leader Kim Il Sung are everywhere; by the end of the twentieth century there were over thirty-five thousand monuments in relatively small North Korea.[8] The patriarchal Korean Confucian legacy, and premodern ancestor veneration, allegedly underlay the extreme form of personality cult that developed around Kim Il Sung.[9] This Korean personality cult echoed the similar cults of Stalin and Mao Zedong, but magnified the impulse even further, turning North Korea into a somewhat bizarre form of "socialist monarchy," in which supreme leadership actually became hereditary. After Kim Il Sung died in 1994, leadership passed to his son Kim Jong Il (Kim Chŏng-il, 1941–2011), and then after Kim Jong Il's death in 2011, again in turn to Kim Jong Il's third son Kim Jong-un (Kim Chŏng-ŭn, 1983–). The Kim family has thus produced three successive generations of North Korean supreme leaders.

Despite the Democratic People's Republic of Korea's apparent early achievements in economic development, these eventually gave way to stagnation and decay. Available resources were diverted to military applications, which, by the late 1960s, consumed some 30 percent of the total national budget.[10] In 1995–1996, serious erosion problems stemming from years of poor land management, combined with the declining availability of fertilizer and a lack of electric power for irrigation pumps, as well as some bad weather, resulted in a truly massive famine that even North Korea could not conceal. Perhaps as many as a million people died from malnutrition (in a country that today has a total population of less than twenty-five million). Economic development has been stunted (see Figure 12.2).

Figure 12.2. Satellite photograph of East Asia at night in 2012, showing a blaze of artificial light everywhere but in North Korea. Planet Observer/UIG/Bridgeman Images.

Tensions between North and South Korea, meanwhile, remain high. The DMZ between the two Koreas is one of the most heavily fortified areas in the world, and remains a potential flashpoint. There continue to be periodic incidents. In 1983, for example, seventeen top South Korean officials were killed, and the president himself only narrowly escaped death, when North Korean commandoes detonated a bomb during their visit to Rangoon, Burma. Most alarmingly, in the early 1990s, North Korea actively embarked on a program to develop an atomic bomb.

In connection with a temporary thaw in relations with the south, in 1992 inspections of North Korean sites by the International Atomic Energy Agency began to be permitted. These inspections had no sooner begun than they were interrupted again the following year, however, and tensions escalated until North Korea announced that any further international sanctions would be considered an act of war. This showdown was defused by a dramatic visit to North Korea by former U.S. President Jimmy Carter, who managed to extract an agreement to resume talks. North Korea agreed to halt its nuclear program in exchange for a U.S. promise to supply fuel and to help North Korea develop light-water nuclear reactors that could not be put to military uses. In 2002, however, North Korea once again expelled its inspectors, withdrew from the Nuclear Nonproliferation Treaty, and openly began trying to develop atomic weapons – in 2006, 2009, and 2013, actually detonating nuclear test devices. North Korea is currently suspected to have enough weapons-grade plutonium for a half-dozen atomic bombs, but probably is not yet capable of launching them by ballistic missile.

Under its youthful new Supreme Leader Kim Jong-un, since 2011 North Korea has appeared, if anything, even more volatile. In 2013, Kim purged and killed his own uncle, who had been the number two leader. In December 2014, the FBI identified North Korea as the culprit behind a cyberattack targeting the Sony Pictures movie "The Interview" – a comedy about a fictional assassination attempt on Kim Jung-un – which included making terroristic threats against movie audiences in the U.S., and which forced Sony to withdraw the film from theatrical release. Even the People's Republic of China, which in 2010 still refused to condemn North Korea after it (was widely suspected of having) torpedoed and sunk a South Korean navy frigate, with considerable loss of life, and shelled a South Korean island causing civilian as well as military casualties, and which is probably North Korea's only significant foreign friend in the world, nonetheless now enjoys vastly greater cultural and commercial ties with South Korea than with the north.

South Korea: Syngman Rhee and the First Republic (1948–1960)

The Republic of Korea (South Korea) was founded in 1948 as a constitutional democracy, but true democracy in South Korea did not flourish immediately, at least not without qualification. Based on a series of major constitutional revisions, and a couple of military coups, South Korea has gone through a succession of six different so-called "Republics" since 1948, the most recent of which began in 1987. Despite a veneer of democracy, the first president of the First Republic, Syngman Rhee, had somewhat authoritarian inclinations. On one occasion, he literally locked up members of the National Assembly until they voted as he desired.[11] Although Syngman Rhee was an undoubted Korean patriot and nationalist hero, he had spent most of his adult life in exile in the United States, where he had obtained a PhD in political science from Princeton. He also had an Austrian wife. This all made him something of a stranger in his own land.

Almost immediately after its formation, his new country had been plunged into a devastating war with the north. Even after the end of active combat, in the 1950s, South Korea long remained one of the poorest countries on earth. Even communist North Korea appeared more economically successful than South Korea until as late as the mid-1970s. A U.S.-backed program of compulsory land redistribution did, however, finally destroy the power base of the old Korean *yangban* aristocracy. This was arguably essential because the modernizing capacity – even the tax-collecting ability – of the late premodern Chosŏn Dynasty had been severely hobbled by the dominance of that landowning-bureaucratic *yangban* elite. According to data collected during the subsequent Japanese colonial period, in the early twentieth century more than three-quarters of all Korean farmers were still tenant farmers who leased part, or all, of their fields. A postcolonial 1949 land distribution law finally limited landholdings to 7.5 acres, but even then it took the mass disruption of the Korean War before this reform could be fully implemented. The tenant-farming rate in South Korea then plunged rapidly from 49 percent to only 7 percent. The Korean War, therefore, finally completed the elimination of the traditional social and economic order in Korea. Korean society was transformed from a highly polarized hierarchy to a relatively egalitarian community – a feature that postwar South Korea also had in common with both postwar Japan and Taiwan.[12]

Even so, the South Korean economy long remained stagnant and heavily reliant on American aid. Between the end of World War II and the mid-1970s, the United States provided more aid to South Korea per capita than to any other country in the world, except Israel and South Vietnam. In the decade following the Korean War, American aid amounted to almost 80 percent of Korea's fixed capital formation.[13]

Allegations of large-scale fraud in the 1960 presidential elections – during which Syngman Rhee claimed to have won almost 90 percent of the vote – ignited student protests. When police in Seoul fired into a crowd outside the presidential office building, killing some 186 student demonstrators, university professors joined the protests, U.S. backing for President Rhee was withdrawn, the Korean army refused to intervene on his behalf, and on April 26 the aging President Rhee was obliged to resign and retire to resumed exile in Hawai'i. After Rhee's resignation, there followed nine months of freewheeling democracy – or leftist anarchy, as others saw it – until a junta from the Military Academy led by Major General Park Chung Hee (Pak Chŏng-hŭi, 1917–1979) stepped in and staged a military coup in the middle of the night on May 16, 1961 (see Figure 12.3).

Figure 12.3. South Korean president Park Chung Hee, 1961. Rene Burri. Magnum Photos.

The military junta then established a Supreme Council for National Reconstruction, suspended the constitution, banned political activities and demonstrations, imposed censorship, and closed down most of Seoul's daily newspapers. For the next thirty-two years, from 1961 until 1993, South Korea would be led in a more or less authoritarian fashion by military men. It was Park Chung Hee's government that also, however, and to its undeniable credit, for the first time firmly set Korea's sights on modern economic development, transformed the Republic of Korea into a classic East Asian-style developmental state, and launched South Korea's dramatically successful period of economic takeoff.

Park Chung Hee and the Industrialization of South Korea

Park Chung Hee, who presided over South Korea from 1961 until his assassination in 1979, had attended a Japanese military academy during the period of Japanese colonial rule, and served as a second lieutenant in the Japanese army in Manchuria during World War II. In Manchukuo, Park encountered the wartime Japanese developmental state model in its most extreme form. Earlier, nineteenth-century Meiji era Japanese success at "enriching the country and strengthening the army" also became an inspiration for Park's Korea, and the exact same Meiji period slogan (written with four Chinese characters that are pronounced *puguk kangbyong* in Korean and *fukoku kyōhei* in Japanese) was even invoked.[14] The roots of a developmental state system – one that could be harsh and exploitative but that also really did deliver rapid rates of industrial growth – had in fact already been planted in Korean soil during the Japanese colonial period.[15] Despite the fact that fifteen years elapsed between the end of Japanese rule in 1945 and the resumption of certain similar developmental patterns under Park Chung Hee, it is probably no coincidence that South Korea's approach to economic development more closely paralleled Japan's model than anywhere else in East Asia did, or that in some ways it more closely resembled the prewar rather than the post-World War II Japanese model.[16]

After seizing power, during his first months in office Park Chung Hee established an Economic Planning Board and announced a five-year plan for economic development. As this first five-year plan was being implemented, beginning in 1962, banking was also placed under the control of the Ministry of Finance and the state-run Bank of Korea. By 1970, 96 percent of all South Korean financial assets were government controlled.[17] This meant that in addition to tax incentives and control over licenses and permits as tools for promoting planned industrialization, the government also held critical control over investment capital. Low-interest bank loans (often even at negative real interest rates – the average net cost to business of loans for heavy industry in the 1970s has been estimated at minus 6.7%[18]) allocated by the government then became a key tool in promoting industrialization.

Such loans were vital to the development of what would become South Korea's distinctively huge *chaebŏl* conglomerates. The Korean word *chaebŏl* is written with the same two Chinese characters as the Japanese word *zaibatsu*, and the two are somewhat similar phenomena: essentially, holding companies controlling a range of highly diversified enterprises. Among the best-known Korean *chaebŏl* are Samsung, Hyundai, and LG. The *chaebŏl* were nearly all new after World War II, and remained largely family owned and managed. The founder of Hyundai, for example, had begun life working at the docks at the port of Inch'ŏn in the 1930s and as an errand boy at a rice mill in Seoul. In 1940, he bought an auto repair shop. After World War II, he developed construction contracts with the U.S. military, eventually including such activities as highway construction for the Americans in Thailand and dredging in Vietnam. By the early 1970s, Hyundai was building the largest shipyard in the world in South Korea (at Ulsan).[19]

Some of these *chaebŏl* became quite astonishingly huge. As of 1991, sales of South Korea's largest five *chaebŏl* amounted to almost 50 percent of total gross national product (GNP). In that year, Samsung's share of Korea's GNP alone was equal to the combined total share of the largest twenty American companies in the U.S.[20] They also became remarkably all encompassing: "The typical Hyundai worker drives a Hyundai car, lives in a Hyundai apartment, gets his mortgage from Hyundai credit, receives health care at Hyundai hospital, sends his kids to school on Hyundai loans or scholarships, and eats his meals at Hyundai cafeterias."[21]

If the *chaebŏl* had the economic resources to extend credit to their employees, though, they themselves needed large infusions of outside investment capital. Like the pre-World War II Japanese *zaibatsu* and the postwar Japanese *keiretsu*, the South Korean *chaebŏl* had highly diversified interests, but unlike the Japanese *keiretsu*, the Korean *chaebŏl* were generally not linked to major banks and were therefore ultimately dependent on outside financing. Because they also normally wished to retain ownership and management privately in the hands of a single family, moreover, Korean *chaebŏl* were usually also reluctant to go public on the stock market. Hyundai Engineering and Construction, for example, made its first public offering of 30 percent of its stock shares in 1984 only after twenty-seven official government requests and attention in the National Assembly.[22] Instead of coming from the stock market, therefore, much capital investment has come in the form of bank loans. Because banking was substantially controlled by the government, these bank loans, together with licensing authority, became key instruments of the South Korean developmental state.

Heavy reliance on bank financing also encouraged South Korean companies to become far more deeply indebted than their counterparts in, for example, Taiwan or the United States. Such debt did not appear threatening at first because, together with government control over the allocation of capital, the government also assumed much of the investment risk. It could be safely assumed that favored *chaebŏl* would never be allowed to go bankrupt. An absolutely critical distinction that set South Korea apart from much of the rest of the developing world, however, was not so much this kind of crony capitalism but the fact that, at least initially, the government was simultaneously also able to demand very high standards of performance and productive discipline from the *chaebŏl*.[23] As these *chaebŏl* increasingly became "too big to fail," however, and under subsequent South Korean presidents with less determination and prestige than Park Chung Hee, in the long run these features of the Korean economy would become problems. In the short term, though, the system seemed to work splendidly. From 1965 to 1990, the Republic of Korea had the second fastest growing economy in the world, after Taiwan.

Park's strategic ambition was not so much to transform Korea into a consumer paradise as to make South Korea a rich country with a strong army. A commitment to the buildup of steel and heavy industrial production, therefore, in spite of Korea's lack of any obvious comparative market advantage in those sectors, became a distinguishing feature of South Korea's approach. As always in South Korea, a major consideration was the ever-looming threat of invasion from the communists in the north. Park Chung Hee felt a deep, and not unreasonable, desire to avoid being entirely dependent on the United States for military protection, and therefore regarded it as essential for South Korea to develop an industrial base that might ensure its own self-defense capability. Especially by the early 1970s, as the United States began transferring its official recognition from the Republic of China on Taiwan to the People's Republic of China on the mainland and disengaging from the war in Vietnam, and as President Richard Nixon announced plans to reduce the American troop presence in Korea, Park increasingly aspired to make Korea self-sufficient in heavy industry. Steel production, chemicals, automobile construction, shipbuilding, machine tools, and electronics were strongly promoted. Hyundai Motors, for example, opened in 1967 with technical assistance from Mitsubishi and other foreign experts, and began producing an automobile of its own design in 1975. Hyundai cars began being exported to the American market in 1986. By the mid-1990s, South Korea was the fifth largest auto maker in the world.

Park Chung Hee had come to power in a military coup, but Park then won election as president in reasonably democratic popular votes in 1963, 1967, and 1971. In the 1971 election, however, an opposition candidate managed to take 45 percent of the vote. Apparently feeling threatened by the strength of the opposition, as well as by the changing international situation of the early 1970s, Park declared martial law, dissolved the National Assembly, and had a new constitution drafted. These 1972 "revitalizing" reforms (the Korean term is *yushin*, which is written with the same two characters – ultimately derived from the Confucian Classic the *Book of Odes* – as the term conventionally translated "restoration" in the 1868 Japanese Meiji Restoration) made the South Korean government significantly more authoritarian. Direct popular election of the president ended, and the president was thereafter selected by an electoral college, one-third of whose members were appointed by the president. Political power was heavily concentrated in the president, who also had the power to appoint cabinet ministers, judges, governors, university presidents, and ranking military officers, to dissolve the National Assembly, and to issue orders having something of the force of law.

Park Chung Hee's South Korean version of the developmental state was, as we have seen, influenced by Japanese models, and the first generation of postwar Korean leaders had mostly been educated under Japanese rule. Many were fluent in the Japanese language. After South Korea reestablished formal diplomatic relations with Japan in 1965, moreover, Japan quickly became South Korea's largest trading partner. But if history explains Korea's close connections with Japan, it also explains deep Korean feelings of bitterness toward their former colonial masters and an understandable desire to assert Korea's own independent national identity. Japanese cultural products were officially banned in South Korea until as late as 1998, and although generic modern Japanese appliances such as TVs might be acceptable, Japanese automobiles were totally excluded. Japanese-language education was also banned in Korea (and not reintroduced into Korean high schools until 1973).

In contrast to Japanese influences, the American presence was not only also very strong but often more welcome, especially in the early years. The Korean army, which long remained under overall U.S. supreme command, was a particularly intense focal point of American influence. As army officer and future president Roh Tae Woo (No T'ae-u, 1932–) later reminisced, "When our Military Academy was founded, all our textbooks were translations of West Point textbooks – some of them were still in English. At first two-thirds of the faculty were American officers. . . . Our cadets were one of the first groups in Korea to study Western institutions this thoroughly."[24] Partly because of its familiarity from American military bases, Spam (a distinctive American brand of precooked canned meat) became uniquely popular in Korea, and American pop culture has become pervasive in the age of globalization, as we will examine further later.

In addition, although it is not a specifically American influence, Christianity has also flourished more spectacularly in Korea than elsewhere in East Asia. The Christian success in Korea may be partially due to a link between Christian churches and anti-Japanese Korean nationalism during the colonial era, and also to Christian support for the causes of democracy and human rights in the authoritarian South Korea of the 1960s–1980s. In Korea, Christmas has been a national holiday since 1945, and by the end of the twentieth century Christianity – especially of the Evangelical Protestant variety – could be called the dominant religion in the Republic of Korea. More than a quarter of the South Korean people are Christians.[25] Only the United States now sends out more Christian missionaries to the rest of the world than South Korea.[26]

Democratization and Globalization

On October 26, 1979, after dinner in a Korean CIA (KCIA) building located near the presidential Blue House in Seoul, President Park Chung Hee was shot to death by his dinner companion, the head of the KCIA – apparently because of a disagreement over how to control recent student and labor unrest. Following the assassination of President Park, on December 12 a gun battle erupted in the streets of Seoul between opposing detachments of South Korean soldiers, which ended with an attack on the Ministry of Defense and the arrest of the defense minister and the martial law commander, ostensibly in connection with President Park's murder. This was the beginning of yet another military coup, this time orchestrated by Major General Chun Doo Hwan (Chŏn Tu-hwan, 1931–). As General Chun gathered the reins of power into his own hands, in May 1980 he declared martial law, closed all universities, and suspended the National Assembly. This sparked protests, notably in the southwestern city of Kwangju. University students were joined in the streets by citizens, and for a few days the demonstrators controlled the city. Army Special Forces were sent in, however, and the disturbance was crushed – with 191 officially acknowledged deaths. Chun's government assumed control over all Korean television networks and began large-scale purges of the bureaucracy.

The climate of world opinion in the 1980s was very different from when Park Chung Hee had seized power in a military coup twenty years before, however. In the Philippines, long-standing dictator Ferdinand Marcos was toppled by a "people power" movement in 1986. In Taiwan, martial law would be lifted, and a successful transition from single-party rule to multiparty democracy began in 1987. By the 1980s, South Korea was also no longer an impoverished, war-ravaged, developing country but a successfully industrialized economic powerhouse, and the expectation was widespread among Korean people that democratization should also be part of this modernization process. Students, in particular, clamored for democracy. Korean workers, whose low wages had helped make Korean industry globally competitive, were increasingly organized and active in demanding pay raises. In the single year 1987, there were 3,749 labor disputes in South Korea – more than in the entire previous history of the republic.[27]

In 1987, with international attention focused on South Korea because of the upcoming 1988 Seoul Olympics, a brutal military crackdown against student demonstrations would have been especially awkward. Weeks of clashes between rock-throwing students and teargas-firing police that year finally ended, therefore, with Chun Doo Hwan's hand-picked successor, Roh Tae Woo, making significant concessions to the demonstrators. In June 1987, Roh publicly promised, among other things, a direct popular presidential election and the release of political prisoners. In December, the promised presidential election duly occurred. Because there were five serious contenders, the ruling party candidate, Roh Tae Woo – President Chun Doo Hwan's chosen successor and another army general – was able to win the election with less than 37 percent of the vote. Nevertheless, he became South Korea's first democratically elected president in years.

Another milestone was passed in 1992 with the election of Korea's first civilian president in three decades (Kim Young Sam, 1927–2015, President 1993–1998). During the 1992 election campaign, all three major candidates had pledged to reduce the level of government intervention in the economy, and the incoming president's new administration was committed to economic liberalization, deregulation, and globalization. As a former dissident (who had, however, now compromised and allied with the ruling party), this new president was also anxious to promote democratizing reforms after he took office in 1993. It is worth noting that his vision of democracy was still strikingly Confucian, however, emphasizing the collective good of the community over selfish individual interests, harmony, national discipline, and the quintessentially Confucian ideal of leadership by virtuous example.[28] In keeping with the goal of implementing democratic reforms, in 1995 former presidents Chun Doo Hwan and Roh Tae Woo were both arrested and placed on trial on charges of mutiny and treason for their role in the 1980 military coup and the Kwangju massacre. Both were convicted, and former president Chun was sentenced to death, although that was commuted to life in prison, and he was eventually pardoned in 1997.

In the early 1990s, the new South Korean administration also made a formal policy commitment to globalization and the dismantling of the Korean developmental state. By the 1990s, the old model of state-guided capitalism was increasingly out of fashion, and it was arguably also starting to become counterproductive. The United States and other trading partners were beginning to apply serious pressure on South Korea to open its domestic markets, while rival exporting countries with even cheaper labor (such as China) were beginning to undercut Korea's competitive edge in cost – just as Korea's own workers' wages were belatedly beginning to shoot up. The idea was that Korea might benefit if inefficiencies resulting from protectionism and tight government regulation could be eliminated. The long series of South Korean government five-year economic plans came to an end, and in 1994 the Economic Planning Board was merged into a new superministry (called the Ministry of Finance and Economy). South Korea also opened up diplomatically, becoming a member of the United Nations in 1991 and normalizing relations with the

Soviet Union in 1990 and with the People's Republic of China in 1992. In 1998, South Korea finally even agreed to begin gradually lifting its ban on the importation of Japanese cultural products, starting with movies and cartoons.

Initially, cheap labor had been South Korea's principal comparative advantage in the global marketplace, and domestic austerity had been strongly encouraged. Neon lights were banned under President Park Chung Hee, and television broadcasts (except for the U.S. Armed Forces network) were only in black and white. Until 1982, a midnight–4:00 A.M. curfew was in effect. Rock and roll music, miniskirts, and long hair for men were banned. Imports of foreign consumer goods were often restricted, and buying foreign was discouraged as being unpatriotic. To protect the domestic automobile industry, the import of finished automobiles was prohibited until 1987.

But, by the 1980s, things had begun to seriously change. In the space of a single generation, South Korea had moved dramatically from what had still been a poor and largely peasant society in the 1940s–1950s to a modern, industrialized, and increasingly affluent urban middle-class society. Something like 42 percent of the South Korean people now lived in the single metropolis of Seoul. These new Korean people were not merely urban but also modern and sophisticated. Seoul boasted strikingly high concentrations of PhDs and especially high levels of broadband computer Internet connections. Koreans were the first in East Asia, for example, to digitize the Buddhist scriptures for CD-ROM distribution.[29] In the 1990s, Korea also became a net investor nation, investing more money abroad than it received.[30]

With the boom of the 1980s, wages went up sharply, automobiles began to fill the once nearly empty streets, and import restrictions finally began to be lifted. Beginning in 1989, for the first time, passports became easily available to South Koreans wishing to leave the country, and foreign travel has since become much more common. Koreans increasingly are inclined to make purchases based on judgments of price and quality rather than for patriotic national considerations. Large Western discount stores such as the American Wal-Mart and the French Carrefour made their appearance, and American music, movies, and cola became the rage among young Koreans. Popular sports, with the exception of the Korean martial art *t'aekwŏndo*, are now almost exclusively Western style. As late as 1995, there had still been only twenty-six golf courses in all of South Korea, but a decade later there were nearly a thousand.[31]

Although the first McDonald's fast-food restaurant opened in Seoul in 1988, McDonald's grew more slowly in South Korea than elsewhere in East Asia. This may have been partly because the hamburger does not fit easily into preexisting Korean food categories, but that was equally true of other East Asian cuisines and is not an entirely adequate explanation for South Korean resistance to McDonald's. But, as a relatively small country with strong recent memories of foreign colonial rule and attempted forced assimilation, many Korean people may understandably have been particularly sensitive to fears of foreign cultural imperialism.[32] As late as 1993, South Korea – "alone in Asia" – still refused to allow the then phenomenally popular American pop music superstar Michael Jackson to perform there.[33]

Although South Korea was opening up to Western culture, in 1996 it was still estimated that only 58 percent of South Koreans ate at Western-style restaurants and only 40 percent said they preferred sleeping on Western-style beds instead of on the floor, Korean style. Through a process of selective amnesia, furthermore, the foreign origins of many of those originally Western items that had been widely accepted, such as computers, blue jeans, and modern commercial pop music, could be conveniently forgotten, and emphasis placed on distinctive Korean national cultural markers such as the eating of *kimch'i* (spicy Korean pickled cabbage) and speaking the Korean language.[34] Yet, success in South Korea has also become closely associated with learning to speak English. It is not considered remarkable for a family in Seoul to spend a third of its income on English lessons for the children. With the turn into the twenty-first century, open multicultural internationalism has rapidly accelerated in South Korea, and defensive nationalism is now perceptibly in decline.[35] And, if South Korea is becoming more open, like Japan before it, South Korea is also becoming a center of globalizing force in its own right.

Despite a public commitment to the ideal of economic globalization (and dismantling the developmental state) in the early 1990s, over the next few years South Korea's global competitiveness rankings actually went down. In 1997, South Korea was obliged to accept the largest bailout (fifty-eight billion dollars) thus far in the history of the International Monetary Fund (IMF) to avoid "financial meltdown."[36] Korea's economic problems in the 1990s may have been less due to inherent defects in the globalization model, however, than to a combination of unfortunate circumstances and remaining imperfections in the reform process. While the *chaebŏl* had continued to grow in size in the 1980s–1990s, liberalization of the economy and deregulation made it simultaneously harder for the government to impose any discipline on them. At the same time, the need of elected politicians for "donations" gave businesses increased leverage over the government itself. In 1995, for example, prosecutors uncovered a secret slush fund of 285 million dollars that had been accumulated by former president Chun Doo Hwan. In the 1990s, deregulation of Korea's financial systems in the name of globalization also brought in a flood of mostly short-term foreign debt, and Korean banks, accustomed to never having to make careful risk assessments because it was assumed they could always rely on government bailouts, permitted some rather dubious investments. Unfortunate circumstances made their appearance at this point, as speculation involving Thailand's currency (known as the baht) in July 1997 touched off a devastating financial crisis that swept across much of Southeast Asia. Most of Confucian East Asia (notably the People's Republic of China) proved relatively immune to this so-called "Asian flu," but South Korea found itself badly exposed. The Korean stock market lost half its value, and by 1998 some twenty thousand Korean firms had gone bankrupt, including ten of the top thirty *chaebŏl*.

This was clearly very bad news, but under the pressure of this crisis and IMF supervision South Korea moved forward quickly with economic liberalization. Although the total number of economic regulations was cut in half, supervisory financial regulations were also effectively tightened. *Chaebŏl* were pushed to become more transparent in their business operations, divest themselves of large numbers of peripheral subsidiaries, and lower their debt-to-asset ratios. Foreign direct investment in Korea was made easier, and even outright foreign acquisition of Korean firms was permitted. The recovery was rapid and successful enough that Korea was able to pay back what it owed the IMF in three and a half years rather than the anticipated four.

One perhaps unexpected result of this 1997 Asian financial crisis was that the South Korean government made a conscious new commitment to emphasize information technology and pop culture as promising future fields for growth. The government has been wiring every household in South Korea for ultra-high-speed Internet, and a billion-dollar investment fund was established to promote pop culture. Most of the investment capital came from private sources, but the fund is coordinated by the Ministry of Culture. Despite liberalization and globalization, the South Korean government apparently still believes it has a role in promoting economic development. As of 2012, more than a quarter of the total venture capital investment in South Korea was government funded. The new pop culture initiative, combined with a global technological digital revolution that caught established Japanese manufacturers somewhat off guard and provided Korean companies with the opportunity to start fresh from a position of relative equality, has helped propel something of a twenty-first-century shift in the center of excitement from Japan to South Korea. As recently as 1993, Samsung's cell phone sales ranked only fourth place in South Korea's own domestic market and were largely unknown outside of Korea, but by 2012 Samsung was number one in global smartphone sales, and even Apple iPhones were being built with Samsung microchips.[37]

Starting in the 1990s, a so-called "Korean wave" (*hallyu*) of fascination for South Korean television programming, movies, music (K-Pop), and other pop cultural items, as well as for the material products of South Korean industry such as cell phones and automobiles, has swept across much of Asia. Although the astonishing worldwide Internet success of Psy's (Park Jae-sang, 1977–) music video "Gangnam Style" might be dismissed as a one-time novelty song fluke, within Asia the Korean wave is real and substantial. For example, especially after the appearance around 2009 of websites providing easy Internet access to a large selection of television programing in the People's Republic of China, South Korean TV dramas (with Chinese-language subtitles) have become enormously popular in China.

Even the domestic Chinese-made reality television program "Where Are We Going, Dad?" (*Baba qu na'er*) – featuring middle-aged Chinese celebrity fathers who take their young children to various scenic locations where they compete in performing amusing "tasks" – which first appeared in 2013 and claims seventy-five million viewers per episode, was based on a South Korean model. Another 2015 Chinese reality TV show, "With You Together on the Road" (*Yi lu shang you ni*), was a joint PRC–South Korean production. This program placed three Chinese couples (two from the PRC and one from Hong Kong) facing challenges in the unfamiliar environment of Seoul, South Korea, with a Korean Boyband host. Such television programs are evidence both of the strength of South Korean popular culture in Asia, and of the swirling complexity of globalization patterns.

Meanwhile, in 1997, opposition party candidate Kim Dae Jung (Kim Tae-jung, 1924–2009, President 1998–2003) won the presidential election in South Korea, marking the first democratic transfer of power to the political opposition in the history of the Republic of Korea. In 2013, Park Geun-hye (Pak Kŭnhye, 1952–), the daughter of former president Park Chung Hee, became the first female president of South Korea. In a patriarchal Confucian society where, as recently as 1991, women could still not legally even be the head of a household, this is impressive. Today, South Korean companies such as Samsung and LG in electronics, and Hyundai and Kia in automobiles, are true global giants, and South Korea is a powerful force in modern Asian pop culture. For a country that had until recently been among the poorest in the world, what South Korea has achieved (mostly through very hard work) since its birth in 1948 has been breathtaking.

For Further Reading

For introductory overviews, see Don Oberdorfer, *The Two Koreas: A Contemporary History* (New York: Basic Books, [1997] 2001), and Michael Edson Robinson, *Korea's Twentieth-Century Odyssey: A Short History* (Honolulu: University of Hawai'i Press, 2007).

A riveting journalistic account of the Korean War is David Halberstam, *The Coldest Winter: America and the Korean War* (New York: Hyperion, 2007).

On North Korea, see chap. 8 of Bruce Cumings, *Korea's Place in the Sun: A Modern History* (New York: W. W. Norton, 1997); Han S. Park, ed., *North Korea: Ideology, Politics, Economy* (Englewood Cliffs, NJ: Prentice Hall, 1996); and Dae-Sook Suh, *Kim Il Sung: The North Korean Leader* (New York: Columbia University Press, 1988).

Concerning South Korea's dramatic economic takeoff, see Alice H. Amsden, *Asia's Next Giant: South Korea and Late Industrialization* (New York: Oxford University Press, 1989); John Lie, *Han Unbound: The Political Economy of South Korea* (Stanford University Press, 1998); and Meredith Woo-Cumings, ed., *The Developmental State* (Ithaca, NY: Cornell University Press, 1999).

On contemporary Korea more generally, see Robert E. Buswell Jr. and Timothy S. Lee, eds., *Christianity in Korea* (Honolulu: University of Hawai'i Press, 2006); Mark L. Clifford, *Troubled Tiger: Businessmen, Bureaucrats, and Generals in South Korea* (Armonk, NY: M. E. Sharpe, 1994); and Carter J. Eckert, "Korea's Transition to Modernity: A Will to Greatness," in *Historical Perspectives on Contemporary East Asia*, ed. Merle Goldman and Andrew Gordon (Cambridge, MA: Harvard University Press, 2000).

For Korea in the age of globalization, see Euny Hong, *The Birth of Korean Cool: How One Nation is Conquering the World through Pop Culture* (New York: Picador, 2014); Young Whan Kihl, *Transforming Korean Politics: Democracy, Reform, and Culture* (Armonk, NY: M. E. Sharpe, 2005); Samuel S. Kim, ed., *Korea's Globalization* (Cambridge University Press, 2000); and James Lewis and Amadu Sesay, eds., *Korea and Globalization: Politics, Economics and Culture* (London: RoutledgeCurzon, 2002).

13 Vietnam since 1945

In 1940, during the early days of WW II, Japan began demanding the cooperation of French colonial authorities in Vietnam as part of the Japanese war effort against China. By the summer of 1941, Japanese military forces had occupied all of Vietnam. Although this led directly to the imposition of Allied sanctions against Japan and the outbreak of a wider war in the Pacific, within Vietnam itself the collaborationist Vichy French regime that was in place by that time did not resist. Despite Japanese occupation, routine French colonial administration of Vietnam continued throughout most of WW II, until March 1945, when the Japanese finally seized power directly and disarmed and interned the French. The following day, the Japanese named the last Nguyen Dynasty ruler, Bao Dai (1913–1997; emperor, 1926–1945; head of state, 1949–1955), emperor of a nominally independent Vietnam, within the Japanese-controlled Greater East Asia Co-Prosperity Sphere.

Meanwhile, the Japanese occupation of Vietnam during WW II had created an opportunity for the Vietnamese communists to call for a united front of all patriotic Vietnamese to resist Japan. After spending thirty years in exile, some time in late 1940 or early 1941 the communist leader Nguyen Sinh Cung returned to Vietnam (where he finally actually assumed his most famous alias, "Ho Chi Minh"). There, at a meeting near the Chinese border in May 1941, a front organization (deliberately intended to downplay the communist leadership role) was formed – called the League for the Independence of Vietnam, but commonly known as the Viet Minh – and it began to conduct guerrilla warfare against the Japanese.

The French Withdrawal, and America's War

The Japanese surrender at the end of WW II, in August 1945, left Vietnam in chaos. Northern Vietnam at the time of surrender was only just beginning to recover from a catastrophic famine that had claimed the lives of one or two million people earlier that spring. Ho Chi Minh and the Viet Minh appeared to be virtually the only forces on the ground that were opposing the Japanese and attempting to deal with the famine – by, for example, leading attacks on warehouses where rice had been diverted and stored for Japanese use. The Viet Minh now stepped into

Figure 13.1. Ho Chi Minh giving a speech to the people of Vietnam on September 2, 1945, declaring the independence of the country from the French Empire. Pictures from History/ Bridgeman Images.

the vacuum created by Japan's surrender, easily occupying Hanoi on August 19 (and Saigon on August 25), and soon thereafter declaring the establishment of a Democratic Republic of Vietnam (see Figure 13.1). On August 30, Emperor Bao Dai formally abdicated, finally ending the old Nguyen Dynasty.

However, the victorious WW II Allied Powers had previously reached an agreement among themselves that Chiang Kai-shek's Chinese Nationalist forces would be responsible for the postwar military occupation of northern Vietnam, and British troops would be responsible for the occupation of the south. The British, some of whom may have still hoped to restore their own prewar empire, were generally sympathetic to the idea of a restoration of French colonial rule in Vietnam. The British commander in the south therefore disarmed the Viet Minh and handed over control to newly arriving Free French troops. In the north, meanwhile, Chinese Nationalist forces, which began arriving in September 1945, were sympathetic neither to European colonialism nor to communism. However, in exchange for the termination of the old French leaseholds and treaty privileges in China, the Chinese Nationalists agreed to return northern Vietnam to the French in February 1946.

Ho Chi Minh, who had made the gesture of officially dissolving the Indochinese Communist Party and calling for general elections, tactically consented to Vietnam's recognition as a "Free State" within the French Union, and even to the return of French forces to the north under the provision that they would only remain for five years. After Ho Chi Minh left for Paris to negotiate in May 1946, however, the French High Commissioner for Indochina unilaterally proclaimed Cochinchina (southern Vietnam) a republic under French control. The return of French armed forces to the north then provoked armed clashes, and open warfare by November 1946. Initially, the French seemed to regain control, and an Associated State of Vietnam (reincorporating Cochinchina) was established in 1949 with the former emperor Bao Dai as head of state, within the French Union, and with continued overall French economic, diplomatic, and military control.

For most of the colonial period the French had been able to hold Vietnam with a surprisingly small force of only about fourteen thousand soldiers.[1] Despite the superficial restoration of French rule after WW II, however, by 1950 Viet Minh guerrillas had gained control over the mountainous border area with China. After Chiang Kai-shek's retreat to Taiwan and the establishment of the communist-ruled People's Republic of China (PRC) in 1949, Beijing began providing the Viet Minh with military assistance. Formal recognition of the Democratic Republic of Vietnam by the PRC in 1950 was soon followed by recognition from the Soviet Union. The Viet Minh guerrillas were simultaneously anti-colonial Vietnamese nationalists seeking independence from French rule, and under fairly tight communist control and direction. While most Americans were not particularly sympathetic to French imperialism, in the wake of the perceived "loss of China" to communism the United States had become strongly resolved to contain any further global communist expansion. By 1950 – the same year the Korean War began – the United States began to provide assistance to the French in Vietnam. By 1954, the United States was covering 80 percent of the French military expenses.[2]

In a campaign that was intended to disrupt the Viet Minh supply lines and engage them in a pitched conventional battle of the type in which superior modern French firepower was expected to prove decisive, in 1953 three battalions of French paratroopers took and fortified a remote northwestern valley called Dien

Bien Phu (which means something like "Office Securing the Border"), located some two hundred miles west of Hanoi near the border with Laos. Unexpectedly, the Viet Minh, who were now supplied with Chinese weapons, were able to laboriously haul some seventy-six anti-aircraft guns to the mountaintops overlooking the French positions, and shut down French air supplies. Cut off and surrounded, the French troops endured a grueling siege for fifty-five days until they ran out of ammunition, and surrendered on May 7, 1954.

On the very next day, at a conference in Geneva that had already been convened to discuss the Korean and Indochinese conflicts, the question of Vietnam was addressed. Following the catastrophic French military defeat at Dien Bien Phu, the Geneva Accords that were finally reached on July 21, 1954, granted independence to Vietnam, Cambodia, and Laos. It was also decided that there would be a temporary division of Vietnam at the seventeenth parallel, between Ho Chi Minh's Democratic Republic of Vietnam in the north, and a regroupment zone for French forces in the south – where the Viet Minh presence was much weaker – and where the former emperor Bao Dai continued to serve as nominal head of state. Democratic elections, and reunification, were expected to follow two years later. Neither the United States nor Bao Dai's government accepted the final agreement, however. (And, in an incident that was bitterly remembered in Beijing for years afterwards, the U.S. Secretary of State conspicuously refused to shake hands with the Chinese Premier Zhou Enlai at the conference in Geneva.)

Bao Dai then appointed the distinguished Vietnamese nationalist Ngo Dinh Diem (1901–1963) as prime minister in 1954, while Bao Dai himself remained in France. Bao Dai never returned to Vietnam. The new Prime Minister, Ngo Dinh Diem, was both anti-French and anti-communist. During the French conflict with the Viet Minh he had spent much of his time abroad, including a stay in a Catholic seminary in the United States. In October 1955, Diem (Vietnamese people are commonly referred to simply by their personal names – which come last in the traditional East Asian word sequence – rather than by their surnames, in contrast to the usual Chinese practice of referring to people by their family names) conducted a referendum vote (which was widely suspected of fraud) that removed Bao Dai as head of state, and Diem became the first president (1955–1963) of a newly proclaimed Republic of Vietnam, in the south. Diem also announced that he would not consult with the north regarding the promised nationwide elections and reunification, on the grounds that any vote conducted in the communist north would not be free and fair. The "temporary" north–south division therefore settled into permanence.

In the north, the Communist government began its envisioned Marxist social revolution, which included Maoist-style land redistribution and collectivization campaigns starting in 1953. By 1959, Hanoi was also committed to a policy of military reunification with the south, and began operations in the south through a new front organization known as the National Liberation Front (NLF). In the south, the NLF was often popularly referred to as the Viet Cong, a contraction of Viet Nam Cong San, or Vietnamese communists. Over the next few years thousands of southern civil servants and teachers were assassinated, and the Viet Cong came to control much of the rural countryside in the Mekong delta — especially at night.[3]

After the Geneva Accords and the French withdrawal in 1954, the United States began to directly support the anti-communist regime in South Vietnam. In 1960, U.S. Army Special Forces began arriving. As of that year, there were approximately four thousand American troops and a few hundred American civilians present in Vietnam. The U.S. emphasis was placed on counter-insurgency tactics against what was then still a relatively small number of guerrillas. One early idea was a "strategic hamlet" program that was intended to relocate and concentrate the rural population of the south in more easily supervised centers, isolated from the insurgents in the countryside (but also from their own old homes).

President Diem unquestionably tried to be a strong leader, but he was also a puritanical man – which was itself not always universally appealing – who came to be surrounded by much alleged corruption and incompetence, and who did not endear himself to large segments of the southern population. As a Catholic, for example, Diem alienated the non-Christian majority. Although there were some two million Catholics in South Vietnam, that was only about 10 percent of the people. Diem, whose brother was a Catholic archbishop, was accused of favoritism. When celebrations of the Buddha's birthday were banned in May 1963, and a Buddhist leader in Hue was denied permission to speak on local radio, Buddhists marched in protest on the radio station. Turned away by police, thousands of protestors massed in the central square, where troops eventually fired into the crowd, killing nine. On June 11, 1963, a Buddhist monk poured gasoline over himself and lit it in protest, sitting in the lotus position in downtown Saigon for ten minutes as the flames consumed his body. An Associated Press news photograph captured the image for a horrified world audience, dramatically demonstrating popular discontent with the Diem regime (see Figure 13.2). This was followed by six more Buddhist self-immolations, and the imposition of martial law.

President Diem lost favor in Washington, DC, and American officials, including the U.S. Ambassador to Vietnam, may have even encouraged a military coup to overthrow him. When the coup came, in November 1963, it ended with Diem's murder, and brought new shocks and instability. Within a little more than a year of Diem's death there were eight more attempted coups, until a final coup in February 1965 brought the generals Nguyen Van Thieu (1923–2001) and Nguyen Cao Ky (1930–2011) into a new military government. In 1967, a new constitution was adopted, beginning the so-called Second Republic of Vietnam, and elections were held, with Thieu elected president (1967–1975) and Ky vice-president.

In August of 1964, three North Vietnamese torpedo boats attacked a U.S. Navy destroyer, the USS *Maddox*, operating in the Gulf of Tonkin off the North Vietnamese coast. Two days later there was an alleged second attack (which was probably an overanxious reaction to stray sonar echoes and radar blips rather than a real attack), after which President Lyndon Johnson ordered airstrikes at military targets in the north, and the U.S. Congress passed the Gulf of Tonkin Resolution which authorized the president to take military action without a formal declaration of war. Soon the U.S. was taking a very active role in combat operations, and President Johnson began an open-ended escalation of the U.S. military commitment.

Figure 13.2. A Buddhist monk burns himself to death in Saigon, 1963. Pictures from History/Bridgeman Images.

In late 1964, meanwhile, the first regular North Vietnamese military units began crossing into the south to join the Liberation Army of the National Liberation Front (popularly known as the Viet Cong). December 1964 saw coordinated communist offensives across the south, and on Christmas Eve a bomb was detonated in a parked car beneath the Brinks hotel in Saigon, which was home to U.S. officers, killing two Americans and wounding fifty-eight. At that time there were some 23,000 U.S. advisors in Vietnam. The first active American combat troops did not arrive until March 1965. By 1967, the United States was delivering a million tons of supplies each month, and South Vietnam's airports were among the busiest in the world.[4] By 1969, there were 541,000 U.S. troops in Vietnam. Altogether, two and a half million Americans served tours of duty in Vietnam, and 58,000 Americans were killed (while nearly four million Vietnamese were killed or wounded). The American presence, both military and civilian, was enormous: at one point there was one American for every fifteen Vietnamese people in Saigon.[5]

The war in Vietnam rapidly became extremely controversial back home in America. At least in the beginning, many Americans had sincerely believed the war effort to be part of a noble cause to save the Free World from communism. But, as the death toll mounted, opposition grew in the U.S. – magnified by a military conscription system that gave American youth (especially those from less privileged backgrounds who were unable to obtain draft deferments) little choice about being sent to war in distant foreign jungles. Massive anti-war demonstrations and student protests erupted, and the war began to have a huge impact on American domestic politics and culture.

On January 30, 1968, at the time of the traditional lunar New Year holiday known as Tet, some 80,000 NLF (Viet Cong) troops and regular North Vietnam army soldiers struck at more than a hundred towns and cities across the south, in a coordinated offensive of unprecedented scale. In Saigon, one small unit even penetrated the U.S. embassy compound for several hours before being killed. In the end, although they held the old imperial capital of Hue for three weeks, the communists suffered heavy casualties, failed to permanently capture any targets, and were not met by the anticipated wave of popular uprisings of support. From a purely military perspective, this "Tet offensive" was a communist defeat; but it also came as a profound shock to American public opinion. Doubt began to grow that the war could be won by American military might. In March, President Johnson announced his desire for a negotiated peace, and withdrew his candidacy from the upcoming U.S. presidential election.

Lyndon Johnson was followed as president of the United States by the newly elected Richard Nixon, who began a drawdown of U.S. forces, and a "Vietnamization" of the war effort. Peace talks had begun in Paris in 1968, and a Paris Peace Accord was eventually signed in January 1973, for which Henry Kissinger (1923–) and Le Duc Tho (1911–1990) were awarded the Nobel Peace Prize. This accord provided a framework for the final withdrawal of American troops. Although a "land to the tiller" program initiated by South Vietnam's President Thieu in 1969, giving ownership of farmland to tenants and government compensation to their former landlords, meant that by 1975 most Mekong delta farmers had become private owners – alleviating some of their old economic grievances – the departure of the free-spending Americans caused the southern economy to deflate dramatically. When a new communist offensive began in 1975, the South Vietnamese army collapsed with surprising speed, Saigon fell, and Vietnam was abruptly reunified under communist rule.

The Socialist Republic of Vietnam

In July 1976, a reunified Socialist Republic of Vietnam was proclaimed, with its capital at Hanoi. Saigon was officially renamed Ho Chi Minh City (although many people still think of it as Saigon). Despite differences in culture, dialect, and ideology, north and south were rapidly reintegrated into a single state. For a short while, existing businesses in the south were permitted to continue, although banks and major institutions were quickly nationalized. Hanoi was determined to achieve a rapid socialist transformation of the south, however, and in early 1978 larger businesses were abruptly nationalized, and an (ultimately unsuccessful) attempt at collectivization of agriculture began. Hundreds of thousands of refugees fled the country, many of them ethnic Chinese (who were particularly likely to be involved in capitalistic commercial activities, and who also fell under Vietnamese nationalist suspicion and pressure to assimilate).

In December 1978, in response to repeated attacks from the Khmer Rouge and reported Khmer Rouge atrocities, Vietnam intervened militarily in neighboring Cambodia. Vietnamese forces did not finally withdraw from Cambodia until 1989. This Vietnamese intervention undoubtedly helped to save many Cambodian people from the murderous regime of the Khmer Rouge, and could be considered justifiable, but it nonetheless triggered an embargo of Vietnam by many foreign countries, including the United States. Vietnam's intervention also angered the People's Republic of China, which had been backing the Khmer Rouge. Earlier that same year, in November, Hanoi had signed a treaty of friendship and cooperation with Moscow, and by this time Vietnam appeared to be more closely aligned with the Soviet Union than with China. Beijing was also concerned about the pervasive mistreatment of ethnic Chinese in Vietnam. To teach Vietnam a lesson, in February 1979 China invaded Vietnam's northern frontier, in what turned out to be a three-week war.

Although the Vietnamese military performed well in the war with China (and China's military performance was widely seen as unimpressive), Vietnam was by this time isolated, and the poorest country in East Asia. By the late 1970s, food had to be rationed and there were serious shortages of consumer goods. Despite a constitutional declaration of gender equality, furthermore, as of 1975 less than a third of Communist Party members were women, and there were no women in the ruling Politburo. The anticipated socialist utopia had not exactly been achieved.

After the collapse of communism in Eastern Europe and the end of the Soviet Union in 1991, Vietnam's leaders reaffirmed their Marxist commitment to the "dictatorship of the proletariat," and realigned themselves somewhat more closely with the still communist-ruled People's Republic of China. By the late 1980s, however, Vietnam had also begun to implement some of the kinds of market-based economic reforms that were already causing spectacular economic takeoff in China. The U.S. finally lifted its trade embargo of Vietnam in 1994, and normalized diplomatic relations in 1995. During the last decade of the twentieth century and the first decade of the twenty-first, Vietnam experienced impressive annual average economic growth of more than 7 percent.[6] Vietnam was beginning to participate in the general East Asian economic miracle.

Vietnam was also beginning to look north again with some apprehension, at the now rapidly rising Chinese giant. More than half of all the world's shipping tonnage today passes through the South China Sea, off Vietnam's coast, whose waters may also contain significant oil and natural gas reserves. China has long claimed that its territorial waters extend deep into the South China Sea, far beyond the limits recognized by most other countries, and Beijing has recently grown much more aggressive in asserting that claim – putting the South China Sea "on the way to becoming the most contested body of water in the world." To counter this potential Chinese threat, Vietnam has recently been pursuing new security arrangements with India, South Korea, Japan, the Philippines, Malaysia, Singapore, Indonesia, and Australia – and, ironically, even with the United States, which has now become Vietnam's largest export market.[7]

Vietnam, East Asia, and the World

Europeans once called it Indochina, and viewed it as the place where ancient Indian and Chinese civilizations met and overlapped. Today, there is disagreement about whether Vietnam should be considered East Asian or Southeast Asian. It has been part of the Chinese Empire (for more than a thousand years), and also part of the French Empire (for less than a hundred). For a few years in living memory its southern half was overrun by Americans. It is today one of the world's last remaining outposts of Marxist communism – a European ideology, by way of Soviet Russia. It is also a deeply Confucian society, where roughly half of the Vietnamese vocabulary derives from the Chinese language. Vietnam's history has arguably been more closely tied to China than Japan's has, yet Vietnam is more likely than Japan to be left out of descriptions of an East Asian region that is supposedly defined in terms of such things as a shared use of the Chinese writing system and Confucianism. And China, above all other countries, is its ancestral adversary. Vietnam fought its most recent war with China (in 1979), and its current tensions are greatest with China. Vietnam is also unique unto itself. In its present configuration, it is a surprisingly new country, yet it has roots in an ancient indigenous Bronze Age civilization.

Like China itself – much of whose history was driven by interactions with Inner Asia, and whose current borders actually straddle (and extend well beyond) the nominal line between traditional Inner Asia and East Asia[8] – and like Japan, whose medieval history in some ways more closely resembled that of western Europe than it did that of either China, Korea, or Vietnam[9] (and which notoriously even contemplated leaving "the ranks of Asian nations" in the late nineteenth century[10]), Vietnam exemplifies both some of the coherence of East Asia as a cultural region, and also some of the inevitable limitations of perhaps all such ultimately arbitrary categories and labels. If East Asia is a coherent cultural sphere, it is a permeable sphere, and only one of many possible ways of conceptualizing the situation. Vietnam is also a reminder that globalization is not really altogether new. In this world, nothing is constant. But it is also often true that the more things change, the more they stay the same. Vietnam remains today part of an enduring East Asian cultural community that does have some compelling significance.

For Further Reading

Much has been written about America's war in Vietnam. One acclaimed example is Neil Sheehan, *A Bright Shining Lie: John Paul Vann and America in Vietnam* (New York: Random House, 1988). Other journalistic accounts include Frances FitzGerald, *Fire in the Lake: The Vietnamese and the Americans in Vietnam* (New York: Vintage Books, [1972] 1989); and Stanley Karnow, *Vietnam: A History* (New York: The Viking Press, 1983).

William J. Duiker delivers a comprehensive academic description of modern Vietnam in *Vietnam: Revolution in Transition*, 2nd ed. (Boulder: Westview Press, 1995). For an attempt to gain a Vietnamese perspective, see Neil L. Jamieson, *Understanding Vietnam* (Berkeley: University of California Press, 1993). Duong Van Mai Elliott's *The Sacred Willow: Four Generations in the Life of a Vietnamese Family* (Oxford University Press, 1999) provides an engagingly personal account of Vietnam since the nineteenth century.

14 China since 1945

The Chinese Civil War

Although China was one of the victors in World War II, conditions in war-ravaged China did not noticeably improve after Japan's defeat. Instead, the catastrophic inflation, corruption, and black marketeering that had begun during the World War only worsened, while the off-again, on-again civil war between the Chinese Nationalists and Communists entered its final phase. In the first months after the war, the U.S. ambassador did succeed in bringing Mao Zedong and Chiang Kai-shek together for face-to-face negotiations. It was reportedly Mao's first ride in an airplane. The American hope was to prevent full-scale civil war and promote democracy in China. For that purpose, in late 1945 President Truman appointed one of America's most distinguished military leaders and statesmen, General George C. Marshall (1880–1959), as a special envoy to China. General Marshall remained in China for a little over a year (December 1945–January 1947), and on his departure, he was able to express cautious optimism that a new Chinese constitution, and democratic elections scheduled for late 1947, might hold.

But General Marshall also expressed concern that efforts at reaching a peace settlement were being frustrated by extremists on both sides. In fact, the bitter antagonism between the Chinese Nationalists and Communists ultimately proved too deep to sustain the uneasy truce. The problems of postwar China in general, moreover, were proving stubbornly intractable. On the island of Taiwan, for example – recently returned to Chinese rule following Japan's surrender – residual damage from World War II, Nationalist Chinese economic policies that restricted the operations of a free market, and the circulation of excessive amounts of currency all combined to foster high unemployment, shortages of goods, and out-of-control inflation. When police attempted to confiscate suspected contraband cigarettes from a middle-aged female street vendor in the provincial capital, Taipei, resulting in a scuffle that killed a bystander, Taiwan erupted into a major island-wide rebellion on February 28, 1947. The rebellion was crushed by Nationalist troops, resulting in the deaths of thousands of Taiwanese.[1] This February

28 Incident (although it was long publicly unmentionable in Taiwan) left a long-festering wound in relations between the Taiwanese people and the ruling Chinese Nationalist government on the island.

Meanwhile, although the Soviet Union did not enter the war against Japan until just six days before Japan's surrender, that was still sufficient time for the Soviets to overrun Manchuria at the end of World War II. The Soviets occupied Manchuria for about a year, retained control over Port Arthur and the China Eastern Railway (running across Manchuria) until 1954, and extracted hundreds of millions of dollars' worth of war reparations from the region. Many Chinese later grumbled about this Soviet looting, but in the short term the massive Soviet military presence gave a boost to the Chinese Communists. The Russians turned over to the Chinese Communists some three-quarters of a million captured rifles, eighteen thousand machine guns, and four thousand pieces of artillery.[2] Manchuria then became the launching pad for the Chinese Communist military reunification of China.

The United States was simultaneously, of course, providing substantial aid to Chiang Kai-shek's Nationalists. The Nationalist armies were initially larger and better equipped than the Communist Red Army (later known as the People's Liberation Army), but the Nationalists fought a static defensive war and were outmaneuvered and defeated unit by unit. In the process, huge amounts of men and material were captured by the Communists. As the Communist offensive began to accelerate in 1948, the last senior American advisor to Chiang Kai-shek's military even complained that "the Communists had more of our equipment than the Nationalists did." Mao Zedong was fond of joking that Chiang Kai-shek "was our supply officer."[3]

Events now began to unfold quickly. Beijing fell to the Communists in January 1949, and by April the Red Army, coming down from the north, was staging assaults across the Yangzi River into south China. Chiang Kai-shek retreated with some two million followers to the island of Taiwan (where the Republic of China at least nominally survives to the present day), and on October 1, 1949, Mao Zedong stood on Tiananmen – the old Gate of Heavenly Peace rather than the new Tiananmen Square, which did not yet exist – and proclaimed the establishment of a new country, called the People's Republic of China (PRC). (See Map 14.1.)

Chairman Mao's New China

Despite the revolutionaries' resentment at what they remembered as a century of Chinese national humiliation at the hands of Western imperialists, Westerners in China were not all immediately expelled after the Communist takeover. The American president, furthermore, even briefly contemplated recognizing the new People's Republic. But, following the outbreak of war in Korea in 1950, the United States firmly recommitted itself to support for Chiang Kai-shek's Nationalist Republic of China on Taiwan, recognizing it as the only legitimate government of China, and the containment of communism emerged as the American grand design. Cold war alignments now rapidly hardened. The new PRC, for its part, adopted a policy of "leaning to one side" by cultivating relatively cordial relations

Administrative Divisions of the
People's Republic of China (PRC)

- Province
- Autonomous Region
- Municipality
- Special Administrative Region

Map 14.1 The People's Republic of China

with the Soviet Union. In December 1949, Mao Zedong went to Moscow on his first ever trip abroad to participate in the celebrations surrounding Joseph Stalin's seventieth birthday. Mao was kept waiting and felt insufficiently well treated, but he did obtain a three hundred million dollar loan, and a (short) period of Soviet assistance to China began that "has been characterized as the largest technology transfer in history."[4]

Following a dozen years of world war and civil war, compounded by decades of previous warlordism and national disintegration, the most urgent immediate priority for the new China was simply to restore order. A new unified national currency was introduced, known as the *renminbi* (the "people's money"; also known, more generically, as the *yuan*), and, through some high-profile executions of currency speculators and the establishment of fixed commodity prices, raging inflation was finally brought under control. The new Communist rulers of China had no intention of merely restoring the status quo, however. The Communist victory in 1949 owed much to the mass mobilization of popular sentiments of patriotic nationalism to save China from foreign threats, perceived or real, but the Communist leaders were also sincerely committed Marxists determined to carry through a Marxist social revolution.

This presented some serious challenges. Although a striking number of early top Chinese Communist leaders had studied in Europe or the Soviet Union, by 1949 the overwhelming majority of party members and cadres (persons in leadership positions) were very poorly educated and unfamiliar with the wider world beyond China. Marxist theory taught that historical progress is driven by class struggle through a regular series of stages, defined in terms of modes of production. The most relevant of these stages were supposed to be the transition from feudalism to capitalism, and then (in the future) from capitalism to communism. Theoretically, therefore, communism was expected to emerge out of the most advanced stage of industrialized capitalism, as a result of class struggle between factory workers (the proletariat) and factory owners. The glaring problem for China, of course, was that factories and factory workers were both quite sparse in the China of 1949. According to theory, China was not yet capitalist but rather still feudal.

Actually, however, conditions in China bore little real resemblance to medieval European feudalism either, and there were some difficulties in applying the feudal model. Tweaking the general theory to better fit Chinese conditions, the specific formula that the Chinese Communists developed was that China was "semi-feudal, semi-colonial." The Marxist revolutionary solution to semi-colonialism, then, was to rise up as a nation and drive out the foreign imperialist exploiters, while the prescription for semi-feudalism was for poor peasants also to rise up, denounce their landlord exploiters, and confiscate and redistribute their land. After the Chinese Communist victory in 1949, anti-landlord struggle sessions were therefore duly encouraged in every village.

The Marxist idea that class exploitation of tenant farmers by landlords was the underlying reason for China's poverty not only came as surprising news to many Chinese farmers but, in many parts of China, it also "distorted reality." In one north Chinese county that has been carefully studied by recent American scholars, for example, 80 percent of the farm households had previously already been owner cultivators (rather than tenant farmers), the recognized existing social divisions had been primarily between families rather than between classes, and there had been a general community-wide spirit of unity in patriotic resistance against Japan and support for the underground Communist Party during the war. Now, however, "suddenly unity was to yield to something called class struggle."[5]

The new class categories that were now obligatorily applied to everyone in China were inevitably therefore often somewhat arbitrary, but land redistribution was nonetheless extensively carried out across the countryside. This was a revolutionary action, but in theory it corresponded to the transition from feudalism to capitalism – what was called the bourgeois-democratic stage of the revolution – rather than from capitalism to communism. Even after redistribution, the land was still private property. Similar land redistribution programs (without the violent struggle) were actively promoted by U.S. advisors in Taiwan, Japan, and South Korea as a way of diminishing the appeal of communism. In theory, furthermore, the subsequent transition from this bourgeois-democratic stage to full-blown communism might still take a long time. But Mao Zedong was impatient. No sooner was the land reform completed, by about 1952, than Mao was ready to initiate the "transition to socialism." Collectivized farming, for example, began to be promoted.

Although Mao had led what was undeniably a rural "peasant revolution," modern (socialist) industrialization nonetheless remained a cherished communist

Figure 14.1. "The Working Class Must Lead Everything." Mao-era propaganda poster, 1970. Stefen R. Landsberger Collection, International Institute of Social History (Amsterdam).

goal. A Soviet Russian model for the development of heavy industry in China was soon adopted, based on centralized planning and a series of Stalinist-style five-year plans, the first of which was implemented in 1953. Although production statistics from China, particularly those from the Mao era, are not always reliable, this first five-year plan does seem to have unleashed considerable real industrialization. Meanwhile, during another visit to Moscow in 1957 on the occasion of the fortieth anniversary of the Bolshevik revolution, Mao was encouraged by the pioneering launch of the Soviet space satellite Sputnik to declare that "the east wind was prevailing over the west wind." It was possible, then, to believe that communism was ascendant throughout the world and was the inevitable future of all mankind. (See Figure 14.1.) Mao was inspired enough by the Soviets' announced goal of overtaking the U.S. economy in fifteen years to call for China overtaking Great Britain in that same length of time.[6]

The Great Leap Forward and the Cultural Revolution

Mao's visit to Moscow may have also struck a spark of Chinese nationalistic competitive rivalry with the Russians. Mao very soon began to contemplate significant departures from the Soviet Russian model. Mao's flash of originality was the idea that industrialization, and economic takeoff, could be achieved through people power, in the form of mass mobilization of labor through "spontaneous" popular enthusiasm rather than through the introduction of new technologies, capital investment, or elitist technocratic Soviet-style centralized planning. Mao, who was particularly fond of a story about a crazy old man who nonetheless eventually moved an entire mountain, bit by bit, was convinced that if sufficiently motivated and determined, people can achieve seemingly impossible goals. This Maoist faith in the capacity of human willpower to overcome all obstacles underlay what came to be known as the Great Leap Forward, beginning in 1958.

The ability to whip up popular enthusiasm and mobilize mass participation is perhaps the single most distinguishing feature of Mao's approach to politics, and one that makes it distinctly modern – there is nothing very "traditional" about Maoism. In addition to energizing an economic takeoff, the expectation was that Mao's Great Leap Forward would also achieve the transition to genuine communism, because newly organized rural people's communes were to become the basic organizational unit in the countryside. Economies of scale were to be achieved on an industrial, or more especially military, model. Much of the language was specifically militaristic. Farmers were to be organized into production brigades, which were divided into platoons and supervised by battalions. Women, too, were to join the labor force, being liberated from household chores by collective nurseries and mess halls.

The Great Leap Forward was announced in early 1958, the first experimental commune was established in April, and by early autumn nearly all of rural China had been convulsed by a wave of literal communization. For a time, even the most cautious of China's leaders were swept away by Mao's enthusiasm for rapid socialist development. But the Great Leap Forward quickly turned into a great disaster. The most notorious examples of this were the so-called backyard steel furnaces that were intended to double China's steel and iron production in a single year. As many as ninety million people were mobilized for some degree of participation in smelting steel, but because there was no coordinated planning, because most of these people had no experience in steel production, and because their equipment was necessarily hastily improvised, the actual results were disappointing.

Even more serious was the disaster in agriculture. Because private ownership was now forbidden, many farmers apparently simply killed their livestock rather than turn it over to the collective. Many felt little incentive to work hard on the new communal farms. Encouraged to believe that the problem now would be what to do with overproduction, and diverted and exhausted by various other mobilization campaigns, farmers sometimes allowed crops to rot unharvested in the fields. In other cases, the yields themselves were meager because of excessive faith in an idea that planting seeds deeper and closer together would increase production. The law of unintended consequences also took its toll: for example, a massive Maoist campaign to kill sparrows, as pests, led to plagues of insects that had previously been eaten by those sparrows. Other Maoist mass mobilization campaigns caused deforestation, soil erosion, and environmental damage. Although the Great Leap Forward began in early 1958 amid great popular enthusiasm, by fall 1958 serious shortages were already becoming apparent. It is now estimated that at least fifteen million people – and possibly a great many more – died of malnutrition during the famine caused by the Great Leap Forward in the years 1958–1962.[7]

Because Mao sometimes encouraged constructive criticism, but also sometimes lashed out unpredictably at anyone who disagreed with him, the people around him were reluctant to tell him anything he did not want to hear. Natural human ambition to always appear successful may have also contributed an incentive to submit glowing false reports. It should be remembered, too, that this was still a China that was largely pre-television and pre-telephone (to say nothing of pre-Internet) – a land where communications were still very poorly developed. Almost no one at the time seems to have fully comprehended the true extent of the disaster, but it was nonetheless soon clear that something had gone wrong, and even Mao came to endorse more realistic corrective measures – but not happily.

At a party meeting held at a retreat on Lu Mountain (Lushan) in 1959, the defense minister, a hero of the Korean War, dared to offer a critique, in a private letter to Mao, of the Great Leap Forward as a violation of the basic laws of economics. Mao had this criticism publicly circulated at the meeting, and denounced it. Even as the hardships caused by the Great Leap Forward were becoming unmistakable, Mao's prestige was still unchallengeable. Mao won this showdown, and the defense minister was purged as a "bourgeois element." Mao did, however, step down as the head of the Chinese government (while retaining his more powerful position as chairman of the Communist Party), and more pragmatic leaders did begin to introduce measures to restore the economy. Over the next few years, Mao was seen so seldom in public that some observers in the West began to speculate that he might even be dead.

But Mao was not dead, and he was apparently growing suspicious that "revisionists" and "capitalist roaders" (contemporary jargon for persons taking the road that led away from socialism back to capitalism) in high positions in the PRC were sabotaging his revolution. This suspicion set the stage for Mao's next, and last, great campaign, which is known as the Great Proletarian Cultural Revolution.[8] The prelude to this Cultural Revolution actually began with a theatrical play about an historical Ming Dynasty official who was dismissed by a despotic emperor, written by a certain vice mayor of Beijing, which was widely interpreted as a thinly veiled allegorical criticism of Mao (as the despotic emperor). Mao responded by orchestrating a campaign to criticize the play, forcing its author to publish a self-criticism and confession by the end of 1965.

By spring 1966, Mao, his wife, and a circle of radical followers were encouraging young students to take to the streets to promote a Maoist vision of revolution. Mao famously told the students, "it is right to rebel." Many of the students organized themselves into groups called Red Guards, the first of which appeared at a Beijing middle school in May 1966. By June, classes in China's schools had been suspended, and millions of students were released to join the action. They were given free rail transportation, and many went to Beijing in the hope of catching a glimpse of the "big red sun," Chairman Mao.

To the extent that the Cultural Revolution was cultural, it represented a rejection of the old feudal (i.e., traditional) and bourgeois (i.e., Western) influences in art, literature, and culture generally (including such things as Western-style haircuts and cosmetics for women), and an attempt to replace these with a new socialist culture, of which the repeated performance of a handful of approved revolutionary model operas was perhaps the most conspicuous example. The main thrust of the Cultural Revolution may be viewed, however, as a power struggle through which Mao intended to regain control over the direction of his revolution.

On July 17, 1966, the seventy-three-year-old Mao Zedong electrified the youth of China by swimming several miles down the Yangzi River. He then returned north to Beijing to attack the party leadership in a Central Committee meeting on July 21. Persons in leadership positions throughout China who were not perceived as being sufficiently Maoist were denounced and publicly struggled against, with the Red Guards serving as the shock troops in this attack. Most prominent among the victims were the president of the PRC (the head of China's government) and another senior leader named Deng Xiaoping. By 1968, the president of the People's Republic had been formally expelled from the Communist Party. He died of pneumonia the following year, in 1969, an "enemy of the people" lying naked on his cement prison floor.[9] The other top-ranking target of the Cultural Revolution, Deng Xiaoping, was comparatively fortunate. He, too, was purged, and endured three years of struggle sessions and solitary confinement, before three more years of internal exile under house arrest working in a tractor repair factory in southeast China.[10] But Deng survived, was eventually rehabilitated, and made a historic comeback.

The Cultural Revolution brought a radical shakeup of the power structure in the People's Republic of China. By 1969, almost half of the original Politburo members and more than half of the original Central Committee members had been purged. However, ever more radical Red Guard factions were also dragging China ever deeper into chaos. Increasingly, there was actual combat between armed factions. Finally, beginning in September 1967, Mao called on the People's Liberation Army to step in and restore order. Beginning in 1968, and continuing until Mao's death in 1976, more than twelve million students were "sent down" to remote rural villages. This was intended both to break up the student concentrations and to acquaint elitist student intellectuals with a taste of hard peasant life. By now, the active phase of the Cultural Revolution was over.

Nixon and Mao

Meanwhile, ironically enough, changing world conditions were leading to a dramatic thaw in relations between the United States and China. Mao had once dismissed U.S. "imperialism" as a "paper tiger" (ferocious looking but harmless) and leaned toward the Soviet Union, but his relationship with Joseph Stalin had also always been distant and rocky, and after Stalin died in 1953, China's relations with the Soviet Union deteriorated rapidly. Beijing denounced the Soviets for revisionism and betrayal of the revolution, while Moscow criticized ultra-radical Chinese Maoists for their extremism. In 1960, there was a complete rupture, and the Soviets withdrew all aid and advisors from China. In 1962, the Soviets supported the Indian side in a minor war between India and China. In 1968, Moscow sent troops into Czechoslovakia and openly asserted Moscow's right to intervene in, and the limited independent sovereignty of, other countries within the Socialist bloc. By this time, the Russians also seemed to be the dominant external supporters of the communist cause in Vietnam, to China's south. The Chinese therefore increasingly felt surrounded with, and threatened by, Russians.

To the north, China and the Soviet Union shared the longest land border in the world – some 4,150 miles. Along this frontier there was a massive Soviet military buildup, with the number of Soviet divisions deployed along the border with China increasing from twenty-five in 1969 to forty-five in 1973. During these years, there were a large number of border incidents, the most serious of which occurred in March 1969 at Damansky Island (called Zhenbao in Chinese) in the Ussuri River, which separates northeastern Manchuria from the Soviet Union. This appears to have begun when the Chinese opened fire in retaliation for an alleged insult to a portrait of Mao, killing some sixty Soviet soldiers. The Soviets responded by introducing tanks and heavy artillery and pounding away at the island and the Chinese shore. A few weeks later, when the Soviet premier tried to telephone Mao Zedong, the Chinese operator hung up on him and would not put his call through.[11] Around this time, Moscow seems to have seriously contemplated waging a preemptive war against China, especially to take out fledgling Chinese nuclear facilities. In view of all these developments, by 1969 many of China's leaders had come to view the Soviet Union as a greater military threat to China than the United States. The preconditions were therefore set on the Chinese side for détente, or a relaxation of tensions, with the United States.

On the American side, the United States had continued to recognize Chiang Kai-shek's Republic of China on the island of Taiwan as the only legitimate government of all China ever since 1949. There were no direct communications between the United States and the PRC (although, after 1954, representatives of the United States and the People's Republic did conduct some limited negotiations in third countries, notably in Warsaw in communist Poland, concerning such pressing issues as exchanges of prisoners of war), and Americans were flatly not permitted to travel to mainland China. In 1969, moreover, the United States had a new president, Richard M. Nixon (1913–1994), who had built much of his early career on vigorous opposition to communism. Nixon was also, however, a brilliant geopolitical realist. As would become clear later, breaking the ice with China was a magnificently effective strategic gambit in Washington's global Cold War rivalry with Moscow. In addition, the United States was then deeply mired in an unpopular war in Vietnam. China appeared to be the only country that might be able to provide some leverage to help the United States extricate itself from Vietnam – and a breakthrough with China would, in any case, shift the spotlight from the unfortunate situation in Vietnam to a new American diplomatic triumph.

Both Mao and Nixon were therefore ready to relax the Sino-American confrontation, and an opportunity presented itself in 1971 in the form of so-called ping-pong diplomacy. During the most feverish years of the Cultural Revolution, China had simply not participated in international athletic events. With Mao's approval, however, a Chinese team attended the 1971 World Table Tennis Championship being held in Japan. Friendly relations between the U.S. and Chinese ping-pong

Figure 14.2. U.S. president Richard M. Nixon meets Chairman Mao Zedong, February 29, 1972. The Nixon Library at College Park/National Archives.

teams prompted an invitation (with top-level approval) to the American team to visit China. A year later, the Chinese team reciprocated with a visit to the United States – becoming the first visitors to America from mainland China in twenty-three years.

Secret negotiations between the Nixon administration and Beijing began, and for a stunning week in February 1972, President Nixon went to China (see Figure 14.2).[12] Aside from the deep ideological divide between communist China and capitalist America, the biggest and most thorny diplomatic issue was the problem of Taiwan. Both Beijing and Taipei (the capital of Taiwan, where Chiang Kai-shek was still alive and still president at the time of the Nixon trip) insisted that they were the only legitimate government of all China. The United States managed to sidestep this impasse in the formal document that resulted from Nixon's visit, known as the Shanghai Communiqué. This document acknowledged that Chinese people on both Taiwan and the mainland agreed that there is only one China and that Taiwan is a part of it, and asserted that the American concern was merely that this issue be settled peacefully by the Chinese people themselves. The Shanghai Communiqué also affirmed the American intention of progressively withdrawing U.S. military forces from Taiwan.

Despite this breakthrough in 1972, the United States did not officially switch recognition from the Republic of China on Taiwan (Taipei) to the PRC on the mainland (Beijing) until 1979. Even after that, the U.S. Congress, which does not always docilely follow the lead of the White House, passed a new Taiwan Relations

Act committing the United States to a high level of continued support for Taiwan (despite official U.S. nonrecognition after 1979). Nonetheless, the 1970s marked the beginning of a new era of friendly feelings between the United States and China.

Deng Xiaoping and Market-Based Economic Reform

This was a People's Republic of China, moreover, that was also now rapidly beginning to be transformed almost beyond recognition. On September 9, 1976, Chairman Mao Zedong, who had long been ill with Lou Gehrig's disease, died. In the wake of Mao's death, there was an alleged attempt by Mao's wife and three of her ultra-radical colleagues – the Gang of Four – to seize power. Instead, however, senior military figures staged a preemptive countercoup. On the night of October 6, elite troops from the State Council Home Guard and PLA unit 8341 – commanded by Mao's own former personal body guard – arrested the Gang of Four in their homes in the Communist Party leadership compound known as Zhongnanhai, adjacent to the old imperial palace in Beijing. There was apparently some fighting involving the Workers' Militia in Shanghai, but the Workers' Militia in Beijing surrendered without a struggle, and the coup succeeded fairly smoothly, although it was not publicly announced for several weeks.[13]

Power therefore passed not to Mao's wife and the Gang of Four but to Mao's own hand-picked successor, Hua Guofeng (1921–2008). Hua was a still relatively young man who had been plucked out of relative obscurity during the Cultural Revolution, and his mandate was therefore based almost entirely on continuing Mao's legacy. Mao's alleged deathbed testimonial, "With you in charge, I'm at ease," was heavily publicized in his support. The problem with relying on Mao's legacy, however, was that after the Cultural Revolution and Mao's death, China was swept with a wave of disillusionment and something of an inevitable counter-reaction. Over time, some three million people who had been purged during the Cultural Revolution were restored to public life. Horror stories of some of the worst excesses of the Cultural Revolution, called the "literature of the wounded," were publicly aired. The senior surviving victim of the Cultural Revolution, Deng Xiaoping – who had joined the Chinese Communist Party (CCP) in the 1920s, participated in the Long March, and been one of the top PRC leaders in 1950s – was not only still alive but also already promoting a relatively appealing program of economic and technological reform.

The Gang of Four, rather than Mao himself (who continued to receive a more qualified public veneration), were blamed for most of the excesses of the Cultural Revolution and placed on a televised show trial. Mao's wife, a former actress, put up a spirited self-defense but was condemned anyway and spent the rest of her life in prison. By 1978, Deng Xiaoping, representing the economic reform faction, had risen to supreme power. Partly because of a conscious desire to avoid a Mao-style cult of personality and to promote a more collective decision-making process (and perhaps also partly because he was constrained by other senior leaders), Deng did not take any top offices or titles for himself, but from this time until his death in

1997 Deng was China's acknowledged paramount leader. Despite his stature, however, Deng never enjoyed the kind of concentrated prestige and power that Mao had once wielded. There remained considerable differences of opinion among China's top leaders, and even for the reformers it was still necessary to cautiously feel their way forward.

The goal of the economic reformers was, very simply, to raise China's standard of living. They had no particular sweeping master plan for achieving this, though, and one of their slogans famously compared reform to wading "across a river by groping for stones." They proceeded, necessarily, through improvisation, and the economic reforms actually began with unauthorized local initiatives in the agricultural sector. In 1979, one commune responded to a drought situation by drawing up individual contracts and basing pay on productivity. The practice quickly spread, despite some criticism from local Communist Party leaders, and turned into a general nationwide abandonment of the communes and a return to the family farm, or individual household, as the basic agricultural unit (although not to actual private property ownership of the land, which remained collectively owned).

Reform of the state-run industrial sector presented a much more complicated problem. China's leaders were especially reluctant to throw large numbers of workers out of their jobs by closing down even the most unproductive state-run factories. It was easier simply to authorize new enterprises outside the existing state-run sector – but the surging growth of this new entrepreneurship then quickly threatened to overwhelm the state-run share. By about 1992, China had become a predominantly market economy. Beginning in 1997, within a five-year period, China actually did lay off more than twenty-five million workers from state-owned enterprises, as it tackled the thorny problem of market-based economic reform. By the early twenty-first century, the former China bureau chief of the *Financial Times* could actually marvel that "China today is a great deal less socialist than any country in Europe."[14]

For orthodox communists, some form of collective ownership of the means of production is supposed to be fundamental. The Chinese translation of the (originally European) word *communism – gongchan-zhuyi* – literally means "collective production-ism." This emphasis on collective ownership was partly an egalitarian ideal, but, theoretically at least, large-scale collective ownership might also enable comprehensive centralized planning and enormous economies of scale, and seemingly did have a rational "scientific" aspect. In historical practice, however, the performance of communist economies in the twentieth century was fairly uniformly less than spectacular, and Deng Xiaoping and the Chinese reformers were open to experimentation. Deng's most distinguishing personal characteristic was pragmatism: he was widely quoted in the English-language press as saying that it does not matter whether a cat is black or white as long as it catches mice, and "seek truth through facts" (*shishi qiu shi*) became the slogan that the reformers themselves heavily promoted in China. Market forces, the pursuit of profit, and even stock exchanges gradually became tolerated. To the extent that some Marxist theoretical justification was still necessary for such apparently capitalist behavior, it came to be argued that because China was still only in the "initial stages of socialism," a little capitalism was only to be expected.[15]

Serious interest in Marxism has, in any case, largely melted away in China since Mao's death. It remains significant, nonetheless, that the new market economy emerged "not *on the ruins*" of communism – sweepingly replacing it – but from within the ruins. New developments were partially shaped by preexisting institutions, habits, and expectations, in an ongoing evolutionary process.[16] As one consequence, actual legal private ownership of property has been slow to develop in China. Many of the new skyscrapers in Shanghai, for example, were built by Hong Kong investors who merely leased the land from the municipal government, which still owned it. Perhaps the most glaringly peculiar historical legacy is that, in the new market-based economy, a third of private business owners in China are now Communist Party members, and even though it became common to joke that the acronym CCP really should now stand for "Chinese Capitalist Party," the (still so-called) Communist Party does remain the sole ruling party.

Outside critics initially objected that China's gradual, piecemeal, hybrid approach to economic reform could not possibly succeed, comparing it to trying to leap over the Grand Canyon in series of small jumps rather than one big leap, but in practice it actually seems to have been more effective than the big-bang sudden shock therapy reform that was attempted in the former Soviet Union, where gross domestic product (GDP) actually contracted sharply after the initial privatization in the 1990s. According to American Central Intelligence Agency (CIA) estimates of purchasing power parity, by 2014 the real size of China's GDP was almost five times that of Russia's, although the Russian economy had originally been much more developed.[17] (China, of course, also has a much larger population than Russia, and per capita GDP in Russia remains significantly higher than in China.)

In terms of sheer economic growth, the market-based reforms in China since 1978 have been spectacularly successful. Although most Chinese people remain poor by the standards of the world's most developed countries, hundreds of millions of Chinese people have been lifted out of the direst poverty, and China's major cities have been utterly transformed. By the end of the twentieth century, China had more television sets than any other country in the world. By the start of the twenty-first century, in 2001, China had the most cell phones in the world. There is now far more Internet use in China than in any other country, and in December 2008 China passed the United States to become the world's largest market for new automobile sales.

The reasons for China's rapid economic takeoff were chiefly the relaxation of central controls; a widespread and obsessive focus on economic growth and money-making; a huge, relatively well-educated, supply of comparatively low-wage labor; and foreign investment. Opening up to foreign trade and investment was critical. Under Chairman Mao, Marxist theories concerning the economic function of imperialism had combined with the memory of a century of perceived national humiliation at the hands of foreigners to put a high priority on national self-sufficiency and independence – and corresponding isolationism. That independence and isolationism then shut China out of the opportunities for export-led economic growth that became a major reason for the economic "miracles" elsewhere in non-communist East Asia. Under Deng Xiaoping, China opened up again.

Indeed, one significant difference between China in the era of market-based economic reform and the developmental state model as seen in Japan and South Korea may actually be China's greater openness to foreign investment. Both Japan and South Korea had promoted exports while simultaneously keeping direct foreign investment in their own domestic economies limited. As of 2003, the foreign direct investment to GDP ratio in China was 35 percent, compared to only 2 percent in Japan. One possibly negative consequence for China of this heavy reliance on direct foreign investment, though, is that an estimated 70 percent of all the value added to China's exports accrues to foreign component makers, brand owners, distributors, and others. Much of the profits, in other words, go to foreigners.[18]

In some respects, post-Mao China ironically seems to be returning to China's late nineteenth and early twentieth-century pattern, even down to the reappearance of something like the old treaty ports in the modified new form of Special Economic Zones (SEZs). Four of these SEZs were initially approved in 1979 (Shenzhen, Shantou, Zhuhai, and Xiamen, all in the southeast), on the model of export processing zones elsewhere in East Asia (such as those established in Taiwan beginning in 1966), offering low taxes and other economic incentives. The SEZ at Shenzhen, near Hong Kong, in particular, then exploded from rural rice paddies into a bustling city that is now home to perhaps fifteen million people.

China's new openness brought in not only foreign investment but also foreign ideas. To hard-line critics, reformers explained that when a window is opened it is impossible to prevent a few flies from coming in too. Many Chinese people actively welcomed the fresh air, however. For some, this rediscovery of the outside world was an exciting time of new possibilities. If the May Fourth era in the early twentieth century had been China's first great experience with Westernization, this was the beginning of a second burst of enthusiasm. But, if "science and democracy" had been the original May Fourth slogan, it was now the science half of the equation that was emphasized. Science has been embraced as a guide to modernization in post-Mao China, and China since 1978 has actively "become a technocracy," where most middle- and top-level leaders have technical training in either engineering or the natural sciences. Amazingly, at the start of the twenty-first century, every single one of China's highest leaders – the nine members of the Politburo Standing Committee – were trained engineers. One of the first concrete results of this new faith in Western-style science, ironically, turned out to be China's controversial one-child policy, which was literally advocated by rocket scientists beginning in the late 1970s.[19]

China's economic growth has been largely fueled by new investment rather than dramatic improvements in productivity. China's level of efficiency in the use of resources such as oil and water has remained low compared with advanced industrialized nations, and China's prohibition of independent labor unions has also helped keep wages low. As a consequence, China's undeniable economic success has also been accompanied by some highly unattractive features such as sweatshops, official corruption, and horrific environmental pollution.

In 2007, China passed the United States to become the world's largest emitter of greenhouse gases. Corruption and abuses of authority have become endemic. To mention only one case, in 2004 some ten thousand farmers in Fujian Province signed petitions calling for the dismissal of local officials. In one of the affected townships, it appears that land use compensation amounting to 240 million *yuan* had been diverted by officials, without consulting the farmers, for the construction of a new technological zone rather than being distributed among the people who had previously tilled the land. In compensation, the farmers were given only 800 *yuan* per year as a dividend and an additional 840 *yuan* per year to purchase the food they could no longer grow themselves on their no-longer-available farmland.[20]

If the economic reforms opened up new entrepreneurial opportunities for some people, they also took away most of the old guarantees for others. China's Mao-era social safety nets quickly evaporated. Rapid urbanization also created a huge underclass of migrant workers, who often face discrimination and harsh working and living conditions. It is also alleged that gender discrimination has actually gotten worse under the market-based reforms, as old patriarchal prejudices revived. Women were often the first to be laid off by unprofitable state industries and the last to be hired for attractive new employment opportunities (while the less desirable sweatshops, on other hand, often preferred to employ young girls). In 1978, on the eve of the market-based reforms, more than 11 percent of the Central Committee members and their alternates had been women, but by 1994, the proportion of women at that level of power had fallen to only 7.5 percent.[21]

Meanwhile, the era of good feelings between China and the United States that was ushered in by President Nixon's visit in 1972 had come under new strains, including a growing trade imbalance, U.S. concern that China was helping Pakistan develop nuclear weapons, and a newly emerging concern for human rights issues. The fall of the Berlin Wall in 1989 and subsequent collapse of the Soviet Union terminated the Cold War anti-Soviet convergence of strategic interests between China and the United States, and the almost simultaneous Tiananmen massacre in Beijing ended any illusions some Americans may have entertained that China was happily on its way to becoming a capitalist democracy just like the United States.

Tiananmen

After Deng Xiaoping became China's paramount leader, he engineered the installation of a (relatively) younger generation of reformers in China's top offices. In the early 1980s, one of these men, Hu Yaobang (1915–1989), was Deng's designated successor and, as secretary general of the Communist Party, the highest ranking person in China. But, in the winter of 1986–1987, Hu Yaobang was accused by hard-liners of being too sympathetic to student demonstrators and the allegedly insidious influences of "bourgeois liberalization," and Hu was compelled to step down. Hu Yaobang was replaced, however, as secretary general by another reformer and Deng protégé, Zhao Ziyang (1919–2005), and this attempted hard-line crackdown on bourgeois liberalization proved to be somewhat abortive.

On the morning of April 15, 1989, former CCP Secretary General Hu Yaobang unexpectedly died in the hospital following a heart attack. Later that same afternoon, mourners began appearing in Tiananmen Square. Their laments for Hu Yaobang offered a pointed criticism of the hard-liners. As one anonymous couplet that appeared on a poster phrased it,

> Those who should have died live,
> Those who should have lived have died.[22]

By the time of Hu Yaobang's funeral, two hundred thousand student demonstrators had gathered in Tiananmen Square. Their demonstrations continued on after the funeral and increasingly included calls for political reforms to complement the existing market-based economic reforms.

An anonymous *People's Daily* newspaper editorial on April 26 threatened the students with harsh reprisals, but the students responded, instead, with defiance. The next day, students staged a huge march on Tiananmen Square from the university campuses that were mostly located in Beijing's northwestern suburbs. The students broke through police barricades and were cheered on by spectators. On May 4, 1989, there was another particularly large student march on Tiananmen Square in commemoration of the seventieth anniversary of the May Fourth Movement, which had begun with student demonstrations against the Versailles peace treaty at Tiananmen in 1919. One Uighur student read a "New May Fourth Manifesto" in the square. On May 13, a smaller group of students began a permanent occupation of the square and a hunger strike. Some of the students claimed that they had consciously chosen to take a nonviolent approach, and a hunger strike was a particularly convincing way of demonstrating self-sacrificing sincerity because it threatened to hurt no one except themselves.

Such massive student demonstrations would have been potent symbols at any time, but their effect was incalculably magnified now because they happened to coincide with the first Sino-Soviet summit meeting in three decades. On May 16, the leader of the Soviet Union arrived in Beijing from Moscow, trailed by over a thousand foreign journalists. As a result of all the world media attention, the student demonstrations in Tiananmen Square became the best-covered political event in the history of the PRC (at least until the 2008 Beijing Olympics). By May 17, there were a million demonstrators in the hundred-acre Tiananmen Square, and their demonstrations completely upstaged the supposedly historic Sino-Soviet summit.

On May 18, Secretary General Zhao Ziyang visited some student hunger strikers recovering in a Beijing hospital and assured them that "the aims of the Party and government are the same as your aims." But, at a meeting of party elders and top officials that very same day, Deng Xiaoping pointedly asked, "What other country in the world would watch more than a month of marches and demonstrations in its capital and do nothing about it?" A decision was reached at that meeting to impose martial law.[23] After the Sino-Soviet summit meeting and the departure of the Russian leader, live satellite television broadcasts were terminated, and on May 20 martial law was formally declared. An ultimatum was issued to the demonstrators: disperse immediately, or be dispersed by force. When troops attempted to move toward the square, however, they were stopped by human barricades formed by the citizens of Beijing. One column of soldiers even turned around, its commanding officer promising never to return. This first attempt to use the army to clear the square had failed.

At the time, many people within the Communist Party itself were sympathetic to the students. It has been claimed that as many as eight hundred thousand Communist Party members actively participated in demonstrations in 123 cities in China in 1989.[24] Sympathizers included even the officially highest-ranking person in China, the secretary general of the Communist Party Zhao Ziyang. Zhao did not attend the meeting declaring martial law, and he eventually went in person to the square, where, shedding tears, he admitted that he had come too late. On May 25, the CCP Secretary General Zhao Ziyang was placed under house arrest, where he remained until his death in 2005.[25]

Student grievances in 1989 included, especially, criticism of widespread official corruption, the often numbing bureaucratic arbitrariness of life in the PRC, the stifling lack of personal freedoms, and frustration with a reform process that had apparently stalled. One student-specific motivation was the fact that college-educated professionals in China at that time were still being assigned jobs by the state, at fixed state salaries. Many students wanted the freedom to choose their careers for themselves. The 1980s were also a time of revived May Fourth-style fascination with Western things. The *Goddess of Democracy* statue that was erected in Tiananmen Square was inspired by, although not an exact copy of, the American *Statue of Liberty*. One of the banners hung in Tiananmen Square proclaimed, "Give me liberty or give me death," which is an obvious allusion to the American Revolution. A Western-influenced rock-and-roll song, Cui Jian's (1961–) "I Have Nothing" (*Yi wu suoyou*), became the "unofficial anthem" of the Tiananmen demonstrations. At the time, someone also even publicly (though anonymously) observed that the inevitable death of capitalism predicted by Karl Marx a century earlier had not only not happened yet, but that the capitalist countries "have turned out to be remarkably healthy," whereas those countries that had taken the socialist cure were "feeling listless and sick to the marrow of their bones."[26]

These were the critical final years when the Cold War was drawing to a close, and there were nearly simultaneous democracy movements in several other parts of the world. "People power" successfully brought down the Filipino dictator Ferdinand Marcos in 1986, student demonstrations in South Korea led to a democratic presidential election in 1987, and in that same year Taiwan repealed martial law and legalized the formation of opposition parties, becoming a genuine multi-party democracy. In 1989, the Berlin Wall fell, beginning the unraveling of the Soviet bloc in Eastern Europe and the collapse of the Soviet Union. But the 1989 Tiananmen Square demonstrations in China ended very differently.

The Australian scholar Geremie Barmé has argued that extremists on both sides shouted down more moderate voices, eliminating the possibility of a compromise and making violent confrontation increasingly unavoidable. One student leader allegedly confessed to a desire for the creation of martyrs, telling an American journalist on May 28:

> My fellow students keep asking me, "what should we do next?" ... I feel so sad, because how can I tell them that what we are actually hoping for is bloodshed.... Only when the square is awash with blood will the people of China open their eyes. Only then will they really be united. But how can I explain any of this to my fellow students?[27]

On the government side, senior leaders were already looking at developments in Eastern Europe as a negative example that they wanted to avoid in China. Deng Xiaoping, who had been a principal target of Red Guard student activism during the Cultural Revolution in the 1960s, distrusted student movements. Deng was a reformer and a pragmatist, but he was also a lifelong communist and former close associate of Mao Zedong, not a liberal democrat. He had previously even been Mao Zedong's chosen instrument to lead the notorious anti-rightist crackdown in 1957. Mao perceptively once compared Deng to "a ball of cotton with a pin inside."[28] Above all else, senior Communist leaders, including Deng Xiaoping, were determined to maintain control.

In the darkness of early Sunday morning, June 4, thousands of fully armed combat troops from the Twenty-Seventh Army, brought in from outside of Beijing for this purpose, and backed by mainline battle tanks and armored personnel carriers, assaulted Tiananmen Square. Around 1:00 A.M., an armored personnel carrier toppled the *Goddess of Democracy* statue, and at 4:30 A.M., the remaining students, after taking a voice vote, withdrew from the square. Hundreds – perhaps thousands – of people had been killed (nearly all of them in the approaches to Tiananmen Square rather than in the square itself), and in the aftermath, the city seethed with discontent, as tanks ominously patrolled the boulevards. For a time, China appeared poised on the brink of civil war.

Debate within the highest reaches of the Communist Party continued until June 7, when a resolution was reached to expel so-called counterrevolutionary elements. On June 8, the Twenty-Seventh Army was pulled out of Beijing, and on June 9, the New China News Agency was able to report that all seven major military zones in China had declared their support for the decision to crack down. The danger of civil war had been avoided, and the CCP had reasserted control. But the cost was high. Many Western observers concluded that the massacre had stripped the CCP of all shreds of legitimacy. Certainly the pervasive image of China's government in American public opinion for a long time after 1989 was one of brutal repression. Since 1989, in China itself, however, the Communist Party has managed to stay in power, suppress unwelcome memories, restart the market-based economic reforms, and deliver surging prosperity. By 2008, a Pew Research Center survey even found that China's rate of popular national satisfaction was the highest in the world, with 86 percent of the Chinese people expressing satisfaction with the direction of their country.[29]

Greater China

China's economic development has been fueled by foreign investment, but a surprising peculiarity of this foreign investment is that much of it – by some estimates perhaps as much as 80 percent – has come from Chinese people.[30] There are approximately fifty million overseas Chinese (*Huaqiao*) who live scattered around the world, in neither the PRC nor the Republic of China on Taiwan, and who have been important sources of investment in China. In some cases, also, there have been PRC-born people who lived abroad long enough to obtain foreign passports or residency permits that, somewhat artificially, qualified them for privileged treatment as "foreign" investors in China. In addition, though, and most pertinently, there are three predominantly Chinese areas lying outside the mainland PRC that together comprise a kind of Greater China: Taiwan, Hong Kong, and Singapore. British colonial Hong Kong, especially, proved critical to the early stages of China's market-based reforms, serving as China's single largest source of foreign direct investment. After Hong Kong reverted to Chinese rule in 1997, Taiwan then replaced it as the major source of foreign investment. Singapore, although more distant and less directly relevant, also merits mention.

Greater China and the overseas Chinese have provided an often underappreciated "secret weapon" in China's economic takeoff. As Chinese-language speakers who have ancestral ties to China, they enjoy certain natural advantages in doing business there. Greater China has a dynamic synergy that is, furthermore, not merely limited to economic activity but also has cultural dimensions. For example, in 1989, nine out of the ten top hit songs in Shanghai came from either Hong Kong or Taiwan.[31] Despite such cultural cross-fertilization, however, all four of these Chinese places – the PRC, Taiwan, Hong Kong, and Singapore – are also significantly different from each other, making them interesting places to explore in their own right.

Singapore

Singapore is the most remote from the PRC of these three predominantly Chinese places, occupying land geographically located in Southeast Asia that has never been part of any country based on mainland China. Singapore also has a larger proportion of non-Chinese people in its population mix than any of the others. Singapore is, accordingly, frequently not even mentioned in discussions of Greater China. Still, about three-quarters of the people in Singapore are ethnic Chinese; Singapore has sometimes been explicitly held up in China as a model for the post-Mao PRC; and since the 1990s, large numbers of Chinese officials have visited Singapore for training. Although it is more peripheral than either Hong Kong or Taiwan, therefore, Singapore is not entirely irrelevant. It is also a spectacularly successful modern place, with a per capita GDP substantially higher than the United States.

Singapore's importance derives mostly from geography. Singapore is located on a tiny island, some twenty-six by seventeen miles in total area, lying at the southern tip of the Malay peninsula. There, it occupies a strategic position dominating the narrow straits of water between the peninsula and the Indonesian island of

Sumatra, which has been a key gateway for shipping coming from the west into the Pacific Ocean for nearly two thousand years. Thanks to this commercial traffic, Singapore is today the world's second busiest container port, after Shanghai. But this now flourishing island was almost entirely uninhabited when the British East India Company first established a base there in 1819.

As the British gradually incorporated Malaya into their empire, large numbers of Chinese people, together with somewhat smaller numbers of Indians, moved into the region to participate in its economic development. After World War II, as part of the general worldwide postwar decolonization movement, British Malaya gained independence in 1957. The problem was that by this time ethnic Chinese were an absolute majority of the population, rather than the supposedly native Malays. The resulting ethnic tensions were severe. Because the Chinese population was especially concentrated in the city of Singapore, these tensions were partially resolved by allowing Singapore to split from Malaysia in 1965, becoming an independent city-state.

Even after independence, Singapore still faced serious challenges. It was necessary to forge a new national identity for an entirely new, and very small, country with a mixed, although majority Chinese, population. The economic outlook was also uncertain on an island where the British naval base had previously been the largest employer. Through low taxes, a strategic location, a skilled and hardworking English-speaking population (English is the only language that all the multiethnic Singaporeans are expected to be able to speak in common, although a local hybrid jokingly called Singlish has emerged in practice on the street), and the embrace of international trade, Singapore prospered. Yet, despite the boast of Singapore's first prime minster that he took Singapore "from third world to first," Singapore had actually already been relatively wealthy even before independence.[32] Singapore's prosperity was rooted in a lengthy British colonial prehistory of active participation in world trade, which was then modified after the end of British rule to include a particularly active new role for government. If markets and global capitalism were essential components in Singapore's success story after independence, Singapore also had a notably interventionist government. "Singapore," it has been said, "is prominent as a country where planning succeeded."[33]

Singapore became arguably the most Westernized place in Southeast Asia, yet it also, paradoxically, became something of a self-conscious spokesman for so-called "Asian values," and a leading example of allegedly Confucian benevolent authoritarianism. An antiseptic, relatively crime-free environment was achieved through notoriously strict measures, such as a stiff $50 (U.S. equivalent) fine for spitting in public, a fine for not flushing public toilets after use, a long-standing (though now somewhat modified) prohibition on chewing gum, a ban on nudity, and a particularly high rate of capital punishment. Despite maintaining many of the forms of political democracy, moreover, an internal security act that was intended to suppress the threat of communism also suppressed most other political opposition to the ruling People's Action Party (PAP). The PAP enjoyed a total monopoly on seats in parliament until 1991, and thereafter continued to limit political opposition to token levels. It is, perhaps, little wonder that Singapore has some-times been invoked as a model by certain leaders of the post-Mao PRC.

Despite the authoritarianism, as of 2014, the World Bank ranked Singapore the number one easiest place in the world to do business, and the free-enterprise-oriented Heritage Foundation named Singapore the second freest economy in the world in 2015.[34] This is clearly a technocratic government that facilitates rather than hinders business. And, in the 2011 elections, although the ruling People's Action Party retained eighty-one of eighty-seven seats in parliament, it did so with only 60 percent of the vote – an unprecedented setback for the ruling party. Although there were predictions that Singapore's future might become less authoritarian, especially after the death in 2015 of its first prime minister and longtime elder statesman Lee Kuan Yew (1923–2015; Prime Minister 1959–1990), however, the ruling party actually regained some of its support in the September 2015 elections, winning 70 percent of the vote and eighty-three of eighty-nine seats in parliament.

Hong Kong

According to the Heritage Foundation, the world's number one freest economy is Hong Kong, for the twenty-first consecutive year in 2015. Hong Kong is a bustling bastion of capitalism and cosmopolitanism. It enjoys a longer average life expect-ancy than the United States, and is a member of that exclusive club of territories with the world's highest per capita incomes. But Hong Kong is also now officially a Special Administrative Region (SAR) of the PRC.

Hong Kong (in Mandarin, *Xiang'gang*, "Fragrant Harbor"), like Singapore, began life as a British colony. In the early nineteenth century there had been literally almost nothing on the island, apart from a scattering of Chinese villagers. When Hong Kong Island was originally won from China at the time of the first Opium War in 1842, it was still such an empty rock that the British foreign secretary, Lord Palmerston, notoriously dismissed the apparently worthless acqui-sition as "a barren island, which will never be a mart of trade."[35] To the original island, Kowloon peninsula (on the mainland across from the island) was added in 1860, and in 1898, an additional 365.5 square miles were leased for ninety-nine years, which came to be known as the New Territories.

Soon after the British acquisition, Chinese people began migrating there in large numbers in search of economic opportunity. Today, Chinese people make up some 95 percent of Hong Kong's total population. Aside from its splendid natural harbor, Hong Kong's initial importance derived mostly from its location, across from Portuguese Macao and near the mouth of the river that leads up to Guang-zhou (Canton), which had been the only Chinese port open to Western shipping. But Guangzhou lost its exclusive monopoly on Western maritime trade at the very moment the British first acquired Hong Kong. Therefore, although British Hong Kong always fared well enough, for the first century of British rule it remained of secondary importance in China – even for the British – to the great treaty port of

Map 14.2 Guangzhou, Hong Kong, and Macao

Shanghai. As Lord Kadoorie once observed, comparing Hong Kong to Shanghai in the days before World War II, Hong Kong was "a nice quiet little place."[36]

That all changed in 1949 when mainland China retreated into self-imposed Maoist isolation. Shanghai moldered for decades after 1949, and much of its business talent fled. Some went to New York, some to Taiwan, and some to various other places, but a disproportionate number came to Hong Kong. Hong Kong remains even today very much an in-migrant society – at the start of the twenty-first century, only about half the people in Hong Kong had actually been born there – although these in-migrants are overwhelmingly Chinese and predominantly Cantonese speaking. Some of these in-migrants came with money, some had prior business experience, but they nearly all brought an anxious, energetic drive to succeed. Hong Kong became a particularly fast-paced society, and flourished as a little enclave of capitalism on the shores of Communist China.

Then, after Chairman Mao's death and the onset of Deng Xiaoping's market-based reforms in the late 1970s, Hong Kong found itself uniquely well positioned to serve as the main doorway through which the outside world reentered China. Most foreign investment in China was soon flowing through Hong Kong (even if it did not all originate there), and before long, a majority of Hong Kong factory workers were actually working on the other side of the border in new factories built in the People's Republic. Much of neighboring Guangdong Province and the Pearl River delta were rapidly transformed into a giant extension of Hong Kong, and Hong Kong entered now into its greatest boom era. Even while still a British colony, per capita income in Hong Kong surpassed that of Great Britain in the 1990s.

Despite Hong Kong's free and prosperous capitalist economy, however, British Hong Kong was not a democracy. There were no elections, and no representative self-government. British Hong Kong was, instead, a direct Crown colony, whose governors – most of them career Foreign Service bureaucrats – were all appointed from London. Recent revelations indicate that British colonial governors had actually contemplated introducing elections as early as the 1950s, but Beijing feared that elections would lead Hong Kong down a path toward permanent independence, and it threatened to invade. The first direct popular democratic election in Hong Kong's history, therefore, was not held until 1991. Those elections were for eighteen of the sixty seats in the relatively weak Legislative Council, the remainder of the seats being either appointed or chosen by professional and industrial groups. The last British colonial governor, Christopher Patten (now Lord Patten, and currently Chancellor of the University of Oxford; 1944–), then came into office in 1992 determined to promote a greater degree of democratization. He succeeded to the extent that by 1995, for the first time, the Legislative Council was wholly elected, though still partially indirectly.[37]

In the meantime, though, people in Hong Kong had always been conscious of living in a "borrowed place," as the famous phrase put it. Although Hong Kong Island had supposedly been awarded to Britain permanently, it had been granted under duress in a moment of Chinese weakness, and remained a sore point in China's memory. The majority of Hong Kong's land area, the New Territories, had merely been leased. That ninety-nine-year lease was due to expire in 1997, and in anticipation of that date, then British Prime Minister Margaret Thatcher (1925–2013) visited Beijing in 1982 in the hope of negotiating an extension. Deng Xiaoping and the Beijing authorities flatly refused to consider any continuation of British administration, however, and the final outcome was a 1984 Sino-British Joint Declaration, under the terms of which all of Hong Kong would revert to Chinese rule at the expiration of the lease. But Beijing also made a significant concession: Hong Kong would become a Special Administrative Region of the People's Republic, and would be allowed to keep its own distinctive capitalist society for at least fifty years, under the formula "one country, two systems" (a formula that PRC authorities also hoped might be used to lure Taiwan back to the motherland).

So, at midnight on June 30, 1997, the Union Jack was brought down for the last time, and 156 years of British colonial rule in Hong Kong finally came to an end. Though officially part of China now, Hong Kong nonetheless does retain a high degree of autonomy. English is still one of its two official languages, the border with the mainland PRC is still monitored, and although pictures of Queen Elizabeth were removed from the coins (paper money in Hong Kong, as befits such a showcase of private capitalism, is issued by banks rather than by the government) Hong Kong retains its own separate money system, known as the Hong Kong dollar.

Since 1997, Hong Kong has generally continued to become ever more prosperous, and it remains a uniquely cosmopolitan success story: "Asia's World City," a place where you can find British-style double-decker buses, a large Indian merchant community, an impressive Islamic mosque near the heart of the Kowloon tourist district, a distinctive local Cantonese version of Chinese cuisine (featuring such delicacies as *dim sum*), and even a Disneyland. As a still relatively free society, Google Internet searches in Hong Kong are uncensored, and Hong Kong is the only place in China today where the Tiananmen massacre can be openly commemorated.

The partially democratic governing system that had been established during the last decade of British colonial rule also remained roughly intact, and a decision of the Standing Committee of the National People's Congress of the PRC even raised the possibility that beginning in 2017 the Chief Executive (or Head) of Hong Kong's government might for the first time ever be directly elected by a universal suffrage democratic vote. At the end of August 2014, however, PRC officials ruled that all candidates for that upcoming election must first be chosen by a nominating committee. This, in effect, meant that all candidates would be Beijing-approved, and protests against this decision erupted immediately in Hong Kong. Largescale street demonstrations continued for some three months, in a movement that came to be dubbed the "umbrella revolution," because protestors used umbrellas to shield themselves from police teargas. Although the protests eventually ended without directly achieving anything, in June 2015 Beijing's proposed electoral procedures were rejected by Hong Kong when they failed to pass a vote in the Legislative Council. The result is an impasse, and as things currently stand this probably means there will simply be no universal suffrage election at all in 2017. Nearly two decades after Hong Kong returned to Chinese rule in 1997, in any case, Hong Kong is proving difficult for the People's Republic to digest.

Taiwan

In 1974, the last surviving unsurrendered Japanese imperial army soldier from World War II was discovered on a remote Indonesian island in the Pacific, after having hidden in the jungle there for three decades, beginning each day with worship of the Shōwa Emperor. Ironically enough, this ultra-loyal Japanese soldier came originally from Taiwan rather than from one of the Japanese home islands. Nor was he "Taiwanese" as that term is narrowly understood; he was, instead, an aborigine from the Ami tribe on Taiwan. His Japanese name was Nakamura Akio (or Teruo), his Chinese name was Lee Kuang-huei, and his Ami name was Suniyon.[38] His story nicely encapsulates some of the complexities of Taiwan's thorny identity problem.

To compound this complexity, incredible though it may seem, a higher percentage of the population on Taiwan today is actually considered to be ethnic Han Chinese (98%) than on mainland China itself (where, officially, 91.5% of the population is ethnic Chinese, and the real proportion is probably even lower). Taiwan's government still calls itself the Republic of China, it still flies the old national flag of the Chinese Republic, "China Airlines" is still today the English name of Taiwan's national flag carrier, and Taiwan still even uses (although less consistently in recent years) the old Chinese Nationalist calendar that counts all dates from the founding of the Chinese Republic on the mainland in 1912 (making, for example, the year 2000 CE the "eighty-ninth year of the Republic" on Taiwan).

For most of Taiwan's history since 1945, furthermore, it has been ruled by the Chinese Nationalist Party. Because Taiwan never conducted a communist revolution against allegedly "feudal" Chinese traditions (as Maoist mainland China did so strenuously in the 1950s–1970s), an argument can even plausibly be made that Taiwan has maintained more continuity with certain aspects of traditional Chinese culture (notably including religion, respect for Confucian values, and the full form of the Chinese writing system) than the mainland PRC has. In perhaps the ultimate paradox, on Taiwan it was actually illegal to advocate Taiwan's independence (from China) until 1992! Yet, on the other hand, Taiwan has never been a part of the People's Republic of China, and there is a sizable segment of the population on Taiwan that denies that they are Chinese.

This bewildering situation is explained by history. There are aborigines on the island, although today they only make up about 2 percent of the population, essentially for the same reason that there are also still aboriginal populations in many of the remote corners of mainland China. Taiwan was simply one of premodern China's last frontiers. Although Taiwan is only about a hundred miles from the mainland, the area on the mainland adjacent to Taiwan was one of the last parts of China proper to be extensively settled by Chinese people. The Taiwan straits are narrow, but navigating those straits in the age of sail was hazardous, due to shallows, strong currents, and often adverse winds. There are relatively few good natural harbors on Taiwan's west coast, and Taiwan is a mountainous, jungle-covered, tropical and subtropical island with limited appeal to early Chinese settlers. Therefore, although there certainly was some Chinese contact from fairly early times, as late as the mid-sixteenth century Chinese sailors landing on the island to trade with the aborigines reported it "uninhabitable."[39] Obviously, this was an exaggeration: there clearly already were inhabitants, and had been for thousands of years. These were the aborigines, who were themselves culturally diverse, speaking numerous different languages, but with broad linguistic and cultural ties to many of the other island peoples of Southeast Asia.

In the seventeenth century, the Dutch established an outpost on the southwest coast of Taiwan (1624–1662), but the Dutch were soon driven off by independent Ming-loyalist Chinese forces (see Chapter 6). In 1683, this independent Chinese base was conquered by the Qing Dynasty, and for the first time Taiwan officially became part of an empire based in China. Over the next two centuries, the island came to be more extensively settled by in-migrants from southeastern coastal China. The largest group came from Fujian Province, directly across the straits. These settlers spoke a dialect of Chinese known as Southern Min, which is today most commonly simply called Taiwanese (*Tai yu*). They now make up roughly three-quarters of the population of Taiwan, and are the so-called "Taiwanese" in the narrowest sub-ethnic sense. Another significant in-migrant group were the Hakka (Mandarin: *Kejia*), who came from farther south in Guangdong Province. The Hakka dialect, Taiwanese, and Mandarin are each significantly different. Hakka people make up roughly 10 percent of the present population of Taiwan.

Taiwan's history also has a substantial Japanese layer. After the Qing Dynasty was defeated by Japan in war in 1895, the island was ceded to Japan, and Taiwan became Japan's first modern overseas imperial colony. Despite an armed insurgency against Japanese occupation that lasted for some twenty years, Japanese rule was eventually consolidated, and – at least compared with other parts of Japan's colonial empire – it was relatively benign. The current presidential palace in Taipei, where the president of the Republic of China now has his office, was constructed by the Japanese. By World War II, most Taiwanese were probably at least functionally literate in the Japanese language, and many were quite fluent in Japanese. Few, on the other hand, would have learned to speak the Mandarin that is the most common tongue on the Chinese mainland, and that has been the favored language of modern Chinese nation building. In 1940, the Japanese colonial government even ordered the Taiwanese to take (quite distinctively different) Japanese names.

After Japan lost World War II in 1945, Taiwan was returned to Chinese rule – but a China that was now Chiang Kai-shek's Nationalist Republic rather than the Manchu-ruled Qing Empire. Four years later, the Chinese Nationalists lost their civil war with the Chinese Communists, and Chiang Kai-shek, the central government of the Republic of China, and roughly two million refugees retreated in 1949 to the island of Taiwan (as well as a scattering of other much smaller off-shore islands including the Pescadores, Quemoy [Mandarin: Jinmen], and Matsu), where the Republic of China has been maintained, at least in name, until the present day. Chiang Kai-shek remained president on Taiwan until his death in 1975, and the government in Taipei long continued to claim that it was the only legitimate government of all China. Until about 1990, Taipei even refused to officially acknowledge the existence of the PRC, referring instead simply to "communist bandits."

The United States supported this claim and continued to officially recognize the government in Taipei as the legitimate government of all China until 1979. (No one, of course, least of all Chiang Kai-shek, ever pretended that the island of Taiwan was the whole of China – only that Taiwan sheltered the supposedly legitimate government of all China.) Because both Taipei and Beijing insisted that they were the only true government of a unitary China that included both the mainland and Taiwan, simultaneous diplomatic recognition of both Taipei and Beijing by foreign governments was not an option. The resulting "one China" formula turned out to be very awkward for Taiwan, however, because, when forced to choose, most of the world eventually opted to recognize the Beijing-based PRC. Great Britain recognized the PRC in 1950, France recognized it in 1964, Canada established diplomatic relations in 1970, and by 1979 even the United States had formally switched its recognition from Taipei to Beijing. Today, the only European state that still officially recognizes the Republic of China on Taiwan is the Vatican. China's seat in the United Nations was eventually awarded to Beijing (in 1971), as was China's position in most other international organizations, leaving Taiwan in considerable formal diplomatic isolation (although it enjoys widespread and cordial unofficial relations).

The split between mainland China and Taiwan is therefore very much a still unresolved holdover from the mid-twentieth-century civil war between the Chinese Communists and Nationalists. The PRC absolutely does claim the island as a "renegade province" and insists that it must be recovered someday, many citizens of the PRC do feel very strongly about the issue, and tensions between Taiwan and the PRC have sometimes run quite high. However, when people speak of friction between mainlanders and Taiwanese, this sometimes refers not to the actual mainland PRC, but rather to the group of "mainlanders" who fled to the island of Taiwan in 1949 together with Chiang Kai-shek. These mainlanders on Taiwan make up roughly 14 percent of the island's population, yet they long dominated the government, the military, and some of the larger businesses. For decades, some Taiwanese felt oppressed by this continuing mainlander rule on the island. This domestic sub-ethnic friction, furthermore, played a role in the development of the Taiwan independence movement.

On Taiwan, the Chinese Nationalist government promoted Mandarin as the so-called "National Language" (*guoyu*), and for a long time required that only Mandarin be spoken in public, even though it is not the mother tongue of the majority of people on the island. Schools on Taiwan taught Chinese history rather than specifically Taiwanese history (but with references to communism long censored out), and under the rule of the Chinese Nationalist Party the government on Taiwan for a long time strenuously tried to promote a Chinese national identity on the island. At the other extreme, however, from the time Taiwan first reverted to Chinese rule in 1945 some of the Taiwanese inhabitants – especially members of the old Taiwanese elite – felt alienated from the new mainlander-dominated government. The lasting memory of the February 28, 1947, island-wide rebellion and massacre of Taiwanese by the Nationalist military governor, in particular, opened a deep and lasting rift between many Taiwanese and the Chinese Nationalist government (see the beginning of this chapter). The prolonged period of martial law, which remained in force from 1948 until 1987, the anti-communist white terror of the 1950s, and long-continued suppression of all political opposition by the ruling Nationalist Party further contributed to simmering resentment.[40]

Despite these problems, however, Taiwan also quickly became a spectacular example of an East Asian "economic miracle," and eventually the first genuine multiparty democracy in Chinese history. When the Nationalist central government first retreated to the island in 1949, Taiwan was war torn, overrun with refugees, and suffering from extremely high unemployment and inflation. By introducing the New Taiwan Dollar (NT) to replace the old currency, and other measures, the government successfully tamed inflation, reducing the inflation rate from a staggering 3,000 percent in early 1949 to only 8.8 percent by 1952.[41] The government also took swift and effective action to end the corruption and warlordism that had plagued the Republic of China on the mainland for so many years, and finally carried out the long-promised farmland redistribution program, under the old Nationalist slogan "land to the tillers." Taiwanese landlords were deprived of their landholdings, but compensated with bonds and stock in government-owned enterprises.

In the 1950s, Taiwan's economic policies emphasized the typical postcolonial developing-world approach known as import substitution, which essentially meant promoting domestically manufactured substitutes for foreign imports, and artificially protecting them with a wall of high import taxes, outright restrictions, and currency controls. But Taiwan then became one of the first developing economies in the world to move away from the import substitution model and concentrate instead on export-led growth, beginning in the early 1960s. Government incentives played a role in this process, such as tax rebates for exporters and the establishment of special duty-free export-processing zones beginning in 1966. But Taiwan's economic takeoff was also accompanied by a general process of deregulation and privatization. In 1952, for example, the government was responsible for 57 percent of Taiwan's industrial production, but by 1987, that figure had fallen to only 14 percent.[42] In striking contrast to South Korea or Japan, where the developmental model featured giant conglomerates with close ties to the government, in Taiwan the source of economic dynamism turned out overwhelmingly to be the independent, small, and often literally family-run "Chinese-style" firm. Ninety-four percent of Taiwan's production was attributable to small enterprises with fewer than fifty employees.[43]

As a consequence of the small scale of these enterprises, Taiwan, unlike South Korea or Japan, has not been globally competitive in heavy industries such as automobile manufacturing. But the flexibility of Taiwan's many small companies correspondingly helped make Taiwan highly competitive in the rapidly changing field of information technology. By 2007, Taiwanese companies were producing an astonishing 90 percent of the world's notebook computers and 98 percent of the world's computer motherboards (often sold under brand names such as Apple or Dell, although local brands such as Acer and Asus have also achieved some global recognition). To keep prices low, however, Taiwan eventually began outsourcing much of the actual manufacturing process to cheaper-labor factories on mainland China. By the early twenty-first century, half of Taiwan's information technology products were being assembled in the PRC, and "Taiwanese controlled around two-thirds of the PRC's output of information technology."[44] Taiwan – which as of 2014 still enjoyed a per capita GDP 3.4 times that of mainland China (and also higher than Canada, France, the UK, Japan, or South Korea)[45] – has thus emerged as a major contributor to the PRC's dramatic economic takeoff.

In a single generation, Taiwan leaped from what had still been a largely pre-industrial peasant economy in 1949 to a modern center of economic globalization in its own right. Taiwan's newfound prosperity, meanwhile, brought a general improvement in the quality of life on the island. The capital city, Taipei, once had the reputation of being a "gray city." The old Japanese colonial era buildings – made of unpainted, weathered, wood which at least had a certain rustic charm – had mostly been torn down and replaced, often by rather ugly naked concrete. More recently, however, Taipei has become an increasingly attractive city. Especially as a splendid new subway system came on-line in the mid-1990s, Taipei now has all the conveniences of a thoroughly modern metropolis. In the towering building known as Taipei 101 – which for a few years in the early twenty-first century was the world's tallest skyscraper – shoppers can stroll in a leisurely fashion from a high-end luxury Armani store to a Cartier store, and then to Fendi, Gucci, Prada, Tiffany, Versace, Louis Vuitton, and so forth.

Following Taiwan's successful economic takeoff, Taiwan also managed the transition to genuine democracy. Since 1949, there had always been at least some of the trappings of democracy on Taiwan, but until 1969 there were only local elections, and until as late as the early 1990s most seats at the national level were simply never up for reelection. This was because those seats were still held by representatives of constituencies on mainland China, elected before 1949, whose continued existence was tied to Taipei's claim to be the legitimate government of all China. Also, until September 1986 (when the first opposition party – the Democratic Progressive Party, or DPP – was formed), Taiwan was always a single-party state. This single ruling party, the Chinese Nationalist Party, had, moreover, been reorganized in 1924 (while still on the mainland) as an explicitly Leninist-model revolutionary party. But, as part of Dr. Sun Yat-sen's legacy, this Nationalist Party had also always been officially committed to an ultimate goal of transition to democracy. Since 1927, under Chiang Kai-shek, it had also always been staunchly anti-communist.[46]

By the 1980s, a majority of Taiwan's population was comfortably middle class, often well educated, intimately familiar with conditions in Japan and the United

States, and increasingly inclined to demand the right to participate in political decision making. The fact that there were significant domestic political dissatisfactions undoubtedly helped fuel this politicization. There may have also simply been something in the global zeitgeist, or spirit of the times, in the late 1980s that favored democratization. We have already examined the democratization of South Korea in 1987 and the Tiananmen Square demonstrations in Beijing in 1989. A generous share of the credit for Taiwan's successful transition to democracy must also go to the leaders of the ruling Nationalist Party, especially President Chiang Ching-kuo (Jiang Jingguo, 1910–1988; President, 1978–1988; see Figure 14.3), Chiang Kai-shek's son and heir, who flatly refused to authorize arrests when told of the (then still technically illegal) formation of the DPP in 1986. "'It is easy to use power,' he told an aide, 'but it is hard to know when not to use it.'"[47] In the following year, 1987, President Chiang Ching-kuo's administration formally repealed martial law, legalized the formation of opposition parties, lifted some of the existing restrictions on the press, and for the first time permitted indirect travel (through another country) to mainland China – thereby beginning a process of dynamic cultural and economic interaction between Taiwan and the PRC.

In the new age of multiparty democracy, a number of political parties formed, but the most important was the DPP. Taiwan seems to be stabilizing into a primarily two-party system, with the DPP and the Nationalist Party as the two major alternatives. As a political party that originated among Taiwanese dissidents

Figure 14.3. Chiang Ching-kuo (on right), President of the Republic of China on Taiwan (1978–1988), with his father, Chiang Kai-shek, and Chiang Kai-shek's second wife, Song Meiling, in 1948. (Chiang Ching-kuo's mother, Mao Fumei, died in 1939.) Pictures from History/Bridgeman Images.

resentful of long-standing mainlander rule through the Nationalist Party, from the start the DPP was closely associated with a platform calling for Taiwan independence, even though openly advocating independence was illegal until 1992. In 2000, the DPP candidate, Chen Shuibian (1950–; President, 2000–2008), actually won the presidential election. This was a true milestone: the first peaceful democratic transfer of power from one political party to another in Chinese history. Chen won the election with only 39.3 percent of the vote, however, thanks to a three-way split within the opposing Nationalist Party. In 2004, Chen Shuibian won reelection for a second four-year term with a slim majority.

As president, although his popular mandate for promoting Taiwan independence was always somewhat qualified, and the danger of provoking war with the mainland made it necessary to proceed with caution, Chen Shuibian did begin gingerly advancing some measures to promote the DPP agenda and to reject the legacy of Chiang Kai-shek and the Chinese Nationalist Party. Notably, the word *China* was dropped from the name of several state-run organizations in Taiwan (such as the Bank of China and China Petroleum), and in 2007 the huge marble Chiang Kai-shek Memorial in downtown Taipei was officially renamed the Taiwan Democracy Memorial Hall. Not only were these moves controversial, however, but during his second term President Chen and his party also became beleaguered by accusations of corruption and incompetence. In November 2008, the by then ex-president Chen was arrested and handcuffed, placed on trial for corruption, and eventually sentenced to life in prison. In the aftermath, the name of the Chiang Kai-shek Memorial in Taipei was officially restored in 2009.

In the 2008 presidential elections, the Nationalist Party candidate Ma Ying-jeou (Ma Yingjiu, 1950–; President, 2008–2016) convincingly won back the presidency with 58.5 percent of the vote. Ma is considered to be a mainlander, having been born in Hong Kong. He holds a doctorate in law from Harvard University, and speaks English fluently. His election, and former president Chen's disgrace, at least temporarily greatly reduced tensions between Taiwan and the PRC and accelerated the pace of interaction with the mainland.

Since the time during the Korean War in 1950 when President Truman committed the U.S. Navy to "neutralizing" the Taiwan Straits, Taiwan has enjoyed an especially close relationship with the United States. Many of Taiwan's leaders have been educated at American universities, the motion pictures advertised on giant billboards at Taipei's many movie theaters have long been disproportionately Hollywood movies (and Taiwan's own best-known director, Ang Lee [Li An, 1954–], has won multiple Oscars and is a familiar figure in Hollywood), a substantial amount of the pop music heard in Taiwan is sung in English (and even the Chinese-language songs are typically in modern Western style), and many young Taiwanese have grown up drinking cola and eating at McDonald's. Yet, the Japanese influence on Taiwan also remains strong (see Chapter 11), and most things in Taiwan merely seem generically modern rather than being copies of any one particular foreign model. Elements of traditional Chinese culture survive, there is a distinctively local Taiwanese variant of Chinese culture, and Taiwan has also generated an exciting new Chinese-language modern pop culture of its own that is extremely popular throughout the whole of Greater China, including the People's Republic.

The PRC has become Taiwan's largest market, and (now that Hong Kong has officially been returned to China) Taiwan has become the PRC's leading source of foreign investment. Taiwan is therefore not only a successful example of Chinese modernization in its own right, but is also actively playing an important role in the continuously unfolding story of the People's Republic of China. Yet, the thorny problem of Taiwan's status and identity remains unresolved. If mainland China now beckons with offers of economic opportunity for many Taiwanese, there is also a clearly perceived danger that if Taiwan gets too close to the mainland it will be sucked into the PRC's huge gravitational field, and absorbed. In early 2014, Taiwanese protestors demonstrating against the ratification of a new free trade agreement negotiated with the PRC (which was intended to allow mutual investment in the service sector) physically occupied Taiwan's Legislature building for twenty-four days. After a florist donated a case of sunflowers to the demonstrators, this became known as the "Sunflower Movement." Later that same year, the Nationalist Party was badly defeated in island-wide local elections, losing half of the mayoral offices it had previously held.

In the January 2016 general election, the DPP candidate Tsai Ing-wen (1956–) won the presidency with 56.12 percent of the vote. In so doing, she became Taiwan's second non-Nationalist Party president, and the first female head of state in Chinese history since the female emperor Wu Zetian in the seventh century. The new president, Tsai, holds a doctorate in law from the London School of Economics, and taught as a university professor before entering public service. For the first time ever, the Nationalist Party also lost its majority in the Legislature in this 2016 election. The election, therefore, seems significant. Taiwan has, thus far, been a remarkable modern success story, and a fascinating part of modern Chinese history, but its future – as ever – remains unpredictable.

China and Globalization

Mainland China's experiment with market-based economic reforms appeared stalled by the mid-1980s, and the shocking events in Tiananmen Square in 1989 ushered in a political chill. But Deng Xiaoping performed a high-profile "southern tour" of the SEZs in 1992, popularly associated with the slogan "to get rich is glorious," which succeeded in explosively restarting the economic reform process. China's emerging new consumer economy initially produced some bizarrely hybrid patterns of consumption, such as commercial sales of Mao memorabilia and pop music remakes of old revolutionary songs. The first television advertisements in the PRC were not broadcast until 1979, and early efforts sometimes produced ads for products such as cement mixers having obviously limited appeal to individual consumers. Initial Chinese attempts to crack the American market also brought some hilariously poorly chosen English brand names, such as White Elephant brand batteries and Maxipuke playing cards (*pu ke* being a Chinese transliteration of the English word *poker*).[48] However, China rapidly adjusted to the new reality of economic globalization, a transition symbolized by China's admission to the World Trade Organization in 2001.

China's economic growth snowballed. If adjusted for purchasing power parity, China probably (as of 2014) already has the world's largest economy (larger than either the U.S. or the European Union as a whole), and also the world's largest reserves of foreign exchange and gold – almost U.S.$4 trillion.[49] There are now more millionaires in China than in any other country in the world – well over a million (U.S. dollar value) – and China is becoming a significant source, as well as recipient, of foreign investment. China also holds approximately $1.6 trillion of U.S. government debt.[50] Despite vehement opposition from the U.S. and Japan, in 2015 fifty-seven countries (including such close American allies as the UK, Germany, Australia, and South Korea) signed on to a new China-sponsored Asian Infrastructure Investment Bank (AIIB), with $100 billion in initial capitalization, intended to rival existing institutions such as the World Bank and to enhance China's global influence. In late 2015, the International Monetary Fund (IMF) also announced its intention to soon admit the Chinese *renminbi* to the elite package of globally traded currencies that includes the U.S. dollar, the Euro, the British pound, and the Japanese yen. From what had been an impoverished, marginalized, Marxist revolutionary Third World country as recently as the 1970s, China has come a long way very fast.

China publicly celebrated its new international prominence by hosting the 2008 Olympics in Beijing. The Opening Ceremonies of the Beijing Olympics invoked China's traditional culture for its world television audience by featuring a quotation from Confucius and three thousand performers dressed as Confucian disciples. This is more than a little ironic, because as recently as the 1970s Confucius was being stridently denounced in the PRC as an odious symbol of "feudalism."[51] While there have been revivals of tradition in recent years, and even during the Mao years ancient Legalism (in pointed contrast to Confucianism) was sometimes praised, nonetheless modern China is hardly a genuinely very traditional society. Invocations of Confucius aimed at foreign audiences today might even seem a little like deceptive advertising, but this is also simply part of the paradox of a People's Republic of China that celebrated its sixtieth birthday in 2009, yet simultaneously likes to claim it has five thousand years of history.

Despite the real antiquity of Chinese civilization, much of China's actual culture today is generically modern, and many aspects are even specifically Western in origin – including, of course, the Olympic Games themselves. At the time of the Tiananmen Square demonstrations in 1989, the cultural influences at work had been a complex mix. As noted above, one of the banners unfurled in Tiananmen Square read "Give me liberty or give me death" in obvious reference to the American Revolution. But the demonstrators also consciously invoked memories of the French Revolution, China's own May Fourth Movement, and world figures such as Mahatma Gandhi as well as the American Dr. Martin Luther King Jr. For the *Goddess of Democracy* statue, the students from the Central Academy of Fine Arts who actually made it explicitly rejected a suggestion to directly copy the

Figure 14.4. Constructing the *Goddess of Democracy* statue in Tiananmen Square, Beijing, 1989. Stuart Franklin. Magnum Photos.

American *Statue of Liberty* in favor of creating "a new work of universal appeal" (see Figure 14.4). As it happened, this was influenced by their prior training in the style of Soviet revolutionary realism. As a result, the head of the *Goddess of Democracy* was arguably inspired more by the monumental statue of a *Collective Farm Woman* from the Soviet Pavilion at the 1937 Paris World's Fair than by the *Statue of Liberty* in New York harbor. Other influences were more specifically East Asian: Chinese student demonstrators got the idea of wearing white headbands bearing slogans from South Korean student demonstrators, who adapted the practice from a Japanese samurai tradition indicating a willingness to fight to the death.[52]

Since 1989, as China has increasingly engaged with the outside world, the Western – and often specifically American – cultural impact has deepened. Half of the top-grossing movies in China have been Hollywood productions. A Disneyland is under construction in Shanghai and expected to open in early 2016 (in addition to the one that is already open in Hong Kong). In 1984, China had no golf courses, but by 2007 China had the fifth largest number of them in the world (and an absolute majority of the world's golf club heads are now made in China). Not only is American-style basketball popular in China, but China has also become the second largest market outside the United States for the actual American National Basketball Association (NBA) itself. Western-style classical music is arguably more flourishing in the PRC than it is in the U.S., and millions of Chinese people are currently taking piano lessons. China also dominates world production of Western-style pianos and violins. A Chinese version of the (originally Dutch) singing competition reality TV show "The Voice" (called "The Voice of China," *Zhongguo hao shengyin*) has been in production since 2012. Christianity may be the most dynamically successful religion in the PRC today. Since the time of Deng Xiaoping, it has been normal for the children of China's elite to study in the U.S. or Europe, and, since 2009, China has provided the single largest group of foreign students studying in American colleges and universities. Some ten thousand people travel between the United States and China every day now.[53] English is the preferred language of international communication, and it is not uncommon to overhear a German businessman in China, for example, conversing with his Chinese counterparts in English.

Yet, the Chinese language is still the world's most commonly spoken native tongue, and its written form dates from the Bronze Age. The depth of recent Westernization and Americanization should not be exaggerated. For example, in 2009 the Mattel corporation opened the world's first entirely Barbie Doll-themed store in Shanghai, China. But it was not a success, and closed within two years. In 2013, Mattel tried to relaunch Barbie in China, and in 2014 the company unveiled a new sales campaign featuring a doll with the face of a famous Chinese actress. This is an example of a process known as localization, through which the products of global business are tailored to appeal to the tastes of local customers.

Even direct European and American influences often go through a filtering process. Many of the outside modern cultural influences on the PRC have come indirectly, through Chinese-language inputs from Hong Kong, Taiwan, and the overseas Chinese. The (South) "Korean wave" has made a very big impact on China, as discussed in Chapter 12. And the People's Republic has been gradually fashioning its own modern Chinese synthesis. To some extent this is an entirely natural process, but open admiration of liberal Western models by Chinese leaders was also largely terminated by the crackdown in Tiananmen Square in 1989, and since 1989 "patriotic education" campaigns have been stepped up in a deliberate effort to shape domestic public opinion and national culture.

In China, the first major political use of the new Internet technology (which is often assumed to be almost synonymous with globalization) involved a newly invented "traditional" Chinese religion. On the tenth anniversary of the Tiananmen Square demonstrations, in April 1999, ten thousand followers of a new religion called Falun Gong suddenly materialized out of nowhere to demonstrate in front of the Communist Party leadership compound northwest of Tiananmen Square in Beijing. Falun Gong is a variant of traditional Chinese therapeutic *qigong* exercises, mixed with Buddhism, which was founded in 1992. In 1999, its followers used computer websites and cell phones to mobilize this impressive mass demonstration, which they evidently hoped would win greater toleration of Falun Gong from the authorities. The attempt backfired badly, however, because party leaders panicked instead and ordered a harsh crackdown on Falun Gong as a supposedly dangerous cult. Other unofficial political uses of the new Internet and cell phone technologies since then have notably included the coordination of large-scale popular demonstrations of anti-Japanese patriotic nationalism. In one case, an Internet campaign was also used to force the closure of an American Starbucks coffee shop inside the Forbidden City in Beijing. The new communications technologies, in other words, can serve indigenous agendas as well as linking China to the outside world.

And, ironically, economic globalization may have only strengthened the rule of the Communist Party, because the Party can plausibly argue that it has successfully delivered prosperity. Certainly, economic growth and increased international integration have not yet triggered automatic democratization in China, frustrating any easy assumption that democracy must be an inevitable part of the post-Cold War globalization process. Surprisingly, the act of voting is actually a familiar part of life in modern China at almost every level from rural villages to the Central Committee of the CCP. Chinese communists themselves have often invoked the word *democracy*. After the establishment of the PRC in 1949, eight so-called democratic parties were also permitted to exist. But they were kept subordinate to the Communist Party and dependent on state funding, and are not genuinely serious opposition parties. Voters in China are rarely offered much substantive choice. In reality, the PRC is a single-party state, which has never tolerated any more than token political opposition or endorsed the idea of direct popular multiparty elections.

Since the time of Deng Xiaoping, leadership succession has been regularized and stabilized (essentially through political bargaining at the top). The unpredictable campaigns and personality cult that had marked the Mao Zedong era are now a thing of the past, but the basic Leninist political structure has not changed much. Communist Party membership has actually grown to what is now some 86 million people, although recent growth in Party membership has little to do with enthusiasm for Marxism and much to do with the CCP being the sole ruling party, "the establishment" in China.

China's newest leader, Xi Jinping (1953–), who took the title President in 2013, has presented himself as perhaps the strongest leader since Deng Xiaoping or Mao Zedong. President Xi has called for renewed economic reforms and an increased role for market forces in the economy, but he has also publicly promoted China's own culture and institutions, created a new National Security Commission with himself in charge, and overseen what may be the most intense crackdown on dissent in recent years. Among other things, there has been a campaign to force Internet users to register using their real names, so that the Internet (which is censored in the PRC behind a so-called "Great Firewall of China") cannot be surfed anonymously. China has also strengthened ties with Russia, in 2014 signing a thirty-year $400 billion gas deal with Moscow.

Although public housing was sold to residents beginning in 1998, and some 80 percent of the Chinese are now homeowners (individual apartment units, for example, can be privately owned), ownership of the land is still held by the state or collectives. After 1998, State Owned Enterprises (SOE) were restructured, and much consumer, light, and export-oriented industry has been consigned to the private sector, which has also created nearly all of China's new jobs. The remaining State Owned Enterprises are, moreover, usually not profitable, if subsidies and other forms of artificial state support are factored out.[54] Nevertheless, the largest and most strategic industries – including things like oil, transportation, communications, and financial services – are mostly still state owned. More than half of China's GDP still derives from state-directed investment.[55] Many observers, moreover, believe that the pace of market-based economic reforms slowed or even reversed somewhat in the early twenty-first century.

After the failure of Lehman Brothers in 2008 and the onset of a major recession in the United States and Europe, state-controlled banks in China doubled the number of new loans they issued in 2009, and in 2008–2009 the combined total value of government stimuli and lending may have been around $1.5 trillion.[56] Much of this went into infrastructure building, including the construction of a network of high-speed rail that went from almost nothing to become the largest in the world by 2015. The fact that China is still only incompletely integrated into international systems, and its currency is still not freely convertible, also may have helped insulate China from the "global" recession. The result has been that China's relative global economic position has been greatly strengthened since 2008.

China has certainly prospered, overall, and in recent years has also begun to show signs of a new assertiveness. After the onset of recession in the U.S. and Europe, it even became possible to imagine China as an attractive model for the world, and to argue that a meritocratic or technocratic form of benevolent authoritarianism may even be more effective than a dysfunctional democracy. Under Deng Xiaoping, China had consciously maintained a low profile and concentrated on economic development. It was claimed that China was pursuing a "peaceful development" that would threaten no one, and be universally beneficial. But, as China's rising economic power has become palpable, there has also been something of a perceptible shift from China simply accepting the rules of the existing world order to China aspiring to play an active part in shaping those rules.[57]

In the early Deng Xiaoping years, the military's share of China's budget actually decreased, but since Tiananmen there have been steady increases in military expenditures, and China's military budget is now the second largest in the world (although still dwarfed by U.S. military spending).[58] China's military capabilities have also been significantly upgraded. Its first aircraft carrier went into service in 2012, an experimental stealth jet fighter and stealth drone have been unveiled, and China appears to have developed sophisticated cyber warfare capability. In the past few years there have been serious tensions between China and Japan over some disputed islands (called Diaoyu in Chinese and Senkaku in Japanese), and between China and several Southeast Asia countries (notably including Vietnam and the Philippines) over disputed claims to territorial waters in the South China Sea. At the same time, though, precisely because of its economic success, China now has a deeply vested interest in global peace and stability.

Some Chinese leaders in recent years have shown an interest in projecting "soft power" – that is, in exerting a global influence that is based not on force, but on the presumed attractiveness of the China model. As of 2011, 350 "Confucius Institutes" had been opened in 105 countries with partial Chinese funding, intended to promote the study of the Chinese language and culture. But, as already noted, Confucius is a somewhat strange choice to represent the modern People's Republic, and not many foreigners are likely to actually become Confucians. Pandas are cute and Confucius may be quaint, but the universal appeal of identifiably Chinese culture and ideals remains limited, thus far. Even China's undeniably successful economy has yet to produce any particularly globally attractive Chinese brands or distinctively Chinese products.[59] (This could change rapidly, though, as we have already witnessed in the case of first Japanese and then South Korean brands, which have become true global powerhouses.)

China may have more than a million millionaires, but, in a country with 1.4 billion people, in per capita terms China is still poorer than Iraq. The gap in wealth between the newly affluent and the still impoverished majority represents a serious potential social problem. Government stimuli may have helped China power through the global recession, but it also created bubbles and inefficiencies and cannot be permanently sustainable. Moreover, the model of manufacturing for export based on low-wage labor and toxic, polluting factories may have reached the limits of its usefulness. Pollution and environmental degradation in China are reaching crisis proportions. According to a much commented-upon report issued in 2014, 64 percent of Chinese millionaires surveyed said that they were either emigrating or planning to do so.[60] When a country's most successful people wish to leave it in large numbers that surely indicates a problem.

China's leaders are aware of all of these issues, and there is a widespread recognition that the country needs to transition to a healthier economic model based more on domestic consumption and services. China may, in fact, be at something of an important crossroads just now. Growth rates have already slowed significantly. The relaxation of the one-child policy in late 2015, permitting married couples to have two children, clearly marks the end of an era. A smooth transition will not be easy – it may even prove impossible. But all East Asian countries have faced daunting challenges in the past century or so, and on balance it has to be said that they have done remarkably well.

For Further Reading

A careful study of the Chinese Nationalist defeat on the mainland in 1949 is provided by Suzanne Pepper, *Civil War in China: The Political Struggle, 1945–1949* (Berkeley: University of California Press, 1978).

For Chairman Mao's revolutionary China, see Frank Dikötter, *The Tragedy of Liberation: A History of the Chinese Revolution, 1945–57* (New York: Bloomsbury Press, 2013); Edward Friedman, Paul G. Pickowicz, and Mark Selden, *Chinese Village, Socialist State* (New Haven, CT: Yale University Press, 1991); and Maurice Meisner, *Mao's China and After: A History of the People's Republic* (New York: Free Press, [1977] 1986). Personal accounts of life in Mao's China are numerous, and include Jung Chang, *Wild Swans: Three*

Daughters of China (New York: Anchor Books, 1992); and Heng Liang and Judith Shapiro, *Son of the Revolution* (New York: Vintage Books, 1984). The best account of the Nixon visit is Margaret MacMillan, *Nixon and Mao: The Week That Changed the World* (New York: Random House, 2007). On relations with the U.S., see Michael Schaller, *The United States and China: Into the Twenty-First Century*, 4th ed. (Oxford University Press, 2016).

On the Deng Xiaoping era and economic reforms, see Richard Baum, *Burying Mao: Chinese Politics in the Age of Deng Xiaoping* (Princeton University Press, 1994), and David L. Wank, *Commodifying Communism: Business, Trust, and Politics in a Chinese City* (Cambridge University Press, 1999). The Deng era origins of China's controversial one-child policy are examined in Susan Greenhalgh, *Just One Child: Science and Policy in Deng's China* (Berkeley: University of California Press, 2008). For an exhaustive biography, see Ezra F. Vogel, *Deng Xiaoping and the Transformation of China* (Cambridge, MA: Harvard University Press, 2011).

A superb collection of documents relating to the Tiananmen democracy movement is Minzhu Han (pseudonym), ed., *Cries for Democracy: Writings and Speeches from the 1989 Chinese Democracy Movement* (Princeton University Press, 1990). Another important (clandestinely released) documentary collection on the events in Tiananmen Square, which purports to include transcripts of discussions among China's top leaders, is Liang Zhang (pseudonym), compiler, *The Tiananmen Papers*, ed. Andrew J. Nathan and Perry Link (New York: PublicAffairs, 2001).

Concerning Greater China, see Willem Van Kemenade, *China, Hong Kong, Taiwan, Inc.*, trans. Diane Webb (New York: Vintage Books, 1998). For Hong Kong, see Frank Welsh, *A Borrowed Place: The History of Hong Kong* (New York: Kodansha International, 1993). For Taiwan, a superb introduction is provided by Shelley Rigger, *Why Taiwan Matters: Small Island, Global Powerhouse* (updated edition; Lanham: Rowman & Littlefield, 2011). On the Chinese Nationalist government in Taiwan, see Jay Taylor, *The Generalissimo's Son: Chiang Ching-kuo and the Revolutions in China and Taiwan* (Cambridge, MA: Harvard University Press, 2000). Johanna Menzel Meskill tells the story of Taiwan's early settlement, in *A Chinese Pioneer Family: The Lins of Wu-feng, Taiwan, 1729–1895* (Princeton University Press, 1979).

On globalization and recent Chinese culture, see Geremie R. Barmé, *In the Red: On Contemporary Chinese Culture* (New York: Columbia University Press, 1999), and Doug Guthrie, *China and Globalization: The Social, Economic, and Political Transformation of Chinese Society* (New York: Routledge, 2006).

For assessments of the current situation, see Geoff Dyer, *The Contest of the Century: The New Era of Competition with China – and How America Can Win* (New York: Alfred A. Knopf, 2014); James Kynge, *China Shakes the World: A Titan's Rise and Troubled Future – and the Challenge for America* (Boston: Houghton Mifflin, 2006); David M. Lampton, *The Three Faces of Chinese Power: Might, Money, and Minds* (Berkeley: University of California Press, 2008); and David Shambaugh, *China Goes Global: The Partial Power* (Oxford University Press, 2013).

Afterword

The new Age of Globalization that followed the end of the Cold War (which was marked by the fall of the Berlin Wall in 1989 and the demise of the Soviet Union in 1991) began on a note of exhilarating optimism for many English-speaking people – sustained by an unprecedented decade-long digital-revolution-fueled economic expansion in the U.S. in the 1990s – that a so-called "Washington consensus" centering around the model of free market capitalism had universally triumphed. Democracy, which was popularly (though mistakenly) assumed to be almost synonymous with capitalism, was spreading globally, and it was even predicted that "the end of history" had been reached, as liberal democracy and free market capitalism promised to become the final stage of human development.[1]

Such predictions may still prove correct in the long term, but the Great Recession of 2008–2009 and growing economic inequality in the developed world have somewhat dampened enthusiasm. Russia is again today led by a strongman, and threatening military expansion. The upsurge of global terrorism since the September 11, 2001, attack on the World Trade Center in New York has chilled the world climate, and may even lead to increased restrictions on travel across national borders, reversing the recent trend towards greater international openness. Meanwhile, economic globalization sometimes benefits multinational corporations and technocratic multinational organizations that are not necessarily directly answerable to democratic electorates, while the looming rise of China – even though it was made possible in the first place by the preexisting international order and in some senses validates its triumph – still poses a challenge to the "Washington consensus," not least because the People's Republic of China remains politically an unreformed Leninist system that shows no sign of embracing multi-party democracy. In addition, the world also now confronts troubling environmental challenges that cast doubt upon the sustainability of prevailing patterns of behavior. It may be that the Age of Globalization will end, and the next historical "age" may prove considerably less attractive.

But the future is unknowable. In many ways, the world today really is more culturally and economically integrated and homogeneous than ever before in history, and the lives of many people are materially much richer. Despite all the globalization and generic modernization, however, multiple layers of culture and identity still continue to coexist, with or without open contradiction. In the tiny but illuminating case of identity-challenged Taiwan, for example, we find a successful, modern, thoroughly Westernized and democratic society that has long enjoyed a particularly close relationship with the United States, but where the Japanese influence has also long been especially strong and allegedly even reemphasized in recent years. In Taiwan, as well, elements of traditional Chinese civilization (such as religion and the writing system) have survived and flourished, arguably even more vigorously sometimes than in mainland China itself, while at the same time there is also undeniably something of a uniquely local Taiwanese culture. Taiwan is simultaneously a "world citizen" poised on the "cutting edge of globalization,"[2] and a place where foreign visitors who manage to escape the cocoon of their Western-style hotels to wander the streets and night markets will also still immediately recognize that, like Dorothy in *The Wizard of Oz*, they are not in Kansas anymore.

East Asia may not be as cohesive and distinctive a region as it once was, and perhaps there is no longer any definable "East Asian civilization." Modernization and Westernization shredded many East Asian traditions beginning as early as the late nineteenth century, and the mid-twentieth-century Cold War divided East Asia between competing outside ideologies and power blocs, whose legacies linger still. Recent East Asian economic takeoff, meanwhile, might be interpreted merely as an extension of a universally successful modern model. Although the various East Asian nations have now all become each other's largest trading partners, and are often enthusiastic consumers of each other's modern pop culture, this new consumer culture is nonetheless unmistakably of a generically modern variety. And East Asian countries are often each other's worst enemies, with rivalries such as those between China and Japan, China and Vietnam, Korea and Japan, North Korea and South Korea, and Taiwan and the People's Republic of China. In the face of ongoing internal East Asian tensions, the continuing external presence of American power remains a welcome stabilizing influence that few East Asians are really eager see disappear anytime soon.

East Asia is not – and actually never has been – a world unto itself. Yet, over the whole of East Asia, the ghost, not so much of Confucius as of the entire East Asian past, still hovers, often invisibly but nonetheless powerfully, especially in the form of the extensively shared vocabulary among the East Asian languages. China (including Greater China), Japan, Korea, and Vietnam are all very different places, but they also literally share many of the same words and ideas. And, if there is any one thing that does seem fairly certain at the start of the twenty-first century, it is that East Asia is once again, as it had been for much of human history prior to the nineteenth century, a major world center.

Character List

Names and terms normally written in Chinese characters, excluding familiar modern place names and such well-known items as the names of Chinese dynasties, but including a few standard modern terms that may be of interest to introductory readers (even when they are normally written in East Asian scripts other than Chinese characters, such as *anime* and *han'gŭl*).

Abe no Nakamaro	阿倍仲麻呂
Abe Shinzō	安倍晋三
Acer (computer company; C: Hongqi)	宏碁
Aguda (Jurchen leader)	阿骨打
Ainu (people)	アイヌ
Aisin Gioro	愛新覺羅
Amaterasu	天照
Ami (aboriginal people)	阿美族
Amitābha	阿彌陀佛
Amoghavajra (C: Bukong)	不空
An Lushan	安祿山
anime (animation)	アニメ
Annam (Vietnam, C: Annan)	安南
Annam quoc vuong	安南國王
Antoku (Emperor)	安德
arahitogami	現人神
Ashikaga Takauji	足利尊氏
Ashikaga Yoshimasa	足利義政
Ashikaga Yoshimitsu	足利義滿
Asuka (Japanese region and historical period)	飛鳥
Asus (computer company; C: Huashuo)	華碩
Au Co	嫗姬
Au Lac	甌駱
Azuchi (castle)	安土

"Baba qu na'er" (TV program)	爸爸去哪儿
Bai Juyi (alternate spelling: Po Chü-I)	白居易
bakufu (Shogunal "tent government")	幕府
bakushu ("native" Japanese word for beer)	麦酒
Bao Dai (Emperor)	保大
be (hereditary production unit)	部
Beiping (Republic of China name for Beijing)	北平
bendi (*punti*)	本地
biiru (beer)	ビール
Bodhidharma (C: Putidamo)	菩提達磨
Bodhisena (J: Bodaisena)	菩提僊那
bunmei kaika	文明開化
bunraku (*jōruri*; puppet theater)	文楽 (淨瑠璃)
bushi (Japanese warrior)	武士
bushido (the Way of the Warrior)	武士道
Cai Hesen	蔡和森
Cao Cao	曹操
chaebŏl (South Korean conglomerate)	財閥
Chajang (Korean Buddhist monk)	慈藏
Chan (J: Zen)	禪
Chang Po-go	張保皋
Chang'an (Chinese capital city)	長安
chanoyu (tea ceremony)	茶の湯
Chen Duxiu	陳獨秀
Chen Shuibian	陳水扁
Chen Yi	陳毅
Chiang Ching-kuo (Jiang Jingguo)	蔣經國
Chiang Kai-shek (Jiang Jieshi)	蔣介石
Chiang Wei-kuo (Jiang Weiguo)	蔣緯國
Chikamatsu Monzaemon	近松門左衛門
Chinggis Khan (C: Chengjisihan)	成吉思汗
chin'gol (true bone rank)	真骨
Chinhan (early Korean community)	辰韓
Chinul (Korean Buddhist monk)	知訥
Ch'oe Che-u	崔濟愚
Ch'oe Sŭng-no	崔承老
Chŏn Namsaeng	泉男生
chōnin (townspeople)	町人
Chōshū (domain)	長州
Chosŏn (Korea)	朝鮮
Chu (kingdom)	楚
chuanshuo (legend)	傳說
Chun Doo Hwan (Chŏn Tu-hwan)	金斗煥
Chunqiu (Spring and Autumn period)	春秋

Chūshingura (*Treasury of Loyal Retainers*)	忠臣蔵
Cixi (Empress Dowager)	慈禧太后
Co Loa	古螺
Cui Jian	崔健
Dadu (early name for Beijing)	大都
Dai (region of northern China)	代
Dai Co Viet	大瞿越
Dai Kui	戴逵
Dai Viet	大越
Daiichi Bank	第一銀行
Daiichi (Life Insurance [building])	第一 (生命保險)
daimyō (Japanese regional lord)	大名
Dalai Lama	達賴喇嘛
Dali (non-Chinese kingdom in southwest China)	大理
Dan no Ura (site of battle)	檀ノ浦
dao (the Way)	道
Dao tong (Transmission of the Dao/Way)	道統
Daoxue (Neo-Confucian "Learning of the Dao")	道學
Daozang (Daoist scriptural canon)	道藏
darughachi	達魯花赤
Daxue (the *Great Learning*)	大學
de (moral force)	德
Deng Lijun (Teresa Teng)	鄧麗君
Deng Xiaoping	邓小平 (鄧小平)
Deshima (island)	出島
di (god)	帝
Di Renjie	狄仁傑
Diaoyu (islands; J: Senkaku 尖閣)	钓鱼 (釣魚台)
Dien Bien Phu	奠邊府
dim sum (Mandarin: *dianxin*)	點心
Ding (legendary cook's name)	庖丁
Dinh Bo Linh	丁部領
Dong Shou	冬壽
Dong Son (prehistoric culture)	東山
Dong Zhongshu	董仲舒
Doraemon (anime)	ドラえもん
Dorgon (Manchu leader)	多爾袞
Dou Yi	竇乂
Du Fu	杜甫
Du Yuesheng	杜月笙
Edo (modern Tōkyō)	江戶
Emishi (people)	蝦夷
enka (music)	演歌
Erlitou (prehistoric culture)	二里頭

Esen (Oirat Mongol leader)	也先
Fajia (Legalism)	法家
Fajing (*Classic of Law*)	法經
Falun Gong (spiritual practice)	法轮功 (法輪功)
Faxian (Chinese Buddhist pilgrim)	法顯
fengshui (geomancy)	風水
Fo xing (Buddha nature)	佛性
Fotucheng (Buddhist monk)	佛圖澄
Fuji Bank	富士銀行
Fujiwara (family)	藤原
Fujiwara Michinaga	藤原道長
Fujiwara Michinori	藤原通憲
fukoku kyōhei	富国強兵
Fukuzawa Yūkichi	福澤諭吉
Funan (early Southeast Asian state)	扶南
Fuxi (legendary emperor)	伏羲
"Gangnam Style" (song title)	江南스타일
Gao Huan	高歡
Gao Xianzhi (K: Ko Sŏnji)	高仙芝
geisha (Japanese female entertainer)	芸者
geming (change of mandate/revolution)	革命
Gempei (war)	源平
Genji monogatari (*Tale of Genji*)	源氏物語
genrō (elder statesmen)	元老
Gia Long (Emperor)	嘉隆
Ginkaku-ji (Silver Pavilion)	銀閣寺
Ginza (district of Tōkyō)	銀座
giri (duty)	義理
Go-Daigo (Emperor)	後醍醐
Go-Sakuramachi (Empress)	後桜町
Go-Shirakawa (Emperor)	後白河
Gong (Prince)	恭親王
gongchan-zhuyi (communism)	共产主义 (共產主義)
Gotō Shimpei	後藤新平
Gu Kaizhi	顧愷之
Guan wu liang shou jing	觀無量壽經
Guangxu (Emperor)	光緒
Guanyin (J: Kannon; K: Kwanŭm)	觀音
Guanzhong ("Within the Passes," Shaanxi)	關中
gunbatsu (warlord)	軍閥
guo (Mandarin pronunciation of "country")	國
Guo Maoqian	郭茂倩
Guomindang (*Kuo-min-tang*, Chinese Nationalist Party)	國民黨

guoyu (national language, i.e. Mandarin)	國語
Hakka (Mandarin: *kejia*)	客家
hallyu (Korean wave)	韓流
Hamaguchi Osachi	濱口雄幸
Han (Chinese)	漢
Han (Korean)	韓
Han Fei(zi)	韓非(子)
Han Gan	韓幹
Han Gaozu (Emperor)	漢高祖
Han Yu	韓愈
Han'guk (Korea)	韓國
han'gŭl (Korean alphabet)	한글
hanzi (Chinese characters)	漢字
Hara Kei (Takashi)	原敬
hashi (chopsticks)	箸
Hayashi Razan	林羅山
he (Chinese word for "river")	河
Heian (city and period)	平安
Heisei (reign period)	平成
Hideyori	秀賴
Hideyoshi	秀吉
(Mt.) Hiei	比叡山
Higashiyama (district of Kyōto)	東山
Himiko	卑彌呼
hiragana (Japanese syllabary)	平仮名
(Andō) Hiroshige	(安藤) 広重
Hizen (domain)	肥前
Ho Chi Minh	胡志明
Ho Quy Ly	胡季犛
hoang de (Vietnamese imperial title, C: *huangdi*)	皇帝
Hōjō (Kamakura regents)	北條
Hōkōji (Asukadera)	法興寺 (飛鳥寺)
(Katsushika) Hokusai	(葛飾) 北斎
Honda (motor company)	本田
Hōnen (Japanese Buddhist monk)	法然
Hong Mai	洪邁
Hong Xiuquan	洪秀全
Hosokawa (*daimyō* family)	細川
Hou Ji	后稷
Hu (northern non-Chinese people)	胡
Hu Yaobang	胡耀邦
Hua Guofeng	华国锋 (華國鋒)
Huaisu (Chinese calligrapher-monk)	懷素
huangdi (Chinese imperial title)	皇帝

Huangpu (Whampoa)	黃埔
Huaqiao (overseas Chinese)	華僑
Huaxia (China/Chinese)	華夏
Huiguo (Chinese Buddhist monk)	惠果
Huineng (Chinese Buddhist monk)	慧能
Hung kings	雄王
Hwabaek (Council of Nobles)	和白
hwangje (Korean imperial title, C: *huangdi*)	皇帝
Hwanung (Korean divinity)	桓雄
Hwarang (Flower Youths)	花郎
Hyegwan (Korean Buddhist monk, J: Ekan)	慧灌
Hyundai (Hyŏndae, conglomerate)	現代
idu (Korean writing)	吏讀
Iemochi (Tokugawa Shogun)	家茂
ikebana (flower arranging)	生け花
Ikkō ikki	一向一揆
Inukai Tsuyoshi	犬養毅
Iryŏn (Korean monk historian)	一然
Ishiwara Kanji	石原莞爾
Ishiyama Honganji	石山本願寺
Isuzu (motors)	いすゞ
Itagaki Taisuke	板垣退助
Itō Hirobumi	伊藤博文
Jia Yi	賈誼
jiang (Chinese word for "river")	江
Jiang Yuan	姜嫄
Jiaoran (Chinese poet-monk)	皎然
Jiaozhi (V: Giao-chi)	交趾
Jiaozhou	交州
Jie (northern non-Chinese people)	羯
Jingdezhen	景德鎮
Jinggang mountains	井岡山
jinshi (examination degree)	進士
Jōdo (Pure Land Buddhism)	淨土
Jōmon (prehistoric culture)	繩文
juche (self-reliance)	主體
jūdō (martial art)	柔道
juntian (equitable fields)	均田
junzi (gentleman)	君子
Jurchen (C: Nüzhen)	女真
Kabo reforms	甲午更張
Kabuki	歌舞伎
Kaitokudō	懷德堂
Kamakura (period and city)	鎌倉

kami (spirit/divinity)	神
kamikaze	神風
kana (Japanese syllabary)	仮名
Kang Youwei	康有爲
Kangxi (Emperor)	康熙
Kantō ("East of the Frontier Passes," a large plain near Tōkyō)	関東
karaoke	カラオケ
katakana (Japanese syllabary)	片仮名
keigo (Japanese honorific speech)	敬語
keiretsu (enterprise group)	系列
kendō (Japanese "way of the sword," fencing)	剣道
keshig (Mongol royal bodyguard)	怯薛
Khitan (C: Qidan)	契丹
Khubilai (C: Hubilie)	忽必烈
Ki no Tsurayuki	紀貫之
Kia (motor corporation)	起亞
Kim Dae Jung (Kim Tae-jung)	金大中
Kim Il Sung (Kim Il-sŏng)	金日成
Kim In-mun	金仁問
Kim Jong Il (Kim Chŏng-il)	金正日
Kim Jong-un (Kim Chŏng-ŭn)	金正恩
Kim Young Sam (Kim Yŏngsam)	金泳三
kimch'i (kimchee, Korean spicy pickled cabbage)	김치
kimono (Japanese-style clothing)	着物
Kinkaku-ji (Gold Pavilion)	金閣寺
Kirin beer	キリンビール
Kishi Nobusuke	岸信介
kobun (Korean "old tombs")	古墳
kofun (Japanese "old tombs")	古墳
Koguryŏ	高句麗
Kojiki (*Record of Ancient Matters*)	古事記
Kojong (King and Emperor)	高宗
Kōken (Empress)	孝謙
Kokinshū (*Collection of Ancient and Modern Poetry*)	古今集
kokka (Japanese word for "country")	国家
kokkai (Diet, the Japanese legislature)	国会
koku (measure of rice)	石
kokugo (national language)	国語
kokutai (national polity)	国体
kolp'um (bone-rank)	骨品
Kong Fuzi (Confucius)	孔夫子
Kong Qiu (Confucius)	孔丘
Kongmin (King)	恭愍

Koryŏ	高麗
kōtei (Japanese imperial title, C: *huangdi*)	皇帝
kuaizi (chopsticks)	筷子
Kūkai (Japanese Buddhist monk)	空海
Kumārajīva (C: Jiumoluoshi)	鳩摩羅什
Kuninaka Kimimaro	國中公麿
Kwantung (Guandong, "east of the passes," i.e. Manchuria)	關東
Lạc (early Viet subgroup)	雒
Laozi (Lao Tzu)	老子
Le Hoan	黎桓
Le Loi	黎利
Lee, Ang (Li An; motion picture director)	李安
Lee Kuan Yew	李光耀
Lee Kuang-huei (a.k.a. Nakamura Akio/Teruo, a.k.a. Suniyon)	李光輝 (中村輝夫)
Lelang (K: Nangnang)	樂浪
LG (conglomerate, formerly called Lucky Goldstar)	(樂喜金星)
li (decorum, rites)	禮
li (unit of distance)	里
li (principle)	理
Li Ao	李翱
Li Bai (alternate spelling: Li Po)	李白
Li Bi (Ly Bi)	李賁
Li Lisan	李立三
Li Yu	李漁
Li Yuan	李淵
Li Zicheng	李自成
liang zhi (innate conscience)	良知
Lin Zexu	林則徐
Lingnan (south of the mountain ranges)	嶺南
Linyi (early state in central Vietnam)	林邑
Liu Bang	劉邦
Liu Yuan	劉淵
Liu Yuxi	劉禹錫
Lu (state)	魯
Lu Fahe	陸法和
Lu Xun	魯迅
Lunyu (Analects)	論語
Lushan (mountain)	廬山
Ly Cong Uan	李公蘊
Ma Ying-jeou (Ma Yingjiu)	馬英九
Ma Yuan	馬遠
Mac Cuu (C: Mo Jiu)	鄚玖
Mac Dang Dung	莫登庸

magatama (prehistoric Japanese curved bead)	勾玉
Mahan (early Korean community)	馬韓
Maitreya (C: Mi le)	彌勒
Mālānanda (missionary monk; C: Moluonantuo)	摩羅難陀
Manchukuo (C: Manzhouguo)	滿洲國
Manchuria (C: Manzhou)	滿洲
manga (comics or cartoons)	漫画
Mantetsu (South Manchurian R.R.)	満鉄
Manyōshū (*Collection of Ten Thousand Leaves*)	万葉集
Mao Mountain	茅山
Mao Zedong	毛泽东 (毛澤東)
maripkan (early Korean title)	麻立干
matsurigoto (Japanese term for "government")	政
Matsushita (electronics corporation)	松下
Meiji Restoration	明治維新
Meishō (Empress)	明正
Mengzi (Mencius)	孟子
Miao (people)	苗
Miao fa lianhua jing	妙法蓮華經
miko (shrine maiden)	巫女
Mimizuka (Mound of Ears)	耳塚
(Southern) Min (dialect)	閩南
Minamoto (family)	源
Minamoto Yoritomo	源頼朝
ming jing (examination degree)	明經
Ming Taizu (Emperor)	明太祖
minjok (Korean pronunciation of "nation")	民族
minzoku (Japanese pronunciation of "nation")	民族
minzu (Mandarin pronunciation of "nation")	民族
Mitsubishi (bank and conglomerate)	三菱
Mitsui (bank and conglomerate)	三井
Mitsukoshi (department store)	三越
mixin (superstition)	迷信
Miyoshi Kiyotsura	三善清行
Mongol (C: Menggu)	蒙古
mono-no-aware	物の哀れ
Motoori Norinaga	本居宣長
Mouzi (Chinese Buddhist master)	牟子
Mozi (classical thinker)	墨子
mudang (shaman)	巫堂
Mulan (storied female warrior)	木蘭
Murakami (Emperor)	村上
Murakami Haruki	村上春樹
Murasaki Shikibu	紫式部

Muromachi (historical period)	室町
Murong Xianbei	慕容鮮卑
Muye (Shepard's Wilderness; battlefield)	牧野
Muyŏl (King)	武烈
Naka no Ōe (Prince)	中大兄
Nakamura Akio/Teruo (a.k.a. Lee Kuang-huei, a.k.a. Suniyon)	中村輝夫 (李光輝)
Nakatomi Kamatari	中臣鎌足
Nam Viet (C: Nan Yue)	南越
namu Amida Butsu	南無阿彌陀仏
Nanzhao (non-Chinese kingdom in southwest China)	南詔
Nara (early Japanese capital)	奈良
Ngo Dinh Diem	吳廷琰
Ngo Quyen	吳權
Nguyen (family)	阮
Nguyen Phuc Anh	阮福日
Nihon (Japan)	日本
Nihon shoki (*Nihongi*; *Chronicles of Japan*)	日本書紀 (日本紀)
Nihonjinron	日本人論
Nikkei (stock index)	日経
Nikon (corporation)	ニコン
ninjō (human feelings)	人情
Nintendō (video game company)	任天堂
Nissan (conglomerate)	日產
Nō (theater)	能
Nom (Vietnamese script)	喃
Nomonhan (C: Nuo men kan)	諾門坎
Nurgaci	努爾哈赤
Oda Nobunaga	織田信長
Odawara (domain)	小田原
Oirat (people; C: Waci)	瓦刺
Okada Keisuke	岡田啓介
Okchŏ (people)	沃沮
Ōkubo Toshimichi	大久保利通
Ōnin War	応仁の乱
onnade ("women's hand," i.e. *hiragana*)	女手
onnagata (performer of female roles)	女形
Ōsaka-ben (Ōsaka dialect)	大阪弁
Paekche	百濟
Pak (royal consort family)	朴
Parhae (kingdom in Manchuria)	渤海
Park Chung Hee (Pak Chŏng-hŭi)	朴正熙
Park Geun-hye (Pak Kŭnhye)	朴槿惠
pinyin (system for spelling Chinese)	拼音

Psy (Park Jae-sang; Korean pop musician)	싸이 (朴載相)
pu ke (poker)	扑克 (撲克)
puguk kangbyong	富国強兵
putonghua (Mandarin)	普通話
Puyi (last Emperor of China)	溥儀
Puyŏ (early state in Manchuria)	夫餘
Pyŏnhan (early Korean community)	弁韓
qaghan (khan, C: kehan)	可汗
qi (substance)	氣
Qi (Warring State)	齊
Qianlong (Emperor)	乾隆
Qieyun (rhyming dictionary)	切韻
Qigong (therapeutic exercise)	氣功
qin (musical instrument)	琴
Qin Shi Huangdi	秦始皇帝
qipao (banner gown)	旗袍
qiren (banner people)	旗人
quoc (Vietnamese word for "country")	國
quoc ngu (alphabetized Vietnamese writing)	國語
ramen (noodles) ラーメン (probably from C: *lamian*)	拉麵)
Rangaku (Dutch studies)	蘭學
ren (humanity)	仁
renga (linked verse)	連歌
renminbi (PRC currency)	人民币 (人民幣)
Rhee, Syngman (Yi Sŭngman)	李承晩
rickshaw (English, from J: *jinrikisha*)	人力車
Rikkokushi (Six National Histories of early Japan)	六國史
ritsuryō jidai	律令時代
Roh Tae Woo (No T'ae-u)	盧泰愚
rōnin (masterless samurai)	浪人
Ru (Confucian scholar)	儒
Ruan Ji	阮籍
Rujiao (Teachings of the Ru, i.e. Confucianism)	儒教
ruyi (scepter)	如意
sadae (serving the great)	事大
Saga (town and prefecture)	佐賀
Saigō Takamori	西郷隆盛
Saitō Makoto	斎藤実
sake (rice wine)	酒
Samguk (Korean Three Kingdoms)	三國
Samguk yusa (*Memorabilia of the Three Kingdoms*)	三國遺事
Samhan (three Han of early southern Korea)	三韓
Samsung (Samsŏng; conglomerate)	三星
samurai	侍

Sanguo zhi (dynastic history of the Chinese Three Kingdoms)	三國志
Sanguo zhi tongsu yanyi (classic novel *The Three Kingdoms*)	三國志通俗演義
sankin kōtai	參勤交代
Sanwa Bank	三和銀行
Sanxingdui	三星堆
Sapporo beer	サッポロビール
Saro (early Korean community)	斯盧
Satsuma (domain)	薩摩
Sei Shōnagon	清少納言
Sei-i tai-shōgun	征夷大將軍
Seiyūkai (political party)	政友会
Sejong (King)	世宗
Sekigahara (battlefield)	關原
semuren (Mongol ethnic category)	色目人
seng (generic Chinese term for Buddhist "monk")	僧
Senkaku (islands; C: Diaoyu 钓鱼 or 釣魚台)	尖閣
seppuku (ritual suicide)	切腹
Shan Yue ("mountain Viet"; people)	山越
Shang Yang (Lord)	商鞅
Shangdi (a supreme deity)	上帝
Shangjun shu (*Book of Lord Shang*)	商君書
Shangshu (*Book of Documents/History*)	尚書
Shatuo (Turkic people)	沙陀
Shennong (legendary ruler)	神農
shi (potential force)	勢
Shi Hu	石虎
Shi Xie	士燮
"Shiawase" ("Xingfu bu er jia," TV program title)	しあわせ
Shijing (*Book of Odes*)	詩經
Shimabara (location of rebellion)	島原
Shingon (Japanese school of Buddhism)	真言
Shintō (Japanese religion)	神道
Shirakawa (Emperor)	白河
Shiseido (Shiseidō; cosmetic company)	資生堂
shishi qiu shi ("seek truth through facts")	实事求是 (實事求是)
shōgun (C: *jiangjun*)	將軍
shōji (paper screen sliding door)	障子
Shōtoku Taishi	聖德太子
Shōwa (reign period of emperor personally named Hirohito 裕仁)	昭和
shu ("book" or "writing"; J: *kaku*)	書
Shu-Han (state)	蜀漢

Shujing (*Book of Documents/History*)	書經
Shun (Sage King)	舜
Silla	新羅
Soga (family)	蘇我
sōjō (head of Japanese Buddhist hierarchy)	僧正
Song (Zhou duchy)	宋
sŏnggol (hallowed-bone rank)	聖骨
sonnō jōi	尊王攘夷
Sony (corporation)	ソニー
Soong May-ling (Song Meiling)	宋美齡
Southern Min dialect	閩南話
sŏwŏn (academy)	書院
Śubhakarasiṃha (C: Shanwuwei)	善無畏
Sugawara Michizane	菅原道真
Sui Wendi (Emperor)	隋文帝
Suiko (Empress)	推古
sukiyaki	すき焼
sumera mikoto	天皇 (スメラミコト)
Sumitomo (bank and conglomerate)	住友
sumō (wrestling)	相撲
Sun Yat-sen (Zhongshan)	孫逸仙 (中山)
Sundo (missionary monk; C: Shundao)	順道
Sunzi bingfa (Sunzi's *Art of War*)	孫子兵法
sushi	寿司, 鮓 or 鮨
Suzuki Kantarō	鈴木貫太郎
T'aebaek Mountain	太白山
T'aejo (King)	太祖
t'aekwŏndo (martial art)	跆拳道
Taewŏn'gun (Lord of the Great Court)	大院君
Tai yu (Taiwanese dialect)	台語
taigi meibun	大義名分
Taihō (reign period)	大寶
taiji (*t'ai-chi*; "supreme ultimate")	太極
Taika (reign period)	大化
taipan (business executive; English, from Cantonese)	大班
Taiping (rebellion)	太平
Taiping tianguo	太平天國
Taiping yulan (encyclopedia)	太平御覽
Taira (family)	平
Taira Kiyomori	平清盛
Taishō (reign period)	大正
Taizu (Emperor)	太祖
Tan Luan (Chinese Buddhist monk)	曇鸞

Tang Taizong (Emperor)	唐太宗
Tan'gun (legendary founder of Korea)	檀君
Tangut (people; C: Dangxiang)	黨項
Tao Qian (a.k.a. Tao Yuanming)	陶潛 (陶淵明)
taotie (ancient bronze design)	饕餮
tatami (floor mats)	畳
Tay Son (rebellion, from Vietnamese place name)	西山
tempura	天麩羅
Tendai (Buddhist school; C: Tiantai)	天台
Teng, Teresa (Deng Lijun)	鄧麗君
Tenji (Emperor)	天智
tennō (Japanese imperial title)	天皇
Tet [nguyen dan] (lunar New Year)	節元旦
Thang-long (modern Hanoi)	昇龍
Tiananmen (Gate of Heavenly Peace)	天安門
tianming (Mandate of Heaven)	天命
tianwang (Heavenly King)	天王
tianxia (All Under Heaven)	天下
tianzi (Son of Heaven)	天子
Tibet (C: Tufan)	吐蕃
Tōdai-ji (Nara temple)	東大寺
Toghan-Temür	妥懽貼睦爾
tokonoma (alcove)	床の間
Tokugawa (family and shogunate)	徳川
Tokugawa Ieyasu	徳川家康
Tomioka silk mill	富岡製系場
Tonghak (Eastern Learning)	東學
Tongmenghui (Revolutionary Alliance)	同盟會
Tongwen guan (College of Foreign Languages)	同文館
Tongzhi (Emperor)	同治
Tongzhi Restoration	同治中興
tonkatsu (breaded pork cutlet)	豚カツ
Tonkin (Dong Kinh)	東京
Tosa (early Japanese province)	土佐
Tōshiba (corporation)	東芝
Tōyō Kanji	当用漢字
Toyota (Motor Corporation)	トヨタ or 豐田
Toyotomi Hideyoshi	豐臣秀吉
Tran (family)	陳
Trinh (family)	鄭
Trung Nhi	徵貳
Trung Trac	徵側
Tsai Ing-wen	蔡英文
tsunami (tidal wave)	津波

tsuwamono (Japanese warrior)	兵
Tuoba Xianbei	拓跋鮮卑
Türk (C: Tujue)	突厥
Uighur (Turkic people; C: Huihe)	回紇
uji (descent group)	氏
ujidera (clan temple)	氏寺
ukiyo (floating world, or entertainment district)	浮世
ukiyoe (pictures from the floating world; woodblock prints)	浮世絵
Vajrabodhi (C: Jin'gangzhi)	金剛智
Van mieu (temple of literature)	文廟
Van-lang kingdom	文郎國
Viet (C: Yue)	越
Vietnam Cong-san (Viet Cong)	越南共產
Wa (Japan)	倭
Wafū (Japanese-style)	和風
Wakō (Japanese pirates; C: *Wokou*)	倭寇
wang (Chinese word for "king" or "prince")	王
Wang Dao	王導
Wang Jingwei	汪精衛
Wang Kŏn	王建
Wang Mang	王莽
Wang Yangming	王陽明
Wang Xizhi	王羲之
wen (literary)	文
Wen (Zhou king)	文
Wen xuan (*Selections of Refined Literature*)	文選
Whampoa (Huangpu)	黃埔
Wiman (founder of historical Chosŏn Kingdom)	衛滿
Wŏn'gwang (Korean Buddhist monk)	圓光
Wu (Zhou king)	武
wu (martial)	武
Wu liang shou jing	無量壽經
Wu Zetian	武則天
Wudi (Emperor Wu)	武帝
Wujing qi shu (*Seven Military Classics*)	武經七書
wuwei (nonaction)	無爲
Xi Jinping	习近平 (習近平)
Xi Xia (state)	西夏
xiao (filial piety)	孝
Xiaojing (*Classic of Filial Piety*)	孝經
Xianbei (people)	鮮卑
Xiaowen (N. Wei Emperor)	孝文
Xiaowu (Liu-Song Emperor)	孝武
xin (new)	新

Xin Qingnian (*New Youth*)	新青年
"Xingfu bu er jia" ("Shiawase," TV program title)	幸福不二家
Xinjing (capital of Manchukuo)	新京
Xiongnu (nomadic empire)	匈奴
Xu Guangqi (Paul)	徐光啟
Xuanwu gate	玄武門
Xuanxue (*Mysterious Learning*)	玄學
Xuanzang (Buddhist pilgrim)	玄奘
Xuanzong (Tang Emperor)	玄宗
Xunzi (classical thinker)	荀子
Yamaga Sokō	山鹿素行
Yamana (*daimyō* family)	山名
Yamatai	邪馬台
Yamato (Japan)	大和
Yan (kingdom)	燕
Yan wang (Yama, King of Hell)	閻王
Yang Guifei	楊貴妃
Yang Jian	楊堅
yangban	兩班
Yangdi (Sui Emperor)	煬帝
Yangshao (Neolithic culture)	仰韶
Yanmen (a place in Shanxi)	雁門
Yao (people)	猺
Yao (Sage King)	堯
Yasuda (conglomerate)	安田
Yawata (steel mill)	八幡
Yayoi (Neolithic culture)	彌生
Ye (city)	鄴
Yemaek (people)	濊貊
yen (Japanese monetary unit)	円
Yi (eastern non-Chinese people)	夷
"Yi lu shang you ni" (TV program)	一路上有你
Yi Sŏng-gye	李成桂
Yi Sun-sin	李舜臣
"*Yi wu suoyou*" (song title)	一无所有 (一無所有)
Yihequan (Boxers)	義和拳
Yijian zhi (*Record of Hearsay*)	夷堅志
Yijing (*Book of Changes*)	易經
yin-yang	陰陽
Ying Zheng	嬴政
Yōfū (Western-style)	洋風
Yŏn Kaesomun	淵蓋蘇文
Yŏngjo (King)	英祖

Yongle (Emperor)	永樂
Yoshida Shigeru	吉田茂
Yoshida Shoin	吉田松蔭
Yoshino (Japanese Southern dynasty capital)	吉野
yŏwang (female king)	女王
Yu (the Great, Sage King)	禹
Yuan (Chinese surname of Tuoba Xianbei ruling family)	元
yuan (Chinese monetary unit)	圓
Yuan Shikai	袁世凱
Yuan Zhen	元稹
Yun'gang (Buddhist grottoes)	雲崗
Yunmeng (archeological site in central China)	雲夢
yushin (revitalization or restoration)	維新
zaibatsu (a type of conglomerate)	財閥
Zen (C: Chan)	禪
Zhang Zuolin	張作霖
Zhao Kuangyin	趙匡胤
Zhao Tuo (V: Trieu Da)	趙佗
Zhao Ziyang	赵紫阳 (趙紫陽)
Zhenbao (Damansky) Island	珍宝岛 (珍寶島)
Zheng Chenggong (Koxinga)	鄭成功
Zheng He	鄭和
zhong (loyalty)	忠
Zhongguo (Central Country, i.e. China)	中國
"Zhongguo hao shengyin" (TV program)	中国好声音
Zhonghua (China)	中華
Zhongnanhai (CCP leadership compound in Beijing)	中南海
Zhou, Duke of	周公
Zhou Enlai	周恩來
Zhu De	朱德
Zhu Xi	朱熹
Zhu Yuanzhang	朱元璋
Zhuang (people)	獞 or 壯
Zhuangzi (*Chuang Tzu*)	莊子
Zongli Yamen	總理衙門
zu (Chinese word for "ethnicity")	族
Zunghar (nomadic people)	準噶爾

Notes

Introduction

1. The top five national economies in 2014 (not counting the European Union as a "nation"), based on estimates of their actual size rather than official statistics, were China, the United States, India, Japan, and Germany, according to the Central Intelligence Agency (CIA), "World Fact Book," country comparison: GDP (purchasing power parity), https://www.cia.gov/library/publications/the-world-factbook/.

2. P. Bairoch, "International Industrialization Levels from 1750 to 1980," *Journal of European Economic History* 11, no. 2 (1982): 296, table 10.

3. Tsuen-Hsuin Tsien, *Written on Bamboo and Silk: The Beginnings of Chinese Books and Inscriptions* (University of Chicago Press, 1962), p. 2.

4. See E. F. Vogel, *Japan as Number One: Lessons for America* (Cambridge, MA: Harvard University Press, 1979).

5. CIA, "World Fact Book" country comparison: GDP-per capita (purchasing power parity), 2014 data.

6. M. W. Lewis and K. E. Wigen, *The Myth of Continents: A Critique of Metageography* (Berkeley: University of California Press, 1997), pp. 16, 21, 53–55. The statistics are from R. B. Marks, *The Origins of the Modern World: A Global and Ecological Narrative from the Fifteenth to the Twenty-First Century*, 2nd ed. (Lanham, MD: Rowman and Littlefield, 2007), pp. 80–81.

7. I-tien Hsing (trans. by W. G. Crowell), "Heracles in the East: The Diffusion and Transformation of his Image in the Arts of Central Asia, India, and Medieval China," *Asia Major*, third series, 18.2 (2005): 126–127. A. E. Dien, *Six Dynasties Civilization* (New Haven: Yale University Press, 2007), pp. 104–105, 288–289. E. Ramírez-Weaver, "Islamic Silver for Carolingian Reforms and the Buddha-Image of Helgö: Rethinking Carolingian Connections with the East, 790–820," in *China and Beyond in the Mediaeval Period: Cultural Crossings and Inter-Regional Connections*, ed. D. C. Wong and G. Heldt (New Delhi: Manohar, 2014), pp. 171, 178.

8. J. K. Skaff, *Sui-Tang China and its Turko-Mongol Neighbors: Culture, Power, and Connections, 580–800* (Oxford University Press, 2012), p. 294. R. von Glahn, "Imagining Premodern China," in *The Song-Yuan-Ming Transition in Chinese History*, ed. P. J. Smith and R. von Glahn (Cambridge, MA: Harvard University Asia Center, 2003), pp. 64–65.

9. This is a major theme of V. Lieberman, *Strange Parallels: Southeast Asia in Global Context, c. 800–1830; vol. II, Mainland Mirrors: Europe, Japan, China, South Asia, and the Islands* (Cambridge University Press, 2009).

10. See for example P. Heather, *Empires and Barbarians: The Fall of Rome and the Birth of Europe* (Oxford University Press, 2009).

11. See W. McCord, *The Dawn of the Pacific Century: Implication for Three Worlds of Development* (New Brunswick, NJ: Transaction, 1993), pp. 28–29, 105–107, 183–184. McCord himself favors structural and policy explanations over those rooted in cultural differences.

12. Guo Maoqian (fl. 1264–1269 CE), *Yuefu shiji* (Collected Music Bureau Poetry) (Taibei: Taiwan Zhonghua shuju, 1965), 44.1a.

13. D. Yen-ho Wu, "The Construction of Chinese and Non-Chinese Identities," in *The Living Tree: The Changing Meaning of Being Chinese Today*, ed. Wei-ming Tu (Stanford University Press, 1994), p. 150.

14. E. H. Schafer, "The *Yeh Chung Chi*," *T'oung Pao* 76, nos. 4–5 (1990): 147–149. See also J. Fitzgerald, "The Nationless State: The Search for a Nation in Modern Chinese Nationalism," in *Chinese Nationalism*, ed. J. Unger (Armonk, NY: M. E. Sharpe, 1996), p. 67.

15. Y. Pines, "Beasts or Humans: Pre-Imperial Origins of the 'Sino-Barbarian' Dichotomy," in *Mongols, Turks, and Others: Eurasian Nomads and the Sedentary World*, ed. R. Amitai and M. Biran (Leiden, Netherlands: Brill, 2005), p. 62.

16. Fang Xuanling, *Jin shu* (The Dynastic History of the Jin) (644 CE) (Beijing: Zhonghua shuju, 1974), 28.844.

17. C. I. Beckwith argues strenuously that the concept of barbarian "does not exist in Chinese" in his *Empires of the Silk Road: A History of Central Eurasia from the Bronze Age to the Present* (Princeton University Press, 2009), pp. 355–362.

18. W. G. Aston, trans., *Nihongi: Chronicles of Japan from the Earliest Times to A.D. 697* (Rutland, VT: Charles E. Tuttle, [1896] 1972), vol. I, p. 1, note 1. See also C. Holcombe, *The Genesis of East Asia, 221 B.C.–A.D. 907* (Honolulu: University of Hawai'i Press, 2001), pp. 72–73.

19. For tea, see D. Keene, *Yoshimasa and the Silver Pavilion: The Creation of the Soul of Japan* (New York: Columbia University Press, 2003), pp. 139–151. For sushi, see S. Issenberg, *The Sushi Economy: Globalization and the Making of a Modern Delicacy* (New York: Gotham Books, 2007), p. xxi. For *jūdō*, see Inoue Shun, "The Invention of the Martial Arts: Kanō Jigorō and Kōdōkan Judo," in *Mirror of Modernity: Invented Traditions of Modern Japan*, ed. S. Vlastos (Berkeley: University of California Press, 1998), pp. 163–173. For the nation-state, see T. Morris-Suzuki, "A Descent into the Past: The Frontier in the Construction of Japanese Identity," in *Multicultural Japan: Palaeolithic to Postmodern*, ed. D. Denoon et al. (Cambridge University Press, 1996), p. 82.

20. A. B. Woodside, *Vietnam and the Chinese Model: A Comparative Study of Nguyên and Ch'ing Civil Government in the First Half of the Nineteenth Century* (Cambridge, MA: Harvard University Press, 1971), p. 120.

21. Pierre Gourou, writing in 1936, quoted in V. Lieberman, *Strange Parallels: Southeast Asia in Global Context, c. 800–1830, vol. I. Integration on the Mainland* (Cambridge University Press, 2003), p. 343.

Chapter 1

1. Technically, the emperor only denied that he was a "manifest deity" and did not renounce the claim to descent from the sun goddess. See J. W. Dower, *Embracing Defeat: Japan in the Wake of World War II* (New York: W. H. Norton, 1999), p. 316.

2. D. E. Mungello, *Curious Land: Jesuit Accommodation and the Origins of Sinology* (Honolulu: University of Hawai'i Press, 1985), pp. 144, 179.

3. Ping-ti Ho, *The Cradle of the East: An Inquiry into the Indigenous Origins of Techniques and Ideas of Neolithic and Early Historic China, 5000–1000 B.C.* (Chinese University of Hong Kong, 1975).

4. A. Sherratt, "The Trans-Eurasian Exchange: The Prehistory of Chinese Relations with the West," in *Contact and Exchange in the Ancient World*, ed. V. H. Mair (Honolulu: University of Hawai'i Press, 2006), pp. 32, 53.

5. S. M. Nelson, "The Politics of Ethnicity in Prehistoric Korea," in *Nationalism, Politics, and the Practice of Archaeology*, ed. P. L. Kohl and C. Fawcett (Cambridge University Press, 1995), p. 221.

6. N. Ostler, *Empires of the Word: A Language History of the World* (New York: HarperCollins, 2005), p. xix.

7. A. P. Smyth, "The Emergence of English Identity, 700–1000," in *Medieval Europeans: Studies in Ethnic Identity and National Perspectives in Medieval Europe*, ed. A. P. Smyth (New York: St. Martin's Press, 1998), p. 25.

8. See J. DeFrancis, *The Chinese Language: Fact and Fantasy* (Honolulu: University of Hawai'i Press, 1984), pp. 54–58.

9. S. R. Ramsey, *The Languages of China* (Princeton University Press, 1987), pp. 21, 24.

10. Chen Shou (233–297 CE), *Sanguo zhi (Chronicles of the Three Kingdoms)* (Beijing: Zhonghua shuju, 1959), 30.852.

11. P. Bellwood, *Prehistory of the Indo-Malaysian Archipelago* (Honolulu: University of Hawai'i Press, [1985] 1997), pp. 97, 110; J. Norman and Tsu-lin Mei, "The Austroasiatics in Ancient South China: Some Lexical Evidence," *Monumenta Serica* 32 (1976).

12. B. G. Trigger, *Understanding Early Civilizations: A Comparative Study* (Cambridge University Press, 2003), pp. 600–602.

13. A. R. Millard, "The Infancy of the Alphabet," *World Archaeology* 17, no. 3 (1986): 394–396.

14. W. C. Hannas, *Asia's Orthographic Dilemma* (Honolulu: University of Hawai'i Press, 1997), p. 28.

15. I. Morris, *The World of the Shining Prince: Court Life in Ancient Japan* (Harmondsworth, UK: Penguin Books, [1964] 1985), p. 207.

16. I. Smits, "The Way of the Literati: Chinese Learning and Literary Practice in Mid-Heian Japan," in *Heian Japan, Centers and Peripheries*, ed. M. Adolphson, E. Kamens, and S. Matsumoto (Honolulu: University of Hawai'i Press, 2007), p. 106; P. Kornicki, *The Book in Japan: A Cultural History from the Beginnings to the Nineteenth Century* (Leiden, Netherlands: Brill, 1998), p. 382; D. Keene, "The Sino-Japanese War of 1894–95 and Its Cultural Effects in Japan," in *Tradition and Modernization in Japanese Culture*, ed. D. H. Shively (Princeton University Press, 1971), pp. 167–172.

17. J. Stanlaw, "'For Beautiful Human Life': The Use of English in Japan," in *Re-made in Japan: Everyday Life and Consumer Taste in a Changing Society*, ed. J. J. Tobin (New Haven, CT: Yale University Press, 1992), pp. 61–62.

18. Kichung Kim, *An Introduction to Classical Korean Literature: From Hyangga to P'ansori* (Armonk, NY: M. E. Sharpe, 1996), p. 5.

19. Hannas, *Asia's Orthographic Dilemma*, p. 183.

20. L. Febvre and H. J. Martin, *The Coming of the Book: The Impact of Printing, 1450–1800*, trans. D. Gerard (London: NLB, [1958] 1976), p. 249.

21. Kwang-chih Chang, *Shang Civilization* (New Haven, CT: Yale University Press, 1980), pp. 38–39, 42–52.

22. S. Allan, "Erlitou and the Formation of Chinese Civilization: Toward a New Paradigm," *Journal of Asian Studies* 66, no. 2 (2007).

23. *Shoku Nihongi* (Continued Chronicles of Japan) (797 CE), Shin Nihon koten bungaku taikei 12 (Tōkyō: Iwanami shoten, 1989), 4.124–127.

24. Trigger, *Understanding Early Civilizations*, p. 79.

Chapter 2

1. G. Shelach-Lavi, "Steppe Land Interactions and their Effects on Chinese Cultures during the Second and Early First Millennia BCE," in *Nomads as Agents of Cultural Change: The Mongols and their Eurasian Predecessors*, ed. R. Amitai and M. Biran (Honolulu: University of Hawai'i Press, 2015), pp. 10–31.

2. Beckwith, *Empires of the Silk Road*, pp. 1–12.

3. Han Yu (768–824 CE), "Yuan dao" (Essentials of the Moral Way), in *Han Changli quanji* (Beijing: Zhongguo shudian, 1991), 11.174. Here *Yi* is translated as "foreign" and *Zhongguo* as "Chinese." For a slightly variant translation, see W. T. de Bary and I. Bloom, eds., *Sources of Chinese Tradition, vol. 1. From Earliest Times to 1600,* 2nd ed. (New York: Columbia University Press, 1999), p. 572.

4. Sanping Chen, *Multicultural China in the Early Middle Ages* (Philadelphia: University of Pennsylvania Press, 2012), pp. 122, 138, 142–146.

5. Y. Pines, *Envisioning Eternal Empire: Chinese Political Thought of the Warring States Era* (Honolulu: University of Hawai'i Press, 2009), pp. 20, 29–30.

6. L. M. Jensen, *Manufacturing Confucianism: Chinese Traditions and Universal Civilization* (Durham, NC: Duke University Press, 1997), p. 5.

7. All quotations from Zhou period texts in this chapter are from de Bary and Bloom, *Sources of Chinese Tradition.*

8. P. Duus, *The Abacus and the Sword: The Japanese Penetration of Korea, 1895–1910* (Berkeley: University of California Press, 1995), p. 31n5.

9. *Shoku Nihongi,* 20.182–183.

10. G. B. Sansom, *Japan: A Short Cultural History* (Stanford University Press, [1931] 1978), p. 109.

11. H. Ooms, *Imperial Politics and Symbolics in Ancient Japan: The Tenmu Dynasty, 650–800* (Honolulu: University of Hawai'i Press, 2009), pp. 165–168, and frequent references to Daoism.

12. D. E. Mungello, *The Great Encounter of China and the West, 1500–1800* (Lanham, MD: Rowman and Littlefield, 1999), pp. 89–90.

13. R. J. Samuels, *"Rich Nation Strong Army": National Security and the Technological Transformation of Japan* (Ithaca, NY: Cornell University Press, 1994), p. 35.

14. See R. D. Sawyer, "Military Writings," in *A Military History of China,* ed. D. A. Graff and R. Higham (Boulder, CO: Westview Press, 2002). See also R. D. Sawyer and Mei-chün Sawyer, trans., *The Seven Military Classics of Ancient China* (New York: Basic Books, [1993] 2007).

15. A. I. Johnston, *Cultural Realism: Strategic Culture and Grand Strategy in Chinese History* (Princeton University Press, 1995), pp. 107–108.

16. Sima Qian (145–90? BCE), *Shi ji* (Records of the Grand Historian) (Beijing: Zhonghua shuju, 1959), 6.245.

17. H. Wang, "How Much for a Camel? A New Understanding of Money on the Silk Road before AD 800," in *The Silk Road: Trade, Travel, War and Faith,* ed. S. Whitfield with U. Sims-Williams (Chicago: Serindia, 2004), p. 27.

18. Chun-shu Chang, *The Rise of the Chinese Empire,* vol. 1. *Nation, State, and Imperialism in Early China, ca. 1600 B.C.–A.D. 8* (Ann Arbor: University of Michigan Press, 2007), p. 58.

19. D. Bodde, "The State and Empire of Ch'in," in *The Cambridge History of China, vol. 1. The Ch'in and Han Empires, 221 B.C.–A.D. 220,* ed. D. Twitchett and M. Loewe (Cambridge University Press, 1986), p. 50.

20. *Lü shi chunqiu, jinzhu jinyi* (The Spring and Autumn of Master Lü, Newly Annotated and Newly Interpreted) (ca. 239 BCE) (Taibei: Taiwan shangwu yinshuguan, 1989), 13.350; Sima Qian, *Shi ji,* 6.238–239.

21. M. J. Puett, *To Become a God: Cosmology, Sacrifice, and Self-Divinization in Early China* (Cambridge, MA: Harvard University Press, 2002), pp. 225, 240.

22. De Bary and Bloom, *Sources of Chinese Tradition,* pp. 228–231.

23. Chang, *Rise of the Chinese Empire,* vol. 1, p. 246.

24. S. A. Queen, *From Chronicle to Canon: The Hermeneutics of the Spring and Autumn, According to Tung Chung-shu* (Cambridge University Press, 1996), p. 115.

25. B. Watson, trans., *Courtier and Commoner in Ancient China: Selections from the* History of the Former Han *by Pan Ku* (New York: Columbia University Press, 1974), pp. 192–193.

26. Feng Yan, *Feng shi wenjian ji, jiaozhu* (A Record of what Mr. Feng Heard and Saw, Revised and Annotated) (ca. 800 CE) (Beijing: Zhonghua shuju, 1958), 2.8.

27. Fan Ye (398–445 CE), *Hou-Han shu* (Dynastic History of the Later Han) (Beijing: Zhonghua shuju, 1965), 84.2801.

28. See H. L. Goodman, *Ts'ao P'i Transcendent: The Political Culture of Dynasty-Founding in China at the End of the Han* (Seattle: Scripta Serica, 1998).

29. Fang Xuanling, *Jin shu*, 69.1848.

Chapter 3

1. The Sixteen Kingdoms were Former Zhao (or Han), Later Zhao, Former Yan, Former Qin, Later Yan, Later Qin, Southern Yan, Xia, Former Liang, Shu (or Cheng-Han), Later Liang, Western Qin, Southern Liang, Western Liang, Northern Liang, and Northern Yan.

2. Sanping Chen, *Multicultural China in the Early Middle Ages* (Philadelphia: University of Pennsylvania Press, 2012), pp. 140–142.

3. The Five Hu peoples were the Xiongnu, the Xianbei, the Di, the Qiang, and the Jie.

4. N. Di Cosmo, *Ancient China and its Enemies: The Rise of Nomadic Power in East Asian History* (Cambridge University Press, 2002), pp. 52, 134–138.

5. See D. A. Graff, *Medieval Chinese Warfare, 300–900* (London: Routledge, 2002), pp. 41–42.

6. Fang Xuanling, *Jin shu*, 101.2649.

7. Sun Sheng (4th century), *Jin yang qiu* (Annals of Jin), quoted in Liu Yiqing (403–444 CE), *Shishuo xinyu, jiaojian* (A New Account of Tales of the World, Revised Commentary), (Hong Kong: Zhonghua shuju, 1987), A.97 (chap. 3, no. 12). Translated slightly differently in R. B. Mather, trans., *Shih-shuo Hsin-yü: A New Account of Tales of the World* (Minneapolis: University of Minnesota Press, 1976), p. 86, no. 12, note 1.

8. For the imperial library, see Xiaofei Tian, *Beacon Fire and Shooting Star: The Literary Culture of the Liang (502–557)* (Cambridge, MA: Harvard University Asia Center, 2007), p. 95. For the *Wen xuan*, see D. R. Knechtges, "Culling the Weeds and Selecting Prime Blossoms: The Anthology in Early Medieval China," in *Culture and Power in the Reconstitution of the Chinese Realm, 200–600*, ed. S. Pearce, A. Spiro, and P. Ebrey (Cambridge, MA: Harvard University Press, 2001), pp. 206, 239.

9. Liu Shufen, "Jiankang and the Commercial Empire of the Southern Dynasties: Change and Continuity in Medieval Chinese Economic History," in Pearce et al., *Culture and Power*, pp. 35 and 254n2.

10. B. Ward-Perkins, *The Fall of Rome and the End of Civilization* (Oxford University Press, 2005), p. 87.

11. Seng You (435–518 CE), *Hong ming ji* (Collection Expanding Illumination) (Taibei: Taiwan Zhonghua shuju, 1983), epilogue, 14.9b. Here translating *Xia* and *Hua* as "China" and *Rong* and *Yi* as "barbarian."

12. Wei Shou, *Wei shu* (Dynastic History of the [Northern] Wei) (554 CE) (Beijing: Zhonghua shuju, 1974), 97.2142.

13. Yu Xin (513–581), in Zhang Zhuo (early eighth century), *Chao ye qian zai* (The Whole Record of Court and Country), preserved in *Taiping guangji* (Extensive Records [Assembled during] the Taiping Era) (978 CE) (Beijing: Zhonghua shuju, 1981), 198.1483.

14. C. Holcombe, "The Xianbei in Chinese History," *Early Medieval China*, 19 (2013): 1–38.

15. J. Holmgren, "The Composition of the Early Wei Bureaucratic Elite as Background to the Emperor Kao-tsu's Reforms (423–490 AD)," *Journal of Asian History* 27 (1993): 115–116.

16. K. A. Lingley, "Naturalizing the Exotic: On the Changing Meaning of Ethnic Dress in Medieval China," *Ars Orientalis*, 38 (2010): 50–80.

17. Wang Tong (ca. 584–617 CE), *Wenzhongzi zhongshuo* (Master Wenzhong's [i.e., Wang Tong's] Discourses on the Mean) (Taibei: Taiwan Zhonghua shuju, 1965), 4.3a.

18. A. F. Wright, "The Sui Dynasty (581–617)," in *The Cambridge History of China, vol. III. Sui and T'ang China, 589–906, Part 1*, ed. D. Twitchett (Cambridge University Press, 1979), p. 49.

19. Li Baiyao (565–648 CE), *Bei-Qi shu* (Dynastic History of the Northern Qi) (Beijing: Zhonghua shuju, 1972), 50.693.

20. A. L. Juliano and J. A. Lerner, eds., *Monks and Merchants: Silk Road Treasures from Northwest China, Gansu and Ningxia, 4th–7th Century* (New York: Harry N. Abrams, 2001), pp. 98–100.

21. A. E. Dien, *Six Dynasties Civilization* (New Haven, CT: Yale University Press, 2007), pp. 71–75; M. E. Lewis, *China between Empires: The Northern and Southern Dynasties* (Cambridge, MA: Harvard University Press, 2009), p. 105.

22. Lewis, *China between Empires*, pp. 196–204; S. R. Bokenkamp, *Ancestors and Anxiety: Daoism and the Birth of Rebirth in China* (Berkeley: University of California Press, 2007), pp. 171–172, 182.

23. Huijiao, *Gao seng zhuan* (Biographies of Eminent Monks) (ca. 530 CE) (Taibei: Huiwentang, 1987), 10.240.

24. See J. A. Millward, *Eurasian Crossroads: A History of Xinjiang* (New York: Columbia University Press, 2007).

25. Mouzi, "Lihuo lun" (On Disposing of Error), *Hong ming ji*, 1.9b.

26. The estimate is from P. L. Swanson, *The Foundations of T'ien-T'ai Philosophy: The Flowering of the Two Truths Theory in Chinese Buddhism* (Berkeley, CA: Asian Humanities Press, 1989), p. 44.

27. Li Yanshou, *Nan shi* (History of the Southern Dynasties) (ca. 629 CE) (Beijing: Zhonghua shuju, 1975), 70.1721–1722.

28. W. G. Aston, trans., *Nihongi: Chronicles of Japan from the Earliest Times to A.D. 697* (Rutland, VT: Charles E. Tuttle, [1896] 1972), vol. II, pp. 66–67.

29. S. M. Nelson, *The Archaeology of Korea* (Cambridge University Press, 1993), p. 147.

30. Hsu Cho-yun (Xu Zhuoyun) and K. M. Linduff, *Western Chou Civilization* (New Haven, CT: Yale University Press, 1988), p. 201.

31. *A Study of the Parhae Kingdom* (Parhae ko), by Yu Tŭk-kong (1748–1807).

32. G. Ledyard, "Galloping Along with the Horseriders: Looking for the Founders of Japan," *Journal of Japanese Studies* 1, no. 2 (1975): 231.

33. K. H. J. Gardiner, *The Early History of Korea: The Historical Development of the Peninsula up to the Introduction of Buddhism in the Fourth Century AD* (Honolulu: University of Hawai'i Press, 1969), pp. 40–42, 53–58. Hyung Il Pai, *Constructing "Korean" Origins: A Critical Review of Archaeology, Historiography, and Racial Myth in Korean State-Formation Theories* (Cambridge, MA: Harvard University Asia Center, 2000), pp. 196, 233–234.

34. Kyeongmi Joo, "The Gold Jewelry of Ancient Silla: Syncretism of Northern and Southern Asian Cultures," in *New Perspectives on Early Korean Art: From Silla to Koryŏ*, ed. Youn-mi Kim (Seoul: Korea Institute, Harvard University, 2013), pp. 243–302.

35. Choi Jongtaik, "The Development of the Pottery Technologies of the Korean Peninsula and Their Relationship to Neighboring Regions," in *Early Korea 1: Reconsidering Early Korean History through Archaeology*, ed. M. E. Byington (Seoul: Korea Institute, Harvard University, 2008), pp. 157, 176–187.

36. The current text of the *Chronicles of the Three Kingdoms* actually reads "Yemayi," but this appears to be a garbling of the original. See W. W. Farris, *Sacred Texts and Buried Treasures: Issues in the Historical Archaeology of Ancient Japan* (Honolulu: University of Hawai'i Press, 1998), p. 22.

37. Kwon Oh Young, "The Influence of Recent Archaeological Discoveries on the Research of Paekche History," in Byington, *Early Korea 1*, pp. 97–102.

38. H. Ooms, *Imperial Politics and Symbolics in Ancient Japan: The Tenmu Dynasty, 650–800* (Honolulu: University of Hawai'i Press, 2009), pp. 102–103.

39. See M. J. Seth, *A Concise History of Korea: From the Neolithic Period through the Nineteenth Century* (Lanham, MD: Rowman and Littlefield, 2006), p. 8

40. D. B. Lurie, *Realms of Literacy: Early Japan and the History of Writing* (Cambridge, MA: Harvard University Asia Center, 2011), p. 92.

41. J. M. Kitagawa, *On Understanding Japanese Religion* (Princeton University Press, [1979] 1987), pp. 71, 117–126.

42. See J. R. Piggott, *The Emergence of Japanese Kingship* (Stanford University Press, 1997), pp. 91–92, 127.

43. Aston, *Nihongi*, vol. II, p. 131.

Chapter 4

1. P. Kennedy, *The Rise and Fall of the Great Powers: Economic Change and Military Conflict from 1500 to 2000* (New York: Random House, 1987), pp. xvi, 515.

2. H. J. Wechsler, *Mirror to the Son of Heaven: Wei Cheng at the Court of T'ang T'ai-tsung* (New Haven, CT: Yale University Press, 1974), p. 31.

3. A. Eisenberg argues that the Tang founder actively anticipated such deadly competition between his sons in chapter 6 of *Kingship in Early Medieval China* (Leiden, Netherlands: Brill, 2008).

4. Wen Daya, *Da-Tang chuangye qiju zhu* (Diary of the Founding of Great Tang) (ca. 626 CE) (Shanghai: Shanghai guji chubanshe, 1983), 1.2.

5. See Yihong Pan, *Son of Heaven and Heavenly Qaghan: Sui-Tang China and Its Neighbors* (Bellingham: Western Washington University, 1997), pp. 179–181.

6. Xuanzang (ca. 596–664 CE) and Bianji (620–648 CE), *Da-Tang xiyu ji* (A Record of the Western Regions in Great Tang) (Taibei: Xinwenfeng chuban gongsi, 1987), 1.78.

7. M. S. Abramson, *Ethnic Identity in Tang China* (Philadelphia: University of Pennsylvania Press, 2008), p. xi.

8. Shao-yun Yang, "Fan and Han: The Origins and Uses of a Conceptual Dichotomy in Mid-Imperial China, ca. 500–1200," in *Political Strategies of Identity Building in Non-Han Empires in China*, ed. F. Fiaschetti and J. Schneider (Wiesbaden: Harrassowitz Verlag, 2014), pp. 18–20.

9. Du You, *Tong dian* (Comprehensive Canons) (801 CE) (Beijing: Zhonghua shuju, 1984), 146.763, panel a.

10. Lu Fahe's biography is in *Bei-Qi shu*, 32.427–431.

11. A. E. Dien, "Civil Service Examinations: Evidence from the Northwest," in *Culture and Power in the Reconstitution of the Chinese Realm, 200–600*, ed. S. Pearce, A. Spiro, and P. Ebrey (Cambridge, MA: Harvard University Press, 2001), pp. 99–121.

12. C. Benn, *China's Golden Age: Everyday Life in the Tang Dynasty* (Oxford University Press, 2002), p. 255.

13. Yuan Zhen, *Yuan shi changqing ji* (The Works of Mr. Yuan [Zhen], Collected in the Changqing Era [821–825 CE]) (Taibei: Taiwan Zhonghua shuju, 1965), 51.1b.

14. Wang Qinruo, *Cefu yuangui* (The Great Tortoise of Archives) (ca. 1012 CE) (Taibei: Taiwan Zhonghua shuju, 1981), 160.1932. Entry dated 835 CE.

15. Ouyang Xiu and Song Qi, *Xin Tang shu* (New Dynastic History of the Tang) (1060 CE) (Beijing: Zhonghua shuju, 1975), 135.4576.

16. R. H. Sharf, *Coming to Terms with Chinese Buddhism: A Reading of the* Treasure Store Treatise (Honolulu: University of Hawai'i Press, 2002), pp. 7–9.

17. H. Dumoulin, *Zen Buddhism: A History, vol. I. India and China*, trans. J. W. Heisig and P. Knitter (New York: Macmillan, 1988), p. 85.

18. S. Owen, *The Great Age of Chinese Poetry: The High T'ang* (New Haven, CT: Yale University Press, 1981), p. 292.

19. See E. G. Pulleyblank, *The Background of the Rebellion of An Lu-shan* (London: Oxford University Press, 1955).

20. M. R. Drompp, *Tang China and the Collapse of the Uighur Empire: A Documentary History* (Leiden, Netherlands: Brill, 2005), pp. 20–38.

21. Abramson, *Ethnic Identity in Tang China*, pp. 179–191.

22. Han Yu (768–824 CE), "Yu Meng Shangshu shu" (Letter to Minister Meng [Jian]), in *Han Changli quanji*, 18.268.

23. Wen Tingyun (mid-ninth century), "Ganzhuanzi" (Master Dried Re-cooked Meat), extracted in *Taiping guangji*, 243.1875–1879.

24. R. M. Hartwell, "Demographic, Political, and Social Transformations of China, 750–1550," *Harvard Journal of Asiatic Studies* 42, no. 2 (1982): 366.

25. Iryŏn, *Samguk yusa* (Memorabilia from the Three [Korean] Kingdoms) (1280 CE), 4; T.49.1002.

26. Kim Pu-sik, *Samguk sagi* (Historical Record of the Three [Korean] Kingdoms) (1145 CE) (Seoul: Hongsin munhwasa, 1994), vol. 1, p. 413 (Koguryŏ Basic Annals 10).

27. Chŏng In-ji, *Koryŏ sa* (History of Koryŏ) (1451 CE) (Seoul: Kyŏngin munhwasa, 1981), 2.15b. Fourth of "Ten Injunctions." Translated more freely in P. H. Lee, ed., *Sourcebook of Korean Civilization*, vol. 1. *From Early Times to the Sixteenth Century* (New York: Columbia University Press, 1993), p. 264.

28. Wei Zheng, *Sui shu* (The Dynastic History of the Sui) (636 CE) (Beijing: Zhonghua shuju, 1973), 81.1827.

29. J. R. Piggott, *The Emergence of Japanese Kingship* (Stanford University Press, 1997), pp. 96–99.

30. H. Ooms, *Imperial Politics and Symbolics in Ancient Japan: The Tenmu Dynasty, 650–800* (Honolulu: University of Hawai'i Press, 2009), p. 51. H. M. Horton, "Literary Diplomacy in Early Nara: Prince Nagaya and the Verses for Envoys from Silla in *Kaifūsō*," in *China and Beyond in the Mediaeval Period: Cultural Crossings and Inter-Regional Connections*, ed. D. C. Wong and G. Heldt (New Delhi: Manohar, 2014), pp. 261, 264.

31. *Ryō no gige* (Commentary to the [Yōrō] Administrative Code [of 718 CE]), Shintei zōho kokushi taikei (fukyūban) (833 CE) (Tōkyō: Yoshikawa kōbunkan, 1972), 6.205.

32. Sugawara no Michizane, compiler, *Ruijū kokushi* (Categorized National Histories), Shintei zōho kokushi taikei (ca. 892 CE) (Tōkyō: Yoshikawa kōbunkan, 1965), 107.59.

33. *Honchō monzui, chūshaku* (The Annotated Essential Literature of Our Dynasty), attributed to Fujiwara no Akihira (989–1066 CE), ed. Kakimura Shigematsu (ca. 1037–45 CE) (Tōkyō: Fuzambō, 1968), 9.210.

34. *Honchō monzui*, 2.285.

35. B. L. Batten, "Cross-border Traffic on the Kyushu Coast, 794–1086," in *Heian Japan, Centers and Peripheries*, ed. M. Adolphson, E. Kamens, and S. Matsumoto (Honolulu: University of Hawai'i Press, 2007), pp. 358–360.

36. W. W. Farris, *Population, Disease, and Land in Early Japan, 645–900* (Cambridge, MA: Harvard University Press, 1985), chap. 2.

37. On early printing, and its massive scale and Buddhist function in this case, see T. H. Barrett, *The Woman Who Discovered Printing* (New Haven, CT: Yale University Press, 2008), p. 94.

38. J. R. Piggott, "Tracking the Wa-Kan Dialectic at Nara," in *China and Beyond in the Mediaeval Period: Cultural Crossings and Inter-Regional Connections*, ed. D. C. Wong and G. Heldt (New Delhi: Manohar, 2014), pp 243, 251.

39. For Japan, see W. R. LaFleur, *The Karma of Words: Buddhism and the Literary Arts in Medieval Japan* (Berkeley: University of California Press, 1983), pp. 9–14.

40. W. H. McCullough, "The Heian Court, 794–1070," in *The Cambridge History of Japan*, vol. II. *Heian Japan*, ed. D. H. Shively and W. H. McCullough (Cambridge University Press, 1999), p. 70.

41. *The Pillow Book of Sei Shōnagon*, trans. I. Morris (early eleventh century) (Baltimore: Penguin Books, 1967), p. 263.

42. *Shoku Nihon kōki* (The Later Chronicles of Japan, Continued), Kokushi taikei (869 CE) (Tōkyō: Keizai zasshisha, 1897), 8.255.

43. McCullough, "Heian Court," pp. 61–62.

44. R. von Glahn, "The Ningbo-Hakata Merchant Network and the Reorientation of East Asian Maritime Trade, 1150–1350," *Harvard Journal of Asiatic Studies* 74, no. 2 (2014): 271–272.

45. M. Collcutt, "Lanxi Daolong (1213–1278) at Kenchōji: Chinese Contributions to the Making of Medieval Japanese Rinzai Zen," in *Tools of Culture: Japan's Cultural, Intellectual, Medical, and Technological Contacts in East Asia, 1000–1500s*, ed. A. E. Goble, K. R. Robinson, and H. Wakabayashi (Ann Arbor, MI: Association for Asian Studies, 2009), pp. 135–138.

Chapter 5

1. Skaff, *Sui-Tang China and Its Turko-Mongol Neighbors*, pp. 257, 270–271.

2. A pioneering study of Xi Xia is R. W. Dunnell, *The Great State of White and High: Buddhism and State Formation in Eleventh-Century Xia* (Honolulu: University of Hawai'i Press, 1996).

3. D. C. Wright, *From War to Diplomatic Parity in Eleventh-Century China: Sung's Foreign Relations with Kitan Liao* (Leiden, Netherlands: Brill, 2005), pp. 36–37.

4. N. Standen, *Unbounded Loyalty: Frontier Crossing in Liao China* (Honolulu: University of Hawai'i Press, 2007), p. 182.

5. Lin Hang, "Conquer and Govern: The Rise of the Jurchen and their Jin Dynasty," in *Political Strategies of Identity Building in Non-Han Empires in China*, ed. F. Fiaschetti and J. Schneider (Wiesbaden: Harrassowitz Verlag, 2014), p. 37.

6. P. K. Bol, "Chao Ping-wen (1159–1232): Foundations for Literati Learning," in *China under Jurchen Rule: Essays on Chin Intellectual and Cultural History*, ed. H. C. Tillman and S. H. West (Albany: State University of New York Press, 1995), p. 127; H. C. Tillman, "Confucianism under the Chin and the Impact of Sung Confucian Tao-hsüeh," in Tillman and West, *China under Jurchen Rule*, pp. 88–89.

7. R. Trauzettel, "Sung Patriotism as a First Step toward Chinese Nationalism," in *Crisis and Prosperity in Sung China*, ed. J. W. Haeger (Tucson: University of Arizona Press, 1975).

8. See M. Elvin, *The Pattern of the Chinese Past: A Social and Economic Interpretation* (Stanford University Press, 1973), part two.

9. D. C. Wong, "An Agent of Cultural Transmission: Jianzhen's Travels to Japan, 743-63," in *China and Beyond in the Mediaeval Period: Cultural Crossings and Inter-Regional Connections*, ed. D. C. Wong and G. Heldt (New Delhi: Manohar, 2014), p. 70.

10. O. W. Wolters, *Early Indonesian Commerce: A Study of the Origins of Śrīvijaya* (Ithaca: Cornell University Press, 1967), p. 250.

11. Tansen Sen, *Buddhism, Diplomacy, and Trade: The Realignment of Sino-Indian Relations, 600–1400* (Honolulu: University of Hawai'i Press, 2003), pp. 232–233.

12. Shiba Yoshinobu, "Sung Foreign Trade: Its Scope and Organization," in *China among Equals: The Middle Kingdom and Its Neighbors, 10th–14th Centuries*, ed. M. Rossabi (Berkeley: University of California Press, 1983), p. 106.

13. P. F. Souyri, *The World Turned Upside Down: Medieval Japanese Society*, trans. Käthe Roth (New York: Columbia University Press, [1998] 2001), pp. 148–149.

14. F. W. Mote, *Imperial China: 900–1800* (Cambridge, MA: Harvard University Press, 1999), p. 165.

15. R. Hartwell, "A Revolution in the Chinese Iron and Coal Industries during the Northern Sung, 960–1126 A.D.," *Journal of Asian Studies* 21, no. 2 (1962): 155; Elvin, *Pattern of the Chinese Past*, pp. 85–86.

16. B. K. So, "Legitimizing New Political Order Legally: Legal Reforms in Northern Song China," in *The Legitimation of New Orders: Case Studies in World History*, ed. P. Y. Leung (Hong Kong: Chinese University Press, 2007), p. 38.

17. The system in its final form, under the Qing Dynasty, is described in Ichisada Miyazaki, *China's Examination Hell: The Civil Service Examinations of Imperial China*, trans. C. Schirokauer (New Haven, CT: Yale University Press, [1963] 1981).

18. P. B. Ebrey, *The Inner Quarters: Marriage and the Lives of Chinese Women in the Sung Period* (Berkeley: University of California Press, 1993), pp. 5–6, 267–270. For the unexpected Mongol role in this process, see B. Birge, "Women and Confucianism from Song to Ming: The Institutionalization of Patrilinealty," in *The Song–Yuan–Ming Transition in Chinese History*, ed. P. J. Smith and R. von Glahn (Cambridge, MA: Harvard University Asia Center, 2003), pp. 212–240.

19. W. T. de Bary, *East Asian Civilizations: A Dialogue in Five Stages* (Cambridge, MA: Harvard University Press, [1988] 1994), p. 62.

20. L. A. Walton, *Academies and Society in Southern Sung China* (Honolulu: University of Hawai'i Press, 1999), pp. 102–103.

21. A. Welter, "A Buddhist Response to the Confucian Revival: Tsan-ning and the Debate over Wen in the Early Sung," in *Buddhism in the Sung*, ed. P. N. Gregory and D. A. Getz Jr. (Honolulu: University of Hawai'i Press, 1999), pp. 37, 48–50.

22. "The Great Learning," in *The Four Books*, trans. J. Legge (repr., Taipei: Culture, 1979), pp. 4–7. Emphasis from original translation.

23. E. L. Davis, *Society and the Supernatural in Song China* (Honolulu: University of Hawai'i Press, 2001), pp. 3–8.

24. Wontack Hong, *Korea and Japan in East Asian History: A Tripolar Approach to East Asian History* (Seoul: Kudara International, 2006), p. 275, margin.

25. See M. Rossabi, *Khubilai Khan: His Life and Times* (Berkeley: University of California Press, 1988).

26. T. T. Allsen, "Population Movements in Mongol Eurasia," in *Nomads as Agents of Cultural Change: The Mongols and Their Eurasian Predecessors*, ed. R. Amitai and M. Biran (Honolulu: University of Hawai'i Press, 2015), pp. 120–123, 130–131, 136.

27. D. M. Robinson, *Empire's Twilight: Northeast Asia under the Mongols* (Cambridge, MA: Harvard University Asia Center, 2009), pp. 11, 118–129, 287.

28. J. W. Dardess, "Did the Mongols Matter? Territory, Power, and the Intelligentsia in China from the Northern Song to the Early Ming," in *The Song–Yuan–Ming Transition in Chinese History*, ed. P. J. Smith and R. von Glahn (Cambridge, MA: Harvard University Asia Center, 2003), p. 116.

29. Hok-Lam Chan, "The 'Song' Dynasty Legacy: Symbolism and Legitimation from Han Liner to Zhu Yuanzhang of the Ming Dynasty," *Harvard Journal of Asiatic Studies* 68, no. 1 (2008): 117. On the choice of the name "Ming," see p. 123.

30. N. Di Cosmo, "Mongols and Merchants on the Black Sea Frontier in the Thirteenth and Fourteenth Centuries: Convergences and Conflicts," in *Mongols, Turks, and Others: Eurasian Nomads and the Sedentary World*, ed. R. Amitai and M. Biran (Leiden: Brill, 2005), pp. 403–404.

31. M. Biran, "The Mongol Empire and Inter-civilizational Exchange," in *The Cambridge World History, vol. v. Expanding Webs of Exchange and Conflict, 500 CE-1500 CE*, ed. B. Z. Kedar and M. E. Wiesner-Hanks (Cambridge University Press, 2015), p. 545.

32. J. Larner, *Marco Polo and the Discovery of the World* (New Haven, CT: Yale University Press, 1999), pp. 153–160.

33. P. D. Curtin, *Cross-cultural Trade in World History* (Cambridge University Press, 1984), p. 121.

34. A. I. Johnston, *Cultural Realism: Strategic Culture and Grand Strategy in Chinese History* (Princeton University Press, 1995), pp. 27, 184.

35. P. C. Perdue, *China Marches West: The Qing Conquest of Central Asia* (Cambridge, MA: Harvard University Press, 2005), pp. 57–60.

36. See L. Levathes, *When China Ruled the Seas: The Treasure Fleet of the Dragon Throne, 1405–1433* (New York: Oxford University Press, 1994).

37. C. Chang, *The Development of Neo-Confucian Thought*, 2 vols. (New York: Bookman Associates, 1962), pp. 2.35, 2.44, 2.52–55, 2.64–65. (Wang Yangming is here referred to by an alternative name, and older spelling, "Wang Shou-jen.")

38. G. Ledyard, "Yin and Yang in the China–Manchuria–Korea Triangle," in Rossabi, *China among Equals*, p. 343.

39. P. H. Lee, ed., *Sourcebook of Korean Civilization, vol. 1: From Early Times to the Sixteenth Century* (New York: Columbia University Press, 1993), p. 284.

40. R. E. Buswell Jr., trans., *The Korean Approach to Zen: The Collected Works of Chinul* (Honolulu: University of Hawai'i Press, 1983), p. 38.

41. M. J. Seth, *A Concise History of Korea: From the Neolithic Period through the Nineteenth Century* (Lanham, MD: Rowman and Littlefield, 2006), pp. 104–106.

42. Robinson, *Empire's Twilight*, pp. 100, 275, 282.

43. Seth, *A Concise History of Korea*, p. 177.

44. M. Deuchler, *The Confucian Transformation of Korea: A Study of Society and Ideology* (Cambridge, MA: Harvard University Press, 1992), p. 134.

45. Yŏng-ho Ch'oe, "Private Academies and the State in Late Chosŏn Korea," in *Culture and the State in Late Chosŏn Korea*, ed. J. K. Haboush and M. Deuchler (Cambridge, MA: Harvard University Asia Center, 1999), p. 28, table 1.

46. J. K. Haboush, "The Confucianization of Korean Society," in *The East Asian Region: Confucian Heritage and Its Modern Adaptation*, ed. G. Rozman (Princeton University Press, 1991), pp. 84–86.

47. On samurai, see W. W. Farris, *Heavenly Warriors: The Evolution of Japan's Military, 500–1300* (Cambridge, MA: Harvard University Press, 1992); K. F. Friday, *Hired Swords: The Rise of Private Warrior Power in Early Japan* (Stanford University Press, 1992); and Takeuchi Rizō, "The Rise of the Warriors," in Shively and McCullough, *Heian Japan*.

48. H. P. Varley, *Warriors of Japan as Portrayed in the War Tales* (Honolulu: University of Hawai'i Press, 1994), p. 5.

49. W. H. McCullough, "The Capital and Its Society," in Shively and McCullough, *Heian Japan*, p. 125.

50. Kitagawa Hiroshi and B. T. Tsuchida, trans., *The Tale of the Heike* (University of Tokyo Press, 1975), p. 18.

51. See J. P. Mass, "The Emergence of the Kamakura *Bakufu*," in *Medieval Japan: Essays in Institutional History*, ed. J. W. Hall and J. P. Mass (Stanford University Press, 1974).

52. H. Ooms, *Imperial Politics and Symbolics in Ancient Japan: The Tenmu Dynasty, 650–800* (Honolulu: University of Hawai'i Press, 2009), pp. xvi, 269n5.

53. See Souyri, *World Turned Upside Down*, chap. 6.

54. Ibid., p. 79.

55. Hayashiya Tatsusaburō, "Kyoto in the Muromachi Age," in *Japan in the Muromachi Age*, ed. J. W. Hall and Toyoda Takeshi (Berkeley: University of California Press, 1977), p. 22.

56. M. E. Berry, *The Culture of Civil War in Kyoto* (Berkeley: University of California Press, 1994), p. 29.

57. D. Keene, *Yoshimasa and the Silver Pavilion: The Creation of the Soul of Japan* (New York: Columbia University Press, 2003), esp. pp. 145–146.

58. Father Alessandro Valignano, quoted in C. R. Boxer, *The Christian Century in Japan, 1549–1650* (Berkeley: University of California Press, 1967), p. 75.

Chapter 6

1. A. Woodside, *Lost Modernities: China, Vietnam, Korea, and the Hazards of World History* (Cambridge, MA: Harvard University Press, 2006), pp. 3–4.

2. See P. Duus, *Feudalism in Japan*, 2nd ed. (New York: Alfred A. Knopf, 1969).

3. R. von Glahn, "Towns and Temples: Urban Growth and Decline in the Yangzi Delta, 1100–1400," in *The Song–Yuan–Ming Transition in Chinese History*, ed. P. J. Smith and R. von Glahn (Cambridge, MA: Harvard University Asia Center, 2003), pp. 205–211. Elvin, *Pattern of the Chinese Past*, pp. 203–204, postulated a "high-level equilibrium trap."

4. T. Brook, *The Confusions of Pleasure: Commerce and Culture in Ming China* (Berkeley: University of California Press, 1998), pp. 211–212.

5. W. T. Rowe, *China's Last Empire: The Great Qing* (Cambridge, MA: Harvard University Press, 2009), pp. 123–124.

6. C. Clunas, *Empire of Great Brightness: Visual and Material Cultures of Ming China, 1368–1644* (Honolulu: University of Hawai'i Press, 2007), p. 67. For the abacus, see p. 119.

7. R. Huang, *1587, a Year of No Significance: The Ming Dynasty in Decline* (New Haven, CT: Yale University Press, 1981), p. 163.

8. C. Clunas, *Superfluous Things: Material Culture and Social Status in Early Modern China* (Honolulu: University of Hawai'i Press, [1991] 2004), pp. 58–59. For sea slugs, see B. W. Andaya, "Oceans Unbounded: Transversing Asia across 'Area Studies,'" *Journal of Asian Studies* 65, no. 4 (2006): 675–676.

9. L. E. Eastman, *Family, Field, and Ancestors: Constancy and Change in China's Social and Economic History, 1550–1949* (New York: Oxford University Press, 1988), p. 124.

10. For firearms, see M. J. Chaiklin, *Cultural Commerce and Dutch Commercial Culture: The Influence of European Material Culture on Japan, 1700–1850* (Leiden, Netherlands: CNWS, 2003), p. 149. For Saint Francis Xavier, see C. R. Boxer, *The Christian Century in Japan, 1549–1650* (Berkeley: University of California Press, 1967), pp. 36–37.

11. Yasuhiro Yokkaichi, "Chinese and Muslim Diasporas and the Indian Ocean Trade Network under Mongol Hegemony," in *The East Asian "Mediterranean": Maritime Crossroads of Culture, Commerce and Human Migration*, ed. A. Schottenhammer (Wiesbaden: Harrassowitz Verlag, 2008), pp. 73–102. Pin-tsun Chang, "The Rise of Chinese Mercantile Power in Maritime Southeast Asia, c. 1400–1700," *Crossroads: Studies on the History of Exchange Relations in the East Asian World*, 6 (2012): 205–230.

12. P. D. Curtin, *Cross-cultural Trade in World History* (Cambridge University Press, 1984), p. 150.

13. A. G. Frank, *ReOrient: Global Economy in the Asian Age* (Berkeley: University of California Press, 1998), pp. xxiii, 5, 142–143.

14. L. Blussé, *Visible Cities: Canton, Nagasaki, and Batavia and the Coming of the Americans* (Cambridge, MA: Harvard University Press, 2008), pp. 23–24.

15. T. Andrade, *Lost Colony: The Untold Story of China's First Great Victory over the West* (Princeton University Press, 2011). J. E. Wills Jr., "The Seventeenth-Century Transformation: Taiwan under the Dutch and the Cheng Regime," in *Taiwan: A New History*, ed. M. A. Rubinstein (Armonk, NY: M. E. Sharpe, 1999).

16. Chun-shu Chang and S. Hsueh-lun Chang, *Crisis and Transformation in Seventeenth-Century China: Society, Culture, and Modernity in Li Yü's World* (Ann Arbor: University of Michigan Press, [1992] 1998), p. 289.

17. J. D. Spence, *The Memory Palace of Matteo Ricci* (Harmondsworth, UK: Penguin Books, 1983), pp. 96, 149, 152.

18. Boxer, *Christian Century*, pp. 134–135.

19. See W. W. Appleton, *A Cycle of Cathay: The Chinese Vogue in England during the Seventeenth and Eighteenth Centuries* (New York: Octagon Books, [1951] 1979); D. E. Mungello, *The Great Encounter of China and the West, 1500–1800* (Lanham, MD: Rowman and Littlefield, 1999), chaps. 4–5; and A. Reichwein, *China and Europe: Intellectual and Artistic Contacts in the Eighteenth Century*, trans. J. C. Powell (New York: Alfred A. Knopf, 1925).

20. Chang and Chang, *Crisis and Transformation*. The quote is from p. 2.

21. Brook, *Confusions of Pleasure*, p. 220.

22. Chang and Chang, *Crisis and Transformation*, p. 273.

23. F. Wakeman Jr., *The Great Enterprise: The Manchu Reconstruction of Imperial Order in Seventeenth-Century China* (Berkeley: University of California Press, 1985), vol. I, p. 42, n43.

24. See P. K. Crossley, *The Manchus* (Oxford: Blackwell, 1997).

25. E. S. Rawski, "Presidential Address: Reenvisioning the Qing: The Significance of the Qing Period in Chinese History," *Journal of Asian Studies* 55, no. 4 (1996): 838, 842. For population, see M. C. Elliott, *The Manchu Way: The Eight Banners and Ethnic Identity in Late Imperial China* (Stanford University Press, 2001), p. 21.

26. P. Berger, *Empire of Emptiness: Buddhist Art and Political Authority in Qing China* (Honolulu: University of Hawai'i Press, 2003), p. 97.

27. See Zhang Fan, "Grass-root Official in the Ideological Battlefield: Reevaluation of the Study of the *Amban* in Tibet," in *Political Strategies of Identity Building in Non-Han Empires in China*, ed. F. Fiaschetti and J. Schneider (Wiesbaden: Harrassowitz Verlag, 2014), pp. 225–253.

28. P. C. Perdue, *China Marches West: The Qing Conquest of Central Asia* (Cambridge, MA: Harvard University Press, 2005), p. 285.

29. Elliott, *The Manchu Way*, pp. 116, 118.

30. E. J. M. Rhoads, *Manchus and Han: Ethnic Relations and Political Power in Late Qing and Early Republican China, 1861–1928* (Seattle: University of Washington Press, 2000), pp. 89–90. For differences between Manchu and Chinese, see pp. 52–63.

31. L. Hostetler, *Qing Colonial Enterprise: Ethnography and Cartography in Early Modern China* (University of Chicago Press, 2001), chap. 2.

32. J. D. Spence, *To Change China: Western Advisers in China 1620–1960* (Boston: Little, Brown, 1969), chap. 1.

33. M. Greenberg, *British Trade and the Opening of China, 1800–42* (Cambridge University Press, [1951] 1969), p. 3.

34. R. B. Marks, *The Origins of the Modern World: A Global and Ecological Narrative from the Fifteenth to the Twenty-First Century*, 2nd ed. (Lanham, MD: Rowman and Littlefield, 2007), p. 106; Bairoch, "International Industrialization Levels from 1750 to 1980," p. 296, table 10.

35. See B. Cumings, *Korea's Place in the Sun: A Modern History* (New York: W. W. Norton, 1997), p. 48.

36. K. M. Swope, *A Dragon's Head and a Serpent's Tail: Ming China and the First Great East Asian War, 1592–1598* (Norman, OK: University of Oklahoma Press, 2009), pp. 3–4.

37. The expression is credited to W. E. Griffis's book *Corea, the Hermit Nation* (New York: Scribner, 1882).

38. J. K. Haboush, "Constructing the Center: The Ritual Controversy and the Search for a New Identity in Seventeenth-Century Korea," in *Culture and the State in Late Chosŏn Korea*, ed. J. Kim Haboush and M. Deuchler (Cambridge, MA: Harvard University Asia Center, 1999), p. 70.

39. D. Baker, "A Different Thread: Orthodoxy, Heterodoxy, and Catholicism in a Confucian World," in Haboush and Deuchler, *Culture and the State*. For saints, see the introduction to ibid., p. 13.

40. Luis Frois, quoted in G. Elison, "The Cross and the Sword: Patterns of Momoyama History," in *Warlords, Artists, and Commoners: Japan in the Sixteenth Century*, ed. G. Elison and B. L. Smith (Honolulu: University of Hawai'i Press, 1981), p. 66.

41. A good study of this remarkable man's career is M. E. Berry, *Hideyoshi* (Cambridge, MA: Harvard University Press, 1982).

42. Blussé, *Visible Cities*, pp. 24, 48.

43. Chaiklin, *Cultural Commerce*, pp. 102, 149–172.

44. M. B. Jansen, *China in the Tokugawa World* (Cambridge, MA: Harvard University Press, 1992), p. 4.

45. See Tetsuo Najita, *Visions of Virtue in Tokugawa Japan: The Kaitokudō Merchant Academy of Osaka* (University of Chicago Press, 1987).

46. J. L. McClain and J. M. Merriman, "Edo and Paris: Cities and Power," in *Edo and Paris: Urban Life and the State in the Early Modern Era*, ed. J. L. McClain, J. M. Merriman, and U. Kaoru (Ithaca, NY: Cornell University Press, 1994), pp. 12–13.

47. See D. H. Shively, "*Bakufu* versus *Kabuki*," in *Studies in the Institutional History of Early Modern Japan*, ed. J. W. Hall and M. Jansen (Princeton University Press, [1955] 1968).

48. D. Keene, *World within Walls: Japanese Literature of the Pre-Modern Era, 1600–1867* (New York: Grove Press, 1976), p. 266.

49. M. E. Berry, *Japan in Print: Information and Nation in the Early Modern Period* (Berkeley: University of California Press, 2006), p. 31.

50. T. C. Smith, *Native Sources of Japanese Industrialization, 1750–1920* (Berkeley: University of California Press, 1988), p. 25.

51. T. Makoto, "Festivals and Fights: The Law and the People of Edo," in McClain et al., *Edo and Paris*, p. 404.

Chapter 7

1. K. W. Taylor, "Surface Orientations in Vietnam: Beyond Histories of Nation and Region," *The Journal of Asian Studies*, 57.4 (1998): 966.

2. C. M. Churchman, *Between Two Rivers: The Rise and Fall of the Bronze Drum Chiefdoms* (Lanham: Rowman & Littlefield, forthcoming).

3. H. R. Clark, *The Sinitic Encounter in Southeast China through the First Millennium* CE (Honolulu: University of Hawai'i Press, 2016), pp. 130–131.

4. See Le Tac, *Annam chi luoc* (A Brief Chronicle of Vietnam) (1340 CE) (Beijing: Zhonghua shuju, 1995), 1.41. See also, H. A. Peters, *Tattooed Faces and Stilt Houses: Who Were the Ancient Yue?*, Sino-Platonic Papers, 17 (Philadelphia: University of Pennsylvania, Department of Oriental Studies, 1990).

5. K. W. Taylor, *The Birth of Vietnam* (Berkeley: University of California Press, 1983), p. 75.

6. Dieu Thi Nguyen, "A Mythographical Journey to Modernity: The Textual and Symbolic Transformations of the Hung Kings Founding Myths," *Journal of Southeast Asian Studies* 44, no. 2 (2013): 315–337.

7. Nam C. Kim, *The Origins of Ancient Vietnam* (Oxford University Press, 2015), especially pp. 235, 281, 283.

8. Kim, *Origins of Ancient Vietnam*, pp. 150, 152, 272–273.

9. Neither the hairstyle nor squatting were especially associated with Viet/Yue culture, and E. F. Brindley questions the historical accuracy of this story, suspecting that it may merely be a Han stereotype for uncivilized behavior. See her *Ancient China and the Yue: Perceptions and Identities on the Southern Frontier, c. 400 BCE–50 CE* (Cambridge University Press, 2015), pp. 155–157, 161–164.

10. Fan Ye, *Hou Han shu* (Dynastic History of the Later Han) (445 CE) (Beijing: Zhonghua shuju, 1965), 86.2836–2837.

11. J. Holmgren, *Chinese Colonization of Northern Vietnam: Administrative Geography and Political Development in the Tongking Delta, First to Sixth Centuries AD* (Canberra: Australian National University, 1980), p. 64.

12. Xiao Zixian, *Nan Qi shu* (Dynastic History of the Southern Qi) (537 CE) (Beijing: Zhonghua shuju, 1972), 58.1017.

13. Di Renjie (607–700), quoted in Ouyang Xiu and Song Qi, *Xin Tang shu* (New Dynastic History of the Tang) (1060 CE) (Beijing: Zhonghua shuju, 1975), 115.4210.

14. Wei Zheng, *Sui shu* (Dynastic History of the Sui) (636 CE) (Beijing: Zhonghua shuju, 1973), 31.887–888.

15. Du You, *Tong dian* (Comprehensive Canons) (801 CE) (Beijing: Zhonghua shuju, 1984), 32.186b.

16. C. Holcombe, "Immigrants and Strangers: From Cosmopolitanism to Confucian Universalism in Tang China," *T'ang Studies*, 20–21 (2002–2003): 72–78.

17. H. R. Clark, "The Southern Kingdoms between the T'ang and the Sung," in *The Cambridge History of China, vol. V, Part 1. The Sung Dynasty and its Precursors, 907–1279*, ed. D. Twitchett and P. J. Smith (Cambridge University Press, 2009), p. 153.

18. Le Tac, *Annam chi luoc*, 16.381.

19. M. Churchman, "Before Chinese and Vietnamese in the Red River Plain: The Han-Tang Period," *Chinese Southern Diaspora Studies*, 4 (2010): 25–37.

20. J. D. Phan, "Re-Imagining 'Annam': A New Analysis of Sino-Viet-Muong Linguistic Contact," *Chinese Southern Diaspora Studies*, 4 (2010): 3–24.

21. M. J. Alves, "What's so Chinese about Vietnamese?," in *Papers from the Ninth Annual Meeting of the Southeast Asian Linguistics Society*, ed. G. W. Thurgood (2001), section 2, pp. 221–242.

22. In the case of Vietnam, premodern dynasties are generally known by the names of their ruling families, unlike in China where the dynasty was the name of the country and not a family name. The latter is generally true of Korean practice as well, although the last Korean dynasty is sometimes alternatively known by the name of its ruling family. In Japan there has only been one dynasty, which therefore needs no name.

23. S. McHale, "'Texts and Bodies': Refashioning the Disturbing Past of Tran Vietnam (1226–1400)," *Journal of the Economic and Social History of the Orient* 42, no. 4 (1999): 494–518; O. W. Wolters, "What Else May Ngo Si Lien Mean? A Matter of Distinctions in the Fifteenth Century," in *Sojourners and Settlers: Histories of Southeast Asia and the Chinese*, ed. A. Reid (Honolulu: University of Hawai'i Press, 1996), pp. 94–114.

24. Kim, *Origins of Ancient Vietnam*, pp. 65–66.

25. I. Glover and Nguyen Kim Dung, "Excavations at Go Cam, Quang Nam, 2000–3: Linyi and the Emergence of the Cham Kingdoms," in *The Cham of Vietnam: History, Society and Art*, ed. Tran Ky Phuong and B. M. Lockhart (National University of Singapore, 2011), p. 54.

26. See Wang Qinruo, *Cefu yuangui* (Outstanding Models from the Archives) (1013 CE) (Taibei: Taiwan Zhonghua shuju, 1981), 959.11287–11288; Li Yanshou, *Nan shi* (History of the Southern Dynasties) (659 CE) (Beijing: Zhonghua shuju, 1975), 78.1949.

27. B. M. Lockhart, "Colonial and Post-Colonial Constructions of 'Champa,'" in *The Cham of Vietnam: History, Society and Art*, ed. Tran Ky Phuong and B. M. Lockhart (National University of Singapore, 2011), p. 28.

28. K. W. Taylor, *A History of the Vietnamese* (Cambridge University Press, 2013), p. 272.

29. L. C. Kelley, *Beyond the Bronze Pillars: Envoy Poetry and the Sino-Vietnamese Relationship* (Honolulu: University of Hawai'i Press, 2005), pp. 178–180.

30. A. B. Woodside, *Vietnam and the Chinese Model: A Comparative Study of Nguyên and Ch'ing Civil Government in the First Half of the Nineteenth Century* (Cambridge, MA: Harvard University Press, 1971), p. 199.

31. Lieberman, *Strange Parallels*, vol. 1, p. 454.

Chapter 8

1. D. R. Headrick, *The Tentacles of Progress: Technology Transfer in the Age of Imperialism, 1850–1940* (New York: Oxford University Press, 1988), pp. 49, 90.

2. H. James, *The End of Globalization: Lessons from the Great Depression* (Cambridge, MA: Harvard University Press, 2001), p. 12.

3. C. Clunas, *Superfluous Things: Material Culture and Social Status in Early Modern China* (Honolulu: University of Hawai'i Press, [1991] 2004), p. 66; F. Dikötter, *Exotic Commodities: Modern Objects and Everyday Life in China* (New York: Columbia University Press, 2006), p. 34.

4. K. Pomeranz, *The Great Divergence: China, Europe, and the Making of the Modern World Economy* (Princeton University Press, 2000), pp. 61–62.

5. Marks, *The Origins of the Modern World*, pp. 108–112.

6. Quoted in S. W. Mintz, *Sweetness and Power: The Place of Sugar in Modern History* (New York: Viking, 1985), p. 116.

7. E. J. Hobsbawm, *The Age of Empire, 1875–1914* (New York: Vintage Books, 1989), p. 59.

8. Pomeranz, *Great Divergence*, pp. 17, 121–122, 138–142.

9. R. Fortune, *A Residence among the Chinese: Inland, on the Coast, and at Sea* (Taipei: Ch'eng Wen, [1857] 1971), pp. 98–99.

10. R. B. Marks, *China: Its Environment and History* (Lanham: Rowman and Littlefield, 2012), pp. 156–161.

11. P. C. Perdue, *China Marches West: The Qing Conquest of Central Asia* (Cambridge, MA: Harvard University Press, 2005), pp. 552–555.

12. A. P. Dudden, *The American Pacific: From the Old China Trade to the Present* (New York: Oxford University Press, 1992), pp. 5–6.

13. See P. W. Fay, *The Opium War, 1840–1842: Barbarians in the Celestial Empire in the Early Part of the Nineteenth Century and the War by Which They Forced Her Gates Ajar* (New York: W. W. Norton, 1975).

14. F. Welsh, *A Borrowed Place: The History of Hong Kong* (New York: Kodansha International, 1993), pp. 310, 318–319.

15. M. S. Erbaugh, "The Secret History of the Hakkas: The Chinese Revolution as a Hakka Enterprise," in *China Off Center: Mapping the Margins of the Middle Kingdom*, ed. S. D. Blum and L. M. Jensen (Honolulu: University of Hawai'i Press, 2002), pp. 186–188. On Hakka origins, see Sow-Theng Leong, *Migration and Ethnicity in Chinese History: Hakkas, Pengmin, and Their Neighbors*, ed. T. Wright (Stanford University Press, 1997).

16. See J. D. Spence, *God's Chinese Son: The Taiping Heavenly Kingdom of Hong Xiuquan* (New York: W. W. Norton, 1996).

17. S. Y. Teng, *The Taiping Rebellion and the Western Powers: A Comprehensive Survey* (Taipei: Rainbow-Bridge, 1972), pp. 212–213.

18. I. C. Y. Hsü, *The Ili Crisis: A Study of Sino-Russian Diplomacy, 1871–1881* (Oxford University Press, 1965), pp. 12–15, 18, 22–44.

19. Quoted in P. K. Cheng, M. Lestz, and J. D. Spence, eds., *The Search for Modern China: A Documentary Collection* (New York: W. W. Norton, 1999), pp. 100–103.

20. A classic study is M. C. Wright, *The Last Stand of Chinese Conservatism: The T'ung-Chih Restoration, 1862–1874* (Stanford University Press, 1957).

21. See P. A. Cohen, *Discovering History in China: American Historical Writing on the Recent Chinese Past* (New York: Columbia University Press, 1984), p. 39.

22. R. Bickers, *The Scramble for China: Foreign Devils in the Qing Empire, 1832–1914* (London: Penguin Books, 2011), pp. 284–285.

23. S. C. M. Paine, *The Sino-Japanese War of 1894–1895: Perceptions, Power, and Primacy* (Cambridge University Press, 2003), pp. 141–145.

24. R. Murphey, *The Outsiders: The Western Experience in India and China* (Ann Arbor: University of Michigan Press, 1977), pp. 122, 192; Welsh, *A Borrowed Place*, p. 235.

25. L. E. Eastman, *Family, Fields, and Ancestors: Constancy and Change in China's Social and Economic History, 1550–1949* (New York: Oxford University Press, 1988), p. 184.

26. Hsü, *The Ili Crisis*, p. 14.

27. N. R. Clifford, *Spoilt Children of Empire: Westerners in Shanghai and the Chinese Revolution of the 1920s* (Hanover, NH: Middlebury College Press, 1991), p. 68.

28. F. Wakeman Jr., *Policing Shanghai, 1927–1937* (Berkeley: University of California Press, 1995), pp. 34–35.

29. See D. Wolff, *To the Harbin Station: The Liberal Alternative in Russian Manchuria, 1898–1914* (Stanford University Press, 1999).

30. J. Davids, ed., *American Diplomatic and Public Papers: The United States and China, Series III – The Sino-Japanese War to the Russo-Japanese War, 1894–1905* (Wilmington, DE: Scholarly Resources, 1981), vol. V (*Boxer Uprising*), document 15, p. 40. On the Boxers, see P. A. Cohen, *History in Three Keys: The Boxers as Event, Experience, and Myth* (New York: Columbia University Press, 1997), and J. W. Esherick, *The Origins of the Boxer Uprising* (Berkeley: University of California Press, 1987).

31. D. J. Silbey, *The Boxer Rebellion and the Great Game in China* (New York: Hill and Wang, 2012), pp. 90–102.

32. M. Deuchler, *Confucian Gentlemen and Barbarian Envoys: The Opening of Korea, 1875–1885* (Seattle: University of Washington Press, 1977), p. 27.

33. Key-Hiuk Kim, *The Last Phase of the East Asian World Order: Korea, Japan, and the Chinese Empire, 1860–1882* (Berkeley: University of California Press, 1980), p. 40.

34. See P. Duus, *The Abacus and the Sword: The Japanese Penetration of Korea, 1895–1910* (Berkeley: University of California Press, 1995), pp. 101, 108–118.

35. See M. E. Robinson, *Cultural Nationalism in Colonial Korea, 1920–1925* (Seattle: University of Washington Press, 1988), chapter 1.

36. See M. B. Jansen, *Sakamoto Ryōma and the Meiji Restoration* (New York: Columbia University Press, [1961] 1994), pp. 41–43.

37. T. C. Smith, *Native Sources of Japanese Industrialization, 1750–1920* (Berkeley: University of California Press, 1988), p. 11, and chap. 7.

38. M. B. Jansen, *The Making of Modern Japan* (Cambridge, MA: Harvard University Press, 2000), pp. 337–339.

39. T. Morris-Suzuki, "A Descent into the Past: The Frontier in the Construction of Japanese Identity," in *Multicultural Japan: Palaeolithic to Postmodern*, ed. D. Denoon, M. Hudson, G. McCormack, and T. Morris-Suzuki (Cambridge University Press, 1996).

40. See D. Keene, "The Sino-Japanese War of 1894–95 and Its Cultural Effects in Japan," in *Tradition and Modernization in Japanese Culture*, ed. D. H. Shively (Princeton University Press, 1971), pp. 169–172.

41. H. M. Hopper, *Fukuzawa Yūkichi: From Samurai to Capitalist* (New York: Pearson Longman, 2005), pp. 121–122.

42. I. P. Hall, *Mori Arinori* (Cambridge, MA: Harvard University Press, 1973), pp. 3–6, 189–195.

43. C. Gluck, *Japan's Modern Myths: Ideology in the Late Meiji Period* (Princeton University Press, 1985), pp. 23, 27.

44. M. B. Jansen, "The Ruling Class," in *Japan in Transition: From Tokugawa to Meiji*, ed. M. B. Jansen and G. Rozman (Princeton University Press, 1986), pp. 89–90.

45. D. H. Shively, "The Japanization of the Middle Meiji," in *Tradition and Modernization in Japanese Culture*, ed. D. H. Shively (Princeton University Press, 1971), p. 85.

46. "Imperial Rescript on Education," in *The Japan Reader 1: Imperial Japan, 1800–1945*, ed. J. Livingston, J. Moore, and F. Oldfather (New York: Pantheon Books, 1973), p. 154.

47. T. C. Smith, *Political Change and Industrial Development in Japan: Government Enterprise, 1868–1880* (Stanford University Press, 1955), pp. 26, 30–31, 34–53, 102–103; E. H. Norman, *Japan's Emergence as a Modern State: Political and Economic Problems of the Meiji Period* (New York: Institute of Pacific Relations, 1940), pp. 117–133; E. S. Crawcour, "Economic Change in the Nineteenth Century," in *The Economic Emergence of Modern Japan*, ed. K. Yamamura (Cambridge University Press, 1997), pp. 41–44, 48–49.

48. J. W. Alexander, *Brewed in Japan: The Evolution of the Japanese Beer Industry* (Honolulu: University of Hawai'i Press, 2013), pp. 6–7, 31–41.

49. R. J. Samuels, *"Rich Nation Strong Army": National Security and the Technological Transformation of Japan* (Ithaca, NY: Cornell University Press, 1994), pp. 84–88.

50. Smith, *Native Sources of Japanese Industrialization*, pp. 42–46.

51. W. D. Wray, "Shipping: From Sail to Steam," in Jansen and Rozman, *Japan in Transition*, pp. 249, 254–259.

52. Akira Iriye, *China and Japan in the Global Setting* (Cambridge, MA: Harvard University Press, 1992), p. 20; W. G. Beasley, *Japanese Imperialism, 1894–1945* (Oxford: Clarendon Press, [1987] 1991), p. 25.

53. S. B. Hanley, "The Material Culture: Stability in Transition," in Jansen and Rozman, *Japan in Transition*, pp. 463, 467–469; E. Seidensticker, *Low City, High City: Tokyo from Edo to the Earthquake* (New York: Alfred A. Knopf, 1983), pp. 42–44, 47–48.

Chapter 9

1. M. Elvin, "The Collapse of Scriptural Confucianism," in *Another History: Essays on China from a European Perspective* (Canberra, Australia: Wild Peony, [1990] 1996), p. 355.
2. Tze-ki Hon, "Zhang Zhidong's Proposal for Reform: A New Reading of the *Quanxue pian*," in *Rethinking the 1898 Reform Period: Political and Cultural Change in Late Qing China*, ed. R. E. Karl and P. Zarrow (Cambridge, MA: Harvard University Asia Center, 2002), pp. 78–79, 86, 91–98.
3. L. Ou-fan Lee, *Shanghai Modern: The Flowering of a New Urban Culture in China, 1930–1945* (Cambridge, MA: Harvard University Press, 1999), p. 44.
4. E. P. Young, "China in the Early Twentieth Century: Tasks for a New World," in *Historical Perspectives on Contemporary East Asia*, ed. M. Goldman and A. Gordon (Cambridge, MA: Harvard University Press, 2000), p. 190.
5. E. J. M. Rhoads, "The Assassination of Governor Enming and Its Effect on Manchu–Han Relations in Late Qing China," in *China's Republican Revolution*, ed. Etō Shinkichi and H. Z. Schiffrin (University of Tokyo Press, 1994), pp. 3, 6, 12, 22–23n29.
6. L. Greenfeld, *Nationalism: Five Roads to Modernity* (Cambridge, MA: Harvard University Press, 1992), pp. 6–7, 47. A particularly influential study is B. Anderson, *Imagined Communities: Reflections on the Origin and Spread of Nationalism* (London: Verso, [1983] 1991).
7. T. Morris-Suzuki, "A Descent into the Past: The Frontier in the Construction of Japanese Identity," in *Multicultural Japan: Palaeolithic to Postmodern*, ed. D. Denoon et al. (Cambridge University Press, 1996), p. 88.
8. L. H. Liu, *Translingual Practice: Literature, National Culture, and Translated Modernity – China, 1900–1937* (Stanford University Press, 1995), appendix B, p. 292.
9. M.-C. Bergère, *Sun Yat-sen*, trans. J. Lloyd (Stanford University Press, [1994] 1998), pp. 6, 31.
10. E. A. McCord, *The Power of the Gun: The Emergence of Modern Chinese Warlordism* (Berkeley: University of California Press, 1993), p. 46.
11. J. W. Esherick, "Founding a Republic, Electing a President: How Sun Yat-sen Became Guofu," in Etō and Schiffrin, *China's Republican Revolution*, p. 146.
12. F. Dikötter, *Exotic Commodities: Modern Objects and Everyday Life in China* (New York: Columbia University Press, 2006), pp. 1, 4, 10, 30–31, 56, 90, 104, 111, 178, 252.
13. Lu Hsun (Lu Xun), "A Madman's Diary," in *Selected Stories of Lu Hsun*, trans. Yang Hsien-yi and G. Yang (Peking: Foreign Language Press, [1918] 1972), p. 10.
14. V. Goossaert, "1898: The Beginning of the End for Chinese Religion?" *Journal of Asian Studies* 65, no. 2 (2006): 308.
15. Bairoch, "International Industrialization Levels from 1750 to 1980," p. 296, table 10.
16. S. Cochran, "Transnational Origins of Advertising in Early Twentieth-Century China," in *Inventing Nanjing Road: Commercial Culture in Shanghai, 1900–1945*, ed. S. Cochrane (Ithaca, NY: Cornell University East Asia Program, 1999).
17. H. Harrison, *China: Inventing the Nation* (London: Arnold, 2001), pp. 158–160.
18. M. B. Jansen, *The Making of Modern Japan* (Cambridge, MA: Harvard University Press, 2000), p. 531.
19. Tse-tsung Chow, *The May Fourth Movement: Intellectual Revolution in Modern China* (Stanford University Press, 1960), pp. 35–40, 42n.
20. J. P. Harrison, *The Long March to Power: A History of the Chinese Communist Party, 1921–72* (New York: Praeger, 1972), p. 23.
21. W. Wei, "'Political Power Grows Out of the Barrel of a Gun': Mao and the Red Army," in *A Military History of China*, ed. D. A. Graff and R. Higham (Boulder, CO: Westview Press, 2002), pp. 231, 234–236.
22. E. Snow, *Red Star Over China* (New York: Grove Press, [1938] 1968), p. 155.

23. See M. L. Cohen, "Cultural and Political Inventions in Modern China: The Case of the Chinese 'Peasant,'" in *China in Transformation*, ed. Tu Wei-ming (Cambridge, MA: Harvard University Press, 1994); B. I. Schwartz, *Chinese Communism and the Rise of Mao* (Cambridge, MA: Harvard University Press, [1951] 1979), pp. 197–199.

24. J. Fitzgerald, *Awakening China: Politics, Culture, and Class in the Nationalist Revolution* (Stanford University Press, 1996), p. 163.

25. J. H. Fincher, *Chinese Democracy: The Self-government Movement in Local, Provincial, and National Politics, 1905–1914* (New York: St. Martin's Press, 1981), p. 223.

26. F. Wakeman Jr., *Policing Shanghai, 1927–1937* (Berkeley: University of California Press, 1995), pp. 124, 259; P. M. Coble Jr., *The Shanghai Capitalists and the Nationalist Government, 1927–1937* (Cambridge, MA: Harvard University Press, [1980] 1986), p. 39.

27. G. McCormack, *Chang Tso-lin in Northeast China, 1911–1928: China, Japan, and the Manchurian Idea* (Stanford University Press, 1977), pp. 120–122.

28. Jui-te Chang, "The National Army from Whampoa to 1949," in Graff and Higham, *Military History of China*, p. 195.

29. M. Atkins, *Informal Empire in Crisis: British Diplomacy and the Chinese Customs Succession, 1927–1929* (Ithaca, NY: Cornell University East Asia Program, 1995), pp. 15, 22.

30. R. Mitter, *A Bitter Revolution: China's Struggle with the Modern World* (Oxford University Press, 2004), pp. 149, 155.

31. Ki-baik Lee, *A New History of Korea*, trans. E. W. Wagner (Cambridge, MA: Harvard University Press, 1984), p. 317.

32. P. Duus, *The Abacus and the Sword: The Japanese Penetration of Korea, 1895–1910* (Berkeley: University of California Press, 1995), pp. 319, 328.

33. M. B. Jansen, "Japanese Imperialism: Late Meiji Perspectives," in *The Japanese Colonial Empire, 1895–1945*, ed. R. H. Myers and M. R. Peattie (Princeton University Press, 1984), p. 78; C. J. Eckert, "Korea's Transition to Modernity: A Will to Greatness," in Goldman and Gordon, *Historical Perspectives*, pp. 136–137.

34. M. E. Robinson, *Cultural Nationalism in Colonial Korea, 1920–1925* (Seattle: University of Washington Press, 1988), pp. 43–46.

35. M. E. Robinson, *Korea's Twentieth-Century Odyssey: A Short History* (Honolulu: University of Hawai'i Press, 2007), pp. 90–91.

36. M. R. Peattie, "Japanese Attitudes toward Colonialism, 1895–1945," in Myers and Peattie, *Japanese Colonial Empire*, pp. 96–98.

37. E. I-te Chen, "The Attempt to Integrate the Empire: Legal Perspectives," in Myers and Peattie, *Japanese Colonial Empire*, p. 242n3.

38. W. G. Beasley, *Japanese Imperialism, 1894–1945* (Oxford: Clarendon Press, [1987] 1991), pp. 152–153.

39. B. Cumings, *Korea's Place in the Sun: A Modern History* (New York: W. W. Norton, 1997), p. 175.

40. E. Seidensticker, *Low City, High City: Tokyo from Edo to the Earthquake* (New York: Alfred A. Knopf, 1983), pp. 95, 101, 110–113, 166.

41. S. B. Hanley, "The Material Culture: Stability in Transition," in *Japan in Transition: From Tokugawa to Meiji*, ed. M. B. Jansen and G. Rozman (Princeton University Press, 1986), pp. 460, 463.

42. D. H. Shively, "The Japanization of the Middle Meiji," in *Tradition and Modernization in Japanese Culture*, ed. D. H. Shively (Princeton University Press, 1971), p. 77.

43. E. S. Crawcour, "Industrialization and Technological Change, 1885–1920," in *The Economic Emergence of Modern Japan*, ed. K. Yamamura (Cambridge University Press, 1997), p. 52.

44. M. Hane, *Peasants, Rebels, and Outcastes: The Underside of Modern Japan* (New York: Pantheon Books, 1982), p. 34.

45. T. Nakamura, "Depression, Recovery, and War, 1920–1945," in Yamamura, *Economic Emergence of Modern Japan*, p. 118.

46. C. Gluck, *Japan's Modern Myths: Ideology in the Late Meiji Period* (Princeton University Press, 1985), p. 12.

47. E. T. Atkins, "Can Japanese Sing the Blues? 'Japanese Jazz' and the Problem of Authenticity," in *Japan Pop! Inside the World of Japanese Popular Culture*, ed. T. J. Craig (Armonk: M. E. Sharpe, 2000), pp. 35, 37.

48. R. H. Mitchell, *Censorship in Imperial Japan* (Princeton University Press, 1983), pp. 196–199.

49. See R. T. Takaki, *Strangers from a Different Shore: A History of Asian Americans*, rev. ed. (Boston: Little, Brown, 1998), pp. 208–210.

50. W. F. Morton, *Tanaka Giichi and Japan's China Policy* (New York: St. Martin's Press, 1980), pp. 130–134, 149–150, 158–160.

51. M. Dietler, "'Our Ancestors the Gauls': Archaeology, Ethnic Nationalism, and the Manipulation of Celtic Identity in Modern Europe," *American Anthropologist*, new series, 96, no. 3 (1994): 590.

52. Duong Van Mai Elliott, *The Sacred Willow: Four Generations in the Life of a Vietnamese Family* (Oxford University Press, 1999), p. 82.

53. D. G. Marr, *Vietnamese Tradition on Trial, 1920–1945* (Berkeley: University of California Press, 1981), pp. 2, 8, 23–4, 40-1, 260, 414.

54. W. J. Duiker, *Vietnam: Revolution in Transition*, 2nd ed. (Boulder: Westview Press, 1995), p. 33.

55. N. L. Jamieson, *Understanding Vietnam* (Berkeley: University of California Press, 1993), p. 91.

56. For Ho Chi Minh's early life, see S. Karnow, *Vietnam: A History* (New York: The Viking Press, 1983), pp. 118–127.

Chapter 10

1. See M. A. Barnhart, *Japan Prepares for Total War: The Search for Economic Security, 1919–1941* (Ithaca, NY: Cornell University Press, 1987).

2. Saburō Ienaga, *The Pacific War, 1931–1945* (New York: Pantheon Books, [1968] 1978), pp. 19–32.

3. J. W. Dower, *War without Mercy: Race and Power in the Pacific War* (New York: Pantheon Books, 1986), pp. 221–222, 238.

4. B.-A. Shillony, *Revolt in Japan: The Young Officers and the February 26, 1936 Incident* (Princeton University Press, 1973), pp. 32–36.

5. S. Pao-San Ho, "Colonialism and Development: Korea, Taiwan, and Kwantung," in *The Japanese Colonial Empire, 1895–1945*, ed. R. H. Myers and M. R. Peattie (Princeton University Press, 1984), p. 352.

6. G. McCormack, *Chang Tso-lin in Northeast China, 1911–1928: China, Japan, and the Manchurian Idea* (Stanford University Press, 1977), p. 8, table 1.

7. W. G. Beasley, *Japanese Imperialism, 1894–1945* (Oxford: Clarendon Press, [1987] 1991), pp. 212–217.

8. M. R. Peattie, *Ishiwara Kanji and Japan's Confrontation with the West* (Princeton University Press, 1975), pp. 32, 56–58, 96–107, 120–123, 319–320.

9. L. Young, *Japan's Total Empire: Manchuria and the Culture of Wartime Imperialism* (Berkeley: University of California Press, 1998), chap. 3.

10. On Xinjing, see D. D. Buck, "Railway City and National Capital: Two Faces of the Modern in Changchun," in *Remaking the Chinese City: Modernity and National Identity, 1900–1950*, ed. J. W. Esherick (Honolulu: University of Hawai'i Press, 2000).

11. Young, *Japan's Total Empire*, pp. 246–247.

12. Prasenjit Duara, *Sovereignty and Authenticity: Manchukuo and the East Asian Modern* (Lanham, MD: Rowman and Littlefield, 2003), pp. 73, 77.

13. See C. D. Musgrove, "Building a Dream: Constructing a National Capital in Nanjing, 1927–1937," in Esherick, *Remaking the Chinese City*.

14. W. C. Kirby, "The Nationalist Regime and the Chinese Party-State, 1928–1958," in *Historical Perspectives on Contemporary East Asia*, ed. M. Goldman and A. Gordon (Cambridge, MA: Harvard University Press, 2000), p. 227.

15. See J. Taylor, *The Generalissimo's Son: Chiang Ching-kuo and the Revolutions in China and Taiwan* (Cambridge, MA: Harvard University Press, 2000).

16. W. C. Kirby, *Germany and Republican China* (Stanford University Press, 1984), pp. 3–5, 262.

17. L. E. Eastman, "Nationalist China during the Nanking Decade, 1927–1937," in *The Nationalist Era in China, 1927–1949*, ed. L. E. Eastman, J. Ch'en, S. Pepper, and L. P. Van Slyke (Cambridge University Press, 1991), p. 9.

18. L. E. Eastman, *Seeds of Destruction: Nationalist China in War and Revolution, 1937–1949* (Stanford University Press, 1984), pp. 10, 41.

19. Harrison, *The Long March to Power*, pp. 19–20.

20. A. Dirlik, *The Origins of Chinese Communism* (New York: Oxford University Press, 1989), pp. 253–273.

21. J. T. Dreyer, *China's Political System: Modernization and Tradition*, 4th ed. (New York: Pearson Longman, 2004), p. 66.

22. E. Snow, *Red Star over China* (New York: Grove Press, [1938] 1968), pp. 165–166.

23. M. Meisner, *Mao's China and After: A History of the People's Republic* (New York: Free Press, [1977] 1986), pp. 43–47.

24. H. E. Salisbury, *The Long March: The Untold Story* (New York: McGraw-Hill, 1985), pp. 10–11.

25. J. D. Spence, *Mao Zedong* (New York: Viking, 1999), pp. 82–86.

26. See I. Chang, *The Rape of Nanking: The Forgotten Holocaust of World War II* (New York: Penguin Books, 1997).

27. T. H. White and A. Jacoby, *Thunder out of China* (New York: William Sloan Associates, [1946] 1961), pp. 70–72.

28. S. Pepper, *Civil War in China: The Political Struggle, 1945–1949* (Berkeley: University of California Press, 1978), p. 95.

29. J. H. Boyle, *China and Japan at War, 1937–1945: The Politics of Collaboration* (Stanford University Press, 1972), pp. 351–352, 361–362.

30. Barnhart, *Japan Prepares for Total War*, pp. 91, 95–96, 101–104.

31. T. R. H. Havens, *Valley of Darkness: The Japanese People and World War Two* (Lanham, MD: University Press of America, 1986), pp. 16, 18, 50.

32. Mikiso Hane, *Modern Japan: A Historical Survey* (Boulder, CO: Westview Press, 1986), p. 297.

33. M. Hastings, *Retribution: The Battle for Japan, 1944–45* (New York: Alfred A. Knopf, 2008), p. 26.

34. M. S. Gallicchio, *The Cold War Begins in Asia: American East Asian Policy and the Fall of the Japanese Empire* (New York: Columbia University Press, 1988), pp. 73–74.

35. See J. W. Dower, *Embracing Defeat: Japan in the Wake of World War II* (New York: W. H. Norton, 1999), pp. 33–39.

36. D. W. White, *The American Century: The Rise and Decline of the United States as a World Power* (New Haven, CT: Yale University Press, 1996), p. 56.

Chapter 11

1. See, for example, O. Statler, *Japanese Inn* (Honolulu: University of Hawai'i Press, [1961] 1982), pp. 3, 321–333, and "About the Author."

2. W. Manchester, *American Caesar: Douglas MacArthur, 1880–1964* (Boston: Little, Brown, 1978), pp. 470–471.

3. J. W. Dower, *Embracing Defeat: Japan in the Wake of World War II* (New York: W. H. Norton, 1999), pp. 96–97.

4. M. B. Jansen, *The Making of Modern Japan* (Cambridge, MA: Harvard University Press, 2000), p. 676.

5. E. O. Reischauer, *My Life between Japan and America* (New York: Harper and Row, 1986), p. 91; E. Terry, *How Asia Got Rich: Japan, China, and the Asian Miracle* (Armonk, NY: M. E. Sharpe, 2002), p. 353.

6. T. J. Pempel, "Prerequisites for Democracy: Political and Social Institutions," in *Democracy in Japan*, ed. T. Ishida and E. S. Krauss (University of Pittsburgh Press, 1989), p. 21.

7. A. Gordon, "Society and Politics from Transwar through Postwar Japan," in *Historical Perspectives on Contemporary East Asia*, ed. M. Goldman and A. Gordon (Cambridge, MA: Harvard University Press, 2000), pp. 279–280.

8. See M. Harries and S. Harries, *Sheathing the Sword: The Demilitarization of Japan* (New York: Macmillan, 1987), p. 307.

9. Yutaka Kosai, "The Postwar Japanese Economy, 1945–1973," in *The Economic Emergence of Modern Japan*, ed. K. Yamamura (Cambridge University Press, 1997), p. 159.

10. Ibid., p. 177.

11. C. Johnson, *MITI and the Japanese Miracle: The Growth of Industrial Policy, 1925–1975* (Stanford University Press, 1982), p. 10.

12. Ibid., pp. 45–46, 102–106, 108–109, 130–132.

13. Ibid., pp. 41, 44, 176.

14. R. Katz, *Japanese Phoenix: The Long Road to Economic Revival* (Armonk, NY: M. E. Sharpe, 2003), p. 166.

15. E. S. Krauss, "Politics and the Policymaking Process," in Ishida and Krauss, *Democracy in Japan*, p. 50.

16. E. F. Vogel, *Japan as Number One: Lessons for America* (Cambridge, MA: Harvard University Press, 1979).

17. C. V. Prestowitz Jr., *Trading Places: How We Allowed Japan to Take the Lead* (New York: Basic Books, 1988).

18. G. McCormack, "*Kokusaika*: Impediments in Japan's Deep Structure," in *Multicultural Japan: Palaeolithic to Postmodern*, ed. D. Denoon et al. (Cambridge University Press, 1996), pp. 274–276.

19. See T. P. Rohlen, "'Spiritual Education' in a Japanese Bank," in *Japanese Culture and Behavior: Selected Readings*, ed. T. Sugiyama Lebra and W. P. Lebra (Honolulu: University of Hawai'i Press, [1973] 1986).

20. E. Seidensticker, *Tokyo Rising: The City since the Great Earthquake* (Cambridge, MA: Harvard University Press, 1991), p. 337.

21. W. I. Cohen, *The Asian American Century* (Cambridge, MA: Harvard University Press, 2002), p. 32.

22. B. R. Barber, *Jihad vs. McWorld: How Globalism and Tribalism Are Reshaping the World* (New York: Ballantine Books, 1996), p. 18; E. Ohnuki-Tierney, "McDonald's in Japan: Changing Manners and Etiquette," in *Golden Arches East: McDonald's in East Asia*, ed. J. L. Watson (Stanford University Press, 1997), p. 181.

23. Cohen, *Asian American Century*, p. 44.

24. M. Y. Brannen, "'Bwana Mickey': Constructing Cultural Consumption at Tokyo Disneyland," in *Re-made in Japan: Everyday Life and Consumer Taste in a Changing Society*, ed. Joseph J. Tobin (New Haven, CT: Yale University Press, 1992), pp. 216–217.

25. J. J. Tobin, "Introduction: Domesticating the West," in Tobin, *Re-made in Japan*, p. 4.

26. Dower, *Embracing Defeat*, p. 182.

27. Terry, *How Asia Got Rich*, pp. 230–231.

28. S. Issenberg, *The Sushi Economy: Globalization and the Making of a Modern Delicacy* (New York: Gotham Books, 2007).

29. D. McGray, "Japan's Gross National Cool (Globalization at Work)," *Foreign Policy* (May 2002).

30. A. Allison, "Sailor Moon: Japanese Superheroes for Global Girls," in *Japan Pop! Inside the World of Japanese Popular Culture*, ed. T. J. Craig (Armonk, NY: M. E. Sharpe, 2000), p. 264.

31. M. Hillenbrand, "Murakami Haruki in Greater China: Creative Responses and the Quest for Cosmopolitanism," *Journal of Asian Studies* 68, no. 3 (2009): 718–719, 739.

32. L. Ching, "Imaginings in the Empires of the Sun: Japanese Mass Culture in Asia," in *Contemporary Japan and Popular Culture*, ed. J. W. Treat (Honolulu: University of Hawai'i Press, 1996), pp. 171, 179–180.

33. J. W. Alexander, *Brewed in Japan: The Evolution of the Japanese Beer Industry* (Honolulu: University of Hawai'i Press, 2013), pp. 1–2, 108–109, 129, 180, 238–239.

34. S. Frühstück and W. Manzenreiter, "Neverland Lost: Judo Cultures in Austria, Japan, and Elsewhere Struggling for Cultural Hegemony," in *Globalizing Japan: Ethnography of the Japanese Presence in Asia, Europe, and America*, ed. H. Befu and S. Guichard-Anguis (London: RoutledgeCurzon, 2001), pp. 86–87.

35. C. R. Yano, *Tears of Longing: Nostalgia and the Nation in Japanese Popular Song* (Cambridge, MA: Harvard University Asia Center, 2002), pp. 3–4, 9 (Teng is here spelled in Japanese, rather than Chinese, as "Ten"), 28–44; A. F. Jones, *Like a Knife: Ideology and Genre in Contemporary Chinese Popular Music* (Ithaca, NY: Cornell University East Asia Program, 1992), p. 16.

Chapter 12

1. M. S. Gallicchio, *The Cold War Begins in Asia: American East Asian Policy and the Fall of the Japanese Empire* (New York: Columbia University Press, 1988), p. 4. D. Oberdorfer, *The Two Koreas: A Contemporary History*, rev. and updated ed. (New York: Basic Books, [1997] 2001), p. 5.

2. B. Cumings, *Korea's Place in the Sun: A Modern History* (New York: W. W. Norton, 1997), p. 192.

3. Gallicchio, *Cold War Begins in Asia*, p. 75.

4. D. Halberstam, *The Coldest Winter: America and the Korean War* (New York: Hyperion, 2007), pp. 366–367.

5. P. West, "Confronting the West: China as David and Goliath in the Korean War," *Journal of American–East Asian Relations* 2, no. 1 (1993): 12, 16.

6. F. Dikötter, *The Tragedy of Liberation: A History of the Chinese Revolution, 1945–57* (New York: Bloomsbury Press, 2013), pp. 130–131.

7. C. J. Eckert, "Korea's Transition to Modernity: A Will to Greatness," in *Historical Perspectives on Contemporary East Asia*, ed. M. Goldman and A. Gordon (Cambridge, MA: Harvard University Press, 2000), p. 146.

8. S. S. Kim, "Korea's *Segyehwa* Drive: Promise versus Performance," in *Korea's Globalization*, ed. S. S. Kim (Cambridge University Press, 2000), p. 277.

9. I. Göthel, "*Juche* and the Issue of National Identity in the DPRK of the 1960s," in *North Korea: Ideology, Politics, Economy*, ed. Han S. Park (Englewood Cliffs, NJ: Prentice Hall, 1996), pp. 25–27.

10. Dae-Sook Suh, *Kim Il Sung: The North Korean Leader* (New York: Columbia University Press, 1988), pp. 219–220.

11. C. J. Eckert, Ki-baik Lee, Young Ick Lew, M. Robinson, and E. W. Wagner, *Korea Old and New: A History* (Seoul: Ilchokak, 1990), pp. 349–350.

12. J. Lie, *Han Unbound: The Political Economy of South Korea* (Stanford University Press, 1998), pp. 11–13.

13. Eckert et al., *Korea Old and New*, p. 396.

14. Young Whan Kihl, *Transforming Korean Politics: Democracy, Reform, and Culture* (Armonk, NY: M. E. Sharpe, 2005), p. 71.

15. Atul Kohli, "Where Do High-Growth Political Economies Come From? The Japanese Lineage of Korea's 'Developmental State,'" in *The Developmental State*, ed. M. Woo-Cumings (Ithaca, NY: Cornell University Press, 1999).

16. E. F. Vogel, *The Four Little Dragons: The Spread of Industrialization in East Asia* (Cambridge, MA: Harvard University Press, 1991), pp. 48–54.

17. Lie, *Han Unbound*, p. 71.

18. Cumings, *Korea's Place in the Sun*, p. 317.

19. M. L. Clifford, *Troubled Tiger: Businessmen, Bureaucrats, and Generals in South Korea* (Armonk, NY: M. E. Sharpe, 1994), pp. 115–118.

20. K. J. Fields, *Enterprise and the State in Korea and Taiwan* (Ithaca, NY: Cornell University Press, 1995), pp. 7, 96.

21. M. Woo-Cumings, "Introduction," *Developmental State*, p. 18.

22. Clifford, *Troubled Tiger*, p. 231.

23. A. H. Amsden, *Asia's Next Giant: South Korea and Late Industrialization* (New York: Oxford University Press, 1989), pp. 145–147.

24. F. Gibney, *The Pacific Century: America and Asia in a Changing World* (New York: Charles Scribner's Sons, 1992), p. 396.

25. J. H. Grayson, "A Quarter-Millennium of Christianity in Korea," in *Christianity in Korea*, ed. R. E. Buswell Jr. and T. S. Lee (Honolulu: University of Hawai'i Press, 2006), pp. 15–17, 21–22.

26. D. Tudor, *Korea: The Impossible Country* (Tokyo: Tuttle Publishing, 2012), p. 63.

27. Kihl, *Transforming Korean Politics*, p. 96.

28. Ibid., pp. 108, 110.

29. Jong-myung Kim, "The Tripiṭaka Koreana: Its Computerization and Significance for the Cultural Sciences in a Modern Globalizing World," in *Korea and Globalization: Politics, Economics, and Culture*, ed. J. Lewis and A. Sesay (London: RoutledgeCurzon, 2002), pp. 154–155.

30. Eun Mee Kim, "Globalization of the South Korean Chaebol," in Kim, *Korea's Globalization*, pp. 109–110.

31. Byong-suh Kim, "Modernization and the Explosive Growth and Decline of Korean Protestant Religiosity," in Buswell and Lee, *Christianity in Korea*, p. 325.

32. Sangmee Bak, "McDonald's in Seoul: Food Choices, Identity, and Nationalism," in *Golden Arches East: McDonald's in East Asia*, ed. J. L. Watson (Stanford University Press, 1997), pp. 138–140, 151, 157, 159.

33. Clifford, *Troubled Tiger*, p. 8.

34. Jeong Duk Yi, "Globalization and Recent Changes to Daily Life in the Republic of Korea," in Lewis and Sesay, *Korea and Globalization*, pp. 11, 16–19, 24, 32.

35. Tudor, *Korea: The Impossible Country*, pp. 202–210, 268–278.

36. S. S. Kim, "Korea and Globalization (Segyehwa): A Framework for Analysis" and "Korea's Segyehwa Drive," in Kim, *Korea's Globalization*, pp. 2, 247–252.

37. E. Hong, *The Birth of Korean Cool: How One Nation is Conquering the World through Pop Culture* (New York: Picador, 2014), pp. 6–7, 91–105, 223–224.

Chapter 13

1. F. FitzGerald, *Fire in the Lake: The Vietnamese and the Americans in Vietnam* (New York: Vintage Books, [1972] 1989), pp. 207, 370.

2. FitzGerald, *Fire in the Lake*, p. 85.

3. "Some estimates place the number of civil servants and teachers murdered between 1959 and 1961 at over ten thousand," according to D. Halberstam, *The Making of a Quagmire: America and Vietnam during the Kennedy Era* (revised edition) (New York: Alfred A. Knopf, [1964] 1988), p. 33.

4. Karnow, *Vietnam: A History*, pp. 436–437.

5. Jamieson, *Understanding Vietnam*, p. 293.

6. Vu Hong Lien and P. D. Sharrock, *Descending Dragon, Rising Tiger: A History of Vietnam* (London: Reaktion Books, 2014), p. 245.

7. R. D. Kaplan, *Asia's Cauldron: The South China Sea and the End of a Stable Pacific* (New York: Random House, 2014), pp. 9–11, 14, 62–63, 175.

8. E. S. Rawski, "Presidential Address: Reenvisioning the Qing: The Significance of the Qing Period in Chinese History," *Journal of Asian Studies* 55, no. 4 (1996): 838.

9. See P. Duus, *Feudalism in Japan*, 2nd ed. (New York: Alfred A. Knopf, 1969), pp. 12–13. More broadly, V. Lieberman contrasts a relatively protected Eurasian outer zone that included Japan, Europe, Russia, and Southeast Asia, with a relatively exposed inner zone that included China, in *Strange Parallels: Southeast Asia in Global Context, c. 800–1830, vol. II. Mainland Mirrors: Europe, Japan, China, South Asia, and the Islands* (Cambridge University Press, 2009).

10. H. M. Hopper, *Fukuzawa Yūkichi: From Samurai to Capitalist* (New York: Pearson Longman, 2005), pp. 121–122.

Chapter 14

1. Lai Tse-han, R. H. Myers, and Wei Wou, *A Tragic Beginning: The Taiwan Uprising of February 28, 1947* (Stanford University Press, 1991), pp. 80–89, 102ff., 159–160.

2. J. D. Spence, *Mao Zedong* (New York: Viking, 1999), pp. 103–104.

3. D. Halberstam, *The Coldest Winter: America and the Korean War* (New York: Hyperion, 2007), p. 235.

4. A. J. Nathan and R. S. Ross, *The Great Wall and the Empty Fortress: China's Search for Security* (New York: W. W. Norton, 1997), p. 39.

5. E. Friedman, P. G. Pickowicz, and M. Selden, *Chinese Village, Socialist State* (New Haven, CT: Yale University Press, 1991), pp. 14, 81–82.

6. F. C. Teiwes and W. Sun, *China's Road to Disaster: Mao, Central Politicians, and Provincial Leaders in the Unfolding of the Great Leap Forward, 1955–1959* (Armonk, NY: M. E. Sharpe, 1999), pp. 70–71.

7. One journalistic exposé of this tragedy is J. Becker, *Hungry Ghosts: Mao's Secret Famine* (New York: Free Press, 1996).

8. There are now numerous firsthand accounts of the Cultural Revolution. One particularly popular memoir of growing up in Mao's China is Jung Chang, *Wild Swans: Three Daughters of China* (New York: Anchor Books, 1992).

9. A. F. Thurston, *Enemies of the People: The Ordeal of the Intellectuals in China's Great Cultural Revolution* (Cambridge, MA: Harvard University Press, 1988), pp. 151–153.

10. D. S. G. Goodman, *Deng Xiaoping and the Chinese Revolution: A Political Biography* (London: Routledge, 1994), pp. 77–78.

11. P. Tyler, *A Great Wall: Six Presidents and China: An Investigative History* (New York: Century Foundation, 1999), pp. 47–49, 59–60. M. Schaller, *The United States and China: Into the Twenty-First Century*, 4th ed. (Oxford University Press, 2016), p. 150.

12. See M. MacMillan, *Nixon and Mao: The Week that Changed the World* (New York: Random House, 2007).

13. R. Baum, *Burying Mao: Chinese Politics in the Age of Deng Xiaoping* (Princeton University Press, 1994), p. 41.

14. J. Kynge, *China Shakes the World: A Titan's Rise and Troubled Future – and the Challenge for America* (Boston: Houghton Mifflin, 2006), p. 99.

15. J. Gittings, *The Changing Face of China: From Mao to Market* (Oxford University Press, 2005), pp. 104–105.

16. D. Stark, cited in D. L. Wank, *Commodifying Communism: Business, Trust, and Politics in a Chinese City* (Cambridge University Press, 1999), p. 32n22.

17. Central Intelligence Agency (CIA), "World Fact Book," country comparison: GDP (purchasing power parity), https://www.cia.gov/library/publications/the-world-factbook/.

18. D. M. Lampton, *The Three Faces of Chinese Power: Might, Money, and Minds* (Berkeley: University of California Press, 2008), pp. 89, 97–98.

19. S. Greenhalgh, *Just One Child: Science and Policy in Deng's China* (Berkeley: University of California Press, 2008), pp. 76, 308, 332–334; J. T. Dreyer, *China's Political System: Modernization and Tradition*, 4th ed. (New York: Pearson Longman, 2004), p. 136, figure 6.2.

20. W. Wo-lap Lam, *Chinese Politics in the Hu Jintao Era: New Leaders, New Challenges* (Armonk, NY: M. E. Sharpe, 2006), p. 89.

21. N. D. Kristof and S. Wudunn, *China Wakes: The Struggle for the Soul of a Rising Power* (New York: Vintage Books, 1995), p. 222.

22. Han Minzhu (pseudonym), ed., *Cries for Democracy: Writings and Speeches from the 1989 Chinese Democracy Movement* (Princeton University Press, 1990), p. 6.

23. Zhang Liang (pseudonym), compiler, *The Tiananmen Papers*, ed. A. J. Nathan and P. Link (New York: PublicAffairs, 2001), pp. 199, 204.

24. Baum, *Burying Mao*, p. 276.

25. Zhao Ziyang's memoirs have been published as *Prisoner of the State: The Secret Journal of Zhao Ziyang*, trans. and ed. Bao Pu, R. Chiang, and A. Ignatius (New York: Simon and Schuster, 2009).

26. Han, *Cries for Democracy*, p. 166.

27. G. R. Barmé, *In the Red: On Contemporary Chinese Culture* (New York: Columbia University Press, 1999), pp. 329–333, 338.

28. O. Schell, *Discos and Democracy: China in the Throes of Reform* (New York: Anchor Books, 1989), p. 251.

29. "The 2008 Pew Global Attitudes Survey in China: The Chinese Celebrate Their Roaring Economy, as They Struggle with Its Costs," http://www.pewglobal.org, under "Reports."

30. Wank, *Commodifying Communism*, p. 228.

31. A. F. Jones, "The Politics of Popular Music in Post-Tiananmen China," in *China Off Center: Mapping the Margins of the Middle Kingdom*, ed. S. D. Blum and L. M. Jensen (Honolulu: University of Hawai'i Press, 2002), p. 302.

32. Kuan Yew Lee, *From Third World to First: The Singapore Story, 1965–2000* (New York: HarperCollins, 2000).

33. W. G. Huff, *The Economic Growth of Singapore: Trade and Development in the Twentieth Century* (Cambridge University Press, 1994), p. 4.

34. World Bank Group, "Doing Business," Economy Ratings, www.doingbusiness.org/rankings. Heritage Foundation, "2015 Index of Economic Freedom," www.heritage.org/index/ranking.

35. F. Welsh, *A Borrowed Place: The History of Hong Kong* (New York: Kodansha International, 1993), p. 1.

36. K. Rafferty, *City on the Rocks: Hong Kong's Uncertain Future* (London: Penguin Books, 1991), p. 139.

37. For the governor's own perspective, see C. Patten, *East and West: China, Power, and the Future of Asia* (New York: Times Books, 1998).

38. Chih-huei Huang, "The *Yamatodamashi* of the Takasago Volunteers of Taiwan: A Reading of the Postcolonial Situation," in *Globalizing Japan: Ethnography of the Japanese Presence in Asia, Europe, and America*, ed. H. Befu and S. Guichard-Anguis (London: RoutledgeCurzon, 2001), pp. 223–224.

39. Wen-hsiung Hsu, "From Aboriginal Island to Chinese Frontier: The Development of Taiwan before 1683," in *China's Island Frontier: Studies in the Historical Geography of Taiwan*, ed. R. G. Knapp (Taipei: SMC, [1980] 1995), pp. 5–11.

40. On "The Origins of Taiwanese Identity," see A. M. Wachman, *Taiwan: National Identity and Democratization* (Armonk, NY: M. E. Sharpe, 1994), pp. 91–124. On

martial law and the "white terror," see P. Chen-main Wang, "A Bastion Created, a Regime Reformed, an Economy Reengineered, 1949–1970," in *Taiwan: A New History*, ed. M. A. Rubinstein (Armonk, NY: M. E. Sharpe, 1999), pp. 323, 330.

41. Wang, "A Bastion Created," p. 324.
42. J. S. Prybyla, "Economic Developments in the Republic of China," in *Democracy and Development in East Asia: Taiwan, South Korea, and the Philippines*, ed. T. W. Robinson (Washington, DC: AEI Press, 1991), p. 54.
43. W. McCord, *The Dawn of the Pacific Century: Implications for Three Worlds of Development* (New Brunswick, NJ: Transaction, [1991] 1993), p. 44.
44. S. Rigger, *Why Taiwan Matters: Small Island, Global Powerhouse*, updated ed. (Lanham: Rowman and Littlefield, 2011), p. 124. Lampton, *Three Faces of Chinese Power*, p. 97.
45. CIA, "World Fact Book," Country comparison: GDP – per capita (purchasing power parity), 2014 data.
46. Hung-mao Tien, *The Great Transition: Political and Social Change in the Republic of China* (Stanford, CA: Hoover Institution Press, 1989), pp. 1–2, 64.
47. J. Taylor, *The Generalissimo's Son: Chiang Ching-kuo and the Revolutions in China and Taiwan* (Cambridge, MA: Harvard University Press, 2000), pp. 405–407.
48. R. E. Stross, *Bulls in the China Shop and Other Sino-American Business Encounters* (New York: Pantheon Books, 1990), p. 244.
49. CIA, "World Fact Book," data for 2014.
50. D. Shambaugh, *China Goes Global: The Partial Power* (Oxford University Press, 2013), pp. 156–157.
51. J. N. Wasserstrom, *China in the 21st Century: What Everyone Needs to Know*, 2nd ed. (Oxford University Press, 2013), pp. 6–7.
52. For the *Goddess of Democracy*, see Han, *Cries for Democracy*, pp. 343–344. For headbands, see O. Schell, *Mandate of Heaven: A New Generation of Entrepreneurs, Dissidents, Bohemians, and Technocrats Lays Claim to China's Future* (New York: Simon and Schuster, 1994), p. 82.
53. Schaller, *United States and China*, p. 217.
54. Hong Sheng and Nong Zhao, *China's State-Owned Enterprises: Nature, Performance and Reform* (Singapore: World Scientific Publishing Company, 2013).
55. J. Osburg, "Global Capitalism in Asia: Beyond State and Market in China," *Journal of Asian Studies* 72, no. 4 (2013): 824.
56. G. Dyer, *The Contest of the Century: The New Era of Competition with China – and How America Can Win* (New York: Alfred A. Knopf, 2014), pp. 244–245; F. Godement, *Contemporary China: Between Mao and Market* (Lanham: Rowman and Littlefield, 2016), p. 104.
57. Dyer, *Contest of the Century*, p. 7.
58. Shambaugh, *China Goes Global*, p. 274.
59. Ibid., pp. 207–268.
60. "Hurun Report Chinese Luxury Consumer Survey 2014." Available at www.hurun.net/en/ArticleShow.aspx?nid=262 (accessed July 12, 2016).

Afterword

1. See F. Fukuyama, *The End of History and the Last Man* (New York: Free Press, 1992).
2. R. Schriver and M. Stokes, "Taiwan's Liberation of China," *Current History* 107, no. 710 (2008): 280.

Index